FOOTBALL

HARVARD VS. McGILL.

Jarvis Field, Cambridge, May 15, 1874

FOOTBALL

THE AMERICAN INTERCOLLEGIATE GAME

BY

PARKE H. DAVIS

MEMBER OF THE INTERCOLLEGIATE RULES COMMITTEE

ILLUSTRATED

NEW YORK
CHARLES SCRIBNER'S SONS
1911

PREFACE

THE football historian who essays to reproduce the battles of the gridiron is more than ordinarily handicapped by the insufficiency of the records. Football, unlike baseball, has not yet evolved the official scorer or reporter. The data of the games consist simply of the contemporaneous accounts in the college and public press. The peculiarities of football, the swift and confusing intricacy of its plays, the substitutions and sudden shifting of players make the work of the reporter excessively difficult and at times more or less inaccurate.

The line-ups and descriptions of games contained in Part II of this book have necessarily been based upon these accounts. The details of play, however, have been submitted for correction to players who participated in the various games, and the lists of players likewise referred for verification to players and officials of the respective institutions, so that, notwithstanding the difficulties, they are substantially accurate. More than this is impossible.

To the many players and officials who have aided in assembling the data of these games a grateful acknowledgment of assistance is made.

P. H. D.

CONTENTS

PART I

ILLUSTRATIONS

CHAPTER I

FOOTBALL IN OLDEN TIME

FOOTBALL, or, as it was called in olden time, camp-ball, camping, or hurling, may be traced from the present backward through century after century until the trail is lost in the remoteness of antiquity. Indeed, abundant evidence may be marshalled to prove that this is the oldest outdoor game in existence.

In the 22d chapter of Isaiah is found the verse, " He will turn and toss thee like a ball." This allusion, slight as it may be, is sufficient unto the antiquary to indicate that some form of a game with a ball existed as early as 750 years before the 'Christian era, the epoch customarily assigned to the Book of Isaiah. A more specific allusion of the same period, however, is the passage in the Sixth Book of the Odyssey of Homer, familiar to all schoolboys: "Then having bathed and anointed well with oil they took their midday meal upon the river's banks and anon when satisfied with food they played a game of ball." This game of Nausicaa and her companions, we are told, was not football, but a dance in which the ball was tossed from hand to hand to the accompaniment of choral singing. This contention may be correct. Another step, however, will bring us to football.

In all Greek lexicons may be found the word "harpaston," usually defined as a game with a ball. Antiquaries have supplemented this meagre definition by asserting that it was a game strikingly similar to modern Rugby football and

3

that it was preceded by three earlier games, traces of which
are preserved in the Greek words phenindra, episkyros,
and epikoinos. Harpaston was a favorite game at Sparta.
It was played upon a rectangular field marked with side
lines, goal-lines, and centre line. There was no limitation
upon the number of players, but these were equally divided
between the two sides. The ball was passed forward by
a man standing at midfield and the game was in action, the
object being to drive the ball by passing, kicking, or carrying across the opposite goal-line. Its progress was impeded
by blocking, holding, and tackling, but here the similarity
to Rugby ends, as this ancient game was a prolonged scrimmage without order or method.

When the Romans came in contact with the Greeks
and seized their novel and admirable institutions they also
adopted this game, slightly Latinizing the name to "harpastum." The Romans, it is true, had at the time a football
game of their own which was called "follis," but which was
not so ingeniously organized as its Spartan counterpart.

These two games existed at Rome for many years, each
having its partisans and each party of partisans clamoring
for the suppression of the other. It would seem that human
nature was not different in 28 B.C. from what it is to-day,
for among the first acts of Augustus after settling his right
to succeed his great uncle, Julius Cæsar, was to demand a
revision of the football rules. Augustus's grievance against
the existing games, however, was their gentleness, which he
considered too childish for Roman youths destined to be
centurions and commanders of legions, thus antedating by
eighteen hundred years a similar thought of the Duke of
Wellington, who said that "England's soldiers are trained
upon England's football fields." The Emperor Augustus
therefore selected a philosopher to effect the revision. This
unknown philosopher, the original member of the Rules

Committee, at last submitted his code of rules and they were approved by Augustus. Their introduction immediately divided the young athletes of Rome into two camps, each raging with debate and discussion, one for the new rules and the other for the old. Thus in the modern light of the controversy over the comparative merits of Rugby and Association football we may appreciate the significance of the familiar verse of Martial, alluding to this controversy over the Roman philosopher's game:

"Folle decet pueros ludere, folle senes."

Julius Pollux, an Egyptian sophist of the second century, who taught at Rome under Commodus, has left among his writings a brief description of this game: "The players divide themselves into two bands. The ball is thrown upon the line in the middle. At the two ends of the field, behind the line where the players are stationed, are two other lines, beyond which these two bands endeavor to carry the ball, a feat that can not be accomplished without pushing one another backward and forward." This description by Pollux does not add much to our detailed knowledge of the Augustan game, but this has escaped oblivion in another way, for it was played throughout Italy after the fall of Rome continuously until the Middle Ages, and, surprising to assert, was revived at Florence as recently as 1898.

With the passing of the Latin language the name harpastum, by which the Augustan game was known, also disappeared, but the game continued under the Italian denomination of "calcio." From the full description extant of this Italian game, even from earliest times, the Augustan game accurately has been reconstructed. It was played upon a square field marked by side lines, goal-lines, and centre line, the goals being marked by posts. The players consisted of twenty-seven on each side, organized in the manner of Roman military tactics, the game being planned as a mimic battle. The tactical arrangement of the players divided each side into fifteen forwards, five defensive backs, four half-backs, and three full-backs. Scoring was accomplished by kicking or carrying the ball across the goal-line between the posts, and two fouls, such as kicking the ball out of bounds, were equivalent to a goal. To equalize any advantage in the ground or wind, sides were changed after each goal. The game was called at sunset and awarded by the six judges, three for each team, to the side having scored the most goals. The partisans of each team, provided with horns and banners, occupied seats behind the goal-posts and paraded at the conclusion of the game, when custom required the vanquished to deliver their banners to the victors. Thus was it truly said that nothing is new under the sun.

In the game of calcio, as played by the mediæval Italians, the artistic feature of colored costumes was introduced, and the officials, as indicative of their honorable and impartial office, were clothed in a garment composed of one half of the costume of each of the rival teams. A celebrated game of this period was played at Florence in 1554, one side being under the captaincy of the Prince of Mantua and the membership of the two forces including the leading members of the great families of Bardolfi, Medici, Ridolfi, Ruccellai, and Strozzi. Antonio Scainio, a Venetian historian writing in 1555, describes a game similar to the Augustan sport, but calls it pallone. This is the same word further immortalized in a book by that name written by Edmondo de Amicis, the eminent Italian writer, who is endeared to all school-boys as the author of "Cuore." This game of pallone also contains the distinctive feature of the old English game of ballown, the batting from one player to another of a ball in the air. Indeed, the similarity of the names and of this feature would indicate that these two games originally were identical.

To many nations may be assigned a share in the honor of founding and fostering this noble sport. The Celts claim that football was once a rite among their ancestors in the worship of the sun-god. The old Teutonic tribes which Cæsar found in Gaul not only used the skulls of their enemies for drinking-cups, but they contemptuously kicked their severed heads about as footballs in a crude and savage game. The earliest explorers of the North found the young Esquimaux playing upon the floes with a cleverly made football sewn with a welt and filled with moss. Travellers in the islands of the South Seas found the natives playing a simple game with a ball made of bamboo fibre, and even stout Cortez has recorded such a game as existing among the Aztecs. Such a primitive diversity throughout the earth of football is not difficult to explain. Child nature is uniform the world over, and children who are forced to find and make their own toys naturally will turn to the same objects. Which of us who was born upon a farm has not awaited eagerly the arrival of "butchering day" in the fall to get the bladder to knead and roll it until pliable, then to inflate it with a quill, for rare sport across the close-cropped fields in the crackling, crisp October air? Yet, Alexander Barclay, an English poet, in his "Ecloges," celebrated this custom of childhood four hundred years ago:

> "And now in winter when men kill the fat swine,
> They get the bladder and blow it great and thine,
> With many beans and peasen put therein
> It rattleth, soundeth and slimeth, clere and fayre,
> While it is thrown and cast up in the ayre,
> Each one contendeth and hath a great delight
> With foote and with hande the bladder for to smite;
> If it fall to the ground they lift it up again,
> And this way to labour they count it no payne."

The bard of Avon, unless he should be indulging in the license of anachronism, would give the game a place even among the Ephesians, for does not Dromio in Scene I of Act II of the "Comedy of Errors" ask Adriana:

"Am I so round with you as you with me,
That like a football you do spurn me thus?"

With more accuracy, however, Shakespeare locates the game during the reign of King Lear, for football unquestionably was brought into England by the Romans. In Scene IV of Act I of the latter play the king says to Oswald, "Do you bandy looks with me, you rascal?" Oswald replies, "I'll not be struck, my lord." Thereupon the Earl of Kent interposes, "Nor tripped, you base football player," and instantly upsets the poor steward by tripping him.

The earliest specific mention of football in the literature of England, and this also is the first mention of any game, is to be found in the "History of London," written by William Fitzstephen in 1175. This genial old chronicler, recording the customs of his day, thus pleasantly pictures our comrades of the game, almost eight hundred years ago:

"After dinner all the youth of the city go into the fields of the suburbs and address themselves to the famous game of football. The scholars of each particular school have their peculiar ball, and the particular trades have, most of them, theirs. The elders of the city, the fathers of the parties, and the rich and wealthy, come to the fields on horseback in order to behold the exercises of the youth, and in appearance are themselves as youthful as the youngest, their natural heat seeming to revive at the sight of so much agility and in a participation in the diversion of their respective sons."

Some of our law students, whose profound incursions into the history of legal institutions have taken them as far

back as the "statutes of nisi prius" enacted in the reign of
Edward II, have returned with the startling information
that the pathway of English legislation is marked by many
a signboard relative to football. The first of these football
laws is denominated in the books as 16 Edward II, enacted April 13, 1314, and runs as follows:

"Forasmuch as there is great noise in the city, caused by
hustling over large footballs from which many evils arise,
which God forbid, we command and forbid on behalf of
the king on pain of imprisonment such game to be played
in the future." The especial grievance that provoked this
repressive proclamation was the persistent custom of the
boys of London of playing their games in the city's streets,
a practice evidently of complete incorrigibility, for Samuel
Pepys in his diary under date of January 2, 1665, three
centuries later, noted "The streets full of footballs, it being
a great frost." Indeed, King Edward's prohibition must
have failed of observance even in his own time, for thirty-
five years later the game became so popular throughout
England that it threatened to submerge the practice of
archery, then the mainstay of a warring nation. Accordingly, Edward III issued an edict which is still extant in
the Close Rolls, 12 Edward III, prohibiting many sports,
among which were "Manualem, pedinam, baculoream et
ad cambucam." Devotees of modern sports afield will
recognize with pain beneath these names in law Latin
their beloved handball, football, hockey, and golf. To the
outlawry of these games must have been credited in no
small portion the marvellous success of the English bow-
men of the period, for in 1389 Richard II forbade "all playing at tennise, football and other such importune games."
During the reign of Henry IV, in the Parliamentary Rolls
for 1410, the proscription against football again appears,
this time being enunciated in Norman French, and four-

teen years later the baby King Henry VI proclaimed in
quaint English, The "King forbiddes that na man play
at the futball." But the game was too strong even for
England's kings, although Henry VII and Elizabeth also
launched against it their royal disfavor.

A recent historian has stated, "James Stuart, the first
King James of England but the sixth of Scotland, was one
of the most foolish and mischievous kings we ever had in
England." Football men throughout the world will be in-
clined to concur in this characterization notwithstanding its
harshness, for James is the man who wrote the "Basilikon
Koron," a ponderous tome on deportment, composed for the
education of his son, Henry, Prince of Wales, in which James
wrote, "From this court I debar all rough and violent exercises, likewise football, meeter for lameing than making able
the users thereof."

Even in the period of rough sport in England, the day
of the quarterstaff of Robin Hood and the justing lance of
the Black Prince, football did not escape the eye of the
gentle moralist. One of these was Sir Thomas Elyote,
author of the "Boke" called the "Gouvernour." Sir John
thus impales three wicked games, of which, of course, our
football is one:

"Some men wolde saye that in the mediocritie, which I
have soo much praysed in shootynge, why should not boul-
ing, claishe pins and koyting be as much commended?
Veryly as for the two last they be utterly objected of all men,
in lyke wyse foote balle, wherein is nothynge but beastie
furie and extreme violence, whereof procedeth hurte and
consequently rancour and malice do remayn with them
that be wounded, wherefore it is to be put in perpetual
sylence."

The two great anatomists of English literature, Robert
Burton and Philip Stubbs, did not overlook football. The

"Yesterday was brave Hallowday,
And above all days in the year,
The school boys all got leave to play
And little Sir Hugh was there.
He kicked the ball with his foote
And kepped it with his knee
And even in at the window
He gart the bonnie ba' flee."

Alexander Barclay, author of the "Shyp of Folys," written in 1508, thus draws a pleasant picture of the game as one of common country recreation:

"The sturdie ploughman, lusty, strong and bold,
Overcometh the winter driving the football,
Forgetting labour and many a grevious fall."

Thomas Tusser, writing a few years later and calling the game by its archaic name of camping, even enthusiastically advocates the game of football as an incidental auxiliary to agriculture:

"In meadow or pasture to grow the more fine
Let campers be camping in any of thine;
Which if ye do suffer when low is the spring,
You gain to yourselves a commodious thing."

In an old comedy, "The Blind Beggar of Bethnal Green," by Thomas Day, an heroic character informs us, "I am Tom Stroud of Hurling. I'll play a gole at camp-ball or wrassel a fall a the hip or the hin turn with ere a Courtroll of ye an match me height for height."

As early as 1609 is to be found a reference to football in America in the "Relation of Virginia," by Henry Spellman. Describing the sports and pastimes of the colony he says: "They vse beside football play wch women and young boys doe much play at. They make their gooles like ours only they never fight nor pull another doone. The men play with a littel ball lettinge it falle out of ther hands and striketh

with the tope of his foote and he that can strike the ball
farthest winnes that they play for." Later in his work Spellman, probably inspired by sentimental memories of boyhood, lapses into poetry on the subject:

> " Football with us may be with them ballown.
> As they at tilt, so we at quintain run."

The refining influence of outdoor sports, of course including football, began to be recognized about this time, for
in 1611 Rowlands, in his "Letting of Humors Blood," represents a swain challenging his rival, not to a murderous duel
with the sword but to a manly and decisive contest in
sports afield:

> "Man, I dare challenge thee to throw the sledge
> To iumpe a leap ouer ditch and hedge,
> To wrassel, play at stoole ball or to runne,
> To pitch the bar or to shoote off a gun,
> To play at loggets, nine holes or pinnes,
> To try it out at football by the shinnes."

Misson, a French writer who visited England during
this period, was much impressed with the game. He says:
"In winter football is a useful and charming exercise. It
is played with a leather ball about as big as one's head,
filled with wind. This is kicked about from one to another
in the streets by him that can get at it and this is all the art
of it." Even the classic John Gay did not overlook the
humor of the game, for in "Trivia" he facetiously writes:

> "When lo, from afar,
> I spy the furies of the football war."

Another poetic allusion, from the pen of Sir Thomas
Wotton, and which is quoted approvingly by Isaak Walton
in the "Compleat Angler," presents a characteristic of the
football man which has survived to the present day:

"Joan takes her neat rubb'd pail and now
She trips to milk the sand red cow,
Where for some sturdy football swain
Joan stirs a syllabub or twain."

But it is to the elegant Edmund Waller, of the writers
of olden time, that the best picture of the sport must be
credited:

"As when a set of lusty shepherds try
Their force at football, care of victory
Makes them salute so rudely breast to breast
That their encounter seems too rough for jest;
They ply their feet and still the restless ball
Tost to and fro is urged by all."

From the pleasant picture conjured by these pastoral
verses it is indeed a lugubrious change to the vision of one of
our fellow-players depicted in an old indictment found in
the Court of the King's Bench at Westminster during the
reign of Henry VIII: "And the Grand Inquest inquiring
upon their oaths for the county of Middlesex do present that
William Wilton, yeoman, at day and place aforesaid did
misbehave himself playing football."

In the days in which the kings of England were assailing
this noble sport, the sport was flouting the kings of England
by passing into proverbs in their English.   "All fellows at
football" runs a saying that has come down from the days
of Edward III, and to the period of 1672 is attributed the
origin of another adage, a portion of which survives to this
very day: "We are hale fellows well met, not only at football but at everything else."   Not only during the period of
the royal proclamations against football did the game un-
restrainedly thrive, but it was played in full view of the very
placards upon which these proclamations were printed.   In
London the apprentices assembled in great numbers to play
on Finsbury Fields.   At Teddington and Twickenham each

Shrove Tuesday prudent householders covered their windows with boards and bushes until the mighty game that roared through the streets for hours was ended. In fact, in all market towns throughout England on this holiday, business was suspended and the afternoon given over to a great game of football, in which his Honor the Mayor invariably kicked off and every able-bodied citizen followed the ball.

Of the ancient game of hurling, which was a form of football, we are indebted for a faithful picture to Richard Carew, who describes this sport in a book entitled "Survey of Cornwall," published in 1602, and dedicated to Cornwall's Lieutenant-General, Sir Walter Raleigh. Sir Richard's pen thus quaintly sets forth the impressive features of hurling:

"Fifteen, twenty, thirty, or more or less players chosen on each side, strip themselves to their slightest apparel and then joyne hands in rank against one another. Out of these rankes they match themselves by payres, one embracing another and so pass away." Is not this a description of a rush-line? Sir Richard then states that two bushes set ten feet apart were used for goals and that the distance between the rival goals was two hundred and fifty feet. Two goal-keepers having taken their stations, one in each goal, "some indifferent person throweth up a ball the which whosoever can catch and carry through his adversaries goale hath won the game. Herein consisteth one of Hercules his labors. As soon as the opponents of the man with the ball essaye to lay hold of him" the runner might ward off with his fist. "Butting" also was a fine point of this play. When the runner was thrown to the ground or his opponents held him and cried "Held," the runner "dealed," that is, passed the ball to an associate of his side for a further advance. It is impressive to observe that this precise play of holding and crying "Held" was a part of intercollegiate football in America as late as 1890. When the runner in the game of hurling passed the "counterwayters" he was tackled by the goal-keepers. Few goals were scored in this game, so that the contest frequently was decided by giving the victory to the side "which keepeth the ball longest, giveth most falls in the hurling and presseth their contrary nearest to their own goale." Carew, however, had stronger liquor than water flowing through his veins, for in summing up the virtues of the game he says: "When hurling is ended you shall see them returning home as from a pitched battle with bloody pates, broken bones and out of joynt, yet all is good playe and never attourney nor crowner troubled for the matter." This was the game which elicited from a French spectator the witticism still frequently quoted in England, "Well, if this is play, then me for France when they begin to fight."

In the year of 1650 football was regarded as a national institution throughout Great Britain. The seventh article of the "Regulations of the Freemen Marblers of Purbeck" provides "That any man in our companie the Shrovetews-daie after his marriage shall paie unto the wardings twelve pence, and the last married man shall bring a football according to the custom of our companie." The annual game thus scheduled was played near Corfe Castle. But the classic game of these times was the contest waged each Shrove Tuesday at Chester, a fixture which antiquaries even of that period claimed had come down the centuries in commemoration of that great day in the year 217 when their ancestors formed a mighty wedge and rushed the Roman garrison out of Chester. Symbolic of that struggle, the goals were the Town Hall and a cross that stood outside of the city in an open space called the Rood Eye, and now known as the Rodehee, thus leaving between a vast space featured with fences, walls, trees, houses, city blocks, and streets, but furnishing nevertheless a playground none too large for the several hundred players who participated. Occasionally in this period one town challenged another or the game would be waged between parish and parish. Upon such occasions the ball would be kicked off midway between the two places and then the game would wax furious by hill and dale until darkness closed down or until one side had kicked the ball into the other's town.

In 1681 the game had so ingratiated itself into the English character that Charles II organized a team and challenged the Duke of Albemarle, the latter winning the ensuing contest. The most momentous circumstance, however, of this time was the adoption of the game by the great schools of England, for it was in the secondary institutions and not in the universities that field-sports originally were cradled. Among the school-boy leaders of the sport was Joseph Addison, of Charterhouse. Years after, when a great man of letters, he wrote an article for the *Spectator* entitled "Rustic Amusements," in which he spoke with pride of the many matches in which he had played. The poet William Cowper, who was a student at Westminster, never ceased to recount his "excellence at football while at school."

The history of the game in Scotland is not dissimilar from that in England. James II prohibited it in 1457 and James IV in 1481 ordered that "football and goff be cried down utterly." But these sports increased in popularity instead. Throughout all Caledonia on Candlemas Day football was the special observance of the occasion. No other festivity could compare with the expectancy and excitement aroused by the approach of the Candlemas Ba'. Sometimes on this day the east end of a town played the west. More often the bachelors were arrayed against the married men. At Jedburg on one occasion the ball accidentally was kicked into the river, but every contestant fearlessly followed the ball and waged the game up and down the river's bed, "amid splashes and bedabblements," to the strident applause of the female inhabitants who lined the river's banks.

The most celebrated game in olden times in Scotland was that held each year at Scone between the married and the unmarried men. The ball would be tossed in the air promptly at two o'clock on Candlemas afternoon. Frederick Eden, in his "Statistical Account of Scotland," thus describes this old game:

"He who got the ball in his hands ran with it until overtaken by an adversary and then if he could shake himself loose he ran on again; if not he passed the ball to another of his side unless it was wrested from him. The object of the married men was to 'hang' the ball, that is to put it three times in a small hole on the moor which was their 'dool' or goal. The bachelors tried to 'drown' it, that is, dip it three times in the river, which was their 'dool.' If neither side won by sun-down the ball was cut in two and half given to each side." From this annual game arose the Scottish proverb: "A' is fair at the ba' o' Scone."

As might be expected, some great games were played along the Scottish border in olden times. One of the most famous of these contests occurred at Kildear Castle between twenty Liddesdale Scots and twenty Englishmen, the latter winning by three goals to two. It was to the general merry-making that accompanied these international struggles that Sir Walter Scott tuned his muse:

> "Some drive the jolly bowl about,
> With dice and draughts some chase the day,
> And some with many a merry shout,
> In riot, revelry and rout
> Pursue the football play."

And now the mention of Sir Walter Scott brings us to one of the most celebrated games in olden or modern times, the game played by the men of Ettrick, under the leadership of their sheriff, against the men of Yarrow, led by the Earl of Horn, at Carterhaugh, December 15, 1815, and won by the sheriff and his men. No detailed account of this game is now extant, but the tales of its individual prowess, its encounters, haps and mishaps, for many years had equal place in Scotia with the legends of Robert Bruce, William Wallace, and Prince Charlie. This game, however, never will pass wholly into oblivion, for its victorious sheriff, who was none other than Sir Walter Scott, has preserved it in immortal verse whose sweet cadence now links football of olden times with football of modern days:

> "From the brown crest of Newark its summons extending,
> Our signal is waving in smoke and in flame,
> And each forester blithe from his mountain descending
> Bounds light o'er the heather to join in the game.
> Then strip lads and to it though sharp be the weather,
> And if by mischance you should happen to fall,
> There are worse things in life than a tumble on heather,
> And life is itself but a game of football."

CHAPTER II

THE BEGINNING OF THE MODERN GAME

THE honor of the invention of modern football belongs to the great secondary schools of England, to Charterhouse, Eton, Forest, Harrow, Rugby, Shrewsbury, Westminster, Winchester, and others. At Oxford and Cambridge that mysterious but powerful influence which among students the world over produces and enforces a conformation to type maintained from the Middle Ages for several centuries a contempt for field sports and games as incompatible with the life of a scholar and an approbation of the pale, thin, and stoop-shouldered youth as a physical ideal for a student. Thus these great universities throbbing to-day with athletic life partake of none of the honors of originating the modern game, even falling in line behind the institutions of America which preceded them fully three years as participants in intercollegiate rivalry.

The development by these schools of football, from a mere sport without rules or organization, into a highly specialized game was wholly inartificial. At no time during its formative period was an interscholastic convention or even a conference held between two schools. The idea of an interscholastic contest did not occur until years after the perfection of the game. This unexpected circumstance is due to the fact that each school originated a style of game peculiar to itself and found sufficient entertainment in the struggles of teams organized within its own walls. A prime factor in the formation of each game was the facilities or difficulties presented in the place of play, for the modern

21

playground, ample and uniform, was not a fixture of football in primitive times. Although the number of these different games is equal to the number of the schools, they easily may be divided into three general classes, best typified at Westminster, Eton, and Rugby. It is a circumstance of more than incidental interest that each one of these schools has contributed its best and most characteristic feature to the evolution of intercollegiate football in America.

At Westminster the crowded conditions of life in the heart of London evolved long prior to 1700 an indoor game of football, played in the cloisters of Westminster Abbey. A stone pavement lay underfoot, pillars, walls, and gates stood at either hand, and a low arched ceiling extended overhead, yet this was the veritable cradle of the modern game of football. Here John Dryden in 1646, Matthew Pryor in 1680, and Joseph Addison in 1684 led the school-boy forces. Indeed, the records of the Abbey disclose that either they or their comrades led so boisterously that the Dean of Westminster was forced to appoint a beadle to keep them quiet during divine service. The Game in Cloister, as it was called, was not intricate. Two goals, known as bases, and a prohibition against the use of the hands either upon opponents or upon the ball comprised the traditional code of their period. About 1800 some old buildings near the Abbey were removed and the space thus obtained became the "Dean's Yard," but the boys promptly pre-empted it for a playground and named it the Green. With this acquisition two games came into being at Westminster, the Game in Cloister and the Game in Green. In the latter game the goals were base-lines equal to the entire width of the Green. In addition to the prohibition against the use of the hands a new restriction was invented which was called "outsiding." This restriction was identical with what to-day is known as "off-side play."

THE WALL GAME AT ETON. A BULLY IN CALX.

It was from this game that the American game derived the principle of limiting the number of players to eleven.

The history of the game at Charterhouse, another London school, is similar to that at Westminster, the game evolving first in Cloisters and with the advent of a playground being transferred to the Green. Consequently the games at each school were almost identical. This circumstance suggested in the fall of 1863 an interscholastic game. This game, the first contest between schools, colleges, or universities in the history of football, was played at Vincent Square and was won by Westminster by two goals to none.

To Eton the American game is indebted for its principle of eleven men. Visitors to Windsor are familiar with the road running from that place to Slough and passing Eton, being separated from the school grounds by a brick wall eight feet in height. Along this wall on the school side originated and still is played the famous Wall Game of Eton. The ground for the game was laid off by drawing a furrow in the turf parallel to the wall and six yards distant. Eighteen yards from either end of the wall was painted perpendicularly upon it a white line, the space thus cut off being called calx. Beyond one calx formerly stood an elm; beyond the other a door in a transverse wall. These two objects, the elm and the door, constituted the goals. In this long, narrow space between the wall and the furrow the two great teams of Eton, the Collegers and Oppidans, annually have met upon St. Andrew's day since 1845. The players, numbering eleven upon a side, put the ball in play by a scrimmage against the wall, by them called a bully. Out of the bully the ball was forced by kicks until it was driven into calx, where the offensive eleven, by a most peculiar play too intricate for description here, endeavored to obtain a "fair shy," which was a free kick at goal. By reason of the great difficulty in hitting the goals these contests usually were decided by the number of shies obtained.

When Eton finally obtained an extensive playing field another game called the Field Game was devised, although the Wall Game has never been abandoned. As one might expect, the Field Game was no less ingeniously organized than the Wall. The ground was 150 yards long and 100 yards broad, the goals being marked with posts connected with a cross-bar. Here again the number of players upon a side was limited to eleven. Off-side play, by the Etonians called "sneaking," was prohibited, as also was the use of hands. The ball was advanced by short kicks, known as "dribbles," and if the defensive side directly or indirectly drove the ball behind their own goal where it was touched by an opponent a "rouge" was scored. A rouge entitled a team to a free kick at goal and three rouges equalled a goal.

On the 17th of November, 1873, a team of Etonians, under the captaincy of G. C. Allen, came to New Haven and played a game with Yale. Those indeed were primitive times, since it was Yale's second season at the game. The contest was waged under mixed rules, one of which called for eleven players, and was won by Yale. Four years later, when Harvard, Princeton, and Yale adopted the Rugby Union game, Yale insisted that the Eton number of eleven should modify the Rugby rule of fifteen. This proposition was defeated, but was renewed each year thereafter with great vigor by Yale, until finally, in 1880, Walter Camp, Yale's delegate, succeeded in persuading the convention to adopt the Eton rule.

There are many places in England so endeared to Americans by the ties of sentiment that we feel an ownership therein by the title of fancy if not by the title of actual fact. Where is the lover of letters that does not claim an interest in the town of Avon? Where is the lawyer that does not believe that he possesses an inalienable right in the Inns of Court? Where is the football man from field, side line, or stand who does not feel that he is an heritor in the glories of Old Bigside at Rugby? It is seventy years since Pater Brooke led out the forces in School-House versus School

and Tom Brown saved the goal in the second half at Rugby. The game long ago outgrew the Close and is now played wherever the English tongue is spoken. In America many of its methods have changed and its name partially has been obliterated, but the time never will come when its first home will be forgotten nor honorable deference not paid to the sweeping sward of Old Bigside at Rugby.

This famous school was founded in 1567. The origin of organized football among its boys is in the eighteenth century, but the precise period has passed into oblivion with those who participated. One of the farthest and most authentic reaches into the past is contained in the recollections of Matthew Bloxam, published in the *Rugby Meteor* for December, 1880. Matthew Bloxam was at Rugby in 1813. Writing of football in his time he says: "The procedure at Bigside of football was as follows. When all had assembled in the Close, two of the best players in the School commenced choosing in, one for each side. After choosing in about a score on each side, a somewhat rude division was made of the remaining fags, half of whom were sent to keep goal on one side, the other half to the opposite goal for the same purpose. Few and simple were the rules of the game. Touch on the sides of the ground was marked out and no one was allowed to run with the ball in his grasp towards the opposite goal. It was football and not handball, with plenty of hacking but little struggling."

From this description it appears that football up to Matthew Bloxam's time had been developing along lines similar to those at Westminster and elsewhere, particularly as to the rule against carrying the ball. But there came a crisp November day in 1823. Over a hundred boys had gathered for Bigside. The game soon was in action and backward and forward surged the ball, but without a score. The time wore on until at last the school-bell trembled on

the first stroke of five, the hour which terminated the game.
A long sailing punt was sent down the field, the last effort
of one side to effect a score. Suddenly out from the mass of
players upon the other side sprang a young Rugbeian by the
name of William Webb Ellis. With arms outstretched and
eyes keenly on the spinning ball he swiftly ranged into position to catch the punt. If he made and heeled it, under
the rules he might fall back, behind his mark, and try for
goal by a free kick. By a violent effort he stoops and
catches the ball just as it is about to strike the ground.
The opponents check their speed in order not to interfere
with the catch and heel, but Ellis, with the inspiration of
desperation, contrary to rule and custom, with increased
speed leaps onward. Five o'clock is now pealing on the
air. With the ball tightly held beneath his arm he dashes
into the ranks of his opponents, who, angered by this flagrant
violation of the rules, roughly seize him and endeavor to
throw him to the ground. Ellis with his free arm wards
them off and zigzagging in and out clears the pack and
crosses the line just as the last stroke of five comes rever-
berating over the Close.

In those days contested points, disputed games, and
changes in the rules were referred to a school judicatory
known as a levee of Bigside, which was held by the football
leaders under the elms between Littleside and Bigside, or
at times on another part of the grounds called the Island.
The sensational performance of Ellis was severely cen-
sured generally throughout the school, but as days came and
went there arose a few who saw in his exploit an opportunity for a great innovation in the game. After a time
the idea was supported by a majority of the school and at
last received the sanction of a Bigside levee. At first the
privilege of carrying the ball was limited to balls obtained
from fair catches in the manner performed by Ellis. Later
the privilege was extended to a ball caught on the bound,

MEMORIAL TO WILLIAM WEBB ELLIS,
The originator of the Rugby game of football, Rugby School, England.

and finally the right to run with the ball without restriction was incorporated as a basic rule in the Rugby game.

The performance of William Webb Ellis, like the exploits of all other heroes, as time passed was questioned by the scoffer and iconoclast and by some was denied altogether, but the Old Rugbeian Society in 1897 collected the personal recollections of the event from the surviving Rugbeians of Ellis's time, which has fairly proved that this tradition is founded upon actual fact.

William Webb Ellis, a town boy of Rugby, entered the school in December, 1816, at the age of eleven years. The school records show that he was a scholar of pronounced ability. Upon leaving the school in 1825, being the second Rugby Exhibitioner of that year, he entered Brasenose College, Oxford. Later he was ordained in the ministry and for several years acted as incumbent of the Church of Saint Clement Danes, Strand, and subsequently served as rector of Laver Magdalen, Essex. He died January 24, 1872.

In an ivy-grown wall at Rugby has been placed a tablet preserving to world-wide football posterity the name and exploit of this school-boy genius. It runs as follows:

> THIS STONE
> COMMEMORATES THE EXPLOIT OF
> ### WILLIAM WEBB ELLIS
> WHO WITH A FINE DISREGARD FOR THE RULES
> OF FOOTBALL
> AS PLAYED IN HIS TIME
> FIRST TOOK THE BALL IN HIS ARMS AND RAN WITH IT
> THUS ORIGINATING THE DISTINCTIVE FEATURE OF
> THE RUGBY GAME
> A. D. 1823

From 1823, the year of the exploit of William Webb Ellis, to the time of the great game of School-House versus School, described in "Tom Brown's School Days," is a space of

twenty years, but in this period the Bigside levies at
Rugby built about the run of Ellis a finished, finely technical game. Its perfection may best be appreciated and
certainly most pleasantly ascertained by now reverting to
boyhood and reading once more in Judge Thomas Hughes's
great book, the description of this game which here is
abridged:

"Old Brooke won the toss with his lucky half-penny and
got the choice of goals and kick-off. But now look, there is
a slight move forward of the School-House wings, a shout
'Are you ready?' and a loud affirmative reply. Old Brooke
takes half a dozen steps and away goes the ball spinning
towards the goal, seventy yards before it touches the ground,
a model kick-off. The School-House cheer and rush on.
The ball is returned. They meet it and drive it back among
the masses in motion. Then follows rush upon rush and
scrummage upon scrummage, and a scrummage, gentlemen,
in a School-House match was no joke in the consulship of
Plancus. Three quarters of an hour are gone, first winds
are failing and weight begins to tell. The School-House
are being pressed now and the ball is behind their goal.
There is a minute's breathing time before Old Brooke
kicks out and he gives the word to play strongly for touch.
Away goes the ball and in another minute there is a shout
of 'In touch' and 'Our ball.' Old Brooke stands with
the ball in his hands while the two sides form in deep lines
opposite one another. He must strike it straight out
between them. Old Brooke strikes it strong. Hurrah!
That rush has taken it right through the School line, far
into their quarters. The School leaders rush back shout-
ing 'Look out in goal.' They strain every nerve to catch
Young Brooke who has the ball, but they are after the fleetest
foot in Rugby. There they go straight for the goal posts.
Young Brooke is down! No! A long stagger but the dan-

ger is past. There is a hurried rush and Young Brooke has touched it right under the School goal posts. The School leaders are furious. They may well be for it is Lombard Street to a china orange that the School-House kick a goal with the ball touched in such a good place. Old Brooke of course will kick it but who shall catch and place it. Call Crab Jones. Here he comes, the coolest fish in Rugby. Old Brooke stands with the ball under his arms motioning the School back. He will not kick it until they are all in goal behind the posts. They are all edging forward inch by inch for the rush at Crab Jones who stands in front of Old Brooke to catch the ball. If they can reach him before he catches the ball the danger is over and with one and the same rush they will carry it right away to the School-House goal. Fond hope! It is kicked out and caught beautifully. Crab strikes his heel in the ground to mark the spot where the ball is caught beyond which the School line may not advance, but there they stand ready to rush forward the moment the ball touches the ground. Take plenty of room. Place it true and steady. Trust Crab Jones for that. He is resting on one knee with his eye on Old Brooke. 'Now!' Crab places the ball at the word. The School rush forward, Old Brooke kicks. A moment's pause and both sides look at the spinning ball. It flies straight between the posts, five feet above the cross-bar. A shout of joy rings out from the School-House players-up and a faint echo of it comes over the Close from the goal keepers. A goal in the first hour! Such a thing hasn't been done in the School-House match these five years!"

After all, is not the author of this famous game of fancy likewise entitled to a place in the hearts of football men with William Webb Ellis? The one performed a deed which gave a great game to Rugby. The other wrote a book which popularized that game and gave it to the world.

In the great wave of popularity that overtook football with the publication of "Tom Brown's School Days," the young Rugbeians were prompted to improve their famous game. Accordingly they introduced the principle of fixed numbers upon a side, twenty in the beginning and eventually fifteen. It was also at this time that the oval ball took the place of the sphere, thus returning to the shape of primitive days when the only ball was an inflated bladder, to which early period we also must go to find the origin of the ball's familiar name of "pigskin."

It was not until 1846 that football made its first appearance in the English universities. In this year two old Westminster boys, H. de Winton and J. C. Thring, were at Cambridge. In company with some boys from other schools they formed a club and played for a time on Parker's Piece. The game did not become popular, however, and so the boys after a few contests under mixed rules disbanded. Two years later the attempt was renewed. At the invitation of H. C. Malden two representatives from each of the schools, fourteen men in all, including Mr. Malden and George Salt, as representatives of the university, met in a conference which lasted six hours, but which resulted in a new code of rules based upon the best points at Eton, Harrow, Rugby, Winchester, and Shrewsbury. The Rugby principle of carrying the ball was rejected in these rules. No copy of this code is in existence, as few games were played thereunder and the movement again failed. The conference was not without influence, however, since its action brought into being a number of outside clubs which were inspired to organize and play, chief among which were Sheffield, in 1855, Hallam, in 1857, and Forest, in 1859, each playing under a variation of the Cambridge code.

In 1863 a third conference was held at Cambridge to draft an improved code of rules. As this conference was successful in launching that style of football now known as "association," it is fitting that the men composing it should have their names here preserved: .

R. Burn (Shrewsbury), R. H. Blake-Humphrey (Eton), W. P. Crawley (Marlborough), M. T. Martin (Rugby), W. R. Collyer (Rugby), J. T. Prior (Harrow), W. T. Trench Eton), H. L. Williams (Harrow), W. S. Wright (Westminster).

A few weeks after the date of this conference a convention was held by the different clubs of London at the Freemason's Tavern in Great Queen Street, at which it was decided to form an association and adopt a uniform code of rules. After a number of meetings, made necessary by a controversy over the adoption or rejection of the Rugby principle of carrying the ball, a code, which was substantially the Cambridge rules, was adopted December 1, 1863, under the title "Football Rules of the London Football Association." In this code players were forbidden to carry the ball. Hence the style of game provided by these rules has since been known as the "association" game. The name of soccer, or socker, as it is sometimes spelled, by which it also is designated, is merely a humorous derivative from the word Association.

The Rugby game now had a great rival competing with it for public favor, but the old school game still held its own. It invaded the universities November 2, 1869. Upon this date a number of old Rugbeians assembled in a room in Balliol College at Oxford and formed a club. During the ensuing three years occasional games were played by teams selected from the membership of this club. It was not until the beginning of 1872 that a proposition was broached to play a match game with Cambridge. This suggestion was enthusiastically approved, and after several conferences between the representatives of the two universities the game was scheduled for February 10, 1872, at Oxford, where it was duly played, Oxford winning by a goal from a try.

The success of the London Football Association in maintaining an orderly, healthy control over its style of game moved the Rugby players also to organize. Accordingly, January 26, 1871, thirty-six representatives from as many clubs in London and vicinity assembled in the Pall Mall Restaurant in Regent Street and organized the Rugby Football Union. Taking the rules of Rugby School as a basis, a number of modifications were introduced which greatly improved the game. These alterations subsequently were accepted at Rugby School. Thus, England in the early '70s presented two great, standard styles of football play, thoroughly organized and perfected and governed by separate but supreme bodies of recognized authority and control, each of which has maintained its sovereignty over its particular game in England unto this day.

CHAPTER III

EARLY FOOTBALL IN AMERICA

FOOTBALL, as a simple campus sport, without rules, without organization, and of course without regular contests, existed at the older American colleges of the East as early as 1800. The ball, it is true, was merely an inflated bladder, the teams were made up of all the fellows at hand, and the game was won merely by driving the ball to a given line, sometimes marked by a campus walk, sometimes indicated by a college wall. Two captains extemporaneously selected tossed up for first choice of men and then alternately chose players for their sides until every man present desirous of playing had been given a place. Frequently the division would be automatic. All men with final initials from A to M would go to the right, all others to the left. Later arrivals at the place of play invariably were given a position on one side or the other. When all were ready the ball was tossed in the air and this ancient game was in motion.

Later the round rubber ball made its appearance. By reason of its symmetrical shape and greater resilience an opportunity was afforded some men by aptitude and practice to excel the others in kicking the ball great distances and with surprising accuracy. It was quickly learned, however, that this individual skill could be offset by driving the ball only short distances with the toe, so that when intercepted by an opponent the ball might be passed deftly to one side to a comrade for a further advance without losing the ball. These features comprised all of the skill and tactics of that early period; but the game was strictly

football—always kicked and never carried.   Let no one
think that these campus struggles, although lacking in
highly specialized skill and intricacy of play, also were lacking in zest and enjoyment.   Shins were barked, noses were
tapped, breath and temper frequently lost.   The players
raced for the ball and blocked their opponents with fearless-
ness and force.   No multitudinous throng cheered the tide
of battle and no newspapers chronicled the achievements
of the day, but these games are still affectionately recalled by
a few hale old survivors who with many a smack of reminis-
cent relish never miss an opportunity to tell the present generation that "football is not as good a game as it used to be."

Antiquaries at Harvard claim that a football was kicked
promiscuously about the Yard in a simple game as early as
1800.   A few years later some genius devised a contest between the Freshmen and Sophomores.   To-day it would be
called a rush instead of a game, but since it possessed a few
crude rules of order and was played with a football it must
be accredited as the lineal progenitor of the fully perfected
organism that to-day is presented upon Soldiers Field.

The older football generation of the present time well
remembers the glories of Jarvis and Holmes Fields, but there
are a few whose recollection can run back to an arena known
as the Delta, now the site of Memorial Hall.   Here seventy
years ago were held Harvard's first football games, the
Freshmen-Sophomore contests aforesaid.   Upon the evening of the match, half-past six being the established hour,
the upper classmen assembled and took seats upon a near-by
fence.   The two lower classes to the last man present were
marshalled in two opposing lines, the sturdiest representative of the Freshmen being in the center of his line with the
ball.   At the signal both lines advanced on the run to the
centre of the Delta, where the Freshmen endeavored to force
their champion with the ball through the Sophomores' ranks

and onward to the line which the Sophomores defended. A copious amount of fisticuffs in this encounter not only was natural but also was permissible. These ebullient young football men, however, eventually became so boisterous and, as confidentially hinted, at times so pugnacious that this sport came under the faculty's displeasure. Periodic were the official prohibitions launched at it, but periodic was its reappearance. About 1845 some improvements were made in the game and regular class contests organized which continued for fifteen years. The pugnacious traditions of the past, however, still were present to keep alive its virile practices. In 1860, bellicose year that it was, these class encounters were waged with unusual vim, prodigious noise, and petty violence, for in the ranks of the combatants were some destined soon for glorious service upon the country's battlefields. In fact, the leading collegian in these games, Henry Ropes, '62, unconsciously was preparing for a greater leadership to terminate in a valiant death at the head of his regiment at Gettysburg. But the faculty were not seers, so they determined to place upon these contests a quietus from which they never should awake. This was done by a resolution vigorous in its English and dire in its provisions for punishment.

The student body at Harvard bowed to the decree, but determined that the event should not pass without being signalized in some extraordinary way. A great funeral celebration, therefore, was organized, the funeral of Football Fightum. A grave was dug in the Delta, a memorial tablet prepared, and a great pageant marshalled. As a capital feature the loudest-voiced if not the best orator at Harvard was chosen to deliver a eulogy. This heroic effort, fortunately for posterity, was rescued from oblivion long years after and preserved in the columns of the *Crimson*, October 14, 1881. Its impressive periods still stir the soul although half a century has elapsed since they were spoken:

"Dearly beloved, we have met together upon this mournful occasion to perform the sad office over one whose long and honored life was put to an end in a sudden and violent manner. Last year, at this very time, in this very place, our poor friend's round, genial appearance and the elasticity of his movements gave promise of many years more to be added to a long life, which even then eclipsed that of the oldest graduate. When he rose exulting in the air propelled by the foot of the valiant Ropes we little thought then that to-day he would lie so low. Exult, ye Freshmen! The wise men who make big laws around a little table have stretched out their arms to protect your eyes and noses. For us there is naught but sorrow, the sweet association and tender memories of eyes bunged up, of noses wonderfully distended and of battered shins, and the many chance blows anteriorly and posteriorly received and delivered,—the rush, the struggle, the victory,—they call forth our deep regret and unaffected tears. The enthusiastic cheers, the singing of 'Auld Lang Syne,' as each stands grasping a brother's hand, all, all have passed away, and will soon be buried with the football beneath the sod, to live hereafter only as a dream in our memories and in the college annals.

"Brothers, pardon my emotion. If I have kept you already too long, pardon me this also. On such an occasion as this few words can be spoken; but they must be spoken, because they are the outcry of grieved spirits and sad hearts. What remains for me to say is short and in the words of a well known poem:

> "' 'Tis time our heavy task were done,
> And I would advise our retiring,
> Or we'll hear the voice of some savage one
> For the ringleader gravely inquiring.' "

An ode specially composed for the occasion then was
sung:

> "Ah! woe betide the luckless time
>   When manly sports decay,
> And football stigmatized as crime
>   Must sadly pass away!
>
> "Beneath this sod we lay you down,
>   This sign of glorious fight;
> With dismal groans and yells we'll drown
>   Your mournful burial rite!
>
> "For 'sixty-three will never see
>   Such cruel murder done
> And not proclaim the deed of shame.
>   No!   Let's unite as one!"

The grave then was closed and a tablet erected bearing
the following inscription:

HIC JACET

FOOTBALL FIGHTUM

Obiit July 2, 1860,

Aet. LX Years.

RESURGAT.

Twelve long years were destined to elapse before this
epitaph was to be realized, but arise at last Football
Fightum did, April 21, 1872, when the Class of 1874
played the Class of 1875 upon Boston Common. From
that day to this Football Fightum has been a hale and
defiant figure at Harvard.

From earliest times young Yale has kicked an inflated
bladder about the Green. About 1840 an organized rivalry
arose between the two lower classes which seized football as
a medium of conclusions. The contest in reality was a
rush, but as a football figured in it the struggle must be
chronicled as football. To New Haven's Green on the af-

ternoon of the fray came the Sophomores in fantastic garb
and painted faces. The Freshmen under the guidance of
the upper classmen were withdrawn to one side and formed
into a great, solid, V-shaped mass, with the most gigantic
Freshman of the class carrying the ball and buried within
the wedge. At the signal this mass started heavily to
plough its way across the Green. A corps of picked Sophomores threw themselves upon its apex and their comrades
fell upon its flanks in a fierce endeavor to reach and capture
the ball.

About 1841 an exciting struggle of this character was
in progress when a firemen's parade was passing. In the
absence of records and at a distance of seventy years it is
impossible to state whether the warlike recreation of the
collegians aroused the primitive fighting lust in the firemen
or whether the ornate costumes of the firemen evoked a
sarcastic vein in the collegians, but in either event a clash
took place between firemen and collegians, that terminated
the game and disrupted the parade. Students will claim
that the fault lay with the firemen, but candor compels an
historian to state that a magistrate in New Haven at that
time thought differently, for he haled into his court Thomas
H. Moody, '43, who like a little John Hampden had stood
in defence of his right to play upon the Green, and fined
him twenty dollars with the imposition of eighty dollars
additional for costs. From the size of the bill of costs
it would seem that the firemen resumed their parade, directing its route to the court-house, where its members
individually filed bills against Moody for witness fees and
mileage.

Eventually an orderliness approaching punctiliousness
crept into these contests. Thus the Freshmen in the fall
of 1857 posted upon the door of the Lyceum the following
challenge:

"*Sophomores:* The Class of '61 hereby challenges the Class of '60 to a game of football, best two in three.

"In behalf of the Class,

> "R. L. CHAMBERLAIN,
> "JAMES W. McLANE,
> "A. SHERIDAN BURT."

Before the day was done upon the door of the Athenæum appeared '60's reply:

> "'Come!
> And like sacrifices in their trim,
> To the fire eyed naiads of smoky war
> All hot and bleeding will we offer you.'

"*To Our Youthful Friends of the Class of '61.*

"We hereby accept your challenge to play the noble and time honored game of football and appoint 2½ o'clock P. M., on Saturday, October 10, 1857, the football grounds as the time and place.

"In behalf of the Class of '60,

> "I. J. POST,
> "E. G. MASSEY,
> "A. C. PALFREY,
> "*Committee.*"

The quotation in the caption of the answer to this challenge, fearful as it is, nevertheless was more gentle than some of its predecessors, to wit:

> "Let them come on, the base born crew,
> Each soiled stained churl, alack.
> What gain they but a splitten skull,
> A sod for their base back!"

As nowadays upper classmen acted as umpires for these under class contests, but the townspeople sometimes constituted themselves a superior judiciary. Thus the struggle of October 19, 1853, was declared a tie by the officials, but

ladies of New Haven who had watched the conflict from
the balconies of the New Haven House, and the steps of
the old State House, reversed the verdict by presenting their
flowers to the Freshmen.

These rushes at last went the way of all good things.
They waxed too rough, and in 1860 were abolished both
by resolution of the faculty and by ordinance of the city of
New Haven. And now football at Yale slept for twelve
years. At length in 1872 a young Rugbeian who had entered Yale in the Class of 1873, David Schley Schaff,
aroused the slumbering football spirit and arranged a game
between '73 and '74 upon the Green. The authorities of
the city, however, had not forgotten their ordinance and
descended upon the game, almost provoking a riot. The
faculty championed the right of the students to use the
Green. Out of the warmth of the altercation was born,
October 31, 1872, the Yale Football Association, with Schaff
as president and captain. Municipal war was averted by
the association leasing a lot on Elm Street. Here beginneth
modern football at Yale, the university's first game being
waged and won with Columbia, under a modification of
Association rules, at Hamilton Park, November 16, 1872.

Traces of play with a football are to be found at Princeton
prior to the Revolution. Fancy pictures as predecessors
of Old Nassau's gridiron stars of to-day, Benjamin Rush,
James Madison, Aaron Burr, and Philip Freneau. Indeed,
the cause of Princeton's great prestige in games afield, notwithstanding its comparatively small numbers, is due to the
fact that upon its campus outdoor sports from the very
beginning vigorously have thrived. The collegians at this
ancient seat of learning, on account of its isolated position
in the country, were deprived of the amusements afforded to
a college in a city and were forced to manufacture their own
means of diversion.

A search of the records discloses this significant minute in the archives of the faculty of the date of November 26, 1787: "It appearing that a play at present much practised by the small boys among the students and by the grammar scholars with balls and sticks, is low and unbecoming gentlemen, and inasmuch as it is attended by alternate heats and colds, and as we are accountable to their parents and liable to be severely blamed by them, therefore the faculty think it incumbent upon them to prohibit the students from playing this game." What was this wicked game? The year of 1787, surprising to state, is not too early for "town ball" or "rounders," the predecessors of baseball. Perhaps it was "tip-cat" and perhaps it was "shinny." Whatever it was it had to go.

During the ensuing twenty years it appears the collegians assuaged their rampant spirits by walking, running, jumping with weights, and other exercises of an individual character. The establishment of organized contests in skill and brawn further was stimulated by the presence in the student body of a preponderance of youths from the South whose racial insistence upon all political subjects of the day called either for acquiescence or a fight. Thus Potter's Woods in the early part of the last century was the ground of many a bloody but fortunately deathless duel. In 1819 the faculty passed a resolution threatening with expulsion every student connected with a duel either as principal or auxiliary.

Forced to further invention the young Princetonians of 1820 adopted the English game of ballown, the batting of a bladder with the fists. The transition to the feet soon ensued and an ingenious set of rules immediately followed, thus placing at Princeton a definitely organized game of football twenty-five years in advance of any other college. The field of play was the entire quadrangle between East and West Colleges, with the walls of these buildings the rival goals. The ball was put in play or "bucked" from an old revolutionary cannon, a relic of the battle of Princeton, that lay midway between.

By 1860 the rules although still traditional called for twenty-five players upon a side, goal-posts twenty-five feet apart, six goals necessary to constitute a game, the ball not to be carried, a ball caught on the fly or first bound to entitle the catcher to a free kick from a clear space of ten feet. No tripping or hacking was allowed, and a ball out of bounds was kicked in at right angles to the side line.

An influential circumstance in the evolution of football from the intracollegiate to the intercollegiate stage was the juxtaposition of Princeton and Rutgers, twenty-five miles apart. Naturally the game had developed at each college along similar lines, and the rules almost were identical. Another highly stimulating element in the birth of intercollegiate football was the spirit of intense rivalry between the two student bodies for the possession of a revolutionary cannon which was captured and recaptured by one college from the other and carried back and forth between Princeton and New Brunswick in a series of sorties which equalled in vigor if not in violence the original fight for this same cannon between General Howe and George Washington. Years afterward Princeton terminated the struggle by craftily sinking the gun up to its trunnions in several hundred pounds of cement. On May 25, 1866, Princeton also had defeated Rutgers 40 to 2 in their first contest in baseball. In the early fall of 1869, therefore, student sentiment at New Brunswick was rife for a further tilt with Princeton and football was selected as the medium of conclusions.

Rutgers was fortunate at this time in having a football leader by the name of "Bill" Leggett, '72. Princeton likewise had a "Bill" for leader, "Bill" Gummere, '70. These men are still leaders, but few people nowadays dare address them as "Bill," for the former is the Reverend William J. Leggett, high in the councils of the Reformed Church, and the other is the Hon. William S. Gummere, Chief Justice of the State of New Jersey.

At Rutgers a challenge was framed in the punctilious language of the day inviting the men of Nassau Hall—for the name Princeton had not become in those days an established university title—to play a series of three games. The receipt of this document aroused great enthusiasm at Princeton. Gummere immediately was selected as captain and empowered to settle the preliminaries. It was agreed that the first game should be played at New Brunswick, November 6, the second at Princeton, November 13, and the third at New Brunswick, November 20; the game at Princeton to be played under Princeton rules allowing a free kick from a catch on fly or first bound, the games at New Brunswick to be played according to the Rutgers code, which did not recognize the free kick or fair catch. With great expectancy these two institutions now awaited the coming of these games.

CHAPTER IV

THE FIRST INTERCOLLEGIATE GAME

In these days of prodigious publicity for the great battles of the gridiron it is startling to realize that up to the present time no account, either by contemporary or historian, has been published of this initial struggle, which by its very priority is entitled to historical precedence over all other celebrated football games. The heroes of the lime-line field to-day may see their faces and read of their exploits in the public prints within one hour after their achievement. The football heroes of 1869 have grown gray with the lapse of years before their deeds have obtained a place in the public chronicles of the game.

Football history, like all other history, must suffer from the uncertainty which invariably cloaks an original occurrence. Thus of this first game it is impossible to-day to compose a complete list of the players participating or to present all of the interesting incidents which were features of this quaint contest. Much, however, has escaped oblivion in the lack of records and the lapse of memory that is worthy of preservation as a most important part in the history of America's major intercollegiate sport. The facts here presented of this first intercollegiate football game have been obtained from the surviving players; for it was the first intercollegiate football game, not only in America, but in the world. In this connection it is interesting to glance at the chronology of the historic "first games."

44

Princeton, 4; Rugters, 6; New Brunswick, Nov. 6, 1869.
Columbia, 3; Rutgers, 6; New Brunswick, Nov. 12, 1870.
Oxford, 1; Cambridge, 0; Oxford, Feb. 10, 1872.
Yale, 3; Columbia, 0; New Haven, Nov. 16, 1872.
Harvard, 3; McGill, 0; Cambridge, May 14, 1874.
Pennsylvania, 0; Princeton, 6; Germantown, Nov. 11, 1876.
Cornell, 10; Union, 24; Ithaca, Nov. 12, 1887.

Those who are familiar with the history of college baseball will be surprised, not at the earliness of the date of this
game, but at its lateness, for the diamond preceded the
gridiron by a full decade, the first intercollegiate baseball
game being the contest between Amherst and Williams
July 1, 1859.   Baseball, however, had in its infancy the stim-
ulus of the sound and uniform set of rules adopted at Cooper
Institute, in New York, March 9, 1859, in the convention at
which came into existence the National Association of Baseball Players.   Football lacked such a guiding influence,
and therefore developed slowly through different rules at
the several colleges of the East.

Notwithstanding the primitiveness of the occasion, the
jerky little "dummy" engine that steamed out of Princeton
on that memorable morning of November 6, 1869, was
crowded to aisles and platforms with a freight of eager
students.   In 1869 and for many years later an unaffected,
old-fashioned hospitality was observed among the colleges
toward one another to a degree that is almost unbelievable
in the rude lack of amenities that characterizes the present
period.   A baseball game was far from the formal fixture it
is to-day.   It was a social event without superior in the life of
a college.   Rutgers accordingly in a mass met their visitors at
the station and devoted the day exclusively to their hearty
entertainment.

The game was called in the afternoon at three o'clock, the

field being laid out on the commons between College Avenue and Sicard Street. The events immediately preceding the game were as primitive as the game itself. The spectators who had arrived early appropriated seats upon the top board of a fence which partly surrounded the field, while the others found places upon the ground. There was no admission fee, no waving of flags. The famous orange and black still was in the forming. But there were college songs, and, strange to say, a college cheer, Princeton's booming rocket call, hissing and bursting just as it does to-day. The players arrived a few minutes before three, and simply laying aside their hats, coats, and vests, stood accoutred for the game, the only touch of costume being red turbans, which were worn by the Rutgers men, a fashion long copied thereafter by other college teams. The Princeton 25 appeared to be much larger and heavier than their opponents. While the spectators were giving the players some preliminary advice the officials and captains were adjusting an objection to the very small size of the ball provided. With these preliminaries out of the way, time was called.

Of the players who lined up only the following can now be recalled:

PRINCETON	RUTGERS
W. S. Gummere, '70.	D. D. Williamson, '70.
W. H. Buck, '70.	E. D. De La Mater, '71.
L. H. Nissley, '70.	S. G. Gano, '71.
H. Oliphant, '70.	W. J. Hill, '71.
C. J. Parker, '70.	W. S. Lasher, '71.
H. D. Boughner, '71.	G. E. Pace, '71.
G. S. Billmeyer, '71.	C. L. Pruyn, '71.
C. W. Darst, '71.	J. H. Wyckoff, '71.
W. C. Chambers, '71.	W. J. Leggett, '72.
W. W. Flagler, '71.	T. W. Clemens, '72.

PRINCETON	RUTGERS
C. M. Field, '71.	E. D. Gillmore, '72.
C. S. Barrett, '71.	J. W. Herbert, '72.
F. C. Burt, '71.	G. H. Large, '72.
J. E. Michael, '71.	G. H. Stevens, '72.
A. Van Rensselaer, '71.	J. A. Van Neste, '72.
T. S. Young, '71.	F. E. Allen, '73.
David Mixsell, '71.	M. M. Ball, '73.
C. S. Lane, '72.	G. R. Dixon, '73.
W. P. Lane, '72.	D. T. Hawxhurst, '73.
J. W. Hageman, '72.	P. V. Huysoon, '73.
J. G. Weir, '71.	A. I. Martine, '73.
	C. Rockefeller, '73.
	J. O. Van Fleet, '73.
	G. S. Willits, '73.
	C. S. Wright, '73.
	W. H. McKee, '73.

The tactical organization of this large number of players was the same on both sides. Two men were selected by each team to play immediately in front of the opponents' goal and were known as "captains of the enemy's goal." These positions for Princeton were filled by H. D. Boughner and G. S. Billmeyer and for Rutgers by G. R. Dixon and S. G. Gano. The remainder of each team was divided into two sections. The players of one section were assigned to certain tracts of the field, which they were to cover and not to leave. These players were known as "fielders." The other section was detailed to follow the ball up and down the field. These latter players were called "bulldogs." They are easily recognizable in the evolution of the game as the forerunners of the modern rush line.

The toss of the coins for advantage gave Princeton the ball and Rutgers the wind. Amid a hush of expectancy among the spectators Princeton "bucked" or kicked the ball, precisely as it is done to-day, from a tee of earth, but the kick was bad and the ball glanced to one side. The light, agile Rutgers men pounced upon it like hounds, and, by driving it by short kicks, or "dribbles," the other players surrounding the ball and not permitting a Princeton man to get near it, quickly and craftily forced it down to Old Nassau's goal, where Dixon and Gano, Rutgers's captains of the enemy's goal, were waiting, and these two latter sent the ball between the posts amid great applause from the fence-top and vicinity.

The first goal had been scored in five minutes of play. During the slight intermission Captain Gummere instructed Michael, a young giant of the Princeton twenty-five, to break up Rutgers's massing around the ball. Sides were changed and Rutgers "bucked." In this period the game was more fiercely contested. Time and time again Michael, or "Big Mike," as he was known, charged into Rutgers's primitive mass play and scattered the players like a burst bundle of sticks. On one of these plays Princeton obtained the ball and by a long, accurate kick scored the second goal.

The third goal, or "game," as it was then called, went to Rutgers. Madison Ball, who had been nonplussing the Princeton men throughout the game by running in the same direction with the ball and upon overtaking it stepping over and kicking the ball behind him, on one of these plays, by a lucky kick, delivered the ball to Dixon, who was standing directly in front of Princeton's goal, and in an instant the ball was through and Rutgers once more was in the lead.

The fourth goal was kicked by Princeton, "Big Mike" again bursting up a mass out of which Gummere gained possession of the ball, and with Princeton massed about him easily dribbled the ball down and through the Rutgers goal-posts, making the score once more a tie.

The fifth goal was kicked by Gano for Rutgers. The sixth goal also went to Rutgers, but the feature of this period of play in the memory of the players after the lapse of forty years is awarded to "Big Mike" and Large. Some one by a random kick had driven the ball to one side, where it rolled against the fence and stopped. Large, of Rutgers, led the pursuit for the ball, closely followed by Michael. Just as to-day a play near the side lines sends an unusual thrill among the spectators, so in this ancient game the crowd of students near the ball started to rise to their feet, but at this instant Large and Michael reached the ball and, unable to check their momentum, in a tremendous impact struck the fence, which gave way with a crash and over went its load of yelling students to the ground.

Every college probably has the humorous tradition of some player who, becoming confused in the excitement of play, has scored against his own team. This tradition at Rutgers almost dated from this first game, for one of her players in the sixth period started to kick the ball between his own goal-posts. The kick was blocked, but Princeton took advantage of the opportunity and soon made the goal. This turn of the game apparently disorganized Rutgers, for Princeton also scored the next goal after a few minutes of play, thus bringing the total up to four all.

As custom, both at Princeton and Rutgers, made a total score of six goals the winning mark, both spectators and players were now aroused to great excitement as the close of the match drew near. At this stage Rutgers resorted to that use of craft which has never failed in the history of forty years to turn the tide of every close battle. Captain Leggett, of Rutgers, had noticed that Princeton obtained a great advantage from the taller stature of their men, which enabled them to reach above the others and bat the ball in the air in some advantageous direction. This was particularly true of Princeton's leader, Captain Gummere. On the resumption of play Rutgers was ordered to keep the ball close to the ground. Following this stratagem, and stimulated by the encouraging shouts of their supporters, the Rutgers men determinedly kicked the ninth and tenth goals, thus winning the match by six goals to four and with it the historic distinction of a victory in the first game of intercollegiate football played in the world.

The memorable day closed with a supper, in which both teams participated together, interspersing songs and speeches with the deliciously roasted game birds from the Jersey marshes and meadows.

The second game of the series was played at Princeton the following Saturday, November 13, 1869, the arena being a field across the street from the famous Slidell mansion, later the home of Grover Cleveland. This second contest, however, was played according to Princeton's custom of free kicks from catch on fly or bound. As Princeton had evolved a high form of strategy in kicking the ball from one to another of their side at close distances, thus creating a series of fair catches and free kicks, Rutgers was wholly outclassed and defeated by eight goals to none.

The third game, owing to the objection of the faculties at Princeton and Rutgers on account of the great and distracting interest aroused, was never played.

CHAPTER V

FOOTBALL IN THE 'SEVENTIES

THE pleasant aftermath which followed the Princeton-Rutgers games of 1869 led to the playing of another series in 1870 and also brought forth a new intercollegiate competitor in Columbia. The rules, however, still remained traditionary at each college and of course were without uniformity. The data of the games waged in this primitive period are:

Princeton, 6; Rutgers, 0; at Princeton, Nov. 10, 1870.
Columbia, 1; Rutgers, 6; at New Brunswick, Nov. 12, 1870.
Princeton, 6; Rutgers, 2; at Princeton, Nov. 23, 1870.

The following year, 1871, no intercollegiate games were played, but evolution, notwithstanding, was strongly in progress. At Princeton, October 15, 1871, a college mass meeting was held, at which formally came into being the Princeton Football Association. Since this is the pioneer organization of its kind in the intercollegiate world the official personnel selected on that occasion is worthy of record: Captain, Arthur Johnson, '72; Committee, Arthur Johnson, '72; D. T. Marvel, '73; T. G. Ricketts, '74; H. Moffat, '75. Another great advance made by this mass meeting was the transference of the ancient rules of play at Princeton from tradition to an authoritative, written code. This code was as follows:

1. The grounds shall be 500 feet in length by 300 feet in breadth.
2. The goal-posts shall be 25 feet apart.

3. The number for match games shall be 25 to the side.

4. To a game 4 of 7 goals are necessary.

5. The winner of the toss shall have the choice of goals.

6. No player shall throw or carry the ball.

7. Any player catching the ball after it has been kicked or knocked and before it touches the ground shall be entitled to a free kick.

8. Any ball passing the boundary lines shall be kicked or knocked in with full force. If passing the side limits, by the player first touching the ball; if passing the goal limits, by a player of the side defending the goal.

9. No holding shall be allowed except when a player has the ball in his possession not caught on the fly.

10. No tripping shall be allowed, nor shall any player use his hands to push an adversary.

The year of 1872 brought a great outburst of football activity. In England, Cambridge and Oxford began a preliminary correspondence which quickly terminated in the arrangement of an inter-university game, which was played at Oxford, February 10, 1872, Cambridge being defeated by a goal from a try, thus establishing this classic series of contests. Resurgat, it will be remembered, was the prayer of the epitaph of Football Fightum when that personage was buried ceremoniously at Harvard in 1860. The early spring of 1872 gave indications that the happy event was soon to occur. Scarcely had the snow melted from the Yard at Cambridge when an agitation arose among the Sophomores and Freshmen for a class contest at football, not such an encounter as those which in bygone days harrowed the sod of the Delta and furrowed the feelings of the faculty, but an orderly game under a set of rational rules. The latter soon were formulated by adopting a modification of the Association code. Thus, April 21, 1872, Football

Fightum arose and afforded a day of rare sport on Boston
Common between the classes of 1874 and 1875, in which the
former achieved the honors of the day. Following this contest a wave of popularity swept over Harvard. The *Advocate* genially expressed the sentiment of the university by
saying:

"We are glad to see that football is being revived once
more. It is hoped that all who feel interested in it will
take an active part and make football what it should be,
one of the most popular of college games." This appeal
evoked a warm response, as the game thrived amazingly
throughout the remainder of the spring and again raged in
the ensuing autumn. With the coming of winter the football genius of the university turned to the subject of organization and thus, December 6, 1872, the Harvard Football
Club was born, the original officers being: President,
Robert Grant, '73; Secretary, Augustus Hemenway, '75;
Treasurer, William C. Sanger, '74; and Captain, Henry
R. Grant, '74; conjuring names, indeed.

At this meeting a playing code was drafted which followed the Association rules excepting three important variations. Rule 1 of the Harvard code provided for not less
than ten nor more than fifteen players upon a side. Rule
8 permitted "any player to catch or pick up the ball but
not to run with it unless pursued by an opponent and then
only so long as pursued." Rule 9 prohibited "any player
from passing or throwing the ball unless pursued by an
opponent." Many games were played under these rules
at Harvard, but, strange to say, the idea of an intercollegiate
contest was not broached, although intercollegiate relationships in baseball at that time were highly developed and the
rivalry was keen.

It was also in this memorable year of 1872 that football
reappeared at Yale, where, as at Harvard, it had slept under
the faculty's quietus since 1860. The cause of this resur-

rection was the presence in the Class of 1873 of a young
Rugbeian by the name of David Schley Schaff. This
genius zealously advocated the re-establishment of football
and spiritedly promoted a class game between 1873 and
1874. This latter contest eventually took place upon New
Haven's Green, but scarcely had the ball been kicked off
when the city's municipal authorities recalled their ordinance
of 1860 prohibiting the game and the police immediately
descended upon the collegians. The attempt to stop the
game almost resulted in a riot. Yale's faculty championed
the ancient prerogative of the collegians to play upon the
the Green and questioned the legality of the city's ordinance.
Debate and discussion raged for several days, and only terminated when the players leased a lot on Elm Street and
abandoned all further claim to the use of the Green. Upon
this lot a game was played in October between the classes
of 1874 and 1875—Sheffield. The effect upon the university of an orderly game was profound. The editor of
"Memorabilia Yalensia," in the *Yale Literary Magazine*,
with the unconscious inspiration of prophecy said of this
contest: "The time is not far distant when the memorabilist
shall be compelled to devote as much space to football as
he now reserves for the two kindred sports." Eight days
later, or, to be precise, as such a notable event deserves, October 31, 1872, a great mass meeting was held at Yale, in
which was organized the Yale Football Association with the
following staff of officers: President, David. S. Schaff, '73;
Secretary, Henry D. Bristol, '74; Captain, David S. Schaff,
'73. Equally important, this meeting also formulated the
following set of rules to govern football at Yale:

1. The grounds shall be 400 feet long by 250 feet broad.
2. The goal-posts shall be 8 paces apart.
3. The number of players in match games shall be 20 to a
side.

4. To a game 5 of 9 goals are necessary. To secure a goal the ball must pass between the posts.

5. No player shall pick up, throw, or carry the ball on any part of the field. Any violation of this regulation shall constitute a foul and the player so offending shall throw the ball perpendicularly into the air from the place where the foul occurred and the ball shall not be in play until it touches the ground.

6. When the ball is caught in the air an adversary may strike it from the hands of the player so catching it.

7. When the ball passes the limits, the person touching it first shall throw it from a spot 6 paces from, and at right angles to, the boundary-line at the place where it went over, and the ball shall not be in play until it has touched the ground. Further, the player throwing the ball shall not play upon it until it has been played upon. When thrown, the players shall be between the ball and their goal.

8. When the ball passes the limits within 6 paces from the goal-posts it shall be carried out by the player first touching it 15 paces in front of the boundary-line and thrown by him into the air under the same conditions as a foul ball (Rule 5).

9. No tripping shall be allowed, nor shall any player use his hands to push or hold an adversary.

10. The winner of the toss shall have first kick-off and choice of goals. The ball shall be placed fifteen paces from the centre of the field toward the starter's goal. In canting the ball must be kicked and not "babied." No player on the canting side shall be in advance of a line passing through the ball and parallel to the base-line, nor shall any player on the opposite side come within 10 paces of the line.

11. No player shall wear projecting nails, iron plates, or gutta-percha on the soles of his shoes.

12. There shall be two judges for each goal, and a referee to whom all disputes shall be referred.

Thus the autumn of 1872 presented football organized and codified at Harvard, Princeton, and Yale. An examination of these three codes discloses that many features at each institution were original, but that Princeton and Yale followed generally the Association rules, while Harvard endeavored to effect a combination of features from the Rugby as well as the Association games. It was now only a step to intercollegiate strife. Princeton challenged Columbia, Rutgers, and Yale. Columbia declined, Rutgers accepted, and while Princeton and Yale were conferring in an attempt to harmonize their respective codes as a basis for a game the faculties at both institutions arose in high indignation at the proposition to take fifteen men away from their studies for an afternoon and peremptorily forbade the contest to take place. To-day when Princeton meets Yale thousands leave their books, business halts, legislatures lack a quorum, courts adjourn, and faculties occupy the front seats. Although a contest between Princeton and Yale was forbidden, peace was made with the powers to such an extent that Princeton was permitted to play Rutgers and Yale was allowed to play Columbia. As this latter game marks the Blue's first appearance in intercollegiate football it presents a contest so historic that it is entitled to reproduction as fully as records and recollections will permit.

COLUMBIA vs. YALE

New Haven, November 16, 1872

COLUMBIA	YALE
G. M. Speir, '73.	C. S. Hemingway, '73.
C. W. R. Moore, '73.	W. F. McCook, '73.
D. Thompson, '73.	E. S. Miller, '73.
P. H. McMahon, '73.	J. P. Peters, '73.
B. M. Whitlock, '73.	J. P. Platt, '73.
A. B. Simons, '73.	H. A. Strong, '73.
B. J. Aymar, '73.	R. D. A. Parrot, '74.

COLUMBIA	YALE
H. M. Webb, '73.	H. D. Bristol, '74.
W. Fales, '73.	R. W. Kelley, '74.
E. I. Frost, '74.	P. A. Porter, '74.
R. C. Cornell, '74.	J. L. Scudder, '74.
E. S. Rapallo, '74.	C. H. Avery, '75.
G. C. Koble, '74.	A. Hotchkiss, '75.
F. Lacey, '74.	J. A. R. Dunning, '74.
T. C. Van Buren, '75.	T. T. Sherman, '74.
T. C. Bach, '75.	H. R. Elliott, '71.
O. D. Smith, '75.	S. L. Boyce, '73.
H. K. Blake, '75.	L. W. Irwin, '73.
C. King, '75.	W. S. Halsted, '74.
F. S. Williams, '75.	H. A. Oaks, '75.
H. R. Marshall, '73.	H. Scudder, '72.

Referees, the Captains: H. R. Marshall, '73, Columbia; H. R. Elliott, '71, Yale. Judges: F. S. Weeks, '73; S. C. Bushnell, '74, Yale. Score: Columbia 0, Yale 3.

The game was played at Hamilton Park. The throng of collegians who began to assemble about half-past two o'clock found a playing space of 400 by 200 feet enclosed with a rope. In a few minutes both teams appeared. It was announced that D. S. Schaff, Yale's captain, would be unable to play because of an injury. The teams were composed of fifteen players upon each side.

The captains call the players together and agree that the match shall be determined by the side first winning five goals out of nine. Thereupon the coin is tossed and H. R. Elliott, the acting Yale captain, sets an illustrious precedent for Yale to follow in years to come by winning the toss. He chooses the south goal. The teams then deploy upon the field. It is at once noticed that each

team presents an entirely different tactical arrangement.
Columbia details four men to guard their goal and masses
the rest of the players in the middle of the field.   Yale stations two men in goal, known as "goal-tends."   Five paces
from them four more are stationed to support the goal-
tends, and some distance farther five other players are
arranged in the shape of a crescent as a further protection
to the goal.   Far down in Columbia's goal also stand two
Yale men to check Columbia's goal-tends when the ball
comes within striking distance.   These two men Yale calls
"peanutters."   The rest of her players, called "rushers,"
are scattered over the field.   Platt for Yale makes a long
kick-off, or "cant."   The rushers immediately follow up
the ball, but Columbia's mass of players surround and
force it close to Yale's goal.   A Yale goal-tend gets it and
kicks it to the side of one of the five supporters, who in the
same way passes it to a fielder and in an instant it is in Columbia's goal, thereby demonstrating the superiority of the
Yale system of team play.   The fielder delivers it to the
"rushers," who drive it down to the "peanutters."   Here
Sherman for Yale lifts the ball straight as a bullet over the
heads of the Columbia men squarely between the goal-posts.
The details of play that ensued throughout the afternoon
have not been recorded, but fancy pictures the sharp cants,
the reckless and random dashes for the ball, the personal
collisions of the players, the long sailing kicks, and the press
of Yale men before Columbia's goal as one and two more
goals are forced through. The chroniclers in the *Yale
Courant* and the *Record* tell us that Columbia's men were
stronger and more athletic, but that Yale's team played
with better craft and precision. Consequently Yale won. At
the close of the game the crowd enthusiastically cheered
both teams and the officials and left the field strong in their
advocacy of football as an additional college sport.   Two

hours later both teams sat down together to a savory supper at Lockwood's.

The spring of 1873 found football at Harvard sharing equally in interest with intra-university baseball. A series of class and club games had been organized under Harvard's peculiar code. These contests were waged upon Boston Common. The keenness of the contests and the enjoyment of the spectators are perhaps best indicated by the fact that the citizens of Boston who resided around the Common presented a petition to the municipal authorities of Boston calling upon them to suppress the "intolerable noises" and "to put down the games." Strange to say, the city fathers of Boston gravely answered this petition by passing a ponderous ordinance that closed the Common to Harvard. Thereupon the collegians transferred their arena to famous old Jarvis Field at Cambridge, where it was to remain for many a long and happy year.

With the arrival of autumn a movement was started at Princeton to form an intercollegiate football league and adopt a uniform code of rules. Accordingly invitations were sent to Columbia, Harvard, Rutgers, and Yale to meet for that purpose at the Fifth Avenue Hotel in New York, October 19, 1873. All of the colleges accepted except Harvard, which courteously answered that its game was so at variance with that played at the other institutions that no advantage could come from their attendance. This convention was held upon the day appointed and the following delegates were present: Princeton, T. G. Ricketts, '74, I. H. Lionberger, '75; Rutgers, Howard N. Fuller, '74, John W. Searing, '74; Yale, William S. Halsted, '74, Peter A. Porter, '74. Columbia had chosen representatives, but the gentlemen did not appear. The convention after a thorough discussion decided not to form a league, but resolved to draft a common code of rules, leaving the scheduling of games thereunder to the independent action of each college represented. This code, consisting of twelve rules, rather a compact body of football law in comparison with the voluminous rule books of modern times, was adopted as follows:

1. The ground shall be 400 feet long by 250 feet broad.

2. The distance between the posts of each goal shall be 25 feet.

3. The number for match games shall be 20 to a side.

4. To win a game 6 goals are necessary, but that side shall be considered the victors which, when the game is called, shall have scored the greatest number of goals. provided that number be 2 or more. To secure a goal the ball must pass between the posts.

5. No player shall throw or carry the ball. Any violation of this regulation shall constitute a foul, and the player so offending shall throw the ball perpendicularly into the air to a height of at least 12 feet and the ball shall not be in play until it has touched the ground.

6. When a ball passes out of bounds it is a foul, and the player causing it shall advance at right angles to the boundary-line, 15 paces from the point where the ball went, and shall proceed as in rule V.

7. No tripping shall be allowed, nor shall any player use his hands to hold or push an adversary.

8. The winners of the toss shall have the choice of first goal, and the sides shall change goals after every successive inning. In starting the ball it shall be fairly kicked, not "babied," from a point 150 feet in front of the starter's goal.

9. Until the ball is kicked no player on either side shall be in advance of a line parallel to the line of his goal and distant from it 150 feet.

10. There shall be two judges, one from each of the con-

testing colleges, and one referee; all to be chosen by the captains.

11. No player shall wear spikes or iron plates upon his shoes.

12. In all match games a No. 6 ball shall be used, furnished by the challenging side and to become the property of the victors.

A comparison of these rules with the former codes indicates a substantial advance in the scientific arrangement of the game. Only three games, however, were played under these rules in 1873. Their data are:

Yale, 3; Columbia, 1; at New Haven, Oct. 25, 1873.
Princeton, 3; Yale, 0; at New Haven, Nov. 15, 1873.
Rutgers, 5; Columbia, 4; at New Brunswick, Nov. 15, 1873.

The game in this list which most impressively attracts the eye is Princeton vs. Yale, the first of America's great football classics.*

But Yale waged another game in this year which also was destined to exercise a profound influence in the development of the intercollegiate game in after years. This was a game with Eton. The latter was a team composed of old Etonians under the captaincy of G. C. Allen, which visited New Haven, November 17, 1873. A special set of rules was devised for the contest, which included portions of Yale's code and portions of the Eton code. Among the latter was a provision that eleven men should constitute a side, that having been the established number at Eton in both the Wall and Field Games from earliest times. An interesting game resulted, which Yale won, two goals to none, but the historical importance of this contest lies in the fact that to

* See Part II, Princeton vs. Yale.

it definitely may be traced the origin seven years later of the famous feature of American football, the eleven.

Although the rules of 1873 had been auspiciously launched the experience of a single season doomed them to failure. No intercollegiate games, therefore, were played thereunder in 1874, but another event occurred in this year to make it one of the most memorable in the annals of American football. The captain of McGill University's team at Montreal in the spring of 1874 was David Rodger. This energetic young Canadian conceived the idea of invading the United States with his team and accordingly sent a courteous challenge to Harvard, inviting the football men thereof to play McGill two games, the first at Cambridge in the following May under the All-Canada code, a modification of Rugby, and the second at Montreal in the fall under the Harvard rules. The receipt of this challenge aroused great enthusiasm at Harvard, but it was ascertained that the faculty would not permit the players to leave Cambridge, during term time. It was suggested to McGill that the two games proposed should be played at Cambridge, and the hope was expressed that in some way an opportunity to return the games might be obtained thereafter. This suggestion Captain Rodger promptly accepted, and both sides commenced preparations for the struggle. The *McGill Gazette* for May, 1874, contains an account of the spirited practice conducted by McGill with the "Banks" of Montreal, in preparation for Harvard, and as a basis upon which to select the players for the team. At Cambridge Henry R. Grant, '74, Harvard's original 'varsity captain, likewise was drilling his men nightly upon Jarvis Field. The *Advocate* published in full the Canadian rules, but said, "These rules apparently are wholly unscientific and unsuited to colleges." Nevertheless interest in the contest grew day by day. The *Magenta*, an obsolete publication at Harvard, thus heralds the coming of McGill: "The McGill University Football Club will meet the Harvard Club on Jarvis Field, Wednesday and Thursday, May 14th and 15th, instant. The game probably will be called at three o'clock. Admittance 50 cents. The proceeds will be devoted to the entertainment of our visitors from Montreal."

Captain Rodger and his players arrived the evening before the game. In the preliminaries it was agreed that the first game should be played under Harvard's rules and that the second, upon the following day, should be played according to the All-Canada code. It is unfortunate for the present generation that the college journalists of that time did not appreciate the importance of these international matches. An examination of the periodicals at Cambridge and Montreal reveals little indeed to reward the antiquary, but the recollections of surviving players have made it possible partially to reconstruct these two famous games. The first contest was played under Harvard's rules. The game was called at four o'clock on Jarvis Field, in the presence of a large throng of collegians, May 14, 1874. Captain Grant, of Harvard, won the toss and chose the north goal, which was backed by a slight wind. The "warnings" were kicked off promptly and Harvard began to work the ball toward McGill's goal. In five minutes Harvard scored. McGill then kicked off, and in this interval improved greatly in its use of the Harvard rules, but their opponents eventually began to increase in strength, and the Canadians once more were beaten into their goal, where Harvard scored. The third clash brought out the best playing of the day, the interval lasting twelve minutes and terminating with a third goal by Harvard. The game then was called.

The following day the second game was played, but according to the All-Canada code, thus presenting the first intercollegiate game of Rugby football in the United States. This historic struggle, so far as it now may be constructed, was played as follows:

HARVARD vs. McGILL
Cambridge, May 15, 1874.

HARVARD		McGILL
H. C. Leeds, '77.	Forward	O'H. Baynes, Law.
F. E. Randall, '74.	"	G. E. Jenkins, Law.
F. Lyman, '74.	"	R. W. Huntington, Law.
H. L. Morse, '74.	"	D. E. Bowie, Law.
W. C. Sanger, '74.	"	H. Joseph, Arts.
A. L. Goodrich, '74.	"	R. P. Pattee, Med.
A. L. Rives, '74.	"	R. A. MacDonald, Med.
A. T. Cabot, '72.	"	E. G. Henderson, Med.
A. B. Ellis, '75.	"	C. R. Jones, Med.
M. L. Cate, '77.	"	P. J. Goodhue, Med.
F. H. Lombard, '74.	Half-back	H. W. Thomas, Arts.
H. R. Grant, '74.	" "	St. G. Boswell, Science.
W. A. Whiting, '77.	Back	David Roger, Science.
R. Gray, '75.	"	J. B. Abbott, Law.
W. R. Tyler, '74.	"	C. J. Fleet, Law.

Judges: H. G. Hubbard, '73, Harvard; Mr. Henshaw, McGill. Score: Harvard 0, McGill 0.

McGill wins the toss and selects the upper goal. The Canadians also win the second toss and take the ball. Owing to this being spherical instead of the usual Rugby oval, the latter not being obtainable in Boston, the visitors experience much difficulty in accustoming themselves to it. The ball is kicked off. Harvard gets it and rushes pell-mell up the field, but the McGill men tackle the runner and bring him quickly to earth. A scrummage forms. Harvard, being unacquainted with the rules, is thrown upon the defensive, the Canadians getting the ball each time out of scrummage, but Harvard's players tackle boldly and well, thus holding the Canadians to little gains. The play is very exciting to the spectators, who frequently rise and cheer the good plays of the day. Harvard's embarrassment wears away, and closely imitating the tactics of McGill, Harvard soon is taking the offensive. The tide of battle surges up and down the field, but the defence on both sides is stubborn, and so the game comes to an end without a score. The spectators cheer both teams and the officials, and the first intercollegiate game under Rugby rules is over.

This game, crude as it was, still was sufficient to demonstrate to all the surpassing superiority of the Rugby rules. In fact the merits of the Canadian's play was the chief topic of discussion at Harvard for many a day. The depth of the impression may be realized from a comment which appeared at that time in the *Advocate*, which reviewed the McGill game: "Football will be a popular game here in the future. The Rugby game is in much better favor than the somewhat sleepy game now played by our men." During the year the Rugby rules thoroughly were tried, and in the fall of 1875 Harvard abandoned its old game and plunged wholly into the Rugby counterpart. So enthusiastic were the players that they eagerly discussed the subject of a game with Yale. Finally this suggestion assumed a definite shape, and a challenge was forwarded to New Haven, inviting the Blue to meet the Crimson under the Rugby Union Rules. Yale promptly accepted the challenge, but demanded certain modifications in that code. As a result conferrees from the two universities met at Springfield, October 16, 1875, and fixed November 13, 1875, as the date of the game and New Haven as the place. The conferrees then proceeded to draft a special set of rules for this game, based upon the Rugby code. From the concessions granted to Yale by Harvard in making these modifications the rules when finally framed were designated as the "Concessionary Rules."

This game was played as scheduled and created great interest at New Haven, Harvard winning by four goals to none.*

The year of 1876, memorable as the centennial of American independence, also marks for the collegian the formal establishment of the present game of intercollegiate football. The "Concessionary Rules" devised by Harvard and Yale in the preceding year appear grotesque now, but they were profoundly impressive to the collegians of that period. Among those who witnessed that original Harvard-Yale game were two Princeton players, W. Earle Dodge, '79, and Jotham Potter, '77. These men perceived beneath the curiosities of the "Concessionary Rules" the meritorious features of the Rugby Union code, upon which the former were founded, and decided that the latter afforded the only set of rules upon which it would be possible for the colleges to unite. It was a difficult labor for these two pioneers to break down the prejudice and sentiment at Princeton in favor of the old rules of 1873, under which Princeton regularly had been victorious. "We stand to lose much and gain little by a change," said the *Nassau Literary Magazine*, ·voicing the college opinion. Nevertheless, the agitation vigorously was maintained until it culminated in a turbulent mass meeting November 2, 1876, at which Princeton voted by a close majority to adopt the Rugby game and to issue an invitation to Columbia, Harvard, and Yale to meet in convention at Springfield for the purpose of forming an intercollegiate association and adopting a uniform modification of the Rugby Union code. Messrs. Dodge and Potter were selected to execute the will of this meeting. These gentlemen immediately sent out the following invitation to the institutions named:

* See Part II, Harvard *vs.* Yale.

*" To the Football Associations of Harvard, Yale, and Co-
lumbia:*

"The Football Association of Princeton College hereby
issues a call, requesting the appointment of delegates to meet
at the Massasoit House, Springfield, Massachusetts, at 3.00
P. M., upon Thursday, the twenty-third of November, for the
purpose of adopting a uniform system of rules, and con-
sidering the advisability of forming an Intercollegiate Football Association. Such Association, if deemed advisable,
to consist of the colleges above named and any others which
they may elect to admit.

"It is generally understood that all the colleges have
adopted the Rugby Union Rules, but that each is playing
them with some slight variations. The specific object of
this call is to establish a system of rules by means of which
the colleges shall be enabled to compete with one another at
football upon a uniform and satisfactory basis. An early
response to this letter of call is especially requested.

"Respectfully,

"JOTHAM POTTER,
"W. EARLE DODGE,
"Delegates.

"PRINCETON, N. J., *Nov.* 7, 1876."

Favorable replies were received from the colleges and in
the meantime attention turned to three great games. The
first of these was the contest between Pennsylvania and
Princeton at Germantown, November 11, 1876. For several years a simple game along Association lines had been
played at Philadelphia by the Red and Blue as an unorganized campus sport. The game with Princeton, however, was the university's first struggle with a rival. It was
played under the rules of 1873 and was won by Princeton,
six goals to none. It was in this game that football costumes
first were worn, the Pennsylvanians appearing in cricket suits

of white flannel and the Princetonians exhibiting an elaborate costume consisting of a black shirt with orange trimming around the neck and wrists and with a large orange P upon the chest.   Black knee pants, black stockings, and baseball shoes completed this primitive but handsome costume.

The Harvard-Yale game was played at New Haven under full Rugby rules, excepting a modification obtained by Yale that the number of players should be limited to eleven upon each side and that touchdowns should not count in the scoring, but that the result should be determined by goals alone.   An incidental feature of interest in this contest was the appearance of a young Yale Freshman at half-back by the name of Walter Camp, '80.   The tactical formation of these eleven men is important, as it was a forerunner of the succeeding evolutions that determined a distinctively American game.   Six of the players formed a line of forwards, or rushers.   Behind them were stationed two players known as half-backs, whose duties resembled those of the modern quarter-back, and behind the half-backs stood three other players designated as backs.   The ball was put in play at the beginning of the game by a kick which might be a punt, place kick, or drop kick.   Thereafter the ball was put in play by a "scrummage," as in English Rugby. This was done by putting the ball on the ground between the two rush lines, no player thereof being permitted to handle the ball.   Each line endeavored to work the ball back to the half-backs with the feet.   The half-back, as soon as he obtained the ball, either ran forward with it or passed it to one of his backs.   In such a game where chance governed the possession of the ball in every scrummage there were no signals, and as there was no advantage in retaining the ball, when the runner was checked the ball invariably was passed to another player for a further advance if possible.   This game was won by Yale, to the great surprise of Harvard, who had previously defeated the leading Rugby teams of Canada. The *Yale Courant* in a column of exultation thus closed its impressions of the Rugby game: "The gay suits of the players, the wrestling, tumbling, and running, the equestrian feat of the Harvard captain and the leap over his shoulders by a hard-pressed Yale man lent a pleasing variety to the scene suggestive of a Roman circus or hippodrome." An addition to the humor of the occasion also is to be found in one of Harvard's periodicals which gravely informs us that Yale's adherents prevented Harvard from converting Herrick's touchdown into a goal by swarming upon the field just as the game was closing and carrying away the goal-posts, a statement albeit that is gravely denied by Yale.

The intercollegiate convention called by Princeton assembled Saturday, November 26, 1876, in the Massasoit House at Springfield. The colleges were represented as follows: Harvard, H. C. Leeds, '77, C. S. Eaton, '78; Columbia, E. W. Price, C. D. H. Brower; Princeton, Jotham Potter, '77, W. Earle Dodge, '79; Yale, E. V. Baker, '77, J. B. Atwater, '77. Mr. Dodge was chosen as chairman and Mr. Baker as secretary. A resolution was then offered that the institutions present form an intercollegiate association for the government of football. Yale stoutly opposed this resolution, urging the individual independence of each college. In the vote that followed Yale alone voted negatively. It was thereupon decided to consider the association as formed subject to the ratification of the action of the delegates by their respective institutions. The great object of the assemblage was then taken up—the adoption of a modification of the Rugby Union code of rules. Section by section the convention patiently and laboriously went through the code. The longest and most vigorous debate perhaps was that over Rule 7, which read: "A match shall be decided by a majority of goals only." Columbia and Yale contended for the adoption of this rule verbatim. Harvard and Princeton advocated making three touchdowns equal to one goal. The issue finally resulted in a compromise as follows: "A match shall be decided by a majority of touchdowns; a goal shall be equal to four touchdowns, but in case of a tie a goal kicked from a touchdown shall take precedence over four touchdowns." Rule 59, making the captains the sole arbiters of disputes, was changed so as to provide for a referee and two judges as the officials, one judge to represent each team and the referee to decide the claims of the rival judges. Two other important subjects of debate in this convention were the size of the field of play, which finally was fixed at 140 yards by 70 yards, and the number of players to constitute a side. Yale, recalling its game with Eton, suggested and vigorously advocated the limit as eleven, but the convention voted to retain the Rugby rule, which provided for fifteen. The convention thereupon adjourned. A few days later a mass meeting was held at Yale, at which the Blue decided not to become a member of the Intercollegiate Football Association. Yale, however, having defeated Harvard, was eager to meet Princeton. This latter battle occurred at St. George's Cricket Grounds in Hoboken, November 30, 1876, and Yale emerged the victor, thus independently winning the championship in this initial year of the intercollegiate game. Many years later a tablet was placed in the trophy-room at Yale commemorating the prowess of Eugene V. Baker, '77, the captain under whom these victories were achieved. This tablet reads as follows:

IN RECOGNITION OF THE SERVICES OF
EUGENE V. BAKER, '77
THE ORGANIZER AND CAPTAIN OF YALE'S FIRST
VICTORIOUS FOOTBALL TEAM
THIS ROOM HAS BEEN FURNISHED AND THIS TABLET
PLACED HERE BY HIS CLASSMATES
1893.

The following year, 1877, brought no changes in the
rules. Yale still remained outside the Association although
playing with its members. Pennsylvania did not put a team
in the field, but the new game appeared at Amherst and
Brown. Two incidental innovations occurred in this year,
however, that are worthy of notice. In the Princeton-
Harvard game, played at Cambridge, April 28, the Princeton players appeared in tightly laced canvas jackets, called
"smocks" after their inventor, Ledru P. Smock, '79, of the
Princeton team. Of greater interest, the Princetonians wore
jerseys of orange and black stripes, thus calling forth from
the jungles of fancy the famous tiger which these orange
and black stripes suggested.

Although the rules remained stationary in 1877, and also
in 1878, the game itself underwent numerous profound
changes. The native genius of the young American for
invention was experimenting in many ways. The most advantageous disposition of the fifteen players received much
attention. The more common formation was a line of
rushers, or forwards, of nine men, with one quarter-back,
two half-backs, one three-quarter-back, and two full-backs.
These names, however, were not used wholly at the time.
At Harvard the full-backs were known as tends and goal-
tends and the half-back as a half-tend. At Princeton the
word backs was in use and at Yale both terms, backs and
tends, are to be found. The greatest change in the game
came in the transition of the English scrummage to the
American scrimmage, both in name and in fact. In the
scrummage the ball was put in play by placing it upon the
ground between the two rush-lines, to be worked out with
the foot to a back for a run, pass, or kick. Under this
style of play the liability of the ball to bound unexpectedly
out of scrummage to either set of backs prevented a prede-
termined plan of play. The collegians, however, quickly

discovered that it was possible to bound or snap back the ball with a deft movement of the foot so as to send it accurately into the hands of a waiting back, or, by craftily making an opening in their line, to draw their opponents into kicking it through for them. This step was a crude one, it is true, but it was the transitional play that preceded the formal snapping back of the ball by a player designated therefor and now known as the snapper-back.

It was in 1878 that football began to attract great crowds of spectators. The Princeton-Yale contest in this year was witnessed by 4,000 persons, an unprecedented assemblage. The cost of the field was $300. Its payment provoked severe criticism in the public and college press as a gross extravagance and a feature of football not to be repeated if the game was to live. Fifteen years later the rental of Manhattan Field in New York for $10,000 for this game did not evoke the incidental notice of a line.

"Football is the grand rage," wrote an enthusiast in the *Princetonian* in September, 1879. The young journalists at New Haven thought no differently, for with the opening of Yale the *News* called for a mass meeting to accomplish certain changes in the rules. This meeting was held October 3. Resolutions were passed advocating the reduction of the players from fifteen to eleven, the counting of safeties in the scoring against the side making them, and the enlargement of the playing field to a rectangle 400 feet by 200 feet. Yale's delegate was instructed to attend the ensuing convention of the Association and vigorously press for these reforms.

This convention was held at Springfield the following day. The colleges were represented as follows: Harvard, Robert Bacon, '80; Princeton, Bland Ballard, '80; and Yale by Walter Camp, '80. Mr. Camp immediately moved the adoption of the changes advocated by Yale, but Harvard

and Princeton voted to make no alterations. Yale then
formally applied for admission to the Association and immediately was made a member.

In the playing season of 1879 the feature of kicking reached
a perfection that has never been surpassed. The ball was
kicked at every opportunity not only by the backs but also
by the forwards. Not only could every player punt, but
he could drop and place-kick with equal facility, and, strange
to assert, many were the brilliant kicks made of a ball that
was bounding along the ground. Many of the backs were
proficient kickers with either foot. It was in this year that
appeared the method of employing the rushers to carry
the ball and the feature of backing one another up so as to
receive the ball on a pass. The practice of previous years
of blindly throwing the ball backward over one's head was
discarded and each player carefully located his associate
before making the pass. But the passing was beautiful and
most clever. The ball traversed the field from side to side
and was delivered with the speed and accuracy of a baseball. Perhaps the most important innovation of the season,
although unrealized at the time, was a method introduced at
Princeton and Yale of protecting the runner, called "guarding," by sending a player at each side of him, although never
in advance, in order to increase the difficulty of tackling,
a play easily recognizable as the forerunner of modern
interference.

In the midst of the popularity of the kicking game, however, a call sounded for a new style of game. An unknown
tactician writing in the *Princetonian* voiced the new idea
as follows: "Keeping the ball and working it by by passing,
running, and rushing is superior to the kicking game now
in vogue. Kicking must be resorted to at times, but to
gain by a long punt depends upon the opposite side's failure
to make a fair catch, which rarely happens, especially under

the non-interference rule. One thing is certain: as long as one side has the ball, the other cannot score, and when one team kicks the ball the other team is extremely sure to get it."

Another feature signalizing the passing of the '70's was the arrival of the germ of the modern training régime, crudely of course, but nevertheless effective, as evidenced by an editorial in the *Yale News* calling upon Yale's players "to reduce their consumption of tobacco and not to stay up late nights lest they be not hardy enough to win."

CHAPTER VI

FOOTBALL IN THE 'EIGHTIES

THE autumn convention of the Intercollegiate Football Association, held at the Massasoit House, Springfield, October 12, 1880, was thrown into consternation by the appearance of Columbia, asking for admission to the league. That such a simple, in fact inevitable, proceeding on the part of a college outside of the circle of membership should cause dismay rather than rejoicing was due to the element of politics which in the late '70s had been introduced into the Association. In those days the great fetich of athletics was the abstract honor of a "championship," and so highly prized was this title and the gilded silk banner which accompanied it that it never was permitted to go to waste even in those years in which a championship was not mathematically apparent. Thus in 1879 Princeton defeated Harvard by one touchdown, but in all the other games between the members of the Association nothing was accomplished but a number of safeties, which, under the rules in that year, did not affect the score. No actual champion, therefore, was in existence. The Association, however, ingeniously devised a championship for that season by selecting the winner of the championship in the preceding year—Princeton—and awarding to that college the championship of 1879 upon the basis of its scores in 1878, thus establishing a precedent that was destined to plague the Association in numerous ways for many years to come. As for Columbia, this institution, it will be remembered, had been one of the original founders of the Association, but subsequently had suffered its membership to lapse. Harvard, Princeton, and Yale, therefore, apprehensively viewed the return of this member to disturb with its vote the political considerations of the league. After a prolonged discussion Columbia finally was admitted, but its power politically was nullified by attaching a condition to its membership that Columbia's vote upon any question should not be counted unless that question could be decided without it, and that the other members might remove Columbia at any time from the Association.

With this peculiar feat in intercollegiate statesmanship accomplished, the convention proceeded to introduce into football two great changes so radically at variance with the rules and traditions of Rugby, and so profoundly momentous in their effects upon its American offspring, that these two changes fairly may be said to mark the establishment of a new style of football, the American intercollegiate game. The first of these was the adoption of the principle so long and stoutly advocated by Yale, that eleven men and not fifteen should constitute a side, and the second was the abolition of the scrummage of the English game and the substitution of the far more ingenious method of putting the ball in play familiar to all to-day as the American scrimmage. This is the device which introduced into our game the principle of an orderly retention of the ball by one side, thereby making possible the use of prearranged strategy, the most distinctive and fascinating characteristic of the American game. It is true that in defining the scrimmage the convention did not invent it, but merely extended to it the recognition of the rules. The play itself had been evolving gradually through the genius of the collegians in actual play.

The immediate result of this legislation was a mighty impetus to the development of tactics. While the rules of

1880 provided for the retention of the ball they did not provide for its surrender. Unless the ball was kicked or fumbled it might be retained indefinitely by the side in possession of it. This precisely was what occurred in the Princeton-Yale game of that year. In the second half Princeton was being hard pressed near its goal. Captain Loney suddenly directed his players not to kick or to pass the ball, but to hold it. Thus, unable to gain a yard of ground, the Orange and Black retained the ball throughout the remainder of the game, thereby forcing the contest to terminate in a draw at 0 to 0. In the struggle Princeton made eleven safeties and Yale six, but safeties were not counted as scoring plays until 1881. As soon as the game had terminated, Princeton disclosed the object of its peculiar tactics, which came to be designated as the "block game," by claiming the championship for 1880 in accordance with the precedent established in 1879. Yale, equally skilful in the casuistry of fine football logic, admitted that the principle of a continuing right by which Princeton claimed the championship was correct, but that Princeton was misapplying it. Since the game of 1880 was played with only eleven men, this right of a championship should revert to the last preceding year in which it had been won with eleven men upon a side, which was the year of 1876. Therefore it was Yale and not Princeton which was entitled to the championship of 1880. The public press took the controversy seriously and joined in the battle of debate. In January, 1881, Princeton issued a ponderous argument in support of its contention, but closed with a curt challenge to Yale to play off the tie in the ensuing month of April. This challenge was not accepted, and so the controversy continued to rage until finally buried beneath the accumulation of time, although among the older generation of football men it occasionally breaks out even to this day.

These were the times in which the names of the positions were originating. As early as 1877 the players at the extremities of the line had been called the "end men," and slightly later the adjacent players as "next to end." The English game had brought with it the names of half-backs and backs, and the rules of 1880 designated formally two players to be known as the snapper-back and the quarter-back, the former of which naturally became located in the center of the line—originally known as forwards and later as rushers—and thus also became known as the centre rush. It was quickly noticed that the two players adjacent to the centre rush guarded him when he snapped the ball, and so these two players were called the guards. Similarly the collegians of the period were not long in observing that the "next to ends" more frequently made tackles than the other players because of the opportunities of their positions, and so these players were designated as tackles. Although these names were in standard use for many years, it was not until 1909 that they were recognized formally by the rules.

In 1881 football might be said to have become a well-established college game, although still confined to the larger institutions. This year particularly is memorable because of the invasion of the east by an eleven from the University of Michigan, which played formidable games with Harvard, Princeton, and Yale. But there were three other incidents to make memorable this season of 1881. The first was the appearance of the professional trainer, a character who caused an avalanche of adverse criticism until he finally passed into the commonplace personages of the sport. The second was the invention by Princeton of the "touch-in-goal" to thwart the new rule which made the safety touchdown count adversely in the scoring, and the third incident was the playing by Princeton and Yale of the famous "block game." The safety originally was merely an incidental play in defensive tactics. When made it in nowise affected the score, but permitted a team to put the ball in play at the 25-yard line. Hence a team which had the ball nearer to its own goal-line deliberately made a safety and then moved out to the 25-yard line. With the passage of the rule making an excess over four safeties a factor in deciding an otherwise tie game, Princeton discovered that this rule could be evaded by touching down in the corners enclosed by a projection of the side line and the goal-line, the touch-in-goal. But it is the "block game" that chiefly made history in 1881. Princeton and Yale had been struggling only four and a half minutes when the former obtained the ball, and the "block game" was in action. The orange-striped runners hit the line and tried the ends, but not a yard could they gain. Not once did the runner pass the ball to an associate or kick it to an opponent, the Tigers thus retaining the ball until the end of the half and without making a total gain of 10 yards in forty minutes of play. Yale started with the ball in the second half, and that period ended as it began, not one Princeton player getting his hands on the ball throughout the half, Yale declining to kick and not having the misfortune to fumble, and not being able to drive the ball forward more than 20 yards throughout the afternoon. This game of course ended in a tie at 0 to 0. Princeton at once claimed the championship on the basis of the last decisive year, 1878. Yale demanded the honor because its record against Harvard was better than that of Princeton, the scores having been: Princeton 1 safety, Harvard 1 safety, Yale 0, Harvard 4 safeties. Yale's theory of the situation prevailed and the Blue was awarded the championship.

But the public desired something more than a political championship. It demanded action, and a great clamor broke out against the "block game." A notable suggestion appeared in a metropolitan newspaper which was widely reprinted in the college press. It was entitled "Letter of an Englishman," and said: "The block-game is an unmitigated evil. It can be remedied by allowing a team only four scrimmages, the ball then to change opponents, who may put it down or punt. A touch-in-goal should count the same as a safety." Another suggestion which furnished the complement to this proposition appeared in the *Princetonian* under the title "Suggestions." Here an unknown football inventor said: "The block game is not football. Further, running and dodging on the part of the backs has become impossible because opponents bring up four backs into the line. The players should be assigned places and made to keep them. It might be agreed that when one side has had the ball twice in succession the halfback on the third down should be compelled either to kick or to forfeit the ball. A game decided by safeties is merely a negative victory."

The pressure became so great that a special convention of the association was called early in 1882, but the representatives failed to agree upon a remedy. However, incidentally they established the famous fixture of a Thanksgiving Day game in New York by ruling that the two leading teams each season should play their championship game in the following year at that time and place. The fall convention of the association met at Springfield, October 14, 1882. Vigorously grappling with the "block game" the collegians quickly put it out of existence by the adoption of a rule which gave the final cleavage to the basic principles of the old Rugby game and established another fundamental underneath the American intercollegiate game. This rule ran as follows: "If on three consecutive fairs and downs a team shall not have advanced the ball five yards or lost ten, they must give up the ball to the other side at the spot where the fourth down was made." Not only did this rule save the game, but it increased its circle of supporters, being adopted at this time by Dartmouth and Lafayette. Sentimentally this great rule also is notable, for it was its operation that brought on the lime-line stripes that have earned for our battle-field the name of gridiron.

Necessity, the mother of football invention, driven by the five-yard rule and invited by opportunity in an undisturbed possession of the ball during the downs, now made a great advance in tactics and strategy. The first improvement to appear was signals. In the beginning these consisted of sentences. Thus Yale's first signals were two sentences, "Play up sharp, Charlie," and "Look out, quick, Deac." Each one of the sentences indicated a play. The signal was disguised by making any portion of the sentence call for the same play. The captain confused his opponents by omitting first one word and then another. At Princeton in this same period letters were used. Thus a sentence beginning with W, as "What's the matter?" indicated that the ball would be passed to the full-back. At Harvard and Pennsylvania both sentences and letters were employed. In fact it was several years before this style of signalling was superseded by the numerical systems which, appearing about 1885, passed from simplicity to complexity until in recent years an accurate application of the prevailing complicated systems has presented a first-class performance in mathematics.

The year of 1882 marked the final settlement of the positions of the players into seven forwards, a quarter-back, two half-backs, and a full-back. Prior to the month of November of this season formations varied not only on different teams but also upon the same team. A frequent arrangement was that of six men on the line, three half-backs and two full-backs; another disposition of the players was that of six forwards, a quarter-back, two half-backs, a three-quarter-back, and a full-back. The Princeton-Yale contest in this year, however, presented the final solution of the problem in the arrangement that has come down to the present time.

A prolific source of disputes was the complicated system of scoring, which in several important games left to the referee the decision as to the proportion in which touch-downs, goals, and safeties should be valued against one another. This grievance the convention of October 17, 1883, removed by assigning a numerical value to the scoring plays as follows:

> Safety 1
> Touchdown 2
> Goal following touchdown 4
> Goal from field 5

These values lasted only one season, when they were amended by increasing the safety to 2, the touchdown to 4, and by decreasing the goal following touchdown to 2, an arrangement that existed without change until 1897.

The playing season of 1884 was opened gayly by the *Harvard Lampoon*, which introduced its team as follows: "Harvard will be represented by a team this fall that is light and portable. It can be packed in a bandbox and shipped to any point at trifling expense. After a good deal of hard training it may be possible to send them even by mail provided permission can be obtained to send live bait through the mail." It was this levity at Cambridge, perhaps, which especially stimulated football that autumn at Pennsylvania and inspired the Red and Blue to make unusual preparations to meet Harvard. Although Pennsylvania had adopted football as early as 1876, and frequently had had the advantage of the presence upon its teams of famous Princeton

THE V.

Princeton's celebrated formation opening the game against Cornell. Princeton, Nov. 14, 1891.

and Yale players who after graduation at their alma mater
had taken professional courses at Pennsylvania, the game
held only a minor position. This was due to the extraordinary interest at the university in rowing and cricket.
The special campaign of 1884 was not without its reward,
for in a great battle with the Crimson at Cambridge, October
22, 1884, Pennsylvania defeated Harvard 4 to 0 and tasted
its first great victory upon the gridiron.

While these signal events were transpiring another notable stride in football was taking place at Lehigh, where
Richard Harding Davis, '86, and Wm. Bradford, '87, were
organizing that university's first team and preparing to meet
Lafayette in the first struggle of these now classic rivals.

Tactically, this was the year that produced the famous
"V Trick," the original wedge and forerunner of the mass
play. Strange to say, this highly ingenious and complicated formation was not the result of long and laborious
study, but was conceived suddenly in the crisis of a close
game and put into immediate execution. This game was
the contest between Pennsylvania and Princeton, October
25, 1884, and the inventor of the play was R. M. Hodge,
'86, of Princeton. The latter has given this account of the
origin of this great formation: "In the middle of the game
Captain Bird, of Princeton, had called upon Baker, '85, a
half-back, to run behind the rush-line, which charged seven
abreast down the field. It was an old play and gained
little ground against Pennsylvania the second time it was
used. It suddenly struck me that if the rush-line would
jump into the shape of a V with the apex forward and with
Baker inside, the formation ought to gain ground. A con-
sultation immediately was held, and upon the next play
the formation tried, Baker ploughing forward within the V
from midfield to the five-yard line. We then reserved this
formation for the Yale game, Lamar making within it a

long gain on the opening play. The next year the V was not used, but was revived in 1886. By 1888 it had come into general use throughout the country and in 1889 was the standard opening play with every eleven."

The V as finally perfected was formed by the eleven players taking positions in a solid V-shaped mass, apex forward, the arms of the players encircling the bodies of one another. The play formed ten yards back from the opponents' rush-line. The player with the ball stood at the apex of the V. When all were ready the ball was technically kicked off by being touched to the toe and ground simultaneously, but without being released. The mass then started heavily forward, the player with the ball disappeared within it, and the opponents charged. Breaking one of these ponderous machines was not gentle play, since this could be accomplished only by throwing oneself directly in front of the mass and upsetting its apex while other players crushed in its flanks. Such a play was in direct disregard of the old rule of off-side play which forbade a player of the offensive side to block an opponent while in advance of the ball, but custom gradually had been nullifying this rule with the evolution of "guarding" and "warding" into "interference." The interferers originally were restrained at the side of the runner, but as officials relaxed in enforcing the rule against off-side play the interferers gradually moved more and more forward until finally they preceded the runner and the rule against such a formation was considered dead.

With the opening of the new year of 1885 football received a great shock at the hands of Harvard's faculty, which abolished the sport. The effect, however, was only momentary, for at the convention of the Association in February both Pennsylvania and Wesleyan applied for admission to the league and both unanimously were accepted. Notwith-

standing the loss of Harvard a substantial increase in public
interest was accorded football in this autumn. Previously
the attendance had been confined to collegians and to a
small portion of the general public. In this year the
Princeton-Yale game for the first time since the inception of
the series was played upon college grounds, the contest being
scheduled in New Haven and not in New York. As a result the game for the first time in its history assumed a decided social feature and attracted many ladies. The good
fortune of the occasion further was augmented by a marvellous game terminating in the celebrated run of Henry
C. Lamar, of Princeton, which converted defeat into victory
at the last moment, thereby affording the spectators a
pleasant and picturesque memory of a meritorious sport
from which to speak its praises through the ensuing winter.
The first effect of this good impression happily was upon
Harvard's faculty, for that august body, January 5, 1886,
removed its ban upon the game and football again was
flourishing at Cambridge.

A picturesque feature of football to pass in 1885 was the
institution of the judges. When the Rugby game was
adopted in 1876, the English rule making the captains the
judges of the play was superseded by an arrangement by
which each team was to be represented by an official of its
own selection to be known as a judge, both teams to select
a third official to be designated as the referee, whose duties
should be to decide the claims and disputes of the judges.
As was natural, the judges soon developed into a pair of
football lawyers, selected as much for their argumentative
ability as for their knowledge of the game. The clamorous
claims of these gentlemen and their continuous counsels
to their clients as to the manner best to circumvent the opposition are recalled with humor by those who remember
this primitive feature of the game. The zeal of the judges

eventually worked their extinction. Thus we find in 1885 and 1886 only one official, the referee, conducting the entire judicial duties of the game. The system of an umpire and a referee dates from 1888. The linesman was added in the great revolution of the game that occurred in 1894. Twice during the history of the game experiments have been made with two umpires. The first was abandoned as a failure years ago and the second, instituted in 1906, also was abolished the following year, but the extra official was preserved in the present field judge. Another spectacular heritage from the old Rugby game that was legislated out of existence in 1885 was the "maul-in-goal." This classical device of old English football is too intricate for description, but suffice it to say that it was as rough as it sounds. Only one event occurred in 1887 to signalize that year in the annals of football, but that event was naught else than the appearance of Cornell in its first gridiron battle, a game waged with Union, at Ithaca, November 12, 1887, upon the site now occupied by Stimson Hall.

The final momentous session of football's legislature in the decade of the '80s was the convention of March 3, 1888. Although this body introduced only four changes in the rules, two of these were of such a character that they radically changed the course of development of the game. These radical amendments was the rule prohibiting the defensive rush-line from clasping hands and stretching out across the field like a chain, and the rule which extended tackling from the waist to the knees. Up to this time rush-lines on offence had stretched across the field so widely that the players could touch one another only with outstretched arms. Occasionally the distance would be greater. The backs played far back and as far out as their ends, taking the ball on long side passes. Defensively the rush-line spread so as to cover opponents. The low tackle had introduced a defensive weapon into the game so powerful that the day of individual rushing and easy dodging was gone. To restore the balance between the offence and defence the rush-line was now contracted until the men stood shoulder to shoulder and the backs were brought up within four yards of the line for the quick plunges into the line that the new game required. And thus passed the beautiful, open style of game recalled so fondly by the older generation of collegians, and in its place came the mass play, ugly and uncouth in construction, but which, designed to be useful rather than handsome, overcame the low tackle and won its long list of victories.

Ingenious indeed were the inventions that immediately appeared along this new line of tactical development. Princeton devised the play now familiarly known as "boxing the tackle," although originally called the "split-the-line-open" play, simple now but surprisingly formidable and effective when first used against Yale in 1888, sending Cowan on the first trial of it to the Blue's five-yard line from midfield, only to be brought back because the officials could not reconcile its strangeness to the rules. Yale, equally constructive, conceived the idea of sending a player in advance of the runner through the line, commonplace now but revolutionary and irresistible when first disclosed, also notable because it abandoned the last vestige of regard for the old Rugby principle forbidding a player to block opponents while in advance of the ball.   On defence a great advance was made by placing a half-back immediately behind each tackle, thus presenting a new invention in the game, a secondary defence.

But if the '80s were to come to a close in a brilliant display of achievements in strategy, this decade was destined to pass out in a still more impressive exhibition of the game's spectacular side features. The playing season of

1889 found Harvard and Princeton facing the campaign
with unusually limited material because of the graduation of
many old players. Within the first few days of the autumn,
however,. two of Princeton's veterans returned for post-
graduate work and two famous football players matriculated as special students. The outlook at Harvard improved
with the accretion of two veterans from the professional
departments and another veteran, a special, who extended
his course of study. At New Haven football also was
stimulated by the recruitment of four veterans who were
pursuing courses in the professional departments. Up
to this time no serious objection had been made to the playing of post-graduates and specials although the subject of
hoary and aged veterans upon rival teams long had been a
prolific source of humorous comment by the college wits.
The presence of such a galaxy of graduates in 1889 created
wide criticism and a stern demand for reform. To sur-
charge the atmosphere rumors of professionalism were rife.
As a result Wesleyan and Yale early in November united
in a call for a special convention of the Association to determine "certain questions of amateur standing." This
meeting was held at the old Fifth Avenue Hotel in New
York, November 4, 1889. In behalf of Yale, Walter Camp
introduced an elaborate set of resolutions on eligibility prohibiting any student from playing upon a team of the Association unless he was attending a certain number of recitations each week, and any student who had participated in
athletics for pay. Duncan Edwards, of Princeton, promptly
moved to amend these resolutions by including all students
in professional departments and all post-graduates. This
amendment if adopted would have disqualified four players
at Harvard, four at Pennsylvania, and four at Yale. H. C.
Leeds, of Harvard, claimed that such an amendment was
out of order because the meeting was called to consider only

questions of amateur standing. This point was sustained. John C. Bell, of Pennsylvania, moved the adoption of that portion of Mr. Camp's resolutions which required a player's attendance upon a certain number of recitations a week. Harvard objected to this because it was not germane to the call of the convention, but the point was not sustained. Princeton then attempted to widen the scope of the resolutions by prohibiting a student at one college from subsequently playing upon the team of another, but a point of order by Harvard was sustained and the amendment was rejected. Thereupon the resolutions were passed.

Slowly and impressively Mr. Leeds now arose and presented protests against fifteen of Princeton's players. The latter's representatives immediately retaliated by filing charges against four of Harvard's men. At this juncture the convention adjourned for ten days in order to afford the protested players opportunity to answer the charges.

The sensation throughout the intercollegiate world produced by this convention was the dominant topic in the interim. In fact the aspects of the controversy, humorously and bitterly treated, occupied more space in the public press than was accorded a complication in international politics that occurred at the same time. As a result the reassembling of this convention upon the date appointed attracted a great crowd of collegians and newspaper men to the corridors of the Fifth Avenue Hotel. The convention was called to order behind closed doors. The protested Harvard players were in attendance for oral examination. No sooner had the convention been called to order than Edwards, of Princeton, jumped to his feet and moved to lay the protests upon the table. F. G. Beattys, who represented Wesleyan, announced that before he voted upon this motion he desired an opportunity to examine the evidence which Harvard would produce against Princeton's players.

Mr. Leeds thereupon invited him to withdraw for that purpose and the convention took a recess. A few minutes later these gentlemen returned and the session was called to order. The motion to table was put and Wesleyan voted to table the protests. Since Pennsylvania and Princeton voted affirmatively and Harvard and Yale negatively, this famous episode ended and the convention adjourned. Two days later Harvard and Princeton met in a great battle on Jarvis Field at Cambridge, the excitement surrounding which had been heightened enormously by these events. From this battle Princeton emerged the victor. Four days later a great mass meeting was held at Harvard, at which it was voted that the university should sever its connection with the Intercollegiate Football Association. The Crimson's resignation immediately was forwarded, thus beginning the disintegration of the association.

PERFECTING THE INTERFERENCE.

Yale at practice, showing W. W. Heffelfinger, the figure to left of centre, with right arm outstretched, reaching back to carry the half-back through the line. Yale Field, 1890.

CHAPTER VII

FOOTBALL IN THE 'NINETIES

THE stirring events which brought to a close the decade of the '80s continued their course unabated in January, 1890. The intercollegiate world was disturbed by persistent rumors that Yale also would withdraw from the Intercollegiate Football Association and with Harvard form a "dual league" in all branches of sport. Color was given to these reports by a number of conferences held at Springfield by these two institutions, but the atmosphere was eventually cleared by the announcement that they had completed an arrangement only for their mutual contests, and this soon was supplemented by a further statement from Yale that the latter had no intention of withdrawing from the league.

Notwithstanding this rupture in the political department of football the season of 1890 brought a remarkable development in the tactics of play. The plan of sending a man through the line in advance of the runner became general. Most memorable of all, however, was the invention by Yale of the most perfect system of interference in end running the game ever has known. The ingeniousness of the Blue's method lay in the employment of a heavy lineman to lead the interference, who sprang from his position in the line at the snap of the ball, but the effectiveness of the play unquestionably lay in the extraordinary skill of the lineman selected, who was none other than W. W. Heffelfinger. This swarthy giant still looms vividly through the lapse of years, his ears protected by a broad white bandage and his great frame ranging swiftly up and down the field, pushing,

pulling, and blocking, continually exhorting his comrades to
action and repeatedly performing the astounding feat of
ripping apart his adversary's rush-line, reaching back for
his runner and carrying him through his own opening and
pell-mell down the field, a veritable Theseus of mental and
physical action. Equally brilliant in the execution of this
play and of a feint for end which terminated in a dash between tackle and end was Lee McClung, the two composing a pair of players whose skill and interaction were the
chief factors in administering to Princeton the heaviest defeat ever suffered by the Tiger team. And yet this great
strategic eleven of Yale was beaten by Harvard, the first
defeat of the Blue by the Crimson excepting their first game
in 1875.

　　This was the year in which appeared that famous curiosity
of the sport, the affectation of long hair by the players.
This custom was defended at the time by the assertion that
it was done for protection. Protection, of course, hair
from four to eight inches long did afford, nevertheless it was
only a fashion. It originated in the humorous proclivities
of a player at Princeton who in 1889 raised an enormous
crop of hair merely as an act of horse-play. Playing a
spectacular game against Harvard, his flaunting, flopping
locks were taken seriously by the spectators, and thus this
comedian unconsciously set a fashion that the next year
swept the country and raged for four years. To such gro-
tesqueness did the chrysanthemum crown of the football
man grow that to-day it is still the comic type of that personage. In 1895 Yale's eleven startled the spectators who
assembled to see the contest with Princeton, by appearing
with locks neatly and closely shorn, and instantly long hair
went out of fashion in imitation of the latest style.

　　Not only did 1890 bring an advance in the scientific
knowledge of the game, but it brought an extension in its

circle of competitors. In the East the Army and Navy, or, as they are popularly known, West Point and Annapolis, played their first contest, thus establishing that great classic series of games. In the Northwest, Minnesota and Wisconsin likewise made their initial appearance in a fixture that never has been broken. Football also invaded the West, resulting in a convention, December 28, 1890, at Kansas City, promoted by Hector W. Cowan, of Princeton, at which Iowa, Kansas, Missouri, and Nebraska formed the Western Intercollegiate Football Association. The advent of so many participants and the keenness of their competition brought forth a brilliant army of football coaches from the older institutions who began to spread far and wide the long-guarded secrets of expert play. At one time in this period there might have been counted no less than 45 former players of Yale, 35 of Princeton, and 24 of Harvard actively engaged in teaching the science of the game.

During the early years of this decade a condition of rest and stability characterized the rules, but the genius of generalship incessantly and brilliantly was active. Of this famous strategic period the month of November, 1892, was by far the most memorable. To begin with, Pennsylvania signalized its advent as a football power by defeating Princeton. With this sensation still in the air Harvard and Yale came together one week later at Springfield. For many years the standard opening play at the beginning of each half had been the old Princeton V, commonly known as the V Trick. With this formation Yale opened the first half against Harvard. At the commencement of the second period Yale's forwards deployed along the 55-yard line to attack a similar formation by Harvard. To the surprise of players and spectators, however, the Crimson did not form a V. Instead, B. W. Trafford, holding the ball, took a position at the centre of Harvard's 45-yard line. The re-

maining 10 men divided into two sections and fell back to
the 25-yard line, each section grouping near the side line,
but at opposite sides of the field. Without putting the ball
in play Trafford waved his hand and the two sections came
swiftly forward in lock step, converging toward Trafford
and gathering tremendous momentum as they ran. Just
as they reached Trafford the latter put the ball in play and
disappeared within the mass of men, thus launching against
the Yale men standing still in their tracks the famous flying wedge, the invention of Lorin F. DeLand. Fearlessly
Yale's rush-line leaped against the mass, finally pulling it
to pieces and bringing down the runner on their 25-yard
line. No play ever has been devised so spectacular and
sensational as this one. It not only was the feature of the
game, although the contest eventually was won by Yale, but
it was the most discussed topic by the country at large
for many days and the central subject of football for several years. To-day the episode is preserved by the passage of the words, "the flying wedge," from a technical
term of football to a standard phrase in the English language.

Less spectacular but equally consequential was an innovation introduced by Yale in this game, the abolition of
sparring in the rush-line. For many years the opposing
forwards had been accustomed to push one another with
the flat of their hands in order to distract their attention
from the ball and to have their opponents off their feet
when the ball was snapped. The effect of this sparring and
counter-sparring was that of seven pairs of windmills. Yale
was the first to observe that a player who stood quietly
in his place, ignoring his opponent and with his eyes fixed
upon the ball, was the man who invariably charged his opponent back. Instantly sparring ceased, thereby incidentally so improving the game as a whole that its rule-makers

prevented a return of the practice by a specific legislation
against it.

The condition of peacefulness which had characterized
the politics of the game for two years was roughly jarred
in January, 1893, by the launching of a movement by Yale
to limit the eligibility of all players upon intercollegiate
teams to undergraduates who were actually candidates for
a degree. This proposition soon became famous far and
wide as the "undergraduate rule." For its consideration a
special session of the Association was held late in January,
at which the rule was adopted by the votes of Princeton,
Wesleyan, and Yale, although vigorously opposed by Pennsylvania. A few weeks later the intercollegiate association
of track athletes assembled at New York, and Yale again
introduced the resolution, thereby producing a great uproar. Pennsylvania led the attack upon the rule and accomplished its defeat. With the arrival of autumn, Pennsylvania renewed its opposition to this rule and began a
campaign to bring about either its repeal or a suspension of
its action for players in college at the time of its adoption.
Public sentiment veered in favor of Pennsylvania when it
was learned that Yale had waived this rule in its agreement
with Harvard, it being stipulated that in these contests
each university should be the judge of its own eligibility
qualifications. With the coming of October, Pennsylvania
aggressively again attacked the rule and called for a convention to consider its repeal. Princeton and Yale would
not recede and the rule remained. Thereupon Pennsylvania
filed its resignation from the Association and soon was followed by Wesleyan, thus substantially disintegrating the
old Association, although Princeton and Yale still maintained its organization.

Turning from intercollegiate politics to the game itself
we find the year of 1893 most brilliant for its great pro-

ductions in strategic play. George W. Woodruff, of Yale, who had been engaged as coach at Pennsylvania, was signalizing his advent by revolutionizing many long-accepted basic theories of the game. Defensively his rush-lines were contracted instead of expanded and his forwards were taught to drive the runner to the side line rather than into the traditional pocket at centre which occasionally proved to be a pocket with a hole. His players also were instructed to disregard the ancient maxim which required a player to fall upon a fumbled ball, Woodruff's idea being to pick it up and take the chance of a fumble against the chance of missing an opportunity for a long run. To his genius also must be credited the origin at this time of the quarter-back kick, the forerunner of the on-side kicking game. Most momentous of all, he introduced the flying principle into all interference, causing the interferers to start before the ball was put in play and the latter to be snapped just as the interference struck the opposing line. Around this feature a great number of variations were evolved which came to be known as momentum mass plays.

At Harvard Lorin F. DeLand was producing one bewildering invention after another. Harvard's opponents lightly called these formations "checker-board plays," but although they did not win for Harvard against Yale, they furnished the basis of nearly all standard formations for ten years. It was in this season that the Harvard eleven startled Yale in their contest, November 25, 1893, by appearing in suits of smooth leather made into a single piece in order to increase the difficulty of tackling. The stratagem was a projection of a similar idea out of which had originated many years before the laced canvas jacket, and it was a saner device than that of the known—but here nameless—genius who once essayed to play half-back in a championship game greased from shoulder to knee, thereby forcing into the rule book that curious section which for many years added interest in its pages, "No sticky or greasy substance shall be used on the persons or clothing of the players." In this game first was seen the "turtle-back," a play executed by forming the eleven men in the shape of a solid oval against a selected point in the rush-line, usually the tackle, and at the snap of the ball into the interior of the oval rolling the mass out around the end, thus unwinding the runner into a clear field. Here also first was seen the "push play," a formation similar to the turtle-back, but in which the runner was lifted on top of the mass and pushed over the opposing rush-line.

Yale with customary genius devised a powerful variation of the momentum mass play. All of the linemen except the centre and guards were withdrawn and with the backs formed into a wedge fifteen yards behind the line. As this wedge started before the ball was put in play, and as the latter was not snapped until the wedge was about to strike its objective point, it is needless to say that the impact was such that the objective point usually remembered it for years. But the most effective formation viewed from the standpoint of results and its influence upon the subsequent development of the game was a play devised at Princeton by Philip King. This famous player conceived the idea of placing the ends with the backs in a straight line behind the tackles, thus originating the tandem-tackle principle of offensive play. Two weeks later Harvard modified this formation by playing the tackles back. From that day to this the tandem-tackle principle has been the chief feature in the invention of offensive tactics.

Unfortunately, this season of exceptional tactical brilliancy was fraught with many mishaps. Perhaps these were due to that peculiar operation of chance which ever seems to accumulate an excess of misfortunes at one time. Perhaps it was due to the fact that the generals of the game had devised plays too powerful for their sturdy soldiers to execute and withstand. Perhaps these accidents were not so numerous or so serious as alleged, but rather were the product of exaggeration. As usual there was much of the latter. The sensational accounts of the season's contests eventually made their way into Europe, and the *Münchener Nachrichten* purveyed the news of battle to its readers thus: "The football tournament between the teams of Harvard and Yale, recently held in America, had terrible results. It turned into an awful butchery. Of twenty-two participants seven were so severely injured that they had to be carried from the field in a dying condition. One player had his back broken, another lost an eye, and a third lost a leg. Both teams appeared upon the field with a crowd of ambulances, surgeons, and nurses. Many ladies fainted at the awful cries of the injured players. The indignation of the spectators was powerful, but they were so terrorized that they were afraid to leave the field."

The sport now faced a serious outcry. The Secretary of the Navy and the Secretary of War abolished the promising Army-Navy series of games by restricting each Academy to its own grounds. Unfortunately for football the game in this crisis had no authoritative governmental head. The old intercollegiate association had dwindled to two members, Princeton and Yale, and the uniformity of the game was threatened by the proposed organization of several "dual leagues" throughout the country. Out of the turmoil eventually came a call from the University Athletic Club of New York requesting Harvard, Pennsylvania, Princeton, and Yale to form a rules committtee and assume the government of the game. These institutions immediately responded by selecting as their representatives, respectively, W. A. Brooks, J. C. Bell, Alexander Moffat, and Walter Camp. These gentlemen extended their numbers

THE PLACE KICK SUPPLANTS THE WEDGE.

Fairchild kicking out for Harvard following a touchback. Harvard vs. Pennsylvania, Nov. 29, 1894.

by inviting P. J. Dashiell to join them, the latter being the game's foremost official at the time. Through Mr. Camp a letter of inquiry was sent to every former football player in the United States requesting answers to a number of specific questions upon the subject of injuries. These answers when compiled and published proved that the charges against the accidents of the sport had been exaggerated so grossly that these accusations subsided and almost ceased. But the committee had gone a step farther. It had invited also from all of the old players suggestions for the improvement of the game. It required many sessions to consider the many meritorious ideas adduced, but at last the committee issued its new rules giving to the sport the most radical revision it had encountered since 1882. The V and the flying wedge were abolished and the old-fashioned kick-off re-established. The momentum plays which depended upon a start in advance of the snap of the ball were prohibited and mass plays were greatly modified by forbidding players to group more than five yards behind the line.

Notwithstanding, the opposition to the game did not cease. The rules committee had only modified the mass plays, whereas the public demanded their complete eradication and the restoration of the open game. To add to the keenness of the situation Harvard and Yale became engaged in an altercation over the unusual vim with which the contest of 1894 had been played, which terminated in a severance of relations between the Blue and the Crimson. Cornell's faculty added a new subject to the rampant debate by adopting a resolution "limiting all contests of Cornell to college grounds." The rules committee organized in 1894 failed to perpetuate itself, and so Alexander Moffat, of Princeton, and Walter Camp, of Yale, as representatives of the old Intercollegiate Association, theoretically still in existence, invited W. A. Brooks, of Harvard, and J. C. Bell, of Pennsylvania, to join in a conference to save the game by revising its rules to meet the public and college demand. This joint conference assembled March 31, 1895. It immediately became apparent that a radical division existed among the members upon the subject of revision. Princeton and Yale stoutly stood for the complete abolition of the momentum mass play. Harvard and Pennsylvania, equally obstinate, insisted upon the retention of this feature. Adjournments from time to time were taken by this committee in an effort to harmonize, but the college year came to an end with no harmony in sight. When the collegians reassembled in the autumn they found an unusual condition. The committee had separated into two factions. Harvard and Pennsylvania had invited Cornell to join them and produce an independent set of rules, which was done, Princeton and Yale likewise drafting a different code. The rules of the last two prohibited more than one man from starting before the ball was in play and forbade more than three men to group behind the line of scrimmage. The other set of rules placed no restrictions upon formations behind the line. Pennsylvania's uncompromising insistence upon unrestricted formations behind the line was due to the great perfection to which George W. Woodruff had brought a marvellous mass play known as guards-back, a formation executed by withdrawing both guards from the line and playing them in tandem style against the objective point, further supported by a powerful arrangement of the backs, one of the most ingenious and effective offensive formations devised in the entire history of the game. These two factions also differed in regard to the manner of continuing play from a fair catch. Princeton and Yale required a heel mark, but the code of their rivals provided that "the player who catches a punt may not run with the ball, but may pass it to another player, who may run with it."

GUARDS—BACK. THE FINAL PLUNGE.

Pennsylvania's famous formation carrying Minds across Harvard's goal-line for a touchdown. Franklin Field, Nov. 20, 1897.

The result of these contending codes of course was chaos. Each institution insisted that its competitors play under its particular code, thus requiring many colleges to be proficient in both. Notwithstanding this the lowest plane to which football has fallen in its long history in this country, the year of 1895 produced one great innovation. From earliest times the ball had been passed from centre to the full-back for a punt by the quarter-back. Yale in this season devised the long pass direct from centre to the full-back, apparently a simple and sound method, yet it invited a storm of hostile criticism as an impracticable manœuvre. Two years later it was used by every team in the United States, and the long, underhand pass of the quarter-back had gone into the lumber-room of discarded plays.

The close of this season found the colleges of the country in rebellion against the further supervision of the game by the major institutions. Disgusted with the quarrels of the East, the Middle West demanded a sectional rules committee of its own and the minor colleges of the seaboard likewise raised a demand for a representative committee to draft a satisfactory and uniform set of rules. The two committees thereupon were forced to coalesce and to stem opposition by inviting all of the colleges to submit their suggestions for reform. The response was immediate. Again the committee was forced to continue in session until midsummer in order to consider the mass of proposed amendments, but at last all were thoroughly debated and the best beaten into a new code. The flying principle was met by legislating that no player of the offensive side might take more than one step towards his opponents' goal before the ball was in play, and the mass feature was modified by prohibiting more than six men from grouping behind the line of scrimmage and further by providing that two of these players should be at least five yards back, or outside of the end men on the line. These changes were supplemented by a number of minor alterations and the game at a bound came back into popular approval. The playing season that ensued was marred by the continuance of the estrangement between Harvard and Yale, but the year was memorable notwithstanding. In October Lafayette surprised the intercollegiate world by playing a draw with Princeton and later defeating Pennsylvania, thereby achieving the honor of being the first minor college to rupture the impregnability of the "big four." Two great plays appeared to add further distinction to this year. The place kick which had lain forgotten for many a long year came back and began to supplant the historic drop kick for goal. At Princeton the old tandem play of 1893 was revived and altered into an irresistible engine of attack that became popularly known as the "revolving tandem." It was executed by swinging one tackle from position at the snap of the ball against the opposite tackle, thereby forming a wedge with the half-backs, one of the latter carrying the ball, and this mass then being whirled by the strong arms of Garret Cochran through the line and over the defensive backs, who vainly fell in front of the play to block it.

Following this season football entered upon four years of stability for the rules, of relief from intercollegiate politics, and of attention to the perfection of play. Great contests were waged, no untoward incidents marred the sport, and a great wave of popular approval was the reward. In this era of good feeling Harvard and Yale resumed their annual game and the interdiction was removed from the Army-Navy struggle, thus permitting the latter with its peculiarly picturesque and social features to leap at a bound into equal importance with the time-honored football classics. Tactically, line and wing shifts made their appearance to delight the strategists and the spectacular hurdle play came into use as one of the game's sensational features.

There is another circumstance which clings in the memory of the older generation making memorable the period whose closing occurred at this time, and that is the Thanksgiving Day game between Princeton and Yale in New York. The advance cohorts of the collegians usually arrived Wednesday afternoon and by evening the rival armies were in the city. From Madison Square to Thirty-third Street the sidewalks of Broadway flashed with blue and orange ribbons and the buildings along the way resounded with the impact of many and diverse college cheers, for the occasion was a convocation of all. Yale's eleven annually was quartered at the Fifth Avenue Hotel and Princeton's was secluded at the Murray Hill. But the forum for all comers were the lobbies of the Hoffman House. The presiding personage here was "Billy" Edwards, a former prize-fighter, raised to the position of guardian genius of the hostelry. Genial, tactful, and popular, Edwards moved among the collegians good-naturedly confining the debates within proper limits of noisiness, acting as stakeholder for that portion of the sporting public which insisted upon a wager and with an eye ever single and alert to the integrity of the glassware.

Owing to the great distance to the field the collegians arose betimes Thanksgiving morning. By ten o'clock the coaching parade was in motion, and the coaching parade was a feature that was second only to the game itself. A full year in advance every drag in the city was engaged, and by the day of the game almost every omnibus, coach, and other vehicle capable of transporting half a dozen or more men upon its roof, for no one rode inside. Flaunting from the tops hung great blankets of blue or orange bunting. Style required the attachment of at least four horses and as many more as the taste and finances of the passengers permitted, the horses being no less ornately and abundantly caparisoned than the coach. Another invariable feature of every equipage was its coaching-horn and hornsman. The latter, it is true, frequently was lacking in skill, but he was most extraordinarily prolific in wind. Starting from Madison Square the route lay up Fifth Avenue to Harlem and thence to the field—the Polo Grounds in the '80s and Manhattan Field in the '90s. The gayety of the drive was augmented by the lavish decorations that were flung from many residences and hotels along the way, each eliciting appreciative salvos of cheers from the collegians whose colors were displayed.

At the field a space was reserved for the coaches directly overlooking the field of play, and here, still upon their coach-tops, these coaching-parties lunched. The great encircling stands did not arrive until the games were transferred to university fields. Indeed even as late as 1891 it was a common sight to find spectators viewing the struggle from boxes and barrels placed against the fence. Those were the days of the overhead sweater, before the blanket made its advent, when teams endeavored, and often succeeded, in playing an entire game without the use of one substitute. It also was the time of the inexpert news reporter who wrote his introduction weeks and months ahead, but who obtained his data of the progress of the battle from the substitutes and later described an important play as " Homans snatched the ball going southbound." Fashionably, it was the period of the ulster and the newmarket, and the neckerchief of colored silk, upon this occasion invariably blue or orange and black.

At the conclusion of the game the great crowd by coach and elevated train made its return downtown, and soon every restaurant and hotel was crowded with happy parties

THE COACHING PARADE TO THE GAME.

Drags of Princeton and Yale leaving the old Fifth Avenue Hotel for the drive up Fifth Avenue to Manhattan Field.
Princeton vs. Yale, New York, Nov. 30, 1893.

partaking of their deferred but now more enjoyable Thanksgiving Day dinner, while the heroes of the day, winners
and losers alike, enjoyed themselves in "breaking training."
During the evening the theatres became the scene of the
day's closing diversions. The play may have been good
or it may have been bad. It mattered not to the audience,
for the best show was given in front of the footlights. The
entrance and the exit of the actors were punctuated with
remarks from the audience and their dialogue with frequent
suddenness was submerged by a tidal wave of noise. No
orchestral leader ever was so witless as to strike up a tune
that the crowd could sing. The theatres over, the crowds
sought their trains for New Haven and for Princeton, giving a parting cheer that almost unroofed the train-sheds,
while New York, which had enjoyed the day immensely,
went home to bed, to resume the following morning its
customary amusements.

CHAPTER VIII

FOOTBALL FROM 1900 TO 1910

EXPERIENCE has proved that the reputation borne by a period of calmness for preceding some signal event is amply justified. With the profound revision of the rules in 1896, and with the invention by Princeton of the revolving wedge, football entered upon four years in which the activities of the collegians seemed to be devoted to the perfection of existing plays rather than to the search for new mechanisms. Thus the decade of the '90s came to a close and the year of 1900 arrived apparently to continue the condition. There was, however, in January, 1900, a little council of football men quietly assembling now and then at Yale to study a novel offensive theory proposed by Walter Camp. From the earliest days of football the defensive rush-line had been taught to play low and to charge their opponents back at the snap of the ball. Camp's theory was that a play could be devised which would take advantage of this forward plunge of the opposing rush-line by getting a play into the opening made by a charging forward and accomplishing a satisfactory gain before that forward could recover his balance and fill up the opening that he himself had made. This theory eventually shaped itself into Yale's famous tackle-back play, thus utilizing an old formation, but executing the play in a wholly new manner. With many misgivings the younger strategists of Yale watched the progress of this play in the early games of the succeeding autumn. As mid-season approached they were demanding its abandonment as a failure, but suddenly the perfection

106

of the play was attained and Yale began to run up large scores and to nonplus their opponents as to the manner in which their attack was made so easily.   November came to a close with Princeton and Harvard defeated by the largest scores ever made against them by Yale, and the country awoke to the realization that another great device of offensive football had arrived.

While this remarkable engine was laying low Yale's adversaries in the East, another highly effective formation was at work in the West. The latter was the "Northwestern tandem," an invention by C. M. Hollister, of Pennsylvania, at that time the coach of Northwestern University.   This play employed three men, one of whom was a heavy forward, arranged in a straight line at a right angle to the rush-line and stationed directly behind the quarter-back.   The effectiveness of the formation lay in its tandem principle, which was accomplished without forming to right or left of centre, thereby obviating a strong and a weak side and making it possible to attack any point in the opponents' line with equal strength.   The shifts in the rush-line produced in this year a great variety of plays, the most unusual of which was the complete separation of the rush-line into two sections, known as a divide, thus permitting the head of tandem plays to come fully into the rush-line.

Few changes in the rules were found necessary in the spring of 1901. One of these, the abolition of throwing the ball into play from the side line when out of bounds, the "fair" of the early game, brought no change in the play since it had gone out of use actually years before, but the dropping from the code of the obsolete legislation on the subject marked the final passing of one of the great features that existed and still exists in the English game.   One recalls this great play as it occurs in the game of School-House vs. School, described in "Tom Brown's School Days."

Time was when it was a centre of strategy in the intercollegiate game. As soon as the ball went out of bounds the opposing side surrounded the point where the ball had crossed the side line and warily watched to see that the ball was not craftily touched into play before the defensive team was ready. "What will you do—take it out or touch it in?" cried the defensive captain. If the answer was "Touch it in," the players took positions in two lines at a right angle to the side line, and one of the players of the side in possession of the ball thereupon touched it in play by touching the ball to the side line and passing it to one of his backs. Many were the stratagems that were devised and executed around the old "fair."

Still enjoying its era of peace the rule-makers found little to command their attention in 1902, and tactics continued as in the two preceding years. This was the season in which occurred G. B. Chadwick's two famous runs in the Princeton-Yale game, each fifty yards and more for a touchdown, by which a victory was achieved by the Blue. The method by which Yale twice divided Princeton's line in this game so widely that Chadwick raced through without being touched by a player has remained one of the secrets of the game. The strategists of Princeton, however, attributed the success of these wonderful and mysterious runs to a change made by Yale from boxing the tackle to boxing the guard. If this is true, then it was an operation of retribution, for it was Princeton which, in 1888, invented this stratagem known as boxing the tackle and tried it first on Yale, sending Cowan in the opening play from midfield to the five-yard line. But in 1888 the officials were overcautious, and not being able to reconcile the method to the rules, Cowan's run went for naught and the play temporarily was outlawed.

Although the season of 1902 had been fraught with no excessive number of accidents nor with any personal mis-

hap of a severe or sensational character, the long-dormant
football reformer awoke. He found ready support in that
portion of the football public which had been exasperated
by the closeness of play and which saw in the agitation an
opportunity to use roughness as a weapon with which to force
the return of open play. The sport thereupon was clam-
orously charged with being intolerably dangerous. At this
juncture came forth Professor Edwin G. Dexter, of the
University of Illinois, who for several years had quietly
been keeping a precise and accurate record of the injuries of
the game and its kindred sports, and who also had compiled
a table of statistics covering the scholarship of the country's
football men. The deductions from these figures were so
strongly in favor of the game and its players that the agitation subsided as quickly as it had arisen.

The Rules Committee, notwithstanding, sensitive to the
situation, decided to revise the game so as to force a more
open style of play. After much discussion it was believed
that this could be accomplished by permitting the player
who received the ball directly from the snapper-back, usually
the quarter-back, to run forward with the ball. Cautious,
however, in their radicalness, the legislators of the game
imposed a condition that such a run must cross the line
five yards distant from the point where the ball was put in
play. But this was a novelty that was not new. The right
of the second man to advance the ball had come in with the
English Rugby game in 1876 and had remained until 1880,
when the evolution of the English scrummage into the
American scrimmage prompted the rule-makers of that day
to establish and name the position of quarter-back and to
prohibit him or the second man from "advancing forward
with the ball under penalty of foul." The imposition of
this five-yard restriction brought in the autumn of 1903 the
lengthwise stripes of the playing-field, thereby changing its

countenance from the classic gridiron to a checker-board. As a further part of their revision and in order to abolish a rough feature of the game the committee made the player who kicks the ball forward ineligible either to recover it or to run forward and put his associates on-side. From earliest times it had been one of the familiar sights of the game after a punt to see the full-back running down the field violently blocked and jostled by his opponents, and to hear him cry when he had passed the ball, "On-side! On-side!" Although this blocking and jostling was rough, it had never been injurious; but it was an incident that frequently had drawn criticism upon the game, and so it had to pass. As a final concession to the public critics of the game the committee at the session of 1903 reduced the value of a goal from the field from five to four points. For many years there had been a contention that the value of a goal from the field which was accomplished by the skill of one man was inadequately high in comparison with the value of a touchdown which was the result of team play and occasionally resulted in a superior eleven being defeated by a superior individual.

Strange to say the satisfaction of the football public over these reforms was short-lived. At the close of the season of 1903 the complaints of 1902 were renewed, and soon in increased volume were sweeping the country. The Middle West began to organize to obtain representation upon the Rules Committee or, failing, to establish a sectional committee. This demand promptly was met by the Rules Committee, which extended its membership to include the University of Chicago, which sent as its representative its professor of physical culture, A. A. Stagg, well remembered as one of Yale's greatest players on diamond and gridiron in the '80s. Still the opposition to the game would not subside. It smouldered throughout the playing season of 1904 and 1905. So acute did the criticism become in the

latter season that Theodore Roosevelt, President of the
United States, in the month of October, called to Washington the representatives in football of Harvard, Princeton,
and Yale, and impressed upon them the necessity of removing every objectionable feature of play, at the same
time giving the sport, if rightly played, the prestige of his
endorsement.   This dramatic episode quelled for a time
the attacks upon football, but at the close of the season
they again burst forth in the most violent storm the game
ever had encountered.   Again the hazards of the game had
accumulated at one time an unusual number of injuries.
The adherents of the open game whom the quarter-back run
had failed to satisfy charged the cause of the accidents to the
closeness of play.   In the midst of the attacks upon the game
the Middle West became rent with dissensions relative to the
eligibility of players.   The first blow at the sport was dealt
by Columbia.   At this institution George Foster Sanford, of
Yale, acting as coach, had brought football from obscurity
to such a state of perfection that Columbia had become a
football power equal with the leaders.   Notwithstanding, its
authorities peremptorily abolished the game.   ¯At the Western institutions similar movements were forming.   Suddenly the attack upon the game was directed against the
Rules Committee.   A number of college heads asked by
what authority this body assumed to legislate for the sport.
The members of the committee promptly replied that they
were acting only for the institutions which they represented,
and that it was optional with other colleges and universities
to accept their rules.

At this juncture, Henry M. MacCracken, chancellor of
New York University, issued an invitation to the colleges
of the country to send representatives to a conference on
football to be held in New York.   Here, December 24,
1905, delegates from twenty-eight institutions assembled,

Harvard being the only member of the Rules Committee to participate in this conference. Out of the mass of suggestions advanced finally issued a plan proposed by Captain Palmer E. Pierce, of the Army, that the conference should appoint a rules committee of seven members, that being the number of the intercollegiate committee, and that this conference committee should sit jointly if possible with the intercollegiate committee and thoroughly revise the game, othewise that it should proceed independently to perform the same service. The intercollegiate committee promptly accepted the proposition of the conference committee, and the two committees thereupon coalesced, January 12, 1906, sitting jointly under the title of the American Intercollegiate Football Rules Committee, although each committee reserved its separate organization. Many were the sessions held by this new tribunal, digesting and testing the multitudinous suggestions presented. At last from its patient deliberations issued a code so thoroughly revised that it presented almost a new game. At the suggestion of John C. Bell, of Pennsylvania, and Paul J. Dashiell, of the Naval Academy, the forward pass was introduced, a play so novel and so at variance with the very traditions of the intercollegiate and Rugby games that for years it has been forced to fight for its existence. And yet nothing is new under the sun, for this forward pass was a feature in the old Spartan game of football, called harpaston, played 2,500 years ago, and which was described in Chapter I. In fact, the name, harpaston, was derived from this very play, the long forward pass with which every contest began. But many other changes marked this revision. The requirement that the offensive eleven must gain five yards on four downs or lose the ball was altered so to require a gain of ten, thus forcing a team if possible to use end runs and other long-distance gaining plays, the open game so long desired. Hurdling, the

spectacular but dangerous play which time and again in the
early years of this decade had brought the stands to their feet
as some daring player by its use turned defeat into victory,
was forbidden. The odious mass play again was suppressed
by commanding six men of the offensive side to play upon the
line of scrimmage and by forbidding the seventh forward, if
playing behind the line, to stand inside the position taken by
the man at the end of the line. Further, linemen were forbidden to interchange with the backs unless the change was
permanent. Even the playing time of the game was reduced ten minutes.

Reform, still on the rampage, continued its course at numerous colleges, which seized the occasion to put their athletic establishments in order. Northwestern University and
Union College abolished the game for one year. Leland
Stanford and California abolished the intercollegiate game
altogether and adopted the Rugby Union game, and then
with the true genius of American invention immediately
started to modify their English rules. Throughout the Middle West training-tables were abandoned, schedules reduced,
and limitations placed upon the retention of professional
coaches. The final blow in this section came in a prohibition of intercollegiate contests between Chicago, Michigan, and Wisconsin for a period of one year. The East was
slightly less turbulent. Harvard, Princeton, and Yale held
a conference at which an agreement was made to prohibit
Freshmen from membership upon university teams, to im-
pose a residence qualification of one year upon a player
coming from another college, and to adopt independently
various high scholastic qualifications for all students desir-
ing to participate in competitive athletics.

Among the new devices created by the Rules Committee, interest of course centred chiefly on the forward pass.
The players treated the play lightly, however, and so the

season disclosed little of its possibilities. It was not until
the Harvard-Yale game that a great forward-pass play
appeared, but with this play Yale won the contest by sending the ball thirty yards to Harvard's three-yard mark, from
which the touchdown was quickly made. This spectacular
victory served to make the public keenly alert for its further development in 1907, but, strange to say, this season
also came and went with no great exposition of the play
until the Princeton-Yale game, in which Yale, starting
in the second half with a score of ten points against them,
won a brilliant victory in which two long forward passes
largely contributed to the result. The tacticians now awoke
to the possibilities of this play. With the arrival of 1908
every team began the season with a large number of variations of the forward pass. The chief value of the play,
however, soon appeared to be in the fear of its use by the
defensive team, which thereby was compelled to spread and
weaken its defence. The two defensive half-backs which
for many years had constituted the secondary defence, supporting the tackles, were sent back to cover the dangerous
forward-pass zone. This weakening of the tackle position
and the necessity of gaining ten yards then invited a development of the very strategic system that the rule-makers
had sought to avoid by the introduction of the forward pass,
a continuous massed attack on the tackles. The tackle of
middle weight instantly disappeared and in his place came
an active giant, the most powerful player in the rush-line.
In the succeeding year, 1909, this style of game, in which
the tackles were heavily and continuously battered, began
with the season's first game. Ingenuity had multiplied the
strength of the attack by reintroducing the revolving principle of play by which the runner was pushed and pulled,
whirled and rammed in the centre of an interlocked mass of
interferers against the tackles. As a result injury followed

RECOVERING AN ON-SIDE KICK.

Kennedy, of Dartmouth, recovers an on-side kick against Harvard. Harvard Stadium, Nov. 14, 1908.

injury, and by the middle of the season some of these, unfortunately, were fatal.   For the first time in the history of the game these serious injuries had occurred to players upon intercollegiate teams.   While there had been fatal injuries in the sport, as there is in every sport, these injuries previously had been confined to unorganized, untrained elevens randomly selected, playing irregular schedules and using improper grounds.   As a result the old cry against the game again was heard and once more football was haled before the bar.   Some demanded its utter abolition, others proposed to substitute for it the Rugby Union game.   Each day in the public press appeared specific suggestions for its reform.   The mass play, interlocked and off-side interference were designated as the chief causes of danger in the intercollegiate game.   In the midst of the uproar the association of colleges formed by Chancellor MacCracken in 1906, now known as the National Collegiate Athletic Association of the United States, assembled in New York.   The game was bitterly assailed, but the association referred the problem of its remedy to the Rules Committee for solution.

This body soon assembled and began a series of sessions the most strenuous in its history.   During the month of May it brought its deliberations to a close and produced a new code.   The five-yard restriction was removed from the quarter-back run and the forward pass, thereby affording the medium of a more open game and incidentally removing the necessity for the lengthwise marking of the field, a change that obliterated the checker-board and brought back the famous gridiron as of yore.   The periods of the game, the halves, which had come down the years since Tom Brown saved the game in the second half at Rugby, were replaced by quarters in imitation of the custom of our Canadian comrades and the playing time was shortened by ten minutes. The privilege of returning a withdrawn player to the game, a custom that came in with the Rugby Union game in 1876 and remained for a few years, was restored. But the most radical and effective alteration made in the rules was that relative to interference. For twenty years the most opposed feature of the intercollegiate game had been the mass play. Those great creations, the V, the flying wedge, the turtle-back, guards-back, the tandem, and the tackle-back, periodically had arisen to win victories for their creators, to be charged with rendering the sport uninteresting and uncouth and with being the cause of its injuries, and eventually to be outlawed, only to be replaced by another great device of coaching genius still constructed along the lines of the mass idea. This time the rule-makers decided to remove the mass play wholly from the game. This was accomplished by prescribing that when the ball was put in play seven men should be on the line of scrimmage and, most revolutionary of all, that no player of the side in possession of the ball should use his hands or arms to assist the player carrying the ball, but that the latter should run unassisted and alone and that the players of the attacking side should not interlock arms or bodies. This final removal of the very core of the mass play prodigiously weakened the offence, necessitating a restoration in some way of the equilibrium of the game, for theoretically the defence and offence must balance in order to present a fair game for the players to play. This was accomplished by forbidding the flying tackle, a spectacular feat, but one frequently provocative of injury, and by permitting the player who received the ball directly from the snapper-back to run forward, a privilege that had been forbidden for thirty years. The problem of providing for an adequate defence of the back field, the attack of which had been so enormously increased by the establishment of the on-side kick and forward pass, was solved by the creation of a zone of twenty yards within which no on-side

"THE MINNESOTA SHIFT."

Yale executing the formation against Harvard. Nov. 19, 1910.

kick might be recovered and beyond which no forward pass might be thrown.   With the exception of this last feature this great change in the game was accomplished without the introduction of one untried or unknown condition, since all of these alterations are recognizable as tactics and methods of former days.

These rules were criticised as all of their predecessors have been criticised, and predictions were made that they would fail to lessen the injuries of the game and to provide an interesting contest for the spectators.   Nevertheless the season of 1910 was awaited eagerly by all to ascertain how the coaching genius was to solve the tactical problems of the new game.   With the single exception of the "Minnesota shift," no new formation or play was presented.   The generals of the gridiron, proceeding cautiously as usual, clung as closely as possible to their old formations, leaving the profound possibilities of the new rules for gradual development, as was done in 1906 and 1907 with the novel forward pass. The "Minnesota shift," the invention of H. L. Williams, of Yale, coach for the University of Minnesota, was new only in its feature of the men forming out of position and leaping into position just before the ball was snapped, thereby masking the attack in order to prevent the defence likewise from shifting to meet the formation.   But the new code surprised its opponents by providing a game that not only was safe but that was still deeply interesting and spectacular. As a result the spring of 1911 produced only one substantial change, and that was in a detail of the forward pass.   Recovering the ball when passed forward and fumbled had been a source of roughness.   This was obviated simply by declaring such a fumbled ball an incompleted forward pass.

Such has been the history of intercollegiate football.   It has been only a sport, but its gridirons have been the training-grounds upon which men have been made.   Where are the players whose names appear in the stories of these games? They are at the head of great business enterprises. They are occupying posts of distinction and honor in our government. They are presiding as judges in our courts, as presidents and professors in our institutions of learning. Transferred from the mimic battles of the lines of lime, they are leading our armies and commanding our warships. Clergymen, merchants, lawyers, authors, doctors, inventors, manufacturers, whatever and wherever they are, they are pursuing their vocations with courage, solving their problems with wisdom, and treating their competitors with honor, worthy soldiers from a worthy school.

PART II

CHAPTER IX

ARMY VS. NAVY

Army vs. Navy
West Point, Nov. 29, 1890

ARMY		NAVY
T. O. Murphy, '91,	Left End,	R. H. Lane, '91.
J. T. Crabbe, '91,	Left Tackle,	H. A. Pearson, '93.
J. T. Moore, '92,	Left Guard,	J. D. Beuret, '92.
S. P. Adams, '92,	Centre,	N. E. Irwin, '91.
J. W. Heavey, '91,	Right Guard,	M. E. Trench, '93.
F. H. Schoeffel, '91,	Right Tackle,	C. F. Macklin, '92.
L. M. Prince, '92,	Right End,	G. W. Laws, '91.
K. Walker, '92,	Quarter-back,	H. E. Smith, '91.
D. M. Michie, '92, Capt.,	Left Half,	C. R. Emrich, '91, Capt.
E. J. Timberlake, '93,	Right Half,	R. J. Hartung, '91.
B. Ames, '94,	Full-back,	A. Althouse, '91.

Substitutions: J. W. Lyon, '91, T. W. Horn, '91, E. W. Clark, '93, Army; H. E. Smith, '91, A. G. Kavanagh, '94, M. K. Johnson, '94, Navy.

Referee: R. R. Belknap, '91, Navy. Umpire: W. H. Hyndman, '84, Yale. Score: Army 0, Navy 24. First Half: Touchdown by C. R. Emrich; touchdown by C. R. Emrich; touchdown by M. K. Johnson. Second Half: Touchdown and goal by C. R. Emrich; touchdown and goal by C. R. Emrich.

First Half: Army wins the toss and takes the south goal. The Navy forms a V and gains 15 yards, Prince bringing down the runner. Sharp tackling by Murphy, and Timberlake forces Navy to punt and Althouse sends the ball down to Ames on Army's 10-yard line. Hard rushing by Michie, and Timberlake works the ball back to midfield, where the

Navy takes it on downs. Emrich and Hartung now alternate in plunges against Army's line and the ball travels steadily to the last line, Emrich crossing the stripe for a touchdown. The goal fails. Army makes 5 yards in the V, but is soon forced to punt. Navy's line attack starts into action and in 10 plunges the ball is placed on the Army's 5-yard line. Emrich bucks the centre and makes a touchdown. The goal is missed. Army puts the ball in play with a wedge, but Navy quickly takes it on downs. The Army line is ripped apart for long gains and Johnson finally skirts the end for 15 yards and a touchdown. No goal.

Second Half: The Army opens with the V, and Michie and Timberlake force the Navy's line for steady gains until the 15-yard line is reached. Laws and Lane tackle sharply and get the ball. Althouse punts out of danger. A brilliant exchange of kicks ensues. Navy renews scrimmage play and again batters the Army line for good gains. In the last space Emrich takes the ball and bucks the Army's centre for a touchdown. He kicks the goal. Play is resumed, but fierce tackling by the Army holds Navy in check. The ball travels back and forth between the 25-yard lines. At last Emrich circles the end and runs 25 yards for a touchdown. Goal. No further scoring.

ARMY vs. NAVY

Annapolis, Nov. 28, 1891

ARMY		NAVY
J. T. Moore, '92,	Left End,	P. Symington, '92.
G. E. Houle, '93,	Left Tackle,	J. D. Beuret, '92.
W. E. Gleason, '92,	Left Guard,	H. A. Pearson, '93.
S. P. Adams, '92,	Centre,	G. L. Holsinger, '93.
	"	C. L. Hussey, '92.
E. W. Clark, '93,	Right Guard,	M. E. Trench, '93.
F. W. Smith, '95,	" "	
D. E. Aultman, '94,	Right Tackle,	C. F. Macklin, '92, Capt.
	" "	W. C. Davidson, '95.

ARMY		NAVY
L. M. Prince, '92,	Right End,	H. L. Ferguson, '92.
F. A. Wilcox, '92,	" "	
K. Walker, '92,	Quarter-back,	W. Bagley, '95.
P. W. Davison, '92,	Left Half,	R. D. Hasbrouck, '92.
	" "	E. H. Campbell, '93.
E. J. Timberlake, '93,	Right Half,	M. K. Johnson, '94.
D. M. Michie, '92, Capt.,	Full-back,	C. Webster, '94.

Referee: G. W. Woodruff, '89, Yale. Umpire: J. N. Thomas, '90, Princeton. Score: Army 32, Navy 16. First Half: Touchdown by E. W. Clark, goal by D. M. Michie; touchdown by C. F. Macklin, goal by P. Symington; touchdown by D. M. Michie. Second Half: Touchdown by D. M. Michie; touchdown by E. W. Clark, goal by D. M. Michie; touchdown by E. J. Timberlake, goal by D. M. Michie; touchdown by R. D. Hasbrouck, goal by P. Symington; touchdown by M. K. Johnson, goal by P. Symington; touchdown by E. J. Timberlake, goal by D. M. Michie.

First Half: Army wins the toss and takes the ball. The game opens with a V, gaining 8 yards. Clark, Michie, and Davidson take the ball to Navy's 20-yard line. Timberlake makes 10 more. Clark goes through for a touchdown. Michie kicks the goal. Navy resumes play with the V, making 15 yards. Johnson skirts the end for 15. The ball goes to the Army on a foul. Timberlake bucks the centre for 10 yards. Navy holds for downs and gets the ball. Althouse punts and Timberlake catches. Timberlake hits the centre for 10. Gleason and Moore make 6. Navy holds for downs. Beuret goes through centre for 15. Webster repeats the play for 15 more. Macklin gets around the end for 20. Army holds and Bagley punts to Michie. Davidson makes 5, but Navy holds for downs. Beuret gets through the line for 5. Johnson circles the end for 20. Hasbrouck pierces the line for 10. Navy fumbles and Army gets the ball. Timberlake gets away for 40 yards. Navy holds and Michie punts. Bagley returns. Army fumbles and Navy gets the ball. Macklin goes through tackle for 20 yards and a touchdown. Symington kicks the goal. Army opens with the V, making 12 yards. The ball goes to Navy on a foul. Bagley, Webster, Hasbrouck, and Johnson force the ball to Army's 20-yard line, where the latter holds for downs. Davidson goes around the end for 20. Michie and Timberlake add 20 more. Davidson again circles the end for 20 and on the next play Michie crosses the line for a touchdown. Time is called for the half.

Second Half: The play is rapid and fierce throughout the second half, each team ripping apart their opponents' line for continual gains. In this period Michie, Clark, and Timberlake score four touchdowns for the Army, from three of which Michie kicks goals. Hasbrouck and Johnson make touchdowns for the Navy, from one of which Symington kicks a goal.

ARMY vs. NAVY

West Point, Nov. 30, 1892

ARMY		NAVY
B. Ames, '94,	Left End,	E. McCauley, '96.
G. E. Houle, '93,	Left Tackle,	C. J. Lang, '93.
A. Laws, '93,	Left Guard,	C. Wells, '93.
T. L. Ames, '95,	Centre	A. G. Kavanagh, '94.
E. W. Clark, '93, Capt.,	Right Guard,	M. E. Trench, '93, Capt.
F. W. Smith, '95,	Right Tackle,	J. M. Reeves, '94.
L. Stacy, '96,	Right End,	M. J. McCormack, '95.
H. H. Stout, '95,	Quarter-back,	C. S. Bookwalter, '94.
E. J. Timberlake, '93,	Left Half,	W. B. Izard, '95.
E. L. King, '96,	Right Half,	M. K. Johnson, '94.
C. W. Kutz, '93,	" "	
H. H. Pattison, '93,	Full-back,	W. Bagley, '95.
T. G. Carson, '94,	"	

Referee: L. T. Bliss, '93, Yale. Umpire: S. V. Coffin, '89, Wesleyan. Score: Army 4, Navy 12. Second Half: Touchdown by W. B. Izard, goal by W. Bagley; touchdown by E. J. Timberlake; touchdown by M. K. Johnson, goal by W. Bagley.

First Half: Navy wins the toss and takes the ball. Bookwalter in the flying wedge gains 5 yards. Izard bucks

the centre for 3. Reeves circles the end for 5. Unable to
make further gains Bagley punts 35 yards, but the ball is
brought back and given to the Army for holding. King
hits the centre for 2. Johnson stops a criss-cross and on
a fumble gets the ball. Izard makes a yard. The Army
gets the ball for holding. Timberlake makes 2 yards,
McCauley tackling. Navy holds for downs. Navy draws
behind the line and forms a flying wedge, in which Bagley
makes 5 yards. Izard and Bagley gain 10. Johnson gets
through the line for 5. Army holds and Bagley punts to
the 10-yard line. The Army cannot gain and Navy takes
the ball on downs. Izard circles the end for 15. The
ball is brought back and given to the Army for holding.
Timberlake, Pattison, and King net 10 yards. Navy holds
for downs. Johnson rounds the end for 20 yards. Army
takes the ball on downs. Pattison makes 30 yards around
the end. Navy holds and takes the ball, but at once is
forced to kick. Smith makes 5 yards around the end.
Timberlake adds 1. Kutz circles the end for 10. Timberlake makes 45 yards, but the ball goes to the Navy on
a fumble. Unable to make first down Bagley punts to
Kutz, who returns. Lang, Reeves, and Johnson fail to gain
first down and Bagley punts. Timberlake goes through
the centre for 2 and time is called for the half.

Second Half: Army in the flying wedge makes 10 yards.
Timberlake and King add 15 more. Smith, Pattison, King,
and Laws advance the ball to the 10-yard line. Navy stops
Clark behind the line. McCauley stops an end run for no
gain. King makes first down. Pattison, in the flying
wedge, adds 4. On the 1-yard line Navy holds 4 downs
for no gain. Bagley punts to Army's 50. Navy holds for
downs and gets the ball. Bagley punts to Army's 25.
Army fumbles and it is the Navy's ball. Johnson goes
through centre for 18 yards. Izard goes through tackle

for a touchdown. Bagley kicks the goal. Army starts play with the flying wedge followed by line plunges which quickly place the ball on Navy's 10-yard line. Stout, Kutz, and Timberlake in 3 downs cross the line for a touchdown. Clark punts out to Timberlake, who heels the catch, but on the try the goal is missed. Navy likewise starts off with a rush and in 10 plays reaches the Army's 5-yard line. Army holds for downs. Kicks are exchanged. Johnson gets away for 35 yards. Bagley and Izard reach the 10-yard line. Johnson is sent over for a touchdown. Bagley kicks the goal. Time soon after is called.

ARMY vs. NAVY
Annapolis, Dec. 2, 1893

ARMY		NAVY
D. E. Nolan, '96,	Left End,	E. McCauley, '96.
A. G. Lott, '96,	Left Tackle,	K. G. Castleman, '96.
J. S. Battle, '94,	Left Guard,	B. Morris, '97.
T. L. Ames, '95,	Centre,	A. G. Kavanagh, '94, Capt.
F. W. Smith, '95,	Right Guard,	F. D. Karns, '95.
D. E. Aultman, '94,	Right Tackle,	J. M. Reeves, '94.
J. P. Harbeson, '94,	Right End,	M. J. McCormack, '95.
S. G. Creden, '95,	Quarter-back,	C. S. Bookwalter, '94.
G. H. Shelton, '96,	Left Half,	H. S. Kimball, '96.
L. Stacy, '96,	Right Half,	W. C. Davidson, '95.
T. G. Carson, '94, Capt.,	Full-back,	W. Bagley, '95.

Referee: W. M. Irvine, '88, Princeton. Umpire: V. C. McCormick, '93, Yale. Score: Army 4, Navy 6. Second Half: Touchdown and goal by H. S. Kimball; touchdown by T. G. Carson.

First Half: Army wins the toss and takes the ball. The flying wedge nets 15 yards, but Navy holds for downs. Bagley punts 50 yards to Shelton, who runs back 20 before being tackled. Army tries the "Woodruff flying interference," but, after shooting Stacy through the centre for 5, Navy gets the ball on downs. The Army immediately recovers on a fumble. Stacy rounds the end for 5, but an attempt to repeat the play results in a loss. Navy gets the ball on downs and Bagley punts 50 yards. Army fumbles and McCauley falls on the ball. Davidson circles the end for 20. Army holds for downs and Carson punts 40. Kimball hits centre for 2, but two more plunges fail to gain. Army gets the ball. Stacy on a triple pass rounds the end for 25 yards. Ames and Smith pierce the centre for 15. A penalty sets the Army back 5. Navy holds for downs and gets the ball. Bookwalter punts 40 yards. Both teams surge back and forth between the 35-yard lines, but cannot get in striking distance of one another's goal. Struggling thus the half closes.

Second Half: The Navy opens with the flying wedge and gains 15 yards. Davidson, Reeves, Kimball, and Bagley now alternate with the ball in rapid succession, making gain after gain, all short but consecutive, until the last yard line is reached, from which Kimball is shot across for the touchdown. A moment later he kicks the goal. Army resumes play with the flying wedge and gains 20 yards. A long struggle now ensues on the 40-yard line. Army plunges and punts, and Navy, unable to gain, sends the ball back. At last Stacy gets around the end for 20 yards, Reeves tackling. On the second play Stacy repeats the play around the opposite end for 20 yards more. Carson makes the last 5 yards through the line for a touchdown. The goal is missed. Play is resumed, but neither goal again is threatened. Time is called.

1894–1898, games not permitted by Army and Navy Departments.

ARMY VS. NAVY

Philadelphia, Dec. 3, 1899

ARMY		NAVY
W. D. Smith, '01, Capt.,	Left End,	B. A. Long, '01.
" "		S. Read, '02.
E. E. Farnsworth, '04,	Left Tackle,	W. K. Wortman, '00, Capt.
C. Enos, '01,	" "	

ARMY		NAVY
W. R. Bettison, '01,	Centre,	G. Whitlock, '01.
N. A. Goodspeed, '02,	Right Guard,	C. Belknap, '03.
P. D. Bunker, '03,	Right Tackle,	R. R. Adams, '02.
C. Burnett, '01,	Right End,	N. E. Nichols, '02.
E. M. Zell, '03,	" "	
F. P. Lahm, '01,	Quarter-back,	B. A. Long, '01.
F. Williams, '03,	"	
A. F. Casad, '02,	Left Half,	O. W. Fowler, '01, Capt.
H. B. Hackett, '04,	" "	
F. W. Clark, '01,	Right Half,	E. S. Land, '02.
F. H. Phipps, '04,	" "	
B. W. Phillips, '03,	Full-back,	C. E. Smith, '03.
W. M. Nichols, '03,	"	

Referee: E. N. Wrightington, '97, Harvard. Umpire: R. D. Wrenn, '95, Harvard. Linesmen: N. Z. Graves, '04, Pennsylvania; W. A. Potter, '02, Pennsylvania. Timekeepers: J. P. Gardiner, '01, Pennsylvania; T. T. Hare, '01, Pennsylvania. Score: Army 7, Navy 11. First Half: Goal from field by F. W. Clark. Second Half: Goal from field by B. A. Long; touchdown by E. S. Land, goal by O. W. Fowler; safety by B. A. Long.

First Half: Navy wins the toss and takes the west goal. Farnsworth kicks to Smith at Navy's 12-yard mark, the ball being run back 15 yards. On the line-up Navy fumbles and Goodspeed gets the ball. Casad makes 5 through the line. Navy stands firm and gets the ball on downs. Belknap punts. Army cannot gain at midfield and Navy gets the ball on downs. Nichols plunges through centre for 15 yards. Navy cannot gain farther and Belknap punts over the goal-line. An exchange of kicks interspersed with rushes lands the ball in the Army's possession on their 25-yard line. On the line-up Army fumbles and Navy recovers the ball at the 19-yard mark. The Navy cannot make an inch and Long tries and misses a drop kick for goal. The Army kicks out and the Navy by short gains rushes the ball back to the 30-yard line, where another drop kick is tried, but fails. The Army kicks out and the Navy again by line plunges forces the ball to the 30-yard line. Long falls back for another drop kick, but Farnsworth is through and blocks the kick.

The ball bounds back to the 45-yard line, where Farnsworth picks it up and with a clear field starts for the goal-line, but is tackled. On the line-up Clark goes around the end for 23 yards. Unable to gain further, Clark tries for a field goal and kicks it from placement. Navy kicks off and Army runs back the kick to the 20-yard line. Unable to gain, the ball is kicked to Navy's 40. By hard plunging the Navy carries the ball to the Army's 20-yard line, where the Navy is forced to try for a field goal. The kick is short and partially blocked, but Navy recovers it. A line plunge carries the ball to the 3-yard mark. Army throws the Navy back and a fumble gives them the ball. Time is then called for the half.

Second Half: Belknap kicks to Goodspeed at 20. The Army adopts a kicking game which lasts for fifteen minutes. At last the Army fumbles a punt and the Navy gets the ball on the former's 10-yard line. Long tries the line, but it is a stone wall. He falls back for a try at goal, but the kick is blocked, Navy recovering the ball. Two line plunges fail to advance the ball and again Long falls back for a try at goal, which he kicks. The Army kicks off and another long kicking duel follows. At last the Army fumbles and Navy gets the ball on the 10-yard line. Land on a delayed pass goes through for a touchdown. Fowler kicks the goal. Army kicks off and Belknap catches. On the line-up Belknap falls back to punt. The kick is blocked and rolls behind the goal-line. A mix-up ensues, Long falling on the ball for a safety. Time soon after is called.

ARMY vs. NAVY

Philadelphia, Nov. 30, 1901

ARMY		NAVY
E. E. Farnsworth, '04,	Left End,	K. Whiting, '05.
T. B. Doe, '05,	Left Tackle,	S. Read, '02.
N. W. Riley, '04,	Left Guard,	R. T. Carpenter, '04.

ARMY		NAVY
R. E. Boyers, '03,	Centre,	P. H. Fretz, '03.
N. A. Goodspeed, '02,	Right Guard,	C. Belknap, '03.
	" "	R. P. Schlabach, '03.
P. D. Bunker, '03,	Right Tackle,	R. R. Adams, '02.
J. A. McAndrew, '04,	Right End,	C. C. Soule, '04.
C. D. Daly, '05,	Quarter-back,	F. V. McNair, '03,
A. F. Casad, '02, Capt.,	Left Half,	F. B. Freyer, '02.
H. B. Hackett, '04,	" "	
H. M. Nelly, '02,	" "	
F. H. Phipps, '04,	Right Half,	E. S. Land, '02, Capt.
E. Graves, '05,	Full-back,	N. E. Nichols, '02.

Referee: E. N. Wrightington, '97, Harvard. Umpire: Evarts Wrenn, '92, Harvard. Linesmen: J. P. Gardiner, '01; S. M. Goodman, '97, Pennsylvania. Timekeeper: T. T. Hare, '01, Pennsylvania. Score: Army 11, Navy 5. First Half: Goal from field by C. D. Daly; touchdown by N. E. Nichols. Second Half: Touchdown and goal by C. D. Daly.

First Half: Navy wins the toss and takes the goal. Graves kicks off to Freyer at 15. Nichols goes through for 15 yards. For twenty minutes the ball travels back and forth between the 25-yard lines, punts following ineffectual plunges by both teams. Graves catches and puts the ball down for a scrimmage on Army's 50-yard line. Army forms in tackle-back formation and by short gains drives the ball to Navy's 25-yard line, where the latter stops the advance. On the last down Daly falls back for a try at goal and drops the ball squarely between the posts. Army kicks off to Navy's 20-yard line. The Navy now opens a brilliant attack, mixing end runs with line plunges, delayed and double passes in rapid succession, thus carrying the ball to Army's 40, where the latter gets the ball on downs. Graves punts. McNair catches on his 15-yard line and by a dodging dash runs 75 yards through the entire Army team, reaching the 10-yard line before he is thrown. Freyer goes around the end to the 5-yard line. Nichols takes the ball over for the touchdown. The punt-out fails. Time is called for the half.

PUNTING OUT OF DANGER.

Navy, driven to its goal-line, momentarily stays the Army's attack.   Philadelphia, Nov. 30, 1901.

Second Half: Belknap kicks off to Daly on the 10-yard line. The latter starts straight up the field, but as he meets the Navy tacklers he turns sharply to the right. The Army blocks off the mass of the Navy players, and Daly, sprinting at great speed, runs around them and covers the 95 yards for a touchdown. The goal is kicked. Navy kicks off. The Army by tackle-back plays hammers its way for 60 yards in short plunges. Navy gets the ball on downs and starts a similar attack upon the Army line. The Army now adopts a kicking game. The Navy again and again slowly works its way for half the length of the field, only to be held at last for downs and the ball punted back by Daly. Thus struggling to overcome the lead time is called.

ARMY vs. NAVY
Philadelphia, Nov. 29, 1902

ARMY		NAVY
E. E. Farnsworth, '04,	Left End,	K. Whiting, '05.
T. W. Hammond, '05,	Left Tackle,	J. Rodgers, '03.
N. W. Riley, '04,	Left Guard,	R. C. Grady, '06.
	" "	H. H. Michael, '04.
R. E. Boyers, '03, Capt.,	Centre,	E. C. Oak, '04.
	"	P. H. Fretz, '03.
C. F. Thompson, '04,	Right Guard,	C. Belknap, '03, Capt.
E. Graves, '05,	Right Tackle,	A. S. Rees, '06.
	" "	L. C. Farley, '05.
J. A. McAndrew, '04,	Right End,	C. C. Soule, '04.
C. D. Daly, '05,	Quarter-back,	F. V. McNair, '03.
	"	R. F. Smith, '06.
H. B. Hackett, '04,	Left Half,	R. B. Strassburger, '05.
P. D. Bunker, '03,	Right Half,	S. Doherty, '06.
	" "	E. S. Root, '05.
H. W. Torney, '06,	Full-back,	V. N. Metcalf, '06.
	"	W. F. Halsey, '04.

Referee: E. N. Wrightington, '97, Harvard. Umpire: J. H. Minds, '98, Pennsylvania. Linesmen: N. Z. Graves, '04; W. A. Potter, '02, Pennsylvania. Timekeepers: Carl Williams, '97; T. T. Hare, '01, Pennsylvania. Score: Army 22, Navy 8. First Half: Touchdown by P. D. Bunker; touchdown by H. B. Hackett; safety by C. D. Daly;

touchdown by R. B. Strassburger, goal by C. Belknap.   Second Half:
Touchdown by H. B. Hackett, goal by H. W. Torney; touchdown by
P. D. Bunker, goal by H. W. Torney.

First Half: Navy wins the toss and takes the ball. Belknap kicks off to Daly at Army's 15-yard line. Army tries
three plunges into the line, but cannot gain, and Daly punts
to Smith, who runs to Army's 40. The Army holds and
Navy punts. Army fumbles and Whiting falls on the ball.
Two hard plunges into the line fail to yield a yard and Strassburger falls back to try a drop kick. The Army line comes
through and the kick is blocked. Army punts and Navy
makes a fierce assault on the line without gain. The ball
is passed to Belknap for a punt, but the kick is partially
blocked, Army securing the ball on their 47-yard mark.
The Army now sets its tackle-back in rapid play, Torney,
Bunker, and Hackett ploughing through for continual gains
and taking the ball to the 5-yard line. Torney makes 3,
and on the next play Bunker goes over for the touchdown.
The punt-out fails. Belknap kicks off to Daly, who runs
back 20 yards. Bunker goes around the end for 18 yards.
The tackle-back again drives the Navy down to their 5-yard
line, where the Army fumbles and Navy gets the ball.
Belknap punts. Hackett catches the ball on the 45-yard
line and runs through the Navy team, 65 yards, for a touchdown. Torney misses the goal. Navy kicks off to Bunker
at Army's 10. The latter runs back the kick 25 yards. On
an exchange of kicks the Army fumbles on their 30-yard
line. Navy hits the line hard, but cannot get through, and
Strassburger tries a drop. The ball is low and Daly catches
it under the bar. Soule throws him across the line for a
safety. Daly kicks out and a long struggle ensues at centre.
At last Strassburger gets away for an end run of 65 yards
for a touchdown. Belknap kicks the goal. Time is then
called for the half.

Second Half: Daly kicks off to McNair at 20. The Navy on the line-up returns the ball. The Army sets its tackle-back again in motion, and Bunker, Daly, Torney, and Hackett by short gains reach the 5-yard line, from which Hackett goes over for the touchdown. Torney kicks the goal. Navy kicks off and Army returns. A long series of kicks ensues. Army puts the ball down for a scrimmage at midfield and rushes the ball to Navy's 30-yard line, where it goes to the Navy on a fumble. On the line-up the Navy fumbles and Bunker gets the ball. The Army now directs a fierce assault upon the Navy line, sending Bunker over the last line for a touchdown, from which Torney kicks the goal. The Navy kicks off to Daly at 10, who runs back the kick to 20. Army puts the ball down for a scrimmage and sets the tackle-back in motion, thus hammering the ball by short plunges 80 yards when time is called.

ARMY vs. NAVY

Philadelphia, Nov. 29, 1903

ARMY		NAVY
T. W. Hammond, '05,	Left End,	D. L. Howard, '06.
T. B. Doe, '05,	Left Tackle,	R. C. Grady, '06.
M. H. Shute, '06,	" "	W. B. Piersol, '08.
C. G. Mettler, '06,	" "	
N. W. Riley, '04,	Left Guard,	C. F. Chambers, '07.
	" "	R. F. Smith, '06.
A. C. Tipton, '05,	Centre,	A. S. Rees, '06.
C. F. Thompson, '04,	Right Guard,	E. C. Oak, '04.
	" "	R. F. McConnell, '07.
E. Graves, '05,	Right Tackle,	S. Doherty, '06.
C. K. Rockwell, '06,	Right End,	C. C. Soule, '04, Capt.
A. G. Gillespie, '06,	" "	K. Whiting, '05.
H. B. Hackett, '04,	Quarter-back,	R. B. Strassburger, '05.
	"	J. W. Wilcox, '05.
F. A. Prince, '06,	Left Half,	E. S. Root, '05.
	" "	J. S. Dowell, '05.
E. E. Farnsworth, '04, Capt.,	Right Half,	W. B. Decker, '06.
V. W. Cooper, '04,	" "	
R. C. Hill, '07,	Full-back,	W. F. Halsey, '04.
R. H. Davis, '08,	"	

Referee: E. N. Wrightington, '97, Harvard. Umpire: J. H. Minds, '98, Pennsylvania. Linesmen: Carl Williams, '97, Pennsylvania; C. B. Marshall, '04, Harvard. Timekeepers: T. T. Hare, '01; C. S. Metzgar, '03, Pennsylvania. Score: Army 40, Navy 5. First Half: Goal from field by C. F. Chambers; touchdown by V. W. Cooper, goal by R. H. Davis; touchdown by R. H. Davis, goal by T. B. Doe; touchdown by F. A. Prince, goal by T. B. Doe. Second Half: Touchdown by F. A. Prince; touchdown by F. A. Prince, goal by T. B. Doe; touchdown by F. A. Prince, goal by H. B. Hackett; goal from field by R. H. Davis.

First Half: Navy wins the toss and takes the goal. Doe kicks off to Navy's 27. A sharp punting exchange ensues marked by many fumbles. After several minutes of such play Army fumbles on their 16-yard mark and Howard falls on the ball. Navy cannot pierce the line. Chambers falls back and drops a goal from the field. Army kicks off to Strassburger at 20. Another kicking duel follows. Army puts down the ball for a scrimmage on their 30-yard line. The ball is rushed 20 yards, when, the Navy line holding for 3 downs, the ball is punted to Navy's 20, where a fumble occurs and Army gets the ball. Cooper in two plunges crosses the line and Davis kicks the goal. Navy kicks off and Army returns. Both teams now adopt a kicking game which wages monotonously until the Navy fumbles a high punt on the 10-yard line and Hammond falls on the ball for the Army. In three plays the Army sends Davis across for the touchdown. Doe kicks the goal. Navy kicks off and the Army returns. Again a kicking exchange opens up and lasts for several minutes. The Navy fumbles on the 10-yard line and Army gets the ball. Prince goes around the end for a touchdown and Doe kicks the goal. On the line-up time is called for the half.

Second Half: Chambers kicks off to Prince at 15. Prince falls back to punt, but Navy blocks the kick and Soule gets the ball. The Navy backs cannot pierce the Army line and Chambers drops back for a try at goal, but Army blocks the kick. A series of kicks ensues, resulting in a fumble by the Navy on their 20-yard line. Army gets the ball. In three plunges Cooper, Davis, and Prince take the ball across for a touchdown. The Navy blocks Doe's try for goal. Navy kicks off and Army returns. The usual punting duel ensues, resulting in a fumble by Navy on the 25-yard line and the recovery of the ball by the Army. Three plunges take the ball to the 5-yard line, from which Prince goes through tackle for the touchdown. Doe kicks the goal. Navy kicks off to Wilcox, who runs the kick back 35 yards. The Army kicks and recovers the ball on a fumble by Navy at the latter's 40. The Army by short gains through the line carries the ball to the last line, where Prince goes over for the touchdown and Hackett kicks the goal. Navy kicks off to Wilcox, who runs back 30 yards. A punt and a fumble gives Army the ball on Navy's 40. Davis kicks a goal from placement. Prince kicks off for Navy, but time is called.

ARMY VS. NAVY

Philadelphia, Nov. 26, 1904

ARMY		NAVY
T. W. Hammond, '05,	Left End,	D. L. Howard, '06.
T. B. Doe, '05, Capt.,	Left Tackle,	L. C. Farley, '05, Capt.
W. W. Erwin, '08,	Left Guard,	N. H. Goss, '05.
H. J. Weeks, '08,	" "	
A. C. Tipton, '05,	Centre	W. S. McClintic, '05.
D. C. Seagrave, '05,	Right Guard,	W. B. Piersol, '08.
C. G. Mettler, '06,	Right Tackle,	R. C. Grady, '06.
	" "	E. B. Woodworth, '06.
A. G. Gillespie, '06,	Right End,	K. Whiting, '05.
	" "	W. H. Dague, '08.
E. B. Garey, '08,	Quarter-back,	H. H. Norton, '07.
	"	J. W. Wilcox, '05.
R. C. Hill, '07,	Left Half,	H. L. Spencer, '07.
	" "	R. F. Bernard, '07.
F. A. Prince, '08,	Right Half,	S. Doherty, '06.
H. W. Torney, '06,	Full-back,	R. F. Smith, '06.
L. H. Watkins, '07.	"	R. L. Ghormley, '06.

Referee: E. N. Wrightington, '97, Harvard. Umpire: Evarts Wrenn, '92, Harvard. Linesman: T. T. Hare, '01, Pennsylvania. Score: Army 11, Navy 0. First Half: Touchdown by H. W. Torney; touchdown by H. W. Torney, goal by T. B. Doe.

First Half: Navy wins the toss and takes the west goal. Torney kicks off to Smith, who runs back to the 25-yard line. Smith goes through the line for 9 and repeats the play for 3 more. Doherty makes 2, and a penalty sets the Navy back 10. Howard punts to Prince at Army's 25. Torney hits the line for 3 and Doe adds 3 more. A penalty loses 15 and Army punts to Smith. Smith makes 5 around the end. Grady doubles the other end for 5 more. Spencer goes through the line for 6. The Army holds and Navy tries a quarter-back kick, but Tipton gets it. The ball is now on Army's 40. On the line-up Army fumbles and Navy recovers the ball at centre. Navy cannot make first down and a quarter-back kick is captured by Army. The Army tries two plunges into the line without gain and then punts to Navy. The ball is fumbled on the 20-yard line. Torney picks it up and runs across the line for a touchdown. The try at goal fails. Navy kicks off and Prince runs the ball back 15 yards. A long punting exchange ensues, ending by the Army putting the ball down for a scrimmage at midfield. Doe make 4, Prince 1, Hill 2, a penalty yields 5, Prince makes 1, Torney 2, and Doe 11, bringing the ball to the 10-yard line. The ball is given to Torney three times in succession and on the third plunge he takes it over for a touchdown. Doe kicks the goal. Navy kicks off to Army at 15. The Army in six plays brings the ball back to midfield, where time is called for the half.

Second Half: Navy kicks to Torney on the 10-yard line and the latter runs back 20 yards. By hard plunging, Torney, Hill, and Doe carrying the ball, the Army reaches Navy's 30-yard line, where the ball is fumbled. Navy can-

not gain and punts. Army returns. Doherty circles the
end and runs to Army's 30-yard line. The Army line does
not yield a yard and Wilcox tries a quarter-back kick, but
the ball goes out of bounds. Army lines up to punt, but
Torney goes through the line for 15 yards. Prince lifts
a long punt to Navy's 23-yard mark. Both teams now
play desperately, each plunging into the other's line without
substantial gain and then punting. The play for the remainder of the game is between the 35-yard lines. Time is
called, with the ball in Army's possession at midfield.

ARMY vs. NAVY
Princeton, Dec. 2, 1905

ARMY		NAVY
C. K. Rockwell, '06,	Left End,	D. L. Howard,'06, Capt.
W. W. Erwin, '08,	Left Tackle,	W. B. Piersol, '08.
	" "	P. W. Northcroft, '09.
H. J. Weeks, '08,	Left Guard,	J. M. O'Brien, '07.
W. H. Moss, '09,	" "	
C. R. Abraham, '06,	Centre,	L. D. Causey, '06.
	"	A. S. Rees, '06.
W. C. Christy, '07,	Right Guard,	J. F. Shafroth, '08.
C. G. Mettler, '06,	Right Tackle,	R. C. Grady, '06.
A. G. Gillespie, '06, Capt.,	Right End,	E. B. Woodworth, '06.
R. D. Johnson, '09,	Quarter-back,	W. B. Decker, '06.
	"	H. H. Norton, '07.
G. W. Beavers, '08,	Left Half,	H. L. Spencer, '07.
R. H. Smith, '08,	" "	A. H. Douglas, '08.
R. C. Hill, '07,	Right Half,	S. Doherty, '06.
H. W. Torney, '06,	Full-back,	R. L. Ghormley, '06.
L. H. Watkins, '07,	"	R. F. Smith, '06.

Referee: E. N. Wrightington, '97, Harvard. Umpire: R. D.
Wrenn, '95, Harvard. Linesman: W. W. Roper, '02, Princeton.
Score: Army 6, Navy 6. First Half: Touchdown by H. J. Weeks,
goal by C. G. Mettler. Second Half: Touchdown by A. H. Douglas,
goal by H. H. Norton.

First Half: Army wins the toss and takes the goal.
Howard kicks off to Torney at 25. Beavers punts to Navy's
50. Several series of kicks are exchanged, resulting in Army

obtaining the ball on Navy's 30-yard line. The Navy
line throws the Army runners back. Torney tries a place
kick, but misses. Navy kicks out and a run and a penalty
put the Army back on the 30-yard line, where a second
try from placement fails. Navy kicks out to midfield.
The Army now, by short gains of Weeks, Hill, and Torney,
reaches the 25-yard line, where Navy holds for downs.
Doherty punts to 48. The Army by short gains forces its
way to the 1-yard mark, from which Weeks is sent over for
a touchdown. Mettler kicks the goal. Navy kicks off and
the Army after a small gain punts. Navy returns. Mettler gets away for a 35-yard run. Torney adds 13. The
ball reaches Navy's 20-yard line. Beavers tries for a goal
from placement, but fails. Navy kicks out and time expires for the half.

Second Half: Army kicks off to Ghormley, who returns.
On a second exchange of kicks Navy recovers a fumble
on Army's 30-yard line. The Navy makes first down, but
Army holds on the 25-yard line and gets the ball. Beavers
punts to Norton, who heels the catch at 40. Navy makes
5 through the line; a penalty adds 15 more. The Army
holds for downs. For several minutes play continues between centre and Army's 20-yard line. The Navy rushes
fiercely, loses the ball on downs, and the Army punts back.
It is getting dark. The Army muffs a punt on their 25-yard
line and Navy gets the ball. Decker makes 2, Doherty 10,
then 2, Spencer 6, Doherty 2, Douglas goes over for a touchdown, and Norton kicks the goal. It is now too dark to
proceed and time is called.

ARMY vs. NAVY

Philadelphia, Dec. 1, 1906

ARMY		NAVY
A. J. Hanlon, '08,	Left End,	R. F. Bernard, '07.
	" "	W. N. Richardson, '09.
H. J. Weeks, '08.	Left Tackle,	P. W. Northcroft, '09.

ARMY		NAVY
W. W. Erwin, '08,	Left Guard,	G. R. Meyer, '10.
D. I. Sultan, '07,	Centre,	F. Slingluff, '09.
W. C. Christy, '07,	Right Guard,	P. T. Wright, '09.
R. F. Fowler, '10,	Right Tackle,	W. B. Piersol, '08.
	" "	G. W. Simpson, '07.
C. P. Stearns, '09,	Right End,	W. H. Dague, '08.
H. M. Hickam, '08,	" "	
R. D. Johnson, '09,	Quarter-back,	H. H. Norton, '07.
F. A. Mountford, '09,	"	
R. H. Smith, '08,	Left Half,	A. H. Douglas, '08.
E. St. J. Greble, '09,	" "	
R. C. Hill, '07, Capt.,	Right Half,	H. L. Spencer, '07, Capt.
G. W. Beavers, '08,	Full-back,	J. H. Ingram, '07.

Referee: W. H. Corbin, '89, Yale. Umpire: A. H. Sharpe, '02, Yale. Linesman: R. G. Torrey, '06, Pennsylvania. Score: Army, 0, Navy 10. Second Half: Goal from field by P. W. Northcroft; touchdown by J. H. Ingram, goal by H. H. Norton.

First Half: Army wins the toss and takes the west goal backed by a strong wind. Norton kicks to Stearns at Army's 15 and the latter runs back 15 yards. A series of kicks terminate by Piersol recovering the ball for Navy on their opponent's 45-yard line. Another exchange of kicks and a forward pass give Army the ball at their opponent's 40. Here Beavers tries for a field goal, but the kick is blocked. Army gets the ball and starts a fierce attack on the Navy line which carries the ball to the 2-yard line, where a forward pass results in a touchback. Navy kicks out and Norton on an on-side kick returns the ball to Navy's 20. Beavers tries for another field goal, but the ball goes beneath the bar. The ball is kicked out, and for several minutes both teams scrimmage and punt without advantage until a long punt by Beavers is fumbled on the Navy's 25-yard line. Smith hits the line for no gain. Hanlon makes 8. Beavers misses a field goal. Douglas kicks out. Beavers runs back 8 yards and then makes 5 more around the end. On a quarter-back kick Stearns gets the ball at

Navy's 20. Dague throws him at the 10-yard line. Before the teams can line up time is called for the half.

Second Half: Beavers kicks to Douglas at Navy's 10. For several minutes the play on both sides becomes a rush, a forward pass, and a punt without successful results. Army at last gets the ball out of bounds at their 25-yard line. On a fake kick Hill makes 10 yards through the centre. Beavers punts and Spencer heels the catch at Army's 45. The angle is wide, but Northcroft kicks a beautiful goal from placement. Beavers kicks off to Navy's 20. Douglas on a fake kick makes 25 yards. Douglas punts to Army's 40 and Dague gets the ball on a fumble. A penalty advances the Navy 5. Smith plunges for 5. Mountford makes the 30-yard line. Norton falls back for a drop kick, but instead shoots a forward pass to Ingram, who goes over for a touchdown. Norton kicks the goal. Beavers kicks off to Navy's 10. Spencer goes around the end for 15. On an exchange of kicks and a block the Navy gets the ball on the Army's 30. Mountford gets an on-side kick at 10. Beavers punts. Both teams, now resort to a kicking game, and time is called, with the ball in the Army's possession at midfield.

ARMY vs. NAVY
Philadelphia, Nov. 30, 1907

ARMY		NAVY
F. S. Besson, '09,	Left End,	M. B. De Mott, '09.
A. R. Underwood, '09,	" "	
E. A. Stockton, '08,	" "	
H. J. Weeks, '08,	Left Tackle,	P. W. Northcroft, '09.
W. W. Erwin, '08,	Left Guard,	G. R. Meyer, '10.
	" "	F. G. Reinicke, '10.
W. C. Philoon, '09,	Centre,	F. Slingluff, '09.
W. H. Moss, '09,	Right Guard,	P. T. Wright, '09.
D. D. Pullen, '10,	Right Tackle,	F. T. Leighton, '09.
R. F. Fowler, '10,	" "	C. W. Magruder, '08.
C. P. Stearns, '09,	Right End,	W. H. Dague, '08.
H. F. Ayres, '08,	" "	

ARMY		NAVY
F. A. Mountford, '09,	Quarter-back,	E. C. Lange, '09.
K. E. Kern, '11,	"	E. W. Strother, '08.
A. D. Surles, 11,	Left Half,	A. H. Douglas, '08, Capt.
E. St. J. Greble, '09,	" "	
G. W. Beavers, '08,	Right Half,	L. F. Reifsnider, '10.
R. D. Johnson, '09,	" "	
R. H. Smith, '08, Capt.,	Full-back,	R. E. Jones, '09.
A. J. Hanlon, '08,	"	H. W. Boynton, '08.

Referee: W. H. Corbin, '89, Yale. Umpire: A. H. Sharpe, '02, Yale. Field Judge: F. D. Godcharles, '93, Lafayette. Linesman: R. G. Torrey, '06, Pennsylvania. Score: Army 0, Navy 6. First Half: Touchdown by A. H. Douglas, goal by P. W. Northcroft.

First Half: Army wins the toss and takes the ball. Beavers kicks off, sending the ball across the goal-line. Navy kicks out to midfield. Army cannot gain and Beavers punts. Navy returns. A kicking duel now lasts for five minutes, the advantage being neutral. Army finally tries a forward pass, but Navy gets it. Douglas kicks to Mountford, who runs back 45 yards. Army is penalized 15 yards. Navy shows amazing defensive strength and throws Army back for a loss of 20 yards. Beavers kicks to Douglas, who returns. Army fumbles and Navy gets the ball. Douglas makes 10 on a delayed pass. Reifsnider cannot gain, but Lange gets around the end and plants the ball 3 yards from Army's goal. Navy fumbles, but recovers the ball. Douglas goes over for a touchdown. Northcroft kicks the goal. Beavers kicks off to Douglas on the 5-yard line. After a double exchange of kicks Douglas circles the end for 10 yards and then kicks to Mountford, who regains 15. The Navy tries two plunges into the line without gain and attempts an on-side kick, which Weeks blocks and then advances the ball 25 yards. Greble goes through tackle for 4 and Smith adds 2 more. Beavers tries a drop kick, but misses the bar. A kicking exchange follows, terminating in a plunge through tackle by Douglas for 5 yards and a for-

ward pass for 10 more. Smith on the next play intercepts
another forward pass and the Navy in turn regains the ball
by intercepting the Army's forward pass. An exchange of
kicks and a fumble puts the Navy on the Army's 15-yard
line. Unable to gain, Lange drops back for a drop kick, but
Weeks blocks it. On the line-up time is called.

Second Half: Douglas kicks off to Beavers, who returns
to Lange, the latter running back 15 yards. Navy makes
15 yards and then loses the ball on a fumble, but on the next
play regains it by intercepting a forward pass. Neither
team can pierce the other's line and kicks are frequent.
Navy kicks to Kern, who makes a brilliant run of 25 yards.
Beavers shoots a long forward pass, 25 yards, to Greble.
The ball is now on Navy's 30-yard line. Army makes 10
yards and Beavers tries for a field goal, but misses. Navy
kicks out to centre and immediately regains the ball on a forward pass. After several minutes of kicking Lange heels a
fair catch. Northcroft tries for a goal from placement, but
fails. Kern kicks out and Navy returns to the 30-yard
line. Greble punts out of bounds at 50 and Navy is penalized for holding. Douglas then punts to Kern at 40,
the latter running back 20 yards. On the line-up time
is called.

ARMY vs. NAVY
Philadelphia, Nov. 28, 1908

ARMY		NAVY
R. D. Johnson, '09;	Left End,	R. E. Jones, '09.
	" "	C. H. Cobb, '11.
A. E. Byrne, '10,	Left Tackle,	P. W. Northcroft, '09, Capt.
F. S. Besson, '09,	" "	
J. L. Wier, '11,	Left Guard,	G. R. Meyer, '10.
	" "	F. G. Reinicke, '10.
W. C. Philoon, '09, Capt.,	Centre,	F. Slingluff, '09.
		C. L. Brand, '10.
W. H. Moss, '09,	Right Guard,	P. T. Wright, '09.
R. R. Nix, '09,	" "	

ARMY		NAVY
D. D. Pullen, '10,	Right Tackle,	F. T. Leighton, '09.
" "	" "	D. H. Stuart, '09.
C. P. Stearns, '09,	Right End,	L. F. Reifsnider, '10.
J. E. Carberry, '10,	" "	L. C. Carey, '11.
R. F. Hyatt, '12,	Quarter-back,	E. C. Lange, '09.
W. Dean, '12,	Left Half,	J. P. Dalton, '12.
" "	" "	I. C. Sowell, '12.
E. St. J. Greble, '09,	Right Half,	H. S. McK. Clay, '11.
H. D. Chamberlin, '10,	Full-back,	W. A. Richardson, '10.
S. M. Walmsley, '12,	"	

Referee: J. A. Evans, '93, Williams. Umpire: A. H. Sharpe, '02, Yale. Field Judge: C. B. Marshall, '04, Harvard. Linesman: R. G. Torrey, '06, Pennsylvania. Score: Army 6, Navy 4. First Half: Touchdown and goal by W. Dean; goal from field by E. C. Lange.

First Half: Navy wins the toss and takes the west goal. Dean kicks off to Richardson at 17. The latter runs back to 30. Dalton punts to Dean. Greble makes 3 on a fake kick and then punts. The ball strikes the ground. Chamberlin, on-side, takes the ball on the run and reaches the 4-yard mark. Dean makes 2 and on the next play crosses the line for a touchdown. Dean also kicks the goal. Northcroft kicks to Hyatt, who runs back 15 yards. Greble punts to Reifsnider at 50. A bad pass loses a down and Dalton punts. Greble starts to run, but the Army is set back 15 on a penalty. Greble punts to Lange, who is downed without gain. Dalton fails to gain on a trick play and then punts. Greble returns to Lange. Clay gets around the end for 5, but fumbles and Greble gets the ball. Hyatt makes 8 and Greble punts to Lange, who heels a fair catch at 30. Dalton is thrown for a loss and then punts to Dean, who runs back 20 yards. Greble fails to gain on a fake kick and punts to Northcroft. Northcroft returns. Dalton makes 8 and then is thrown for a loss of 4. A long punting series opens up, finally resulting in Greble kicking to Lange at midfield, who runs out of bounds at Army's 35. Clay gets around the end for 3. Leighton goes through the line for 7. Dalton, Clay, and Leighton make 15 yards. On a double pass Lange circles the end for 6. Army holds and Navy tries a goal from placement, which Lange makes. Dean kicks off to Dalton at 25. Both teams try a plunge into the line, followed by a punt, as neither can gain against the other consistently, and thus the half closes.

Second Half: Northcroft kicks off to Hyatt, who returns to the 25-yard line. Chamberlin makes 2 yards. Dean punts to Lange and Dalton returns on the line-up to Hyatt. Stearns stops Clay on a double pass. Hyatt makes 10 around the end and Chamberlin adds 2 more. Dean lifts a punt 75 yards. Lange gets it behind the goal and runs it out to the 7-yard line. Dalton punts to 35. Dean makes 3 and Chamberlin 4. Navy recovers a forward pass on their 12-yard line. Dalton punts to Dean. Greble punts to Richardson. Dalton runs across the field on a fake kick, but there is no gain. Hyatt heels a fair catch at 45. Greble tries the end for no gain. Lange gets an on-side kick, and on the line-up goes around the end for 20 yards. Clay tries the other end without gain and Dalton punts. Navy now begins to send in substitutions. For several minutes the game becomes merely a punting contest between Dalton and Greble. Dalton makes 1 yard around the end and then Lange shoots a forward pass to Clay, which nets 12 yards. Dalton again gets round the end for 1, but Lange punts to Dean. Hyatt goes around the Navy's end for 15 yards. Greble makes 8 more. Chamberlin on a fake kick gets through the line for 2. Dalton recovers a fumble and with a clear field starts for the goal, but Chamberlin throws him out of bounds. Lange punts and time is called.

There was no game in 1909.

Army vs. Navy
Philadelphia, Nov. 26, 1910

ARMY		NAVY
J. S. Wood, '12,	Left End,	D. W. Hamilton, '12.
" "		R. E. P. Elmer, '12.
L. S. Devore, '12,	Left Tackle,	H. L. Merring, '11.
H. D. Douglas, '11,	" "	
H. Huston, '14,	Left Guard	C. Q. Wright, '11, Capt.
A. V. Arnold, '12,	Centre,	P. Van H. Weems, '12.
J. L. Wier, '11, Capt.,	Right Guard,	J. H. Brown, '14.
R. McG. Littlejohn, '12,	Right Tackle,	F. Loftin, '11.
J. B. Gillespie, '13,	Right End,	K. P. Gilchrist, '14.
R. F. Hyatt, '12,	Quarter-back,	I. C. Sowell, '12.
W. Dean, '12,	Left Half,	H. S. McK. Clay, '11.
C. J. Browne, '12,	Right Half,	J. P. Dalton, '12.
A. D. Surles, '11,	Full-back,	P. P. Rodes, '13.
J. E. McDonald, '12,	"	

Referee: A. H. Sharpe, '02, Yale. Umpire: M. J. Thompson, '01, Georgetown. Field Judge: D. L. Fultz, '98, Brown. Linesman: A. L. Smith, '05, Pennsylvania. Score: Army 0, Navy 3. Fourth Quarter: Goal from field by J. P. Dalton.

First Quarter: Army wins the toss and selects the west goal. Dalton kicks off. Many exchanges of kicks ensue, the Navy steadily gaining, notwithstanding the wind. Army is eventually forced to punt from behind their goal-line. Rodes catches on Army's 40-yard line and runs to 25. Army holds and Dalton tries for a goal from the field, but the kick is blocked. Navy recovers the ball, but is held after a short gain. Dalton again tries for a goal, but misses. The ball is put in play on the 25-yard line and Army unable to gain punts. Many punts follow, the Navy slowly gaining by the exchanges. Dalton at last catches on his 40 and runs to the Army's 40. A bad pass sets the Navy back to midfield. Dalton punts to Army's 20. Dean makes 6 on a fake kick. Dean punts to Clay, who runs the ball back 15 yards. Dalton punts to Surles and the quarter ends.

Second Quarter: Army starts play at midfield. Dean makes 1 and then punts. Navy returns. The Army by a

few short gains reaches Navy's 45-yard line. Nine more are
made and Dean tries for a goal from placement, which fails.
Dalton kicks to Navy's 45. On an exchange of kicks
Army fumbles and Navy gets the ball on their opponents'
35-yard line. Unable to gain, Dalton tries for a goal, but
misses. Scrimmage begins on the 25-yard line and Dean
gets around the end for 5 yards. Several kicks are exchanged. Clay finally heels a fair catch on Army's 40-yard
line. Dalton tries for a goal from placement, but the kick
is short. Hyatt circles the Navy's end for 9 yards. Kicks
are exchanged and a penalty gives Army the ball on their
40. Several sharp exchanges of kicks follow, the Army
fumbling and Gilchrist getting the ball on Army's 10-yard
line. Here time is called for the half.

Third Quarter: Dalton kicks to Hyatt. Browne goes
around the end for 10. A long punting duel follows, which
terminates by Browne heeling a fair catch at Navy's 44.
Dean tries for a goal from placement, but misses. Navy
punts to midfield, Army fumbles, and Navy gets the ball.
Rodes makes 5, Dalton 5, Dalton 4, Sowell 6, Clay 2.
Army holds. Navy forms for a place kick, but shoots a
forward pass to Army's 20-yard line. Dalton goes through
for 5. Army holds and Dalton tries for a goal, but misses.
Army puts the ball in play at 25. Navy blocks the kick and
gets the ball. Unable to gain, a place kick is tried, which
fails. Dean punts on the line-up. Clay runs the kick back
10 yards and the quarter ends.

Fourth Quarter: For five minutes the game is limited to exchanges of punts, Dalton from a fake-kick formation finally
circling Army's end for 11 yards and putting the ball down
on the latter's 30-yard line. Rodes makes 2, Dalton adds
3. Navy forms for a place kick and Dalton drives the
ball squarely between the posts for a field goal. Dean
kicks to Clay and the latter runs back 20 yards. Navy is

A TIMELY GOAL FROM THE FIELD.

Dalton, of the Navy, breaks a scoreless contest with the Army by kicking a goal from the field just as the game is closing.
Philadelphia, Nov. 26, 1910.

penalized and Dalton punts.   The ball now surges back and forth between the 30-yard lines in a succession of punts. Army is penalized 5 yards.   Clay goes through centre for 4 and the ball is on the Army's 30-yard line.   Navy forms for a place kick, but Sowell shoots a forward pass which the Army gets.   Dean kicks on the line-up and Clay returns the punt.   Browne fails to gain and Dean kicks out of bounds at midfield.   Time now is called.

CHAPTER X

CHICAGO VS. WISCONSIN

CHICAGO VS. WISCONSIN
Chicago, Oct. 20, 1894

CHICAGO		WISCONSIN
E. R. Yundt,	Left End,	W. H. Sheldon, '96.
G. N. Knapp,	Left Tackle,	T. P. Silverwood, '96.
N. D. Flint,	Left Guard,	F. W. Bolzendahl, '95.
R. L. Parker,	" "	W. Alexander, '97.
W. Rullkoetter,	Centre,	N. A. Comstock, '97.
C. W. Allen, Capt.,	Right Guard,	H. H. Jacobs, '93.
C. F. Roby,	Right Tackle,	G. W. Bunge, '95.
W. E. Garrey,	Right End,	J. C. Major, '96.
R. N. Tooker,	" "	
F. E. Hering,	Quarter-back,	T. U. Lyman, '94, Capt.
H. I. Coy,	Left Half,	F. W. Nelson, '97.
W. E. Garrey,	" "	
F. D. Nichols,	Right Half,	J. C. Karel, '95.
H. G. Gale,	Full-back,	J. R. Richards, '96.

Referee: Herbert Alward, '92, Harvard. Umpire: N. N. Young, Northwestern. Score: Chicago 0, Wisconsin 30.

First Half: Chicago wins the toss and takes the wind. Wisconsin kicks off. Allen gets around the end for a run of 35 yards. Wisconsin holds and Gale punts. Wisconsin fumbles and Allen carries the ball to Wisconsin's 15-yard line. Here the latter takes the ball on downs and by steady line plunges carries the ball the length of the field for a touchdown. Lyman kicks the goal. Allen kicks off to Karel and the latter runs 50 yards. On the line-up Karel goes through tackle for 40 yards, but the ball is given to Chicago for a foul. Nichols makes 20 yards around the end. Gale bucks the line for 5 and Nichols for 7, but failing to gain farther

150

Gale kicks across Wisconsin's goal-line. Richards kicks out. Nichols circles the end for 10, and then repeats the play for 20. Chicago by short gains now advances the ball to Wisconsin's 3-yard line, where the latter holds for downs. Time is soon called for the first half.

Second Half: Wisconsin becomes very aggressive and Chicago weakens. In this half Wisconsin makes 4 touchdowns and Lyman kicks the goals.

CHICAGO VS. WISCONSIN
Chicago, Nov. 2, 1895

CHICAGO		WISCONSIN
H. G. Leighton,	Left End,	W. H. Sheldon, '96.
E. V. Williamson,	Left Tackle,	W. Alexander, '97.
W. Rullkoetter,	Left Guard,	J. P. Riordan, '98.
P. S. Allen,	Centre,	F. Kull, '94.
T. L. Ketman,	Right Guard,	N. A. Comstock, '97.
C. W. Allen, Capt.,	Right Tackle,	J. F. A. Pyre, '92.
C. F. Roby,	Right End,	E. S. Anderson, '99.
A. A. Ewing,	Quarter-back,	G. H. Trautman, '96.
H. G. Gale,	Left Half,	G. Thompson, '99.
F. D. Nichols,	Right Half,	J. C. Karel, '95.
C. B. Neel,	Full-back,	J. R. Richards, '96, Capt.

Referee: R. D. Wrenn, '95, Harvard. Umpire: F. M. Gould, '93, Amherst. Linesman: H. L. Pike. Score: Chicago 22, Wisconsin 12. First Half: Touchdown by J. F. A. Pyre, goal by J. R. Richards; touchdown and goal by J. R. Richards; touchdown by H. G. Gale, goal by C. B. Neel; touchdown by F. D. Nichols, goal by C. B. Neel; touchdown by E. V. Williamson, goal by C. B. Neel. Second Half: Touchdown by C. W. Allen, goal by C. B. Neel.

First Half: Wisconsin wins the toss and takes the goal. Chicago kicks off. Wisconsin starts in with a rush and scores two touchdowns in fifteen minutes, Pyre and Richards taking the ball across, from both of which Richards kicks the goals. Chicago braces and Nichols, Neel, Gale, and Allen rush the ball by long gains and score three touchdowns, the latter being made by Gale, Nichols, and William-

son.   Neel kicks the goals.   Karel on a fake kick runs 65
yards, but is stopped on Chicago's 15-yard line.

Second Half: In this half both teams play stubbornly,
the ball surging back and forth across the centre line, punts
following rushes in rapid succession. At last Chicago
rushes the ball into Wisconsin's goal, where C. W. Allen
scores a touchdown. The try for goal fails.

CHICAGO vs. WISCONSIN

Madison, Nov. 7, 1896

CHICAGO		WISCONSIN
E. D. K. Leffingwell,	Left End,	W. H. Sheldon, '96.
W. S. Kennedy,	Left Tackle,	W. A. Atkinson, '97, Capt.
J. E. Webb,	Left Guard,	J. P. Riordan, '98.
W. J. Cavanagh,	Centre,	N. A. Comstock, '97.
R. N. Tooker,	Right Guard,	J. E. Ryan, '95.
C. F. Roby, Capt.,	Right Tackle,	J. F. A. Pyre, '92.
R. C. Hamill,	Right End,	C. L. Brewer, '99.
	" "	E. S. Anderson, '99.
M. G. Clarke,	Quarter-back,	J. P. Gregg, '99.
J. S. Johnson,	Left Half,	J. C. Karel, '95.
H. I. Coy,	Right Half,	F. W. Nelson, '97.
W. T. Gardner,	Full-back,	J. R. Richards, '96.

Referee: C. M. Hollister, '95, Pennsylvania. Umpire: F. M.
Gould, '93, Amherst. Linesmen: Messrs. Jones and Anson. Score:
Chicago 0, Wisconsin 24. Second Half: Touchdown and goal by J.
R. Richards; touchdown by J. C. Karel, goal by J. R. Richards;
touchdown by J. C. Karel, goal by J. R. Richards; touchdown by F.
W. Nelson, goal by J. R. Richards.

First Half: Chicago wins the toss and selects the goal.
Richards kicks to Hamill. Gardner at once punts to Karel,
who runs back 5 yards. Wisconsin by line plunges advances the ball to Chicago's 40-yard line, where it is lost on
downs. Chicago immediately punts to Karel, who runs
back 10 yards. Wisconsin fumbles. Roby makes 20 yards.
Chicago punts to Karel on the 10-yard line. Karel hits
centre for 5 and then rounds the end for 25. Nelson makes

5, Atkinson 17. Karel takes ball to 5-yard line. The ball is given to Chicago on a foul. Gardner punts to Wisconsin's 40. Karel runs back 10. The ball for the remainder of the half travels back and forth across the centre without substantial advantage to either team.

Second Half: Chicago kicks to Riordan. Wisconsin fumbles and regains the ball. Richards kicks to 20-yard line. Chicago returns. Wisconsin by short line plunges takes the ball to Chicago's goal-line for a touchdown and goal by Richards. Gardner kicks off and Wisconsin returns. After a few short gains Gardner punts. Wisconsin catches at 35 and again by short line plays reaches the 5-yard line, from which Karel is sent across for the touchdown. Richards kicks the goal. Gardner kicks to Richards, who returns. Chicago makes 10 yards, but is forced to kick. Wisconsin starts in motion its line-plunging plays and reaches the 10-yard line. Karel goes through centre for a touchdown. Richards kicks the goal. Gardner kicks to Gregg, who runs back 10 yards. Richards punts to Chicago's 30-yard line. The latter returns the kick to centre. Karel makes 10, Pyre 12, Gregg 5. Six more plunges take the ball to the 5-yard line. Nelson goes through tackle for a touchdown. Richards kicks the goal. Gardner kicks to Pyre, who runs back 15 yards. Richards punts to Chicago's 15-yard line. Chicago rushes for 20 yards and then kicks to Wisconsin's 10. Karel makes 5 through centre. Gregg adds 5 more. Richards on a fake kick runs to Chicago's 20-yard line. Time is called.

CHICAGO VS. WISCONSIN
Chicago, Nov. 13, 1897

CHICAGO		WISCONSIN
H. Fox,	Left End,	J. Dean, '01.
T. W. Mortimer,	Left Tackle,	H. R. Holmes, '99.
K. Speed,	Left Guard,	J. P. Riordan, '98, Capt.

CHICAGO		WISCONSIN
N. K. Anderson,	Left Guard,	
W. J. Cavanagh,	Centre,	W. C. Hazzard, '97.
A. C. Bowdish,	Right Guard,	N. A. Comstock, '97.
J. E. Webb,	Right Tackle,	H. G. Forrest, '98.
R. C. Hamill, Capt.,	Right End,	W. Fugitt, '01.
G. H. Garrey,	Quarter-back,	J. P. Gregg, '99.
W. S. Kennedy,	Left Half,	H. J. Peele, '99.
	" "	W. M. Joliffe, P. G.
M. G. Clarke,	Right Half,	H. F. Cochems, '97.
W. T. Gardner,	Full-back,	P. J. O'Dea, '00.

Referee: R. D. Wrenn, '95, Harvard. Umpire: R. T. Hoagland, '95, Princeton. Score: Chicago 8, Wisconsin 23. First Half: Touchdown by H. R. Holmes; goal from field by P. J. O'Dea; touchdown by H. J. Peele. Second Half: Touchdown by M. G. Clarke, goal by W. T. Gardner; touchdown by J. P. Gregg; safety by Wisconsin; touchdown by W. M. Joliffe, goal by P. J. O'Dea.

First Half: Chicago wins the toss and takes the ball. Wisconsin rushes the ball well back and, unable to advance farther, O'Dea tries a long drop kick, which fails. Gardner gets the ball and is tackled on the 17-yard mark. Chicago rushes to Wisconsin's 35, where a penalty gives the ball to the latter. Wisconsin cannot gain and O'Dea tries a long drop kick, which falls short, but rolls over the line for a touchback. Gardner punts out. Wisconsin returns, and Chicago by line plunges carries the ball to their opponent's 35-yard line, where it is lost on downs. Kicks are exchanged. Holmes breaks through and, blocking a kick, picks up the ball and runs 50 yards for a touchdown. O'Dea misses the goal. Gardner kicks off to O'Dea and the latter runs back to midfield. O'Dea punts. After several exchanges, Wisconsin is held for third down on Chicago's 50-yard line. O'Dea drops a goal from the field. Chicago kicks off, and following an exchange of kicks, Wisconsin works the ball to Chicago's 5-yard line, from which Peele is sent across for a touchdown.

Second Half: O'Dea kicks off and Gardner is tackled on the 25-yard line. Wisconsin recovers the ball at centre. Unable to gain, O'Dea tries a drop kick, but the try is blocked. A kicking duel ensues, resulting in a fumble by Wisconsin. Clarke gets the ball and runs 55 yards for a touchdown. Gardner kicks the goal. Wisconsin kicks off, and after several plays, Gregg, on a trick play, circles the end and runs 35 yards for a touchdown. O'Dea misses the goal. Gardner kicks off, and after several unimportant plays Wisconsin gets the ball on a fumble on Chicago's 40-yard line. Chicago tackles sharply and O'Dea punts. A succession of fumbles ensues, one of which results in a safety by Wisconsin. Wisconsin punts out and soon gets the ball on the return, O'Dea running it back 50 yards. Joliffe and Cochems by line plunges reach Chicago's 10-yard line. Joliffe goes across for a touchdown. O'Dea kicks the goal.

CHICAGO vs. WISCONSIN
Chicago, Nov. 12, 1898

CHICAGO		WISCONSIN
B. J. Cassells,	Left End,	E. B. Cochems, '00.
T. W. Mortimer,	Left Tackle,	H. R. Holmes, '99.
M. A. Cleveland,	" "	
O. S. Burnett,	Left Guard,	H. R. Chamberlain, '99.
W. J. Cavanagh,	Centre,	A. A. Chamberlain, '99.
C. J. Rogers,	Right Guard,	M. M. Beddall, '97.
J. E. Webb,	Right Tackle,	A. H. Curtis, '02.
R. C. Hamill,	Right End,	E. S. Anderson, '99.
W. S. Kennedy, Capt.,	Quarter-back,	P. H. Tratt, '01.
J. R. Henry,	Left Half,	W. M. Joliffe, P. G.
C. B. Herschberger,	Right Half,	A. F. Larson, '02.
F. L. Slaker,	Full-back,	P. J. O'Dea, '00, Capt.

Referee: J. F. Darby, '95, Grinnell. Umpire: W. O. Hickok, '95, Yale. Score: Chicago 6, Wisconsin 0. First Half: Touchdown by W. S. Kennedy, goal by C. B. Herschberger.

First Half: Chicago wins the toss and takes the ball. O'Dea kicks to the 10-yard line and Slaker runs back to the 25. Wisconsin gets the ball on a fumble and a penalty sets them 10 yards forward. Chicago holds for downs and Herschberger punts to Wisconsin's 20-yard line. Slaker makes 3, and on the next play reaches midfield on an end run. Kennedy hits centre for 3, and then, by 2- and 3-yard gains, Slaker, Kennedy, and Herschberger reach the 3-yard line, from which Kennedy is shot through centre for a touchdown. Herschberger kicks the goal. Wisconsin kicks off and Chicago by short gains rushes the ball to Wisconsin's 40. Kicks are exchanged and Chicago gets the ball at 35 on a fumble. Unable to gain, Herschberger tries a drop kick, but misses the goal. Similar plays soon put Wisconsin on Chicago's 40-yard line and O'Dea tries and misses a field goal. Just before the half closes Herschberger tries at 45 yards to drop a goal, but fails.

Second Half: Herschberger kicks off and O'Dea punts to centre. After two plunges into the line without gain Herschberger punts to Wisconsin's 20, where the latter fumbles and Slaker falls on the ball. In five plunges Chicago reaches the 2-yard line, where Wisconsin holds for downs. O'Dea punts. Herschberger returns. Another fumble gives Chicago the ball and Herschberger tries for a goal, but Wisconsin blocks the kick. O'Dea punts. A brisk kicking duel ensues, Chicago continually threatening Wisconsin's goal. O'Dea runs a kick to 35 and punts to Chicago's 40. Wisconsin holds for downs and O'Dea punts to Chicago's 20. The remainder of the game becomes a contest between O'Dea and Herschberger, and time is called with the ball in Wisconsin's possession on their 10-yard line.

CHICAGO vs. WISCONSIN
Madison, Dec. 9, 1899

CHICAGO		WISCONSIN
J. M. Sheldon,	Left End,	E. B. Cochems, '00.
F. Feil,	Left Tackle,	E. R. Blair, '03.
H. F. Ahlswede,	Left Guard,	A. C. Lerum, '03.

CHICAGO		WISCONSIN
K. Speed,	Centre,	A. A. Chamberlain, '99.
C. G. Flannagan,	Right Guard,	C. W. Rodgers, P. G.
J. E. Webb,	Right Tackle,	A. H. Curtis, '02.
B. J. Cassells,	Right End,	F. S. Hyman, '02.
W. S. Kennedy, Capt.,	Quarter-back,	P. H. Tratt, '01.
"		G. H. Wilmarth, P. G.
J. R. Henry,	Left Half,	H. J. Peele, '99.
C. B. Herschberger,	Right Half,	A. F. Larson, '02.
F. L. Slaker,	Full-back,	P. J. O'Dea, '00, Capt.

Referee: Evarts Wrenn, '92, Harvard. Umpire: R. D. Wrenn, '95, Harvard. Score: Chicago 17, Wisconsin 0. First Half: Touchdown by F. L. Slaker, goal by C. B. Herschberger; touchdown by F. Feil, goal by C. B. Herschberger. Second Half: Touchdown by F. L. Slaker.

First Half: Chicago wins the toss and selects the goal. O'Dea kicks to Slaker, who runs back to the 20-yard line. By short plunges Chicago rushes the ball to Wisconsin's 8-yard line, where the latter takes it on downs and O'Dea punts, but a series of short gains by Chicago brings it back to the 10-yard line, where in two plunges Slaker goes over for a touchdown and Herschberger kicks the goal. On the kick-off Chicago runs the ball out to the 7-yard line. Feil makes 20 yards, Kennedy kicks to Tratt. O'Dea returns. Chicago now starts a steady advance which reaches their opponent's 5-yard line. Feil is sent across for a touchdown. Herschberger makes the goal. Wisconsin kicks off, Chicago returns and recovers the ball on a fumble. Line plunges reach Wisconsin's 35-yard line, where time is called for the half.

Second Half: Kennedy kicks off to Larson, who runs back 5 yards. Wisconsin by short plunges rushes 40 yards. Chicago holds for downs and punts. Wisconsin fumbles and Chicago takes the ball on their opponent's 30-yard line. Wisconsin holds for downs and O'Dea punts. A long run by Slaker and a series of short gains bring the ball to Wisconsin's 10-yard line. Slaker breaks through the

line for ten yards and touches down. The try at goal fails.
O'Dea kicks off and Herschberger returns. O'Dea heels
the catch and tries a place kick at 50 yards, but fails. Chicago by short plunges carries the ball 65 yards, but is about
to be held for downs and takes a 20-yard loss to hold the
ball. Wisconsin gets the ball on a fumble. Larson makes
3, Blair 2. Chicago takes the ball on downs. Six plunges
net 20 yards and time is called.

CHICAGO vs. WISCONSIN
Chicago, Nov. 17, 1900

CHICAGO		WISCONSIN
F. Feil,	Left End,	A. C. Abbott, '04.
O. E. Atwood,	Left Tackle,	A. A. Chamberlain, '99, Capt.
C. W. Ervin,	Left Guard,	J. P. Riordan, '98.
K. Speed, Capt.,	Centre,	E. Scow, '01.
C. G. Flannagan,	Right Guard,	A. C. Lerum, '03.
J. G. MacNab,	Right Tackle,	A. H. Curtis, '02.
Z. R. Pettet,	Right End,	W. J. Juneau, '03.
J. M. Sheldon,	Quarter-back,	P. H. Tratt, '01.
J. R. Henry,	Left Half,	E. B. Cochems, '00.
F. O. Horton,	Right Half,	A. F. Larson, '02.
A. B. Snider,	Full-back,	S. E. Driver, '03.

Referee: Evarts Wrenn, '92, Harvard. Umpire: R. D. Wrenn, '95,
Harvard. Score: Chicago 5, Wisconsin 39. First Half: Touchdown
by E. B. Cochems, goal by P. H. Tratt; goal from field by F. Feil.
Second Half: Touchdown by A. F. Larson, goal by P. H. Tratt; touchdown by A. H. Curtis; touchdown by A. H. Curtis, goal by P. H. Tratt;
touchdown by J. P. Riordan; touchdown by A. F. Larson; touchdown
by E. B. Cochems, goal by P. H. Tratt.

First Half: Chicago wins the toss and takes the goal.
Cochems kicks to Chicago's 18-yard line. Unable to make
first down Chicago punts. Larson, Cochems, and Driver
by short, steady gains reach the 3-yard line, from which
Cochems goes over for the touchdown and Tratt kicks the
goal. Following the kick-off neither team develops plunging
power sufficient to gain consecutively. Wisconsin fumbles
one of the punts on the 30-yard line. Feil tries a place
kick, but misses. In five plays Feil gets another oppor-

tunity from the same distance and kicks the goal.   Following the kick-off and a return Wisconsin starts a steady advance, and by short gains reaches Chicago's 10-yard line,
where time is called.

Second Half: Feil kicks to Tratt, who runs back to the
20-yard line. The ball changes hands several times on punts
and downs. Starting from centre, Wisconsin gains steadily,
and on the 5-yard line sends Larson across for a touchdown,
from which Tratt kicks the goal.   Chicago kicks off, and
after many exchanges a punt puts the ball in Chicago's possession on their 20-yard line.   Curtis blocks Feil's kick
and falls on the ball for a touchdown.   No goal.   Chicago
kicks off.   After many exchanges of the ball without substantial advantage to either, Wisconsin puts the ball down
for a scrimmage on the 55-yard line.   Driver, Curtis,
Cochems, Larson, and Chamberlain by short gains advance
the ball to Chicago's 5-yard line.   On the next play Curtis
is sent across for a touchdown and Tratt kicks the goal.
Chicago kicks off.   Wisconsin puts the ball down for a
scrimmage on the 10-yard line.   Without once being held
for downs the ball reaches Chicago's goal-line, which Riordan crosses for a touchdown.   No goal.   Chicago kicks off,
and Wisconsin by rapid gains quickly reaches the 5-yard
line from which Larson is sent through the center for a
touchdown. The goal fails. Once more Chicago kicks off
and again Wisconsin plunges steadily down to the goal-line.
Cochems takes the ball over in the last minute of play and
Tratt kicks the goal.

CHICAGO VS. WISCONSIN
Chicago, Nov. 28, 1901

CHICAGO		WISCONSIN
F. A. Speik,	Left End,	A. C. Abbott, '04.
C. G. Flanagan,	Left Tackle,	E. J. Haumerson, '03.
R. L. Knapp,	Left Guard,	A. C. Lerum, '03.

CHICAGO		WISCONSIN
A. C. Ellsworth, Capt.,	Centre,	E. Scow, '01.
M. M. Beddall,	Right Guard,	W. C. Holstein, '04.
E. B. Cooke,	" "	
R. B. Kennedy,	Right Tackle,	A. H. Curtis, '02, Capt.
J. G. MacNab,	Right End,	W. J. Juneau, '03.
G. H. Garrey,	Quarter-back,	A. L. Marshall, '04.
L. W. Maxwell,	"	J. G. Fogg, '04.
E. E. Perkins,	Left Half,	E. B. Cochems, '00.
M. S. Dondanville,	" "	
F. O. Horton,	Right Half,	A. F. Larson, '02.
G. H. Garrey,	" "	
B. Strauss,	Full-back,	S. E. Driver, '03.

Referee: Mr. McLean, Michigan. Umpire: G. W. Walbridge, '98, Lafayette. Score: Chicago 0, Wisconsin 35. First Half: Touchdown by E. B. Cochems, goal by W. Juneau; touchdown by E. B. Cochems, goal by W. Juneau. Second Half: Goal from field by W. Juneau; touchdown by S. E. Driver, goal by W. Juneau; touchdown by A. F. Larson, goal by W. Juneau; touchdown and goal by W. Juneau.

First Half: Chicago wins the toss and selects the goal. Driver kicks off, sending the ball over the goal-line. Chicago kicks out to Wisconsin's 50-yard line. Larson, Cochems, and Driver, alternating rapidly with the ball in line plunges, carry the ball to the 3-yard line, where Cochems rounds the end for a touchdown. Juneau kicks the goal. Ellsworth kicks to Larson, who makes a run of 85 yards. Chicago holds for downs. Two downs fail to gain and Strauss punts. Catching the return of the punt Chicago opens an attack on the Wisconsin line mingled with quarter-back kicks and carries the ball to Wisconsin's 30-yard line, where a place kick for goal fails. Cochems runs the ball out to the 2-yard line, where it is put down for a scrimmage. By short gains and without a check Wisconsin now advances down the field to the 1-yard mark, where Chicago gets the ball on downs, but immediately loses it on a foul. Cochems then makes a touchdown and Juneau kicks a goal. Ellsworth kicks off. Play crosses and recrosses the centre without threatening the goal of either team.   Time is called for the half.

Second Half: Strauss kicks off and Driver returns. Chicago, unable to advance, punts and Wisconsin starts its line attack, which takes the ball steadily down the field to the 30-yard line, from which Juneau drops a goal.   Play for some time becomes a series of rushes and punts near the centre until Wisconsin is given the ball on a foul on Chicago's 20-yard line.   Larson makes 5, Driver 2, Driver 4, and on the next play Driver breaks through for a touchdown. Juneau kicks the goal.   Fogg returns Ellsworth's kick to the 35-yard line.   On an exchange of kicks Juneau makes a run of 35 yards.   Unable to advance farther he tries but misses a drop kick.   Chicago kicks out, and Wisconsin, catching at centre, by short plunges brings the ball to Chicago's 20-yard line.   Larson circles the end for a touchdown. Juneau kicks the goal.   Ellsworth kicks off to Juneau, who runs 100 yards for a touchdown and then kicks the goal. During the remainder of the half Wisconsin rushes the ball well into Chicago's territory, but cannot score, being held for downs near the 25-yard line.

CHICAGO VS. WISCONSIN
Chicago, Nov. 27, 1902

CHICAGO		WISCONSIN
F. A. Speik,	Left End,	A. C. Abbott, '04.
	" "	A. R. Findlay, '05.
J. P. Koehler,	Left Tackle,	F. A. Long, '05.
R. C. Tripp,	" "	
H. F. Ahlswede,	Left Guard,	W. A. Berthke, '06.
A. C. Ellsworth,	Centre,	E. Scow, '01.
L. W. Maxwell,	Right Guard,	A. C. Lerum, '03.
E. W. Farr,	Right Tackle,	E. J. Haumerson, '03.
M. S. Catlin,	Right End,	J. I. Bush, '06.
R. W. Maxwell,	Quarter-back,	J. G. Fogg, '04.
G. E. Schnur,	"	
J. M. Sheldon, Capt.,	Left Half,	W. F. Moffat, '02.

CHICAGO		WISCONSIN
G. E. Ivison,	Left Half,	W. J. Juneau, '03, Capt.
E. E. Perkins,	" "	E. J. Vanderboom, '06.
H. F. Bezdeck	Right Half,	
	" "	C. D. Marsh, '06.
S. H. Wightman,	Full-back,	S. E. Driver, '03.
	"	W. F. Moffat, '02.

Referee: G. A. Huff, '96, Dartmouth. Umpire: J. W. Beacham, '97, Cornell. Score: Chicago 11, Wisconsin 0. First Half: Goal from field by S. H. Wightman. Second Half: Touchdown by G. E. Schnur, goal by A. C. Ellsworth.

First Half: Chicago wins the toss and takes the goal. Abbott kicks to Catlin, who runs back 15 yards. Unable to advance farther, Ellsworth punts to Wisconsin's 15-yard line. Wisconsin by line plunges gains 8 yards and then punts. Sheldon, Schnur, and Wightman bring the ball to the 30-yard line, from which Ellsworth makes a place kick, scoring a goal. During the remainder of this half the ball changes hands frequently on downs and punts, but neither team can pass the other's 25-yard line.

Second Half: Chicago kicks off and Wisconsin returns. A poor punt on the next exchange gives Chicago the ball on Wisconsin's 15-yard line. Schnur breaks through for a touchdown. Ellsworth kicks the goal. During the remainder of the half the ball crosses and recrosses the centre line, the play being marked by many penalties. Neither goal again is threatened.

CHICAGO vs. WISCONSIN
Madison, Oct. 31, 1903

CHICAGO		WISCONSIN
F. A. Speik,	Left End,	A. C. Abbott, '04, Capt.
H. F. Ahlswede,	Left Tackle,	A. R. Findlay, '06.
S. H. Wightman,	Left Guard,	W. A. Berthke, '06.
F. G. Burrows,	" "	
A. C. Ellsworth, Capt.,	Centre,	R. W. Remp, '05.
J. F. Tobin,	Right Guard,	H. R. Chamberlain, 06.

CHICAGO		WISCONSIN
B. P. Gale,	Right Guard,	J. Price, '06.
L. W. Maxwell,	Right Tackle,	C. Washer, '05.
R. B. Kennedy,	Right End,	J. I. Bush, '06.
W. H. Eckersall,	Quarter-back,	J. G. Fogg, '04.
G. E. Schnur,	Left Half,	E. J. Vanderboom, '06.
G. E. Ivison,	Right Half.	W. M. Baine, '07.
C. H. Hitchcock,	" "	V. Wrabetz, '03.
M. S. Catlin,	Full-back,	E. S. Perry, '07.
H. F. Bezdeck,	"	A. S. Peterson, '07.
G. E. Ivison,	"	
—— Harvey,	"	

Referee: T. L. Burkland, '99, Illinois. Umpire: C. R. Rinehart, '98, Lafayette. Score: Chicago 15, Wisconsin 6. First Half: Goal from field by W. H. Eckersall. Second Half: Goal from field by W. H. Eckersall; touchdown by E. J. Vanderboom, goal by C. Washer; goal from field by W. H. Eckersall.

First Half: Chicago wins the toss and takes the goal. Abbott kicks to Eckersall, who runs back to the 20-yard line. Throughout the first twenty minutes the play is characterized by the ability of each team to advance the ball about 20 yards by short plunges, and then the inability to make the succeeding first down, thus forcing a kick. In this manner the ball travels back and forth between the 25-yard lines several times. Finally Eckersall tries but misses a drop kick from the 45-yard line. Wisconsin kicks out. Schnur makes 2, Catlin 1, Catlin 5, Ivison 9, Schnur 1, Catlin 4, and Wisconsin holds for two downs. Eckersall falls back and drops a field goal from the 25-yard line. Wisconsin kicks off, but time is soon called for the half.

Second Half: Play in the second half returns to the tactics of the first period—substantial gains by both teams between the 25-yard lines, but inability to advance farther. On one of these advances Eckersall tries for a field goal at 50, but misses. Abbott punts to midfield. Schnur makes 6, Catlin 2, Bezdeck goes in at full-back for Chicago. Wisconsin holds and Eckersall punts to the 15-yard line. Wisconsin fumbles and Chicago gets the ball. Bezdeck cannot gain. Eckersall kicks a field goal from the 25-yard line. Peterson returns the kick-off. Wisconsin, on an exchange of kicks, gets the ball and puts it down for a scrimmage on the 50-yard line. Sperry, Peterson, Vanderboom, and Wrabetz make yard after yard until the 3-yard line is reached, where Chicago stiffens and takes the ball on downs. Eckersall punts and Vanderboom returns. Wisconsin again rushes the ball into Chicago's goal; but fumbles. Eckersall punts out. Wrabetz, Vanderboom, and Perry tenaciously force back the ball to the 15-yard line. Wrabetz reaches the 3-yard line. Vanderboom goes over for the touchdown. Washer kicks the goal. Chicago kicks off and Wisconsin returns. Chicago rushes ball to 35-yard line, from which Eckersall kicks a goal from the field. Time soon after is called.

CHICAGO vs. WISCONSIN
Chicago, Nov. 26, 1904

CHICAGO		WISCONSIN
F. A. Speik, Capt.,	Left End,	A. R. Findlay, '06.
M. A. Hill,	Left Tackle,	W. A. Berthke, '06.
J. F. Tobin,	Left Guard,	L. P. Donovan, '06.
B. P. Gale,	Centre,	R. W. Remp, '05.
A. H. Badenoch,	Right Guard,	J. E. O'Brien, '05.
W. J. Boone,	Right Tackle,	T. L. St. Germaine, '05.
	" "	F. E. Hunt, '08.
R. B. Kennedy,	Right End,	J. I. Bush, '06, Capt.
W. H. Eckersall,	Quarter-back,	A. B. Melzner, '06.
L. C. De Tray,	Left Half,	E. J. Vanderboom, '06.
W. C. Speidel,	Right Half,	W. H. Schneider, '08.
M. S. Catlin,	" "	
H. F. Bezdeck,	Full-back,	L. Stromquist, P. G.

Referee: G. W. Walbridge, '98, Lafayette. Umpire: N. W. Snow, '02, Michigan. Score: Chicago 18, Wisconsin 11. First Half: Touchdown by L. Stromquist; touchdown by H. F. Bezdeck, goal by R. B.

Kennedy. Second Half: Touchdown by L. C. De Tray, goal by R. B. Kennedy; touchdown by W. H. Eckersall, goal by R. B. Kennedy; touchdown by E. J. Vanderboom, goal by J. I. Bush.

First Half: Wisconsin wins the toss and takes the goal. Tobin kicks to Findlay, who runs back 10 yards. Stromquist makes 3 and then Wisconsin punts. Chicago fumbles and Vanderboom gets the ball. Two penalties set the latter back and Stromquist punts. Eckersall returns. Vanderboom makes 25 yards. Small gains bring the ball to Chicago's 30-yard line, where Melzner tries for a field goal, but fails. Chicago punts out and Wisconsin sends Stromquist, Vanderboom, and Schneider into the line, for steady gains. Stromquist bursts through centre for a touchdown. The goal is missed. Chicago kicks off. Wisconsin makes a few gains but is forced to punt. Chicago's rushing game now grows stronger. The ball is taken to Wisconsin's 35-yard line, where it is lost on downs. Catching the punt, Chicago sends Bezdeck, Catlin, and Spidell into the line for small but steady gains. On the 5-yard line Wisconsin holds for three downs without gain, but on the last attempt Bezdeck goes over for a touchdown. Kennedy kicks the goal. Time is called for the half immediately after the kick-off.

Second Half: Eckersall returns the kick-off to the 20-yard line. After a gain of 12 yards in two plunges, Eckersall falls back to punt. The kick is blocked and Wisconsin gets the ball. Unable to pierce the line, Melzner tries a drop kick for goal, but fails. Chicago kicks out and Schneider sends the ball back. Catlin goes through tackle for 30 yards. Chicago punts to Wisconsin's 30-yard line. Wisconsin makes a first down. On the line-up the ball is fumbled. De Tray picks up the ball and runs the length of the field for a touchdown. Kennedy kicks the goal. Melzner kicks off to Eckersall on the 4-yard line and the latter runs 106 yards for a touchdown. Kennedy kicks the goal. Chicago kicks off and Wisconsin shows amazing strength. The Chicago line is pierced repeatedly for steady gains. On the 20-yard line Vanderboom circles the end for a touchdown. Bush kicks the goal.

CHICAGO vs. WISCONSIN
Madison, Oct. 21, 1905

CHICAGO		WISCONSIN
E. E. Parry,	Left End,	T. H. Brindley, '03.
M. A. Hill,	Left Tackle,	W. A. Berthke, '06.
J. B. Meigs,	Left Guard,	L. P. Donovan, '06.
B. P. Gale,	Centre,	R. W. Remp, '05.
L. D. Scherer,	Right Guard,	W. A. Gelbach, '07.
A. H. Badenoch,	Right Tackle,	A. A. Johnson, '07.
	" "	C. N. Dering, '06.
M. S. Catlin, Capt.,	Right End,	J. I. Bush, '06.
W. H. Eckersall,	Quarter-back,	A. B. Melzner, '06.
L. C. De Tray,	Left Half,	E. J. Vanderboom, '06, Capt.
F. M. Walker,	Right Half,	A. R. Findlay, '06.
	" "	F. M. Clark, '07.
H. F. Bezdeck,	Full-back,	L. E. Roseth, '08.

Referee: H. B. Hackett, '04, Army. Umpire: C. R. Rinehart, '98, Lafayette. Score: Chicago 4, Wisconsin 0. Second Half: Goal from field by W. H. Eckersall.

First Half: Chicago wins the toss and selects the goal. Melzner kicks to the 20-yard line, Eckersall running back 10 yards. An exchange of kicks follows, Wisconsin fumbling and Chicago taking the ball. Line plunges net 20 yards and then Wisconsin holds for downs, punting to Chicago's 15-yard line. Chicago returns and blocks Wisconsin's kick on the latter's 35-yard line. Eckersall takes the ball to the 8-yard line. Wisconsin throws the next two runners for a loss and Eckersall tries a drop kick, but fails. Wisconsin kicks out and Eckersall tries another drop kick, but misses. Wisconsin kicks out. Chicago begins a hard attack on Wisconsin's line, sending the ball along by small gains to the 25-yard line. Here Wisconsin holds for downs and punts. During the remainder of the half the ball is near midfield, neither team getting within striking distance of their opponent's goal.

Second Half: Findlay runs back the kick-off to the 33-yard line. By kicks and rushes Wisconsin transfers the play into Chicago's territory. Melzner falls back for a drop kick at goal, but Chicago blocks the kick. Wisconsin gets the ball and rushes to the 27-yard line, where Chicago holds for downs. On a quarter-back kick Bezdeck makes 13 yards. Eckersall goes around the end for 30 more. Line plunges, each netting 10 yards, quickly take the ball to Wisconsin's 10-yard line. Unable to advance farther Eckersall drops a field goal. Bezdeck runs back the kick-off to the 35-yard line. Catlin and Eckersall make 20 yards, but a fumble gives the ball to Wisconsin. Bush punts to Chicago's 28-yard line. Eckersall returns to Wisconsin's 45. The game becomes wholly a kicking contest, each side catching cleanly. Time is called with the ball in Wisconsin's possession on their 25-yard line.

1906, 1907, no games.

CHICAGO VS. WISCONSIN
Madison, Nov. 21, 1908

CHICAGO		WISCONSIN
J. J. Schommer,	Left End,	H. B. Rogers, '09, Capt.
A. C. Hoffman,	Left Tackle,	F. E. Boyle, '10.
H. J. Ehrhorn,	Left Guard,	J. Messmer, '09.
B. H. Badenoch,	Centre,	E. O. Steihm, '09.
M. A. Hirschl,	Right Guard,	C. E. Dreutzer, '09.
T. Kelley,	" "	
T. Kelley,	Right Tackle,	O. P. Osthoff, '10.
L. T. Falk,	" "	
H. O. Page,	Right End,	J. P. Dean, '11.
W. P. Steffen, Capt.,	Quarter-back,	J. Moll, '11.
W. L. Crawley,	"	
H. G. Iddings,	Left Half,	H. Culver, '10.
W. L. Crawley,	Right Half,	C. J. Cunningham, '09.
O. W. Worthwine,	Full-back,	J. W. Wilce, '10.

Referee: W. S. Langford, '96, Trinity. Umpire: W. H. Edwards, '00. Princeton. Field Judge: E. K. Hall, '92, Dartmouth. Linesman: H. B. Hackett, '04, Army. Score: Chicago 18, Wisconsin 12. First Half: Touchdown by W. P. Steffen, goal by J. J. Schommer; touchdown by J. W. Wilce, goal by J. Moll; touchdown by H. G. Iddings, goal by J. J. Schommer; touchdown and goal by J. J. Schommer. Second Half: Touchdown by J. W. Wilce, goal by J. Moll.

First Half: Chicago wins the toss and takes the goal. Stiehm kicks to Steffen, who runs 100 yards for a touchdown. Schommer kicks the goal. Stiehm kicks off. Chicago, by a series of line plays for short gains, takes the ball to Wisconsin's 20-yard line, where the latter holds for downs. Wisconsin punts to midfield and Chicago rushes back to the 25-yard line, where Wisconsin again secures the ball on downs and putting it down for a scrimmage by short-line plunges, advances to Chicago's 30-yard line. Wilce, on a forward pass, reaches the 1-yard mark. On the next play he is sent over for a touchdown. Moll kicks the goal. A sharp exchange of punts succeeds the kick-off. Wisconsin takes the ball on the 30-yard line and by line-plunging reaches Chicago's 40. Culver, on a forward pass, reaches the 15-yard line. Moll tries a drop kick for goal, but misses. Chicago punts out and Wisconsin returns. Page dashes around the end to the 45-yard line. Steffen reaches Wisconsin's 30. An on-side kick places the ball on the 5-yard line. Iddings, in three plunges, goes over for a touchdown, and Schommer kicks the goal. Stiehm kicks to Chicago's 5-yard line. A run reaches the 30-yard line and Chicago punts. Wisconsin returns. Worthwine, Iddings, and Crawley carry the ball to midfield. Two forward passes, Crawley to Page, reach the 20-yard line. Schommer goes over for a touchdown and kicks the goal. Time is called for the half.

Second Half: Wisconsin runs back the kick-off to the 30-yard line. By penalties and plunges Chicago takes the ball to Wisconsin's 1-yard line. Chicago is set back 5 yards on a penalty. Wisconsin intercepts a forward pass. An exchange of kicks gives Wisconsin the ball on the 20-yard line. By a brilliant series of forward passes the ball is carried to Chicago's 25-yard line. An on-side kick fails and Chicago gets the ball, but loses it on a fumble. Wisconsin, in two end runs, reaches the 20-yard line. Moll sends a short kick over the goal-line. Chicago punts out to the 40-yard line. A penalty yields 15 yards. Wilce makes 10 yards and then goes over for a touchdown. Moll kicks the goal. Schommer kicks off. By line plunges and forward passes Wisconsin reaches Chicago's 15-yard line, where the ball is lost on downs. An exchange of kicks and a fumble give Chicago the ball on Wisconsin's 30-yard line. Schommer misses a place kick. For several minutes play remains at midfield, the ball changing hands several times on punts and downs. Short rushes then take it to Wisconsin's 30, where it is lost on downs. Neither goal is again threatened.

CHICAGO vs. WISCONSIN
Chicago, Nov. 20, 1909

CHICAGO		WISCONSIN
C. G. Sauer,	Left End,	J. P. Dean, '11.
W. J. Sunderland,	" "	
A. C. Hoffman,	Left Tackle,	O. P. Osthoff, '10.
	" "	A. G. Zander, '12.
D. E. Smith,	Left Guard	A. L. Buser, '12.
A. H. Badenoch,	Centre,	H. A. Arpin, '11.
M. A. Hirschl,	Right Guard,	W. F. Mackmiller, '12.
T. Kelley,	Right Tackle,	F. E. Boyle, '10.
M. S. Gerend,	" "	
H. J. Ehrhorn,	Right End,	E. F. Bunker, '11.
	" "	H. Rau, '11.
H. O. Page, Capt.,	Quarter-back,	R. A. Fucik, '10.
R. B. Rogers,	Left Half,	C. J. Jacobson, '11.
	" "	F. R. Petersen, '10.
W. L. Crawley,	Right Half,	E. Jacob, '10.
J. A. Menaul,	" "	
C. G. Sauer,	" "	
O. W. Worthwine,	Full-back,	J. W. Wilce, '10, Capt.

Referee: A. W. Kelly, '98, Princeton. Umpire: Evarts Wrenn, '92, Harvard. Field Judge: A. B. Fleager, '94, Northwestern. Lines-

man: A. P. Jamison, '95, Purdue.   Score: Chicago 6, Wisconsin 6.
First Half: Touchdown by H. A. Arpin, goal by J. W. Wilce; touchdown
by O. W. Worthwine, goal by H. O. Page.

First Half: Wisconsin wins the toss and takes the goal.
Page kicks to Dean at 20.   Several fumbles transfer the ball
from team to team, giving Andersen a chance at a drop
kick from 35 yards, which fails.   A long kicking duel now
ensues, resulting in a fumble by Chicago on the 20-yard
line.   Arpin picks up the ball and dashes across the line for
a touchdown.   Wilce kicks the goal.   Andersen runs back
Page's kick-off 25 yards.   Unable to gain, Wisconsin punts
to midfield.   Crawley makes 8, Worthwine 10, Crawley 5.
Kelley, on a forward pass, reaches Wisconsin's 10-yard line.
Worthwine makes 5 and on the next play crosses the line
for a touchdown.   Page kicks the goal.   The remaining
time is used in futile rushing by each team.   Wisconsin
tries several forward passes, but neither team again threatens
the other's goal.

Second Half: Worthwine runs back the kick-off to the
30-yard line.   During this half play is confined to the space
between the 30-yard lines.   Each team tries a few line
plunges, but unable to gain consecutively soon punts.   The
play occasionally is varied by a forward pass and marred by
several fumbles.   Thus playing monotonously the time
expires.

CHICAGO vs. WISCONSIN
Madison, Nov. 19, 1910

CHICAGO		WISCONSIN
W. S. Kassulker,	Left End,	F. G. Carter, '11.
C. M. Rademacher,	Left Tackle,	W. F. Mackmiller, '12.
	" "	P. J. Murphy, '11.
C. P. Sawyer,	Left Guard,	S. Neprud, '12.
L. H. Whiting,	Centre,	H. A. Arpin, '11.
	"	R. E. Branstad, '12.
H. E. Whiteside,	Right Guard,	M. C. Pierce, '12.

A LONG END RUN.

Gillette, of Wisconsin, getting off for a run of 75 yards and a touchdown. Chicago vs. Wisconsin, Nov. 19, 1910.

OF
RNIA

CHICAGO		WISCONSIN
H. M. Carpenter,	Right Tackle,	A. L. Buser, '12.
	" "	E. J. Samp, '13.
N. C. Paine,	Right End,	E. F. Bunker, '11.
J. A. Menaul,	" "	
E. I. Wilson,	Quarter-back,	J. P. Dean, '11, Capt.
R. B. Rogers,	Left Half,	E. S. Gillette, '12.
	" "	A. Birch, '11.
W. L. Crawley, Capt.,	Right Half,	R. R. Newman, '13.
R. H. Young,	Full-back,	E. J. Samp, '13.
	"	C. F. G. Wernicke, '12.

Referee: A. W. Kelly, '98, Princeton. Umpire: R. D. Wrenn, '95, Harvard. Field Judge: W. T. Fishleigh, '02, Michigan. Linesman: L. E. Endsley, '01, Purdue. Score: Chicago 0, Wisconsin 10. Second Quarter: Touchdown by A. L. Buser. Fourth Quarter: Touchdown by E. S. Gillette.

First Quarter: Chicago wins the toss and selects the west goal. Pierce kicks to Crawley and the latter is forced out of bounds at 28. Wilson makes 8 on a fake kick. Wilson rounds the end for 10 more. Rogers breaks through the line for 40. Wisconsin holds for downs. Two plays net 25 yards, but a penalty sets Wisconsin back 15. Line plays take the ball to Chicago's 35 and Gillette tries a drop for goal, but misses. Chicago kicks out and several sharp scrimmages ensue, netting 15 yards for Wisconsin. Time is called.

Second Quarter: Young makes 2 and Whiting takes a forward pass. Wilson tries a drop kick, but the kick is short. Wisconsin rushes 20 yards and Chicago holds for downs at midfield. Chicago cannot gain and Wilson punts. Gillette returns. Chicago's next attempt at a punt is blocked and it is Wisconsin's ball at centre. Buser and Newman in two plunges carry the ball to Chicago's 10-yard line. Gillette makes 8 and Buser goes over for the touchdown. Pierce misses the goal. Kicks are exchanged and Wilson tries a drop from 50, but misses. Wisconsin kicks out and then intercepts a forward pass. Time is called for the half.

Third Quarter: Wilson kicks off to Newman. Wisconsin fumbles and Chicago gets the ball. Newman intercepts a forward pass. Neither team can make substantial gains. Line plays are ineffectual and both sides resort to punting. The ball travels back and forth between the 35-yard lines without advantage to either side.

Fourth Quarter: Gillette opens the last quarter with a drop kick, but it fails. Chicago now makes some brilliant gains through the dashes of Crawley, but are finally held for downs. Wisconsin lines up on its 40-yard line. Gillette skirts the end and runs the length of the field for a touchdown. The try at goal fails. Pierce kicks off to R. H. Young, who runs back 15. Wilson's punt is blocked, but Chicago recovers the ball. Kicks are exchanged and time is called.

CHAPTER XI

CORNELL VS. PENNSYLVANIA

CORNELL VS. PENNSYLVANIA
Philadelphia, Nov. 28, 1893

CORNELL		PENNSYLVANIA
E. P. Young, '94,	Left End,	R. H. Simmons, '93.
P. Deeming, '94,	" "	C. L. Upton, '96.
A. C. Freeborn, '95,	Left Tackle,	H. A. Mackie, '93, Capt.
G. S. Warner, '94,	Left Guard,	H. D. Oliver, '96.
	" "	W. G. Woodruff, '97.
A. H. Barnhisel, '94,	Centre,	H. W. Thornton, '94.
E. U. Henry, '95,	Right Guard,	F. Ellsler, '94.
C. J. Barr, '93, Capt.,	Right Tackle,	O. F. Wagenhurst, '96.
J. H. Taussig, '97,	Right End,	S. B. Newton, '94.
O. L. Hunter, '97,	" "	M. G. Rosengarten, '95.
J. W. Beacham, '97,	Quarter-back,	Carl Williams, '97.
P. A. Robbins, '94,	Left Half,	A. A. Knipe, '94.
G. P. Dyer, '95,	Right Half,	W. D. Osgood, '95.
W. F. Ohl, '97,	Full-back,	G. H. Brooke, '95.

Referee: H. L. Williams, '91, Yale. Umpire: W. A. Brooks, '87, Harvard. Score: Cornell 0, Pennsylvania 50. First Half: Touchdown by S. B. Newton, goal by G. H. Brooke; touchdown by W. D. Osgood; touchdown by A. A. Knipe, goal by G. H. Brooke; touchdown and goal by G. H. Brooke. Second Half: Touchdown by A. A. Knipe, goal by G. H. Brooke; touchdown by A. A. Knipe, goal by G. H. Brooke; touchdown by A. A. Knipe, goal by G. H. Brooke; touchdown by W. D. Osgood, goal by G. H. Brooke; touchdown by A. A. Knipe.

First Half: Pennsylvania wins the toss and takes the ball. Knipe makes 20 yards in the flying wedge. Osgood goes through centre for 5. Knipe follows for 5 more. Newton gets around the end for a long run, ending in a touchdown. Brooke kicks the goal. Cornell opens with the flying wedge. After several minutes of ineffective play Pennsylvania secures the ball on a fumble at midfield. Knipe makes 5, Newton 8, Knipe 20, Brooke 8, and Osgood goes around the end for a touchdown. The goal is missed. Cornell resumes with the flying wedge, making 20 yards. Kicks are exchanged. Brooke catches on the 45-yard line. Knipe hits the line for 10 and then rounds the end for 20. Three plunges into the line by Osgood net a first down. Knipe circles the end for a touchdown. Brooke kicks the goal. After several minutes of fluctuating play Pennsylvania holds for downs on the 55-yard line. Rosengarten doubles the end for 10. Knipe hits the line for 4 and then Osgood dashes through tackle for 40 yards. Brooke takes the ball over and kicks the goal. Time is called for the half.

Second Half: Cornell opens play with the flying wedge, gaining 15 yards. The Red and Blue line is punctured for a few small gains by Robbins, Dyer, and Ohl. The latter gets away for a long run, taking the ball to the 25-yard line. On the next play Rosengarten gets the ball away from the runner. Osgood makes 8 through the line. On the line-up Knipe goes around the end for a 70-yard run and touchdown. Brooke kicks the goal. Cornell starts with the flying wedge and makes 20. Dyer hits centre for 5 and Robbins adds 10 more. Pennsylvania tightens and Ohl is forced to punt. Short rushes by Pennsylvania bring the ball to centre. Knipe rounds the end for 20 yards and on the next play circles the opposite side for a touchdown. Brooke kicks the goal. Cornell's wedge nets 10 yards. Ohl adds 5, Robbins 10, Dyer 5, and other short plunges take the ball to the 3-yard mark. Here Pennsylvania holds for downs. After a few line plays Osgood is sent around the end for 30 yards. Knipe duplicates the play at the other end for a touchdown. Brooke kicks the goal. In the remaining period of play touchdowns are made by Osgood and Knipe, from the former of which Brooke kicks the goal.

CORNELL VS. PENNSYLVANIA
Philadelphia, Nov. 17, 1894

CORNELL		PENNSYLVANIA
J. W. Beacham, '97,	Left End,	C. L. Upton, '96.
F. C. Hall, '98,	Left Tackle,	W. M. Farrar, '96.
G. S. Warner, '94, Capt.,	Left Guard,	W. G. Woodruff, '97.
T. F. Fennell, '97,	Centre,	A. E. Bull, '96.
A. J. Colnon, '93,	Right Guard,	C. M. Wharton, '97.
C. E. Rogers, '96,	Right Tackle,	J. H. Minds, '98.
E. P. Van Mater, '96,	" "	
J. H. Taussig, '97,	Right End,	M. G. Rosengarten, '95.
A. S. Downey, '96,	" "	
C. R. Wyckoff, '96,	Quarter-back,	Carl Williams, '97.
C. B. Mason, '95,	Left Half,	W. D. Osgood, '95.
G. P. Dyer, '95,	Right Half,	C. S. Gelbert, '97.
W. F. Ohl, '97,	Full-back,	G. H. Brooke, '95, Capt.

Referee: Alex. Moffat, '84, Princeton. Umpire: P. J. Dashiell, Navy. Linesman: M. Newell, '94, Harvard. Score: Cornell 0, Pennsylvania 6. Second Half: Touchdown and goal by G. H. Brooke.

First Half: Cornell wins the toss and takes the ball. Ohl kicks to Brooke on Pennsylvania's 6-yard line and Brooke returns the kick to midfield. Mason, Dyer, Ohl, Taussig, and Beacham rush the ball quickly to Pennsylvania's 8-yard mark. Pennsylvania tightens and holds for downs. Osgood hits the line for 15 and then Brooke punts to Cornell's 45. Mason and Ohl by hard plunges work the ball back to Pennsylvania's 20-yard line. Pennsylvania again holds for downs. The remainder of the half is characterized by large gains by each team between the 25-yard lines and the inability of each one to advance farther. The half closes with the ball in Cornell's possession on Pennsylvania's 20-yard line.

Second Half: Brooke kicks to Cornell's 10-yard line. Ohl on the line-up punts back to centre. Wharton goes

through tackle for 8. Cornell holds for downs. Ohl
punts out of bounds. Upton, Wharton, and Osgood by line
plunges gain 10 yards. A penalty gives the ball to Cornell
but a fumble returns it again to Pennsylvania. Gelbert,
Woodruff, and Osgood by plays against tackle reach the
8-yard line. Woodruff and Brooke gain 6 through centre.
Wharton reaches the 6-inch mark. Gelbert goes over, but
is brought back for holding and the ball given to Cornell on
the 8-yard mark. Ohl makes 10 around the end and then
punts to 50. Brooke gets through for 15. Gelbert adds
15 more. Osgood and Wharton make 9. Pennsylvania
fumbles and the ball is recovered by Cornell. A penalty
transfers the ball to Pennsylvania on Cornell's 25-yard line.
Osgood rounds the end for 15. Brooke hits the line for 2
and on the next play dashes across for a touchdown. A
moment later he kicks the goal. Cornell kicks off and Pennsylvania returns. Time is called.

CORNELL VS. PENNSYLVANIA
Philadelphia, Nov. 28, 1895

CORNELL		PENNSYLVANIA
H. H. Lyle, '98,	Left End,	C. S. Gelbert, '97.
E. H. Fitch, '97,	Left Tackle,	O. F. Wagenhurst, '96.
F. W. Freeborn, '97,	Left Guard,	W. G. Woodruff, '97.
L. M. Schoch, '97,	Centre,	A. E. Bull, '96.
C. E. Rogers, '96,	Right Guard,	C. M. Wharton, '97.
E. R. Sweetland, '99,	Right Tackle,	W. M. Farrar, '96.
J. H. Taussig, '97,	Right End,	B. W. Dickson, '97.
C. R. Wyckoff, '96, Capt.,	Quarter-back,	Carl Williams, '97, Capt.
J. W. Beacham, '97,	Left Half,	J. E. Blair, '95.
F. W. Cool, '95,	Right Half,	J. H. Minds, '98.
D. R. Richie, '97,	Full-back,	G. H. Brooke, '95.

Referee: L. T. Bliss, '93, Yale. Umpire: P. J. Dashiell, Navy.
Linesmen: M. Newell, '94, Harvard; C. H. Schoff, '93, Pennsylvania.
Score: Cornell 2, Pennsylvania 46. First Half: Touchdown by J.
H. Minds, goal by G. H. Brooke; touchdown by J. H. Minds, goal
by G. H. Brooke, goal from field by G. H. Brooke. Second Half:
Touchdown by B. W. Dickson; safety by G. H. Brooke; safety by D. R.

Richie; touchdown by J. H. Minds, goal by G. H. Brooke; touchdown by B. W. Dickson, goal by G. H. Brooke; touchdown by J. H. Minds, goal by G. H. Brooke; goal from field by G. H. Brooke.

First Half: Cornell wins the toss and takes the ball. After an exchange of kicks following ineffective rushing, Pennsylvania obtains the ball on a fumble on Cornell's 25-yard line. Pennsylvania on the first play also fumbles, but Williams recovers the ball 15 yards nearer Cornell's goal. Wharton makes 3, Brooke 2. Williams tries a quarter-back kick across the line, which Minds recovers for a touchdown. Brooke kicks the goal. Cornell kicks off and the ball fluctuates back and forth across the centre line for some time. At last Gelbert gets away for a run of 25 yards. Minds and Brooke add 20 more and Minds, on the next play, makes a touchdown. Brooke kicks the goal. After a succession of plays Pennsylvania punts into Cornell's goal. The latter rushes it out to the 25-yard line, but upon a third down Wyckoff punts to Brooke, who heels a fair catch at 45, from which he kicks a goal from placement.

Second Half: An exchange of punts follows the kick-off, Pennsylvania finally catching on their 40-yard line. Minds makes 20 through tackle, Brooke 20 more on the opposite side, Blair 5, and Wharton 3. On the line-up Dickson gets around the end for a long run, ending in a touchdown. Cornell kicks off and Pennsylvania, in several minutes, by rushes and punts places the ball well into Cornell's goal. Cornell by hard rushing transfers the play into Pennsylvania's goal and forces Brooke to kick out from behind his goal. Cornell blocks the kick, but Brooke recovers the ball for a safety. Brooke kicks off and Richie returns after an exchange of kicks. Richie is forced to make a safety. Pennsylvania starts a series of line plays on their 40-yard line, which reaches Cornell's goal-line, where the ball is fumbled on the final play. Sweetland falls on it for a touchback.

Schoch kicks off for Cornell. Brooke circles the end for 25 and Minds rounds the opposite side for 40 more and a touchdown. Brooke kicks the goal. Cornell kicks off to Pennsylvania's 25, and the Red and Blue, by short line plunges, slowly returns to Cornell's goal-line, where Dickson is sent across for a touchdown. Brooke kicks the goal. Freeborn kicks off. Brooke, Minds, Wharton, Gelbert, and Williams, by steady gains, force the ball to Cornell's goal-line, where Minds makes a touchdown. Goal. Cornell kicks off. Pennsylvania resumes its line battering tactics, but is stopped by a fumble. Recovering the ball by a blocked kick, Brooke drops a goal from the field and the game ends.

CORNELL VS. PENNSYLVANIA

Philadelphia, Nov. 26, 1896

CORNELL		PENNSYLVANIA
L. S. Tracy, '98,	Left End,	S. A. Boyle, '98.
H. Lee, '97,	" "	
H. E. White, '98,	Left Tackle,	L. J. Uffenheimer, '99.
E. H. Fitch, '97,	" "	
D. A. Reed, '98,	Left Guard,	W. G. Woodruff, '97.
T. F. Fennell, '97,	Centre,	P. D. Overfield, '01.
J. W. Clark, '97,	Right Guard,	C. M. Wharton, '97, Capt.
E. R. Sweetland, '99,	Right Tackle,	W. M. Farrar, '96.
J. H. Taussig, '97,	Right End,	B. W. Dickson, '97.
K. K. Bossfed, '97,	Quarter-back,	D. F. Weeks, '98.
J. W. Beacham, '97, Capt.,	Left Half,	C. S. Gelbert, '97.
W. McKeever, '98,	Right Half,	W. N. Morice, '99.
D. R. Richie, '97,	Full-back,	J. H. Minds, '98.

Referee: P. D. Mills, '97, Yale. Umpire: P. J. Dashiell, Navy. Linesman: F. D. Conden. Score: Cornell 10, Pennsylvania 32. First Half: Safety by J. H. Taussig; touchdown by C. S. Gelbert, goal by J. H. Minds; touchdown by J. W. Beacham; touchdown and goal by J. H. Minds. Second Half: Touchdown and goal by D. R. Richie; touchdown by S. A. Boyle, goal by J. H. Minds; touchdown by W. N. Morice, goal by J. H. Minds; touchdown by W. G. Woodruff, goal by J. H. Minds.

First Half: Cornell wins the toss and takes the ball. The play soon forces Cornell into goal, where Taussig is forced

to punt from behind the line. Gelbert is through and
tackles him with the ball, scoring a safety. After the kick-
off an exchange of kicks gives Pennsylvania the ball at 50.
Wharton makes 5, Minds 5, Boyle 10, Uffenheimer 8, Gelbert 8. On the next play Gelbert crosses the line for a
touchdown. Goal by Minds. Cornell kicks off. After
several minutes of rushing Pennsylvania fumbles on the 45-
yard line. White gets it. Beacham circles the end for 20
yards. A penalty yields ten more. McKeever and Richie
in two plunges make the 20-yard line. McKeever goes
through centre for 4. Beacham circles the end for a touchdown. The goal fails. Play for some time remains at
midfield. Richie punts to Pennsylvania's 45. Minds
rounds the end for 15. Woodruff hits the line for 2, Uffenheimer 25, Boyle 2. A penalty sets Pennsylvania forward
10 yards. Minds doubles the end for a touchdown and
kicks the goal.

  Second Half: Pennsylvania kicks off. An exchange of
kicks gives Pennsylvania the ball on the 10-yard line.
Rushes reach the 25-yard line. Three downs fail by six
inches and Pennsylvania takes the chance. Cornell holds
and gets the ball. Beacham makes 4, Richie 5, McKeever
10, Beacham 2. Richie across for a touchdown. Richie
also kicks the goal. Play is resumed at centre. After
several rushes and punts Pennsylvania gets the ball at midfield. Minds circles the end for 10. Gelbert makes 8
through tackle. Woodruff hits the line for 3, Morice 4.
Cornell stops the advance and Minds punts. Cornell fumbles and Boyle, picking up the ball, dashes across the line
for a touchdown. Goal. Pennsylvania, again taking the
ball from kick-off by line plays, reaches the 15-yard line,
from which Morice circles the end for a touchdown. Minds
kicks the goal. Cornell has the ball on Pennsylvania's
45-yard line, where it is given to the latter for holding. Gel-

bert makes 8, Uffenheimer 5. Cornell holds for two downs.
On the next play Woodruff gets free and with compact interference races for the line and touches down.   Goal.

CORNELL vs. PENNSYLVANIA
Philadelphia, Nov. 25, 1897

CORNELL		PENNSYLVANIA
L. S. Tracy, '98,	Left End,	S. A. Boyle, '98.
A. B. Lueder, '99,	Left Tackle,	S. M. Goodman, '97.
C. H. Tangeman, '01,	" "	
D. A. Reed, '98,	Left Guard,	T. T. Hare, '01.
L. M. Schoch, '97,	Centre,	P. D. Overfield, '01.
M. R. Faville, '01,	Right Guard,	J. C. McCracken, '01.
D. M. McLaughlin, '98,	Right Tackle,	J. H. Outland, '00.
W. McKeever, '98, Capt.,	Right End,	J. Hedges, '01.
C. V. P. Young, '99,	Quarter-back,	D. F. Weeks, '98.
A. E. Whiting, '98,	Left Half,	M. R. Jackson, '98.
P. B. Windsor, '00,	Right Half,	W. N. Morice, '99.
C. W. Wilson, '00,	Full-back,	J. H. Minds, '98, Capt.

Referee: M. McClung, '94, Lehigh. Umpire: P. J. Dashiell, Navy.
Linesmen: E Hill, '99, Cornell; G. R. Fortesque, '99, Pennsylvania.
Timekeeper: W. L. McCauley, '94, Princeton. Score: Cornell 0,
Pennsylvania 4. Second Half: Touchdown by J. C. McCracken.

First Half: Cornell wins the toss and takes the wind.
Morice kicks off to Cornell's 20-yard line, Young catching
and running the kick back 20 yards. Pennsylvania holds
for downs and Cornell punts to Pennsylvania's 10-yard
line. Pennsylvania by short gains rushes the ball to midfield, where Cornell stops the advance and Minds kicks.
Cornell now opens a rapid attack on the Pennsylvania line,
Whiting, Windsor, and Wilson crossing stripe after stripe.
Pennsylvania stands firm on the .10-yard line and takes
the ball on downs. Minds at once punts to centre. Again
the Cornell attack starts in motion and reaches the 6-yard
mark. Pennsylvania's line will not yield and Cornell loses
the ball on downs. Minds punts to centre. For the third
time Cornell hammers its way to Pennsylvania's 10 line.

On the third down, and 3 yards to go, Young tries a drop
kick, but misses by an inch.   Play for the remainder of the
half fluctuates between the 25-yard lines.   The half closes
with the ball in Cornell's possession at centre.

Second Half: Cornell kicks off and Pennsylvania runs
the kick back to the 25-yard line.   Pennsylvania in 8
plunges gains 15 yards, but is then forced to punt.   Cornell
by hard rushes, using 4 downs for every 5 yards, works the
ball to Pennsylvania's 40-yard line, where Pennsylvania
holds for downs.   Thus the play continues until the half
lacks ten minutes of expiration.   Pennsylvania, by plunges
of Jackson, Weeks, Morice, and Minds, carries the ball to
Cornell's 1-yard line, where Cornell throws the Red and Blue
runners back for a loss and takes the ball.   Young kicks
to 40.   Kicks are exchanged.   Pennsylvania catches at midfield.   Goodman goes through tackle for 4.   Outland gets
around the end for 27.   Goodman again pierces tackle
and reaches Cornell's 10-yard line.   Outland bursts centre
for 3.   McCracken goes through for a touchdown.   The
punt out is missed.   Neither team again gets within striking
distance of their opponent's goal and the game ends.

CORNELL VS. PENNSYLVANIA
Philadelphia, Nov. 24, 1898

CORNELL		PENNSYLVANIA
H. J. Davall, '01,	Left End,	P. J. McMahon, '00.
C. W. Wilson, '00,	" "	
M. M. Wyvill, '01,	Left Tackle,	J. M. Reugenberg, '99.
D. A. Reed, '98,	Left Guard,	T. T. Hare, '01.
W. F. Dorner, '01,	Centre,	P. D. Overfield, '01.
	"	J. F. McCloskey, '01.
A. B. Lueder, '99,	Right Guard,	J. C. McCracken, '01.
E. R. Sweetland, '99,	Right Tackle,	J. B. Carnett, '99.
C. W. Cross, '01,	Right End,	J. Hedges, '01.
F. G. Grimshaw, '00,	" "	
G. H. Young, '00,	Quarter-back,	J. P. Gardiner, '01.
J. C. Short, '00,	"	J. H. Outland, '00, Capt.

CORNELL		PENNSYLVANIA
A. E. Whiting, '98, Capt.,	Left Half,	W. J. Coombs, '00.
P. Will, '00, Capt.,	" "	
C. V. P. Young, '99,	Right Half,	J. H. Outland, '00.
P. B. Windsor, '00,	" "	J. P. Gardiner, '01.
R. D. Starbuck, '00,	Full-back,	N. T. Folwell, '00.
F. C. Perkins, '00,	"	

Referee: M. McClung, '94, Lehigh. Umpire: P. J. Dashiell, Navy. Timekeeper: W. H. Lewis, '95, Harvard. Score: Cornell 6, Pennsylvania 12. First Half: Touchdown by E. R. Sweetland, goal by G. H. Young. Second Half: Touchdown by J. H. Outland, goal by T. T. Hare; touchdown by J. Hedges, goal by T. T. Hare.

First Half: Cornell wins the toss and takes the west goal. Pennsylvania kicks off. Cornell tries the line, but, unable to gain consecutively, punts to midfield. Coombs and Outland circle Cornell's ends in succession for 20 yards. A fumble gives the ball to Cornell. The entire half is now consumed by the struggles of each team to get within striking distance of the other's goal, each eleven advancing a few yards into the other's territory only to be held for downs. Just as the half closes a long punt places Pennsylvania in possession of the ball on its 15-yard line. Hare falls back to punt. Sweetland breaks through and blocks the kick, falling on the ball across the line for a touchdown. G. H. Young kicks the goal. Time soon after is called for the half.

Second Half: Cornell kicks off. The elevens again play ineffectively for several minutes, the defence of each being too strong to be overcome. Pennsylvania at last by short gains reaches the 25-yard line. Cornell stops the advance for 2 downs, but on the third attempt Outland goes around the end and dashes 25 yards across the line for a touchdown. Hare kicks the goal. Cornell kicks off. The play for some time surges back and forth across the centre line. Towards the close Hare's punting drives Cornell into goal. Young stands on the 25-yard line to return the kick. Hedges breaks through and blocks the ball. Picking it up he runs 25 yards for a touchdown. Hare again kicks the goal and the game soon closes.

CORNELL VS. PENNSYLVANIA
Philadelphia, Nov. 30, 1899

CORNELL		PENNSYLVANIA
H. J. Davall, '01,	Left End,	W. J. Coombs, '00.
F. S. Porter, '00,	Left Tackle,	J. B. Snover, '00.
W. J. Warner, '03,	Left Guard,	T. T. Hare, '01, Capt.
J. C. Pierson, '02,	Centre,	P. D. Overfield, '01.
W. A. Caldwell, '01,	Right Guard,	J. C. Teas, '02.
W. F. Dorner, '01,	" "	
E. R. Alexander, '01,	Right Tackle,	C. E. Wallace, '01.
C. A. Taussig, '02,	Right End,	J. H. Outland, '00.
G. H. Young, '00,	Quarter-back,	A. R. Kennedy, '01.
G. B. Walbridge, '00,	Left Half,	W. A. Potter, '01.
P. B. Windsor, '00,	" "	
A. B. Morrison, '01,	Right Half,	J. P. Gardiner, '01.
R. D. Starbuck, '01,	Full-back,	J. C. McCracken, '01.

Referee: R. D. Wrenn, '95, Harvard. Umpire: P. J. Dashiell, Navy. Linesmen: C. W. Wilson, '00, Cornell; F. E. Woodley, '01, Pennsylvania. Timekeepers: H. H. Tuller, '00, Cornell; J. Hedges,' 01, Pennsylvania. Score: Cornell 0, Pennsylvania 29. First Half: Touchdown by W. A. Potter; touchdown by J. C. McCracken, goal by J. H. Outland. Second Half: Touchdown by T. T. Hare, goal by J. H. Outland; touchdown by J. C. McCracken, goal by J. H. Outland; touchdown and goal by J. H. Outland.

First Half: Cornell wins the toss and takes the west goal. Kicks are exchanged, Pennsylvania catching at 40. McCracken, Hare, and Gardiner drive the ball to the 30-yard line. On the next play Potter circles the end for a touchdown. No goal. Cornell kicks off. Pennsylvania with guards-back steadily drives the ball, yard after yard, 85 yards. Within 5 yards from the goal-line the ball is given to McCracken, who in guards-back formation bursts through for a touchdown. Outland kicks the goal. During the remainder of the half Pennsylvania's guards-back makes great gains, but Cornell's stubborn defence checks the advance each time when driven to the 25-yard line.

Second Half: Cornell kicks off. Pennsylvania, forming guards-back in rapid succession right and left, forces the ball 80 yards, Hare taking it over for a touchdown and Outland kicking the goal. Cornell kicks off and after a succession of unimportant plays Pennsylvania secures the ball on a fumble on Cornell's 15-yard line. Cornell puts up an impregnable defence and takes the ball on downs. The ball is punted to midfield. Potter and Gardiner by long end runs work it back to Cornell's 5-yard line. Guards-back is formed on the right and McCracken is sent over for a touchdown. Outland kicks the goal. Cornell kicks off and after a long series of kicks Pennsylvania catches the ball on the 5-yard line. Coombs circles the end for 25 yards. Gardiner and Potter by short gains through the line advance 20 more. Outland goes around the end for 15. Potter takes the ball to the 10-yard line. Guards-back in four attempts sends Outland across for the touchdown. A moment later he kicks the goal and the game ends.

CORNELL VS. PENNSYLVANIA
Philadelphia, Nov. 29, 1900

CORNELL		PENNSYLVANIA
C. A. Taussig, '02,	Left End,	H. B. Hodge, '01.
C. A. Lueder, '02,	Left Tackle,	J. M. Horner, '01.
W. J. Warner, '03,	Left Guard,	T. T. Hare, '01, Capt.
W. H. Namack, '01,	Centre,	J. F. McCloskey, '01.
W. F. Dorner, '01,	Right Guard,	J. C. Teas, '02.
S. H. Hunt, '04,	" "	
E. R. Alexander, '01,	Right Tackle,	C. E. Wallace, '01.
C. W. Cross, '01,	Right End,	W. G. Gardiner, '03.
A. A. Brewster, '04,	Quarter-back,	J. P. Gardiner, '01.
T. R. Finucane, '03,	"	
H. Purcell, '03,	Left Half,	W. A. Potter, '01.

CORNELL

A. B. Morrison, '01, — Right Half, — W. S. Davidson, '01.
" " — W. G. Baird, '03.
R. D. Starbuck, '00, Capt., — Full-back, — J. C. McCracken, '01.
H. Schoellkopf, '02, — "

PENNSYLVANIA

Referee: M. McClung, '94, Lehigh. Umpire: P. J. Dashiell, Navy. Linesmen: H. J. Davall, '01, Cornell; F. E. Woodley, '01, Pennsylvania. Timekeeper: P. D. Mills, '97, Yale. Score: Cornell 0, Pennsylvania 27. First Half: Touchdown by T. T. Hare; touchdown and goal by T. T. Hare. Second Half: Touchdown by C. E. Wallace, goal by T. T. Hare ; touchdown by T. T. Hare; touchdown by W. S. Davidson.

First Half: Cornell wins the toss and selects the east goal. Pennsylvania kicks off. The ball is rushed a few yards by each team and then punted, neither being able to gain consistently. At last Cornell punts to Potter at 20, the latter runs the kick back to midfield. Pennsylvania sets in motion a mass play against the tackle, alternating right and left, which rapidly forces the ball down to the 5-yard line, where Hare is sent across for a touchdown. No goal. Cornell kicks off and Pennsylvania at once calls into play its mass play of guards-back. Slowly but steadily the ball creeps 72 yards, Hare being again sent over for the touchdown and later kicking the goal. Cornell kicks off and Pennsylvania, unable to gain, punts. Cornell hits the line hard and works the ball to Pennsylvania's 30-yard line, where it goes to opponents on a fumble. Pennsylvania is slowly but surely forcing the ball toward Cornell's goal when time is called for the half.

Second Half: Cornell kicks off. After a series of ineffective rushes by each team and a series of punts Pennsylvania secures the ball on its 50-yard line. Guards-back sends runner after runner into the line for small but sufficient gains until the 5-yard line is reached, from which Wallace is sent across for a touchdown. Hare kicks the goal. A few

moments after the succeeding kick-off Hare gets around the
end and runs 65 yards for a touchdown. No goal. Cornell
kicks off. Pennsylvania, after several advances, the ball
being lost on downs, finally sends Potter around the end
twice in succession for gains of 20 yards, bringing the ball
to the midfield, where Davidson goes around the end 55
yards for a touchdown. No goal.

CORNELL VS. PENNSYLVANIA
Philadelphia, Nov. 28, 1901

CORNELL		PENNSYLVANIA
C. A. Taussig, '02,	Left End,	
R. A. Turnbull, '04,	" "	C. A. Nelson, '03.
C. A. Lueder, '02,	Left Tackle,	F. A. Piekarski, '03.
	" "	R. Brenton, '02.
	" "	C. S. Mitchell, '04.
W. J. Warner, '03,	Left Guard,	M. S. Bennett, '03.
R. S. Kent, '02,	Centre,	J. McCabe, '05.
S. H. Hunt, '04,	Right Guard,	J. C. Teas, '02.
M. Smith, '04,	Right Tackle,	W. G. Baird, '03.
W. A. Tydeman, '03,	Right End,	W. G. Gardiner, '03.
A. A. Brewster, '04,	Quarter-back,	T. Howard, '03.
H. Purcell, '03,	Left Half,	M. S. Reynolds, '05.
	" "	C. S. Townsend, '04.
T. R. Finucane, '03,	" "	J. C. Ludes, '03.
A. R. Coffin, '04,	Right Half,	D. Dale, '04.
W. J. Warner, '03, Capt.,	" "	T. Snook, '02.
H. Schoellkopf, '02,	Full-back,	H. A. Davidson, '02, Capt.

Referee: E. N. Wrightington, '97, Harvard. Umpire: P. J. Dashiell, Navy. Linesmen: E. J. Snow, '04, Cornell; C. S. Metzger, '03,
Pennsylvania. Timekeepers: E. Metcalf, Cornell; L. de P. Vail,
'94, Pennsylvania. Score: Cornell 23, Pennsylvania 6. First Half:
Touchdown by A. R. Coffin; touchdown and goal by H. A. Davidson;
touchdown by R. A. Turnbull, goal by A. R. Coffin. Second Half:
Touchdown and goal by A. R. Coffin; touchdown by A. A. Brewster,
goal by A. R. Coffin.

First Half: Pennsylvania wins the toss and takes the
west goal. Cornell kicks off. Pennsylvania cannot gain
and is forced to punt. Cornell opens up the Pennsylvania
line for several gains. Kicks are exchanged. Pennsylvania

ADDING A POINT TO THE SCORE.

Coffin, of Cornell, kicking the goal following a touchdown against Pennsylvania.   Franklin Field, Nov. 28, 1901.

gets the ball at midfield and by short gains forces the ball to Cornell's 5-yard line, where the ball is lost on downs. Purcell goes through the line on a fake kick for 20 yards. Coffin, on another trick play, clears the line and runs 84 yards for a touchdown. Pennsylvania kicks off, and after several unimportant plays Cornell punts, Pennsylvania catching at 50. Dale circles the end for 30 yards. Short plunges net five more. Davidson goes over for a touchdown and kicks the goal. Cornell kicks off, and after a series of kicks Turnbull catches the ball on the 40-yard line. He starts straight up the field, dodging brilliantly among the Pennsylvania forwards, in and out, until he clears the backs and thus covers 84 yards for a touchdown. Coffin kicks the goal. Soon after time is called for the half.

Second Half: Pennsylvania kicks off to Cornell on the 15-yard line. The latter by straight line plunges, short gains at a time without losing the ball, drives the play to Pennsylvania's 15-yard line. Cornell masses to attack centre, but Coffin dashes around the end for a touchdown. Goal. Pennsylvania kicks off to Cornell on the 5-yard line and the latter again forces its way by short gains to Pennsylvania's 10-yard line, where the ball is lost on a penalty. Davidson, Reynolds, and Teas by line plays advance the ball 50 yards, but are finally held for downs at centre. Kicks are exchanged which with a fumble places Pennsylvania in its own goal to punt. Brewster catches on the 35-yard line and runs through the Pennsylvania team for a touchdown. The goal is again made.

CORNELL VS. PENNSYLVANIA
Philadelphia, Nov. 27, 1902

CORNELL		PENNSYLVANIA
P. E. Larkin, '06,	Left End,	D. L. Richardson, '04.
	" "	B. A. Thomas, '03.
C. A. Lueder, '02,	Left Tackle,	R. G. Torrey, '06.
J. H. Costello, '06,	" "	

CORNELL		PENNSYLVANIA
W. J. Warner, '03, Capt.,	Left Guard,	H. C. Hoffman, '05.
J. A. Davitt, '03,	Centre,	J. F. McCabe, '05.
S. H. Hunt, '04,	Right Guard,	F. A. Piekarski, '03.
E. O. P. Waud, '04,	" "	C. S. Mitchell, '04.
M. Smith, '04,	Right Tackle,	W. G. Baird, '03.
W A. Tydeman, '03,	Right End,	V. S. Metzger, '03.
A. A. Brewster, '04,	Quarter-back,	D. Dale, '04.
H. Purcell, '03,	Left Half,	H. L. Fortiner, '05.
J. H. Sheble,	" "	
W. G. Snider, '04,	Right Half,	W. G. Gardiner, '03, Capt.
A. R. Coffin, '04,	Full-back,	M. S. Bennett, '04.
E. Burns, '03,	"	G. W. Weschler, '05.
S. B. Hunt, '04,	"	

Referee: E. N. Wrightington, '97, Harvard. Umpire: P. J. Dashiell, Navy. Linesmen: H. G. Webb, '03, Cornell; T. T. Hare, '01, Pennsylvania. Score: Cornell 11, Pennsylvania 12. First Half: Touchdown by H. Purcell, goal by A. R. Coffin; goal from field by A. R. Coffin. Second Half: Touchdown by R. G. Torrey, goal by W. G. Gardiner; touchdown by M. S. Bennett, goal by W. G. Gardiner.

First Half: Cornell wins the toss and takes the ball. Kicks are exchanged. Cornell at once forces Pennsylvania back, making repeated gains through the Red and Blue line. After several exchanges of kicks interspersed with numerous hard line plunges Pennsylvania is forced to punt from behind the goal-line. The kick is high and Cornell recovers it on Pennsylvania's 33-yard line. The ball is worked to the 10-yard line. Here Pennsylvania plays spiritedly and takes the ball on downs. Bennett punts to the 30-yard line, where Brewster heels a fair catch. Coffin kicks a goal from placement. Gardiner kicks off to Warner. For several minutes play moves back and forth across the centre line without advantage to either side. Two long punts by Coffin send the ball well into Pennsylvania's territory. Bennett returns and Cornell catches the ball on Pennsylvania's 40-yard line. By trick plays Cornell reaches the 15-yard line. Purcell now circles the end for a touchdown. Coffin kicks the goal. There is no further scoring in this half.

Second Half: Gardiner kicks off. Cornell makes a small gain and punts. Pennsylvania with difficulty makes a first down and is soon forced to punt. Play of this character ensues for several minutes. Cornell catches a punt at 35 and by short rushes makes 35 yards. Pennsylvania holds for downs. On the first plunge Pennsylvania gains 10 yards. The Red and Blue shows great improvement and rapidly rushes Cornell down the field. At the 30-yard line Cornell stops the advance for 3 downs, but on the last trial Gardiner gets off a quarter-back kick which Pennsylvania captures on the 10-yard line. Two line plunges reach the 5-yard line, from which Torrey is sent over for a touchdown. Gardiner kicks the goal. Cornell kicks off. The game becomes almost wholly kicks, Cornell being driven steadily back. Gardiner catches at 55 and runs back 30 yards. Dale rounds the end for 15, Mitchell duplicates the play on the opposite side for 10. Bennett goes through the line for a touchdown. The score now is a tie at 11 to 11. Gardiner carefully points the ball for the try. As he kicks the great crowd rises to its feet. The goal is made and Pennsylvania leads by 1 point. Pennsylvania kicks off and Cornell fumbles. The Red and Blue forces the ball to the 10-yard line, where time is called.

CORNELL VS. PENNSYLVANIA
Philadelphia, Nov. 26, 1903

CORNELL		PENNSYLVANIA
F. W. Hackstaff, '05,	Left End,	G. W. Weede, '05.
J. H. Costello, '06,	Left Tackle,	T. A. Buthiewicz, '05.
" "		A. B. Ziegler, '07.
W. S. Voris, '04,	Left Guard,	F. A. Piekarski, '05.
J. A. Davitt, '03,	Centre,	H. B. Taylor, '05.
W. S. Newman, '07,	"	
S. H. Hunt, '04, Capt.,	Right Guard,	H. C. Hoffman, '05.
" "		D. B. Kase, '06.
M. S. Halliday, '06,	Right Tackle,	R. G. Torrey, '06.
J. E. Forgy, '06,	Right End,	C. S. Metzger, '03, Capt.

CORNELL		PENNSYLVANIA
A. A. Brewster, '04,	Quarter-back,	A. L. Mulford, '04.
J. Lynah, '05,	"	C. S. Corson, '07.
L. J. Rice, '07,	Left Half,	M. S. Reynolds, '05.
W. G. Snider, '06,	Right Half,	G. R. Drake, '05.
A. R. Coffin, '04,	Full-back,	M. S. Bennett, '04.

Referee: E. N. Wrightington, '97, Harvard. Umpire: W. H. Edwards, '00, Princeton. Linesman: R. P. Kernan, '03, Harvard. Score: Cornell 0, Pennsylvania 42. First Half: Touchdown by G. R. Drake, goal by M. S. Bennett; touchdown and goal by M. S. Bennett. Second Half: Touchdown by F. A. Piekarski, goal by M. S. Bennett; touchdown by M. S. Reynolds, goal by M. S. Bennett; touchdown by M. S. Reynolds, goal by M. S. Bennett; touchdown by F. A. Piekarski, goal by M. S. Bennett; touchdown and goal by M. S. Bennett.

First Half: Cornell wins the toss and takes the west goal. An exchange of kicks with some rushing gives Pennsylvania the ball at 40. Bennett and Piekarski pierce the Cornell line for great gains. Mulford skirts the end for 10. Torrey goes through tackle for 8, Piekarski makes 7, then 9, and Drake crosses the line for the touchdown. Bennet, kicks the goal. Cornell kicks off. For several minutes play is near centre without advantage. Long punts drive Cornell back and Brewster punts out of bounds at 30. Bennett hits the line for 5. Piekarski goes through tackle for 15 and Bennet through centre for a touchdown, also kicking the goal. The half soon after closes.

Second Half: Pennsylvania kicks off. Rushes and a punt by Cornell give Pennsylvania the ball at 40. Bennett rounds the end for 20 yards. Torrey duplicates the play for 20 more. Mulford gets off a quarter-back kick on the third down, with 2 yards to gain, which Pennsylvania recovers on the 1-yard line. Piekarski goes through the line for the touchdown and Bennett kicks the goal. Cornell kicks off. After a few small gains through the line Pennsylvania sends Metzger around the end for 40 yards. Reynolds in a line plunge reaches the 2-yard line. Bennett takes the ball over and kicks the goal. Cornell kicks off and holds Pennsylvania for downs. Play for some time surges back and forth between the 25-yard lines. At last Cornell fumbles on the 25-yard line and Pennsylvania gets the ball. In two plays Reynolds crosses the line for a touchdown. Bennett kicks the goal. Upon resumption of play a punting exchange ensues. Cornell again fumbles on the 15-yard line and Pennsylvania gets the ball. Piekarski is forced through the line for a touchdown. Bennett kicks the goal. Cornell kicks off. Pennsylvania is unable to gain and punts. Cornell fumbles at centre and Pennsylvania secures the ball. Mulford gets around the end for a run of 35 yards. Bennett goes through the line for a touchdown and kicks the goal. Times is then called.

CORNELL VS. PENNSYLVANIA
Philadelphia, Nov. 24, 1904

CORNELL		PENNSYLVANIA
F. W. Hackstaff, '05,	Left End,	G. R. Drake, '05.
C. B. Goodspeed, '08,	" "	J. Hollenback, '06.
R. A. Smith, '05,	Left Tackle,	T. A. Buthiewicz, '05.
H. H. Downes, '08,	Left Guard,	F. A. Piekarski, '05.
C. C. Oderkirk, '08,	" "	D. B. Case, '06.
G. M. Chapman, '05,	Centre,	R. G. Torrey, '06, Capt.
L. A. Wilder, '06,	"	H. B. Taylor, '05.
F. J. Furman, '06,	Right Guard,	A. B. Ziegler, '07.
J. H. Costello, '06, Capt.,	Right Tackle,	O. F. Lamson, '07.
M. S. Halliday, '06,	" "	
R. Van Orman, '08,	Right End,	W. Sinkler, '06.
	" "	G. W. Weede, '05.
E. J. Bird, '07,	Quarter-back,	V. M. Stevenson, '08.
	"	C. S. Corson, '07.
L. J. Rice, '07,	Left Half,	M. S. Reynolds, '04.
	" "	J. H. Sheble, '08.
	" "	W. M. Hollenback, '06.
E. T. Gibson, '07,	Right Half,	E. L. Greene, '08.
	"	E. M. Bennis, '08.
M. S. Halliday, '06,	Full-back,	A. L. Smith, '06.
H. E. Davis, '07,	"	R. C. Folwell, '08.

Referee: W. H. Corbin, '89, Yale. Umpire: W. H. Edwards, '00, Princeton. Linesman: J. J. Hogan, '05, Yale. Score: Cornell 0,

Pennsylvania 34. First Half: Touchdown by F. A. Piekarski, goal by M. S. Reynolds; touchdown by F. A. Piekarski, goal by M. S. Reynolds; touchdown by F. A. Piekarski, goal by M. S. Reynolds; touchdown by V. M. Stevenson; goal by M. S. Reynolds. Second Half: Touchdown by C. S. Corson; touchdown by C. S. Corson.

First Half: Cornell wins the toss and selects the west goal. Reynolds kicks off to Rice. Cornell advances the ball to the 35-yard line. Here, on the third down, with 6 inches to go, a line plunge is made, but the runner is thrown for a loss and Pennsylvania takes the ball. Smith, Ziegler, and Lamson in three plunges reach the 10-yard line. Smith makes 4 and Piekarski goes over for a touchdown. Reynolds kicks the goal. Cornell kicks off. After a succession of unimportant plays Cornell has the ball for third down on the 20-yard line, with 1 foot to go. Again a line plunge is made, but once more Pennsylvania throws the runner for a loss and takes the ball. Smith, Ziegler, and Lamson, by a long series of short gains, reach the 5-yard line. Piekarski goes over for a touchdown. Reynolds again kicks the goal. Following the kick-off both teams resort to punting. Finally Furman punts to Reynolds on Pennsylvania's 10-yard line. Pennsylvania puts the ball down for a scrimmage. Folwell, Piekarski, Reynolds, Ziegler, and Lamson, by hard but short line plunges, carry the ball 90 yards. Piekarski then takes it over for a touchdown and Reynolds kicks the goal. Pennsylvania scores another touchdown just before the close of the half. Obtaining the ball on a fumble on Cornell's 20-yard line, Stevenson dashes around the end for a touchdown. Reynolds makes the goal.

Second Half: After the kick-off by Cornell and an exchange of punts, Pennsylvania catches the ball on Cornell's 40-yard line. In three plays Pennsylvania reaches the 8-yard mark, from which Corson is sent across for a touchdown. Reynolds kicks the goal. Cornell stops Pennsylvania's rushes until the close of the half, although unable to get near the latter's goal. Cornell punts to Folwell at the latter's 30. Sheble gets away for a long run to Cornell's 30-yard line. Weede makes 15, Folwell 3, Piekarski 1. On the next play a quarter-back kick is placed across the line and Corson falls on the ball for a touchdown. The goal is missed. Time soon after is called.

CORNELL vs. PENNSYLVANIA
Philadelphia, Nov. 30, 1905

CORNELL		PENNSYLVANIA
C. L. Roadhouse, '06,	Left End,	I. G. Levene, '07.
G. T. Cook, '08,	Left Tackle,	W. J. Rooke, '07.
E. I. Thompson, '09,	Left Guard,	J. L. Junk, '07.
C. L. Downes, '06,	" "	F. H. Hobson, '08.
W. S. Newman, '07,	Centre,	R. G. Torrey, '06, Capt.
B. J. O'Rourke, '09,	Right Guard,	J. L. Robinson, '09.
J. H. Costello, '06, Capt.,	Right Tackle,	O. F. Lamson, '07.
C. A. Lyon, '05,	" ";	
R. Van Orman, '08,	Right End,	H. W. Scarlett, '07.
J. A. Pollak, '07,	" "	
J. Newhall, '06,	Quarter-back,	V. M. Stevenson, '08.
G. H. Walder, '09,	Left Half,	J. H. Sheble, '08.
E. T. Gibson, '07,	Right Half,	E. L. Greene, '08.
M. S. Halliday, '06,	Full-back,	R. C. Folwell, '08.

Referee: W. H. Corbin, '89, Yale. Umpire: W. H. Edwards, '00, Princeton. Linesman: A. H. Sharpe, '02, Yale. Score: Cornell 5, Pennsylvania 6. Second Half: Touchdown by G. H. Walder; touchdown by O. F. Lamson, goal by J. H. Sheble.

First Half: Pennsylvania wins the toss and takes the west goal. Walder kicks off to Greene. Pennsylvania cannot gain consecutively and Sheble punts. Cornell fumbles at 35 and Pennsylvania secures the ball. Rooke, Robinson, and Folwell take the ball to the 15-yard line. Rooke makes 5 more, but Pennsylvania is penalized 10. Stevenson regains 15 yards. Pennsylvania fumbles and the ball goes to Cornell. Thompson, Gibson, and Halliday, by hard plunges and short gains, take the ball to Pennsylvania's 35-yard line. Here Pennsylvania holds for downs and takes the ball. A long punting duel ensues. Pennsylvania again puts the ball down on its 35-yard line and by sharp line plays rushes to Cornell's 35, where time stops the half.

Second Half: Sheble kicks off to Walder. An exchange of kicks ensues, terminating in Pennsylvania starting a scrimmage on its 20-yard line. Lamson, Rooke, and Robinson plough through the Cornell line to the latter's 45-yard line. Cornell captures a short kick. Another punting duel follows which terminates in a fumble by Pennsylvania on its 15-yard line, Cornell getting the ball. Twice Pennsylvania stops the Cornell backs without gain, but on the third attempt Walder breaks through and crosses the line for a touchdown. The goal is missed. Sheble kicks across the goal-line on the kick-off. Cornell kicks out. Sheble, Lamson, and Folwell rush the ball to the 28-yard line, where it goes to Cornell on a fumble. Walder punts to Greene. Pennsylvania now sets in motion a hard and rapid line attack which takes the ball without a check to Cornell's 5-yard line. Lamson in two plays makes the goal-line for a touchdown. Amid great excitement Sheble kicks the goal. Cornell kicks off, but time soon expires.

CORNELL vs. PENNSYLVANIA
Philadelphia, Nov. 29, 1906

CORNELL		PENNSYLVANIA
C. H. Watson, '09,	Left End,	I. G. Levene, '07.
L. Babcock, '09,	" "	
G. T. Cook, '08, Capt.,	Left Tackle,	D. W. Draper, '09.
E. I. Thompson, '09,	Left Guard,	P. J. Gallagher, '09.
W. S. Newman, '07,	Centre,	J. K. Dwyer, '08.
B. J. O'Rourke, '09,	Right Guard,	A. B. Ziegler, '07.
C. C. Brinton, '08,	Right Tackle,	F. H. Gaston, '07.

CORNELL		PENNSYLVANIA
R. Van Orman, '08,	Right End,	H. W. Scarlett, '07.
J. H. Jamieson, '09,	Quarter-back,	G. J. Lawrence, '07.
F. E. Gardner, '09,	"	
E. Earle, '08,	Left Half,	R. C. Folwell, '08.
E. T. Gibson, '07,	Right Half,	E. L. Greene, '08, Capt.
G. H. Walder, '09,	Full-back,	W. M. Hollenback, '08.

Referee: W. H. Corbin, '89, Yale. Umpire: W. H. Edwards, '00, Princeton. Linesman: A. H. Sharpe, '02, Yale. Score: Cornell 0, Pennsylvania 0.

First Half: Cornell wins the toss and takes the ball. Walder kicks off to Pennsylvania's 10-yard line, but the ball goes out of bounds. A second kick results similarly and the kick-off goes to Pennsylvania. Hollenback kicks to Walder. The play of the first half is characterized by an absence on both sides of line-plunging and end runs. Each team resorts to forward passes and punts. Many of the passes are successful, but the inability to gain by the play consecutively forces each team to kick. Several punts are blocked on each side, but neither team comes within scoring distance of the other's goal.

Second Half: Pennsylvania kicks off. Cornell tries the line, but, unable to advance the ball consistently, punts. Hollenback gets away for a 30-yard run. Folwell and Greene hit the line for 12 yards and then Cornell holds for downs. Hollenback punts. Walder cannot make first down and Cornell kicks. In this half the two teams resort to line-bucking, but neither side is able to gain consecutively or to come within striking distance of the other's goal. Outside of a few long runs by Hollenback the play is without individual brilliance. Much kicking is done and the punts well caught, thus keeping the play between the 25-yard lines without a score. The game thus comes to an end.

CORNELL VS. PENNSYLVANIA
Philadelphia, Nov. 28, 1907

CORNELL		PENNSYLVANIA
C. H. Watson, '10,	Left End,	S. H. Pauxtis, '10.
" "	" "	A. C. Miller, '10.
J. A. Lynch, '08,	Left Tackle,	D. W. Draper, '09.
E. I. Thompson, '09,	Left Guard,	P. J. Gallagher, '09.
" "	" "	J. F. Macklin, '10.
C. C. May, '10,	Centre,	J. K. Dwyer, '08.
J. J. Cosgrove, '09,	Right Guard,	A. B. Ziegler, '07.
C. C. Brinton, '08,	" "	
B. J. O'Rourke, '09,	Right Tackle,	F. H. Gaston, '07.
R. Van Orman, '08,	Right End,	H. W. Scarlett, '07.
A. F. Tydeman, '10,	" "	
W. Harris, '09,	" "	
F. E. Gardner, '09,	Quarter-back,	C. Keinath, '09.
R. K. Caldwell, '09,	"	C. W. Reagan, '08.
E. Earle, '08,	Left Half,	E. L. Greene, '08.
" . "		C. D. Dwyer, '07.
E. L. McCallie, '09,	Right Half,	R. C. Folwell, '08, Capt.
G. H. Walder, '09,	Full-back,	W. M. Hollenback, '08.
F. O. Ebeling, '09,	"	

Referee: A. H. Sharpe, '02, Yale. Umpire: W. H. Edwards, '00, Princeton. Field Judge: H. B. Hackett, '04, Army. Linesman: W. H. Corbin, '89, Yale. Score: Cornell 4, Pennsylvania 12. First Half: Touchdown by R. C. Folwell, goal by H. W. Scarlett. Second Half: Touchdown by D. W. Draper, goal by H. W. Scarlett; goal from field by R. K. Caldwell.

First Half: Cornell wins the toss and takes the west goal. Hollenback kicks off to Walder. Cornell tries the line, but unable to gain punts on the third down. Pennsylvania returns the kick and a sharp kicking duel ensues. Finally Pennsylvania catches the ball on Cornell's 40-yard line. Pauxtis throws a forward pass to Draper, netting 40 yards. Hollenback gets around the end for 12 more. Cornell holds for 2 downs and then Keinath shoots a forward pass to Pauxtis, placing the ball 3 yards from Cornell's goal-line. A penalty sets Pennsylvania back 15 yards. Keinath sends a forward pass to Draper on the 8-yard mark. Hollenback makes 3 yards around the end. Greene goes through the line for 4, and on the next play Folwell dashes through tackle for the touchdown. Scarlett kicks the goal. Cornell kicks off. The play remains at centre for several minutes. At last Cornell recovers a fumble in Pennsylvania's territory and reaches the 30-yard line by hard rushes. Pennsylvania holds for downs and time is called.

Second Half: Cornell kicks off and Pennsylvania returns. A sharp kicking exchange commences, in which Cornell has the advantage. The latter fumbles on the 40-yard line. Draper picks up the ball and races 75 yards for a touchdown. The goal is made by Scarlett. Cornell kicks off. Pennsylvania tries rushing, but Cornell's defence stiffens and Hollenback punts. Cornell now tries two plays into the line without gain. On the next play Caldwell throws a long forward pass to Ebeling, which puts the ball down on the 30-yard line. Pennsylvania does not yield an inch. Caldwell falls back in drop-kick formation and sends the ball between the posts for a field goal. Pennsylvania kicks off, but there is no further scoring.

CORNELL VS. PENNSYLVANIA
Philadelphia, Nov. 26, 1908

CORNELL		PENNSYLVANIA
R. B. Hurlburt, '10,	Left End,	H. P. Braddock, '10.
E. I. Bayer, '09,	" "	T. Crooks, '10.
C. A. Franke, '11,	" "	S. Townsend, '09.
R. L. Leventry, '11,	Left Tackle,	D. W. Draper, '09.
J. J. Cosgrove, '09,	Left Guard,	G. A. Dietrich, '10.
H. C. Wight, '09,	Centre,	W. Le R. Marks, '11.
	"	E. B. Cozens, '11.
J. G. McCollum, '09,	Right Guard,	R. E. Lamberton, '10.
	" "	C. H. Pike, '11.
B. J. O'Rourke, '09,	Right Tackle,	F. H. Gaston, '08.
F. W. Bell, '11,	" "	
E. G. McArthur, '11,	Right End,	H. W. Scarlett, '07.
E. S. Crosby, '10,	" "	

CORNELL		PENNSYLVANIA
B. B. Wood, '11,	Quarter-back,	C. Keinath, '09.
F. E. Gardner, '09,	"	A. C. Miller, '10.
R. K. Caldwell, '09,	"	
A. F. Tydeman, '10,	Left Half,	J. O. Manier, '09.
H. G. Mowe, '10,	" "	
A. H. Hutchinson, '10,	Right Half,	J. W. Means, '10.
G. K. Shearer, '09,	" "	
S. G. Hoffman, '10,	" "	
G. H. Walder, '09, Capt.,	Full-back,	W. M. Hollenback,'08, Capt.

Referee: A. H. Sharpe, '02, Yale. Umpire: W. H. Edwards, '00, Princeton. Field Judge: W. S. Langford, '96, Trinity. Linesman: W. R. Okeson, '96, Lehigh. Score: Cornell 4, Pennsylvania 17. First Half: Goal from field by H. G. Mowe; touchdown by W. M. Hollenback, goal by H. W. Scarlett. Second Half: Touchdown by J. O. Manier; touchdown by A. C. Miller, goal by H. W. Scarlett.

First Half: Cornell wins the toss and takes the ball. Pennsylvania kicks off. Cornell at once resorts to a kicking game and after a few exchanges forces Pennsylvania to kick out behind the line. The ball goes out of bounds at 25. A penalty sets Cornell forward upon the 15-yard line. Unable to break the Red and Blue line, Mowe kicks a goal from the field. Pennsylvania kicks off. Cornell cannot gain consistently and punts. Pennsylvania now plays a kicking game and recovers a fumble on Cornell's 35-yard line. Cornell stands firm and Pennsylvania tries a forward pass, Miller to Draper, which places the ball on the 7-yard mark. On the second play Hollenback breaks through for a touchdown. Scarlett kicks the goal. There is no further scoring in this half.

Second Half: Cornell kicks off. Play for some time is confined between the 25-yard lines, owing to the inability of both teams to force it beyond except by kicking. Pennsylvania picks up a fumble on Cornell's 40-yard line. By straight line plays Manier, Means, and Hollenback rush the ball to the 5-yard line, from which Manier goes over for a

Photograph by F. R. Bushnell.

A POWERFUL ATTACK AND A SHARP DEFENCE.

MacArthur, of Cornell, having pierced Pennsylvania's heavy interference, tackles Hollenback.   Franklin Field, Nov. 26, 1908.

touchdown. The goal fails. Cornell kicks off. Pennsylvania returns and Cornell, by rushing, forces the ball into Pennsylvania's territory. A forward pass is tried which Pennsylvania intercepts on the 40-yard line, Miller taking it and then running the distance for a touchdown. Scarlett kicks the goal. Cornell kicks off. Play deadlocks and a punting exchange ensues. Thus the game ends.

CORNELL VS. PENNSYLVANIA
Philadelphia, Nov. 25, 1909

CORNELL		PENNSYLVANIA
H. K. Seeley, '10,	Left End,	H. P. Braddock, '10.
E. H. Teagle, '12,	" "	
R. B. Hurlburt, '10,	" "	
P. S. Munk, '12,	Left Tackle,	J. L. Fretz, '12.
T. H. Farrington, '10,	" "	R. B. Burns, '10.
G. S. Donnan, '12,	Left Guard,	G. A. Dietrich, '10.
	" "	R. E. Lamberton, '10.
	" "	G. Burdick, '11.
C. H. Seagrave, '11,	Centre,	E. B. Cozens, '11.
K. E. Pfeiffer, '12,	"	
J. J. O'Connor, '12,	Right Guard,	C. H. Pike, '11.
C. P. Weekes, '12,	Right Tackle,	P. A. Ferrier, '11.
E. S. Crosby, '10,	Right End,	P. B. Kauffman, '11.
S. H. Sutton, '11,	" "	W. Le. R. Marks, '11.
C. C. Owen, '10,	Quarter-back,	D. L. Hutchinson, '12.
B. B. Wood, '11,	"	
S. E. Robb, '11,	Left Half,	F. Sommer, '11.
A. F. Tydeman, '10, Capt.,	" "	W. J. Young, '11.
S. G. Hoffman, '10,	Right Half,	P. C. Irwin, '11.
A. Krutzsch, '11,	" "	A. G. Heilman, '12.
L. D. Simson, '11,	Full-back,	F. L. Ramsdell, '11.
	"	A. C. Miller, '10, Capt.
	"	J. H. Scott, '11.

Referee: A. H. Sharpe, '02, Yale. Umpire: W. H. Edwards, '00, Princeton. Field Judge: W. S. Langford, '96, Trinity. Linesman: W. R. Okeson, '96, Lehigh. Score: Cornell 6, Pennsylvania 17. First Half: Touchdown by S. E. Robb, goal by J. J. O'Connor; touchdown by F. L. Ramsdell, goal by H. P. Braddock. Second Half: Touchdown by P. C. Irwin, goal by H. P. Braddock; touchdown by A. G. Heilman.

First Half: Pennsylvania wins the toss and takes the west goal. O'Connor kicks to Hutchinson at 15. Following a fake kick Hutchinson punts. Tydeman catches and runs the ball to the 42-yard mark. Cornell cannot gain and Simson kicks. Pennsylvania fumbles and the ball goes to Cornell. Simson goes through the line to the 15-yard line. A penalty takes the ball 10 yards farther. Robb goes through the right wing for a touchdown and O'Connor kicks the goal. The ball now changes hands several times on punts following ineffectual rushes. Sommer catches at midfield. Ramsdell hits centre for 15. A delayed pass sends Sommer for an additional yard. Hutchinson sends an on-side kick to Cozens at 14. Irwin in two plunges through centre advances 9 yards. Ramsdell goes over for the touchdown and Braddock kicks the goal. During the remainder of this half Pennsylvania twice, by hard line plunges, works the ball to Cornell's 5-yard line, but each time is held for downs. Time is called without further scoring.

Second Half: Both teams appear in fresh uniforms, as the game is being played in rain and sleet. Hutchinson kicks to Wood. Simson returns the punt and Hutchinson runs to Cornell's 45-yard line. Irwin makes 9, but Cornell holds and Hutchinson punts to 15, where Cozens recovers a fumble. Pike rounds the end for 9. Fretz gains 2 more. Irwin makes a touchdown and Braddock kicks the goal. Play surges back and forth at Cornell's 40-yard line. Finally Simson is forced to punt from his 5-yard line. Heilman blocks the kick and the ball bounds across the line. Heilman makes the touchdown. The try at goal fails. During the remainder of the game play does not pass either 25-yard line, being for the most time in Cornell's territory. The latter, however, holds for downs when their goal is threatened and punts the ball back to centre.

CORNELL VS. PENNSYLVANIA
Philadelphia, Nov. 24, 1910

CORNELL		PENNSYLVANIA
H. R. Eyrick, '13,	Left End,	W. Le R. Marks, '11.
E. H. Teagle, '12,	" "	
P. S. Munk, '12,	Left Tackle,	H. E. Rodgers, '12.
D. K. Champaign, '13,	" "	
E. H. O'Rourke, '12,	Left Guard,	C. C. Wolferth, '12.
	" "	H. B. Patterson, '12.
J. S. Whyte, '13,	Centre,	E. B. Cozens, '11, Capt.
C. Delano, '12,	Right Guard,	J. M. Cramer, '13.
C. P. Weekes, '12,	Right Tackle,	H. H. Morris, '12.
	" "	T. F. Dillon, '13.
C. H. Seagrave, '11,	Right End,	L. W. Jourdet, '13.
L. B. Pitcher, '13,	" "	P. B. Kauffman, '11.
E. W. Butler, '13,	Quarter-back,	J. H. Scott, '11.
K. W. Gass, '12,	"	W. J. H. Hough, '11.
	"	E. Thayer, '12.
	"	J. J. Keough, '12.
S. E. Robb, '11, Capt.,	Left Half,	F. L. Ramsdell, '11.
R. B. Whyte, '13,	" "	J. P. Harrington, '13.
B. O'Connor, '13,	" "	
J. S. Nichols, '12,	Right Half,	F. Sommer, '11.
E. S. Bates, '13,	" "	L. M. Kennedy, '13.
E. P. Wilson, '13,	Full-back,	E. L. Mercer, '13.
	"	W. J. Young, '13.

Referee: J. B. Pendleton, '90, Bowdoin. Umpire: A. H. Sharpe, '02, Yale. Field Judge: W. S. Langford, '96, Trinity. Linesman: C. J. McCarthy, Germantown Acad. Score: Cornell 6, Pennsylvania 12. First Quarter: Touchdown by E. L. Mercer, goal by F. L. Ramsdell. Second Quarter: Goal from field by E. W. Butler; touchdown by F. Sommer, goal by F. L. Ramsdell; goal from placement by E. W. Butler.

First Quarter: Pennsylvania wins the toss and selects the east goal. Mercer kicks across the goal-line and Cornell puts the ball in play on its 25-yard line. A quarter-back run is stopped and Butler punts to 32. Mercer makes 7 yards, Ramsdell 5. Eyrick stops Mercer, but Sommer nets 5 through the line. A forward pass, Scott to Marks, places the ball on the 8-yard line. Another forward pass is tried, but Whyte gets the ball for Cornell. Butler kicks from behind the goal-posts to Scott, who races forward 15 yards. Mercer goes around the end for 30 yards and a touchdown. Ramsdell kicks the goal. Butler kicks across the goal-line and Pennsylvania starts a scrimmage on the 25-yard line. Mercer skirts the end for 20 yards. Scott punts to midfield. Butler punts, Whyte gets the ball and runs 35 yards across the goal-line, but a touchdown is not allowed. Kicks are exchanged and Cornell gets the ball on Pennsylvania's 30-yard line. Butler tries for a field goal, but the ball strikes the post. An exchange of kicks again gives the ball to Cornell on their opponent's 40-yard line, where another field goal is attempted but missed. Kicks ensue. Munk recovers the ball and runs to Pennsylvania's 21-yard line. O'Connor makes 4 and time is called.

Second Quarter: Cornell resumes play 19 yards from Pennsylvania's goal-line. O'Connor makes 3. Pennsylvania holds and Butler tries a place kick which scores. Mercer kicks off and O'Connor runs the ball back 10 yards. Neither team can gain consecutively and punting frequently follows short gains. Pennsylvania gets the ball out of bounds at her 25-yard line. Hough goes in at quarter. He gets off for 20 yards and repeats the play for 9 more. Mercer adds a first down. The ball is on Cornell's 6-yard mark. Pennsylvania tries a fake end run, terminating in a forward pass to Sommer, who plunges through the centre for a touchdown. Goal.

Third Quarter: Patterson kicks to Robb. A long series of kicks intermingled with penalties finally gives Cornell the ball on her 45-yard line. Nichols circles Pennsylvania's end and reaches the 35-yard line. Butler drops back to the 45-yard line and kicks a difficult goal from placement. A brilliant series of kicks and passes ensues, closing by Cornell intercepting a pass on her 35-yard line. Butler shoots another forward pass for 25 yards. Butler gets off a long kick, which strikes the ground and Eyrick gets it on Pennsylvania's 15-yard line. Butler tries a field goal, but fails. Pennsylvania kicks and recovers the ball. Plunges carry it to Cornell's 18-yard line, where time is called.

Fourth Quarter: A line plunge fails and Cornell gets a forward pass on the 15-yard line. Butler kicks and Seagrave recovers the ball. Kicks and penalties terminate in giving Pennsylvania the ball on Cornell's 45-yard line. Kauffman makes 9, Sommer 2, Young 7, and a forward pass takes the ball to Cornell's 7-yard mark. Cornell stands firm and Ramsdell tries for a field goal, but fails. Butler kicks to midfield. Pennsylvania cannot gain and punts. Nichols makes 14 around the end. Pennsylvania stops the next plunge for a 10-yard loss. Pitcher reaches Pennsylvania's 45-yard line and the quarter closes.

CHAPTER XII

DARTMOUTH VS. PRINCETON

DARTMOUTH VS. PRINCETON
Princeton, Oct. 30, 1897

DARTMOUTH		PRINCETON
C. J. Boyle, '00,	Left End,	W. B. Schwartz, '98.
	" "	S. G. Craig, '95.
J. H. Putnam, '01.	Left Tackle,	E. G. Holt, '00.
F. W. Lowe, '01,	Left Guard,	I. R. Dickey, '98.
R. Jackson, '00,	Centre,	W. C. Booth, '00.
C. C. Walker, '98,	Right Guard,	W. H. Edwards, '00.
J. H. Edwards, '99,	Right Tackle,	A. R. T. Hillebrand, '00.
	" "	H. Potter, '98.
F. W. Cavanaugh, '99,	Right End,	G. Cochran, '98, Capt.
	" "	H. R. Lathrope, '00.
J. Wentworth, '00,	Quarter-back,	J. Baird, '99.
J. B. C. Eckstorm, '98, Capt.,	Left Half,	H. R. Reiter, '98.
	" "	J. L. Crane, '99.
F. J. Crolius, '99	Right Half,	A. W. Kelly, '98.
	" "	H. R. Reiter, '98.
	" "	G. H. Lathrope, '00.
D. C. McAndrew, '98,	Full-back,	H. Wheeler, '00.
W. Stickney, '00,	"	

Referee: W. H. Andrus, '97, Princeton. Umpire: J. Parker, '89, Cornell. Linesmen: F. E. Jennings, '00, Dartmouth; S. P. Hayward, '98, Princeton. Score: Dartmouth 0, Princeton 30. First Half: Touchdown by A. W. Kelly, goal by H. Wheeler; touchdown by A. W. Kelly, goal by H. Wheeler; touchdown by A. R. T. Hillebrand, goal by H. Wheeler. Second Half: Touchdown by H. R. Reiter, goal by H. Wheeler; touchdown and goal by H. Wheeler.

First Half: Princeton wins the toss and takes the north goal. Dartmouth kicks to Cochran. Princeton kicks and soon recovers the ball on downs on the 40-yard line. From here Princeton by straight football rushes the ball to Dartmouth's 5-yard line, from which Kelly goes over for a touchdown. Wheeler kicks the goal. Dartmouth kicks off and after an exchange of kicks Princeton gets the ball on a fumble on Dartmouth's 30-yard line. Reiter, Wheeler, and Kelly take the ball across for a touchdown. Goal by Wheeler. After the kick-off and several minutes of rushing, Booth blocks Dartmouth's kick on the latter's 30-yard line. Hillebrand gets the ball and runs 75 yards for a touchdown. Goal.

Second Half: Princeton kicks off and Dartmouth, unable to gain, punts to Princeton's 40. Reiter rounds the end for 30 yards. He skirts the other end for 30 more. On the next play he goes over for a touchdown. Goal. Dartmouth kicks off. Holt, Reiter, Lathrope, and Wheeler alternating with the ball, carry the ball 70 yards for a touchdown. Wheeler kicks the goal. No further scoring.

1898–1902, no games.

DARTMOUTH vs. PRINCETON
Princeton, Oct. 24, 1903

DARTMOUTH		PRINCETON
M. W. Bullock, '04,	Left End,	R. T. Davis, '04.
W. H. Lillard, '05,	" "	
F. H. Brown, '05,	Left Tackle,	J. L. Cooney, '07.
J. T. Gilman, '05,	Left Guard,	H. L. Dillon, '07.
H. J. Hooper, '07,	Centre,	H. H. Short, '05,
J. W. Gage, '06,	Right Guard,	J. R. De Witt, '04, Capt.
L. C. Turner, '04,	Right Tackle,	H. R. Reed, '04.
R. Glaze, '06,	Right End,	H. H. Henry, '04.
E. A. Herr, '06,	" "	
M. E. Witham, '04, Capt.,	Quarter-back,	J. R. Vetterlein, '07.
	"	T. J. Burke, '05.
W. S. Dillon, '05,	Left Half,	R. R. Hart, '04.
D. J. Main, '06,	" "	
J. A. Vaughan, '05,	Right Half,	J. D. Kafer, '05.
H. W. Colburn, '06,	" "	C. G. Stevens, '04.
J. W. Knibbs, '05,	Full-back,	S. Rulon-Miller, '07.
W. A. Conley, '05,	"	S. W. McClave, '03.

Referee: N. W. Snow, '02, Michigan. Umpire: S. A. Boyle, '98, Pennsylvania. Linesmen: I. J. French, '01, Dartmouth; W. Pell,

'02, Princeton. Score: Dartmouth 0, Princeton 17. First Half: Touchdown by J. D. Kafer, goal by J. R. Vetterlein. Second Half: Touchdown by J. L. Cooney, goal by J. R. Vetterlein; touchdown by S. W. McClave.

First Half: Princeton wins the toss and takes the north goal. Dartmouth kicks to Princeton's 20. Princeton fumbles and Dartmouth gets the ball. Dartmouth tries a wing shift and makes 5 yards. Princeton holds for downs and De Witt punts 60 yards. A long series of kicks ensues. Dartmouth puts the ball down for a scrimmage on their 20-yard line. Dillon breaks through and gets the ball. Four tackle-back plays reach the goal-line, Kafer touching down. Vetterlein kicks the goal. Dartmouth kicks off and Princeton returns. Glaze on a double pass goes around the end and runs past the Princeton team. Rulon-Miller catches him after a sprint of 60 yards and brings him down on the 20-yard line. Dartmouth, by a wing-shift, ploughs through for 13 yards. Princeton holds for downs and De Witt punts to Dartmouth's 45. Play remains near centre for some time, and time is called for the half.

Second Half: Dartmouth kicks to De Witt at Princeton's 10-yard line. De Witt runs 80 yards. Short plunges into the line by Cooney and Hart take the ball to the 5-yard line, from which Cooney goes over for a touchdown. Vetterlein kicks the goal. Princeton kicks off and Dartmouth, by the wing-shift, rushes the ball back to midfield. Here the ball surges back and forth for several minutes without advantage. Princeton holds for downs at Dartmouth's 40. Kafer circles the end for 25 yards. De Witt makes 5 more. McClave gets around the end for a touchdown. De Witt misses the goal. Princeton kicks off and Dartmouth by short rushes makes 35 yards. Time is called.

1904, no game.

DARTMOUTH VS. PRINCETON
Princeton, Nov. 7, 1905

DARTMOUTH		PRINCETON
G. F. Kennedy, '09,	Left End,	N. B. Tooker, '06.
D. J. Church, '08,	" "	
G. N. Bankart, '06,	Left Tackle,	W. J. Phillips, '08.
	" "	J. L. Cooney,' 07, Capt.
A. H. Thayer, '09,	Left Guard,	E. L. Rafferty, '06.
	" "	H. L. Dillon, '07.
J. T. Griffin, '06,	Centre,	J. C. Waller, '06.
J. W. Gage, '06,	Right Guard,	P. E. Waller, '10.
J. T. Smith, '06,	Right Tackle,	D. G. Herring, '07.
R. Glaze, '06,	Right End,	G. H. Fryer, '09.
J. B. Glaze, '08,	Quarter-back,	E. A. Dillon, '09.
	"	H. S. Tenney, '07.
D. J. Main, '06, Capt.,	Left Half,	R. A. Bard, '06.
	" "	J. R. Munn, '06.
E. A. Herr, '06,	Right Half,	W. H. Daub, '07.
	" "	L. H. Simons, '06.
E. D. Rich, '08,	Full-back,	J. B. McCormick, '08.

Referee: E. N. Wrightington, '97, Harvard. Umpire: J. H. Minds, '98, Pennsylvania. Linesmen: W. P. White, '00, Lehigh, S. S. Feagles, '00, Princeton. Score: Dartmouth 6, Princeton 0. First Half: Touchdown by G. N. Bankart, goal by D. J. Main.

First Half: Princeton wins the toss and takes the north goal. Dartmouth kicks off to E. A. Dillon at 10, who runs back to 25. Bard punts to midfield. Dartmouth opens up a steady attack of line plunges, which takes the ball to Princeton's 10-yard line. Princeton holds for downs and gets the ball. McCormick punts to 40. Dartmouth again hammers the ball to the 30-yard line, where Princeton holds for downs. Bard goes around the end for 8. Daub rounds the opposite end for 25. Princeton fumbles and Dartmouth gets the ball. Upon several rushes and an exchange of kicks Dartmouth gets the ball on their 40-yard line. From here, by a steady attack of line plunges aided by a total of 25 yards in penalties Dartmouth reaches the 8-yard line, where Princeton holds for downs. McCormick falls behind the line to punt, but Dartmouth blocks the kick. Bankart falls on the ball for a touchdown and Main kicks the goal. Time soon after is called.

Second Half: Tooker kicks off to Dartmouth's 10, and the latter, unable to gain on the last down, punts back. Princeton fumbles and Dartmouth gets the ball. Princeton stands firm and Dartmouth again punts to Princeton's 20-yard line. Princeton cannot pierce the Green line and Bard kicks, the ball going out of bounds at 35. Dartmouth hits the line for 5 and then Main tries for a goal from placement, but misses. Princeton kicks out and Dartmouth returns. Dillon gets away on a quarter-back run for 30 yards. Line plunges take the ball to midfield, where Dartmouth holds for downs. Simons skirts the end for 20 yards. Munn in three plunges gains 17 yards, but Dartmouth takes the ball on downs. The remainder of the game becomes a deadlock between the two teams, neither able to get within striking distance of the other's goal, but punting after a few short gains.

DARTMOUTH vs. PRINCETON
Princeton, Nov. 3, 1906

DARTMOUTH		PRINCETON
W. Jennings, '07,	Left End,	L. C. Wister, '08.
G. F. Kennedy, '09,	" "	H. N. Shaw, '07.
C. L. De Angelis, '08,	" "	
C. K. Pevear, '10,	Left Tackle,	W. J. Phillips, '08.
H. H. Hobbs, '10,	" "	S. Rheinstein, '07.
J. A. McDonald, '07,	Left Guard,	H. L. Dillon, '07, Capt.
J. T. Smith, '06,	" "	
J. C. Brusse, '09,	Centre,	D. G. Herring, '07.
	"	M. K. Cameron, '08.
M. K. Smith, '07,	Right Guard,	E. Stannard, '08.
C. K. Pevear, '10,	" "	
C. W. Tobin, '10,	" "	J. Martin, '07.
B. Lang, '10,	Right Tackle,	J. L. Cooney, '07.
R. P. Pritchard, '07,	Right End,	A. N. Hoagland, '06.
M. Stearns, '08,	" "	K. B. Warden, '08.

DARTMOUTH		PRINCETON
R. Glaze, '06, Capt.,	Quarter-back,	E. A. Dillon, '09.
	"	H. L. Dowd, '09.
E. G. Stuart, '10,	Left Half,	S. Rulon-Miller, '07.
H. H. Driver, '10,	" "	N. R. Cass, '09.
H. R. Heneage, '07,	Right Half,	E. H. W. Harlan, '08.
	" "	F. M. Tibbott, '09.
I. A. Greenwood, '07,	Full-back,	J. B. McCormick, '08.
H. C. Storrs, '07,	"	A. A. Little, '09.

Referee: J. H. Minds, '98, Pennsylvania. Umpire: Evarts Wrenn, '92, Harvard. Head Linesman: O. F. Lamson, '07, Pennsylvania. Assistant Linesmen: F. E. Jennigs, '00, Dartmouth; A. De C. O'Brien, '07, Princeton. Score: Dartmouth 0, Princeton 42. First Half: Touchdown by L. C. Wister, goal by J. B. McCormick; touchdown by D. G. Herring, goal by J. B. McCormick. Second Half: Touchdown by L. C. Wister; touchdown and goal by J. B. McCormick; touchdown by S. Rulon-Miller, goal by J. B. McCormick; touchdown by F. M. Tibbott, goal by J. B. McCormick.

First Half: After several minutes of play with even advantage, Dillon catches a punt and runs 55 yards for a touchdown. McCormick kicks the goal. A few moments later Wister takes a forward pass and runs 42 yards for a touchdown. Goal by McCormick. Dartmouth kicks off. Princeton works the ball gradually into Dartmouth's goal, but being held for two downs without gain, Harlan drops a short kick over the line, which is fumbled. Herring gets it and makes a touchdown. Goal.

Second Half: For several minutes play remains at centre, the ball changing hands on punts and downs. Harlan sends a long punt to Dartmouth on the 10-yard line which the latter fumbles. Wister gets it and runs across the line for a touchdown. McCormick kicks the goal. Dartmouth kicks off to Princeton's 5-yard line. Princeton opens up a series of straight line plays, which takes the ball by short gains steadily down the field to the 5-yard line, from which McCormick is sent through centre for a touchdown. Goal. Dartmouth kicks off and Princeton repeats the long gain, this time sending Rulon-Miller across for the touchdown. Goal. Dartmouth kicks off and a series of punts are exchanged. Tibbott catches on his 15-yard line and brilliantly runs through the entire Dartmouth team for a touchdown. McCormick kicks the seventh and last goal.

1907, no game.

DARTMOUTH vs. PRINCETON

New York, Nov. 7, 1908

DARTMOUTH		PRINCETON
G. F. Kennedy, '09, Capt.,	Left End,	H. L. Dowd, '09.
E. J. Daly, '12,	" "	
R. W. Sherwin, '11,	Left Tackle,	R. C. Siegling, '10.
	" "	F. C. Bamman, '10.
C. W. Tobin, '10,	Left Guard,	P. E. Waller, '10.
J. C. Brusse, '09,	Centre,	D. M. MacFadyen, '10.
H. R. Bankart, '09,	Right Guard,	H. G. Buckingham, '10.
E. D. Rich, '09,	Right Tackle,	A. E. Booth, '09.
G. H. Schildmiller, '09,	Right End,	T. H. Welch, '10.
L. H. Bankart, '10,	" "	N. R. Cass, '09.
	" "	H. E. Gill, '10.
	" "	R. R. Meigs, '10.
S. Pishon, '10,	Quarter-back,	E. A. Dillon, '09, Capt.
	"	F. S. Bergin, '10.
J. B. Hawley, '09,	Left Half,	F. M. Tibbott, '09.
W. D. Stewart, '10,	" "	W. D. Sparks, '11.
	" "	H. W. Bishop, '09.
J. E. Ingersoll, '11,	Right Half,	F. B. Read, '10.
J. J. Ryan, '11,	" "	T. N. Pfeiffer, '08.
	"	L. Cunningham, '11.
J. Marks, '11,	Full-back,	J. M. McCrohan, '11.
G. W. Hoban, '12,	"	
I. A. Greenwood, '07,	"	

Referee: C. A. Taussig, '02, Cornell. Umpire: N. P. Stauffer, '96, Pennsylvania. Field Judge: Carl Williams, '97, Pennsylvania. Linesman: W. R. Okeson, '96, Lehigh. Score: Dartmouth 10, Princeton 6. First Half: Goal from field by R. W. Sherwin. Second Half: Touchdown by L. Cunningham, goal by P. E. Waller; touchdown by G. H. Schildmiller, goal by L. H. Bankart.

First Half: Princeton wins the toss and takes the north goal. Dartmouth punts to Princeton's 10. Princeton cannot make first down and Buckingham punts. The ball goes out of bounds at 10. A penalty sets Dartmouth back to the 25-yard line. Princeton holds firm and gets the ball on downs. Buckingham punts to midfield. Play alternates back and forth for a long time between centre and Princeton's 25-yard line without advantage or material gain to either team. At last Princeton by runs and punts sends the ball down to Dartmouth's 25-yard line. On the return Princeton fumbles and the ball goes to Dartmouth at midfield. Hawley circles the end for 30 yards. Princeton holds for downs on the 25-yard line and gets the ball. Buckingham punts to centre. Dartmouth again works the ball to the 25-yard line and Princeton again stops the advance, but on the third down Sherwin drops a field goal. Dartmouth kicks off and Princeton by hard line work and brilliant end runs takes the ball to Dartmouth's 5-yard line, where the ball is lost on downs. Time soon after is called for the half.

Second Half: Waller kicks off to Hoban, who runs back 15 yards. A loss of 5 yards forces Sherwin to punt. A penalty of 15 yards for Dartmouth and an exchange of punts gives the ball to Princeton on Dartmouth's 30-yard line. Gains by Tibbott and McCrohan and two penalties place the ball 1 yard from the line. Cunningham is sent over for a touchdown and Waller kicks the goal. Princeton kicks off. For a long time the teams are deadlocked, the play becoming a rush and a punt without advantage to either. Toward the close of the second half a misjudged punt and a penalty forces Princeton to punt out from behind the goal-line. The kick is partially blocked and Dartmouth recovers the ball on the 17-yard mark. A forward pass to Schildmiller makes the touchdown. The goal fails.

In the remaining time Princeton forces the ball to Dartmouth's 3-yard mark, but fails on the last plunge to cross the line.

DARTMOUTH vs. PRINCETON

Princeton, Nov. 6, 1909

DARTMOUTH		PRINCETON
E. J. Daley, '12,	Left End,	C. Ballin, '10.
R. W. Sherwin, '11,	Left Tackle,	R. C. Siegling, '10, Capt.
W. B. Elcock, '12,	"	
C. W. Tobin, '10, Capt.,	Left Guard,	P. E. Waller, '10.
E. Needham, '11,	Centre,	F. C. Bamman, '10.
R. E. Farnum, '12,	Right Guard,	C. McCormick, '12.
B. Lang, '10,	Right Tackle,	A. MacGregor, '11.
L. H. Bankart, '10,	Right End,	T. H. Welch, '10.
C. P. Dodge, '12,	" "	
F. A. Brady, '10,	Quarter-back,	F. C. Bergin, '10.
S. Pishon, '10,	"	
S. J. Boylan, '12,	"	
J. E. Ingersoll, '11,	Left Half,	E. J. Hart, '12.
H. W. Smith, '12,	" "	
W. W. Dudley, '10,	" "	
J. J. Ryan, '11,	Right Half,	F. B. Read, '10.
	" "	W. R. Sparks, '11.
	" "	R. E. Bard, '11.
J. Marks, '11,	Full-back,	L. Cunningham, '11.
	"	F. T. Dawson, '10.

Referee: J. B. Pendleton, '90, Bowdoin. Umpire: H. M. Nelly, '02, Army. Field Judge: J. H. Minds, '98, Pennsylvania. Linesman: G. H. Young, '00, Cornell. Score: Dartmouth 6, Princeton 6. First Half: Goal from field by L. Cunningham; goal from field by L. Cunningham. Second Half: Touchdown by J. Marks, goal by C. W. Tobin.

First Half: Dartmouth wins the toss and selects the north goal. Waller kicks off and Dartmouth returns. A long exchange of kicks follows. Hart recovers a fumble on Dartmouth's 35-yard line. A forward pass to Ballin nets 10 yards, but Hart and Read on end runs are thrown for losses. Cunningham drops a goal from the field. Dartmouth kicks off, and after 10 minutes of ineffective rushing by both teams, Dartmouth in an exchange of punts is forced down into goal. Read catches a punt on Dartmouth's 40-yard line. Two downs fail to gain, and Cunningham, falling back, drops another field goal. This terminates the scoring for the first half.

Second Half: Dartmouth kicks off. An exchange of kicks forces Princeton into goal, and in attempting to punt back Lang blocks the kick and recovers the ball on the 3-yard mark. Ryan, in a powerful plunge, crosses the line for the touchdown and Tobin, at a most difficult angle, kicks the goal. During the remainder of the half the ball constantly shifts back and forth on downs and punts, but play is confined between the 25-yard lines, neither team being able to force the other back within striking distance of the goal-line.

DARTMOUTH VS. PRINCETON
New York, Oct, 29, 1910

DARTMOUTH		PRINCETON
E. J. Daley, '12,	Left End,	S. B. White, '12.
G. C. Lewis, '12,	" "	J. Bredemus, '12.
R. W. Sherwin, '11,	Left Tackle,	E. J. Hart, '12, Capt.
N. M. Whitmore, '12,	Left Guard,	T. S. Wilson, '13.
	" "	C. McCormick, '12.
E. Needham, '11,	Centre,	A. Bluethenthal, '13.
R. L. Bennett, '13,	"	
W. B. Elcock, '12,	Right Guard,	W. McLean, '12.
R. E. Farnum, '12,	" "	C. McCormick, '12.
L. E. Lovejoy, '11,	Right Tackle,	A. MacGregor, '11.
J. T. Cottrell, '12,	Right End,	C. C. Dunlap, '13.
	" "	G. K. Wight, '13.
J. E. Ingersoll, '11,	Quarter-back,	V. Ballou, '13.
D. B. Morey, '13,	Left Half,	T. T. Pendleton, '13.
G. W. Hoban, '13,	" "	
J. J. Ryan, '11, Capt.,	Right Half,	W. R. Sparks, '11.
	" "	H. M. Sawyer, '12.
H. A. Barends, '13,	Full-back,	C. E. Brown, '13.

Referee: W. S. Langford, '96, Trinity. Umpire: A. E. Whiting, '98, Cornell. Field Judge: W. N. Morice, '99, Pennsylvania. Linesman: C. R. Rinehart, '98, Lafayette. Score: Dartmouth 0, Princeton 6. Third Quarter: Touchdown and goal by T. T. Pendleton.

First Quarter: Princeton wins the toss and selects the south goal. Ballou kicks off to Ryan, who runs back 15 yards. Ingersoll punts to Pendleton at centre, the latter being tackled by Morey. Princeton cannot gain and a penalty transfers the ball to Dartmouth. Princeton holds and Ingersoll punts, Princeton getting the ball on the 45-yard line. Sparks makes 10 yards and a penalty adds 15. A forward pass, Sparks to Pendleton, advances the ball 10 yards. Princeton tries another forward pass, which Dartmouth intercepts. The latter cannot gain and punts, Princeton catching the ball on their opponent's 35-yard line. A penalty and two line plunges take the ball to the 5 yard-line. Ballou tries a forward pass, which Daley intercepts and, breaking through into a clear field, dashes for Princeton's goal-line. Pendleton catches him from behind and stops him at midfield. The quarter ends.

Second Quarter: Several minutes elapse in a brilliant punting exchange. At last Ingersoll, catching a punt from Pendleton, runs through the Princeton team and reaches the 10-yard line, where he is tackled by Ballou. Princeton stands firm and Barends essays a place kick, which goes wide.

Third Quarter: A long exchange of punts terminates in an attempt by Barends to kick a goal from placement on the 45-yard line, which fails. The ball again is forced into Princeton's territory and Barends misses another goal from placement, the ball being blocked by MacGregor. On the line-up Needham blocks Ballou's punt, but the latter saves the ball. Ballou punts to Dartmouth's 45. Dartmouth cannot gain through the line and Ingersoll lifts a long punt to Pendleton on the latter's 10-yard line. Side-stepping Cottrell and Daley, Pendleton dashes sharply to the left and, dodging and twisting, sifts through the Dartmouth forwards. Running parallel and close to the left side line, he races at great speed until at midfield he meets the opposing backs, whom he evades by sprinting sharply to the right for

100 YARDS FOR A TOUCHDOWN AND THE GAME.

Pendleton, of Princeton, catching a punt on his 10-yard line, runs through Dartmouth's eleven for the only touchdown of the game. Polo Grounds, New York, Oct. 29, 1910.

a touchdown, from which a goal is kicked. Dartmouth kicks off, and recovering the ball Barends again tries for a goal from placement on the 40-yard line, but misses. Soon a fumbled punt gives Dartmouth the ball on Princeton's 10-yard line. A plunge at tackle gains 1 yard and on a wide quarter-back run Ingersoll is tackled by Sawyer for no gain. The quarter ends.

Fourth Quarter. Dartmouth puts the ball in play on Princeton's 9-yard line. Barends and Ingersoll fall back into place-kick formation. Instead Ingersoll shoots a forward pass over the line, but the ball is fumbled, Hart falling on it for a touchback. The game becomes a punting duel, Pendleton and Ryan each getting off for a 30-yard run, but neither goal again is threatened. Thus the game ends.

CHAPTER XIII

HARVARD VS. PRINCETON

HARVARD VS. PRINCETON
Cambridge, April 28, 1877

HARVARD		PRINCETON
L. Cushing, '79, Capt.,	Forward,	E. H. Nicoll, '80.
J. B. Keyes, '77,	"	W. D. Van Dyke, '78.
B. S. Blanchard, '79,	"	J. Potter, '77.
F. G. Perry, '79,	"	B. Ballard, '80.
J. B. Holmes, '79,	"	A. T. Enos, '78.
F. A. Houston, '79,	"	T. M. McNair, '79.
H. W. Cushing, '77,	"	A. Wylly, '79.
E. H. Herrick, '77,	Half-back,	B. Nicoll, '77.
W. R. Austin, '77,	"	D. Stewart, '78.
N. Curtis, '76,	"	L. P. Smock, '79.
Robert Winsor, '77,	"	E. S. McCalmont, '77.
W. S. Seamans, '80,	"	A. J. McCosh, '77.
G. R. Sheldon, '79,	Back,	W. E. Dodge, '79, Capt.
E. F. Thomas, '77,	"	H. B. Thompson, '77.
G. B. Faucon, '75,	"	H. M. Cutts, '80.

Referee: Mr. Harrington, Tufts. Judges: W. E. Russel, '79, Harvard; E. O. Roessle, '79, Princeton. Score: Harvard 2 touchdowns, 1 goal, Princeton 1 touchdown. First Half: Touchdown by L. Cushing. Second Half: Touchdown by L. Cushing, goal by W. S. Seamans; touchdown by T. M. McNair.

NOTE.—For system of scoring see Rule 7, convention Nov. 26, 1876, Appendix.

First Half: Princeton startles Harvard by appearing in tight-fitting canvas jackets to make tackling more difficult. Princeton wins the toss and takes the goal, backed with a slight breeze. Harvard kicks off. The ball oscillates back and forth for some time until Cushing makes a long run. In the next scrimmage he again gets the ball and runs

across the line for a touchdown. Seamans misses the goal.
Princeton improves in play and withstands Harvard's
sharp attack. Harvard at last forces the ball well into
Princeton's quarters. Ballard gets it out by a long run and
McCosh follows the play with a long punt, transferring the
play into Harvard's goal, where time is called.

Second Half: Princeton kicks off and Harvard rushes the
ball back to midfield, where it remains for several minutes.
Cushing, '79, finally gets away and, dodging sharply, crosses
the line for a touchdown. Seamans kicks the goal. Sides
are changed and Princeton fights fiercely. McNair finally
breaks through and makes a touchdown. The goal is
missed. In the next period Harvard presses Princeton back
into their goal, but cannot get the ball across the line.
Thus the game closes.

HARVARD vs. PRINCETON

Hoboken, Nov. 23, 1877

HARVARD		PRINCETON
L. Cushing, '79, Capt.,	Forward,	T. B. Bradford, '81.
F. W. Thayer, '78,	"	B. Ballard, '80.
L. N. Littauer, '78,	"	H. Stevenson, '78.
F. G. Perry, '79,	"	C. C. Clarke, '78.
J. Holmes, '79,	"	F. Loney, '81.
J. Swift, '79,	"	H. K. Devereux, '80.
H. W. Cushing, '77,	"	B. Lee, '80.
	"	A. T. Enos, '78.
	"	A. Wylly, '79.
W. R. Austin, '79,	Half-back,	D. O. Irving, '78.
B. S. Blanchard, '79,	"	W. E. Dodge, '79, Capt.
C. Harrington, '78,	"	T. M. McNair, '79.
F. A. Houston, '79,	"	
F. W. Holden, '80,	"	
W. B. Lombard, '78,	Back,	W. D. Van Dyke, '78.
Robert Bacon, '80,	"	H. M. Cutts, '80.
J. A. Wetherbee, '78,	"	H. L. Minor, '79.

Referee: W. S. Seamans, '80, Harvard. Judges: P. T. Barlow, '79,
Harvard; E. O. Roessle, '79, Princeton. Score: Harvard 2 touch-

downs, Princeton 1 touchdown, 1 goal. First Half: Touchdown by J. Holmes. Second Half: Touchdown by B. Ballard, goal by H. M. Cutts; touchdown by L. Cushing.

NOTE.—For system of scoring, see Rule 7, convention Nov. 26, 1876, Appendix.

The game is played at St. George's Cricket Grounds. The day is faultless, with little wind, but the ground is very heavy from the recent rains. Owing to the disability of a player on each side the game is played with fourteen men upon each team.

First Half: Princeton wins the toss and takes the wind. Blanchard kicks off for Harvard. Princeton begins a steady advance, Dodge, McNair, Wylly, and Enos making good gains, with Cutts backing up with long kicks. Harvard is forced to touchdown for safety. The ball is immediately kicked and rushed to the centre of the field. On the next play Cushing, of Harvard, recovers the ball from a kick and when tackled passes to Holmes, who makes a brilliant run, ending in a touchdown. The try at goal falls short. Princeton at once works the ball into Harvard's goal, but is stopped by the call of time and the end of the half.

Second Half: The intermission of fifteen minutes having expired, time is called for the beginning of the second half of forty-five minutes. McNair kicks off or Princeton. Harrington catches and starts on a spectacular run, shaking off one forward after another until stopped by Dodge and Van Dyke. A rough mix-up ensues, in which many players participate for several minutes. Order at last is restored, Dodge coming out of the tangle with his shirt split to ribbons. The ball and play have been forgotten, but suddenly Ballard, realizing that the ball throughout the affair has not been dead, picks it up and starts for Harvard's goal with the Harvard men in keen pursuit. Ballard is overtaken, but shakes himself loose from his tacklers and in a final superb dash crosses the line and touches down the ball. Dodge places the ball for Cutts to kick. A bard at Princeton has best described the ensuing play:

"'Then for a little moment all people held their breath,
And 'mid the anxious multitude was a stillness as of death;
And in another moment broke forth from one and all,
The well-known rocket cheer from the men of Nassau Hall."

The goal has been squarely kicked and Princeton has scored.

Amid great excitement play is resumed. Each side strives with the final ounce of power and grit, making run after run and kick after kick, but in vain. At last Cushing, by a great dodging effort, swings loose from the Princeton pack and heads for the goal. Ballard brings him down on the line, but Cushing squirms across for a touchdown. The punt-out fails. A few moments later Princeton is brought to its feet by Dodge kicking the ball across the bar, but the kick was a punt and the goal does not count. Shortly after the game closes and the throng of collegians disperses, realizing that they have seen the greatest game played in America up to this time.

HARVARD VS. PRINCETON
Boston, Nov. 16, 1878

HARVARD		PRINCETON
H. W. Cushing, '77,	Forward,	F. T. Bryan, '80.
J. Swift, '79,	"	F. Loney, '81.
T. C. Thacher, '82,	"	H. McAlpin, '81.
J. E. Cowdin, '79,	"	H. K. Devereux, '80.
J. Holmes, '79,	"	B. Ballard, '80, Capt.
F. G. Perry, '79,	"	H. H. Brotherlin, '80.
E. W. Morse, '78,	"	H. McDermott, '81.
	"	T. B. Bradford, '81.
B. S. Blanchard, '79,	Half-back,	J. B. Waller, '79.
F. C. Warren, '79,	"	T. M. McNair, '79.
L. Cushing, '79, Capt.,	"	H. L. Minor, '79.

HARVARD		PRINCETON
Robert Winsor, '80,	Half-back,	I. P. Withington, '80.
F. A. Houston, '79,	"	
J. A. Wetherbee, '78,	Back,	F. Larkin, '79.
Robert Bacon, '80,	"	H. M. Cutts, '80.
H. D. Sedgwick, '82,	"	W. Miller, '80.

Referee: A. Wylly, '79, Princeton. Judges: R. W. Thayer, '78, Harvard; W. E. Dodge, '79, Princeton. Score: Harvard 0, Princeton 1 touchdown. First Half: Touchdown by F. Loney.

NOTE.—For system of scoring, see Rule 7, convention Nov. 26, 1876, Appendix.

First Half: Princeton wins the toss and takes the wind. Warren kicks off for Harvard. Minor makes a long run, being stopped by Warren. In the next scrimmage Minor again gets away for another good run. Harvard gets the ball on a short kick. Houston attempts a long pass, but McNair gets the ball and makes a brilliant run. Kicks are exchanged, Holmes getting the ball and starting on a long run. On a kick McNair gets the ball and runs it back again into Harvard's territory. After some sharp passing Blanchard gets away for a 30-yard run, but is stopped by Ballard. Harvard kicks and Bryan secures a fair catch. McNair kicks far down the field. Harvard works the ball back. Waller gets the ball in a scrimmage, makes a beautiful long pass to Minor, who is thrown after a small gain. The ball is now passed back to Cutts, who kicks out of bounds. Cushing runs the ball up the field. Harvard kicks, Devereux gets the ball and starts at sharp speed a dodging run. He clears the entire Harvard team except Bacon. As the latter reaches to tackle, Devereux passes the ball to Loney, who races with it across the line for a touchdown. The try at goal fails. Wetherbee runs the ball out. Harvard kicks, Princeton returns, Blanchard lifts a long, high kick for Harvard and time is called for the half with the ball in midfield.

Second Half: Minor kicks off for Princeton. Morse runs the ball back. A great kicking duel follows, Princeton finally being forced to touchdown for safety. Cutts sends a kick well into Harvard's territory. Bacon makes a great run on the recovery, being sharply tackled by McNair. Wetherbee duplicates Bacon's feat and Withington brings him down. Princeton now gets the ball and makes big gains. McNair carries the ball within 10 feet of the Harvard line, but is stopped by Sedgwick. McNair tries for a field goal, but misses by an inch. Harvard touches down for safety. Harvard kicks out, but McNair, by a drop, kicks the ball back again, missing the goal. Harvard again touches down for safety. Princeton repeats the play on the kick-out, but cannot make the goal. Wetherbee by a prodigious kick-out gets Harvard out of difficulties. Princeton returns the kick, Harvard sends it back. Cutts and McNair outkick Harvard and the latter tries a scrimmage. Princeton gets the ball, Withington passes to McNair, but Holmes intercepts the pass and runs to Princeton's goal-line, where he is downed by Larkin. On the next play Princeton stops Harvard and gets the ball. Princeton is driving the ball rapidly down the field when time is called.

HARVARD VS. PRINCETON

Hoboken, Nov. 15, 1879

HARVARD		PRINCETON
E. W. Morse, '78,	Forward,	F. T. Bryan, '80.
W. H. Manning, '82,	"	E. C. Peace, '83.
L. Cushing, '79,	"	F. Loney, '81.
J. S. Tebbets, '80,	"	B. Ballard, '80, Capt.
F. C. Warren, '79,	"	H. K. Devereux, '80.
H. W. Cushing, '77,	"	H. H. Brotherlin, '80.
J. T. Howe, '80,	"	H. McDermott, '81.
T. C. Thacher, '82,	"	T. B. Bradford, '81.
T. W. Nickerson, '80,	"	
Robert Winsor, '80,	Half-back,	I. P. Withington, 80.
Robert Bacon, '80, Capt.,	"	B. Lee, '80.

HARVARD		PRINCETON
F. E. Cabot, '80,	Half-back,	T. M. McNair, '79.
F. A. Houston, '79,	"	T. H. P. Farr, '81.
	"	M. R. Ely, '82.
G. H. Leatherbee, '82,	Back,	W. S. Horton, '80.
A. B. Shattuck, '81,	"	H. M. Cutts, '80.
	"	A. B. Duncan, '80.

Referee: Walter Camp, '80, Yale. Judges: W. S. Seamans, '80, Harvard; A. McLaren, '80, Princeton. Score: Harvard 0, Princeton 1 goal. First Half: Goal from field by T. M. McNair.

First Half: Princeton wins the toss and selects the goal. Warren kicks off for Harvard. Princeton returns the kick. An exchange of kicks follows, Cutts and Wetherbee punting. Cutts makes a fair catch of one of Harvard's punts and tries a place kick, the ball missing the post by inches. Harvard touches the ball down for safety and punts out. Princeton makes a fair catch and Cutts again tries a place kick, which again misses and forces Harvard to touchdown for safety. Brotherlin catches the kick-out, but passes to McNair, who tries a drop kick. Once more Harvard makes a safety. The kick-out is returned by Cutts across the goal-line, and for the fifth time Harvard makes a safety. Harvard punts out, Princeton returns and Harvard tries a scrimmage. Bacon and Cabot make good gains, but Princeton gets the ball and, with a strong wind, immediately kicks. Again Harvard forces the ball down and again Princeton kicks. Up to this point Princeton has not tried to rush the ball. After a scrimmage without gain Wetherbee punts to Cutts. Princeton now lines up for scrimmage. Withington gets the ball and passes it to McNair, who, while running, drops a goal from the field. Walter Camp objects to Princeton's style of "guarding" * the runner. He

* Placing a player at each side of the runner, but not in advance, thereby making tackling from the side difficult. This was the play out of which eventually developed "interference."

notifies Ballard that if it is persisted in he will rule on it as
a foul. Cushing makes a long zigzag run, butting over
two Princeton men with his head, but Lee brings him down.
The half closes with the ball in midfield.

Second Half: Princeton kicks off in the face of a strong
wind. Harvard returns the kick. Princeton resorts to a
scrimmage, but loses the ball at the outset. Wetherbee
attempts to kick, but Bradford blocks. Princeton recovers
the ball. Withington gets the ball out of a scrimmage,
makes a sharp dash to the right, and as he is about to be
tackled, passes the ball to Cutts, who is tackled by Howe.
McNair adds 20 yards. Ballard and Withington reel off
25 more. The ball is now within 10 yards of Harvard's
goal-line. Harvard obtains the ball out of scrimmage and
Bacon lifts a tremendous kick far into Princeton's territory.
Princeton works the ball back to midfield, where Bacon
again gets it and sends it down into Princeton's goal. Repeated runs by Lee, Farr, and Ely work the ball back to centre field. McNair carries it 20 yards into Harvard's territory and tries a goal from the field. The ball falls short
and Bacon kicks. McNair tries another drop kick from
midfield, but the ball again falls short. Thereupon the
game closes.

HARVARD VS. PRINCETON
New York, Nov. 13, 1880

HARVARD		PRINCETON
H. M. Atkinson, '84,	Forward,	T. B. Bradford, '81.
F. H. Clark, '82,	"	H. K. Devereux, '80.
A. Boyd, '82,	"	C. McKee, '81.
F. E. Cabot, '80,	"	E. C. Peace, '83.
	"	L. Riggs, '83.
F. A. Houston, '79, Capt.	"	F. Loney, '81, Capt.
E. S. Perin, '82,	"	P. T. Bryan, '82.
	"	J. P. Flint, '83.
T. C. Thacher, '82,	Half-back,	I. P. Withington, '80.
G. P. Keith, '83,	"	B. G. Winton, '82.

HARVARD		PRINCETON
E. G. Kent, '82,	Half-back,	
C. H. W. Foster, '81,	Back,	D. P. Morgan, '83.
W. O. Edmands, '83,	"	J. S. Harlan, '83.
	"	T. W. Cauldwell, '81.

Referee: R. W. Watson, '81, Yale. Judges: L. N. Littauer, '78, Harvard; H. McAlpin, '81, Princeton. Score: Harvard 1 touchdown, 1 goal, Princeton 2 touchdowns, 2 goals. First Half: Touchdown by F. Loney, goal by B. G. Winton; touchdown by H. M. Atkinson, goal by W. O. Edmands. Second Half: Touchdown and goal by B. G. Winton.

First Half: Princeton wins the toss and takes the wind. Keith kicks off for Harvard. Princeton fumbles and Harvard gets the ball on the 25-yard line. Princeton gets the ball on a foul, but on the first play is forced to touch down for safety. Harlan kicks out for Princeton, Cabot blocks the kick and Princeton makes another safety. The play goes to the centre of the field. Harlan lifts a great punt which Harvard fumbles and Loney gets the ball. He springs out of the clutches of two Harvard men and dashes across the line for a touchdown, from which Winton kicks the goal. Harvard claims a foul, the crowd break upon the field, and the game is delayed several minutes. The foul is not allowed. On resumption of play a kicking duel ensues. Keith kicks for Harvard. The ball hits a spectator and bounds back into the field. Atkinson picks it up and touches down behind the Princeton goal. Princeton claims Atkinson was off-side, but the claim is not allowed. Edmands kicks the goal. Princeton commences a fierce attack on Harvard, which carries the ball down into the Harvard goal, where the latter is forced to make several safeties in succession. Peace and Bryan retire; L. Riggs, '83, and J. P. Flint, '83, take their places. Boyd, Cabot, and Houston are tackling very sharply and Princeton is held in check. Keith makes one long kick after another. Morgan runs the ball back time and again. And so the half closes.

Second Half: Harvard has the wind in this half. The ball is kicked into Princeton's territory, where sharp work by Harvard forces Princeton to touch down for safety. Withington, Winton, and Morgan make a series of great runs, transferring the ball into Harvard's territory. Keith lifts a number of long punts, relieving the danger, but Princeton each time works it back. Perin and Houston are fighting hard for Harvard, making rush upon rush. Peace gets the ball and splits the Harvard line in two, making a touchdown. The ball is brought back for a foul. After a few gainless rushes Winton gets away and, dashing and dodging down the field, plants the ball behind Harvard's goalline. Darkness has now closed down and the ball is at a wide angle to the posts. Winton sights the leather carefully and sends it squarely between the posts. Play is resumed and Princeton drives the ball by short gains again down into Harvard's goal, but the game is called with the goalline ten yards away.

HARVARD VS. PRINCETON
New York, November 19, 1881

HARVARD		PRINCETON
A. Boyd, '82,	Forward,	W. H. Stone, '84.
L. W. Kendall, '84,	"	S. H. Benton, '82.
E. T. Cabot, '83,	"	J. H. Bryan, '82.
R. M. Appleton, '84,	"	L. Riggs, '83.
F. A. Houston, '79,	"	J. T. Haxall, '83.
W. H. Manning, '82, Capt.,	"	P. T. Bryan, '82, Capt.
T. C. Thacher, '82,	"	
F. A. Mason, '84,	Half-back,	T. A. C. Baker, '83.
G. P. Keith, '83,	"	E. C. Peace, '83.
W. A. Henry, '85,	"	A. F. Burt, 82.
W. O. Edmands, '83,	Back,	J. S. Harlan, '83.
H. R. Woodward, '84,	"	A. S. Bickham, '82.
	"	W. Shaw, P. G.

Referee: Walter Camp, '80, Yale. Judges: L. N. Littauer, '78, Harvard; B. J. Winton, '84, Princeton. Score: Harvard 1 safety,

Princeton 1 safety. First Half: Safety by W. A. Henry; Second Half: Safety by W. Shaw.

NOTE.—For system of scoring, see Amended Rule 5, convention Oct. 8, 1881, Appendix.

First Half: Princeton wins the toss and takes the wind. Edmands kicks off for Harvard and Baker returns the kick. A further exchange of kicks ensues, terminating in a fumble by Harvard. Bryan gets the ball, races down the field, and touches down behind Harvard's goal-posts, but the ball is brought back because of a foul. Princeton forces the ball to Harvard's 10-yard line, where several scrimmages follow, but the ball cannot be driven farther. Harvard gets the ball and punts, Princeton returns the kick, Henry catches behind his goal-posts and is thrown by Riggs for a safety. Manning now lifts some long punts down the field and the play transfers to Princeton's goal. Henry tries a place kick, but misses by an inch. Two plays later he again tries a place kick for goal, but the ball goes wild and hits a policeman. Kicks are exchanged and for a third time Henry tries for the goal. Haxall blocks the kick and the half closes.

Second Half: Bryan kicks off in the second half for Princeton. Manning returns, Harlan makes a fair catch and tries a place kick for the goal, but misses. Harvard kicks out and Harlan, Bryan, and Peace break through for good gains, but Manning offsets their work by his long kicks. Harvard attempts a rushing game and discloses some brilliant passing from one side of the field to the other, but Riggs tackles sharply and the attack fails. Edmands gets the ball and by a long kick lands the ball in Princeton's goal. Stone and Bryan are down on the ball, but Harvard forces a safety by W. Shaw. Princeton makes a great fight to get the ball out of danger without kicking, but Henry, Manning,

and Keith stop every advance. At last Peace gets away for
a long run. Cabot tackles, but Peace passes the ball to Har-
land, who plants it on Harvard's 25-yard line. Harvard
stands firm and drives the ball back to midfield. Manning
kicks over Princeton's goal-line. Harlan is so hard pressed
by the Harvard ends that he is forced to throw the ball out
of bounds to Baker, who makes a touch-in-goal to avoid a
safety. Harlan kicks and Henry catches. Keith tries for
a field goal, but misses. A long kick transfers the play into
Harvard's goal. Princeton touches down behind the line,
but the play is not allowed. The game closes. Extra
halves are called for by the referee, and the teams resume
play. The play is confined to kicks. At the end of fifteen
minutes darkness has settled down so completely that the
game cannot be continued and the extra halves are post-
poned. (These were never played. The game, therefore,
was a draw.)

HARVARD vs. PRINCETON
Cambridge, Nov. 18, 1882

HARVARD		PRINCETON
R. M. Appleton, '84,	Forward,	E. S. Belknap, '84.
E. T. Cabot, '83, Capt.,	"	J. T. Haxall, '83.
L. W. Kendall, '84,	"	G. R. Fleming, '83.
G. B. Morison, '83,	"	C. W. Bird, '85.
C. H. Hammond, '83,	"	E. C. Peace, '83, Capt.
G. D. Ayers, '82,	"	L. Riggs, '83.
W. F. Wesselhoeft, '84,	"	
F. A. Mason, '84,	Quarter-back,	D. P. Morgan, '83.
G. P. Keith, '83,	Half-back,	T. A. C. Baker, '83.
W. H. Coolidge, '81,	"	A. T. Baker, '85.
	Three-quarter-back,	Alex. Moffat, '84.
W. O. Edmands, '83,	Full-back,	H. P. Toler, '86.

Referee: R. W. Watson, '81, Yale. Judges: F. A. Houston, '79,
Harvard; D. M. Look, '84, Princeton. Score: Harvard 1 touchdown,
1 goal from the field. Princeton 1 touchdown and 1 goal from

touchdown. First Half: Touchdown and goal by J. T. Haxall; touchdown by F. A. Mason. Second Half: Goal from field by F. A. Mason; safety by Princeton; safety by Princeton.

NOTE.—For system of scoring, see Amended Rule 5, convention Oct. 8, 1881, and Amended Rule 7, convention Oct. 14, 1882, Appendix.

First Half: Harvard wins the toss and takes the ball. Appleton dribbles, picks up the ball and passes it to Mason, standing 10 yards back, Mason punting down to Keith. Princeton's line closes in on Keith, who completes the beautiful play by passing clear across the field to Wesselhoeft, who runs in for a touchdown. But the ball is brought back, as Wesselhoeft was off side. Moffat punts and Harvard fumbles. Haxall falls on the ball and squirms with it across the line, scoring a touchdown. Princeton punts out, Haxall makes a fair catch and immediately kicks the goal.

Harvard kicks off, Princeton makes a fair catch, and Moffat makes a long punt down the field. This play is repeated several times in succession, the ends on both sides getting down the field well and holding the runner in his tracks. Princeton fumbles in their goal, but recovers the ball. Peace breaks through and by a long run takes the ball to midfield. Moffat lifts a high punt. Mason catches the ball on the run and, without stopping, races through the Princeton team, being brought down by Morgan just as he crossed the line, thus forcing the touchdown to be made in the extreme corner of the field. The ball is brought out and Keith tries for a difficult goal, but fails. The half then ends.

Second Half: In the second half Princeton sends Toler to the rush-line and plays Peace at half-back, Moffat being sent to full-back. Princeton then kicks off. Harvard rushes the ball quickly down into Princeton's quarters. Peace, Baker, and Moffat fight grimly to get the ball out, but Harvard tackles hard and sharp and Princeton is forced to make two safeties. Princeton fumbles. Mason picks up the ball and from his tracks drops a goal from the field. Princeton kicks off and follows up the ball. Harvard now commences a block game, voluntarily losing 10 yards time after time in order to gain a first down and hold the ball, thus exhausting the time, which plan is successful, Princeton regaining the ball only twice up to the end of the game. The referee awards the game to Harvard. Princeton makes a vigorous protest, claiming that a touchdown followed by a punt-out and a goal is equivalent to a goal and touchdown; that the score is a tie and that supplementary halves should be played. Watson overrules the objection, and awards the game to Harvard.

HARVARD VS. PRINCETON
Princeton, Nov. 17, 1883

HARVARD		PRINCETON
G. C. Adams, '86,	End,	J. M. T. Finney, '84.
L. W. Kendall, '84,	Next-to-end,	R. J. Travers, '84.
L. Bonsal, '84,	Guard,	C. W. Bird, '85.
R. M. Appleton, '84, Capt.,	Center,	J. M. Harlan, '84.
E. T. Cabot, '83,	Guard,	T. H. Harris, '86.
R. E. Hartley, '86,	Next-to-end,	L. R. Wanamaker, '86.
C. F. Gilman, '85,	End,	C. M. De Camp, '86.
M. M. Kimball, '86,	Quarter-back,	P. T. Kimball, '84.
F. B. Austin, '86,	Half-back,	Alex. Moffat, '84, Capt.
H. E. Peabody, '87,	"	H. C. Lamar, '86.
J. V. Cowling, '87,	Full-back,	A. T. Baker, '85.

Referee: R. Tompkins, '84, Yale. Judges: L. N. Littauer, '78, Harvard; D. M. Look, '84, Princeton. Score: Harvard 7, Princeton 26. First Half: Touchdown by J. M. T. Finney, goal by Alex. Moffat; goal from field by J. V. Cowling; touchdown by L. W. Kendall. Second Half: Goal from field by Alex. Moffat; goal from field by Alex. Moffat; goal from field by Alex. Moffat; goal from field by Alex. Moffat.

NOTE.—For system of numerical scoring see convention, Oct. 17, 1883, Appendix.

First Half: Harvard wins the toss and takes the goal, with a strong wind. Princeton takes the ball. Moffat opens by a dribble, ending in a pass to Kimball for a kick. Austin returns for Harvard and Lamar catches and runs, but as he is about to be tackled he passes to Baker. Baker by a magnificent burst of speed cuts through the Harvard forwards, but is brought down by Austin. A long exchange of punts ensues, which the strong wind turns to Harvard's favor, although Moffat returns gamely. Princeton changes the kicking policy and commences scrimmaging. Lamar, Baker, and De Camp force the Harvard line for good gains and the ball is in Harvard's goal. Cowling punts back again, Moffat returns. Wanamaker gets the ball and makes a touchdown, but the ball is brought back for off-side play. Austin attempts to punt, Harris blocks the kick, and Finney gets the ball and crosses the line for a touchdown. Moffat kicks the goal. Austin kicks off for Harvard, Kimball gets the ball and dashes brilliantly through the forwards, but Cabot brings him down. Baker gets away for a long run, but is stopped by Cowling. Princeton fumbles and Harvard gets the ball. Cowling, standing at midfield, drops a phenomenal goal. Princeton kicks off. Harvard returns. Princeton fumbles and Harvard gets the ball. Cowling sends a long high one behind Princeton's goal-line. Baker catches and attempts to run the ball out, fiercely tackled by Appleton. The ball is dropped and Kendall falls upon it for a touchdown for Harvard. The goal fails. Here the half ends.

Second Half: The second half finds the sides reversed, Princeton having a strong wind behind them. Moffat dribbles and makes 10 yards before being downed. On the next play, standing 46 yards from the Harvard cross-bar, he drops the ball squarely over. Harvard kicks off and Lamar, catching the ball on his 5-yard line, starts upon the most brilliant run of the game, dodging from right to left, slowing up and springing forward until he clears the entire Harvard eleven and starts unopposed for the goal.   Hartley overtakes him from behind and down he goes.   Harvard soon after gets the ball.   Bonsal gets away for a run, but is tackled by Baker.   Princeton gets the ball and Moffat, at a distance of 40 yards, drops his second goal.   This style of scoring apparently disorganizes Harvard, for after their kick-off and a return by Moffat, they lose the ball.   Moffat, standing 40 yards from the line, drops a third field goal. Harvard now uncovers a complicated series of trick passes which takes the ball well into Princeton's territory.   Baker by a clever run gets the ball out again, being tackled by Gilman.   The ball is now 38 yards from the line and to the extreme side of the field.   Moffat falls back for a drop kick. He gets the ball, but instantly is smothered by Adams, Kendall, and Appleton, who are upon him.   To the amazement of the crowd, the unmistakable sound of a drop kick is heard and through a slit of daylight between two crimson jerseys shoots the ball straight and low.   Princeton holds its breath lest the kick fall short, but with wonderful momentum the ball continues to rise and crosses the bar with three feet to spare, thus making the unparalled feat of four drop kicks in one half of a game from difficult distances and angles.   The game shortly after closes.

HARVARD VS. PRINCETON
Cambridge, Nov. 15, 1884

HARVARD		PRINCETON
E. M. Hurd, '88,	End,	H. L. Hodge, '86.
W. P. Homans, '85,	Tackle,	W. M. Irvine, '88.
C. F. Gilman, '85,	Guard,	C. W. Bird, '85, Capt.
S. E. Winslow, '85,	Center,	C. E. Griffith, '86.
W. A. Brooks, '87,	Guard,	T. H. Harris, '86.
W. B. Phillips, '86,	Tackle,	L. R. Wanamaker, '86.
J. E. Thayer, '85,	End,	C. M. De Camp, '86.

HARVARD		PRINCETON
J. Simpkins, '85,	End,	
J. W. Bemis, '85,	Quarter-back,	R. M. Hodge, '86.
W. W. Willard, '87,	Half-back,	A. T. Baker, '85.
M. M. Kimball, '86, Capt.,	"	H. P. Toler, '86.
	"	H. C. Lamar, '86.
H. E. Peabody, '87,	Full-back,	Alex. Moffat, '84.

Referee: L. K. Hull, '83, Yale. Judges: G. C. Adams, '86, Harvard; W. W. Connor, '85, Princeton. Score: Harvard 6, Princeton 34. First Half: Touchdown by A. T. Baker, goal by R. M. Hodge; touchdown by W. M. Irvine, goal by R. M. Hodge; touchdown by J. E. Thayer, goal by J. W. Bemis. Second Half: Touchdown by H. C. Lamar, goal by A. Moffat; touchdown by T. H. Harris; touchdown by L. R. Wanamaker, goal by A. Moffat; touchdown by C. M. De Camp, goal by A. Moffat.

NOTE.—For system of scoring, see Amended Rule 6, convention Dec. 5, 1883, Appendix.

First Half: Harvard kicks off. Princeton at once opens a rushing game. Baker, Lamar, and Irvine hit the line hard, but Harvard throws them back. Princeton punts. Harvard attacks the Princeton line, but Harris, Bird, and Wanamaker allow no gains. Peabody punts. Baker catches the ball at midfield and sharply springing to the right, skirts the Harvard line. Swerving swiftly to the left he dodges Willard and Kimball and crosses the line for a touchdown. Hodge kicks the goal. Harvard kicks off and Princeton returns, Moffat lifting a long, swirling high one. Harvard lines up and Willard punts to midfield. Princeton fumbles and Brooks falls on the ball. Kimball lifts another punt, which lands in Moffat's arms on Princeton's 10-yard line. Princeton tries a rush, but the ball is fumbled. Hurd gets it, sprints around the end and crosses the goal-line, but the ball is brought back, as Hurd has run out of bounds. Kimball drops back to kick. Harris and De Camp are on him with the ball and the try for goal fails, De Camp falling on the ball for Princeton. The Orange and

Black now directs a hard attack against the Harvard line. Baker, Lamar, and Harris break through for long gains and the ball is carried to Harvard's 5-yard line. Homans, Brooks, and Thayer then throw the Princeton runners for a loss and Harvard gets the ball. Peabody immediately punts to midfield. Lamar catches and by a brilliant dash returns the ball back to the 5-yard line. Irvine is called upon for a run. He splits the Crimson line in two and touches down. Moffat kicks the goal. Harvard kicks off. A series of rushes ensues in which the ball is fumbled and Winslow gets it. Harvard cannot gain and Peabody tries a drop. The goal is missed, but the ball is fumbled and Thayer falls on it behind the line for a touchdown for Harvard. Bemis kicks the goal. The half closes.

Second Half: A sharp exchange of kicks opens the second half which lasts for several minutes. Finally Lamar catches and runs 40 yards. Hodge follows it up with 30 more. Lamar covers the remaining distance and touches down. Moffat makes a difficult goal. Peabody kicks off and Moffat returns the ball by a sharp dash to the 40-yard line. Irvine and Bird advance the ball 20 more. Harris splits the line and scores a touchdown. The goal is missed. Harvard shows a great burst of strength. Brooks, Winslow, Kimball, and Willard make good gains and the ball is travelling rapidly toward Princeton's goal. It is now on the 5-yard line. It is carried over, but fumbled. Moffat picks up the ball and carries it to the 25-yard line before being brought down by Hurd. Baker is hurt and retires, Toler taking his place. Princeton now opens up a brilliant passing and running game. The backs and linemen alternate in receiving the ball and all as tackled make long passes to others of their team. Wanamaker, from the 15-yard line, takes the ball over. Moffat kicks the goal. Heavy kicking and a bad fumble soon gives the ball again to Princeton on Harvard's

5-yard line. Hodge tries for a field goal, but fails. De Camp is on the ball, however, and touches down for Princeton. Moffat makes the goal. Another exchange of kicks intermingled with sharp rushing by Harris, Bird, and Irvine again lands the ball on Harvard's 5-yard line. Brooks, Gilman, and Simpkins throw Princeton for a loss and Harvard gets the ball. Willard is forced to punt from behind the line. Irvine and Wanamaker are on him and the punt is shot straight overhead. Lamar gets it standing on the 20-yard line and leaps for the goal. Just as he crosses the line Brooks tackles and Bemis, punching the ball out of Lamar's arms falls on it. Harvard lines up and punts, but time expires.

HARVARD VS. PRINCETON

Princeton, Nov. 13, 1886

HARVARD		PRINCETON
A. F. Holden, '88,	End,	H. L. Hodge, '86.
F. Remington, '87,	Tackle,	F. Moore, '89.
F. C. Woodman, '88,	Guard,	H. W. Cowan, '88.
W. A. Brooks, '87, Capt.,	Centre,	W. J. George, '89.
T. P. Burgess, '87,	Guard,	W. M. Irvine, '88.
A. P. Butler, '88,	Tackle,	W. J. Cook, '89.
V. M. Harding, '89,	End,	E. O. Wagenhurst, '88.
J. B. Fletcher, '87,	Quarter-back,	R. M. Hodge, '86.
A. T. Dudley, '87,	"	
C. A. Porter, '88,	Left Half,	L. E. Price, '88.
J. H. Sears, '89,	Right Half,	K. L. Ames, '90.
H. E. Peabody, '87,	Full-back,	H. S. Savage, '87, Capt.

Referee: Walter Camp, '80, Yale. Score: Harvard 0, Princeton 12. First Half: Touchdown by K. L. Ames, goal by R. M. Hodge; touchdown by K. L. Ames, goal by R. M. Hodge.

First Half: Harvard wins the toss and takes the ball. Brooks dribbles and passes to Sears. Sears runs, but is tackled by Cowan. The ball is passed to Porter, who makes 20 yards before being thrown by Irvine. Brooks gets the ball and by a double pass carries it to Princeton's 20-

yard line.   Princeton stands like a wall, George, Cook, and
Hodge throwing back the Crimson backs and the Orange
and Black gets the ball.   Ames punts to midfield, where
Harvard fumbles.   H. Hodge falls on the ball.   Ames
breaks Harvard's centre for 15 yards.   Cowan hits the right
side of the line for 10 more.   Ames crashes through centre
and crosses the line for a touchdown.   Hodge makes the goal.
On the kick-off Brooks again dribbles and passes to Sears,
who makes 20 yards before being downed by Price.   Moore,
Cook, and Cowan stop the Harvard backs and Princeton gets
the ball.   Harvard holds and recovers.   Peabody punts,
Savage returns.   On the line-up Peabody punts, Princeton
fumbles, and Holden gets the ball.   He starts to run, but
Cowan brings him down.   Fletcher sends a long side pass
to Burgess, who makes 20 yards, Price tackling.   Porter
gets through the line for 20 yards, being tackled by H. Hodge.
Harvard fumbles and Cowan, picking up the ball, makes a
run of 40 yards before being thrown by Brooks.   Hodge,
Ames, Irvine, and Price in succession carry the ball to Harvard's 10-yard line.   As Price is falling he passes the ball
to Moore, who makes 5 yards more.   Ames breaks the centre for the touchdown.   Hodge kicks the goal.

Second Half: Princeton opens the second half with a
dribble to Ames, who runs brilliantly to the 15-yard line,
being tackled by Porter.   Three downs yield no further
gain and Savage touches down 10 yards back in order to
hold the ball for a first down.   Cook, Ames, and Price advance the ball 5 yards.   Savage tries for a field goal, but
misses.   Porter punts out from the 25-yard line and Moore
makes the catch.   Princeton cannot gain and Savage punts.
Harvard tries the Princeton line without results and Porter
punts out of bounds at 35.   Price recovers the ball.   Fletcher
is hurt and Dudley takes his place.   The Orange and Black
can make no impression on the Crimson line and Ames

punts. Sears catches and returns the kick. Irvine, Cowan, and Ames, by hard rushing, work the ball to midfield. Price goes round the end for 20 yards. Cowan splits the line for 10 more. Price again gets round the end and takes the ball to Harvard's 5-yard line, but on the next play a penalty sets Princeton back 5 yards. Savage tries for a goal from the field, but misses. Numerous fumbles mar the ensuing plays, the ball changing from side to side several times. Sears lifts a high punt, which Princeton fumbles, and Harding gets the ball on Princeton's 15-yard line. Princeton does not give an inch and gets the ball on the fourth down. Cowan goes through tackle for 20 yards. Irvine, Ames, and Price, in three plays, plant the ball at midfield. Harvard stops the advance and gets the ball. Sears punts. Princeton in a series of brilliant plays rapidly works the ball to Harvard's 23-yard mark. Savage tries a drop kick, but misses the .post. The two teams are played to a deadlock. The play becomes a series of ineffectual rushes and punts on each side. Price gets away for a 30-yard run. Ames follows with a dash for 30 more, placing the ball on Harvard's 30-yard line, where time is called.

HARVARD vs. PRINCETON
Cambridge, Nov. 12, 1887

HARVARD		PRINCETON
A. J. Cumnock, '91,	Left End,	D. Bovaird, '89.
L. A. Piper, '90,	" "	
P. D. Trafford, '89,	Left Tackle,	R. E. Speer, '89.
J. W. Appleton, '88,	" "	
J. B. Markoe, '89,	Left Guard,	W. M. Irvine, '88.
F. C. Woodman, '88,	Centre,	W. J. George, '89.
A. P. Butler, '88,	Right Guard,	H. W. Cowan, '88.
	" "	W. T. Chapin, '90.
W. Alexander, '87,	Right Tackle,	J. R. Church, '88.
W. D. Bancroft, '88,	Right End,	E.O. Wagenhurst, '88, Capt.
V. M. Harding, '89,	Quarter-back,	J. Hancock, '88.

HARVARD		PRINCETON
A. F. Holden, '88, Capt.,	Half-back,	L. E. Price, '88.
J. A. Saxe, '88,	"	W. C. Price, '88.
C. A. Porter, '88,	"	R. H. Channing, '91.
R. W. Boyden, '85,	Full-back,	K. L. Ames, '90.

Referee: Walter Camp, '80, Yale. Umpire: W. Terry, '85, Yale. Score: Harvard 12, Princeton 0. Second Half: Touchdown by C. A. Porter, goal by J. A. Saxe; touchdown by R. W. Boyden, goal by J. A. Saxe.

First Half: Princeton wins the toss and takes the upper goal, with a strong wind. Harding dribbles and runs, but is tackled by Irvine. Butler makes a gain of 3 yards. Holden gets away for a long run and plants the ball on Princeton's 20-yard line. Bovaird and Wagenhurst tackle sharply and Princeton gets the ball on downs. Ames punts 40 yards, but Holden runs the ball back to the 10-yard line. Here Harvard fumbles and Cowan gets the ball. Harvard holds for downs. Cowan goes out and Chapin takes his place. Porter and Boyden in two rushes take the ball within 3 yards of the line. Speer, Church, and Bovaird throw the crimson runners back for losses and it is Princeton's ball. Ames punts. Harvard fumbles and Price picks up the ball and runs to Harvard's 10-yard line. On the next play Harding intercepts a pass and gets the ball. Porter and Boyden break through for good gains. Princeton holds for downs, but cannot gain, and Ames punts. Bancroft, Trafford, Boyden, and Porter begin a heavy attack on Princeton's line and work the ball yard after yard until the leather rests on Princeton's 15-yard line. Boyden tries for a field goal, but misses. Ames runs the ball out from behind the line and time is called for the half.

Second Half: Princeton opens with the V trick and Price gains 20 yards. Cumnock and Bancroft tackle sharply and it is Harvard's ball on their 35-yard line. Porter and Butler gain 10. A double run and pass, Porter to Butler and

Butler to Bancroft, takes the ball to the 25-yard line Holden makes 10 yards through the line. Trafford gains 5 more. A fumble occurs and Bovaird gets the ball. Bancroft goes out and Alexander takes his place. Ames punts and Harvard gets the ball on the 45-yard line. Porter, Piper, and Saxe force it to the 10-yard line. Porter splits the line for a touchdown and Saxe kicks the goal. Price goes out and is succeeded by his brother, W. C. Price. Princeton opens with the V and makes 10 yards. Channing makes 10 more. Harvard holds and Princeton kicks. Harvard scrimmages, but Irvine and Speer stop the Crimson for no gain. Boyden punts. Cumnock goes off and Piper takes his place. For a long time play remains upon Princeton's 45-yard line, being a succession of plunges, stops, kicks, and returns. Boyden at last breaks through and races the length of the field for a touchdown. Saxe again kicks the goal. Play is resumed, but becomes a kicking contest between Ames and Boyden. The game closes.

HARVARD VS. PRINCETON
Princeton, Nov. 17, 1888

HARVARD		PRINCETON
A. J. Cumnock, '91,	Left End,	J. B. Riggs, '92.
F. C. Woodman, '88,	Left Tackle,	W. J. Cook, '89.
	" "	R. E. Speer, '89.
E. H. Carpenter, '93,	Left Guard,	W. M. Irivne, '88.
J. S. Cranston, '92,	Centre,	W. J. George, '89.
P. D. Trafford, '89,	Right Guard,	H. H. Janeway, '90.
J. T. Davis, '89,	Right Tackle,	H. W. Cowan, '88, Capt.
V. M. Harding, '89,	Right End,	David Bovaird, '89.
S. V. R. Crosby, '91,	" "	
G. F. Harding, '89,	Quarter-back,	R. M. Hodge, '86.
J. P. Lee, '91,	Half-back,	J. S. Black, '91.
C. A. Porter, '88,	"	L. D. Mowry, '91.
J. H. Sears, '89, Capt.,	Full-back,	K. L. Ames, '90.

Referee: Walter Camp, '80, Yale. Umpire: W. H. Corbin, '89, Yale. Score: Harvard 6, Princeton 18. First Half: Touchdown by

W. J. Cook; touchdown by J. S. Black; touchdown by H. W. Cowan.
Second Half: Touchdown by D. Bovaird, goal by R. M. Hodge;
touchdown by J. T. Davis, goal by J. H. Sears.

First Half: Harvard opens with the V and Lee makes
5 yards. Sears punts. Cowan, Janeway, and Cook in
succession make 20 yards. Ames makes 25 around the
end. Black breaks the line for 10 more. Mowry carries
the ball to Harvard's 10-yard line. Sharp tackling by Cumnock, Trafford, and Davis gets the ball for Harvard. Harding passes back to Sears for a punt, but Cook is through
and gets the ball, touching it down for Princeton. Ames
misses the try at goal. Harvard sends Porter in the V for
12 yards, Janeway getting him. Bovaird and Riggs throw
Lee and Porter sharply and Princeton gets the ball on downs.
Ames and Sears exchange punts. Janeway gets the ball
for Princeton on Harvard's 40-yard line. Ames falls back
for a drop kick, but Cumnock blocks the kick. Ames gets
the ball. Black hits the centre hard and it breaks in two.
Black leaps past the backs, and dashing sharply to the
right, crosses the goal-line and touches down. Ames kicks
the goal. Harvard sends Lee in the wedge for 20 yards.
Gains by Woodman, Carpenter, and Davis land the ball on
Princeton's 15-yard line. Bovaird, Janeway, and Riggs
stop the advance and get the ball. Ames punts. Harvard
fumbles and Cowan gets the ball. Ames goes round the
end for 20 yards and follows it up for 7 more around the
opposite side. Black dives through tackle for 5. The ball
is now on the 10-yard line. Cowan runs from tackle position, swinging in on the opposite side and goes through
for a touchdown. Ames again makes the goal. Time is
called for the half.

Second Half: Princeton opens with the V, Black making
15 yards. Ames punts. Harvard now commences a brilliant attack. Lee and Porter alternate running the ends
with Sears and Woodman, Carpenter, Trafford, and Davis

running from line position. Without a check the ball travels down to Princeton's 10-yard line. Here Bovaird and Riggs throw the Harvard backs for a big loss and Princeton gets the ball. Ames immediately punts. Sears sends it back to Princeton's 15-yard line. Black strikes through tackle for 10 yards. Off-side play gives Harvard the ball. A drop kick is attempted, but Cook breaks it up. Cook goes off and Speer takes his place. Mowry makes a touchback of the drop kick. Ames punts out, Sears returns. Ames again punts and Harvard fumbles. Bovaird gets the ball and with a clear field races down the field for a touchdown. Ames kicks the goal. Harvard opens with the V and makes 15 yards. Princeton holds and Sears punts. On the line-up Princeton springs a trick play, a V-shaped mass, splitting the line between end and tackle, the Princeton end coming in against the Harvard tackle and the half carrying the opposing end out. The backs running in the form of a triangle give the play the appearance of a V. Princeton calls it a "split-the-line-open play," or "boxing the tackle." Ames gains 45 yards on the play. Harvard stops Princeton's advance on the 25-yard line. Unable to gain, Sears punts; Princeton returns. Sears takes the ball on the bound and runs through the Princeton team, being brought down on the 3-yard mark. Princeton makes a spirited stand and takes the ball. Kicks are exchanged. A fumble occurs, and Davis coming up on the run, picks up the ball and dashes across the line for a touchdown. Sears kicks the goal and time is called.

HARVARD vs. PRINCETON
Cambridge, Nov. 16, 1889

HARVARD		PRINCETON
A. J. Cumnock, '91, Capt.,	Left End,	B. Donnelly, '90.
" "		R. Furness, '91.
J. D. Upton, '93,	Left Tackle,	H. W. Cowan, '88.
J. S. Cranston, '92,	Left Guard,	H. H. Janeway, '90.

HARVARD		PRINCETON
B. T. Tilton, '90,	Centre,	W. J. George, '89.
P. D. Trafford, '89,	Right Guard,	J. B. Riggs, '92.
	" "	P. C. Jones, '91.
H. H. Stickney, '93,	Right Tackle,	W. S. Cash, '90.
S. V. R. Crosby, '91,	Right End,	R. H. Warren, '93.
D. S. Dean, '91,	Quarter-back,	E. A. Poe, '91, Capt.
J. P. Lee, '91,	Left Half-back,	R. H. Channing, '91.
J. A. Saxe, '88,	Right Half-back,	J. S. Black, '91.
G. R. Fearing, '93,	" "	
B. W. Trafford, '93,	Full-back,	K. L. Ames, '90.

Referee: G. W. Woodruff, '89, Yale. Umpire: H. Beecher, '88, Yale. Score: Harvard 15, Princeton 41. First Half: Touchdown by S. V. R. Crosby; touchdown by R. H. Channing, goal from field by B. W. Trafford; touchdown by R. H. Channing, goal by K. L. Ames; touchdown by J. P. Lee. Second Half: Safety by B. W. Trafford; goal from field by K. L. Ames; touchdown and goal by K. L. Ames; touchdown by H. W. Cowan; touchdown by R. H. Channing; touchdown by H. W. Cowan; touchdown by W. S. Cash; goal by K. L. Ames.

First Half: Princeton wins the toss and takes the ball. The game opens with a V, in which Channing makes 10 yards. On the line-up Princeton fumbles and Crosby, getting the ball, dodges the entire Princeton team and makes a touchdown. Trafford misses the goal. Princeton resumes play with a V, Black making 12 yards. Harvard holds for downs and gets the ball. Lee is sent into the line without gain. Harvard fumbles and Channing gets the ball. Princeton sends a play right and left of centre, which Harvard stops. Channing gets through the line and races off for a touchdown. Ames misses the goal. Harvard sends the wedge to the right and Cowan smashes it. Trafford and Ames exchange kicks, on one of which Trafford recovers the ball 35 yards from Princeton's goal-line. He drops back for a field goal and sends the ball squarely between the posts. Princeton resumes play with a V, gaining 15 yards. Black, Channing, and Cowan hit the line hard and gain consecutively. The ball has reached the 10-yard line.

Harvard contracts the line, the ball is snapped, Channing swings around from place and hitting the line just inside of end breaks across for the touchdown. Ames kicks the goal. Harvard starts off with the wedge, from which Lee makes 20 yards. On the line-up he rounds the end for 20 more. Again he is called to take the ball, and, dashing for the end, suddenly cuts through tackle and crosses the line. Trafford kicks the goal and the half closes.

Second Half: Harvard opens the second half with a V, which gains 5 yards. Riggs, Janeway, and Cash throw the Harvard runners back and Trafford punts. Ames gets the ball and runs it back 10 yards before being thrown. Princeton now attacks the Harvard line, Riggs, Cash, and Cowan breaking through for good gains, alternating with Black and Channing. Harvard is forced back, but gets the ball in her own goal. Trafford drops back to punt, but Cowan and Furness are on him and he makes a safety. Trafford punts out. Ames runs the ball back 10 yards and then drops a goal from the field. Harvard starts the wedge at centre, but cannot gain and punts. Ames catches the ball and by a brilliant dash, dodging from left to right, slips through the Harvard team and crosses the line for a touchdown. A moment later he kicks the goal. Harvard again launches a V, but, unable to gain, punts. Ames returns and several kicks are exchanged, Cowan finally getting the ball. In a burst of speed he crashes through and over the Harvard players for a touchdown. Trafford punts out from the 25-yard line and Poe catches and runs the ball back 25 yards. Harvard holds for downs and gets the ball. Riggs and Poe make great tackles and Princeton recovers the ball. A play is sent against centre, Channing carrying the ball, gaining 5 yards. Cowan breaks away and, dragging several players clinging to him, crosses the line. Harvard starts the ball, but cannot gain. Trafford punts.

Channing makes a run of 25 yards. Harvard holds and Princeton punts. Trafford returns, landing the ball in Ames's arms beneath the cross-bar. Ames starts swiftly forward, but at the 20-yard line slips and falls. Cumnock is upon him, but, shaking him off, Ames springs to his feet and dashes down the side line. Swerving to the right he threads his way by sharp dodging through the Harvard forwards, then suddenly crossing the field he eludes the Harvard backs and once more turns to the right. Dodging tackler after tackler he turns toward the goal, only 15 yards away. At the 5-yard line he slips and falls to one knee. Before he can rise Trafford is upon him and his great run is ended. Harvard stands like a wall. Upton, Crosby, and Dean throw the Orange and Black runners back and Harvard gets the ball. The Crimson cannot gain and punts. Channing brings the ball back and on the next play takes it over for a touchdown. The play resumes and Harvard punts. Darkness is coming on and the spectators are crowding upon the field. Ames receives Trafford's kick and once more comes swiftly down the side line, carrying the ball to the 15-yard line. On the next play Cash breaks through and scores a touchdown. Ames kicks the goal. Soon after time is called.

HARVARD VS. PRINCETON
Princeton, Nov. 2, 1895

HARVARD		PRINCETON
N. W. Cabot, '96,	Left End,	W. P. Hearn, '96.
R. H. Hallowell, '96,	Left Tackle,	W. W. Church, '97.
T. G. Stevenson, '96,	" "	
S. W. Wheeler, '98,	" "	
E. G. Holt, '99,	Left Guard,	D. Riggs, '97.
	" "	P. Wentz, '99.
F. G. Shaw, '97,	Centre,	R. R. Gailey, '97.
J. E, N. Shaw, '98,	Right Guard,	J. M. Rhodes, '97.
M. Donald, '99,	Right Tackle,	L. Lea, '96, Capt.
	" "	A. C. Tyler, '97.

HARVARD		PRINCETON
A. H. Brewer, '96, Capt.,	Right End,	G. Cochran, '98.
G. Newell, '98,	" "	
A. Borden, '96,	Quarter-back,	H. M. Suter, '99.
E. N. Wrightington, '97,	Left Half,	A. H. Rosengarten, '97.
J. A. Sullivan, '97,	" "	
M. G. Gonterman, '96,	" "	
C. Brewer, '96,	Right Half,	H. C. Armstrong, '98.
	" "	W. H. Bannard, '98.
J. C. Fairchild, '96,	Full-back,	J. Baird, '99.
J. W. Dunlop, '97,	"	

Referee: H. L. Pratt '95, Amherst. Umpires: P. J. Dashiell, Navy; F. de P. Townsend, '95, Williams. Linesmen: M. A. Kennedy, Stanford; V. M. Coyne, E. A. C. Score: Harvard 4, Princeton 12. Second Half: Touchdown by A. H. Rosengarten; touchdown by F. G. Shaw; touchdown by A. H. Rosengarten; touchdown by H. M. Suter.

First Half: Harvard wins the toss and selects the north goal. Lea kicks off and C. Brewer returns. On the line-up Baird punts and Harvard returns the kick. Lea swings into tackle for 7 yards. The play is reversed, gaining 4 more. Rosengarten bucks the line for 3, Church 3, Armstrong 3, and Rosengarten 5. The ball is fumbled and Wrightington gets it. Harvard cannot gain an inch and C. Brewer kicks over the goal-line. Princeton punts out and Harvard returns. Princeton tries the line, but cannot advance and Baird punts. Harvard again sends back the ball on the line-up. Baird attempts to skirt the end, but is tackled on the 10-yard line. On the next play he kicks to 45. Harvard holds in the line and the ball goes to Princeton. Armstrong splits the tackle for 5. Harvard holds for downs and gets the ball. Church stops Wrightington and Lea does the same for C. Brewer. C. Brewer kicks down to Princeton's 5-yard line. Princeton tries to punt, but the kick is bad and Harvard gets the ball on the 12-yard line. Harvard plunges hard and is taking the ball across the line when a fumble occurs. Suter picks it up and dashes for the Harvard goal, 110 yards away. The two teams give chase, but Suter, closely pursued by C. Brewer, draws away. The white lines are flying under feet, but Brewer is gaining. As Suter crosses the 20-yard line Brewer springs through the air and brings him down 15 yards from Harvard's goal-line. Rosengarten breaks through the centre for 5. Cabot and Holt throw back the next two runners and Harvard gets the ball. Brewer kicks to 40. Princeton by small gains works the ball to Harvard's 40. Baird tries a drop, but the kick is blocked. Harvard by a series of runs and double passes now quickly advances the ball to Princeton's 25-yard line. Fairchild tries for a field goal, but his kick is blocked. Princeton kicks out and Harvard works back to the 35-yard line. Again Fairchild tries for a goal, but Lea blocks the kick. Time is called for the half.

Second Half: Harvard kicks down to Princeton's 20. Princeton lines up to punt back, but the kick is blocked, Harvard getting the ball. The Crimson cannot gain and tries for a field goal, but the kick is blocked. Princeton punts and Harvard fumbles. Princeton punts again. Harvard lines up to punt, but the kick is blocked and it is Princeton's ball on Harvard's 3-yard line. Rosengarten in one plunge goes over for a touchdown. C. Brewer kicks off to Princeton's 20-yard line. Princeton tries a fake kick and gains 5 yards. Baird then attempts to punt, but Shaw blocks the kick, which rolls across the goal-line, where he falls on it for a touchdown for Harvard. The goal is missed. Harvard kicks off. Princeton returns over the heads of the Harvard men and the ball rolls almost to Harvard's goal. The Crimson lines up and C. Brewer, standing on his 10-yard line, prepares to punt. The kick is blocked and rolls across the line, where Rosengarten falls on it for a touchdown for Princeton. Suter misses the goal. Harvard kicks off and Princeton returns. Harvard tries the line, but cannot make first down. C. Brewer drops back to punt and again the kick is blocked. Wrightington recovers the ball. Harvard again tries the line without gain and drops back to punt, but once more the Princeton forwards crash through and the kick is blocked. This time Princeton gets the ball on the 10-yard line. Bannard shoots a double pass to Suter and the latter goes around the end for a touchdown. No goal. The remainder of the time is spent in useless line-bucking by Harvard and long punts by Princeton.

HARVARD VS. PRINCETON
Cambridge, Nov. 7, 1896

HARVARD		PRINCETON
A. H. Brewer, '96,	Left End,	H. C. Brokaw, '97.
N. W. Cabot, '98,	" "	S. H. Thompson, '97.
S. W. Lewis, '00,	" "	
C. O. Swain, '00,	Left Tackle,	W. W. Church, '97.
G. W. Bouvé, '98,	Left Guard,	E. G. Crowdis, '99.
F. G. Shaw, '97,	Centre,	R. R. Gailey, '97.
A. E. Doucette, '95,	"	
J. E. N. Shaw,	Right Guard,	H. C. Armstrong, '98.
J. H. Lee, '00,	Right Tackle,	A. R. T. Hillebrand, '00.
J. E. Moulton, '98,	Right End,	G. Cochran, '98, Capt.
A. M. Beale, '97,	Quarter-back,	F. L. Smith, '97.
G. F. Cozzens, '96,	Left Half,	W. H. Bannard, '99.
	" "	H. Wheeler, '00.
J. W. Dunlop, '97, Capt.,	Right Half,	A. W. Kelly, '98.
J. A. Sullivan, '97,	" "	H. R. Reiter, '98.
	" "	N. Poe, '97
R. W. P. Brown, '98,	Full-back,	J. Baird, '99.
B. H. Dibblee, '99,	"	

Referee: W. O. Hickok, '95, Yale. Umpire: P. J. Dashiell, Navy. Linesman: C. R. Wyckoff, '96, Cornell. Score: Harvard 0, Princeton 12. Second Half: Touchdown by W. H. Bannard, goal by J. Baird; touchdown by H. C. Brokaw, goal by J. Baird.

First Half: Harvard wins the toss and takes the west goal. Baird kicks off for Princeton, sending the ball to Harvard's 10-yard line. On the line-up Brown returns

A LINE PLUNGE.

Kelly, of Princeton, breaking through Harvard's line, is tackled by B__le and T__nley. Cambridge, Nov. 7, 1896.

the kick to midfield. Kelly goes through the centre for 3.
Bannard rounds the end for 10. Two downs fail to make
the required distance and Harvard gets the ball. Brown
punts to Princeton's 30. Smith goes through tackle for 2.
Three revolving tandem plays net 15 yards. Harvard
holds for downs. Brown punts 35 yards. Kelly hits the
centre for 5. Church splits the tackle for 3. Harvard
holds and Baird punts to Harvard's 48. Dunlop circles
the end for 15 yards. Several exchanges of punts ensue.
Brown tries for a field goal, but misses. Baird kicks out
to midfield. Reiter takes the place of Kelly. Brown
punts over Princeton's goal-line. Princeton kicks out, but
Brown returns. Princeton opens up the revolving tackle play
and gains 15 yards. Harvard holds for downs and Brown
punts. Smith makes 5. Two plunges into the line fail
to gain and Baird drops back to punt. Brown returns the
kick. Reiter goes through the line for 4. Harvard holds
and Baird again falls back to punt. Bouvé blocks the kick.
Moulton picks up the ball and with a clear field starts for
the goal, but slips on the 20-yard line and loses the ball.
Baird gets it for Princeton. Punts are exchanged. Beale
tries a quarter-back kick, but Brokaw gets the ball. Baird
goes through the line for 4. Time is called for the half.

Second Half: Brown kicks to Princeton's 25. Baird returns. Brown punts, but the Princeton forwards are on
him and the ball goes straight into the air, Baird catching
it on Harvard's 35. Cabot takes the place of Brewer. The
teams line up, the ball is snapped, and Bannard dashes
around the end for a touchdown. Baird kicks the goal.
Brown kicks off for Harvard, sending the ball to Princeton's
10-yard line. Baird returns to midfield. Brokaw tackles
Cabot for no gain. Punts are exchanged. Sullivan recovers ball for Harvard at 53. Brown punts to Princeton's
35-yard line. Another exchange of punts follows. Smith

heels a fair catch for Princeton 50 yards from the Crimson goal. Baird attempts a place kick, but misses. Harvard kicks out and Princeton gets the ball at 40. The revolving tandem again starts in motion. Harvard stops the advance on the 25-yard line. Wheeler replaces Bannard. Brown punts and Baird catches at 45. Church and Hillebrand each make 10 yards. Baird punts to Harvard's 20. A penalty sets Princeton back 10 yards. Sullivan takes the place of Dunlop. Brown falls back to punt, but Church blocks the kick. The ball bounds back over Harvard's goal-line, where Brokaw falls on it for a touchdown. Baird kicks the goal. Harvard kicks off. Princeton quickly works the ball into Harvard's territory. Poe replaces Reiter and Lewis takes the place of Cabot. Dibblee relieves Brown. Princeton commences a fierce attack on the Harvard line. The ball rapidly, but by short gains, advances toward the Crimson goal. As it reaches the 15-yard line the strains of "Fair Harvard" float from a cornet in the east stand. The Crimson stands firm and the attack is stopped. Harvard punts and once more Princeton forces the ball steadily toward the goal. The ball reaches the 30-yard line. Time is called.

1897–1910 no games.

CHAPTER XIV

HARVARD VS. YALE

HARVARD vs. YALE
New Haven, Nov. 13, 1875

HARVARD		YALE
H. C. Leeds, '77,	Rusher,	M. H. Phelps, '76.
M. L. Cate, '77,	"	W. J. Wakeman, '76.
J. B. Keyes, '77,	"	J. P. Peters, '73.
B. S. Blanchard, '79,	"	C. C. Camp, '77.
A. C. Tower, '77,	"	G. T. Elliott, '77.
	"	G. V. Bushnell, '74.
	"	O. D. Thompson, '79
J. A. Wetherbee, '78,	Half-tender,	D. T. Trumbull, '76.
H. L. Morse, '77,	"	F. W. Vaille, '76.
	"	D. R. Alden, '76.
E. C. Hall, '76,	Tender,	William Arnold, '76, Capt.
W. S. Seamans, '80,	"	C. Johnson, '76.
N. Curtis, '77, Capt.,	"	W. L. R. Wurts, '78.
D. C. Bacon, '76,	"	
E. H. Herrick, '77,	"	

Referee: R. C. Cornell, Columbia. Judges: W. A. Whiting, '77, Harvard; E. J. McKnight, '76, Yale. Score: Harvard 4 goals, Yale 0. First Half Hour: Goal by H. C. Leeds; goal by W. S. Seamans. Second Half Hour: Goal by B. S. Blanchard. Third Half Hour: Goal by A. C. Tower. (Score by goals only.)

This game was played at Hamilton Park under a code of rules known as the "concessionary rules," so called because of certain concessions in the Rugby Union code granted by Harvard to Yale. At noon on the day of the game the train from Boston arrived with a throng of 150 collegians, chronicled at the time as "the biggest crowd from Boston ever seen in New Haven."

First Half Hour: Harvard wins the toss and selects the wind. Arnold kicks off for Yale, sending a long kick down the field. Leeds springs a trick not known at Yale: he kicks the ball back again. Yale again kicks and Leeds, catching, runs in for a touchdown. He kicks the goal. The ball is kicked off and Harvard soon has it in touch near Yale's goal. It is thrown in to Seamans, who kicks a goal from the field. Yale kicks off. Seamans almost runs in to Yale's goal, but stops 35 yards away and tries a drop kick. The ball sails squarely for the posts, but Trumbull jumps in the air and stops it with his hand just as it is crossing the cross-rope. Yale kicks out and the half hour terminates with the ball 10 yards from Yale's goal.

Second Half Hour: Bacon sends a long kick down the field for Harvard. Arnold returns and Herrick, catching, almost runs in for a touchdown, being stopped by Bushnell. On the next play Cushing gets away and makes a touchdown. The goal fails. Yale kicks off. After a few plays Wetherbee gets the ball, and as he is about to be tackled, passes to Blanchard, who kicks a goal from the field. Yale kicks off, Cate catches and runs, but is brought down by Elliott. The ball is in touch with a pile of men upon it. The referee finds several pairs of hands holding the ball, but gives it to Harvard. The ball is thrown in and time is called.

Third Half Hour: Yale kicks off. Harvard runs back, but Yale now shows greater familiarity with the game and tackles strongly. The runner is stopped and the whole Yale team pile on him. When they are taken off the ball is found a flattened sheet of rubber at the bottom. It is blown up again and the game proceeds. Blanchard gets the ball and runs in for a touchdown. The goal is missed. Play is resumed, and after a few runs and tackles Tower kicks a goal from the field. Yale kicks off and forces the

ball into Harvard's quarters. The latter transfers the play
to the other end of the field, where just as the game closes
Seamans makes a touchdown. The goal fails.

HARVARD vs. YALE

New Haven, Nov. 18, 1876

HARVARD		YALE
H. W. Cushing, '77,	Forward,	N. U. Walker, '77.
L. Cushing, '79,	"	W. V. Downer, '78.
F. A. Houston, '79,	"	W. H. Taylor, '78.
J. B. Keyes, '77,	"	G. H. Clark, '80.
F. W. Rollins, '77,	"	C. C. Camp, '77.
	"	E. L. Morse, '78.
	"	W. L. R. Wurts, 78.
N. Curtis, '77, Capt.,	Half-back	Walter Camp, '80.
E. H. Herrick, '77,	"	W. D. Hatch, '79.
W. S. Seamans, '80,	"	
G. P. Faucon, '75,	Back,	E. V. Baker, '77, Capt.
F. D. Jordan, '80,	"	W. I. Bigelow, '77.
J. A. Wetherbee, '78,	"	O. D. Thompson, '79.

Referee: G. V. Bushnell, '74, Yale. Judges: W. E. Russell, '77,
Harvard; G. T. Elliott, '77, Yale. Score: Harvard 0, Yale 1 goal.
Second Half: Goal from field by O. D. Thompson.

NOTE.—At the request of Yale an agreement was made
preliminary to this game that touchdowns should not count
in the scoring, but that the latter should be computed by
goals alone. At the request of Harvard the game was
played with ten men only upon a side.

First Half: Harvard wins the toss and takes the upper
goal. The two teams, composed of ten men each, deploy
upon the field. It is noticed that they present two different
tactical dispositions of the men. Harvard is playing three
men at half-back, or, as the position is known at Cambridge,
as "half-tend," while Yale uses only two, thus throwing
an extra man for Yale in the line of forwards, or, as Har-

vard denominates the position, "rushers." Each side is
playing three men at "back," or "tend." Baker kicks off
and Faucon returns the kick. For half an hour the play
is even, kicks and scrummages following in rapid succession to the advantage of neither. Houston at last gets away
for a long run and makes a touchdown, but the try at goal
fails. The half comes to an end without further features
of record.

Second Half: Yale opens the second half by quickly rushing the ball into Harvard's quarters, but sharp work by Seamans and Herrick gets it back again. After thirty minutes of
varying play O. D. Thompson gets the ball and, standing on
the 35-yard mark and at a wide angle, cleverly sends a drop
kick squarely over the bar and between the posts. Harvard
resumes play desperately and forces Yale back. Three
seconds before the expiration of time Herrick runs in for
a touchdown, but time expires while he is in flight and the
try at goal is not allowed. The referee awards the game to
Yale by 1 goal to 0.

1877, no game.

HARVARD VS. YALE
Boston, Nov. 23, 1878

HARVARD		YALE
H. W. Cushing, '77,	Rusher,	J. V. Farwell, '79.
J. Swift, '79,	"	P. C. Fuller, '81.
W. D. Holden, '82,	"	J. S. Harding, '80.
F. G. Perry, '79,	"	L. K. Hull, '83.
F. C. Warren, '79,	"	P. King, '80.
T. C. Thacher, '82,	"	F. M. Eaton, '82.
J. E. Cowdin, '79,	"	W. I. Badger, '82.
E. W. Morse, '78,	"	W. A. Peters, '80.
B. S. Blanchard, '79,	Half-back	O. D. Thompson, '79.
L. Cushing, '79, Capt.,	"	R. W. Watson, '81.
H. D. Sedgwick, '82,	"	Walter Camp, '80, Capt.
Robert Winsor, '80,	"	

HARVARD		YALE
J. A. Wetherbee, '78,	Back,	W. W. K. Nixon, '81.
F. L. Eldridge, '82,	"	W. J. Wakeman, '77.
F. A. Houston, '79,	"	C. W. Lyman, '82.
J. Holmes, '79,	"	

Referee: B. Ballard, '80, Princeton. Judges: W. A. Whiting, '77, Harvard; G. H. Clark, '80, Yale. Score: Harvard 0, Yale 1 goal. Second Half: Goal from field by O. D. Thompson.

NOTE.—At the request of Yale an agreement was made preliminary to this game that touchdowns should not count in the score, but that the latter should be computed by goals alone.

First Half: Harvard wins the toss and takes the wind. Yale kicks off. Harvard at once works the ball, by runs of Wetherbee, Cushing, and Houston, into Yale's goal. Camp gets the ball and runs it out of danger. Sedgwick runs it back again. A random kick sends the ball into a small pond of water near the field of play, but both teams plunge in after it to the huge merriment of the spectators. W. Camp gets it. The ball is now worked back to centre by Thompson, Watson, and Wakeman. L. Cushing gets it out of a scrimmage and makes 20 yards, kicking just as he is about to be tackled. Wetherbee takes it down into Yale's goal. Yale gets the ball and by long runs of Thompson, Watson, and W. Camp carries it within 20 yards of Harvard's goal. W. Camp drops a goal from the field, but time expires while the ball is in flight and the goal does not count.

Second Half: Warren kicks off to Yale in the second half. Yale plays up strong and works the ball quickly down into Harvard's goal, where Holmes runs it out, delivering a long punt while on the run. Thompson catches, and eluding the Crimson tacklers, runs with the ball, also kicking when about to be tackled. The ball is again in Harvard's goal, but rush upon rush cannot get it over.

Holmes again gets the ball and saves Harvard by running it out to midfield. Thompson runs 15 yards into Harvard's territory. W. Camp tries a long drop, but misses the posts. Winsor and Wetherbee by long runs transfer the play to Yale's side, where it remains for some time. Camp and Lyman get it back to midfield. Thompson runs the ball to the 40-yard mark, and stopping suddenly, tries a drop for the goal. The ball shoots between two Harvard men and sails squarely between the posts for a goal. Play is resumed. The ball remains at centre for several minutes and time is called.

HARVARD vs. YALE
New Haven, Nov. 8, 1879

HARVARD		YALE
E. W. Morse, '78,	Rusher,	L. K. Hull, '83.
W. H. Manning, '82,	"	C. S. Beck, '83.
L. Cushing, '79,	"	F. R. Vernon, '81.
E. Brooks, '80,	"	B. B. Lamb, '81.
F. C. Warren, '79,	"	J. S. Harding, '80.
J. S. Tebbets, '80,	"	F. Remington, '80.
T. C. Thacher, '82,	"	F. M. Eaton, '82.
T. W. Nickerson, '80,	"	J. Moorehead, '80.
Robert Bacon, '80, Capt.,	Quarter-back,	
Robert Winsor, '80,	Half-back,	Walter Camp, '80, Capt.
W. R. Austin, '77,	"	W. A. Peters, '80.
	"	W. I. Badger, '82.
	"	G. H. Clark, '80.
F. E. Cabot, '80,	Three-quarter-back,	B. W. Bacon, '81.
G. H. Leatherbee, '82,	Back,	W. W. K. Nixon, '81.
A. B. Shattuck, '81,	"	C. W. Lyman, '82.

Referee: B. Ballard, '80, Princeton. Judges: F. A. Houston, '79, Harvard; W. C. McHenry, '80, Yale. Score: Harvard 0, Yale 0.

NOTE.—For system of scoring see Rule 7, convention Nov. 26, 1876, Appendix.

First Half: Harvard wins the toss and takes the south goal. Yale kicks off. Harvard, by runs of Cabot and

Austin, works the ball back to midfield, where it remains for twenty minutes. Runs by Camp, Peters, and Badger then take it down near Harvard's goal. Long kicks by Cabot and Shattuck suddenly transfer play into Yale's goal, where Nixon gets the ball and by a long run followed by a kick by Camp the ball is placed 40 yards from Harvard's goal. Here Eaton is fouled and Yale is given a free kick as a penalty. The ball goes to the left of the posts. Harvard punts well down the field and Yale returns. Lamb gets the ball and runs across the line for a touchdown, but the play is not allowed on account of a foul. The ball is directly in front of Harvard's goal. Harding passes to Camp, who drops a goal from the 45-yard line, but again the play is not allowed on account of holding by Yale. Time is then called for the half.

Second Half: Harvard opens the second half by a long kick. Moorehead gets the ball and almost covers the field for a touchdown, but is stopped when near the goal. Harvard puts up a strong fight to save their goal-line, but cannot get the ball out, although they prevent it from being rushed over. Camp tries for a field goal, but misses. Harvard makes a safety. Shattuck by a long run and kicks gets the ball near Yale's goal. Yale gets the ball, but is forced to touch down twice for safety. At last Camp punts far down the field and time then is called.

HARVARD VS. YALE
Boston, Nov. 20, 1880

HARVARD		YALE
H. M. Atkinson, '84,	Forward,	P. C. Fuller, '81.
F. C. Warren, '79,	"	C. S. Beck, '83.
F. A. Houston, '79,	"	B. B. Lamb, '81.
W. H. Manning, '82, Capt.,	"	J. S. Harding, '80.
Alex. Boyd, '82,	"	C. B. Storrs, '82.
G. B. Morison, '83,	"	F. R. Vernon, '81.
T. C. Thacher, '82,	"	W. L. Adams, '83.

HARVARD		YALE
	Quarter-back,	W. I. Badger, '82.
W. O. Edmands, '83,	Half-back,	R. W. Watson, '81, Capt.
C. H. W. Foster, '81,	"	Walter Camp, '80.
G. P. Keith, '83,	"	
H. M. Cutts, '83,	Full-back,	B. W. Bacon, '81.

Referee: F. Loney, '81, Princeton. Judges: R. Winsor, '80, Harvard; G. H. Clark, '80, Yale. Score: Harvard 0, Yale 1 field goal, 1 touchdown. Second Half: Goal from field by Walter Camp; touchdown by R. W. Watson.

NOTE.—For system of scoring see Rule 7, convention Nov. 26, 1876, Appendix.

First Half: Yale wins the toss and takes the south goal, favored by a light wind. Keith kicks off for Harvard, whose players follow up the ball and force Yale to make a safety. A great kicking exchange follows, the field being too slippery for good rushing. By kicks of Camp and Watson the ball is transferred into Harvard's territory. The ball is now within 20 yards of the goal. Camp tries to run in for a touchdown, but Keith stops him. He tries for a field goal, but the slippery ball glances to one side. Harvard is in straits and makes four safeties. Harvard by long runs of Edmands, Foster, and Keith works the ball back to Yale's side and carries it within 5 yards of the goal. Several rushes fail to advance it an inch and Edmands prepares for a drop at goal. The kick misses the post by inches. Watson makes two long runs in succession, getting the ball to midfield. Camp follows with another of 25 yards and Adams gets away in a clear field, but slips and falls on the 5-yard-line mark. Time is then called for the half.

Second Half: Harding kicks off for Yale. Manning is hurt in the scrimmage and retires, Boyd taking his place. Boyd soon after also is injured and goes off, Manning, who has recovered, coming back in his place. Yale is playing strong now and the ball is travelling rapidly down the field. It is within 6 paces of the goal. Watson is hurt, but resumes playing. Yale makes a number of downs in front of the goal, gaining a few inches. Cutts gets the ball and pretends to make a safety, but instead runs the ball out and kicks. Bacon gets it and kicks it back. Only five minutes are left to play. The referee awards a foul to Yale in front of the goal-posts. Yale takes a free kick and draws back. The ball is carefully placed and Camp sends it squarely between the posts. Harvard kicks off at centre and Watson, catching the ball, runs through the entire Harvard team, making a touchdown. Before the try at goal can be made time expires and the great game is at an end. In the evening the Harvard team entertained their opponents with a dinner at Young's. Speeches were made by Coolidge, Lamb, Manning, Loney, and Watson, and the company was entertained by the singing of Atkinson, Edmands, and Merrill.

HARVARD vs. YALE

New Haven, Nov. 12, 1881

HARVARD		YALE
W. H. Manning, '82, Capt.,	Forward,	H. H. Knapp, '82.
E. T. Cabot, '83,	"	A. L. Farwell, '84.
F. A. Houston, '79,	"	R. Tompkins, '84.
T. C. Thacher, '82,	"	L. K. Hull, '83.
L. W. Kendall, '84,	"	C. B. Storrs, '82.
R. M. Appleton, '84,	"	C. S. Beck, '83.
E. S. Perin, '82,	"	B. B. Lamb, '81.
F. A. Mason, '84,	Quarter-back,	W. I. Badger, '82.
W. A. Henry, '85,	Half-back,	Walter Camp,'80, Capt.
G. P. Keith, '83,	"	E. L. Richards, '85.
W. O. Edmands, '83,	Full-back,	B. W. Bacon, '81.

Referee: P. T. Bryan, '82, Princeton. Score: Harvard 4 safeties, Yale 0. First Half: 3 safeties by Harvard. Second Half: 1 safety by Harvard. (Names of judges and makers of safeties not on record.)

NOTE.—For system of scoring see Rule 5, convention Oct. 8, 1881, Appendix.

First Half: Harvard wins the toss and takes the south goal. Camp kicks off. Harvard is taken by surprise, as the kick is to the side, which Knapp, running forward, recovers. On the scrimmage Badger sends a long side pass to Lamb, but Houston prevents a gain. Badger then passes the ball to Camp, who kicks. During the rest of this half the ball is kept inside of Harvard's 25-yard line by rush upon rush, resulting only in slight gains for Yale. Harvard at last gets the ball on a foul. A long pass is sent to the side, but Badger intercepts it and gets the ball. Hull snaps to Badger, who passes to Lamb. Lamb is forced out of bounds. Harvard gets the ball, but is forced to make a safety. The ball after the kick-out is forced back into Harvard's goal, where a second safety is made. Henry punts out, Lamb catches and runs in until tackled, when the ball is passed to Camp. Camp is stopped. A try at goal fails and Harvard for the third time touches down for safety. Henry punts out to Hull, who runs, but is thrown by Cabot. Hull then passes the ball sideways to Storrs, who crosses the line, but the referee refuses to allow the touchdown and time is called for the half.

Second Half: Keith kicks off at the opening of the second half to Bacon, who stands underneath the cross-bar. Bacon returns the kick. The ball oscillates back and forth near midfield without advantage to either side. Richards, Camp, and Keith commence a brisk kicking duel which terminates in a long run by Camp. Another exchange of kicks follows and Hull gets away for a long run. Harvard gets the ball and Manning immediately runs it back into Yale's territory. Camp sends two kicks which take the ball into Harvard's goal and the Crimson makes its fourth safety. Henry punts out, Bacon returns, and Badger recovers the ball. Camp, Badger, and Lamb try to force a touchdown, but cannot get through the Harvard line.

Manning gets the ball on a fumble and makes 40 yards. Knapp stops him from reaching the clear field. Keith, Richards, and Henry get in some long kicks, terminating in a great run by Keith which seems good for a touchdown, when Lamb forces him out of bounds. Yale gets the ball and Camp sends it out of danger by a long kick. Time is then called.

HARVARD VS. YALE

Cambridge, Nov. 25, 1882

HARVARD		YALE
G. B. Morison, '83,	Rusher,	H. H. Knapp, '82.
L. W. Kendall, '84,	"	W. H. Hyndman, '84.
E. T. Cabot, '83, Capt.,	"	R. Tompkins, '84, Capt.
C. M. Hammond, '83,	"	L. K. Hull, '83.
R. M. Appleton, '84,	"	F. G. Peters, '86.
G. D. Ayers, '82,	"	C. S. Beck, '83.
W. F. Wesselhoeft, '84,	"	A. L. Farwell, '84.
G. C. Adams, '86,	"	
F. A. Mason, '84, ·	Quarter-back,	H. B. Twombly, '84.
W. H. Coolidge, '81.	Half-back,	W. Terry, '85.
G. P. Keith, '83,	"	E. L. Richards, '85.
W. O. Edmands, '83,	Back,	B. W. Bacon, '81.

Referee: C. J. Winton, '84, Princeton. Judges: F. A. Houston, '79, Harvard; W. I. Badger, '82, Yale. Score: Harvard 2 safeties, Yale 4 touchdowns, 1 goal from touchdown. First Half: Touchdown by L. K. Hull; safety by Harvard; touchdown by C. S. Beck. Second Half: Touchdown by C. S. Beck; goal by E. L. Richards; touchdown by A. L. Farwell; safety by Harvard.

NOTE.—For system of scoring see Rule 5, convention Oct. 8, 1881, and Rule 7, convention Oct. 14, 1882, Appendix.

First Half: Yale wins the toss and selects the goal backed by a strong wind. Edmands kicks off for Harvard and lands the ball in Yale's goal. Richards kicks it back and Edmands returns. Yale puts the ball in play by a scrimmage and the play for several minutes is at midfield. Bacon punts and Edmands again returns. On the second scrimmage Hull gets through, and dashing swiftly to the right, dodges Keith and Edmands and touches down. Richards tries for goal at a difficult angle, but misses. Harvard puts the ball in play by a dribble and run. Tompkins tackles for no gain. Scrimmage now follows scrimmage. Harvard is forced to make a safety. Yale gets the ball and slowly forces it down the field, Beck taking it across for Yale's second touchdown. Richards again misses the goal. On resumption of play Wesselhoeft is injured and Adams takes his place. Bacon and Edmands commence a punting duel. Time for the half expires with the ball in midfield.

Second Half: The strong wind that favored Yale in the first half has died down. Richards kicks off, sending the ball over Harvard's goal-line. Harvard fumbles and Beck is down on the ball for a touchdown. The ball is punted out and caught. Richards kicks the goal. Bacon sends the ball on the kick-off into Yale's goal. Bacon runs it out 15 yards. Yale now commences a fierce attack. Richards, Hull, and Twombly alternate with the ball. Appleton, Kendall, and Cabot tackle desperately, but slowly the ball travels down the field. It is now on the 10-yard line. A pass is made out to Farwell, who takes it over for a touchdown. The goal is missed. Harvard kicks off and Yale commences another vigorous attempt to score. The time is growing short. The Yale backs cut through Harvard's line for big gains, but Mason and Coolidge finally stop the onslaught. Harvard makes another safety and punts. Yale also is soon forced to kick, and the time expires.

HARVARD vs. YALE

New York, Nov. 29, 1883

HARVARD		YALE
J. Simpkins, '85,	Rusher,	L. F. Robinson, '85.
R. E. Hartley, '86,	"	W. P. McCrorey, '84.
C. F. Gilman, '85,	"	R. Tompkins, '84, Capt.
R. M. Appleton, '84, Capt.,	"	W. H. Hyndman, '84.

HARVARD		YALE
L. Bonsal, '84,	Rusher,	F. G. Peters, '86.
L. W. Kendall, '84,	"	S. R. Bertron, '85.
J. Codman, '85,	"	A. L. Farwell, '84.
A. R. Crane, '84,	Quarter-back,	H. B. Twombly, '84.
W. A. Henry, '85,	Half-back,	E. L. Richards, '85.
J. V. Cowling, '87,	"	W. Terry, '85.
H. E. Peabody, '87,	Full-back,	S. H. Deneen, '87.

Referee: E. C. Peace, '83, Princeton. Judges: L. N. Littauer, '78, Harvard; F. Kellogg, '83, Yale. Score: Harvard 2, Yale 23. First Half: Safety by Harvard; goal from field by E. L. Richards; touchdown by W. H. Hyndman, goal by E. L. Richards. Second Half: Touchdown by J. Codman; goal from field by H. B. Twombly; touchdown by A. L. Farwell, goal by W. Terry.

NOTE.—For system of scoring see convention Oct. 17, 1883, Appendix.

First Half: Yale wins the toss and takes the goal with the wind. Harvard kicks off and Richards returns, landing the ball 20 yards from Harvard's goal, where Harvard fumbles and Yale gets the ball. Terry tries a drop kick, missing the goal. Harvard kicks out and on the return shows amazing strength. Henry gets the ball and breaks through the line for a long run. Yale tackles sharply and Harvard punts. Richards catches the ball and runs it back. Farwell follows it up by another brilliant dash. Harvard holds and Richards tries for a field goal, but misses. Henry punts out lifting the ball 60 yards. Richards sends it back. Cowling attempts to punt, but the kick is blocked. The ball is 5 yards from Harvard's goal-line. A maul in goal ensues, the spectators screaming with excitement. Harvard gets out of the predicament with a safety. Cowling kicks out and Twombly takes the ball on the run, bringing it back through the entire Harvard team to the 35-yard line. Harvard holds. Richards kicks a goal from the field. Harvard kicks off. Yale rushes and Terry misses a long drop

kick for goal. Harvard kicks out and on the next play
Terry gets away and runs 85 yards, being brought down by
Cowling on Harvard's 5-yard line. Hyndman gets the ball,
and with the entire Harvard team on his back staggers
across the line for a touchdown. Richards kicks the goal
and the half ends.

Second Half: During the first half Henry's punting has
been the chief feature of Harvard's play. In the second
half he has the additional aid of a strong wind. Henry
feints to kick off but dribbles and sends a long pass out to
Cowling, who dashes down the field to Yale's 30-yard line.
Yale tightens up and gets the ball. Richards immediately
lifts the ball back to midfield. Henry catches at full
speed, and when hard pressed lifts a magnificent punt while
running, sending the ball over the side line close to Yale's
goal-line. Yale fumbles and Harvard gets the ball. Harvard lines up for a drop kick. The Yale line comes through
upon Henry, but the play has been a feint, for the ball is
shot out to the side to Codman, who leaps across the line
for a touchdown. Cowling tries for goal, but the ball strikes
the post, bounding back upon the field, where Bonsal is
through and on it. Yale stands like a stone wall and stops
another touchdown, getting the ball. A heavy attack is now
directed against the Harvard rushers, which carries the ball
down into Harvard's goal. The Crimson line plays with
desperation and gets the ball. Henry and Peabody lift two
great kicks in succession and the ball is in Yale's goal.
Deneen makes a long run, Codman tackling. Twombly
follows it up with another and again Codman saves Harvard's line. The ball is exchanged on kicks. Twombly
gets it and, standing on the 45-yard line, and at a wide
angle drops a difficult goal from the field. Harvard kicks
off. Yale lifts a tremendous punt, which the wind catches
and whirls over Harvard's line. Henry kicks out from

the 25-yard line. The ball is returned, Kendall gets it
and dashes down the field for 35 yards. Yale holds and
gets the ball. They line up for a punt, but the ball is shot
to the side, where Farwell gets it and with a clear field
dashes down the side line 50 yards for a touchdown. Terry
kicks the goal. The ball is kicked off, but time is called.

HARVARD VS. YALE

New Haven, Nov. 22, 1884

HARVARD		YALE
E. M. Hurd, '88,	Rusher,	L. F. Robinson, '85.
J. E. Thayer, '85,	"	S. R. Bertron, '85.
C. F. Gilman, '85,	"	H. R. Flanders, '85.
T. P. Burgess, '87,	"	R. S. Storrs, '85.
W. A. Brooks, '87,	"	F. G. Peters, '86.
W. P. Homans, '85,	"	A. B. Coxe, '87.
J. M. T. Finney, '89,	"	R. Ronalds, '86.
	"	W. N. Goodwin, '88.
J. W. Bemis, '85,	Quarter-back,	T. L. Bayne, '87.
W. W. Willard, '87,	Half-back,	E. L. Richards, '85, Capt.
M. M. Kimball, '86, Capt.,	"	W. Terry, '85.
H. E. Peabody, '87,	Full-back,	M. H. Marlin, '86.

Referee: D. M. Look, '84, Princeton. Judges: G. C. Adams, '86,
Harvard; L. K. Hull, '83, Yale. Score: Harvard 0, Yale 48. First
Half: Touchdown by A. B. Coxe, goal by E. L. Richards; touchdown
by H. R. Flanders, goal by W. Terry; touchdown by T. L. Bayne,
goal by E. L. Richards; touchdown and goal by E. L. Richards.
Second Half: Touchdown by F. G. Peters; touchdown by A. B. Coxe;
touchdown by A. B. Coxe; touchdown by E. L. Richards, goal by W.
Terry; touchdown by T. L. Bayne, goal by W. Terry.

NOTE.—For system of scoring see Rule 6, convention
Dec. 5, 1883, Appendix.

First Half: Harvard wins the toss and selects the goal
backed by a slight wind. Yale kicks off, Terry dribbling,
but quickly passes the ball out to Coxe, who runs, but is
downed by Burgess. The ball is then passed to Richards,
who sends a long punt down to Peabody. On the line-up

Harvard fumbles and it is Yale's ball 5 yards from the line. Coxe throws his 230 pounds against the Harvard line, and it breaks in two, letting him over with the ball for a touchdown. Richards kicks the goal. Harvard dribbles and runs. Willard, Kimball, and Thayer work the ball down to Yale's 10-yard line, where the Blue holds and gets the ball. Terry kicks and Peabody returns. Yale fumbles and it is Harvard's ball 10 yards from the line. They form for a drop kick. Flanders gets through and intercepts the pass. Shaking loose the backs he starts for the goal-line 100 yards distant, with the whole Harvard team in pursuit. Hurd gets him just as he crosses the line, but Flanders goes over for the touchdown. Terry makes the goal. Peabody kicks off for Harvard and Hurd is down, getting the ball. On the first play the ball is fumbled. Yale sends Terry on a run of 35 yards: Bemis stops him with a hard tackle. Harvard gets the ball and punts. The kick is high and Bayne makes a fair catch for Yale. Richards tries for goal, but fails. Terry picks up the ball on the ground and attempts to leap across the line, but Finney throws him back. Harvard gets the ball and tries to punt. The Yale men are through and the ball goes straight into the air. Richards makes a fair catch on the 35-yard line. He draws the Yale team 10 yards back and tries for a place kick. Terry kicks, but misses. On the kick-out Yale gets the ball and lines up for a punt, but a long pass is sent to the side to Bayne, who races 45 yards for a touchdown. Richards kicks the goal. Harvard kicks off. Richards runs back the kick 15 yards. Bayne gets off on the first play for 40 more. On the next line-up the ball is passed to Richards, who covers the remaining distance and touches down. He kicks the goal and time is called for the half.

Second Half: Flanders has been relieved by Storrs. Harvard kicks off, Richards catches, but is thrown in his tracks. Terry punts. Yale gets the ball and Richards lifts one across Harvard's line. Harvard kicks out from the 25-yard line. Terry catches and dashes for the line. Brooks tackles, but the ball is passed to Richards, who makes 10 yards and then passes to Peters as Homans tackles. Peabody tackles Peters, but the burly Yale man drags him across the line and makes a touchdown. The try for goal fails. Harvard punts out and Terry runs the ball back 10 yards. Coxe gets the ball and starts down the field close to the side line, Peters blocking off. The referee awards a foul for such interference. Yale quickly recovers the ball and forces it down to Harvard's goal-line. Coxe is sent across for the touchdown. The try for goal fails. Yale quickly works the ball again into Harvard's 5-yard line. Harvard masses for an attack on centre. Coxe hits the line, but cannot get through. He rolls around the end for a touchdown. The goal is missed. Again Harvard punts out and Terry almost runs the ball back to the line. Richards is sent across for the touchdown and Terry kicks the goal. Harvard kicks off. Coxe gets the ball on the first down and rolls around the end for 5 yards. Richards skirts the opposite side for 40. Bayne goes over for a touchdown and Terry kicks the goal. Harvard kicks off, but time is soon called.

1885 no game. Harvard's faculty abolished football Jan. 6, 1885, but re-established the sport Jan. 5, 1886.

HARVARD VS. YALE
Cambridge, Nov. 20, 1886

HARVARD		YALE
G. C. Adams, '86,	Rusher,	F. W. Wallace, '89.
F. Remington, '87,	"	C. O. Gill, '89.
F. C. Woodman, '88,	"	G. R. Carter, '88.
T. P. Burgess, '87,	"	J. J. Buchanan, '89.
W. A. Brooks, '87, Capt.,	"	W. H. Corbin, '89.
J. W. Wood, '88,	"	G. W. Woodruff, '89.

HARVARD		YALE
A. P. Butler, '88,	Rusher	E. L. Burke, '87.
V. M. Harding, '89,	"	R. N. Corwin, '87, Capt.
A. T. Dudley, '87,	"	
J. B. Fletcher, '87,	Quarter-back,	H. Beecher, '88.
C. A. Porter, '88,	Half-back,	G. A. Watkinson, '89.
R. W. Boyden, '85,	"	S. B. Morison, '91.
A. F. Holden, '88,	"	
J. H. Sears, '89,	"	
H. E. Peabody, '87,	Full-back,	W. T. Bull, '88.

Referee: Walter Camp, '80, Yale. Score: Harvard 4, Yale 29. First Half: Touchdown by S. B. Morison, goal by G. A. Watkinson; touchdown by H. Beecher, goal by G. A. Watkinson; touchdown by H. Beecher, goal by G. A. Watkinson; touchdown by A. F. Holden. Second Half: Touchdown by C. O. Gill, goal by G. A. Watkinson; goal from field by G. A. Watkinson.

First Half: Harvard wins the toss and takes the wind. Corbin dribbles, picks up the ball and runs 20 yards. Watkins, Beecher, and Corbin in three rushes reach the 5-yard line. Morison is sent across for a touchdown on the next play. Watkinson kicks the goal. Holden opens for Harvard with a rush of 20 yards. Wallace, Gill, and Woodruff hold Harvard for downs. Woodruff cannot gain and Watkinson punts. Peabody returns the kick. Gill and Woodruff in a series of rushes force the ball to Harvard's 10-yard line. Beecher is sent across for a touchdown. Watkinson makes the goal. Harvard resumes play with a long kick-off which Bull returns. Holden, Brooks, and Porter hit the line hard, but Yale does not give way. Porter is relieved by Boyden. Peabody punts. Woodruff catches and makes a brilliant run to Harvard's 20-yard line. On the next play Beecher dashes through the line and makes a touchdown. Watkinson again kicks the goal. Boyden opens play for Harvard, but cannot gain. Adams and Holden break Yale's line for long gains and plant the ball on the latter's 10-yard line. Holden again hits the centre, which gives way and he crosses the line for a touchdown. The goal is missed. Play is resumed, but time soon after is called.

Second Half: Watkinson opens for Yale by sending a long kick almost to Harvard's goal. The ball is fumbled. Gill is down and gets it, diving across the line for a touchdown. Watkinson kicks the goal. Harvard kicks off. Yale by strong rushing gets the ball within the 35-yard line, but Harvard holds and Watkinson is forced to try a drop kick for goal, which fails. Harvard kicks out and Yale again works the ball back to the 35-yard line, where Harvard again stiffens and Watkinson misses another try at goal. The series of plays are repeated, but this time, standing on the 40-yard line and well to the side Watkinson kicks a goal from the field. Peabody kicks off for Harvard, punting over Yale's goal-line. Yale, by strong rushing of Wallace, Gill, Woodruff, and Corbin, drives the ball by short gains to Harvard's 15-yard line. As the teams line up time is called and the game is over.

HARVARD VS. YALE

New York, Nov. 24, 1887

HARVARD		YALE
A. J. Cumnock, '91,	Left End,	F. W. Wallace, '89.
J. W. Appleton, '88,	" "	
F. C. Woodman, '88,	Left Tackle,	C. O. Gill, '89.
J. W. Wood, '88, Capt.,	Left Guard,	G. R. Carter, '88.
J. B. Markoe, '89,	Centre,	W. H. Corbin, '89.
P. D. Trafford, '89,	Right Guard,	G. W. Woodruff, '89.
A. P. Butler, '88,	Right Tackle,	S. M. Cross, '88.
W. D. Bancroft, '88,	Right End,	F. C. Pratt, '88.
V. M. Harding, '89,	Quarter-back,	H. Beecher, '88, Capt.
R. W. Boyden, '85,	Left Half,	W. P. Graves, '91.
C. A. Porter, '88,	Right Half,	W. C. Wurtenberg, '89.
J. H. Sears, '89,	Full-back,	W. T. Bull, '88.
J. A. Saxe, '88,	"	

Referee: J. Hancock, '88, Princeton. Umpire: A. T. Baker, '85, Princeton. Score: Harvard 8, Yale 17. First Half: Goal from field by W. T. Bull; touchdown by W. H. Corbin, goal by W. T. Bull.

Second Half: Safety by W. P. Graves, touchdown by C. A. Porter, goal by J. A. Saxe; touchdown by W. C. Wurtenberg, goal by W. T. Bull.

First Half: Yale wins the toss and takes the ball. Corbin dribbles, runs, and passes to Beecher. Yale cannot gain and Bull punts. Porter and Sears by hard rushing work the ball back to midfield. Yale gets the ball on a foul. Graves gets through for a gain of 25 yards. Harvard holds and gets the ball on downs. Porter rounds the end for 25 yards; Boyden adds 10 more through the line. The ball is fumbled and Wallace gets it. Beecher gets through for 10 yards. Harvard stops the next two rushes and Bull punts. Boyden catches and runs, passing the ball to Sears as he is tackled, Sears making 25 yards. A long exchange of punts mixed with short gains ensues. The ball is in midfield in Yale's possession. Corbin suddenly dribbles the ball a few inches, picks it up and dodges through the Harvard line for 25 yards. Beecher follows it up with a gain of 20 more, placing the ball on the 15-yard line. Harvard stops the attack and Bull, dropping back to the 25-yard line, kicks a goal from the field. Harvard kicks off and Bull returns. Beecher and Gill in two great runs bring the ball to Harvard's 25-yard line. Corbin is unguarded and suddenly putting the ball in play by a short dribble he springs through the Harvard line for a touchdown. Bull kicks a difficult goal. Harvard kicks off and after some unimportant scrimmaging gets the ball. Boyden, Trafford, and Sears beat Yale down to the 15-yard line. Porter makes 2; Sears adds 2 more. An off-side penalty gives Harvard 5 more and Sears runs through the centre for a touchdown. This does not count, as time has expired during the play.

Second Half: Harvard opens the second half by a dribble and run by Harding, gaining 10 yards. Sears and Porter by good runs work the ball to Yale's 15-yard line. Yale tackles sharply and gets the ball on downs. Bull punts 50 yards. Boyden and Porter run the ball back again in four dashes. Cumnock is hurt and goes off, Appleton taking his place. Yale breaks through and throws the Crimson backs for a loss, getting the ball on the fourth down. Bull drops back for a punt. The ball is kicked low, striking Woodman in the chest and bounding behind the Yale line, where Graves falls on it for a safety. Corbin dribbles and passes to Gill, who makes 5 yards. Kicks are exchanged. Wurtenberg, Woodruff, and Graves make good gains, but Bull is finally forced to punt. Sears leaves and Saxe takes his place. Kicks are exchanged and Harvard gets the ball on a fumble on Yale's 10-yard line. Porter hits the line for no gain. The ball again is given to Porter, and the latter, leaping through the line, dodges Yale's backs and by a marvellous burst of speed runs the remaining length of the field for a touchdown. Saxe kicks a difficult goal. Yale kicks off by dribbling and commences a series of terrific rushes. Gill, Beecher, Woodruff, and Graves hit the Harvard line in rapid succession, carrying the ball to the Crimson's 20-yard line. Harvard here stops the advance by holding Yale for 4 downs. Saxe immediately punts. Yale once more starts in motion its great attack and fights the ball to Harvard's 5-yard line. Harvard makes a great rally and holds 4 downs. Saxe punts. The two teams line up on Harvard's 45-yard line. The ball is passed to Bull, who again passes to Wurtenberg and the latter runs 35 yards. Time is nearly up. A plunge at the line yields no gain. The game almost has ended, when the ball is passed to Wurtenberg. By brilliant dodges he runs 35 yards and touches down at the corner of the field. Bull, standing on the 35-yard line at the extreme side of the field, kicks the ball squarely between the posts. Time soon after is called.

1888. No game.

HARVARD VS. YALE
Springfield, Nov. 23, 1889

HARVARD		YALE
A. J. Cumnock, '91, Capt.,	Left End,	A. A. Stagg, '88.
J. D. Upton, '93,	Left Tackle,	C. O. Gill, '89, Capt.
J. S. Cranston, '92,	Left Guard,	W. W. Heffelfinger, '91.
B. T. Tilton, '90,	Centre,	B. Hanson, '90.
	"	H. T. Ferris, '91.
P. D. Trafford, '89,	Right Guard,	A. B. Newell, '90.
	" "	L. Heyworth, '90.
H. H. Stickney, '93,	Right Tackle,	W. C. Rhodes, '91.
J. A. Blanchard, '91,	" "	
H. Hutchinson, '93,	Right End,	J. A. Hartwell, '89.
F. W. Hallowell, '93,	" "	
D. S. Dean, '91,	Quarter-back,	W. C. Wurtenberg, '89.
J. P. Lee, '91,	Left Half,	Lee McClung, '92.
J. A. Saxe, '88,	Right Half,	S. B. Morison, '91.
B. W. Trafford, '93,	Full-back,	H. McBride, '90.

Referee: C. A. Porter, '88, Harvard. Umpire: E. C. Peace, '83, Princeton. Score: Harvard 0, Yale 6. First Half: Touchdown and goal by Lee McClung.

First Half: Harvard wins the toss and takes the wind. Yale opens with the V, sending Gill for a gain of 15 yards. Harvard stops the next two rushes without gain and Mc-Bride punts. Trafford returns and McBride again sends the ball down to Harvard. Stickney breaks through tackle for 20 yards. Lee doubles the end for 10 more. Yale stiffens and throws back Saxe and Trafford for a loss and the latter punts. McBride returns the kick and Harvard fumbles. Stagg gets the ball. McClung bucks the line for 8, Wurtenberg for 5, and Morison for 3. Cumnock drops McClung for a loss and McBride punts. Trafford returns the ball to Yale's 10-yard line, the kick going over the heads of the Yale backs. Newell goes off and Heyworth takes his place. The ball changes sides several times at this point on fumbles. Hanson goes off and Ferris is substituted. Trafford kicks and Yale fumbles, Cumnock getting

the ball at midfield. Three times the Crimson backs hit
the line, but Gill and Rhodes throw them back. Trafford
punts, but Heffelfinger blocks the kick. McClung makes
18 yards through centre. Stickney and Upton break up the
next two plays and McBride punts. Trafford sends it back
and Harvard holds for downs. Lee rounds the end for
10 and adds 10 more through the line. Stickney gets through
tackle for 10 and Trafford in two rushes gains 15. Hartwell
stops a rush at him for a loss and Stagg tackles behind the
line. Kicks are exchanged and the play is very rapid.
Stickney leaves and Blanchard takes his place. Gill gets
through the line for 20 yards and McClung adds 5 more.
Heffelfinger swings round the end for 5 and McClung plants
the ball on the 25-yard line. Cranston and Hutchinson
stop the next three plays and Harvard gets the ball on downs.
Yale immediately gets the ball for holding. McClung
and Morison bend back the line for 2 yards each. Mc-
Clung splits the centre in two for 15, and on the next play
is sent over the line on a blue mountain of jerseys for a
touchdown. A moment later he kicks the goal.

Second Half: In the intermission Harvard substitutes
Hallowell for Hutchinson. Harvard opens with the V,
sending Lee for a gain of 15 yards. Upton and Lee then
make 5 each on line plays. Lee adds 8 more around the
end. Yale holds and Trafford punts. Yale fumbles and
Cumnock gets the ball on Yale's 25-yard line. Harvard
also fumbles on the first play and Heyworth gets the ball
for Yale. McBride kicks. The ends are down and there
is no run back. Lee gets around the end for 15 yards.
Hartwell and Stagg throw Harvard for a loss and Trafford
tries a drop kick. The goal is missed and Yale touches
back. Yale kicks out. Harvard cannot gain and punts.
Yale returns and with one or two rushes kicks again are
exchanged. McClung tries for a goal from the 45-yard

line, but cannot make it. Hard scrimmaging, with punts
and returns, takes place for nearly twenty minutes on Harvard's 25-yard line, but Harvard's ends prevent Yale from
advancing beyond that mark. Trafford finally punts.
McClung gets around the end for a long run, bringing the
ball to Harvard's 5-yard line, where time is called.

HARVARD vs. YALE

Springfield, Nov. 22, 1890

HARVARD		YALE
A. J. Cumnock, '91, Capt.,	Left End,	J. A. Hartwell, '89.
J. D. Upton, '93,	Left Tackle,	A. H. Wallis, '93.
J. R. Finlay, '91,	Left Guard,	W. W. Heffelfinger, '91.
J. S. Cranston, '92,	Centre,	W. M. Lewis, '91.
P. D. Trafford, '89,	Right Guard,	S. N. Morison, '91.
M. Newell, '94,	Right Tackle,	W. C. Rhodes, '91, Capt.
F. W. Hallowell, '93,	Right End,	B. L. Crosby, '92.
D. S. Dean, '91,	Quarter-back,	F. E. Barbour, '92.
J. Corbett, '94,	Left Half,	Lee McClung, '92.
E. J. Lake, '92,	Right Half,	H. L. Williams, '91.
J. P. Lee, '91,	" "	L. T. Bliss, '93.
B. W. Trafford, '93,	Full-back,	S. B. Morison, '91.

Referee: W. M. Irvine, '88, Princeton. Umpire: W. J. George, '89,
Princeton. Score: Harvard 12, Yale 6. Second Half: Touchdown
by J. P. Lee, goal by B. W. Trafford; touchdown by D. S. Dean, goal
by B. W. Trafford; touchdown and goal by Lee McClung.

First Half: Yale wins the toss and chooses the south goal.
Harvard opens with the V and gains 5 yards. Corbett and
Lake each gain 10 yards more. Harvard fumbles and
Hartwell gets the ball. B. Morison goes around the end,
Heffelfinger interfering, and 40 yards are covered before
Lake brings him down. Cumnock drops McClung for no
gain. Williams carries the ball three times in succession,
covering 20 yards. Yale fumbles, but recovers the ball.
Morison punts and Trafford catches. Harvard tries the
line three times, but is piled up underneath a mountain of
blue jerseys for no gain. Trafford punts and McClung

catches on the 20-yard line. Williams and Morison each
hit the line for 5 yards and then Yale fumbles. Corbett
makes 10 yards around the end. Lake tries the line for
no gain and Trafford punts. McClung catches and runs
across the field, but cannot gain, Cumnock tackling hard.
Harvard gets the ball on downs. McClung goes around
the end and passes the entire team except Trafford, covering
35 yards, but Trafford brings him down. Williams makes
4, 5, and then loses 6, Cranston and Cumnock making the
tackles. Harvard gets the ball on downs. Lake hits centre
for 3, Corbett makes 3, and Trafford punts. Morison
returns the kick. Corbett makes 25 yards through Yale's
centre, but the ball is brought back. McClung is hurt, but
resumes playing. Harvard fumbles and Williams gets the
ball. Williams makes 4 and then Harvard holds for downs.
Lake and Corbett cannot gain and Trafford punts. Mc-
Clung catches, but Cumnock downs him in his tracks.
Rhodes tries a run from position, but Newell stops him.
Williams rounds the end for 20 yards. McClung, with a
strong wind, tries for a field goal at 50 yards, but fails. Corbett, Upton interfering, runs the ball back 20 yards. They
both go down underneath a mass near the side line and
Upton comes out with his jersey torn to ribbons. Harvard
punts and Yale returns, but the latter's kick is high and
Corbett catches. Lake and Corbett split the tackle for 6
yards, Crosby bringing them down. Harvard punts and
McClung makes a fair catch and tries for a field goal, but
the kick is short, both teams piling up 6 feet high on the
ball as the whistle blows for the half.

Second Half: Yale opens the second half with a V and
makes 10 yards. Williams is injured and Bliss takes his
place, a long wrangle ensuing between the captains and doctors over Yale's right to make the substitution. Trafford
and Morison now exchange kicks, Corbett catching and

running forward for 12 yards. Harvard cannot gain and
Yale hits the centre for 3 downs without making an inch.
Harvard gets the ball, and on the first play Corbett goes
through for 40 yards; McClung tackles hard and both are
laid out, but quickly recover. The ball is taken back for
an off-side play. McClung opens up the Harvard centre
for 20 yards. McClung rounds the end, with Heffelfinger interfering, and Cumnock tackles both and brings them down.
Lake downs Bliss in his tracks for a loss. McClung tries a
difficult drop kick, but fails. Lake rounds the end for 20
yards. Corbett adds 3 more and then Trafford punts.
Yale fumbles, and Newell, on the run, picks up the ball and
races across the line for a touchdown, but the ball is brought
back on a foul. McClung breaks through Harvard's centre
for 35 yards. Harvard stiffens and gets the ball on downs.
Trafford punts. Yale catches and after one try at the line,
Bliss making 3 yards, returns the kick, Hartwell downing
Corbett without a gain. Lake now in a great burst of speed
circles the end for 25 yards, Barbour tackling so sharply
that both are laid out. Lake is compelled to retire, Lee
taking his place, but Barbour resumes. Yale tightens up
and gets the ball. McClung splits the tackle for 2 yards.
Yale fumbles and Dean gets the ball. Corbett makes 2
yards through centre, but here is stopped. Trafford punts.
Wallis and Bliss hit the line for 4 yards each. On the next
play Yale fumbles. Lee picks up the ball, the Yale men are
on him, but wriggling loose he sprints at great speed toward the side-line, then turning sharply down the field he
races and dodges through the Yale team for 40 yards, making a touchdown. Trafford kicks the goal. Yale starts
play with the V, making 11 yards. On the line-up the ball
is fumbled. Dean gets it. Hartwell leaps for him, but
falls short. Dean springs away, and with the Yale team
following him he outruns his pursuers except Hartwell, who

has regained his feet and again leaps for Dean just as he
dives headlong between the posts for a touchdown. Trafford again kicks the goal. Yale resumes with the V,
ploughing ahead for 10 yards. Wallis and Rhodes run
from position and make steady gains; McClung and Bliss
alternate likewise, breaking the line for yardage. Corbett
is playing strong, but Harvard seems to be weakening.
Yale is playing fiercely now. Without a stop the ball travels
by slow gains to Harvard's 10-yard line. The moon has
risen and twilight is deepening. The lines tighten and
quiver from end to end, the ball is snapped to McClung
and with a crash he throws himself against the Harvard
centre, bursting it in two and crossing the line for a touchdown. The goal is made. Harvard kicks off. Yale resumes its desperate, smashing attack, but with the ball
travelling rapidly down the field the whistle sounds and
this great game is over.

HARVARD vs. YALE
Springfield, Nov. 21, 1891

HARVARD		YALE
R. W. Emmons, '95,	Left End,	F. A. Hinkey, '95.
B. G. Waters, '94,	Left Tackle,	W. C. Winter, '93.
S. Dexter, '93,	Left Guard,	W. W. Heffelfinger, '91.
F. R. Bangs, '91,	Centre,	G. F. Sanford, '95.
W. C. Mackie, '94,	Right Guard,	S. N. Morison, '92.
M. Newell, '94,	Right Tackle,	A. H. Wallis, '93.
F. W. Hallowell, '93,	Right End,	J. A. Hartwell, '89.
W. B. Gage, '94,	Quarter-back,	F. E. Barbour, '92.
E. J. Lake, '92,	Left Half,	Lee McClung, '92, Capt.
J. Corbett, '94,	Right Half,	L. T. Bliss, '93.
B. W. Trafford, '93, Capt.,	Full-back,	V. C. McCormick, '93.

Referee: Alex. Moffat, '84, Princeton. Umpire: S. V. Coffin, '89,
Wesleyan. Score: Harvard 0, Yale 10. First Half: Touchdown by
S. N. Morison. Second Half: Touchdown by L. T. Bliss, goal by
V. C. McCormick.

First Half: Yale wins the toss and takes the ball. Sanford makes 7 in the V. Bliss goes through centre for 2 more.
McClung rounds the end and runs to the 10-yard line aided
by the magnificent interference of Heffelfinger and Bliss.
Heffelfinger hits the line for no gain. McCormick gets to
the 5-yard line through centre and again taking the ball he
makes 4 more around the end. Morison is pushed through
tackle for the touchdown. The goal fails. Lake makes
9 in the V, Corbett adds 2, Lake 6, and Hinkey makes a
tackle behind the line, forcing Trafford to punt. McClung
gets a fair catch for interference by the Harvard ends. The
V is tried, but Winter makes no gain. McClung punts and
Harvard returns the kick. Sanford picks up a fumble and
runs around the end for 13 yards. McClung breaks the
centre for 15. Morison, Winter, and Bliss add 5 each.
Emmons, Waters, and Newell hold for downs and get the
ball. Hartwell throws the Harvard backs for a loss and
Trafford punts to Yale's 25-yard line. The ball is fumbled
and Hallowell gets it. Hinkey stops Lake and Hartwell
holds Corbett for no gains. Heffelfinger stops an attack
on centre and Yale gets the ball. McClung doubles the
end for 20. Bliss and Morison in two plunges add 10. The
ball goes to Harvard for holding in the line. Bliss tackles
Corbett for no gain. Trafford punts to McCormick.
McClung bucks the centre for a great run of 30 yards. The
next 3 downs fail to gain and McCormick kicks. Harvard tries the Yale line, but cannot get through and punts.
McClung catches, standing close to the side line. Heffelfinger interferes and McClung, running close to the line,
covers 34 yards before being thrown by Trafford. Harvard holds for downs and time is called.

Second Half: Lake makes 5 yards in the V. Bliss throws
Corbett behind the line and Trafford punts. Yale cannot make an inch and McCormick punts. Harvard fumbles

and Wallis gets the ball on the 45-yard line. Heffelfinger hits the centre for 2. Bliss rounds the end for 10. McClung doubles the other end for 15 more. Dexter and Bangs tackle for a loss and Yale punts. Harvard can make no impression on the Yale line and punts. Yale, after trying to gain without success, also kicks. The ball goes out of bounds at Harvard's 25-yard line. The teams line up. Gage passes the ball to Corbett, who starts for the end. Hinkey tackles him fiercely and the ball rolls upon the ground. Trafford jumps for it, but McCormick blocks him. Bliss picks up the ball and leaps across the four remaining lines for a touchdown. McCormick kicks the goal. Harvard resumes play desperately. Lake and Corbett in rapid plunges carry the ball to Yale's 10-yard line. Unable to advance farther Trafford tries a drop, but misses. Yale punts out and Harvard rushes the ball within kicking distance. Trafford again tries for a field goal, but Hinkey and Heffelfinger block the kick. Hallowell recovers the ball. Time is then called.

HARVARD VS. YALE

Springfield, Nov. 19, 1892

HARVARD		YALE
R. W. Emmons, '95,	Left End,	F. A. Hinkey, '95.
F. Mason, '92,	" "	
J. D. Upton, '93,	Left Tackle,	W. C. Winter, '93.
L. T. Shea, '96,	" "	
B. G. Waters, '94,	Left Guard,	J. A. McCrea, '95.
W. H. Lewis, '95,	Centre,	P. T. Stillman, '95.
W. C. Mackie, '94,	Right Guard,	W. O. Hickok, '95.
M. Newell, '94,	Right Tackle,	A. H. Wallis, '93.
F. W. Hallowell, '93,	Right End,	J. C. Greenway, '95.
B. W. Trafford, '93, Capt.,	Quarter-back,	V. C. McCormick, '93, Capt.
G. A. Gray, '94,	Left Half,	L. T. Bliss, '93.
E. J. Lake, '92,	Right Half,	C. D. Bliss, '93.
C. Brewer, '96,	Full-back,	F. S. Butterworth, '95.

Referee: Alex. Moffat, '84, Princeton. Umpire: S. V. Coffin, '89, Wesleyan. Score: Harvard 0, Yale 6. Second Half: Touchdown by C. D. Bliss, goal by F. S. Butterworth.

First Half: Yale wins the toss and takes the ball. Mc-
Cormick makes 15 yards on the V. Harvard holds and
Yale punts. Harvard at once adopts kicking tactics.
Yale makes several fumbles and Emmons falls on the ball
behind Yale's goal line, but interference is awarded and the
ball brought out and given to Yale. Yale now starts a heavy
attack on the Harvard line. The two Blisses and Butterworth, relieved by Wallis and Winter, buck right and left.
Emmons, Upton, and Newell prevent any large gains, but
the ball travels continually down to Harvard's 3-yard line,
where time is called.

Second Half: Harvard opens the second half with a new
and startling formation. Trafford stands 10 yards back
from midfield with the ball. The Harvard team divides into
two parts, each part drawing back 20 yards and taking a
position at opposite sides of the field near the side lines.
Trafford signals and the Harvard men come forward rapidly, converging toward Trafford. As they reach him he
touches the ball in play and disappears into the mass, which
has now formed into a wedge. This formation, the famous
"flying wedge," goes crashing into the Yale men with a
tremendous impact, taking the ball to the 25-yard line.
Sensation runs through the stands at the novel play, which
is the most original and beautiful ever seen upon a football
field. Yale holds and Brewer punts. Butterworth attempts
to return, but the kick is blocked and Harvard gets the ball.
Hinkey, McCrea, and Hickok stop Harvard on the 7-yard
line and get the ball. The Yale backs carry the ball to the
centre of the field, but lose it here on a fumble. Upton
makes 20 yards. Yale holds and Brewer punts out of
bounds. Emmons and Upton retire and Shea and Mason
come on. An exchange of kicks follows and L. Bliss gets
around the end for 35 yards. Yale now starts a series of
quick plays through the line, the two Blisses and Butterworth carrying the ball. The gains are short but consecu-

THE ORIGINAL FLYING WEDGE.

Harvard's famous formation about to attack Yale. Springfield, Nov. 19, 1892.

tive. Gradually Harvard is being beaten back and weakening. The ball is on the 2-yard line. The lines contract at centre. C. D. Bliss takes the ball and, lifted upon a wave of blue jerseys, is carried over the centre and across the line for a touchdown. Butterworth kicks the goal. In the remaining minutes of play Harvard blocks Butterworth's punt and gets the ball on the 15-yard line. Three downs are tried for no gain. Winter stops Trafford's try for a goal from the field and time is called.

HARVARD VS. YALE

Springfield, Nov. 25, 1893

HARVARD		YALE
R. W. Emmons, '95,	Left End,	F. A. Hinkey, '95, Capt.
T. J. Mannahan, '96,	Left Tackle,	F. T. Murphy, '97.
R. Acton, '94,	Left Guard,	J. A. McCrea, '95.
W. H. Lewis, '95,	Centre,	P. T. Stillman, '95.
W. C. Mackie, '94,	Right Guard,	W. O. Hickok, '95.
M. Newell, '94,	Right Tackle,	A. McC. Beard, '95.
R. H. Stevenson, '97,	Right End,	J. C. Greenway, '95.
A. M. Beale, '97,	Quarter-back,	G. T. Adee, '95.
E. N. Wrightington, '97,	Left Half,	S. B. Thorne, '96.
B. G. Waters, '94, Capt.,	Right Half,	R. Armstrong, '95.
J. W. Dunlop, '97,	" "	
C. Brewer, '96,	Full-back,	F. S. Butterworth, '95.

Referee: C. H. Schoff, '93, Pennsylvania. Umpire: Alex. Moffat, '84, Princeton. Score: Harvard 0, Yale 6. Second Half: Touchdown by F. S. Butterworth, goal by W. O. Hickok.

First Half: Yale wins the toss and takes the north goal. Harvard makes 25 yards with the flying wedge. Waters and Wrightington in two plays through the line make 5 yards. Greenway and Hinkey hold the Harvard backs for downs and Yale gets the ball. Butterworth punts. Harvard now discloses a series of intricate formations and plays evolved by Lorin F. Deland, the inventor of the flying wedge. The Yale ends are alert, however, and nip the Harvard backs for no gain. Brewer punts. Butterworth

returns to Harvard's 10-yard line.   Brewer sends it back on
the second down.   Thorne rounds the end for 10.   On the
next play the ball is fumbled and Emmons gets it.   Brewer
punts.   Yale fumbles and Stevenson falls on the ball.   Newell
strikes the opposite tackle for 3.   Waters, Dunlop, and
Brewer in the new Deland mass play, an oval formation
called a "turtle-back," work the ball to Yale's 35-yard line.
Murphy, McCrea, and Hickok hold for downs and Yale
gets the ball.   Butterworth lifts the leather 70 yards down
the field.   On the line-up Brewer punts, but the kick is high
and Yale gets the ball on Harvard's 25-yard line.   Three
plunges into the line do not yield a first down and it is
Harvard's ball.   Harvard uses a flying interference play for
consecutive gains of 40 yards, which Hinkey and Murphy
finally check by sharp tackling.   Yale uses a revolving
wedge that gains 5 yards and then loses 3.   Butterworth
tries for a long field goal, but cannot make it.   Harvard
punts out and time is called for the half.

Second Half: Yale opens with the flying wedge, making
10 yards.   Hinkey nets 6 around the end and Thorne duplicates the run around the other end.   By a series of mass
plays Thorne, Armstrong, and Butterworth, alternating with
the ball, advance by gains of 6, 6, 3, 15, and 7 yards to the
2-line mark, where Butterworth is rammed across the line
for a touchdown.   Hickok kicks the goal.   Harvard resumes
play with the flying wedge and makes 15 yards.   Waters,
Newell, and Brewer are sent into the line on flying plays
for steady gains to the 35-yard line, where Hinkey and
Greenway break them up and get the ball.   Yale punts
and Brewer returns.   Thorne catches and runs back the
kick 35 yards.   Unable to gain farther, Butterworth punts.
Harvard resumes its flying plays, in which the interference
starts before the ball is in play.   Wrightington skirts the
end for 15, Brewer doubles the other for 15.   Yale stops the

advance on their 35-yard line and Thorne and Butterworth in four rushes take the ball back to centre. Waters goes off and Dunlop takes his place. Harvard attempts a double pass, but McCrea gets it. Kicks are exchanged. Thorne and Butterworth by great work hammer the ball to Harvard's 5-yard line, Lewis, Mackie, and Newell hold for downs. Brewer from behind the line punts to Butterworth at 40. Armstrong and Thorne rush it back to Harvard's 15-yard line, where it goes to Harvard on fourth down. Brewer punts to Yale's 45-yard line and time is called.

HARVARD VS. YALE
Springfield, Nov. 24, 1894

HARVARD		YALE
N. W. Cabot, '98,	Left End,	F. A. Hinkey, '95, Capt.
	" "	L. M. Bass, '97.
R. H. Hallowell, '96,	Left Tackle,	A. McC. Beard, '95.
S. W. Wheeler, '98,	" "	
W. C. Mackie, '94,	Left Guard,	J. A. McCrea, '95.
F. G. Shaw, '97,	Centre,	P. T. Stillman, '95.
J. E. N. Shaw, '98,	Right Guard,	W. O. Hickok, '95.
B. G. Waters, '94,	Right Tackle,	F. T. Murphy, '97.
	" "	C. Chadwick, '97.
A. H. Brewer, '96,	Right End,	L. Hinkey, '97.
R. D. Wrenn, '95, Capt.,	Quarter-back,	G. T. Adee, '95.
E. N. Wrightington, '97,	Left Half,	S. B. Thorne, '96.
P. W. Whittemore, '95,	" "	
C. Brewer, '96,	Right Half,	A. N. Jerrems, '96.
J. J. Hayes, '96,	" "	R. Armstrong, '95.
M. G. Gonterman, '96,	" "	
J. C. Fairchild, '96,	Full-back,	F. S. Butterworth, '95.
	" "	H. W. Letton, '97.

Referee: D. Bovaird, '89, Princeton. Umpire: Alex. Moffat, '84, Princeton. Linesman: H. L. Pratt, '95, Amherst. Score: Harvard 4, Yale 12. First Half: Touchdown by P. T. Stillman, goal by W. O. Hickok; touchdown by J. J. Hayes; touchdown by S. B. Thorne, goal by W. O. Hickok.

First Half: Harvard wins the toss and takes the south goal. Hickok kicks off to Brewer and the latter runs the ball back 20 yards, being tackled by Beard. Stillman blocks Wrightington's kick. The ball rolls across Harvard's goal-line. Stillman falls on it for a touchdown. Hickok kicks the goal. On the kick-off Harvard dribbles the ball to the right and Brewer falls on it. Wrightington and Brewer hit the centre for 6 yards. Wrightington rounds the end for 10 yards, but Yale gets the ball for off-side play. Harvard regains it immediately for holding. The ball changes sides several times for downs. Fairchild tries for a field goal, but the ball hits the cross-bar. Thorne punts. C. Brewer is hurt and Hayes takes his place. Harvard starts a lively attack on Yale's line, Wrightington, Hayes, and Fairchild breaking through for consecutive gains. Hayes gets around the end for 17 yards and a touchdown. The punt-out is fumbled. The ball is kicked off and Wrightington is injured. Whittemore takes his place. Thorne misses a field goal. Hayes catches the ball on the 5-yard line. Yale blocks the kick and gets the ball. On the first play Thorne is pushed over for the touchdown. Hickok kicks the goal.

Second Half: Chadwick takes the place of Murphy. Armstrong is substituted for Jerrems and Letton for Butterworth. Fairchild kicks off. The playing during this half is fierce and vigorous. Smash after smash is made against the opposing lines, but neither side can score. Thorne tries for a field goal, but misses. Hallowell is injured and Wheeler takes his place. Harvard drives the ball down to the 27-yard line. The signal is given for a punt. The whistle sounds, the ball is passed back to Fairchild, who drops a goal from the field. Harvard claims the goal, but Bovaird rules that time was called. The game closes.

1895. No game.

1896. No game.

HARVARD VS. YALE
Cambridge, Nov. 13, 1897

HARVARD		YALE
N. W. Cabot, '98, Capt.,	Left End,	J. J. Hazen, '98.
C. O. Swain, '00,	Left Tackle,	J. O. Rodgers, '98, Capt.
S. W. Wheeler, '98,	" "	
G. W. Bouvé, '98,	Left Guard,	C. Chadwick, '97.
A. E. Doucette, '95,	Centre,	G. L. Cadwalader, '01.
H. B. Haskell, '99,	Right Guard,	F. G. Brown, '01.
J. E. N. Shaw, '98,	" "	
M. Donald, '99,	Right Tackle,	B. C. Chamberlin, '97.
S. F. Mills, '99,	" "	
J. E. Moulton, '98,	Right End,	J. A. Hall, '97.
W. L. Garrison, '97,	Quarter-back,	C. A. H. De Saulles, '99.
B. H. Dibblee, '99,	Left Half,	A. F. Corwin, '99.
L. Warren, '00,	Right Half,	H. F. Benjamin, '99.
G. S. Parker, '00,	" "	
P. D. Haughton, '99,	Full-back,	M. L. McBride, '00.

Referee: M. McClung, '94, Lehigh.   Umpire: P. J. Dashiell, Navy.
Score: Harvard 0, Yale 0.

NOTE.—See amended rule of scoring, session Feb. 19, 1897, Appendix.

First Half: Yale wins the toss and takes the west goal. Haughton kicks off to Hazen on the 25-yard line. Corwin makes 5. Cabot and Moulton tackle behind the line and Chamberlin punts to Harvard's 20-yard line. Dibblee rounds the end for 17. Harvard sends a guards-back formation into the line twice, and not making first down Haughton punts. Corwin makes 1, Benjamin adds another, and Chamberlin lifts a kick into Harvard's goal. Haughton punts out from the 25-yard line. Yale fumbles and Haskell gets the ball. Warren splits the line for 5 and immediately repeats the play for 5 more. Cabot gets through for 4, and then Rodgers and Brown throw Harvard for a loss and Yale gets the ball on downs. McBride immediately punts. Harvard lines up and Warren rounds the end for 12. Cabot plunges through centre for 7, but Yale gets the ball on a penalty. McBride drops back to punt, but Haskell blocks the kick. Harvard hits the line hard, but Hall, Chamberlin, and Chadwick stop the Crimson backs for no gain and Yale gets the ball. McBride falls back to kick on the first down. The kick again is blocked. Warren gets around the end for 12, Cabot doubles the other end for 7, but the ball goes to Yale on a foul. McBride punts and Haughton returns. Yale cannot gain. For the third time Harvard blocks the kick and gets the ball. Two plunges into the line fail to gain and Haughton kicks to De Saulles. Several scrimmages ensue without gain. McBride kicks to Haughton, who returns. Yale starts a series of hard rushes. Corwin makes 4 through tackle. Benjamin breaks the centre for 4. Corwin rounds the end for 4. Chamberlin plunges into the line for 6. McBride adds 5 and Corwin 5. The ball is now on Harvard's 15-yard line. Cadwalader snaps the ball, but there is a mistake in the signals and Swain falls on the ball for Harvard. Harvard puts it down for a scrimmage. Dibblee, Haughton, and Parker buck the line for good gains and the ball advances back to centre. Here kicks are exchanged and time is called, with the ball in Harvard's possession on the 45-yard line.

Second Half: Yale kicks off and Haughton returns. Yale kicks out of bounds at Harvard's 50-yard mark. Dibblee and Parker plunge into the line for 4 yards. Parker tries the end and in a magnificent dash takes the ball to Yale's 5-yard line, where he is stopped by Chamberlin. Rodgers and Brown throw Dibblee and Cabot for a loss of 5 yards. Haughton tries to make it up, but is tackled by Hazen and Yale gets the ball on fourth down. McBride from behind the line punts out to the 30-yard line. Harvard makes a desperate effort to score, but cannot make the first down. Yale prepares to punt, but the kick is

partly blocked. Yale recovers it. A long series of kicks
are exchanged in which Yale gains. De Saulles finally
catches on his 30-yard line and runs back to centre. Yale
cannot gain and punts. Haughton runs back the kick and
punts. McBride, on the line-up, tries to punt, but the kick
is blocked, De Saulles recovering. Yale cannot gain and
drops back to kick, but time is called.

HARVARD VS. YALE

New Haven, Nov. 19, 1898

HARVARD		YALE
F. D. Cochrane, '99,	Left End,	G. W. Hubbell, '01.
J. W. Farley, '99,	" "	
M. Donald, '99,	Left Tackle,	G. S. Stillman, '01.
W. D. Eaton, '02,	" "	
W. A. Boal, '00,	Left Guard,	F. G. Brown, '01.
P. M. Jaffray, '99,	" "	
F. L. Burnett, '02,	Centre,	G. B. Cutten, '99.
W. A. M. Burden, '00,	Right Guard,	E. E. Marshall, '99.
P. D. Haughton, '99,	Right Tackle,	B. C. Chamberlin, '97, Capt.
J. W. Hallowell, '01,	Right End,	E. M. Eddy, '99.
	" "	L. M. Thomas, '01.
C. D. Daly, '01,	Quarter-back,	M. U. Ely, '98.
B. H. Dibblee, '99, Capt.,	Left Half,	C. T. Dudley, '00.
	" "	E. M. Eddy, '99.
L. Warren, '00,	Right Half,	A. H. Durston, '99.
W. T. Reid, '01,	Full-back,	R. Townshend, '00.
	" "	M. L. McBride, '00.

Referee: M. McClung, '94, Lehigh. Umpire: P. J. Dashiell, Navy.
Linesmen: F. B. Talbot, '00, Harvard; D. R. Francis, '00, Yale.
Score: Harvard 17, Yale 0. First Half: Touchdown by W. T. Reid;
touchdown by B. H. Dibblee, goal by P. D. Haughton. Second Half:
Touchdown by W. T. Reid, goal by P. D. Haughton.

First Half: Yale wins the toss and takes the ball. Chamberlin kicks off and Reid returns to midfield. Yale tries a
buck at the line, but cannot gain. The backs drop back
for a punt, but a line play is sent instead, gaining 3 yards.
Harvard stops the next play and gets the ball. On the first

down a Crimson player is off side and the ball goes back to
Yale. Two cracks against the line fail to yield an inch and
Townshend punts to Daly, who instantly sends the ball back
to Yale's 45-yard line. Two trials at the line by Yale net
3 yards and Townshend again lifts the leather to Harvard's
35-yard line. Haughton drops back for a punt and sends the
ball over Yale's goal-line. It is brought out to the 25-yard
line. Townshend kicks it to Harvard's 45-yard line, but
Daly catches and runs it to midfield. Dibblee and Reid hit
the line right and left for 10 yards. Dibblee gets through
tackle for 5 more. Reid and Warren pierce the centre
for 7. Harvard now has the ball on Yale's 45-yard line.
Dibblee advances it through centre 20 yards. He takes it
around the end for 10 more. Reid splits the tackle for 5.
The Crimson team masses toward centre and shoves Yale
back for 5 yards. Reid tries for the last 5, but is stopped.
He again hits the line and goes over at the extreme corner
of the field for a touchdown. The ball is punted out and
kicked from placement, but it strikes the goal-post. Chamberlin kicks off for Yale and Haughton returns the ball to
midfield. Durston makes a yard, but Yale is forced to kick.
Dibblee runs the ball back 10 yards. Haughton punts to
Ely, who brings the ball back to centre. Yale cannot gain
and Chamberlin punts. Off-side play is given and Harvard gets the ball. The ball changes sides without substantial gains. Harvard gets the ball on a foul on Yale's
20-yard line. Reid plunges through centre and plants the
ball on the 12-yard line. Townshend is hurt and McBride
goes to full-back. Reid adds 3 more through the line, and
Dibblee, dashing between guard and tackle, covers the remaining distance and touches down. Haughton kicks the
goal. Yale kicks off and Harvard returns. The ball is
fumbled and Harvard gets it. On the first down Dibblee
gets around Yale's end for 40 yards, placing the ball on the

10-yard line. Yale stops the Crimson for downs without a
gain and gets the ball. McBride punts to the 40-yard line,
where Daly heels for a fair catch. Haughton tries a place
kick, but misses. McBride kicks out to midfield and Daly
returns to Yale's 5-yard line, where the ball is fumbled
and rolls over the line, being touched down by Ely. Harvard claims a safety, but it is not allowed. The ball is
kicked out and Dibblee runs it back 10 yards. Harvard
cannot gain and Yale gets the ball, punting on the first
down to Harvard's 20-yard line. Dibblee returns the punt
to midfield and time is called for the half.

Second Half: Haughton kicks off to McBride. On the
first line-up Yale returns. Harvard puts the ball down for
a scrimmage at midfield. Dibblee rounds the end for 5 and
Reid duplicates the play on the opposite side for 5 more.
An attempt to go through centre results in a fumble and
Yale takes the ball on the 40-yard line. By a mass play on
tackle the Blue sends Durston, Stillman, and McBride for
short but steady gains for a total of 60 yards. Harvard
now holds for downs and Reid punts back to midfield.
An exchange of kicks follows, resulting in Yale punting
out of bounds through a high punt being blown back by
the wind, sending the ball out at the 10-yard line. Dibblee
circles the end for 4 yards. Daly tries to round the opposite
side, but Chamberlin throws him for a loss. Yale takes
the ball on downs and Chamberlin punts. Haughton
returns the kick and Yale fumbles on the 15-yard line.
Warren goes through centre for 4. Dibblee makes 3 and
Warren gains 8 more. Reid hits the line and bursts through
for a touchdown. Haughton kicks the goal. Yale kicks
off and Harvard returns. For a long time neither team is
able to make a substantial advance, the play becoming a
series of unsuccessful line plunges followed by punts. Yale
sends a long pass to the side, Durston to Ely, and the latter

carries the ball to Harvard's 25-yard line. Two line plunges fail to gain and Chamberlin falls back to try a goal from placement. The Harvard forwards hurry the kick and the try fails. Time soon after is called.

HARVARD vs. YALE
Cambridge, Nov. 18, 1899

HARVARD		YALE
D. C. Campbell, '02,	Left End,	G. W. Hubbell, '01.
A. W. Ristine, '02,	" "	
M. Donald, '99,	Left Tackle,	D. R. Francis, '00.
W. D. Eaton, '02,	" "	
A. R. Sargent, '00,	Left Guard,	F. G. Brown, '01.
F. L. Burnett, '02,	Centre,	P. T. W. Hale, '00.
W. A. M. Burden, '00, Capt.,	Right Guard,	H. P. Olcott, '01.
J. Lawrence, '01,	Right Tackle,	G. S. Stillman, '01.
J. W. Hallowell, '01,	Right End,	E. N. Snitjer, '00.
	" "	P. J. Gibson, '01.
C. D. Daly, '01,	Quarter-back,	W. M. Fincke, '01.
E. H. Kendall, '02,	Left Half,	A. H. Sharpe, '02,
G. A. Sawin, '01,	" "	G. B. Chadwick, '03.
G. S. Parker, '00,	Right Half,	R. B. Keane, '02.
	" "	H. Richards, '00.
S. G. Ellis, '01,	Full-back,	M. L. McBride, '00, Capt.
W. T. Reid, '01,	"	

Referee: M. McClung, '94, Lehigh. Umpire: P. J. Dashiell, Navy. Linesmen: G. M. Thompson, '99, Harvard; R. J. Schweppe, '00, Yale. Timekeeper: F. A. Wood, B. A. C. Score: Harvard 0, Yale 0.

First Half: Francis kicks off for Yale. Harvard brings the ball out, and a try at the line failing, Hallowell punts to Yale's 45-yard line, Sharpe making the catch and running the ball back 3 yards. Yale cannot gain and McBride sends the ball down to Harvard's 10-yard line. Daly skirts the end for 10. A centre play fails and Hallowell punts to Yale's 40-yard line. Fincke catches and attempts to run, but Campbell tackles him. Two plunges into the line are tried without a gain and McBride punts. Harvard cannot make a foot in three attempts and punts. Yale gains

3 yards, but McBride punts on the third down. The ball is out of bounds. It is brought in and Kendall gets away on a double pass for 20 yards, placing the ball on Yale's 45-yard line, Francis making the tackle. Daly gets around the opposite end and is not stopped until he reaches the 17-yard mark. By short gains of Daly and Kendall the ball is advanced to the 7-yard line, where it is third down, with 1 yard to gain. Ellis by a great effort makes it. Again the Harvard backs strike the line and the Yale men tackle desperately. Three downs are required to get the 4 yards, and on the last attempt Yale stops the advance and gets the ball. Sharpe from behind the line punts out to the 35-yard line. Daly signals for a fair catch, but is thrown. Burnett drops back and sights the ball for a place kick from the 25-yard line. The ball misses by inches. Play starts at the 25-yard line and Francis punts. Sawin runs back the kick 5 yards, landing the ball on the 40-yard line. Hallowell kicks out of bounds. The ball is brought in and Yale punts. Harvard cannot gain and again kicks the ball down into Yale's goal. Fincke runs it back 10 yards. McBride punts to Harvard's 45-yard line and Sawin runs it back 20 yards. Time is called for the half.

Second Half: Burnett kicks for Harvard to Sharpe on the 10-yard line. Yale lines up and McBride returns to midfield. Sawin goes through centre for 1, Kendall follows for 1. Hallowell punts. McBride returns. On a double pass Sawin goes round the end for 20 yards. The ball is brought back and given to Yale. Chadwick takes the place of Sharpe and the ball is put in play. Keane makes 1, Chadwick 1. Yale sends McBride 20 yards back and touches down for the full loss of 20 yards, thereby holding the ball under the rule for first down. Yale commences a hard attack. Keane, Chadwick, and McBride, alternating with Francis and Stillman, by short gains advance the ball to

Yale's 25-yard line. Here Campbell and Lawrence stop the Yale backs for a loss and once more McBride deliberately marks off a loss of 20 yards in order to hold first down. On the next play Yale fumbles and Harvard gets the ball. Reid replaces Ellis. Hubbell and Snitjer stop a run at the ends and Reid punts. Eaton replaces Donald. Keane and Chadwick by short gains place the ball on the 30-yard line. Lawrence and Sargent stop the attacks and Harvard gets the ball. Harvard now commences a fierce assault on Yale's line. The ball moves forward line by line until it is down on Yale's 30-yard line. A fumble occurs and Chadwick gets the ball. McBride immediately kicks to Daly, who runs the ball back 20 yards. Reid lifts a prodigious punt to Yale's 15-yard line, where it is fumbled and Ristine gets the ball. Two plunges into Yale's line do not gain and Hallowell drops back for a try for goal, but misses. The ball is punted out and time is called.

HARVARD vs. YALE

New Haven, Nov. 24, 1900

HARVARD		YALE
D. C. Campbell, '02,	Left End,	C. Gould, '02.
E. Bowditch, '03,	" "	
J. D. Clark, '03,	" "	
W. D. Eaton, '02,	Left Tackle,	J. R. Bloomer, '05.
T. H. Graydon, '03,	" "	
W. C. Lee, '01,	Left Guard,	F. G. Brown, '01, Capt.
F. L. Burnett, '02,	" "	
C. S. Sargent, '02,	Centre,	H. P. Olcott, '01.
C. A. Barnard, '02,	"	H. C. Holt, '03.
H. K. Roberts, '00,	Right Guard,	R. Sheldon, '02.
J. S. Lawrence, '01,	Right Tackle,	G. S. Stillman, '01.
J. W. Hallowell, '01,	Right End,	S. L. Coy, '01.
A. W. Ristine, '02,	" "	
C. D. Daly, '01, Capt.,	Quarter-back,	W. M. Fincke, '01.
R. Fincke, '01,	"	

HARVARD		YALE
G. A. Sawin, '01,	*Left* Half,	A. H. Sharpe, '02.
W. S. Gierasch, '01, .	" "	
E. H. Kendall, '02,	Right Half,	G. B. Chadwick, '03.
S. G. Ellis, '01,	" "	
A. Stillman, '03,	Full-back,	P. T. W. Hale, '00.

Referee: M. McClung, '94, Lehigh. Umpire: P. J. Dashiell, Navy. Linesmen: B. G. Waters, '94, Harvard; T. B. Hull. Score: Harvard 0, Yale 28. First Half: Touchdown by J. R. Bloomer, goal by P. T. W. Hale; touchdown by W. M. Fincke, goal by P. T. W. Hale. Second Half: Touchdown by G. B. Chadwick, goal by P. T. W. Hale; touchdown by S. L. Coy; goal from field by A. H. Sharpe.

First Half: Harvard wins the toss and takes the north goal, with a slight wind. Hale kicks to Sawin on Harvard's 10-yard line. The ball is returned to Sharpe at Yale's 50-yard line, Hallowell tackling. Hale hits the centre for 3 yards and then the tackle for 3 yards more. Chadwick gets through centre for 2. A delayed pass sends Sharpe around the end and down to Harvard's 30-yard line, where Sawin brings him down. Yale forms a tackle-back against Hallowell. Chadwick takes the ball and rounds the end for 5 yards. Yale hits the line right and left in rapid succession, making short gains and planting the ball 3 yards from the line. Yale masses for the final thrust, but the ball is fumbled and Campbell gets it. The pass to Ellis is high and the kick goes out of bounds at the 23-yard mark. Hale makes 2 through the centre and Sharpe adds three more through tackle. Chadwick and Bloomer take the ball to the 6-yard line. Harvard stops Chadwick on the next rush. Sharpe makes the 3-yard line, third down, and 1 to gain. Hale makes first down. On the next play Bloomer gets across for a touchdown. Hale kicks the goal. Kendall kicks off to Fincke at the 10-yard mark. The ball is run back 15 yards. Sawin stops Sharpe with a gain of 2 yards around the end.

Kendall does the same for Chadwick, with 1 yard gain around the other extremity. Hale punts to Daly on the 52-yard mark. Ellis makes 3 yards through the centre. Sawin adds 3 more and Ellis duplicates the gain. Sawin punts out of bounds at the 6-yard mark. Stillman and Chadwick make 2 each through tackle. Sharpe gets around the end for 10 yards and then on a double pass gets 2 more. Bloomer, Chadwick, and Hale on tackle plays gain 20 yards. Hale gets through the centre for 20 more. Harvard gets the ball for holding. Sawin punts. Fincke picks up the ball from the ground and, with great interference, runs through the Crimson players for a touchdown. Hale kicks the goal. During the remainder of this half Yale steadily punctures Harvard's line for steady gains, being checked only once by failure to make the distance. Sawin immediately lifts a long punt to Yale's 20-yard line and the Blue again starts to hammer its way steadily down the field until stopped by the call of time.

Second Half: Burnett kicks off, sending the ball across the goal-line. Hale punts out, kicking down to Daly on Harvard's 35-yard line. The latter runs back 20 yards. Sawin goes through centre for 1. Yale is penalized 10. Line plunges bring the ball to Yale's 40-yard line, where Gould throws Stillman for a loss. Sawin tries for a field goal, but misses. Fincke rounds the end for 13, Hale adds 3, Stillman 3, and Sharpe 1. Sharpe gets off a quick kick. Sawin catches it on the 20-yard line. On the line-up Harvard fumbles and Yale gets the ball. Hale and Bloomer, alternating with Stillman, Sharpe, and Chadwick, drive the ball by short but consecutive gains to Harvard's 16-yard line. Yale feints to strike the centre, but sends Chadwick outside of tackle for the touchdown. Goal. Bowditch replaces Campbell and Fincke takes the place of Daly. Roberts also is sent on in place of Barnard. Harvard kicks off and

THE TACKLE—BACK IN ACTION.

Yale's famous formation defeats Harvard. Yale Field. Nov. 24, 1900.

Sharpe runs the ball back to the 25-yard line. Chadwick makes 6 and on the next play adds 6 more. Harvard holds and Sharpe punts to Harvard's 40. Sawin rounds the end for 15. On the line-up there is a mistake in the Harvard signals, which leaves a pass uncovered in the air. Coy gets it and runs 50 yards for a touchdown. Hale misses the goal. Gierasch takes the place of Sawin. Harvard kicks off and Yale returns. Harvard punts and again Yale returns, the ball being fumbled by Harvard on their 32-yard mark and recovered by Brown. Two line plunges fail to gain and Sharpe tries for a goal, but misses. Harvard kicks out to Hale at centre. Yale by short rushes returns it to the 20-yard line. Unable to advance farther Sharpe drops back and kicks a goal from the field. Hallowell and Bowditch are hurt, and Ristine and Clark take their places. The game now develops into an exchange of punts mixed with a few short runs. Olcott goes off and Holt takes his place. On a double pass R. Fincke gets away for 20 yards, but Harvard can go no farther. Stillman punts and the game ends with the ball at midfield.

HARVARD VS. YALE

Cambridge, Nov. 23, 1901

HARVARD		YALE
D. C. Campbell, '02, Capt.,	Left End,	C. Gould, '02, Capt.
	" "	C. D. Rafferty, '04.
C. Blagden, '02,	Left Tackle,	G. A. Goss, '03.
W. C. Lee, '01,	Left Guard,	H. P. Olcott, '01.
E. H. Greene, '02,	Centre,	H. C. Holt, '03.
C. A. Barnard, '02,	Right Guard,	C. J. Hamlin, '03.
	" "	T. R. Johnson, '04.
O. F. Cutts, '03,	Right Tackle,	J. J. Hogan, '05.
E. Bowditch, '03,	Right End,	J. R. Swan, '02.
C. B. Marshall, '04,	Quarter-back,	J. L. De Saulles, '04.
	"	H. G. Metcalf, '04.
R. P. Kernan, '03,	Left Half,	J. B. Hart, '02.

HARVARD		YALE
A. W. Ristine, '02,	Right Half,	G. B. Chadwick, '03.
	" "	J. E. Owsley, '05.
T. H. Graydon, '03,	Full-back,	C. A. Weymouth, '03.
	"	S. O. Van der Poel, '03.

Referee: M. McClung, '94, Lehigh. Umpire: P. J. Dashiell, Navy. Linesmen: J. S. Lawrence, '01, Harvard; T. B. Hull. Timekeeper: F. A. Wood, B. A. C. Score: Harvard 22, Yale 0. First Half: Touchdown by C. Blagden, goal by O. F. Cutts; touchdown by A. W. Ristine, goal by O. F. Cutts; goal from field by C. B. Marshall. Second Half: Touchdown by T. H. Graydon.

First Half: Harvard wins the toss and takes the east goal, with the wind. Olcott kicks to the 15-yard line to Campbell. Harvard opens with a tackle-back and gains 5 yards. The ball is fumbled and Yale gets it. De Saulles drops back for a try for goal, but misses. Harvard punts to the 50-yard line. Yale loses ground on three plays and punts. Harvard gains 35 yards, but Yale gets the ball on the fourth down at midfield. Harvard twice stops Yale without a gain, but a quarter-back kick takes the ball to the 22-yard line. De Saulles tries for a goal, but the kick is blocked. Harvard works the tackle-back for 19 yards, but finally is forced to kick. De Saulles returns and Kernan in turn lifts the ball over Yale's goal-line. De Saulles kicks out to midfield, but Kernan runs it down to Yale's 22-yard line, but the plays are for naught, as Kernan is caught out of bounds. De Saulles again kicks out. Cutts and Ristine in successive plays bring the ball to Yale's 10-yard line, where De Saulles by a great tackle saves a touchdown. Blagden hits the line for a gain of 6. Ristine makes 3 and Blagden takes the ball over for a touchdown. Cutts kicks the goal. Yale kicks off and Harvard returns. A series of scrimmages and kicks ensue, the play being at Harvard's 40-yard line. On a line play Cutts reaches Yale's 33-yard mark. Graydon advances 10 more. Ristine hits one tackle

for 3 and Cutts the opposite tackle for 2.   Cutts reaches the
13-yard mark and Graydon goes to the 10 and then to the 6.
Yale makes a desperate stand.   One down and no gain;
second down 4 yards to gain.   On the third down a revolving play on the tackle is sprung which whirls Ristine
just over the line.   Touchdown.   Cutts kicks the goal.
Olcott kicks to Harvard's 20-yard line, where Marshall,
aided by great interference, catches and runs back to Yale's
45-yard line.   Harvard's play is very quick now—Kernan 2,
Blagden 4, Graydon 6, Kernan 5, Blagden 1, Graydon 1.
Yale holds.   Marshall drops back to the 45-yard line for a
try at goal, and sends the ball squarely between the posts
for a goal.   Yale kicks off, Harvard returns, and time is
called for the half.

   Second Half: Marshall kicks off for Harvard, sending
the ball down to Weymouth at 25.   Yale lines up and De
Saulles punts.   Graydon is downed in his tracks.   On the
line-up the ball goes to Yale for a foul.   Campbell and
Bowditch stop Yale's attacks and De Saulles punts.   Graydon makes 5, Cutts adds 4 more.   Rafferty and Hogan
tackle for losses and Kernan punts to Yale's 50.   Weymouth
rounds the end for 11 yards.   Hart and Chadwick hit the
line, but cannot get through.   De Saulles tries a quarter-
back kick, but Marshall makes the catch and runs to Yale's
45.   De Saulles makes the tackle, but is hurt.   Metcalf takes
his place.   Ristine goes through tackle for 5, Cutts splits the
opposite position for 6, Graydon gets around end for 15, and
Cutts adds 7 more.   Ristine plunges into the line for 7.
Graydon and Cutts in three plunges plant the ball on the
6-yard line.   Cutts gets 4 more.   The lines mass toward
centre, the ball is snapped, and Graydon is rammed through
centre for the touchdown.   The goal fails.   Van der Poel
takes the place of Weymouth.   Yale kicks down to Graydon,
who runs back 5.   On the line-up he skirts the end for 8.

He tries the end again, but is thrown for an 8-yard loss.
Kernan punts and Van der Poel returns. Cutts and Graydon hit the line in rapid succession for good gains, but Yale
finally holds on the 43-yard mark. The Blue immediately
punts down into Harvard's goal. Harvard fumbles and
Hogan gets the ball. Hart hits the line for 3, and on the next
plunge takes the ball to the 10-yard line. Harvard tackles
sharply and holds for downs. Kernan punts out of danger.
Owsley is substituted for Chadwick. Harvard gets the ball
on the line-up for a foul. The Harvard backs commence a
terrific assault on Yale's line, breaking it in two for consecutive gains until 60 yards have been covered. Yale stops the
advance on the 35-yard line. Marshall drops back to try
for a field goal, but misses. Yale punts out. Harvard now
adopts a kicking game and Yale does likewise. Thus the
game comes to a close.

HARVARD vs. YALE
New Haven, Nov. 24, 1902

HARVARD		YALE
P. O. Mills, '05,	Left End,	C. D. Rafferty, '04.
C. A. Shea, '04,	Left Tackle,	R. P. Kinney, '05.
C. A. Barnard, '02,	Left Guard,	E. T. Glass, '04.
W. S. Sugden, '03,	Centre,	H. C. Holt, '03.
A. Marshall, '04,	Right Guard,	G. A. Goss, '03.
	" "	C. J. Hamlin, '03.
D. W. Knowlton, '03,	Right Tackle,	J. J. Hogan, '05.
E. Bowditch, '03,	Right End,	T. L. Shevlin, '06.
W. J. Clothier, '04,	" "	
C. B. Marshall, '04,	Quarter-back,	F. H. Rockwell, '06.
R. P. Kernan, '03, Capt.,	Left Half,	G. B. Chadwick, '03, Capt.
E. T. Putnam, '01,	Right Half,	H. G. Metcalf, '04.
T. H. Graydon, '03,	Full-back,	M. H. Bowman, '05.
D. J. Hurley, '05,	"	S. O. Van der Poel, '03.
	"	M. Farmer, '04.

Referee: M. McClung, '94, Lehigh. Umpire: P. J. Dashiell, Navy.
Linesmen: N. W. Cabot, '98, Harvard, T. B. Hull. Time-keeper:
J. C. McCracken, '01, Pennsylvania. Score: Harvard 0, Yale 23.
First Half: Touchdown by J. J. Hogan, goal by M. H. Bowman;

touchdown by H. G. Metcalf, goal by M. H. Bowman. Second Half:
Touchdown by R. P. Kinney, goal by H. G. Metcalf; touchdown by
J. J. Hogan.

First Half: Harvard wins the toss and takes the south
goal. Bowman kicks off to Putnam on the 10-yard line.
Harvard makes 3 yards in 2 downs and Kernan kicks to the
50-yard line. Two downs for Yale result in no gain, but
on the third attempt a tackle-back sends the ball to the 20-
yard line. Three downs with the same play nets another
5 yards. Metcalf gets through the line for 3 yards. Bowman and Chadwick make the 10-yard line and first down.
Four plays take the ball to the 5-yard line, from which
Hogan on the next play makes a touchdown and Bowman
kicks the goal. Marshall kicks to Yale's 5-yard line, Shevlin runs it back 20 yards. Bowman kicks to Marshall and
the ball is down at midfield. By steady mass plays and short
gains Harvard advances the ball to Yale's 40-yard line, where
a fumble gives the ball to Yale. Bowman punts. Harvard
sends five plays into the line, taking the ball to Yale's 35-
yard line, where a fumble again gives the leather to the Blue.
On the line-up the Harvard line is split in two and Metcalf
runs 73 yards for a touchdown. Bowman kicks the goal.
Harvard kicks off and a series of scrimmages and exchanges
of kicks puts the ball in Harvard's hands at midfield.
Kernan and Graydon advance the ball 20 yards. Putnam
adds 5 more. Graydon and Putnam through centre take
the ball to the 28-yard line. Kernan adds 2 through tackle.
Graydon gets to the 15-yard line. Putnam on a mass play
makes the 9-yard mark. Harvard fumbles, but Sugden
recovers the ball. Two plunges at the line fail and it is
Yale's ball. A trick play by the Blue loses 3 yards. Bowman punts high and Harvard gets the ball on the 35-yard
line. Putnam and Kernan bring it down to the 20-yard line,
where Yale gets it on a fumble. Yale makes 10 yards by

rushes of Chadwick and Kinney, and Bowman punts to
the 50-yard line. Harvard loses 5 on a trick play. Kernan
punts and Bowman runs it out to the 25-yard line, where
time is called for the half.

Second Half: Van der Poel replaces Bowman. Harvard
kicks to Yale's 10-yard line. Metcalf runs the kick back
15 yards. Glass makes 8 through tackle. An off-side play
yields 5 more. Glass again hits the line for 8. Kinney
rounds the end for 30 and Chadwick does the same for 10.
Kinney goes through tackle for 5. Yale now has the ball
on Harvard's 15-yard line. Hogan splits the tackle for 3,
Metcalf plunges for 12. On the line-up Kinney breaks
through for a touchdown. Metcalf kicks the goal. Harvard kicks off to Yale's 12-yard line. By line-plunging
Harvard works the ball back to Yale's 45, where the Blue
holds for downs. Marshall tries for a field goal, but misses.
Yale punts out and again Harvard tries in vain to break the
Blue line. Goss is hurt and Hamlin takes his place. Harvard punts. Yale gets the ball on the 20. Chadwick goes
through tackle for 4. Kinney adds 4 more. Van der Poel
makes 4. Metcalf rounds the end for 18. Chadwick hits
the line for 7 and Hogan repeats the play for 3 more. Hogan
again takes the ball and gains 4 yards. Van der Poel adds
7. Harvard makes a determined stand on their 25-yard
line and Bowditch and Mills throw the Yale backs for no
gain and get the ball. Graydon punts to Yale's 45 and
Metcalf runs back the kick 20 yards. Yale now opens a
rapid attack on the Harvard line, Van der Poel, Hogan, and
Chadwick taking the ball to the 4-yard mark, from which
Hogan is shot across for a touchdown. The goal fails.
Harvard kicks off and both teams resort to a punting game
without further scoring until the close of the game.

HARVARD VS. YALE
Cambridge, Nov. 21, 1903

HARVARD		YALE
W. J. Clothier, '04,	Left End,	C. D. Rafferty, '04, Capt.
R. A. Derby, '05,	Left Tackle,	R. P. Kinney, '05.
B. H. Squiers, '06,	" "	L. F. Bissell, '04.
	" "	S. B. Morton, '00.
H. LeMoyne, '07,	Left Guard,	H. S. Batchelder, '05.
J. Parkinson, '06,	Centre,	J. C. Roraback, '03.
A. Marshall, '04,	Right Guard,	J. E. Miller, '04.
	" "	R. P. Kinney, '05.
D. W. Knowlton, '03,	Right Tackle,	J. J. Hogan, '05.
E. Bowditch, '03,	Right End,	T. L. Shevlin, '06.
J. M. Montgomery, '06,	" "	
C. B. Marshall, '04, Capt.,	Quarter-back,	F. H. Rockwell, '06.
	"	W. B. Soper, '04.
J. D. Nichols, '06,	Left Half,	W. L. Mitchell, '04.
F. A. Goodhue, '06,	" "	
D. J. Hurley, '05,	Right Half,	H. G. Metcalf, '04.
H. Schoellkopf, '01,	Full-back,	M. Farmer, '04.
P. O. Mills, '05,	"	J. E. Owsley, '05.
	"	M. H. Bowman, '05.

Referee: M. McClung, '94, Lehigh. Umpire: P. J. Dashiell, Navy. Linesman: A. E. Whiting, '98, Cornell. Score: Harvard 0, Yale 16. First Half: Touchdown by R. P. Kinney. Second Half: Touchdown by J. J. Hogan; touchdown by J. J. Hogan, goal by W. L. Mitchell.

First Half: Schoellkopf kicks off for Harvard to Shevlin on the 5-yard line and the ball is run back 10 yards. Yale tries the Harvard line, but cannot gain, and Mitchell kicks. Harvard has the ball on Yale's 45-yard line. Marshall goes around the end for 25 yards. A tackle behind the line and a penalty give Yale the ball on their 30-yard line. Mitchell punts down to Marshall on the latter's 25-yard stripe, but the ball is run back 20 yards. Harvard rushes vigorously, but a penalty forces Marshall to kick. A bad pass forces him to run across the field without gain and it is Yale's ball. Hogan drops back and ploughs through to the 28-yard line. Three plunges take the ball to the 3-yard mark.

A tackle-back is formed. Kinney takes the ball and splits
the Harvard line in two, crossing the line for a touchdown.
Mitchell misses a difficult goal. Harvard kicks off. An
exchange of kicks and a fumble gives Harvard the ball on
Yale's 25-yard line. Three mass plays take the ball to the
15-yard line and two more reach the 5. Harvard tries a
fake end run and loses 3 yards. It is third down and 2 yards
to gain. Marshall drops back for a kick. The pass is bad
and the kick is blocked, but Harvard gets the ball on the
30-yard line. A tandem on the left nets 3 yards. A delayed pass gains 1 more. Nichols gets around the end for 6.
Two more plunges plant the ball on the 10-yard line. Yale
is penalized 5 yards. Nichols makes the 5-yard line. On
the next play the ball is fumbled and Yale gets it. The
kick is weak and it is again Harvard's ball on the 20-yard
line. Marshall tries a delayed pass, but is thrown for a loss.
He drops back for a goal, but misses. Yale punts out to
the 50-yard line. Here rush follows rush by Harvard, ending on each third down with a kick and a return by Yale,
and playing thus the half closes.

Second Half: Mitchell kicks down to Bowditch at 25.
Le Moyne on the line-up punts to Farmer at Yale's 25. An
exchange of kicks between Le Moyne and Marshall places
the ball in Harvard's possession on the latter's 15. Harvard forms to punt. Rafferty breaks through and blocks
the kick. Hogan falls on the ball behind the line for a
touchdown. The goal is missed. Le Moyne kicks off for
Harvard, sending the ball across the goal-line. Mitchell
punts out to Marshall on Harvard's 50. A brisk kicking
exchange ensues. Harvard on a fumble gets the ball on
Yale's 40. Mills gets away for a run to Yale's 20-yard line.
Mills and Nichols in two plunges gain 6 yards. Nichols
adds 3 more. Mills and Nichols then advance the ball to
the 2-yard mark. Rafferty, Kinney, and Shevlin throw

Harvard back and get the ball on downs. Farmer in three plunges makes 15 yards. Mitchell kicks to Nichols at Yale's 50. Harvard tries the line in vain and forms to punt. Mitchell blocks Le Moyne's kick and Bissel, diving for the ball, gets it on Harvard's 30-yard line. Mitchell skirts the end for 15. Metcalf goes through the line for 5. Hogan makes 5 yards twice in succession and then crosses the line for a touchdown. Mitchell kicks the goal. Harvard kicks off. Each team now tries scrimmage after scrimmage, but cannot make a substanial gain and so resorts to kicking. Harvard at last puts the ball down for a try at the line, but on the plunge the ball is fumbled and Shevlin races down the field and across the goal-line. The touchdown is not allowed. The teams resort to kicking and thus the game ends.

HARVARD vs. YALE
New Haven, Nov. 19, 1904

HARVARD		YALE
C. W. Kendall, '05,	Left End,	T. L. Shevlin, '06.
W. C. Matthews, '05,	" "	
F. Pruyn, '04,	" "	
K. F. Brill, '08,	Left Tackle,	J. R. Bloomer, '05.
F. H. White, '06,	Left Guard,	R. P. Kinney, '05.
B. Parker, '08,	Centre,	J. C. Roraback, '03.
J. Parkinson, '06,	"	
B. H. Squires, '06,	Right Guard,	R. C. Tripp, '06.
F. H. White, '06,	" "	
R. A. Derby, '05,	Right Tackle,	J. J. Hogan, '05, Capt.
J. M. Montgomery, '06,	Right End,	C. T. Neal, '05.
D. P. Starr, '08,	Quarter-back,	F. H. Rockwell, '06.
S. H. Noyes, '05,	"	
R. E. Sperry, '06,	Left Half,	L. Hoyt, '06.
J. D. Nichols, '06,	" "	
D. J. Hurley, '05, Capt.,	Right Half,	S. F. B. Morse, '07.
P. O. Mills, '05,	Full-back,	A. R. Flinn, '06.

Referee: M. McClung, '94, Lehigh. Umpire: P. J. Dashiell, Navy. Linesman: J. C. McCracken, '01, Pennsylvania. Score: Harvard 0, Yale 12. First Half: Touchdown by S. F. B. Morse, goal by L. Hoyt. Second Half: Touchdown by A. R. Flinn, goal by L. Hoyt.

First Half: Harvard wins the toss and takes the south goal. Roraback kicks to Harvard's 15-yard line, Kendall running the kick back to the 30-yard line. A double pass is shot to Sperry for an end run, but the play fails. A line plunge into centre results similarly and Sperry punts to Rockwell. Yale now starts in motion its tackle-back play, alternating rapidly from right to left, in which Rockwell gains 3, Flinn 6, Morse 3, Hogan 5, Flinn 10, Hogan 10, and with other gains taking the ball to Harvard's 20-yard line. Here the Crimson holds for downs. On a tandem Harvard makes 4 through tackle, but the next play fails and a long punt takes the ball to Hoyt at Yale's 45, the latter running 10 yards before being tackled. Morse, Flinn, Bloomer, and Hogan by short, quick plunges return the ball to Harvard's 25, where it goes to Harvard on a fumble, Mills picking it up and running 30 yards before being stopped by Hogan. Two line plays fail to yield a first down and Sperry punts. Yale returns on the first line-up and Harvard fumbles. Hogan recovers the ball at 32. Flinn, Morse, Bloomer, and Hogan advance the ball to the 15-yard line. Flinn makes 2 through centre, but a penalty sets the Blue back 15 yards. Hoyt falls back for a drop kick, but Harvard blocks it and gets the ball. Sperry punts to midfield. Yale, by tackle-back formations, in ten plays returns the ball to the Crimson's 25-yard line. Flinn makes 1. A penalty gives Yale half the distance to the goal-line. Hogan hits the line for 5, and on the next play Morse goes the remaining distance for a touchdown. Hoyt kicks the goal. Sperry kicks to Shevlin on the 15-yard line and the latter runs 32 yards before being stopped. Yale cannot pierce the Crimson line and Hoyt punts to Sperry at 25. Time is now called for the half.

Second Half: Sperry kicks off to Shevlin at 10, the latter running the kick out to 33. Two line plunges fail to gain and Hoyt punts 40 yards and Harvard fumbles, Shevlin getting the ball. Again Yale fails to gain consecutively and Hoyt punts to Harvard's 20. For a long time the two teams play without substantial advantage to either, line plays failing to gain consistently and being followed by punts, the play being confined between the 25-yard lines. At last Tripp blocks a kick on Harvard's 25. Bloomer picks up the ball and runs to the 3-yard mark, where Mills brings him down. Flinn in a tackle-back formation crosses the line for the touchdown. Hoyt kicks the goal. Play is resumed, but no further scoring occurs.

HARVARD VS. YALE

Cambridge, Nov. 25, 1905

HARVARD		YALE
L. H. Leary, '05,	Left End,	J. M. Cates, '06.
	" "	H. H. Jones, '08.
K. F. Brill, '08,.	Left Tackle,	R. W. Forbes, '07.
J. M. Montgomery, '06,	" "	
F. H. Burr, '09,	Left Guard,	A. G. Erwin, '07.
	" "	C. W. Hockenberger, '07.
B. Parker, '08,	Centre,	C. S. Flanders, '06.
H. B. Barney, '08,	"	P. C. Smith, '06.
H. E. Kersburg, '06,	Right Guard,	R. C. Tripp, '06.
B. H. Squires, '06,	Right Tackle,	L. H. Biglow, '08.
D. W. Knowlton, '03, Capt.,	Right End,	T. L. Shevlin, '06, Capt.
D. P. Starr, '08,	Quarter-back,	T. A. D. Jones, '08.
M. L. Newhall, '08,	"	G. Hutchinson, '06.
H. Foster, '07,	Left Half,	H. L. Roome, '07.
J. D: Nichols, '06,	" "	W. F. Knox, '07.
J. W. Wendell, '08,	Right Half,	S. F. B. Morse, '07.
	" "	L. Hoyt, '06.
W. Z. Carr, '06,	Full-back,	J. J. Quill, '06.
	"	J. N. Levine, '07.
	"	A. R. Flinn, '06.

Referee: M. McClung, '94, Lehigh. Umpire: P. J. Dashiell, Navy. Linesman: A. E. Whiting, '98, Cornell. Score: Harvard 0, Yale 6. Second Half: Touchdown by R. W. Forbes, goal by L. Hoyt.

First Half: Harvard wins the toss and takes the goal. Biglow kicks to Starr at Harvard's 7 and the latter runs the kick back 10 yards. Harvard tries the tandem on the tackles, but cannot gain, and Burr punts to Roome at Yale's 49. The Blue sets in motion its tackle-back play, but cannot gain consecutively, and Roome punts to Harvard's 35. The Crimson again calls for the tandem and by short plunges takes the ball to Yale's 43-yard mark, where the latter holds for downs and takes the ball. Quill circles the end for 20 yards and on the next play doubles the other end for 10 more. Roome and Biglow by line plunges reach the 16-yard mark. Here Harvard holds for downs. The Crimson tries a trick play, but Yale nips the runner behind the line. For several minutes play becomes a series of punts between the 25-yard lines, neither eleven being able to pierce the other's line consecutively. The half closes with the ball at midfield, the advantages of the half being neutral.

Second Half: Burr kicks to Shevlin on Yale's 5-yard line. Shevlin runs back the kick 10 yards. A line plunge fails to gain and a long punt reaches Harvard's 50-yard line. The Crimson attempts to run the Yale end, but loses ground and a line plunge fares no better. Burr then punts. Jones catches on the 15-yard line and by a brilliant dodging run carries the ball out to 40. The Harvard line does not yield to the following attack by Yale and Roome sends the ball to Harvard's 10-yard line. The Crimson now uncovers a rapid, brilliant attack, taking the ball by tandem plays to Yale's 25-yard line. Here Yale, stiffens and holds for 3 downs without gain. Burr tries a short kick over the line, but Yale gets it. Hoyt punts and Burr returns. Another exchange of kicks follows and Harvard fumbles. Shevlin gets the ball and reaches Harvard's 31-yard mark before being stopped. Five plunges put the ball on the Crim-

son's 5-yard line, from which Forbes takes it over for a
touchdown. Hoyt kicks the goal. Harvard kicks off and
after several exchanges of kicks time is called for the game.

HARVARD VS. YALE
New Haven, Nov. 24, 1906

HARVARD		YALE
J. F. Macdonald, '08,	Left End,	R. W. Forbes, '07.
V. P. Kennard, '09,	" "	C. B. Stuart, '07.
C. G. Osborne, '07,	Left Tackle,	H. R. Paige, '08.
F. H. Burr, '09,	Left Guard,	A. E. Brides, '09.
B. Parker, '08,	Centre,	C. W. Hockenberger, '07.
S. Fraser, '07,	"	
H. E. Kersburg, '07,	Right Guard,	A. G. Erwin, '07.
W. Pierce, '07,	Right Tackle,	L. H. Biglow, '08.
D. P. Starr, '08,	Right End,	H. H. Jones, '08.
G. M. Orr, '08,	" "	C. F. Alcott, '08.
	" "	S. F. B. Morse, '07.
M. L. Newhall, '08,	Quarter-back,	T. A. D. Jones, '08.
	"	T. M. Dines, '08.
H. Foster, '07, Capt.,	Left Half,	P. L. Veeder, '07.
C. E. Lincoln, '08,	Right Half,	W. F. Knox, '07.
	" "	H. L. Roome, '07.
	" "	W. P. Bomar, '08.
	" "	H. Linn, '07.
J. W. Wendell, '08,	Full-back,	S. F. B. Morse, '07, Capt.
	"	F. E. Werneken, '07.

Referee: E. K. Hall, '92, Dartmouth. Umpire: W. H. Edwards, '00,
Princeton. Linesmen: H. B. Hackett, '04, Army; E. A. Everett,
Groton. Timekeeper: F. A. Wood, B. A. C. Score: Harvard 0,
Yale 6. First Half: Touchdown by H. L. Roome, goal by P. L.
Veeder.

First Half: Yale wins the toss and takes the north goal.
Burr kicks off to Veeder, who runs the ball back 20 yards.
On the line-up Veeder drops back to punt, but Macdonald
gets through and blocks the kick, recovering the ball. Harvard feints into the line, but sends a forward pass to Starr,
who makes 20 yards. Lincoln goes through tackle for 5.
Newhall adds 3 more. Yale stops the next play and New-

hall falls back for a drop at goal. Yale blocks the kick
and Forbes gets the ball.. The Blue cannot gain and a penalty sets them back 15. Veeder punts to Harvard's 48.
Lincoln on a triple pass makes 10 yards. He gains 5 more
through the line, but a penalty sets Harvard back 5. Burr
punts to Yale's 35. The Blue fumbles and Harvard·
gets the ball. The ball is taken back and Harvard is
penalized 15 yards. Several exchanges of kicks ensue.
Biglow gets the ball at Yale's 50. Knox tries an on-side
kick, which Forbes recovers on Harvard's 30-yard line.
Roome replaces Knox. Roome fails to gain. Yale is
penalized 5 yards. Veeder sends a forward pass 30 yards
to Forbes on Harvard's 4-yard mark. Yale tries a mass
play into the line, but Harvard stops it. Roome is sent
against tackle and rammed through for a touchdown.
Veeder kicks the goal. Harvard kicks off. T. Jones runs
the ball back 30 yards. Yale punts. Harvard tries a
scrimmage without substantial gain and punts. The half
closes with the ball on Yale's 35-yard line.

Second Half: Yale kicks off to Macdonald at 20. Burr
punts to Yale's 35. Veeder catches and runs the ball back
to midfield. By a series of fast and smashing line plays
Yale forces the ball down to Harvard's 25-yard line. Fraser
takes the place of Parker. Harvard stops the advance and
Veeder tries a drop kick, but misses. Harvard punts. On
the line-up Veeder returns. Starr tries a forward pass from
the 48-yard mark, but Yale gets it. The Blue makes 10
around the right end and then 20 around the left. Roome
gets through the line for 10 more. Yale is penalized 15.
Veeder tries for a goal from the field, but fails. Orr takes
the place of Starr. Harvard gets the ball at 45 and Burr
punts to Yale's 15. Bomar replaces Roome. Sharp tackling sets the Blue back 15 yards. A penalty causes the loss
of 5 more. Veeder kicks from behind his goal-line to

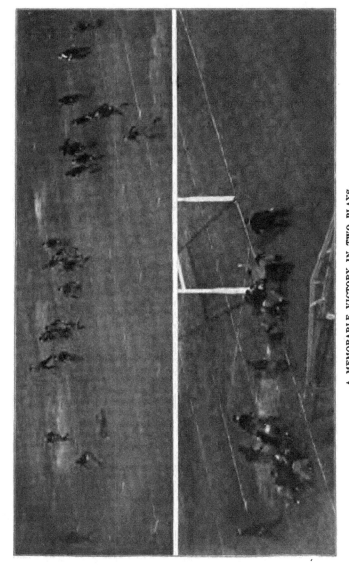

A MEMORABLE VICTORY IN TWO PLAYS.

Veeder, of Yale, sends a forward pass 30 yards to Forbes, placing the ball 3 yards from Harvard's goal-line. Roome then plunges through Harvard's line for a touchdown, which wins the game. Yale Field, Nov. 24, 1906.

Newhall at 45. Harvard cannot gain and Burr punts.
The kick is low and Jones gets it, running it out to 45.
Jones punts. On the line-up Burr punts to Yale's 18.
The Blue is penalized 15. Kennard replaces Macdonald.
Veeder punts from the line out to 40. Harvard tries a forward pass, Newhall to Orr, and the latter gains 8 yards.
On the next play Yale throws the Crimson for a loss. Harvard tries a double pass. The ball is fumbled and Forbes
gets it. Linn replaces Bomar. Yale opens a fierce attack
on the Harvard line, the ball being carried by line plunges
from line to line until the 10-yard line is reached, where
time is called.

HARVARD VS. YALE
Cambridge, Nov. 23, 1907

HARVARD		YALE
D. P. Starr, '08,	Left End,	H. H. Jones, '08.
G. G. Browne, '10,	" "	R. B. Burch, '09.
F. H. Burr, '09,	Left Tackle,	H. R. Paige, '08.
	" "	G. Foster, '07.
B. Parker, '08, Capt.,	Left Guard,	C. T. Cooney, '10.
S. Hoar, '08,	" "	H. M. S. Dunbar, '08.
P. Grant, '08,	Centre,	E. Congdon, 08.
W. Pierce, '08,	Right Guard,	W. A. Goebel, '10.
H. Fish, '10,	Right Tackle,	L. H. Biglow, '08, Capt.
J. F. Macdonald, '08,	Right End,	C. F. Alcott, '08.
M. L. Newhall, '08,	Quarter-back,	T. A. D. Jones, '08.
	"	T. M. Dines, '08.
J. W. Wendell, '08,	Left Half,	A. E. Brides, '10.
J. H. Rand, '08,	" "	R. Beebe, '08.
P. C. Lockwood, '08,	Right Half,	W. P. Bomar, '08.
	" "	S. H. Philbin, '10.
	" "	H. M. Wheaton, '09.
C. Appollonio, '08,	Full-back,	E. H. Coy, '10.
	"	E. A. Wylie, '08.

Referee: M. J. Thompson, '01, Georgetown. Umpire: W. H. Edwards, '00, Princeton. Field Judge: H. B. Hackett, '04, Army. Head
Linesman: W. S. Langford, '96, Trinity. Assistant Linesmen: D. J.

Hurley, '05, Harvard; J. J. Hogan, '05, Yale. Score: Harvard 0, Yale 12. First Half: Touchdown by E. H. Coy, goal by L. H. Biglow. Second Half: Touchdown by E. H. Coy, goal by L. H. Biglow.

First Half: Yale wins the toss and takes the south goal. Burr kicks to Coy on the 10-yard line and the latter runs back the kick 15 yards. On the line-up Yale punts and Harvard returns the kick. Another exchange of punts follows, resulting in a fumble by Yale and the recovery of the ball by Harvard on the former's 25-yard line. The Blue line stops two plunges without gain and Parker tries for a goal from placement, but misses. Yale kicks out and Harvard again returns. Brides catches the kick and runs 30 yards. A sharp attack on the Harvard tackles nets 20 yards. Harvard holds for three downs and Yale gets off a short on-side kick which is recovered at Harvard's 23-yard mark. The Crimson line will not yield a foot and Coy tries for a goal from placement, but is hurried in his kick and misses. Harvard kicks out. Coy on fake kick formations tries to run the Harvard ends, but is stopped for no gains. Following a series of kicks Coy catches at 45. Bomar and Coy make 20 yards through the line. Philbin adds 10 more. Coy gains 2, and on the next play Philbin reaches Harvard's 2-yard mark. On the line-up Coy bursts through centre for a touchdown and Biglow kicks the goal. Harvard kicks off and Yale returns. Harvard tries a number of line plays for short gains and then Wendell shoots a forward pass to Starr, which places the ball on Yale's 30-yard line. Unable to advance farther by rushing, Newhall tries for a goal from placement, but misses. Yale punts out and Harvard in several line plunges again places the ball on Yale's 25-yard line, from which a second try by placement is made and lost. Time soon after is called.

Second Half: Yale kicks off and Harvard, after an ineffectual attack on the line, punts. Coy catches at 40.

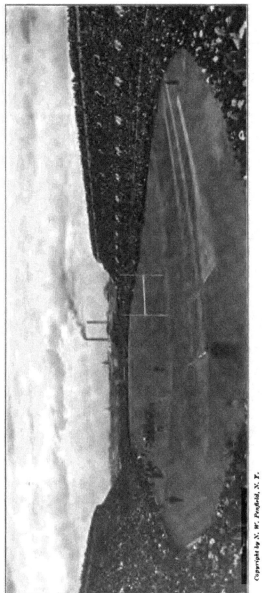

FOOTBALL IN HARVARD STADIUM.
Harvard vs. Yale, Nov. 23, 1907.

Copyright by N. W. Penfield, N. Y.

A FAMOUS GOAL FROM THE FIELD.

With the ball in Harvard's possession on Yale's 15-yard line and the Crimson unable to advance, Kennard, of Harvard, is called into the game at full-back. On the first play he kicks a goal from the field, winning the game. Yale Field, Nov. 21, 1908.

suddenly is withdrawn and Kennard called from the bench
and placed at full-back. Harvard forms for a try at goal.
The ball immediately is passed to Kennard, and the latter,
standing on the 30-yard line, drops a goal from the field.
Time soon after is called.

Second Half: McKay kicks off and Daly runs the kick
back 42 yards. Harvard holds and Coy punts. Harvard
tries the line without gain and Kennard kicks to Coy at
midfield. Daly and Coy in two plunges advance 17 yards.
From a kicking formation Coy runs the end for 20 yards.
A forward pass to Coy places the ball on Harvard's 8-yard
line, but the play is not allowed, Harvard getting the ball.
Cutler punts, and Yale from midfield by hard line-plunging
works the ball to the 35-yard line. Here Harvard holds
for 2 downs and an on-side kick is tried, which Harvard
captures on the 15-yard line. The game now becomes
largely one of kicks and play is confined thereafter between
the 25-yard lines. .

HARVARD VS. YALE

Cambridge, Nov. 20, 1909

HARVARD		YALE
L. D. Smith, '12,	Left End,	J. R. Kilpatrick, '11.
F. de H. Houston, '10,	" "	
R. G. McKay, '11,	Left Tackle,	H. H. Hobbs, '10.
L. Withington, '11,	Left Guard,	H. F. Andrus, '10.
P. Withington, '09,	Centre,	C. T. Cooney, '10.
R. T. Fisher, '12,	Right Guard,	W. A. Goebel, '10.
H. Fish, '10, Capt.,	Right Tackle,	T. Lilley, '10.
	" "	C. H. Paul, '12.
	" "	J. B. Spencer, '10.
G. G. Browne, '10,	Right End,	E. Savage, '11.
H. A. Rogers, '11,	" "	J. W. Field, '11.
	" "	H. J. Holt, '10.
	" "	H. Vaughn, '11.
D. V. O'Flaherty, '11,	Quarter-back,	A. Howe, '12.
R. B. Wigglesworth, '12,	"	
H. F. Corbett, '11,	Left Half,	F. J. Daly, '11.

HARVARD		YALE
T. Frothingham, '12,	Left Half,	F. J. Murphy, '10.
H. C. Leslie, '11,	Right Half,	S. H. Philbin, '10.
P. D. Smith, '11,	" "	
W. M. Minot, '11,	Full-back,	E. H. Coy, '10, Capt.

Referee: W. S. Langford, '96, Trinity. Umpire: W. H. Edwards, '00, Princeton. Field Judge: E. K. Hall, '92, Dartmouth. Linesman: J. B. Pendleton, '90, Bowdoin. Score: Harvard 0, Yale 8. First Half: Safety by W. M. Minot; goal from field by E. H. Coy. Second Half: Goal from field by E. H. Coy.

NOTE.—See amended rule of scoring, session March 27, 1909, Appendix.

First Half: Yale wins the toss and takes the south goal. Withington kicks off for Harvard. A penalty and Philbin's run of 5 yards returns the ball to midfield. Coy punts, Harvard fumbles, and Yale gets the ball. Two plunges at tackle fail to gain and Coy tries for a field goal, but misses. Harvard puts the ball in play at 25, but, unable to rush, punts. Yale fumbles and Browne gets it. The Crimson makes 20 yards in four plunges, but loses the ball on an intercepted forward pass. Coy, failing to gain, punts to Harvard's 25. Harvard, in four plays, gains 55 yards, two of which are end runs by Leslie and Corbett, 25 and 18 yards. A penalty sets Harvard back 15. Minot is stopped in the centre and the latter punts to Philbin, who returns to Harvard's 40. Yale can make no impression on the Harvard line and Coy sends a long punt down the field. An exchange of kicks terminates in Cooney recovering a short one, on side, for Yale on Harvard's 35-yard line. Coy plunges through centre for 8. He repeats the play for 1. Philbin makes 5, 2, and Coy 3. The latter tries a drop kick, but misses. Harvard puts the ball down at 25 and gains 5 yards, Minot then punting to Daly at centre. A forward pass hits the ground and Yale is set back to 40.

Coy punts to Minot at Harvard's 42. Howe gets Harvard's short kick and reaches his 45-yard line. Philbin on a wide end run fails to gain and Coy punts. Minot falls back to punt, but Cooney blocks the kick. The ball rolls behind the goal line. Minot falls on it for a safety. Harvard tries a forward pass on the 25-yard line, which fails, and on the next play Minot punts from behind his goal-posts. Daly makes a fair catch at 40 and Hobbs tries for a goal from placement, but misses. An exchange of kicks gives Yale the ball on Harvard's 46-yard line. Philbin and Coy gain 6 yards, and then Coy tries a drop kick, which misses. Minot punts and Philbin runs back the kick to Harvard's 15-yard line. On the line-up Coy kicks a goal from the field. Yale kicks off, Harvard catches and returns. Time is called for the half.

Second Half: Cooney kicks off to McKay at 20. Minot cannot gain and punts to Philbin at Yale's 38. Murphy makes 3 yards, and a forward pass, Howe to Savage, advances the ball to 42, where Coy punts to O'Flaherty at Harvard's 24. Leslie makes 5 yards through tackle, Minot 10, and Frothingham 6. Harvard tries an on-side kick, but Howe gets the ball and runs the length of the field. The touchdown is not allowed, as the ball was dead. Yale puts the ball down for scrimmage. Coy makes 9 and then 7, Philbin 3, Murphy 3, and Coy 5. Coy now punts to O'Flaherty at 14. Harvard makes a few short gains, reaching the 25-yard line. From here Frothingham makes 5, Minot 12, Houston 7, and Minot 2. A penalty sets the Crimson back 15 yards. Minot punts to Coy at centre and the latter returns to him at 10. Brown tries the line, but a penalty sets Harvard within 1 foot of the goal-line. Minot punts to Philbin at 38. Murphy makes 8, and then Coy tries an on-side kick, which Frothingham gets. Minot plunges into the line for 5. Wigglesworth skirts the end for 13. Frothingham and Houston fail to gain and Minot punts out of bounds at 50. A run from a fake kick by Coy fails and the latter gets off an on-side kick to Hobbs, which the latter gets at Harvard's 41. Coy now resorts to short punts to keep the ball continually in front of Harvard's goal. After two exchanges of punts Minot tries an on-side kick from the 15-yard line, which Howe secures at 30. Murphy makes 5. Coy falls back and drops a goal from the field. Time soon after is called.

HARVARD vs. YALE

New Haven, Nov. 19, 1910

HARVARD		YALE
R. P. Lewis, '13,	Left End,	J. R. Kilpatrick, '11.
R. G. McKay, '11,	Left Tackle,	J. W. Scully, '12.
W. M. Minot, '11,	Left Guard,	M. E. Fuller, '12.
	" "	C. C. Childs, '11.
J. G. B. Perkins, '11,	Centre,	E. B. Morris, '12.
P. D. Smith, '11,	"	
R. T. Fisher, '12,	Right Guard,	E. W. McDevitt, '12.
L. Withington, '11, Capt.,	Right Tackle,	C. H. Paul, '12.
L. D. Smith, '12,	Right End,	S. H. Brooks, '11.
	" "	H. Vaughn, '11.
R. B. Wigglesworth, '12,	Quarter-back,	A. Howe, '12.
R. S. Potter, '12,	"	
H. B. Gardner, '13,	"	
S. M. Felton, '13,	Left Half,	J. W. Field, '11.
P. L. Wendell, '13,	" "	A. L. Corey, '11.
H. F. Corbett, '11,	Right Half,	F. J. Daly, '11, Capt.
T. J. Campbell, '12,	" "	
H. C. Leslie, '11,	Full-back,	E. O. Kistler, '11.
G. E. Morrison, '12,	"	

Referee: W. S. Langford, '96, Trinity. Umpire: D. L. Fultz, '98, Brown. Field Judge: J. B. Pendleton, '90, Bowdoin. Linesman: W. N. Morice, '99, Pennsylvania. Score: Harvard 0, Yale 0.

First Quarter: Harvard wins the toss and takes the north goal. Paul kicks to Felton on the 10-yard line and the latter runs out 12 yards. Leslie makes 2 and Felton punts to

Howe on the latter's 45.   Field fails to gain and Howe punts.
Corbett catches on his 30 and runs back 25 yards.   Corbett
adds 15 more through the line, but Harvard is forced to punt,
the ball going over the line.   Yale starts a scrimmage on the
25.   Howe is thrown for a loss and punts to Wigglesworth
at centre.   Corbett makes 15 on a line plunge.   Wigglesworth makes 2 more, but Harvard is forced to kick.   Howe
punts from the 25 yard line, Brooks getting the ball at 45.
Following a few unimportant plays ending in a kick and a
penalty, Yale gets the ball on their 35-yard line.   Failing to
gain, Howe punts to Wigglesworth at Harvard's 40.   Corbett makes 6, Leslie 7, Corbett 3.   Yale holds and Felton
punts.   Howe returns and the quarter closes.

Second Quarter: Harvard resumes play with the ball on
their 45-yard line.   Punts are exchanged, Yale gaining 10
yards.   Corbett goes through centre for 8.   Field recovers
a fumble at centre.   Howe skirts the end for 15 yards.
Yale is penalized 15 yards.   Daly repeats the formation
and circles the end for 25 yards.   Harvard holds for downs.
Wendell replaces Felton.   Wendell makes 8, 3, 5, and 8.
Corbett hits the line for 4.   Wendell dodges for 15 yards.
A penalty sets the Crimson back 15.   Wigglesworth punts
to Howe.   A long punting duel ensues.   Wendell gets
through tackle for 10.   Corbett adds 15 more.   Potter replaces Wigglesworth.   Harvard lines up and Potter sends
a forward pass to Corbett for 4 yards.   Kicks follow and
the half closes.

Third Quarter: Wigglesworth returns to the game, relieving Potter.   Morrison goes in for Leslie at full-back.
Paul kicks to Wendell and the latter runs out 30 yards
Wendell makes 4 more and Corbett punts to Howe.   Yale
tries the line shift and Kistler makes 10, Daly 8, Kistler 10,
Field 6.   Howe punts to Wigglesworth, who heels a fair
catch.   The play is recalled.   A penalty puts Yale with the

ball on Harvard's 40-yard line. Yale fumbles and Corbett gets the ball. Punts are exchanged and Howe intercepts Wigglesworth's forward pass. Kistler and Howe fail to gain and the latter punts. Campbell replaces Corbett. Wendell makes 5. Harvard tries a drop kick from the 45-yard line, but the ball falls short. Howe gets the ball on Yale's 12-yard line. Kistler and Daly make 9 yards and Howe punts. Wendell gets the ball on Harvard's 45-yard line and the quarter closes.

Fourth Quarter: Corbett replaces Campbell and makes 4 yards. Wendell adds 6 more. Corbett nets 2 on a delayed pass. Wendell hits tackle for 6. Wigglesworth punts to Howe on his 3-yard line. Howe punts out of bounds at 23. Wendell makes 5 and then 8. Harvard fumbles and Howe gets the ball on the 13-yard mark. Howe punts to Corbett at 40. Harvard is penalized. Corey replaces Field. Wigglesworth punts and Howe quickly returns. Wendell makes 2 and a forward pass adds 20 more. Howe recovers a punt on his 30-yard line. Kicks and short gains terminate in giving the ball to Yale on Harvard's 34-yard line, Minot having punted out of bounds. Daly misses a drop kick from the 45-yard line. Harvard puts the ball in play on the 25-yard line and the game closes.

CHAPTER XV

MICHIGAN VS. PENNSYLVANIA

MICHIGAN vs. PENNSYLVANIA

Philadelphia, Nov. 11, 1899

MICHIGAN		PENNSYLVANIA
C. F. Juttner, '00,	Left End,	F. Stehle, '01.
H. White, '02,	" "	
C. G. McDonald, '00,	Left Tackle,	J. B. Snover, '00.
R. J. Siegmund, '02,	Left Guard,	T. T. Hare, '01, Capt.
C. L. Bliss, '02,	" "	
W. R. Cunningham, '99,	Centre,	P. D. Overfield, '01.
R. R. France, '02,	Right Guard,	J. C. Teas, '01.
W. C. Steckle, '01,	Right Tackle,	C. E. Wallace, '01.
	" "	J. H. Outland, '00.
N. W. Snow, '02,	Right End,	W. J. Coombs, '00.
C. E. Street, '02,	Quarter-back,	F. E. Woodley, '01.
J. F. McLean, '00, Capt.,	Left Half,	A. R. Kennedy, '01.
C. M. Leiblee, '03,	Right Half,	J. P. Gardiner, '01.
H. S. Weeks, '02,	" "	
H. White, '02,	Full-back,	J. C. McCracken, '01.
E. M. Sweeley, '03,	"	

Referee: W. H. Corbin, '89, Yale. Umpire: W. A. Brooks, '77, Harvard. Linesmen: Mr. Bliss, Michigan; J. de Silver, '00, Pennsylvania. Timekeeper: L. T. Bliss, '93, Yale. Score: Michigan 10, Pennsylvania 11. First Half: Touchdown by J. F. McLean. Second Half: Touchdown by T. T. Hare; touchdown by G. C. McDonald; touchdown by T. T. Hare, goal by P. D. Overfield.

First Half: Pennsylvania wins the toss and takes the ball. Hare kicks off to Leiblee at 20, Leiblee running back the kick 12 yards. McLean skirts the end for 15 yards. Pennsylvania holds for downs and gets the ball. From this point by short gains through the line Pennsylvania works the ball to Michigan's 35-yard line. Here Michigan secures the ball. Leiblee, Steckle, McDonald, and McLean by plunges take the ball back to midfield, where it is fumbled. Pennsylvania tries two plunges at the line for a 4-yard gain, but the ball goes to Michigan on a foul. Steckle and McLean by end runs advance the ball to the 20-yard line. McLean again rounds the end and makes a touchdown. The try at goal fails. Hare kicks off to Michigan's 20, McLean running the ball back to the 45-yard line. Pennsylvania holds for downs and gets the ball, but immediately loses to Michigan, also on downs. Michigan now rushes the ball to Pennsylvania's 15-yard line, where it is lost on a foul. Pennsylvania develops sudden strength and by short plunges takes the ball to Michigan's 35-yard line, where it is lost on downs. McLean goes around the end for 40 yards. Michigan reaches the 30-yard line, where the ball goes to Pennsylvania on a quarter-back kick. The ball travels back and forth for some time until McCracken heels a fair catch on Michigan's 40-yard line. The try for goal is missed. Michigan rushes the ball out to the 45-yard line, where time is called for the half.

Second Half: Sweeley kicks off to Outland on Pennsylvania's 15-yard line, Outland running back the kick 10 yards. Pennsylvania carries ball to midfield and fumbles. Coombs gets ball on a fumble and on the first play goes around the end for 25 yards. The ball by short gains now travels to Michigan's 25-yard line, where Michigan recovers it on a fumble. Michigan gets off a bad punt, and Woodley, catching at 30, runs 25 yards. McCracken, Teas, and Hare by yard plunges take the ball over for a touchdown. No goal. Michigan punts to Pennsylvania at 37. Pennsylvania works the ball out to 40, where Michigan takes it on downs. McLean goes around the end for 20 yards. Steckle, McLean, and McDonald reach the 10-yard line. McDonald goes over for a touchdown. No goal.

Hare kicks off to McDonald at 30, the latter running back 25 yards. Overfield gets the ball at 45. Coombs punts down to 23. Sweeley kicks to Gardiner at centre. Mc-Cracken, Hare, and Teas by short gains reach Michigan's 20-yard line. Hare makes 8 around the end and then plunges through centre for a touchdown. The ball is punted out to Overfield, who kicks the goal. Michigan kicks off, but time soon after is called.

1900 to 1906 no games.

MICHIGAN vs. PENNSYLVANIA
Philadelphia, Nov. 17, 1906

MICHIGAN		PENNSYLVANIA
J. L. Loel, '09,	Left End,	I. G. Levene, '06.
W. L. Eycke, '07,	Left Tackle,	D. W. Draper, '09.
S. J. Davidson, '08,	Left Guard,	P. J. Gallagher, '09.
C. H. Clement, '07,	Centre,	J. K. Dwyer, '08.
W. D. Graham, '08,	Right Guard,	A. B. Ziegler, '07.
F. B. Newton, '08,	Right Tackle,	F. H. Gaston, '08.
	" "	U. V. Lavery, '07.
H. S. Hammond, '08,	Right End,	H. W. Scarlett, '07.
H. A. Workman, '07,	Quarter-back,	G. J. Lawrence, '07.
P. P. Magoffin, '08,	Left Half,	R. C. Folwell, '08.
H. S. Bishop, '09,	Right Half,	E. L. Greene, '08, Capt.
M. P. Rumney, '08,	" "	
J. C. Garrels, '07, Capt.,	Full-back,	W. M. Hollenback, '08.

Referee: W. S. Langford, '96, Trinity. Umpire: A. W. Kelly, '98, Princeton. Linesman: D. L. Fultz, '98, Brown. Score: Michigan 0, Pennsylvania 17. First Half: Touchdown by R. C. Folwell, goal by W. M. Hollenback. Second Half: Touchdown by E. L. Greene, goal by W. M. Hollenback; touchdown by E. L. Greene.

First Half: Michigan wins the toss and takes the goal. Pennsylvania kicks off and Michigan fumbles, but Garrels recovers the ball. On the line-up Garrels punts. Greene makes 2, but Michigan stops the next play and Pennsylvania punts to Magoffin at 35. The latter runs the kick back to midfield. Here Pennsylvania holds and Garrels punts. An exchange of kicks, a fumble, and a penalty sets Michi-

gan with the ball on Pennsylvania's 35-yard line. Garrels
tries to round Levene, but is thrown for a loss. Bishop tries
to gain on a trick play, but is stopped, and Pennsylvania
takes the ball. Greene punts to midfield. Michigan cannot
pierce the Red and Blue line and Garrels kicks. Another
fumble and a penalty brings Michigan back to Pennsylvania's 35-yard line, from which Garrels misses a goal from
placement. A kick-out and a run back gives Michigan
again a place on Pennsylvania's 35-yard line. Magoffin
makes 5. Michigan fumbles and Pennsylvania punts to
Michigan's 45, where another fumble gives Pennsylvania
the ball. Lawrence, on a quarter-back run terminating in
a forward pass to Levene, sends the ball to Michigan's 3-yard
line. Hollenback makes 2, and on the next play Folwell
goes over for the touchdown. Hollenback kicks the goal.

Second Half: Garrels kicks off, sending the ball to Lawrence at 35. Hollenback hits centre for 5. Michigan takes
the ball on downs. Garrels falls back to punt, but Gas-
ton blocks the kick and Gallagher gets the ball. An exchange of punts gives Pennsylvania the ball on Michigan's
35-yard line. Greene makes 6 and then 10, Folwell gets
through for 5. Michigan holds for downs and punts.
Ziegler catches and runs back to the 35-yard line. Hollenback from a kicking formation runs to the 15-yard line.
Folwell makes 8 and follows it for 6. Greene goes over for
the touchdown and Hollenback kicks the goal. Michigan
kicks off. A long kicking exchange ensues. At last Hollenback gets away for a 55-yard run, putting the ball on Michigan's 25-yard line. Ziegler makes 7, but Michigan takes
the ball on downs. Garrels punts. Lawrence and Hollenback by a double pass bring the ball to Michigan's 40-yard
line. Lavery recovers a short kick at 20. Folwell, Hollenback, and Greene in three plunges make a touchdown.
The goal is missed.

A STUBBORN DEFENCE.

Michigan holds Pennsylvania on the 1-yard line. Franklin Field, Nov. 17, 1906.

MICHIGAN VS. PENNSYLVANIA   321

MICHIGAN vs. PENNSYLVANIA
Ann Arbor, Nov. 16, 1907

MICHIGAN		PENNSYLVANIA
M. P. Rumney, '08,	Left End,	S. H. Pauxtis, '10.
W. M. Casey, '09,	Left Tackle,	D. W. Draper, '09.
W. J. Embs, '09,	Left Guard,	P. J. Gallagher, '09.
A. W. Schulz, '09,	Centre,	J. K. Dwyer, '08.
W. D. Graham, '08,	Right Guard,	A. B. Ziegler, '07.
W. Rheinschild, '08,	Right Tackle,	F. H. Gaston, '08.
H. S. Hammond, '08,	Right End,	H. W. Scarlett, '07.
W. S. Wasmund, '09,	Quarter-back,	C. Keinath, '09.
P. P. Magoffin, '08, Capt.,	Left Half,	R. C. Folwell, '08, Capt.
D. W. Allerdice, '10,	Right Half,	E. L. Greene, '08.
J. J. Miller, '10,	" "	
J. K. Watkins, '09,	Full-back,	W. M. Hollenback, '08.
J. L. Loell, '09,	"	

Referee: F. W. Murphy, '99, Brown. Umpire: H. M. Nelly, '02, Army. Field Judge: W. S. Langford, '96, Trinity. Linesman: W. E. McCormack, '97, Dartmouth. Score: Michigan 0, Pennsylvania 6. First Half: Touchdown by P. J. Gallagher, goal by H. W. Scarlett.

First Half: Michigan wins the toss and takes the west goal. Hollenback kicks off to Allerdice at 15. Michigan sends Watkins into the line for a gain of 10 yards in two plunges, but Pennsylvania holds and Hammond punts. Michigan holds Pennsylvania for no gain and Hollenback returns the kick. Magoffin catches on the 1-yard line and is thrown by Pauxtis 1 inch from the goal-line. Hammond punts to Keinath at 55. Hollenback circles the end for 10 and follows it up with another run for 8. A forward pass is tried, but Magoffin gets it. Michigan tries the Red and Blue line in vain and punts. The Pennsylvania forwards get through and the kick is high, Pennsylvania getting it on the 30-yard line. Hollenback and Greene make first down. Keinath falls back for a drop kick. Instead a short kick is sent over the rush line, which Gallagher gets and plants behind the line for a touchdown. Scarlett kicks the goal.

Second Half: Michigan kicks off and both teams settle down to a hard game, neither eleven being able to make consecutive gains, but punting after each second or third down. A punt from Pennsylvania goes out of bounds. Michigan on the run takes the ball quickly in, the rush line forming out of customary positions with one end back. The ball is put in play and a double pass occurs behind the line followed by a long pass forward down the field to the tackle, who carries it across the line and touches down. The touchdown is not allowed. Neither goal thereafter is threatened, although the ball several times reaches the 35-yard lines.

MICHIGAN vs. PENNSYLVANIA
Ann Arbor, Nov. 14, 1908

MICHIGAN		PENNSYLVANIA
W. J. Embs, '09,	Left End,	H. P. Braddock, '10.
" "	" "	T. Crooks, '10.
W. M. Casey, '09,	Left Tackle,	D. W. Draper, '09.
A. Benbrooke, '11,	Left Guard,	G. A. Dietrich, '10.
A. W. Schulz, '09, Capt.,	Centre,	W. Le R. Marks, '11.
H. A. Brennan, '09,	"	E. B. Cozens, '11.
J. Riley, '09,	Right Guard,	R. E. Lamberton, '10.
" "	" "	C. H. Pike, '11.
M. E. Crumpacker, '09,	Right Tackle,	F. H. Gaston, '08.
F. H. Linthicum, '10,	Right End,	H. W. Scarlett, '07.
W. S. Wasmund, '09,	Quarter-back,	C. Keinath, '09.
"	"	A. C. Miller, '10.
P. P. Douglas, '09,	Left Half,	J. W. Means, '10.
D. W. Allerdice, '10, Capt.,	Right Half,	J. O. Manier, '09.
S. J. Davison, '09,	Full-back,	W. M. Hollenback, '08, Capt.

Referee: W. S. Langford, '96, Trinity. Umpire: W. H. Edwards, '00, Princeton. Field Judge: G. Stahl, '03, Illinois. Linesman: A. C. Lerum, '03, Wisconsin. Score: Michigan 0, Pennsylvania 29. First Half: Touchdown by D. W. Draper, goal by H. W. Scarlett. Second Half: Touchdown by W. M. Hollenback, goal by H. W. Scarlett; touchdown by W. M. Hollenback, goal by H. W. Scarlett; touchdown by J. W. Means; touchdown by W. M. Hollenback, goal by H. W. Scarlett.

First Half: Pennsylvania wins the toss and selects the north goal. Allerdice kicks off to Hollenback. Pennsylvania makes a short gain and then punts. Michigan tries the Pennsylvania line for a first down, but, unable to advance consecutively, kicks. The play is now confined between the 25-yard lines, neither eleven being able to advance against the other. Toward the close of the half Pennsylvania springs a triple pass—Keinath, Means, and Draper —the latter running 45 yards for a touchdown. Scarlett kicks the goal. There is no further scoring in this half.

Second Half: Pennsylvania kicks off. After a series of kicks interspersed with a number of unimportant scrimmages Means gets off a short on-side kick to Braddock on Michigan's 40-yard line. On the next play Means shoots a forward pass to Braddock, which places the ball on the 10-yard line. Hollenback goes over for a touchdown and Scarlett kicks the goal. After kick-off play surges back and forth across the centre line for several minutes. At last Allerdice punts to Hollenback at Pennsylvania's 45-yard line. The latter runs brilliantly through the Michigan team 65 yards for a touchdown. Scarlett kicks the goal. A few minutes later Miller catches Allerdice's punt at midfield. Hollenback circles the end for 20. Means makes 10 through tackle. Hollenback gains 8, Means 5, and on the next play Hollenback reaches the 5-yard line. Means makes a touchdown. The goal is missed. Pennsylvania secures its last touchdown just before the close of the game by recovering a fumble on Michigan's 30-yard line. Hollenback makes 5, Manier 20, and Hollenback crosses the line for a touchdown. Scarlett kicks the goal.

MICHIGAN VS. PENNSYLVANIA
Philadelphia, Nov. 13, 1909

MICHIGAN		PENNSYLVANIA
F. J. Conklin, '12,	Left End,	H. P. Braddock, '10.
R. W. Ranney, '11,	" "	H. K. Cornell, '10.
W. M. Casey, '09,	Left Tackle,	J. L. Fretz, '12.
	" "	R. B. Burns, '10.
A. Benbrooke, '11,	Left Guard,	G. A. Dietrich, '10.
A. W. Smith, '12,	Centre,	E. B. Cozens, '11.
	"	W. W. Philler, '11.
W. P. Edmunds, '12,	Right Guard,	R. E. Lamberton, '10.
	" "	C. H. Pike, '11.
S. M. Wells, '11,	Right Tackle,	P. A. Ferrier, '11.
J. J. Miller, '11,	Right End,	S. S. Large, '11.
	" "	P. B. Kauffman, '11.
	" "	A. C. Miller, '10, Capt.
W. Wasmund, '09,	Quarter-back,	A. D. Thayer, '10.
J. Magidsohn, '11,	Left Half,	W. J. Young, '11.
	" "	F. Sommer, '11.
D. W. Allerdice, '10, Capt.,	Right Half,	A. G. Heilman, '12.
	" "	P. C. Irwin, '10.
F. G. Clark, '12,	Full-back,	D. L. Hutchinson, '12.
	"	J. H. Scott, '11.

Referee: W. S. Langford, '96, Trinity. Umpire: J. W. Beacham, '97, Cornell. Field Judge: D. L. Fultz, '98, Brown. Linesman: F. A. Hinkey, '95, Yale. Score: Michigan 12, Pennsylvania 6. First Half: Touchdown by J. Magidsohn, goal by D. W. Allerdice; touchdown by J. Magidsohn, goal by D. W. Allerdice; touchdown by D. L. Hutchinson, goal by H. P. Braddock.

First Half: Michigan wins the toss and takes the ball. Allerdice kicks to Braddock, who runs back 20 yards. Pennsylvania fumbles and Michigan gets the ball. Two attempts at end fail, but the ball is placed directly in front of the goal-posts. Allerdice falls back to try a drop kick, but the play is a feint, as the ball is passed forward to Conklin, who reaches the 8-yard line. On the second down Magidsohn is sent across for a touchdown and Allerdice kicks the goal.   Hutchinson kicks off for Pennsylvania an sends the ball to the 25-yard line.   Allerdice kicks to Pennsylvania's 45-yard line and Miller runs the ball back to Michigan's 50 before being downed.   Hutchinson makes 3 yards through the line and then 12 around the end.   Heilman makes 5 more, but a fumble gives the ball to Michigan.   Wasmund ploughs forward for 12 yards.   Magidsohn reaches Pennsylvania's 33-yard line and on a delayed tripple pass gets away for a touchdown.   Allerdice kicks the goal.   Hutchinson kicks over the goal-line.   Clark attempts to run it out, but is thrown on the 1-yard line.   Michigan punts from behind the goal-line, sending the ball out of bounds at 30.   Pennsylvania fails to make first down and Allerdice punts to 35.   Young and Heilman make first down.   A forward pass strikes the ground and Michigan takes the ball at 15.   Allerdice punts.   After several exchanges of kicks and rushes Pennsylvania shoots a forward pass from 50 to 35, Hutchinson to Cozens.   A second forward pass fails and Pennsylvania is penalized.   An on-side kick is recovered by Cozens at 20.   Heilman and Young make a first down.   Hutchinson crosses the remaining 13 yards for a touchdown.   Braddock kicks the goal.

Second Half: Hutchinson kicks over the goal-line.   Michigan puts the ball in play at 25.   Allerdice punts to Hutchinson at 43.   Pennsylvania rushes the ball to the 20-yard line, where · Michigan holds for downs.   After the ball changes hands several times on kicks and downs Wasmund runs around the end for 45 yards, placing the ball at midfield.   Michigan cannot gain farther and punts.   Neither team in the remainder of this half seriously threatens the other's goal, the play consisting of ineffective gains followed by punts.

MICHIGAN vs. PENNSYLVANIA
Philadelphia, Nov. 12, 1910

MICHIGAN		PENNSYLVANIA
W. P. Edmunds, '12,	Left End,	W. Le R. Marks, '11.
	" "	E. Thayer, '12.
F. J. Conklin, '12,	Left Tackle,	L. L. Rodgers, '12.
A. Benbrooke, '11, Capt.,	Left Guard,	C. C. Wolferth, '12.
A. B. Cornwell, '13,	Centre,	E. B. Cozens, '11, Capt.
C. P. Quinn, '13,	Right Guard,	J. M. Cramer, '13.
W. D. Cole, '12,	Right Tackle,	H. H. Morris, '12.
	" "	T. F. Dillon, '13.
S. M. Wells, '11,	Right End,	L. W. Jourdet, '13.
N. McMillan, '13,	Quarter-back,	J. H. Scott, '11.
	"	W. J. H. Hough, '11.
J. Magidsohn, '11,	Left Half,	F. L. Ramsdell, '11.
	" "	J. P. Harrington, '13.
	" "	W. J. Young, '11.
V. C. Pattingill, '11,	Right Half,	F. Sommer, '11.
	" "	L. M. Kennedy, '13.
G. C. Thompson, '12,	Full-back,	E. L. Mercer, '13.

Referee: W. H. Eckersall, '07, Chicago. Umpire: C. B. Marshall, '04, Harvard. Field Judge: W. G. Crowell, '06, Swarthmore. Linesman: J. W. Beacham, '97, Cornell. Score: Michigan 0, Pennsylvania 0.

First Quarter: Michigan wins the toss and elects to receive the kick-off. Mercer kicks to Pattingill. Magidsohn makes 5, Thompson 5, Cozens throws the next runner for a loss, and Thompson punts. Mercer makes 5, but Scott is forced to kick. Several plays on each side are limited to a short line plunge and a necessary kick. Thompson tries a place kick on the 40-yard line, but Marks blocks the ball. Michigan recovers the ball at 50. Magidsohn hits the line for 10. McMillan adds 12 more. Magidsohn reaches the 35-yard line. Pennsylvania holds for downs. Unable to gain, Scott punts. By hard plunges Magidsohn and Pattingill advance the ball 25 yards, when Pennsylvania again holds for downs. A bounding kick crosses the line. Pennsylvania brings the ball out to the 25-yard line and the quarter closes.

Second Quarter: Scott sends a long punt to McMillan. Magidsohn hits centre for 5. Michigan is penalized and fumbles, but recovers the ball. Thompson punts to Scott. Mercer circles the end for 15 yards. Kennedy breaks through into a clear field, but slips and falls. Scott punts to McMillan on Michigan's 40. Several exchanges of punts, with a long run by Mercer, brings the ball to Michigan's 30-yard line. Mercer plunges to the 15-yard mark. He adds 5 more. Michigan throws the next runner for a 20-yard loss. Thayer is sent back to try for a field goal, but the kick is blocked, Cozens getting the ball. A forward pass is stopped and the half closes.

Third Quarter: Mercer kicks to Edmunds, who runs back 15 yards. Thompson punts out of bounds. Michigan fumbles the return and Cozens gets the ball on Michigan's 15-yard line. Michigan holds for downs and takes the ball. An exchange of punts places the ball on Michigan's 12-yard line, in the latter's possession. Several kicks now are exchanged and Wells gets away on a forward pass and races to Pennsylvania's goal-line, but is put back to the 12-yard mark, having stepped out of bounds. Pennsylvania holds for downs. Mercer makes 5 on a double pass. Scott punts. Further kicks are exchanged and the quarter closes.

Fourth Quarter: Marks throws Magidsohn for a loss of 2 yards on Michigan's 45-yard line. An exchange of punts and a fumble by Pennsylvania gives Michigan the ball on the former's 40-yard line. Magidsohn gets around the end for 15 yards. McMillan's forward pass hits the ground and Pennsylvania takes the ball on the 20-yard line. Scott punts. Kicks are exchanged. Edmunds shoots a forward pass 20 yards to Wells. A long punting duel follows, terminating in a run back of 35 yards by Mercer placing the ball on Pennsylvania's 40-yard line. Mercer punts. Michigan fumbles, but Cornwell recovers the ball. The game now ends.

CHAPTER XVI

MINNESOTA VS. WISCONSIN

MINNESOTA VS. WISCONSIN
Minneapolis, Nov. 15, 1890

MINNESOTA		WISCONSIN
J. A. Harris,	Left End,	T. P. Loope,'91.
W. C. Muir,	Left Tackle,	W. C. McNaught, '93.
C. J. Flannagan,	Left Guard,	J. D. Freeman, '94.
J. E. Maddigan,	Centre,	H. Oppenheim, '91.
S. S. Start,	Right Guard,	M. R. Wiener, '91.
G. C. Sikes,	Right Tackle,	E. H. Ahara, '92.
C. E. Guthrie,	Right End,	R. J. Logeman, '92.
A. F. Pillsbury,	Quarter-back,	J. B. Kerr, '89, Capt.
W. J. Leary,	Left Half,	L. D. Sumner, '93.
E. L. Patterson,	Right Half,	F. W. Prael, '91.
G. K. Belden,	Full-back,	J. H. McNaught, '91.

Substitutions by Minnesota: G. B. Rossman, H. E. White, D. R. Burbank. Referee: L. K. Hull, '83, Yale. Umpire: G. P. Kletsch. Score: Minnesota 63, Wisconsin 0.

First Half: Touchdown by Patterson. Touchdown by Harding and goal by Belden. Touchdown by Patterson. Touchdown by Patterson and goal by Belden.

Second Half: Touchdown by Patterson and goal by Belden. Touchdown by Leary and goal by Belden. Touchdown by Leary and goal by Belden. Touchdown by Leary. Touchdown by Patterson and goal by Belden. Touchdown by Patterson and goal by Belden. Touchdown by Patterson. Goal from the field by Belden.

MINNESOTA VS. WISCONSIN
Minneapolis, Oct. 24, 1891

MINNESOTA		WISCONSIN
L. C. Edson,	Left End,	D. H. Walker, '92.
E. C. Bisbee,	" "	
R. C. Dewey,	Left Tackle,	J. D. Freeman, '94.
C. J. Flannagan,	Left Guard,	G. N. Knapp, '95.
J. E. Madigan,	Centre,	F. Kull, '94.
E. P. Harding,	Right Guard,	L. B. Flower, '92.
G. C. Sikes,	Right Tackle,	J. F. A. Pyre, '92.
D. R. Burbank,	Right End,	J. B. Kerr, '89.
A. F. Pillsbury,	Quarter-back,	E. H. Ahara, '92, Capt.
W. J. Leary,	Left Half,	H. M. Coleman, '95.
E. L. Patterson,	Right Half,	R. C. Thiele, '93.
G. K. Belden,	Full-back,	L. D. Sumner, '93.
C. S. Hale,	"	

Score: Minnesota 26, Wisconsin 12. No record of officials. First Half: Touchdown by H. M. Coleman, goal by J. F. A. Pyre; touchdown by W. J. Leary, goal by G. K. Belden; touchdown by L. D. Sumner, goal by J. F. A. Pyre. Second Half: Touchdown by E. L. Patterson, goal by G. K. Belden; touchdown by A. F. Pillsbury, goal by G. K. Belden; touchdown by W. J. Leary; touchdown by A. F. Pillsbury.

First Half: Minnesota wins the toss and takes the ball. Starting with the V, Minnesota makes 15 yards. A run by Leary and a line plunge by Harding takes the ball to Wisconsin's 5-yard line, where Minnesota fumbles. Coleman gets the ball and runs 105 yards for a touchdown. Pyre kicks the goal. Minnesota starts off with the wedge and by rapid line plays carries the ball to Wisconsin's 5-yard line, from which Leary is sent over for a touchdown. Belden kicks the goal. Wisconsin makes 15 yards in the V. The ball changes sides frequently on punts and downs without substantial advantage to either eleven. Just as the half is closing Sumner catches a punt on his 25-yard line and runs through the entire Minnesota team for a touchdown. Pyre kicks the goal.

Second Half: Wisconsin opens play with the V and makes 2 yards. Minnesota holds for downs and Wisconsin punts. Minnesota opens a fierce line attack and rapidly carries the ball by plunges of Harding and Pillsbury to their opponent's 5-yard line, from which Patterson is sent across for a touchdown. Belden kicks the goal. Wisconsin makes 10 yards in the V, but is soon forced to punt. Minnesota again carries the ball the length of the field by line plays and sends Pillsbury across the last line for the touchdown. Goal. Wisconsin gains 15 yards in the V and by line plays reaches Minnesota's 10-yard line, where the ball is lost on downs. Minnesota starts an attack on the tackles and reaches the 10-yard line. Leary gets across for a touchdown. A sixth touchdown is scored for Minnesota by Pillsbury. No goal.

MINNESOTA vs. WISCONSIN
Madison, Oct. 29, 1892

MINNESOTA		WISCONSIN
W. F. Dalrymple,	Left End,	C. C. Case, '93.
G. C. Sikes,	Left Tackle,	J. H. Francis, '94.
A. T. Larson,	Left Guard,	T. P. Krenshaw, '95.
J. E. Madigan,	Centre,	F. Kull, '94.
E. P. Harding,	Right Guard,	H. H. Jacobs, '93.
C. Larson,	Right Tackle,	T. P. Silverwood, '96.
E. C. Bisbee,	Right End,	J. R. Richards, '96.
A. F. Pillsbury,	Quarter-back,	T. U. Lyman, '94, Capt.
E. L. Patterson,	Left Half,	J. C. Karel, '95.
D. R. Burbank,	Right Half,	R. C. Thiele, '93.
R. H. Folewell,	Full-back,	F. H. Dillon, '95.

Score: Wisconsin 4, Minnesota 32. No record of officials and makers of scores.

First Half: Minnesota wins the toss and takes the ball. The V gains 20 yards. Line plays by Larson and Patterson carry the ball to Wisconsin's 20-yard line, from which a criss-cross sends Patterson around the end for a touchdown.

Wisconsin gains 15 yards in the V. By end runs Karel and
Thiele reach the 10-yard line. Thiele again circles the end
for a touchdown. Minnesota gains 5 in the V. Both teams
now play hard, but cannot come within striking distance of
each other's goal.

Second Half: Wisconsin opens with the V for 15 yards.
Thiele, Karel, and Dillon by line plunges reach the 4-yard
line. Here Minnesota holds for downs. Minnesota now
opens up a game largely of trick plays, double passes, criss-
crosses, fake runs, line and position shifts, which completely bewilders their opponents, by which 6 touchdowns
are scored. Folewell also kicks a goal from the field.

MINNESOTA vs. WISCONSIN

Minneapolis, Nov. 11, 1893

MINNESOTA		WISCONSIN
W. F. Dalrymple,	Left End,	W. H. Sheldon, '96.
C. Larson,	Left Tackle,	J. D. Freeman, '94.
A. T. Larson,	Left Guard,	C. W. Bunge, '95.
J. E. Madigan,	Centre,	F. Kull, '94.
E. P. Harding,	Right Guard,	H. H. Jacobs, '93.
W. C. Muir,	Right Tackle,	P. H. Davis, '94.
E. C. Bisbee,	Right End,	H. F. Dickinson, '96.
C. H. Van Campen,	Quarter-back,	T. U. Lyman, '94, Capt.
C. Adams,	Left Half,	F. W. Nelson, '97.
A. F. Pillsbury,	Right Half,	J. C. Karel, '95.
H. C. Cutler,	Full-back,	J. R. Richards, '96.

Score: Wisconsin 0, Minnesota 40. No record of officials. First
Half: Touchdown by C. Adams; touchdown by A. F. Pillsbury, goal
by H. C. Cutler. Second Half: Touchdown by E. P. Harding, goal by
H. C. Cutler; touchdown by A. F. Pillsbury, goal by H. C. Cutler;
touchdown by C. Adams, goal by H. C. Cutler; touchdown by A. F.
Pillsbury, goal by H. C. Cutler; touchdown by C. Adams, goal by
H. C. Cutler.

First Half: Minneapolis wins the toss and takes the ball.
The game starts with a flying wedge, Davis stopping Pills-

bury for no gain.   Wisconsin takes the ball on downs.   The latter sends several plays in succession against Minnesota's tackles and the ball reaches the 3-yard mark, where it is fumbled.   Cutler punts.   Wisconsin cannot gain consecutively and Richards punts.   Minnesota by line plays reaches their opponent's 25-yard line.   Adams circles the end for a touchdown.   Wisconsin gains 10 yards in the flying wedge and Karel and Nelson force the ball to Minnesota's 5-yard line.   Minnesota takes the ball on downs and by line plays takes the ball the length of the field, where Pillsbury makes a touchdown.   Cutler kicks the goal.   Wisconsin, starting with the flying wedge, advances the ball to Minnesota's 10-yard line, where the ball is lost on a fumble. Minnesota drives it to Wisconsin's 12-yard line and time is called for the half.

Second Half: Wisconsin gains 10 yards in the wedge, but is then held for downs.   Pillsbury makes two long end runs terminating in a touchdown.   Obtaining the ball on downs on the 40-yard line Minnesota hammers Wisconsin's line until the ball rests on the 25-yard line.   Harding goes around the end for a touchdown.   Pillsbury makes the next touchdown by securing the ball on a fumble and running 40 yards.   Goal.   Wisconsin is held for downs at the 35-yard line and Pillsbury and Adams on trick plays double the ends for the distance and a touchdown.   Goal. Wisconsin carries the ball to Minnesota's 10-yard line, where the latter takes the ball on downs.   Line plays reach Wisconsin's 10-yard line and Pillsbury gets across for a touchdown.   Goal.   Just as time is expiring Adams gets away for a 45-yard run and touchdown.   Goal.

MINNESOTA VS. WISCONSIN
Madison, Nov. 17, 1894

MINNESOTA		WISCONSIN
O. K. Harrison,	Left End,	W. H. Sheldon, '96.
" "	" "	J. C. Major, '96.
J. S. Dalrymple,	Left Tackle,	W. Alexander, '97.
A. T. Larson,	Left Guard.	G. W. Bunge, '95.
G. A. Finlayson,	Centre,	F. Kull, '94.
E. P. Harding,	Right Guard,	J. E. Ryan, '95.
W. J. Walker,	Right Tackle,	J. F. A. Pyre, '92.
W. F. Dalrymple,	Right End,	H. F. Dickinson, '96.
C. H. Van Campen	Quarter-back,	T. U. Lyman, '94, Capt.
C. Adams,	Left Half,	F. W. Nelson, '97.
W. N. Southworth,	Right Half,	J. C. Karel, '95.
H. C. Cutler,	Full-back,	J. R. Richards, '96.
H. A. Parkyn,	"	

Referee: H. H. Stepp, '96, Grinnell. Umpire: F. M. Gould, '93, Amherst. Score: Wisconsin 6, Minnesota 0. Second Half: Touchdown by J. C. Karel, goal by T. U. Lyman.

First Half: Wisconsin wins the toss and takes the goal. Minnestoa kicks off and Wisconsin rushes the ball by line plays to their opponent's 30-yard line, where the latter holds for downs. Minnesota drives the ball to Wisconsin's 30-yard line and there loses on downs. Karel and Nelson by end runs reach Minnesota's 2-yard mark, where the ball is fumbled. Cutler punts to centre. Wisconsin fumbles and Minnestoa gets the ball. Cutler again punts. Several exchanges of kicks follow and time for the half is called.

Second Half: Richards kicks to Minnesota's 25-yard line. Minnesota reaches midfield on line plunges, but there is held for downs. Karel gets around the end for 50 yards and a touchdown. Lyman kicks the goal. Minnesota kicks off and Karel returns. Larson makes 15 yards and line plays carry the ball to Wisconsin's 35-yard

line. Parkyn tries a drop kick, but misses. Karel gets
around the end for 40 yards. Minnesota takes the ball
on downs and Parkyn punts. The play remains near centre during the remainder of the half.

MINNESOTA vs. WISCONSIN
Minneapolis, Nov. 16, 1895

MINNESOTA		WISCONSIN
J. M. Harrison,	Left End,	W. H. Sheldon, '96.
J. S. Dalrymple,	Left Tackle,	W. Alexander, '97.
A. T. Larson,	Left Guard,	J. P. Riordan, '98.
J. C. Fulton,	Centre,	F. Kull, '94.
G. A. Finlayson,	Right Guard,	N. A. Comstock, '97.
W. J. Walker,	Right Tackle,	J. F. A. Pyre, '92.
T. M. Kehoe,	Right End,	H. F. Dickinson, '96.
C. Adams,	Quarter-back,	G. H. Trautman, '96.
H. C. Loomis,	Left Half,	J. P. Gregg, '99.
	" "	G. Thompson, '99.
	" "	F. W. Nelson, '97.
H. B. Gilbert,	Right Half,	J. C. Karel, '95.
H. A. Parkyn,	Full-back,	J. R. Richards, '96, Capt.

Referee: H. H. Stepp, '96, Grinnell. Umpire: H. Cornish, C. A. A.
Linesmen: E. P. Harding, Minnesota; A. R. Smith, Wisconsin.
Score: Wisconsin 10, Minnesota 14. First Half: Touchdown by J. F.
A. Pyre, goal by J. R. Richards; touchdown by T. M. Kehoe; touch-
down by J. R. Richards. Second Half: Touchdown by H. B. Gilbert;
touchdown and goal by H. B. Gilbert.

First Half: Minnesota wins the toss and takes the goal.
Wisconsin kicks to Minnesota's 10-yard line and Parkyn
runs back the kick 10 yards. Wisconsin takes the ball on
downs and Minnesota immediately recovers it likewise.
Parkyn punts. Wisconsin opens a rapid attack on the line
and carries the ball to Minnesota's 2-yard mark, where
the latter holds for downs. Parkyn kicks to Karel. Wisconsin now attacks the centre and creeps forward line
after line until Pyre is sent through for the last 5 yards

and a touchdown. Richards kicks the goal. Parkyn kicks
off and Richards returns. Minnesota advances 20 yards,
but the ball goes to Wisconsin on downs. A fumble occurs
and Kehoe gets the ball and runs for a touchdown. The
goal is missed. Wisconsin kicks off and Adams runs back
the kick 10 yards. Wisconsin gets the ball on a punt.
Alexander makes 5, Karel 30, Karel 5, bringing the ball to
the 10-yard line. Richards goes through centre for the
touchdown. The goal is missed. Time is called for the
half.

Second Half: Minnesota kicks off and Karel runs the
kick back 10 yards. Karel circles the end for 40 yards.
Minnesota takes the ball on downs. Parkyn, Larson, Gilbert, and Loomis now hit the line in rapid succession, sending the ball forward line after line until a touchdown is made.
Wisconsin kicks off and Minnesota again hammers the ball
the length of the field, but is held for downs on Wisconsin's
10-yard line. Minnesota recovers the ball and Gilbert
makes a touchdown. Goal. Wisconsin kicks off. Minnesota returns. Karel and Nelson in end runs take the
ball to centre and a fierce attack on the line advances the
ball to Minnesota's 20-yard line, where time is called.

MINNESOTA VS. WISCONSIN
Madison, Nov. 21, 1896.

MINNESOTA		WISCONSIN
J. M. Harrison,	Left End,	W. H. Sheldon, '96.
A. N. Smith,	Left Tackle,	W. A. Atkinson, '97, Capt.
G. A. Finlayson,	Left Guard,	J. P. Riordan, '98.
J. C. Fulton,	Centre,	N. A. Comstock, '97.
E. P. Harding,	Right Guard,	J. E. Ryan, '95.
I. A. Parry,	Right Tackle,	J. F. A. Pyre, '92.
H. A. Scandrett,	Right End,	C. L. Brewer, '99.
G. E. Cole,	Quarter-back,	J. P. Gregg, '99.
	"	C. W. McPherson, '99.

MINNESOTA		WISCONSIN
S. W. Bagley,	Left Half,	F. W. Nelson, '97.
" "	" "	H. J. Peele, 99.
M. Teigen,	Right Half,	J. C. Karel, 95.
H. C. Loomis,	Full-back,	J. R. Richards, '96.

Referee: C. F. Roby, '99, Chicago. Umpire: R. D. Wrenn, '95, Harvard. Score: Minnesota 0, Wisconsin 6. Second Half: Touchdown and goal by J. R. Richards.

First Half: Minnesota wins the toss and takes the goal. Richards kicks to Bagley, who runs back 5 yards. Minnesota tries two line plays with a small gain and then punts to Wisconsin's 25. A penalty advances the latter 10 yards. Karel makes 5, Nelson 2, and Richards 5. Other line plays net 20 yards, but the ball is lost on downs. Minnesota rushes 20 yards and fumbles. Wisconsin in brilliant line plays reaches their opponent's 8-yard line, where it goes to Minnesota on a fumble. Harding goes through centre for 5 yards. Loomis circles the end for 25 more. Minnesota now steadily advances the ball to Wisconsin's 25-yard line, where they are held for downs. Wisconsin punts to Minnesota's 45. The latter returns to Wisconsin's 40. Wisconsin fumbles and the ball goes to Minnesota. The ball by short gains reaches Wisconsin's 25-yard line, where it is fumbled. Richards punts to centre and time is called.

Second Half: Loomis kicks off and Pyre runs the kick back 15 yards. Wisconsin fumbles and it is Minnesota's ball on their opponent's 30-yard line. Wisconsin holds for downs and takes the ball. Richards punts to centre. On the first play Minnesota fumbles and Richards on lining up punts across the goal-line. Minnesota kicks out. A series of kicks are exchanged which with a fumble gives Minnesota the ball on Wisconsin's 35-yard line. The latter holds for downs. A punt and a fumble give Wisconsin the ball at centre. Minnesota does not yield and Richards punts across the goal-line. Loomis kicks out and Karel runs the ball back 15 yards. A centre play yields 5 and then the ball goes to Minnesota on a fumble. Minnesota by line plunges reaches the centre of the field, where Wisconsin takes the ball and rushes to the 25-yard line to lose on downs. Minnesota makes 10, but Wisconsin holds for fourth down. Brewer circles the end for 25. Karel reaches Minnesota's 10-yard line. Atkinson makes 3, Peele 1, Richards to the 1-foot mark. Minnesota holds for downs. The ball is recovered on a fumble. Atkinson makes 1 yard, Karel 3, Richards over for a touchdown and goal.

MINNESOTA VS. WISCONSIN
Minneapolis, Oct. 30, 1897.

MINNESOTA		WISCONSIN
J. M. Harrison,	Left End,	J. Dean, '01.
G. A. Finlayson,	Left Tackle,	H. R. Holmes, '99.
A. N. Smith,	Left Guard,	J. P. Riordan, '98, Capt.
J. G. Winkjer,	Centre,	W. C. Hazzard, '98.
A. K. Ingalls,	Right Guard,	N. A. Comstock, '97.
C. Nicoulin,	Right Tackle,	H. G. Forrest, '98.
G. R. Shepley,	Right End,	E. S. Anderson, '99.
G. E. Cole,	Quarter-back,	J. P. Gregg, '99.
G. W. Evans,	Left Half,	H. F. Cochems, '97.
S. W. Bagley,	Right Half,	H. J. Peele, '99.
	" "	W. M. Joliffe, P. G.
H. C. Loomis,	Full-back,	P. J. O'Dea, '00.

Referee: L. Stacey, '96, Army. Umpire: R. D. Wrenn, '95, Harvard. Score: Minnesota 0, Wisconsin 39. First Half: Touchdown by H. J. Peele, goal by P. J. O'Dea; touchdown by H. J. Peele, goal by J. P. Gregg; touchdown by J. P. Riordan, goal by J. P. Gregg; goal from field by P. J. O'Dea. Second Half: Touchdown by J. P. Riordan; touchdown by H. J. Peele, goal by J. P. Gregg; touchdown by W. M. Joliffe, goal by P. J. O'Dea.

First Half: Wisconsin wins the toss and takes the goal. Cochems runs back the kick-off 15 yards. O'Dea punts to Minnesota's 20-yard line, where Wisconsin takes the ball on

a fumble. Minnesota regains the ball on downs and punts.
Wisconsin returns. Further kicks are exchanged and Wisconsin finally gets the ball at midfield. Wisconsin now
opens up a sharp attack on their opponent's rush-line and
the ball creeps forward line by line until it reaches the 10-
yard line. Riordan makes 5 and Peele goes across for the
touchdown. O'Dea kicks the goal. Minnesota kicks off
and Wisconsin soon is forced to punt. Wisconsin does not
yield a yard and Minnesota punts. Riordan, Forrest, and
Cochems make steady gains until the ball rests on the 3-yard
line. Peele goes around the end for a touchdown. Gregg
kicks the goal. Minnesota kicks off and O'Dea returns.
Wisconsin holds for downs at centre. Line plays again
send the ball steadily down the field and Riordan is shot
across the last line for a touchdown. Gregg kicks the goal.
Minnesota kicks off and Wisconsin rushes the ball to Minnesota's 30-yard line, where the ball is lost on a fumble. Minnesota cannot gain and punts to O'Dea at 45. A line
plunge reaches the 35-yard line, where Minnesota holds for
two downs. O'Dea falls back and kicks a goal from the
field.

Second Half: Wisconsin kicks off, and Minnesota, failing
to pierce the line, punts to 40. Wisconsin cannot get in
motion and O'Dea punts to opponent's 5-yard line. Wisconsin holds for two downs and Loomis falls behind his
goal-line to kick, sending the ball out to the 35-yard
line. Cochems, Holmes, and Gregg by line plays carry the
ball to the 10-yard line. Peele gets through for 6 and
Riordan covers the remaining distance for a touchdown.
The try at goal fails. Minnesota kicks off and O'Dea returns. Minnesota fumbles and Wisconsin gets the ball on
their opponent's 35-yard line. Minnesota puts up a stubborn defence and O'Dea tries a drop kick, but misses.
Loomis kicks out to O'Dea and the latter runs back 30

yards. Forrest, Peele, and Gregg reach the 4-yard line. Peele is sent through centre for a touchdown. Gregg kicks the goal. Minnesota kicks off and Wisconsin rushes the ball to Minnesota's 40-yard line, where it is lost on downs. Minnesota is soon forced to punt. Wisconsin starts a fierce attack on their opponent's line and steadily forces the ball to the last line, which Joliffe crosses for a touchdown. O'Dea kicks the goal.

MINNESOTA VS. WISCONSIN

Madison, Oct. 29, 1898

MINNESOTA		WISCONSIN
V. Von Schlegel,	Left End,	E. B. Cochems, '00.
R. Gray,	Left Tackle,	A. H. Curtis, '02.
	" "	I. Mather, '01.
A. N. Smith,	Left Guard,	H. R. Chamberlain, '99.
L. A. Page,	Centre,	A. A. Chamberlain, '99, Cpt.
C. Nicoulin,	Right Guard,	C. Yeager, '01.
G. Anderson,	Right Tackle,	J. T. S. Lyle, '00.
H. A. Scandrett,	Right End,	W. Fugitt, '01.
H. C. Adams,	Quarter-back,	P. H. Tratt, '01.
	"	H. E. Bradley, '01.
G. Otte,	Left Half,	W. M. Joliffe, P. G.
G. B. Coleman,	Right Half,	A. F. Larson, '02.
G. R. Shepley,	Full-back,	E. S. Anderson, '99.

Referee: Evarts Wrenn, '92, Harvard. Umpire: R. D. Wrenn, '95, Harvard. Score: Minnesota 0. Wisconsin 28. First Half: Touchdown by A. F. Larson, goal by E. S. Anderson; touchdown by A. F. Larson, goal by E. S. Anderson; touchdown by H. R. Chamberlain; touchdown and goal by E. S. Anderson. Second Half: Touchdown by E. B. Cochems.

First Half: Minnesota wins the toss and takes the goal. Anderson kicks off, Minnesota fumbles, Larson gets the ball and crosses the line for a touchdown. Anderson kicks the goal. Minnesota kicks off and then holds Wisconsin for no gain. Anderson punts. For a long time play swings back and forth between the 35-yard lines. At last Larson

gets around Minnesota's end and runs 35 yards for a touchdown. Anderson makes the goal. Minnesota kicks off and
Wisconsin puts the ball down for a scrimmage on the 20-
yard line. End runs, line plunges, and trick plays follow
one another in rapid succession and the ball is carried to
Minnesota's 3-yard line, where the latter takes the ball on
downs. The ball is kicked out to the 20-yard line. Larson makes 5, Joliffe 5, Larson 3, and Joliffe reaches the 2-
yard mark. H. R. Chamberlain breaks through centre for a
touchdown. The goal is missed. Minnesota kicks off
and Anderson runs the ball back 20 yards. Tratt circles
the end for 20 more. Joliffe and Anderson hit the line for
continual gains until the 5-yard line is reached. Anderson
is shot through centre for a touchdown. A moment later
he kicks the goal. Minnesota kicks off and Wisconsin,
putting the ball down for scrimmage at 20, forces the way
by short line plunges until Minnesota's 3-yard mark is
reached, where time is called for the half.

Second Half: Wisconsin kicks off and Shepley runs the
kick back 10 yards and then punts. The ball for some time
changes sides frequently on punts and downs and play does
not pass either 35-yard line. Minnesota forms to punt on
the 45-yard line. The Wisconsin forwards come through
and the kick is blocked. Anderson gets the ball and runs
20 yards. Another end run and a penalty place the ball
on Minnesota's 10-yard line. Cochems skirts the end for
a touchdown. Anderson kicks the goal.

MINNESOTA vs. WISCONSIN
Minneapolis, Nov. 18, 1899

MINNESOTA		WISCONSIN
G. Dobie,	Left End,	E. B. Cochems, '00.
	" "	W. Juneau, '04.
G. Otte,	Left Tackle,	E. R. Blair, '03.
B. Aune,	Left Guard,	A. C. Lerum, '03.

MINNESOTA		WISCONSIN
L. A. Page,	Centre,	A. A. Chamberlain, '99.
F. Tift,	Right Guard,	C. W. Rodgers, P. G.
R. Gray,	Right Tackle,	A. H. Curtis, '02.
H. A. Scandrett,	Right End,	F. S. Hyman, '02.
G. E. Cole,	Quarter-back,	G. H. Wilmarth, P. G.
G. W. Evans,	Left Half,	H. J. Peele, '99.
	" "	G. Senn, '01.
W. Keinboltz,	Right Half,	S. E. Driver, '03.
F. Cameron,	" "	W. M. Joliffe, P. G.
W. C. Knowlton,	Full-back,	P. J. O'Dea, '00, Capt.

Referee: W. W. Heffelfinger, '91, Yale. Umpire: W. B. Burtt, '99, Army. Score: Minnesota 0, Wisconsin 19. Second Half: Goal from field by P. J. O'Dea; touchdown by E. B. Cochems, goal by P. J. O'Dea; touchdown by F. S. Hyman, goal by P. J. O'Dea; safety by W. C. Knowlton.

First Half: Wisconsin wins the toss and takes the goal. Knowlton kicks off and Wilmarth runs the ball back 10 yards. O'Dea punts and Wisconsin recovers the kick on Minnesota's 40-yard line. Unable to gain by rushing, O'Dea tries a drop kick, but misses the post. Knowlton kicks out to centre and O'Dea runs the ball back 20 yards. O'Dea tries another drop, but again misses. Minnesota gets the ball on the 15-yard line. Aune gets through for a run of 30 yards. Wisconsin stands firm and Minnesota punts. Several kicks are exchanged and a fumble gives Minnesota the ball on Wisconsin's 30-yard line. The latter takes the ball on downs. Play during the rest of this half is confined between the 35-yard lines.

Second Half: O'Dea kicks off and Knowlton returns the kick to centre. Driver, Peele, and Curtis advance the ball to Minnesota's 20-yard line. O'Dea on a fake kick makes 10 yards more. Two plunges into the line net 5. Minnesota holds for downs and takes the ball on the 2-yard mark. Knowlton punts and O'Dea heels a fair catch on the 35-yard line. The try at goal is missed. Minnesota kicks out and Wisconsin recovers the ball on the 25-yard line. Unable to gain by rushing, O'Dea falls back and drops a goal from the field. Minnesota kicks off and O'Dea returns the kick to centre. Punts are exchanged. Minnesota puts the ball down for scrimmage on their 5-yard line. Knowlton falls behind the line to punt. Cochems is through and blocks the kick, falling on the ball for a touchdown. O'Dea kicks the goal. Minnesota kicks off and O'Dea returns. Minnesota tries the line, but is forced to punt. Hyman blocks the kick and picking up the ball runs 40 yards for a touchdown. O'Dea kicks the goal. Minnesota kicks off and Wisconsin by several rushes and kicks transfers the ball into Minnesota's territory. O'Dea tries a drop kick from the 45-yard line, but misses. Knowlton catches on his 5-yard line. Minnesota fumbles and the ball rolls behind the goal-line. Knowlton recovers it for a safety. Time is then called.

MINNESOTA vs. WISCONSIN
Minneapolis, Nov. 3, 1900

MINNESOTA		WISCONSIN
B. Aune, '01,	Left End,	E. B. Cochems, '00.
	" "	A. C. Abbott, '04.
C. S. Fee,	Left Tackle,	A. A. Chamberlain, '99, Cpt.
P. S. Smith,	" "	
J. G. Flynn,	Left Guard,	J. P. Riordan, '98.
L. A. Page,	Centre,	E. Scow, '01.
G. F. Mueller,	Right Guard,	A. C. Lerum, '03.
H. C. Tweet,	Right Tackle,	A. H. Curtis, '02.
C. Hoyt,	Right End,	W. Juneau, '04.
G. Dobie,	Quarter-back,	P. H. Tratt, '01.
W. S. Lafans,	Left Half,	A. L. Marshall, '04.
H. Van Valkenburg,	Right Half,	A. F. Larson, '02.
W. C. Knowlton,	Full-back,	W. E. Schreiber, '04.
	"	S. E. Driver '03.

Referee: R. D. Wrenn, '95, Harvard. Umpire: Evarts Wrenn, '92, Harvard. Score: Minnesota 6, Wisconsin 5. First Half: Touchdown by E. B. Cochems; touchdown by B. Aune, goal by W. C. Knowlton.

First Half: Minnesota wins the toss and takes the wind. Wisconsin kicks off and Knowlton runs the kick back 10 yards. By mass plays Minnesota sends Lafans and Van Valkenburg forward 15 yards, where they are held for downs. Wisconsin cannot gain and Minnesota takes the ball on downs. A fumble at once transfers it back to Wisconsin. Marshall and Larson hit the line for 15 yards. Several penalties take the ball to Minnesota's 5-yard line. Minnesota holds until the last down, when Wisconsin gets off a quarter-back kick, which Cochems recovers and secures a touchdown. The try at goal fails. Minnesota kicks off, sending the ball across the goal-line. Wisconsin kicks out. Minnesota puts the ball down for a scrimmage at midfield. Van Valkenburg, Lafans, and Knowlton hit the centre for repeated gains, taking the ball to Wisconsin's 5-yard line. Aune goes through for a touchdown. Knowlton kicks the goal. Wisconsin kicks off and Minnesota returns the kick. Wisconsin hits their opponent's line for a total of 25 yards and then are held for downs. Van Valkenburg circles the end for 30 yards. Wisconsin takes the ball on downs on its 10-yard line. Driver punts.

Second Half: Knowlton kicks off. Wisconsin starts upon the 20-yard line, and hitting the line for continual gains of 5 yards, carries the ball to Minnesota's 18-yard mark, Larson and Marshall being used repeatedly. Minnesota stands firm and takes the ball on fourth down. Knowlton punts. Wisconsin fumbles, and Minnesota, regaining the ball, again punts. Wisconsin returns the kick to Minnesota's 40. Knowlton punts to Wisconsin's 25. Again Wisconsin starts a heavy attack on the Minnesota line and carries the ball to their opponent's 15-yard line, where the ball is lost on downs. Minnesota tries three plunges into the line, netting 30 yards, and then punts to Wisconsin's 35. Punts are exchanged and Tratt tries a drop kick for goal, but misses. Wisconsin rushes the ball to Minnesota's 35-yard line, where time is called.

MINNESOTA vs. WISCONSIN

Madison, Nov. 16, 1901

MINNESOTA		WISCONSIN
E. L. Rogers,	Left End,	A. C. Abbott, '04.
C. S. Fee,	Left Tackle,	E. J. Haumerson, '03.
J. G. Flynn,	Left Guard,	A. C. Lerum, '03.
L. A. Page,	Centre,	E. Scow, '01.
M. L. Strathern,	Right Guard,	W. A. Wescott, '03.
F. Schacht,	Right Tackle,	A. H. Curtis, '02, Capt.
B. Aune,	Right End,	W. Juneau, '03.
G. Dobie,	Quarter-back,	A. L. Marshall, '04.
W. W. Thorpe,	Left Half,	E. B. Cochems, '00.
W. S. Lafans,	Right Half,	A. F. Larson, '02.
W. C. Knowlton,	Full-back,	S. E. Driver, '03.

Referee: R. T. Hoagland, '95, Princeton. Umpire: W. S. Kennedy, '00, Chicago. Score: Minnesota 0, Wisconsin 18. First Half: Safety by G. Dobie; touchdown by A. H. Curtis, goal by W. Juneau; touchdown by A. F. Larson; touchdown by A. H. Curtis.

First Half: Minnesota wins the toss and takes the goal. Driver kicks off and Knowlton runs the ball back 20 yards. Knowlton punts to centre. Wisconsin hits the line twice without gain and Driver returns the ball. Minnesota is forced to punt from behind the line. Haumerson blocks the kick, but Dobie falls on it for a safety. Minnesota kicks out to centre and recovers ball on a fumble. Flynn runs to the 15-yard line. Wisconsin takes ball on downs at 8-yard mark. Driver punts to centre. Minnesota by mass plays forces the ball to the 10-yard line, where Knowlton is forced to try for a field goal, but misses. Wisconsin kicks out and recovers ball on the 45-yard line. Driver kicks to Minnesota's 25-yard line and again recovers the ball on a fumble. Minnesota holds for downs and punts to centre.

Larson skirts the end for 25 yards. Larson plunges through
the line and reaches the 5-yard line. Minnesota holds for
downs and takes the ball 1 yard from the line. Knowlton
punts to the 55-yard line and Larson runs the kick back
to the 2-yard line. Curtis goes over for a touchdown.
Juneau kicks the goal. Knowlton kicks off and Wisconsin
runs the kick out to the 40-yard line. Larson circles the
end for 30 yards. Kicks are exchanged, and Cochems,
catching the return, runs to the 10-yard line. Juneau tries
for a field goal, but misses. Minnesota kicks out, Wisconsin returns and recovers a fumble on their opponent's
20-yard line. Larson breaks through for a touchdown.
Juneau misses the goal. Knowlton kicks off and Driver
runs the kick off to Minnesota's 35-yard line. Minnesota
takes the ball on downs, but fumbles on the first line-up.
Curtis gets the ball and dashes across the line for a touchdown. No goal.

Second Half: Minnesota kicks off and Marshall runs the
ball out to the 35-yard line. Driver punts to Minnesota's
35. The latter by line plays reaches Wisconsin's 40-yard
line, where the ball is lost on a fumble. Larson skirts the
end for 35 yards. Wisconsin punts. Minnesota forces it
back by line plays to Wisconsin's 35, where the latter takes
the ball on downs and Driver punts. A long punting duel
now ensues. Wisconsin begins a scrimmage on the 45-
yard line. Larson makes 25. Kicks again are exchanged
and time is called.

MINNESOTA VS. WISCONSIN
Minneapolis, Nov. 15, 1902

MINNESOTA		WISCONSIN
E. L. Rogers,	Left End,	A. C. Abbott, '04, Capt.
	" "	A. R. Findlay, '06.
J. B. Warren,	Left Tac.ke,	F. A. Long, '05.
J. G. Flynn,	Left Guard,	W. A. Berthke, '06.

MINNESOTA		WISCONSIN
M. L. Strathern,	Centre,	E. Scow, '04.
P. S. Smith,	Right Guard,	A. C. Lerum, '03.
F. Schacht,	Right Tackle,	E. J. Haumerson, '03.
R. Gray,	Right End,	J. I. Bush, '06.
S. Harris,	Quarter-back,	J. G. Fogg, '04.
O. N. Davies,	Left Half,	E. J. Vanderboom, '06.
H. Van Valkenburg,	" "	
J. B. Irsfield,	Right Half,	C. D. Marsh, '06.
W. W. Thorpe,	" "	W. F. Moffatt, '02.
W. C. Knowlton,	Full-back,	W. F. Moffatt, '02.
	"	W. E. Driver, '03.

Referee: T. L. Burkland, '99, Illinois. Umpire: B. P. Gale, '06, Chicago. Score: Minnesota 11, Wisconsin 0.

First Half: Minnesota wins the toss and takes the goal. Wisconsin kicks off and Minnesota by mass plays rushes the ball to centre, where Wisconsin holds and Knowlton punts. Kicks are exchanged and the ball goes to Wisconsin on a fumble. Minnesota at once takes the ball on downs. Van Valkenburg hits Wisconsin's line for repeated gains and reaches their 45-yard line, where the latter holds. A punting duel now ensues which lasts throughout the remainder of the half.

Second Half: Minnesota kicks off and Fogg runs the ball back 15 yards. Minnesota holds and Wisconsin punts. Harris circles the end for 15 yards. Van Valkenburg gains three yards in two plunges. Schacht skirts the end for 15. Van Valkenburg goes through centre for 8. The ball is now on Wisconsin's 2-yard mark. Van Valkenburg goes through tackle for a touchdown. Knowlton kicks the goal. Wisconsin kicks off and Harris runs the ball out 10 yards. Van Valkenburg makes 5 through the line. Wisconsin takes the ball on a fumble. Vanderboom circles the end for 30 yards. Moffat and Vanderboom alternate rapidly on each side of the line and take the ball to Minnesota's 5-yard line, where the latter holds for downs. Knowlton punts. Minnesota

recovers the ball and Thorpe and Schacht make 15 yards.
Van Valkenburg makes 8, Warren 3, Van Valkenburg 12.
The ball reaches Wisconsin's 35-yard line, where the latter
holds for 2 downs and Knowlton tries a place kick, but
misses. Minnesota gets the ball and on a fumble Strathern
picks up the ball and runs 10 yards for a touchdown. The
try at goal fails.

MINNESOTA VS. WISCONSIN
Madison, Nov. 26, 1903

MINNESOTA		WISCONSIN
E. L. Rogers,	Left End,	A. C. Abbott, '04, Capt.
G. B. Webster,	Left Tackle,	A. R. Findlay, '06.
J. B. Warren,	Left Guard,	W. A. Berthke, '06.
M. L. Strathern,	Centre,	R. W. Remp, '05.
W. W. Thorpe,	Right Guard,	H. R. Chamberlain, '06.
F. Schacht,	Right Tackle,	C. Washer, '05.
U. L. Burdick,	Right End,	J. I. Bush, '06.
S. Harris,	Quarter-back,	J. G. Fogg, '04.
O. N. Davies,	Left Half,	E. J. Vanderboom, '06.
J. B. Irsfield,	Right Half,	W. M. Baine, '07.
E. H. Current,	Full-back,	H. A. Schofield, '04.
	"	F. M. Clark, '07.

Referee: T. L. Burkland, '99, Illinois. Umpire: B. P. Gale, '06,
Chicago. Score: Minnesota 17, Wisconsin 0. Second Half: Touchdown by F. Schacht, goal by E. L. Rogers; touchdown by F. Schacht,
goal by W. W. Thorpe; touchdown by U. L. Burdick.

First Half: Minnesota wins the toss and takes the goal.
Wisconsin kicks off and Harris runs the kick back 20 yards.
Line plays take the ball to Wisconsin's 45-yard line, where
the ball goes to the latter on a fumble. Bush punts to midfield. Wisconsin gets the ball on a fumble and Bush punts
to Minnesota's 10. Minnesota rushes the ball back to midfield and again fumbles. Bush punts and again Minnesota
by line plunges brings the ball back to centre, where this
time Wisconsin holds for downs. The latter cannot gain
and Bush punts. Several series of kicks are exchanged and

Wisconsin secures the ball on a fumble on Minnesota's 35. Baine misses a place kick. Following the kick-out and a return Wisconsin takes the ball on downs on Minnesota's 35-yard line. Two rushes fail to gain and Baine tries but misses a drop kick for goal. Time is called for the half.

Second Half: Minnesota kicks off and Vanderboom runs the ball back 18 yards. Bush punts to centre. Schacht makes 8, Irsfield 4, Davies 3, Schacht 10, and by short gains the ball travels rapidly to Wisconsin's 10-yard line. Davies makes 1, Irsfield 4, and Schacht covers the remaining distance for a touchdown. Rogers kicks the goal. Wisconsin kicks off and Minnesota punts to midfield. Kicks are exchanged. Minnesota gets ball at centre. Schacht circles the end and reaches the 8-yard line. He again gets away and crosses the line for a touchdown. Thorpe kicks the goal. Wisconsin kicks off and Burdick runs the kick back 20 yards. Kicks are exchanged. Haines and Schacht in 4 long runs carry the ball 65 yards, planting it on Wisconsin's 20-yard line. Davies makes 3, Schacht 4, Burdick 6, Davies 4, Burdick over for a touchdown. The try at goal fails. Following the kick-off the ball is rushed into Wisconsin's territory, where Harris and Davies each try a place kick for goal, but fail. Time is called with the ball at centre.

MINNESOTA vs. WISCONSIN

Minneapolis, Nov. 12, 1904

MINNESOTA		WISCONSIN
R. Marshall,	Left End,	A. R. Findlay, '06.
" "		C. S. Perry, '07.
T. Vita,	Left Tackle,	W. A. Berthke, '06.
G. L. Case,	" "	F. E. Hunt, '08.
W. W. Thorpe,	Left Guard,	L. P. Donovan, '06.
M. L. Strathern,	Centre,	R. W. Remp, '05.
M. W. Ricker,	Right Guard,	H. Fleischer, '07.

MINNESOTA		WISCONSIN
	Right Guard,	J. E. O'Brien, '05.
P. P. Brush,	Right Tackle,	T. H. Brindley, '03.
F. P. Burgan,	Right End,	J. I. Bush, '06, Capt.
S. Harris,	Quarter-back,	G. W. Jones, '07.
F. Hunter,	Left Half,	E. J. Vanderboom, '06.
O. N. Davies,	" "	
G. E. Kremer,	Right Half,	V. Wrabets, '03.
	" "	D. Stromquist, P. G.
E. H. Current,	Full-back,	F. M. Clark, '07.

Referee: R. C. Hamill, '99, Chicago. Umpire: S. C. Williams, '01, Iowa. Score: Minnesota 28, Wisconsin 0. First Half: Touchdown by G. E. Kremer, goal by E. H. Current; touchdown by O. N. Davies, goal by S. Harris. Second Half: Touchdown by E. H. Current; touchdown by G. E. Kremer; touchdown by G. E. Kremer, goal by E. H. Current.

First Half: Minnesota wins the toss and takes the goal. Wisconsin kicks off and Current runs the kick back 10 yards. Davies makes 20 around the end. Six plunges take the ball to the 5-yard line, from which Kremer goes over for a touchdown and Current kicks the goal. Wisconsin kicks off and recovers the ball on a fumble. Jones tries a drop kick for goal, but misses. Minnesota gets the ball before it crosses the line and starts a scrimmage. By line plays the ball is carried to Wisconsin's 20-yard line, where the latter takes the ball on downs. Line plays yield 35-yards and an on-side kick is recovered by Wisconsin on Minnesota's 35-yard line. Minnesota holds and Jones tries a place kick, but misses. Minnesota rushes the ball to Wisconsin's 15-yard line, where it is lost on downs. Several kicks are now exchanged. Minnesota gets ball at centre and Davies circles the end for 50 yards. On the next play he breaks through the centre for a touchdown. Harris kicks the goal. Wisconsin kicks off and Minnesota carries the ball to Wisconsin's 30-yard line, where, being held for 2 downs, Harris tries a drop kick for goal, but misses. Jones punts out and Minnesota puts the ball down for a scrimmage on the 45-yard line as time is called.

Second Half: Minnesota kicks off and recovers the ball on a fumble on their opponent's 30-yard line. Davies makes 15 yards around the end. Three plunges reach the 5-yard line. Current goes over for the touchdown. The try at goal fails. Wisconsin kicks off and Davies runs the ball back 20 yards. Minnesota now begins a steady advance down the field yard by yard until Kremer crosses the last line for a touchdown. The goal is missed. Wisconsin kicks off and Bush returns the kick. Minnesota gets the ball at centre and again starts a steady advance down the field, Kremer finally being pushed through centre for a touchdown. Current kicks the goal.

MINNESOTA vs. WISCONSIN
Minneapolis, Nov. 4, 1905.

MINNESOTA		WISCONSIN
R. Marshall,	Left End,	T. H. Brindley, '03.
W. Ittner,	Left Tackle,	W. A. Berthke, '06.
T. Vita,	Left Guard,	L. P. Donovan, '06.
J. A. Kjelland,	Centre,	R. W. Remp, '05.
D. D. Smith,	Right Guard,	W. A. Gelbach, '07.
P. P. Brush,	Right Tackle,	C. N. Dering, '06.
F. P. Burgan,	Right End,	J. I. Bush, '06.
G. F. Weisel,	Quarter-back,	A. B. Melzner, '06.
A. Larkin,	"	
J. P. Cutting,	Left Half,	E. J. Vanderboom, '06, Capt.
G. E. Kremer,	Right Half,	A. R. Findlay, '06.
E. H. Current,	Full-back,	L. E. Roseth, '08.

Referee: H. B. Hackett, '04, Army. Umpire: T. L. Burkland, '99, Illinois. Score: Minnesota 12, Wisconsin 16. First Half: Touchdown by W. Ittner, goal by J. P. Cutting; touchdown by A. R. Findlay, goal by J. I. Bush; touchdown by A. R. Findlay, goal by J. I. Bush. Second Half: Goal from field by A. B. Melzner; touchdown and goal by J. P. Cutting.

First Half: Wisconsin wins the toss and takes the goal. Minnesota kicks off and Findlay runs the ball back 10 yards. After a few short gains Bush punts 40 yards. Kicks are exchanged and Minnesota puts the ball down for a scrimmage on the 50-yard line. Short line plunges by Cutting, Current, and Kremer carry the ball to the 7-yard mark, from which Ittner breaks through for a touchdown. Cutting kicks the goal. Minnesota kicks off and Vanderboom runs the kick back 3 yards. Wisconsin by line plays advances the ball to midfield, where Minnesota takes it on downs and punts to Wisconsin's 20-yard line. Findlay gets around the end on the second down and runs 85 yards for a touchdown. Bush kicks the goal. Wisconsin kicks off and Minnesota runs the ball out 10 yards. Unable to pierce the line Current punts to midfield. Bush punts back to the 10-yard line. Wisconsin gets the ball on a fumble. Minnesota holds and Melzner misses a drop kick. Minnesota punts out. Kicks are exchanged. Wisconsin puts the ball down for a scrimmage on the 25-yard line. Findlay circles the end and runs 80 yards for a touchdown. Bush kicks the goal.

Second Half: Wisconsin kicks off and Kremer runs the kick back 20 yards. Larkin punts to midfield. Wisconsin runs the ball back 20 yards and Melzner tries but misses a drop kick for goal. Larkin punts to centre. Bush returns the kick and Wisconsin gets the ball on a fumble on Minnesota's 5-yard line. Minnesota holds for downs and takes the ball. Kremer kicks to midfield. Wisconsin runs the ball back 15 yards. Melzner drops a field goal from the 40-yard line. Wisconsin kicks off and Larkin runs the kick back 30 yards. Minnesota punts and Wisconsin by line plays carries the ball to their opponents' 20-yard line, where the ball is lost on downs. Minnesota punts to the 45-yard line. Bush returns the kick. Cutting gets through the line and runs 80 yards for a touchdown. He also kicks the goal. Wisconsin kicks off, and getting the ball on the return, Melzner tries a drop kick for goal, but misses. Time is soon called.

1906, no game.

MINNESOTA vs. WISCONSIN

Madison, Nov. 23, 1907

MINNESOTA		WISCONSIN
E. T. Chestnut,	Left End,	H. B. Rogers, '09.
J. P. Young,	Left Tackle,	F. E. Boyle, '10.
A. G. Molstad,	Left Guard,	L. H. Huntley, '08.
J. A. Kjelland,	Centre,	E. O. Stiehm, '09.
W. J. Bandelin, '	Right Guard,	T. R. Davidson, '08.
G. L. Case,	Right Tackle,	P. J. Murphy, '10.
	" "	F. A. Dittman, '08.
W. H. Radermacher,	Right End,	J. Messner, '09, Capt.
E. D. Coughlan,	Quarter-back,	C. J. Cunningham, '09.
G. Capron,	Left Half,	R. A. Fucik, '10.
J. R. Schuknecht,	Right Half,	R. W. Mucklestone, '09.
N. Dunn,	Full-back,	J. W. Wilce, '10.

Referee: A. W. Kelly, '98, Princeton. Umpire: N. W. Snow, '02, Michigan. Score: Minnesota 17, Wisconsin 17. First Half: Touchdown by J. W. Wilce, goal by R. W. Mucklestone; touchdown by N. Dunn; touchdown and goal by R. W. Mucklestone; goal from field by G. Capron; goal from field by G. Capron; touchdown by R. W. Mucklestone. Second Half: Goal from field by G. Capron.

First Half: Minnesota wins the toss and takes the goal. Wisconsin kicks off and Capron runs the ball back to the 20-yard line. Capron punts to centre. Wisconsin returns. Minnesota fumbles and the ball goes to opponents. Mucklestone recovers a forward pass and gains 25 yards. Fucik and Wilce plunge forward to the 10-yard line. Wilce makes 5 and on the next play crosses the line for a touchdown. Mucklestone kicks the goal. Minnesota kicks off and Wisconsin punts and recovers the ball on the 45-yard line. Minnesota immediately recovers on a fumble. A long forward pass takes the ball to Wisconsin's 15-yard line.

Schuknecht is sent twice into the line, netting 5 yards on each plunge. Dunn goes over for a touchdown. The goal is missed. Wisconsin kicks off and Schuknecht runs back 15 yards. Unable to gain Dunn punts. Mucklestone recovers a long forward pass and reaches Minnesota's 10-yard line. Wilce makes 5 and Mucklestone takes the ball across and also kicks the goal. Minnesota kicks off and recovers the ball on a fumble on their opponent's 30-yard line. Schuknecht makes 10. Capron drops a field goal. Wisconsin kicks off and Schuknecht runs the ball back 20 yards. On the line-up he circles the end for 30 more. Capron drops another field goal from the 45-yard line. Wisconsin kicks off and Minnesota returns the kick. Mucklestone in two attempts at end gains 35 yards and on a third trial makes a touchdown. The goal is missed.

Second Half: Minnesota kicks off and Mucklestone runs the ball back 20 yards and then punts to Minnesota's 45. Capron goes through the line for 5. Schuknecht makes 5 more. Capron adds 15 and then drops a field goal from the 45-yard line. Wisconsin kicks off and Minnesota by kicks and runs transfers the play into their opponent's territory. Capron three times tries for further field goals. Two of his tries are blocked and the third misses the post. Both teams punt continually, but neither goal is again threatened.

MINNESOTA VS. WISCONSIN
Minneapolis, Nov. 7, 1908

MINNESOTA		WISCONSIN
L. Pettijohn, '10,	Left End,	F. E. Rogers, '09, Capt.
J. P. Young,	Left Tackle,	F. E. Boyle, '10.
P. M. Ostrand, '10,	Left Guard,	J. Mesmer, '09.
O. E. Safford, '10,	Centre,	E. O. Stiehm, '09.
R. M. Rosenwald, '13,	Right Guard,	C. E. Dreutzer, '09.
H. E. Farnam, '10,	Right Tackle,	O. P. Osthoff, '10.
W. H. Radermacher, '10,	Right End,	J. P. Dean, '11.

MINNESOTA		WISCONSIN
J. F. McGovern,	Quarter-back,	J. Moll, '11.
L. Johnson,	Left Half,	C. J. Cunningham, '09.
	" "	R. W. Mucklestone, '09.
F. Hubbard,	Right Half,	H. Culver, '10.
A. F. Plankers,	Full-back,	J. W. Wilce, '10.

Referee: H. Haddon, Michigan. Umpire: N. W. Snow, '02, Michigan. Score: Minnesota 0, Wisconsin 5. First Half: Touchdown by J. Moll.

First Half: Minnesota wins the toss and takes the ball. Wilce kicks off and Pettijohn runs the ball back 15 yards. On the line-up he punts to centre. Moll returns. Minnesota makes 10 yards on a forward pass. Johnson adds 10, Hubbard 5, and then the ball is worked to Wisconsin's 5-yard line, where the latter takes it on downs. Wilce punts and Wisconsin recovers the ball. Minnesota secures a forward pass and punts. Moll returns. Pettijohn punts. Osthoff rounds the end for 15 yards. Culver takes a forward pass for 20 yards. Cunningham makes 5 and then Culver takes another long forward pass for a touchdown. No goal. Minnesota kicks off and Cunningham runs the ball out to the 40-yard line. Punts are exchanged. Moll heels a fair catch at centre and tries for a place kick, but misses. Punts are exchanged and Moll again heels a fair catch at 50 and tries for a field goal, but misses.

Second Half: Minnesota kicks off and Moll runs back the kick 20 yards. Unable to gain Wisconsin punts. Pettijohn returns. Wisconsin now opens a hard line attack and carries the ball by short gains 40 yards, but is finally held. Punts are exchanged. Johnson, for Minnesota, three times circles the end and plants the ball on Wisconsin's 25-yard line, but each time the latter holds for downs and Moll by a long punt returns the ball to midfield. The game is called with the ball in Wisconsin's possession on Minnesota's 8-yard mark.

MINNESOTA vs. WISCONSIN
Madison, Nov. 13, 1909

MINNESOTA		WISCONSIN
J. H. Vidal, '10,	Left End,	R. Fucik, '10.
G. A. Schain, '11,	" "	
J. C. Walker, '12,	Left Tackle,	F. E. Boyle, '10.
A. Molstad, '10,	Left Guard,	A. L. Buser, '12.
H. E. Farnam, '10,	Centre,	H. A. Arpin, '11.
H. Powers, '12,	Right Guard,	W. F. Mackmiller, '12.
J. A. McCree,	Right Tackle,	R. Iakisch, '10.
W. H. Radermacher, '10,	Right End,	J. P. Dean, '11.
	" "	O. P. Osthoff, '10,
L. Pettijohn, '10,	Quarter-back,	J. Moll, '11.
R. M. Rosenwald, '13,	Left Half,	H. Culver, '10.
L. Erdahl, '11,	Right Half,	S. W. Andersen, '12.
L. C. Stevens, '12,	" "	
E. Pickering, '11,	Full-back,	J. W. Wilce, '10, Capt.

Referee: G. W. Beavers, '08, Army. Umpire: N. W. Snow, '02, Michigan. Field Judge: A. B. Fleager, '94, Northwestern. Linesman: J. W. Esterline, '97, Purdue. Score: Minnesota 34, Wisconsin, 6. First Half: Touchdown by L. C. Stevens; touchdown by R. Fucik, goal by J. Moll; touchdown by L. Erdahl, goal by E. E. Farnam. Second Half: Touchdown by E. Pickering, goal by H. E. Farnam; touchdown by L. C. Stevens, goal by H. E. Farnam; touchdown by J. P. Rosenwald, goal by H. E. Farnam; touchdown by E. Pickering.

First Half: Minnesota wins the toss and takes the goal. Wisconsin kicks off and Pettijohn runs the ball back 15 yards. Minnesota opens a series of wing shifts and forward passes, by which the ball is carried to Wisconsin's 15-yard line. Stevens circles the end for a touchdown. The try at goal fails. Minnesota kicks off and Wisconsin returns the kick, recovering the ball on the 45-yard line. Moll and Fucik work 2 forward passes for 18 yards each, and an on-side kick following gives Wisconsin the ball on their opponent's 6-yard mark. Another forward pass, Moll to Fucik, scores a touchdown and Moll kicks the goal. Wisconsin kicks off. Minnesota, by a brilliant series of line plays, forward passes, and on-side kicks, carries the ball to Wisconsin's 5-yard line, where it is lost on downs. Culver doubles the end for 30 yards. Minnesota recovers the ball on downs at midfield and Pettijohn punts. Wisconsin returns and gets the ball on a fumble. Culver again punts. Starting from the 40-yard line Minnesota takes the ball by steady gains the length of the field for a touchdown.

Second Half: Minnesota kicks off and Anderson runs the ball back 15 yards. Kicks are exchanged. Minnesota starts a line attack at midfield. Rosenwald, Stevens, and Rademacher make repeated gains and at last plant the ball 4 yards from Wisconsin's goal. Pickering goes through the centre for a touchdown and Farnam kicks the goal. Minnesota kicks off and Wisconsin returns the kick. Minnesota again starts a line attack, by which Pickering, Stevens, and Rosenwald reach the 3-yard mark, from which Stevens goes across for the touchdown and Farnam kicks the goal. Wisconsin kicks off. Minnesota works the ball out to the 30-yard line. Rosenwald gets around the end and runs 70 yards for a touchdown. Farnam kicks the goal. Wisconsin kicks off. On the line-up Pickering breaks through and runs 80 yards for a touchdown. No goal. Time soon after is called.

MINNESOTA vs. WISCONSIN
Minneapolis, Nov. 12, 1910

MINNESOTA		WISCONSIN
L. A. Smith, '12.	Left End,	C. C. Chambers, '13.
E. Pickering, '11.	" "	F. G. Carter, '11.
J. C. Walker, '12.	Left Tackle,	W. F. Mackmiller, '12.
G. F. Bromley, '12.	Left Guard,	M. C. Pierce, '12.
C. Morrell, '14.	Centre,	H. A. Arpin, '11.
	"	R. E. Branstad, '12.
C. J. Robinson, '13.	Right Guard,	S. Neprud, '12.
	" "	P. J. Murphy, '12.
J. P. Young, '14.	Right Tackle,	A. L. Buser, '12.

MINNESOTA		WISCONSIN
L. Frank, '12.	Right End,	E. F. Bunker, '11.
J. F. McGovern, '11.	Quarter-back,	J. P. Dean, '11, Capt.
R. Johnson,	"	
R. M. Rosenwald, '13.	Left Half,	E. S. Gillette, '12.
	" "	R. R. Newman, '13.
S. A. Hill,	" "	
G. Vanstrum,	" "	
L. C. Stevens, '12.	Right Half,	A. Birch, '11.
A. C. Erdahl,	" "	C. S. Gilbert, '13.
L. Johnson, '12.	Full-back,	E. J. Samp, '13.
L. T. Erdahl, 11.	"	

Referee; L. E. Endsley, '01, Purdue. Umpire: N. M. Snow, '02, Michigan. Linesman: F. S. Porter, '00, Cornell. Field Judge: A. B. Fleager, '94, Northwestern. Score: Minnesota 28, Wisconsin 0. First Quarter: Touchdown by L. C. Stevens, goal by J. F. McGovern; touchdown by R. Johnson; touchdown by R. Johnson, goal by J. F. McGovern. Second Quarter: Touchdown and goal by J. F. McGovern. Third Quarter: Touchdown by R. M. Rosenwald.

First Quarter: Wisconsin fumbles at outset of game, giving Minnesota the ball on the 15-yard line. In three plays the latter sends Stevens over for a touchdown. McGovern kicks the goal. Pierce kicks to McGovern at 15. By short gains Minnesota reaches midfield, where a penalty sets the ball back 5 yards. On the next play Rosenwald breaks through the line and reaches Wisconsin's 37-yard mark. Plays and penalties place the ball on Wisconsin's 30-yard line. Rosenwald skirts the end to the 2-yard mark. Johnson is sent across for a touchdown. The goal is missed. Pierce kicks off and Johnson returns. Minnesota takes the ball by short plunges to Wisconsin's 20-yard line, where the latter takes the ball on downs. Gillette kicks and McGovern runs the kick back to the 25-yard line. Rosenwald pierces centre for 5. McGovern makes 5 more and Johnson rounds the end for a touchdown. McGovern kicks the goal. Pierce kicks off, but time is called soon after.

Second Quarter: Gillette loses 5 yards and kicks to Minnesota's 35. McGovern runs the kick back to midfield. Short plunges take the ball to Wisconsin's 8-yard mark. McGovern from kick formation goes through centre for a touchdown. Goal.

Third Quarter: Wisconsin's defence strengthens, but Minnesota slowly forces the line, carrying the ball by short gains to the 5-yard line, from which Rosenwald is sent across for a touchdown. The try for goal fails.

Fourth Quarter: Pierce kicks off. Minnesota puts ball down for scrimmage on the 25-yard line. Rosenwald kicks. Gillette makes 25 yards. Other gains take the ball to Minnesota's 15-yard line, where the ball is lost on downs. Kicks are exchanged. During the remainder of this half play is confined between the 25-yard lines.

CHAPTER XVII

PRINCETON VS. YALE

PRINCETON VS. YALE

New Haven, Nov. 15, 1873

PRINCETON	YALE
C. O. Dershimer, '74, Capt.,	W. S. Halsted, '74, Capt.
H. C. Beach, '74,	H. C. Deming, '72.
H. C. Bittenbender, '74,	J. P. Peters, '73.
S. P. Cook, '74,	W. E. D. Stokes, '74.
H. Huston, '74,	J. L. Scudder, '74.
J. H. Vandeventer, '74,	C. D. Waterman, '74.
C. F. Whittlesey, '74,	C. E. Humphrey, '74.
R. Boyd, '74,	G. V. Bushnell, '74.
F. Biddle, '75,	E. D. Robbins, '74.
G. R. Elder, '75,	T. T. Sherman, '74.
S. B. Hutchinson, '75,	H. D. Bristol, '74.
I. H. Lionberger, '75,	L. Mellick, '74.
H. Moffat, '75,	W. O. Henderson, '74.
R. C. Rodgers, '75,	G. M. Munn, '74.
C. Denny, '76,	J. A. R. Dunning, '74.
T. R. Sheets, '76,	P. A. Porter, '74.
J. M. Woods, '76,	H. J. McBirney, '75.
S. C. Cowart, '76,	E. V. Baker, '77.
J. Chambers, '72,	F. L. Grinnell, '75.
Wm. Martin, Sem.,	W. H. Hotchkiss, '75.

Referee: J. M. Harvey, '75, Princeton. Judges: J. W. Peckett, 74, Princeton; W. Kelley, '74, Yale. Score: Princeton 3 goals, Yale 0.* Goals by H. C. Beach, H. C. Beach, G. R. Elder.

The game was played at Hamilton Park. At precisely two o'clock the officials called together the contesting captains and tossed the coin. Princeton won the first toss and chose the south goal. Yale correctly called the second toss

* This game was played under the " Rules of 1873," a modification of the " Association Code."

and elected to give Princeton the kick-off, or "cant," as it
was called at Yale and "buck" at Princeton. Moffat
carefully adjusted the ball, drew back a few steps, and then
at full speed lifted the ball a prodigious cant, far down the
field. Dershimer, the Princeton captain, ranged up and
down the field and from side to side, getting into every play.
In fact the whole Princeton team excelled in following the
ball. Not only did they kick the ball, but they batted it
as well. For the first few minutes the ball hovered in front
of Yale's goal, but to no avail, as the Yale men stood firm
and drove it repeatedly back. Suddenly a heavier press of
Princeton players rallied before the posts. From the mass
suddenly issued a sharp report and the football lay a flattened piece of rubber upon the ground. Two stout toes
had struck it squarely at the same time and the ball had ex-
ploded. A half hour was required to obtain another ball.
During the interim Dershimer took his men to one side and
coached them in a new style of tactics. Some men were
detailed to follow the ball and others were directed to ward
off the Yale players. The new ball having arrived, play was
resumed at ten minutes past three. Princeton's new tactics worked well, but Yale fought gamely. After an hour
and twenty minutes of stiff play Princeton forced Yale's
goal, the ball being kicked through by Beach. A second
goal was made twenty minutes later, Beach again making
the final play. Princeton's machine was running well now,
and in twenty-three minutes Elder shot another ball between
the posts. But Yale was growing stronger as the game pro-
gressed and now transferred the play to Princeton's goal.
The latter stoutly fought it back until time was called. Although suffering their first defeat at football, Yale's followers
lustily cheered the victors as well as the vanquished, and
then dispersed jubilant in the zest of a good game, well
played by two great teams.

Princeton vs. Yale
Hoboken, Nov. 30, 1876

PRINCETON		YALE
B. Nicoll, '77,	Forward,	W. V. Downer, '78.
E. H. Nicoll, '80,	"	C. C. Camp, '77.
H. Stevenson, '78,	"	W. L. R. Wurts, '78.
J. Potter, '78,	"	W. H. Taylor, '78.
E. S. McCalmont, '77,	"	F. W. Davis, '77.
S. B. Johnston, '77,	"	N. U. Walker, '77.
D. Stewart, '78,	Half-back,	Walter Camp, '80.
J. O'H. Denny, '77,	"	W. D. Hatch, '79.
A. J. McCosh, '77, Capt.,	Back,	E. V. Baker, '77, Capt.
H. B. Thompson, '77,	"	O. D. Thompson, '79.
W. E. Dodge, '79,	"	W. I. Bigelow, '77.

Referee: G. V. Bushnell, '74, Yale. Judges: E. W. Price, Columbia; G. T. Elliott, '77, Yale. Score: Princeton 0, Yale 2 goals. First Half: Goal by W. I. Bigelow. Second Half: Goal from field by O. D. Thompson.

NOTE.—At the request of Yale this game was played with 11 men on a side instead of 15; and also at the request of Yale an agreement was made preliminary to the game that touchdowns should not count in computing the score, but that the latter should be based upon goals alone.

First Half: Princeton wins the toss and chooses the goal with the wind, thus forcing Yale to play with their backs to the club-house, facing a keen, biting wind. Captain Baker kicks off for Yale, but Stewart and Denny, for Princeton, quickly run the ball back to midfield. Dodge punts and Downer catches, Johnston tackling. Camp gets the ball out of scrimmage and makes a long run. On being tackled he passes the ball to Thompson, who runs in for a touchdown. Princeton claims that the pass was a forward one. The referee is requested to end the dispute, by tossing a coin. Yale correctly calls the turn and the touchdown is allowed. Bigelow kicks the goal. McCosh kicks off for Princeton and sends the ball over Yale's goal-line.

Yale brings it out to the 25-yard line and punts. Baker is down on the ball, but Nicoll gets him. Hatch gets the ball on a play from the side line, but is stopped by McCalmont. The ball is fumbled. McCalmont picks it up and with a clear field starts for the goal-line, but is stopped by the expiration of time.

Second Half: Bigelow opens the second half by a long kick-off for Yale, which Dodge returns. Thompson catches, but C. Camp throws him. As Thompson is falling he passes the ball to Camp, who carries it within 20 paces of Princeton's goal. Here Stewart gets the ball and makes a brilliant dash for Yale's goal, but Hatch, coming up from behind, gets the ball away from him and races almost to Princeton's line. In the next scrimmage Bigelow passes the ball to Thompson, who kicks a beautiful goal from the field. Sides are reversed and Princeton shows an improvement in play. The ball changes rapidly from side to side without advantage. Time at last is called with the ball in midfield. Soon spectators and players are off for a Thanksgiving dinner in New York, enthusiastic in their praise of the new game and keen in the relish of the afternoon's sport.

PRINCETON vs. YALE
Hoboken, Dec. 8, 1877

PRINCETON		YALE
T. B. Bradford, '81,	Forward,	B. B. Lamb, '81.
B. Lee, '80,	"	W. L. R. Wurts, '78.
A. T. Enos, '78,	"	J. S. Harding, '80.
A. Wylly, '79,	"	W. V. Downer, '78.
C. C. Clarke, '78,	"	W. A. Peters, '80.
B. Ballard, '80,	"	F. J. Brown, '78.
F. Loney, '81,	"	W. H. Smith, '79.
H. K. Devereux, '80,	"	H. Ives, '81.
H. Stevenson, '78,	"	
W. E. Dodge, '79, Capt.,	Half-back,	O. W. Brown, '78.
T. M. McNair, '79,	"	O. D. Thompson, '79.
D. O. Irving, '78,	"	G. H. Clark, '80.

PRINCETON		YALE
	Half-back,	Walter Camp, '80.
H. M. Cutts, '80,	Back,	D. T. Trumbull, '76.
H. L. Minor, '79,	"	W. J. Wakeman, '76.
L. P. Funkhouser, '78,	"	E. V. Baker, '77, Capt.

Referee: W. N. Elbert, '79, Trinity. Judges: E. O. Roessle, '79, Princeton; W. I. Bigelow, '77, Yale. Score: Princeton 0, Yale 0.

At the suggestion of Yale, as in 1876, this game was played under a special agreement that touchdowns should not be counted in computing the score, but that this should be based upon goals alone. The safety did not affect the score in the Princeton-Yale series until 1881. See college press of the period.

"At the suggestion of Yale an agreement was entered into by the two captains before the game that the game should be decided by goals and that no touchdowns should count."—*Princetonian*, Dec. 8, 1877.

"Although, according to the rules, we did not win, we at least were not vanquished. Unfortunately the preliminaries of the game were so arranged that after a valiantly fought contest neither party was left victor."—*Yale Record*, Dec. 15, 1877.

"The game lasted about two hours and nominally was a draw."—*Yale Literary Magazine*, Dec., 1877.

First Half: Princeton wins the toss and selects the south goal. Baker kicks off, sending the ball to Princeton's goal-line. Dodge recovers the ball and passes it to McNair, who kicks. Yale drives the ball by short rushes and a kick into Princeton's territory, where Dodge touches down for safety. Princeton reverses the situation and works the ball into Yale's goal. Baker by a long kick returns it. Camp receives the ball and by a long, brilliant run makes a touchdown. The try at goal fails. Dodge kicks. Yale works the ball well into Princeton's goal. Princeton becomes aggressive and forces the ball into Yale's goal, where the Blue is compelled to touch down twice for safety. The half ends with the ball near Yale's goal-line.

Second Half: Cutts kicks off for Princeton. Thompson gets the ball and makes a great run for Yale, bringing the ball dangerously near Princeton's line. Camp takes the ball, but as he is about to cross the goal-line is tackled by McNair, Minor, and Clarke. He rises to his feet, however, shakes off his tacklers and crosses over for a touchdown. The try for goal fails. Princeton forces the ball into Yale's quarters, but Trumbull extricates his team by long kicks, thereby forcing Princeton to touch down for safety. Princeton works the ball back to midfield, where the two teams play one another to a deadlock. Time is called and the game declared a draw at 0 to 0.

PRINCETON vs. YALE

Hoboken, Nov. 28, 1878

PRINCETON		YALE
T. B. Bradford, '81,	Forward,	J. V. Farwell, '79.
H. McDermott, '81,	"	P. C. Fuller, '81.
H. H. Brotherlin, '80,	"	L. K. Hull, '83.
B. Ballard, '80, Capt.,	"	J. S. Harding, '80.
H. K. Devereux, '80,	"	B. B. Lamb, '81.
H. McAlpin, '81,	"	P. King, '80.
F. Loney, '81,	"	F. M. Eaton, '82.
F. T. Bryan, '80,	"	
J. B. Waller, '79,	Half-back,	F. J. Brown, '78.
H. L. Minor, '79,	"	W. A. Peters, '80.
T. M. McNair, '79,	"	O. D. Thompson, '79.
I. P. Withington, '80,	"	R. W. Watson, '81.
F. Larkin, '79,	Back,	Walter Camp, '80, Capt.
H. M. Cutts, '80,	"	W. J. Wakeman, '77.
W. Miller, '80,	"	W. W. K. Nixon, '81.
	"	W. I. Badger, '82.

Referee: L. N. Littauer, '78, Harvard. Judges: W. E. Dodge, '79, Princeton; G. H. Clark, '80, Yale. Score: Princeton 1 touchdown, 1 goal, Yale 0. Second Half: Touchdown by I. P. Withington, goal by T. M. McNair.　　　•

NOTE.—For system of scoring see Rule 7, convention Nov. 26, 1876, Appendix. Safeties did not affect the score in the Princeton-Yale series until 1881.

First Half: Princeton wins the toss and takes the wind. Camp kicks off for Yale. Princeton returns the kick. Camp obtains a free kick. Waller tries to return Camp's kick, but Yale blocks the ball and forces Princeton to touch down for safety. The ball is brought out and kicked off. Yale returns the kick, forcing Princeton to make another safety. McNair tries a long drop kick at Yale's goal, Camp catches, but is immediately thrown. Minor gets the ball on a fumble and makes a long run, being tackled by Badger. The ball is now in midfield. Yale attempts long passes. Camp races through the Princeton players, but is stopped by Waller. Some sharp scrimmages ensue in which Yale gains ground. Camp tries a drop kick, but the ball is blocked by Loney. Thompson recovers the ball and makes a run, Bryan tackling sharply. Princeton gets the ball behind the line from a kick and touches down for safety. On the kick-out a punting duel ensues, the ball changing fields several times, finally going behind Princeton's goal-line where Larkin touches down for safety, and a moment later touches down again as time is called for the half.

Second Half: McNair kicks off by a drop kick. Camp catches, but is thrown in his tracks. Camp now kicks, Mc-Nair catches and makes a brilliant run, taking the ball close to Yale's goal. Camp gets the ball from a scrimmage and tries to get around the forwards, but is thrown by Bradford. Withington gets ball out of a scrimmage and carries it close to Yale's goal-line, where he makes a long pass to McNair, who tries for a drop kick, but fails. Loney falls on the ball for a touchdown. Yale protests and the touchdown is not allowed. Play is resumed a few feet from the goal-line. The ball is passed to McNair, who kicks across the line, forcing Yale to make a safety. Camp kicks out, Princeton forces the ball back again by a clever pass. The scrimmage is formed 20 feet from Yale's goal-line. Withington breaks through for a touchdown. McNair kicks the goal. Camp kicks off for Yale, Princeton returns the kick. Yale starts from midfield, Camp, Thompson, and Farwell carrying the ball, and forces the fighting well down into Princeton's territory, where the latter makes a safety. Princeton kicks out, the ball is returned, McNair catches it and gets away for a long run, being downed by Hull at midfield, when the game ends.

PRINCETON vs. YALE

Hoboken, Nov. 27, 1879

PRINCETON		YALE
F. T. Bryan, '80,	Forward,	C. B. Storrs, '82.
E. C. Peace, '83,	"	J. Moorehead, '80.
F. Loney, '81,	"	B. B. Lamb, '81.
B. Ballard, '80, Capt.,	"	L. K. Hull, '83.
H. K. Devereux, '80,	"	J. S. Harding, '80.
H. H. Brotherlin, '80,	"	F. Remington, '81.
T. B. Bradford, '81,	"	H. H. Knapp, '82.
	"	F. R. Vernon, '81.
L. P. Withington, '80,	Half-back,	C. S. Beck, '83.
B. Lee, '80,	"	W. A. Peters, '80.
T. M. McNair, '79,	"	Walter Camp, '80, Capt.
T. H. P. Farr, '81,	"	R. W. Watson, '81.
M. R. Ely, '82,	"	W. I. Badger, '82.
W. S. Horton, '80,	Back,	W. W. K. Nixon, '81.
H. M. Cutts, '80,	"	C. W. Lyman, '82.
A. B. Duncan, '80,	"	

Referee: Robert Bacon, '80, Harvard. Judges: A. McLaren, '80, Princeton; W. C. McHenry, '80, Yale. Score: Princeton 0, Yale 0.

NOTE.—For system of scoring see Rule 7, convention Nov. 26, 1876, Appendix. Safeties did not affect the score in the Princeton-Yale series until 1881.

First Half: Yale wins the toss and gets both the wind and the sun. Ballard kicks off for Princeton and Yale rushes the ball back to Princeton's 40-yard mark. Camp tries two drop kicks in succession. Neither makes a goal, but they force the play near Princeton's goal-line. McNair,

Loney, and Cutts tackle sharply and save the goal-line, but are forced to touch down three times for safety during the half.

Second Half: Camp opens the second half by a dribble to Harding. Again the ball is rushed well into Princeton's territory. Cutts makes a prodigious kick and lands the ball in front of the Yale posts. The scrimmages are very severe and neither side seems able to advance the ball more than a few feet against the clean, hard tackling of the other. The ball goes frequently into touch in Yale's territory. Princeton invariably puts it in play by taking it out 15 paces and putting it down for a scrimmage. Yale, however, in her own territory throws the ball out or makes a quick pass. After twenty minutes of monotonous play of this character Princeton begins to force Yale back, Lee, Withington, and Farr making good gains. The ball is now within kicking distance of the goal. A quick pass is made to McNair, who drops a goal from the 45-yard line, but it crosses the goal above the posts (a "poster"), and does not count. Yale touches down for safety. Camp now proposes to make some substitutions for Yale, but Ballard will not permit it, claiming that the Yale players are not injured. A long dispute ensues and the substitutions are not made. Beck, Peters, and Camp now start a series of rushes which takes the ball well down to Princeton's line. Camp tries another drop kick, but misses. Princeton, however, is forced to touch down for safety. Soon after time is called.

PRINCETON VS. YALE
New York, Nov. 25, 1880

PRINCETON		YALE
T. B. Bradford, '81,	Forward,	P. C. Fuller, '81.
H. McDermott, '81,	"	C. S. Beck, '83.
C. McKee, '81,	"	F. R. Vernon, '81.
E. C. Peace, '83,	"	J. S. Harding, '80.
F. Loney, '81, Capt.,	"	B. B. Lamb, '81.

PRINCETON		YALE
J. P. Flint, '83,	Forward,	C. B. Storrs, '82.
	"	W. L. Adams, '82.
D. P. Morgan, '83,	Quarter-back,	W. I. Badger, '82.
B. G. Winton, '82,	Half-back,	
J. Chetwood, '82,	"	R. W. Watson, '81, Capt.
	"	Walter Camp, '80.
T. W. Cauldwell, '81,	Back,	B. W. Bacon, '81.
J. S. Harlan, '83,	"	

Referee: W. H. Manning, '82, Harvard. Judges: H. McAlpin, '81,
Princeton; G. H. Clark, '80, Yale. Score: Princeton 0, Yale 0.

NOTE.—For system of scoring see Rule 7, convention
Nov. 26, 1876, Appendix.

First Half: Princeton wins the toss and takes the wind.
Camp kicks off for Yale and Harlan returns. Rushes are
followed by kicks and the ball is forced down into Yale's
goal, where it is touched down for safety. The ball is
brought out and punted down the field. Harlan sends it
back. Camp makes a long, brilliant run, carrying the ball
almost to Princeton's line, but is stopped by Harlan. Princeton is in straits and makes several safeties. Snow is falling
heavily, but play follows play in rapid succession. Storrs
is tackling sharply, thus checking Peace and Flint, who are
hammering hard for Princeton. The half ends with the
ball in midfield.

Second Half: Winton opens the second half by a long kick
for Princeton. Camp returns the kick and Cauldwell
sends it back. Camp attempts to kick, but Peace blocks,
and Morgan gets the ball. With a clear field he starts for
the Yale line, but slips and falls five yards away. Before
he can rise Camp is on him. Yale gets the ball out of
scrimmage and touches down for safety. Camp kicks out.
Great running, passing, and tackling now break forth on
each team and the ball traverses up and down the field

with brilliant rapidity.   Again it is down in Yale's goal and
the Blue makes another safety.   The ground has now become heavy and slippery and the ball is covered with sleet.
Yale drives the ball back and for fifteen minutes maintains
a fierce attack on Princeton's line, the Orange making six
safeties in succession to hold their adversaries back.   Captain Loney, for Princeton, shrewdly directs his half-back,
Chetwood, to rush instead of kicking or passing.*   Fortune
also is with Princeton in getting the ball out of the mauls.
Princeton works out to the 25-yard line, where Yale holds the
Orange for scrimmage after scrimmage, Princeton still holding the ball without passing or kicking.   Yale is chagrined
at these novel tactics of blocking their attack by withholding
the ball, but the stratagem succeeds and the game ends in
a draw.   In the attacks of the game Princeton has touched
down for safety eleven times and Yale six, but safeties do
not count in the scoring.

PRINCETON vs. YALE

New York, Nov. 24, 1881

PRINCETON		YALE
J. P. Flint, '83,	Forward,	B. B. Lamb, '81.
S. H. Benton, '82,	"	C. S. Beck, '83.
J. H. Bryan, '82,	"	R. Tompkins, '84.
L. Riggs, '83,	"	L. K. Hull, '83.
J. T. Haxall, '83,	"	C. B. Storrs, '82.
P. T. Bryan, '82, Capt.,	"	A. L. Farwell, '84.
	"	H. H. Knapp, '82.
	Quarter-back,	W. I. Badger, '82.
T. A. C. Baker, '83,	Half-back,	Walter Camp, '80, Capt.
E. C. Peace, '83,	"	E. L. Richards, '85.
A. F. Burt, '82,	"	
J. S. Harlan, '83,	Back,	B. W. Bacon, '81.
W. McD. Shaw, '82,	"	
A. S. Bickman, '82,	Substitute,	C. S. Hebard, '82.

* This style of play became known as the "block game."

PRINCETON		YALE
G. R. Fleming, '83,	Substitute,	H. B. Twombly, '84.
A. W. McMillan, '84,	"	F. E. Beach, '83.
J. L. Woolston, '84,	"	F. A. Benedict, '84.
O. Rafferty, '82,	"	

Referee: W. H. Manning, '82, Harvard. Judges: B. G. Winton, '82, Princeton; R. W. Watson, '81, Yale. Score: Princeton 0, Yale 0.

First Half: Yale wins the toss and takes the goal with a fair wind. Harlan surprises Yale by dribbling instead of kicking, then quickly picking up the ball and running with it. Tompkins stops him for a small gain. Riggs tries to pierce the line, but is thrown by Storrs. On the next play the ball is fumbled. Richards kicks it while bounding on the ground. Camp overtakes it and lifts a high sailing punt from the ground which the wind takes to Princeton's goal-line. Lamb and Farwell are down with the ball and Harlan is forced to throw the ball to Burt for a touch-in-goal to avoid a safety. The ball is taken to the 25-yard line, where Princeton elects to put it in play by a scrimmage. The play indicates that Princeton is about to launch the "block game" *. The indications are correct. Peace hits the Yale line, but Storrs throws him back. Baker repeats the attempt and Tompkins stops him. Harlan dashes for the end, but Lamb gets him. The plays are repeated, but without gain. Princeton now directs play after play against the line, but Yale does not give an inch. For nearly twenty minutes the ball hits the Yale line without an impression, the 25-yard line gleaming continually beneath the feet of the players. The crowd

* The "block game" designated the persistent retention of the ball by one side. This was possible under the rules of the period, which did not require a team to surrender the ball upon failure to gain a certain number of yards. Thus if a team did not kick or fumble it might retain the ball indefinitely. For explanation of extra periods see Rule 5, convention Oct. 8, 1881, Appendix.

yells in derision at Princeton's tactics in holding the ball
and not kicking, but the attack on the line monotonously
keeps up. Out on the end Flint and Lamb are engaged in
a personal encounter that greatly amuses the crowd. At
every move of the Yale man Flint endeavors to block him.
Frequently their arms are intertwined or wrapped around
one another's body. Suddenly Peace gets past the Yale
line with the ball. Lamb gets loose from Flint and makes
the tackle. Harlan takes the ball, but cannot gain, as
Camp throws him heavily. The ball is dropped and Camp
picks it up and starts for Princeton's goal. The entire
Princeton team pile upon him and bury him beneath a
struggling mass, beneath which Flint steals the ball away.
On the next play Baker gets by the line, but Storrs brings
him down with a wonderful tackle with one hand. Time
is now called for the half. Princeton has had the ball
throughout the entire half with the exception of four and a
half minutes. There have been only four kicks.

Second Half: Yale opens the second half with the ball.
Camp dribbles and runs, indicating that Yale is now to play
the "block game," and play it Yale did, not once losing or
surrendering the ball throughout the entire second half of
forty-five minutes. Storrs and Hull are given the ball repeatedly, but Princeton's line is the same stone wall on defence that Yale's was in the first half. Bryan, Flint,
Riggs, and Peace balk every attack. The assault monotonously keeps up and the defence meets it at every point.
Forty minutes have thus been expended and the ball has not
been twelve yards from the centre of the field. Time is
about to expire as Storrs at last gets free. He starts on a
wide run across the field, circles the end and clears for the
goal-line. Riggs catches him on the 25-yard line and
brings him down. Before play can be resumed the time is
up. The referee notifies the two captains to be ready
for the extra periods at five o'clock. On the hour the

teams take the field. Camp kicks over Princeton's goal-line.
Harlan runs the ball out and Princeton starts in play on the
25-yard line, resuming the tactics of the "block game."
At the expiration of the half it is too dark to continue and
time is called. The game ends in a draw at 0 to 0.

PRINCETON vs. YALE
New York, Nov. 30, 1882

PRINCETON		YALE
F. R. Wadleigh, '83,	End,	H. H. Knapp, '82.
P. T. Kimball, '84,	Next to End,	W. H. Hyndman, '84.
J. T. Haxall, '83,	Next to Centre,	R. Tompkins, '84, Capt.
G. F. Fleming, '83,	Centre,	L. K. Hull, '83.
C. W. Bird, '85,	Next to Centre,	F. G. Peters, '86.
E. C. Peace, '83, Capt.,	Next to End,	C. S. Beck, '83.
L. Riggs, '83,	End,	A. L. Farwell, '84.
D. P. Morgan, '83,	Quarter-back,	H. B. Twombly, '84.
T. A. C. Baker, '83,	Half-back,	E. L. Richards, '85.
S. J. Poe, '84,	"	W. Terry, '85.
Alex. Moffat, '84,	Full-back,	B. W. Bacon, '81.

Referee: E. T. Cabot, '83, Harvard. Judges: D. M. Look, '84,
Princeton; W. I. Badger, '82, Yale. Score: Princeton 1 goal, 1 safety;
Yale 2 touchdowns, 2 goals, 1 safety. First Half: Touchdown by
C. S. Beck, goal by E. L. Richards, goal from field by J. T. Haxall. Sec-
ond Half: Safety by A. Moffat; touchdown by R. Tompkins, goal by
B. W. Bacon; safety by Yale.

NOTE.—For system of scoring see Amended Rule 5, convention Oct. 8, 1881, and Amended Rule 7, convention
Oct. 14, 1882, Appendix.

First Half: Princeton wins the toss and takes the goal
backed by a strong breeze. Yale dribbles and rushes the
ball by gains of Twombly, Richards, and Terry down to
Princeton's quarters. Princeton is in straits, but fights
gamely. Poe, Bird, and Riggs tackle fiercely and Moffat
lifts tremendous kicks. Gradually the ball comes closer
and closer to the line. At last Richards drops a field goal,
but his men were off side and the ball is brought out.
Moffat lifts it far down the field, but the Yale men rush it

back, Twombly making the distance in two attempts. Beck now bursts through for a touchdown. Richards kicks the goal. Time, thirty-two minutes.

Princeton kicks off, Yale returns, and Princeton makes a fair catch. Haxall lifts the ball down to Yale's 30-yard line. Richards takes the ball on the run and, with increased speed, kicks it while running far down into Princeton's territory, where Moffat cleanly catches it and heels for a free kick. The ball is then returned into Yale's quarters. Bacon immediately returns it to midfield. The duel is continued. Baker makes a fair catch on his 45-yard line. On the next play Haxall, standing 65 yards distant from Yale's goal and 15 yards to the side of centre, lifts a mighty place kick squarely between the posts, thus scoring the longest place kick on record. The half now ends.

Second Half: The second half opens and Princeton immediately takes the aggressive, Yale being willing to hold its lead. Princeton dribbles and Bird, picking up the ball, punts. Richards returns the ball and Moffat heels a fair catch. The kick is fumbled, but Richards soon gets the ball and punts almost to Princeton's goal-line. Moffat sends it back to centre. Poe gets the ball and runs 40 yards. On the next play the ball is lost and Hull brings it back to midfield. Farwell now sends a long kick behind Princeton's line and Moffat touches down for safety. A great kicking duel breaks out, which lasts for five minutes, the ball being continually in the air and the forwards running back and forth from end to end. The ball goes out of bounds, and Princeton, to avoid making safeties, is forced to touch three times in goal. Tompkins gets the ball and rolls across the line. The crowd, in great excitement, breaks out upon the field. Princeton claims a foul. An attempt is made to clear the field. The referee allows the touchdown and Bacon kicks the goal. Princeton renews the contest with increased vigor, rushing the ball down to Yale's

goal, where it is pushed over. The referee decides that
Yale was holding the ball at the time for a down and the
play goes as a touch in goal by Yale. Princeton at once
forces Yale to make a safety. The ball is kicked to midfield. Poe, by a great run, makes 20 yards and repeats
the performance on the next play, landing the ball on Yale's
5-yard line. Farwell gets it and punts back to midfield.
Poe, Baker, and Moffat again take the ball up to the Yale
line, but the latter holds in the last ditch and Bacon gets the
ball, and sends it out of danger. The time is getting short
now, and the Orange jerseys are steaming with the final
efforts to beat the Blue. Again the ball is driven to Yale's
goal, but Terry sends it back. Once more Poe, Fleming,
and Moffat reel off long runs. The ball is fumbled. Richards gets it, but before it can be kicked time is called, the
game ends, and victory is awarded to Yale.

PRINCETON VS. YALE

New York, Nov. 24, 1883

PRINCETON		YALE
J. M. T. Finney, '84,	End,	H. H. Knapp, '82.
M. C. Kennedy, '84,	Next to End,	W. H. Hyndman, '84.
T. H. Harris, '86,	Guard,	F. G. Peters, '86.
J. M. Harlan, '84,	Centre,	L. K. Hull, '83.
C. W. Bird, '85,	Guard,	R. Tompkins, '84, Capt.
L. R. Wanamaker, '86,	Next to End,	S. R. Bertron, '85.
R. J. Travers, '84,	End,	A. L. Farwell, '84.
P. T. Kimball, '84,	Quarter-back,	H. B. Twombly, '84.
Alex. Moffat, '84, Capt.,	Half-back,	W. Terry, '85.
H. C. Lamar, '86,	"	E. L. Richards, '85.
A. T. Baker, '85,	Back,	B. W. Bacon, '81.

Referee: R. M. Appleton, '84, Harvard. Judges: D. M. Look, '84,
Princeton; F. Kellogg, '83, Yale. Score: Princeton 0, Yale 6. First
Half: Touchdown by F. G. Peters, goal by E. L. Richards.

NOTE.—For system of scoring see convention Oct. 17,
1883, Appendix.

First Half: Princeton wins the toss and takes the wind. Terry kicks off by a dribble to Twombly, who picks up the ball and runs. Succeeding rushes by Yale carry the ball within 10 yards of Princeton's goal. Princeton gets the ball and Moffat punts. Peters catches and by hard rushing and brilliant dodging takes the ball through the entire Princeton eleven and over the line for a touchdown, which is followed by a goal by Richards. Princeton kicks off. Lamar gets the ball and makes 35 yards. The ball is lost on a fumble and Knapp and Farwell by short rushes work it back to midfield. Here Princeton stops the advance and gets the ball. Moffat lifts the leather to Yale's goal-line. Richards runs it back 10 yards and punts and Hull recovers the ball. Terry by a long run carries the ball to the 35-yard line. Hull follows with a rush to the 10-yard mark, where Bird stops him from a touchdown. Sharp rushing and tackling ensue here, but the ball is lost, and Moffat sends it back to midfield, where time soon after is called.

Second Half: In the second half Travers takes Wanamaker's place. Moffat opens the game with a long kick, which Richards returns. Moffat again sends the ball down the field. Twombly makes the catch and on the ensuing kick lifts the ball well into Princeton's quarters. Moffat gets it and runs it out, kicking magnificently while at full speed. Yale fumbles and Harris gets the ball. Unable to gain by scrimmaging, Moffat tries for a field goal, but misses the post by an inch. Yale punts out and Lamar, catching, runs 20 yards. Here Yale stops the advance and gets the ball. On the line-up the ball is dribbled and passed to Richards, who is far out to the side. He reaches the 15-yard line before being thrown. On the next play Richards, standing near the side line, prepares for a difficult try at goal. Princeton's ends rush, run at him and, by clever body-checking, block the kick and get the ball.

Moffat at once punts out of danger. Richards and Knapp
quickly rush it back. Richards again tries for a goal, and
the Princeton ends, by their beautiful body-checking, again
block the kick, Moffat getting the ball. On the next play,
to avoid a safety, Moffat touches down the ball in goal.
The ball is then brought out to the 25-yard line and Moffat
punts to midfield, where the game ends.

PRINCETON vs. YALE

New York, Nov. 27, 1884

PRINCETON		YALE
C. M. De Camp, '86,	End,	W. N. Goodwin, '85.
L. R. Wanamaker, '86,	Tackle,	L. F. Robinson, '85.
T. H. Harris, '86,	Guard,	A. B. Coxe, '87.
J. C. Adams, '86,	Centre,	F. G. Peters, '86.
C. W. Bird, '85, Capt.,	Guard,	H. R. Flanders, '85.
W. M. Irvine, '88,	Tackle,	S. R. Bertron, '85.
H. L. Hodge, '86,	End,	F. W. Wallace, '89.
D. Edwards, '85,	"	R. Ronalds, '86.
R. M. Hodge, '86,	Quarter-back,	T. L. Bayne, '87.
H. P. Toler, '86,	Half-back,	E. L. Richards, '85, Capt.
H. C. Lamar, '86,	"	O. G. Jennings, '87.
	"	W. Terry, '85.
Alex. Moffat, '84,	Back,	M. H. Marlin, '86.

Referee: R. M. Appleton, '84, Harvard. Judges: W. W. Connor,
'85, Princeton; L. K. Hull, '83, Yale. Score: Princeton 0, Yale 0.

First Half: Yale wins the toss and takes the ball. Coxe
gets the ball and runs 10 yards, passing to Bayne as he is
about to be tackled. Princeton intercepts the pass and gets
the ball. Hodge, on the line-up, sends a long pass out to
the end rush, but Yale in turn intercepts and gets the ball.
Coxe makes 2 yards through the centre. Bayne runs 10,
and as he is about to be tackled, passes to Richards, who continues for 40 more. Yale's heavy centre now forces the ball
to the 5-yard line. Bertron takes it over for a touchdown

and Terry kicks the goal. Princeton kicks off by a dribble and quick passes to Lamar, who dodges and dashes to Yale's 25-yard line. Moffat tries for a field goal at a difficult angle, but misses. De Camp gets the ball behind the line and makes a touchdown. Hodge makes the kick for goal, but the ball glances to the side. Yale brings the ball out to the 25-yard line and Richards makes a long punt down the field. Moffat sends it back to the 30-yard line. Yale starts a series of hard rushes. Peters makes 20, Terry adds 20 more, and Bayne another 20. Princeton intercepts a side pass and Moffat gets away for a 45-yard run. Yale stops the attack and gets the ball. Richards gets away on the first down for a long run, but is injured. Jennings takes his place. Kicks are now exchanged, Terry and Moffat doing the kicking. The punting duel terminates by a 20-yard run by Moffat. Lamar duplicates the feat by carrying the ball to Yale's 25-yard line. Moffat tries for a goal from the field, but fails. De Camp is hurt and goes off. Moffat gets another chance at a field goal, but the ball falls short. Wallace catches it and runs out 20 yards. Terry carries it to Princeton's 40-yard line, where the half ends.

Second Half: Princeton opens the second half with a dribble, pass to Lamar, and a run by the latter of 25 yards. Moffat then kicks. Wallace and Terry by short rushes work the ball back to Princeton's 25-yard line. Here Princeton recovers the ball and Harris and Bird get away for long gains. Moffat from the 45-yard line drops a field goal. A prolonged dispute ensues between the rival judges. Finally the referee refuses to allow it. Yale punts out from the 25-yard line. A few plays later Terry gets the ball and dashes for 35 yards. The ball is fumbled and Princeton carries it back to Yale's 40-yard line. Moffat tries for another goal, but misses. A few minutes later he drops back for another try, but Ronalds blocks the kick. Wallace and Terry by two magnificent runs carry the ball to Princeton's 25-yard line. Here sharp tackling by Princeton gets the ball and Moffat lifts it 65 yards down the field. Terry catches on the run, and eluding the entire Princeton team except Moffat, brings it back to the 25-yard line, Moffat tackling. On the next play Edwards leaps through the line and takes the ball from Yale's quarter-back, advancing 25 yards. Yale's judge claims that Edwards was off-side. A long wrangle ensues terminating in a decision by the referee that Edwards was off-side and that the ball shall go to Yale at midfield. The game has been so prolonged by the various altercations of the contending teams that it has now become dark. Eighteen minutes still remain to play. The referee calls the game on account of darkness. Yale claims the victory upon the points scored, 6 to 4.* Princeton contends that the game must be declared a tie at 0 to 0 under Rule 22 of the intercollegiate code requiring a championship game to consist of two halves of forty-five minutes each. The referee reserves his decision until he can examine the rules. The teams and crowds thereupon leave the field. Subsequently the referee declares the contest no game and the score as 0 to 0.

NOTE.—Late in the evening following this game the Intercollegiate Convention assembled at the Fifth Avenue Hotel, in New York. Yale appealed from the decision of Mr. Appleton, the referee, in declaring this contest "no game and the score as 0 to 0." The convention voted, however, to sustain the decision of the referee. See convention of Nov. 27, 1884, Appendix.

* See amended rule of scoring, No. 6, convention of Dec. 5, 1883, Appendix.

PRINCETON VS. YALE
New Haven, Nov. 21, 1885

PRINCETON		YALE
C. M. De Camp, '86, Capt.,	Right End,	R. N. Corwin, '87.
W. J. Cook, '89,	Right Tackle,	H. L. Hamlin, '87.
	" "	C. O. Gill, '89.
T. H. Harris, '86,	Right Guard,	G. W. Woodruff, '89.
J. C. Adams, '86,	Centre,	F. G. Peters, '86, Capt.
H. W. Cowan, '88,	Left Guard,	A. C. Lux, '88.
W. M. Irvine, '88,	Left Tackle,	G. R. Carter, '88.
H. L. Hodge, '86,	Left End,	F. W. Wallace, '89.
R. M. Hodge, '86,	Quarter-back,	H. Beecher, '88.
H. C. Lamar, '86,	Right Half-back,	W. T. Bull, '88.
H. P. Toler, '86,	Left Half-back,	G. A. Watkinson, '89.
H. S. Savage, '87,	Full-back,	E. L. Burke, '87.

Referee: Walter Camp, '80, Yale. Score: Princeton 6, Yale 5. First Half: Goal from field by G. A. Watkinson. Second Half: Touchdown by H. C. Lamar, goal by R. M. Hodge.

First Half: Princeton wins the toss and takes the ball. The game opens by a dribble and pass to Cowan, who makes a slight gain. The ball is passed out to De Camp, who makes 5 yards. Beecher stops Lamar by a sharp tackle. Two more rushes without gain give the ball to Yale. Watkinson lifts a tremendous kick over Princeton's goal-line. R. M. Hodge punts out from the 25-yard line, and Wallace, catching, runs it back 5 yards before De Camp brings him down. Watkinson gets away for a run of 20 yards and kicks on the run, Savage catching. A dribble to Lamar results in no gain. The play is repeated and Peters stops him by a hard tackle. Princeton abandons rushing and turns to a kicking game. Watkinson catches the ball. Beecher in two runs gains 10 yards. Bull adds 20 more. Wallace plants the ball on the 35-yard line, but De Camp and Hodge stop the advance. Yale forms for a try at goal. Cowan breaks through and blocks the kick. A great punting duel ensues. Scrimmaging is resumed. Watkinson tries for another goal from the field, but misses.

Princeton punts out. Corwin dashes for 25 yards, being at last stopped by Harris. Watkinson and Beecher take the ball to the 5-yard line. Watkinson tries for another goal, but misses it by a foot. Savage punts out. Beecher, standing on the side at the 45-yard line, catches the ball. He starts diagonally across the field and by a series of beautiful dodges crosses the line. The touchdown is not allowed, however, as he has run out of bounds. Princeton stops the attack and gets the ball. Savage punts. Watkinson catches and runs the ball back to the 25-yard line, from which he cleverly kicks a field goal. Princeton punts out, Beecher runs the ball back 20 yards, and time is called.

Second Half: Yale opens the second half by a dribble and pass to Watkinson for a kick. Toler catches and returns. Yale fumbles and Harris gets the ball. On the snap, Peters, at centre, seizes the ball from Adams. Beecher on the first play takes it to the 25-yard line. Princeton's line will not yield an inch and Yale loses the ball. Lamar kicks and Watkinson returns. Princeton, by a series of sharp rushes, now works the ball well into Yale's territory, Harris and Lamar making good gains. The ball then changes sides frequently. Harris gets out of a scrimmage and runs to the 15-yard line. Lamar reaches the 5-yard line. Three hard rushes fail to gain and Yale gets the ball. Peters, Watkinson, and Beecher work the ball back to the centre. Hamlin is hurt and Gill takes his place. The ball remains here for a long time, oscillating back and forth from side to side, interrupted only by a kick and a return. Only ten minutes are left to play. Yale starts a steady but slow advance toward Princeton's goal. Peters calls for a kick. The ball is passed to Watkinson, who sends a long, high punt down the field. The ball strikes the ground and bounds toward the side line. Lamar seizes it on the bound and, with a peculiar loping but swift motion,

darts between Corwin and Wallace. Turning sharply he
runs along the southern side line. Bull and Beecher mass
to tackle or to force him out of bounds. With incredible
swiftness he turns suddenly to the right, and as Beecher
leaps to tackle, dodges beneath him and thus dives into a
clear field. Peters, coming up swiftly from behind, is overtaking him. As they reach the last line Peters dives, but
Lamar springs away and crosses the line for a touchdown.
R. M. Hodge kicks the goal. Yale kicks off and Princeton
at once commences an attack that steadily forces the Blue
back, but time is nearly up, and as the ball comes to midfield the game is called.

PRINCETON vs. YALE

Princeton, Nov. 25, 1886

PRINCETON		YALE
H. L. Hodge, '86,	Left End,	F. W. Wallace, '89.
F. Moore, '89,	Left Tackle,	C. O. Gill, '89.
H. W. Cowan, '88,	Left Guard,	J. J. Buchanan, '89.
W. J. George, '89,	Centre,	W. H. Corbin, '89.
W. M. Irvine, '88,	Right Guard,	G. W. Woodruff, '89.
W. J. Cook, '89,	Right Tackle,	G. R. Carter, '88.
E. O. Wagenhurst, '88,	Right End,	R. N. Corwin, '87, Capt.
R. M. Hodge, '86,	Quarter-back,	H. Beecher, '88.
K. L. Ames, '90,	Half-back,	G. A. Watkinson, '89.
L. E. Price, '88,	"	S. B. Morison, '91.
T. H. Savage, '87, Capt.,	Full-back,	W. T. Bull, '88.

Referee: T. H. Harris, '86, Princeton.   Score: Princeton 0, Yale 0.

First Half: The game is called nearly two hours late
through inability to obtain a referee, Mr. Harris, of Princeton, finally consenting to act. A heavy rain is falling.
Yale wins the toss and takes the ball. Corbin dribbles to
Beecher, who gains 10 yards. Yale fumbles and Princeton
gets the ball. Hodge sends a pass to Ames, who starts for
the end, but is downed by Wallace. On the third down
Savage touches down for a loss of 10 yards, to make first

down under the rules. On the next play he attempts to
punt, but is thrown in his tracks by Gill. Savage then lifts
a punt down to Yale's 30-yard line. A sharp exchange
of kicks follows. Princeton begins rushing tactics, sending Ames and Price into the line in rapid succession for
repeated gains, carrying the ball to Yale's 10-yard line.
Here Yale holds. On the fourth down Savage again touches
down 10 yards back to gain a first down. On the line-up
Savage drops back for a try at goal, but Woodruff is through
and prevents the kick. Hodge makes 20 yards, but Ames
on the next play is thrown by Wallace for a loss of ten.
Savage again kicks. Yale gets the ball and punts. Several
scrimmages ensue, resulting in Yale getting the ball. Gill,
Watkinson, and Morison are sent against the line. Twice
Yale is compelled to touch down for a 10-yard loss in order
to hold the ball. The play suddenly shifts by a long kick
to Princeton's goal, Hodge being thrown by Beecher on the
4-yard line. On the next play Princeton fumbles and Corwin gets the ball and crosses the line. The play is not allowed, as the Yale centre has kicked the ball in play instead
of its being snapped by Princeton. Princeton punts to
midfield and time is called.

Second Half: The second half opens as darkness is closing
down and the rain is falling in increased torrents. Princeton opens with the V and makes 10 yards. Yale punts and
gets the ball near Princeton's goal. Watkinson tries for a
field goal, but fails. The ball goes over the line, having been
touched by Savage. Wallace falls on it for a touchdown.
The goal is missed. The crowd breaks upon the field in
great excitement and fifteen minutes elapse before play
can be resumed. Play is resumed for five minutes without
further result. Owing to the delay in starting this game
it has now become dark. Twenty minutes still remain
to play. The referee calls the game and declares it "no

game and the score as 0 to 0." Captain Corwin demands
that the game shall be awarded to Yale by a score of 4 to 0.
Princeton claims that the decision shall stand in accordance
with the precedent of 1884. The referee maintains his
decision of no game.

NOTE.—At the ensuing intercollegiate convention Yale
claimed the championship, but the convention declined to
award it. See convention of Nov. 28, 1886, Appendix.
Also see report of Committee on Championships, convention
of Oct. 4, 1890, Appendix.

PRINCETON VS. YALE

New York, Nov. 19, 1887

PRINCETON		YALE
S. C. Hodge, '88,	Left End,	F. W. Wallace, '89.
J. R. Church, '88,	Left Tackle,	C. O. Gill, '89.
H. W. Cowan, '88,	Left Guard,	G. R. Carter, '88.
	" "	C. T. Brooks, '89.
W. J. George, '89,	Centre,	W. H. Corbin, '89.
W. M. Irvine, '88,	Right Guard,	G. W. Woodruff, '89.
	" "	W. C. Rhodes, '91.
R. E. Speer, '89,	Right Tackle,	S. M. Cross, '88.
E. O. Wagenhurst, '88,	Right End,	F. C. Pratt, '88.
J. Hancock, '88,	Quarter-back,	H. Beecher, '88, Capt.
L. E. Price, '88,	Left Half,	W. P. Graves, '91.
W. C. Price, '88,	" "	
R. H. Channing, '91,	Right Half,	W. C. Wurtenberg, '89.
K. L. Ames, '90,	Full-back,	W. T. Bull, '88.

Referee: W. A. Brooks, '87, Harvard. Umpire: R. F. Fiske, '87,
Harvard. Score: Princeton 0, Yale 12. First Half: Touchdown by
W. P. Graves, goal by W. T. Bull. Second Half: Touchdown by
W. H. Corbin, goal by W. T. Bull.

First Half: Princeton wins the toss and takes the ball.
The ball is dribbled to Hancock, who runs, but passes to
Ames for 15 yards. Three rushes more take the ball to
Yale's 25-yard line. Yale gets it on downs and Graves
punts. Price and Ames advance it 10 yards, but Princeton

is forced to punt. Both sides are fumbling frequently. Channing, Ames, and Cowan force it well down into Yale's territory, but Ames is forced to kick. Yale returns, Princeton fumbles, and Gill gets the ball. Yale cannot gain and Bull punts. Ames catches on Princeton's 25-yard line. Princeton prepares to kick, but Wurtenberg gets the ball and crosses the line. The ball is brought back for holding. Princeton punts, Gill rushes it back. Yale is held for downs and Princeton again punts. Yale by short gains forces it back to the 5-yard line, but cannot get it across. Ames once more lifts the ball far down the field. Graves, Gill, and Bull start the advance again and reach the 10-yard line. Graves this time gets it over for a touchdown and Bull kicks the goal. Princeton kicks off and several minutes of fierce scrimmaging ensues on the 40-yard line, which ends by the call of time for the first half.

Second Half: W. C. Price takes the place of L. E. Price for Princeton and Yale opens with a rush by Woodruff, followed by Gill, Graves, and Wurtenberg, taking the ball to the 20-yard line, where the advance is checked. Bull punts. Princeton makes a short gain, but Ames is compelled to kick. Gill and Woodruff alternate with Wurtenberg and Graves, and the ball is steadily pushed down the field toward Princeton's goal. Corbin finally takes it over for a touchdown. Bull kicks the goal. Brooks takes Carter's place for Yale. Princeton dribbles to Price, who makes a run of 25 yards. No further gain can be made and Ames punts. Bull returns. Cowan gets the ball and ploughs solidly through the Yale team, Beecher saving Yale from the touchdown. Yale gets the ball and Woodruff on the line-up gets away for the longest run of the game, 60 yards, being tackled by Price. Woodruff is hurt and Rhodes takes his place. Wallace and Graves make 25 yards, the latter interfering finely. Wurtenberg and

Graves carry the ball within 2 yards of Princeton's goal. Princeton holds for downs and Ames punts to midfield, where time is called.

PRINCETON VS. YALE

New York, Nov. 24, 1888

PRINCETON		YALE
R. E. Speer, '89,	Left End,	F. W. Wallace, '89.
W. J. Cook, '89,	Left Tackle,	C. O. Gill, '89.
W. M. Irvine, '88,	Left Guard,	W. W. Heffelfinger, '91.
W. J. George, '89,	Centre	W. H. Corbin, '89, Capt.
H. H. Janeway, '90,	Right Guard,	G. W. Woodruff, '89.
H. W. Cowan, '88, Capt.,	Right Tackle,	W. C. Rhodes, '91.
J. B. Riggs, '92,	" "	
D. Bovaird, '89,	Right End,	A. A. Stagg, '88.
R. M. Hodge, '86,	Quarter-back,	W. C. Wurtenberg, 89.
J. S. Black, '91,	Left Half,	W. P. Graves, '91.
R. H. Channing, '91,	Right Half,	Lee McClung, '92.
	" "	P. W. Harvey, '91.
K. L. Ames, '90,	Full-back,	W. T. Bull, '88.

Referee: W. A. Brooks, '87, Harvard. Umpire: R. F. Fiske, '87, Harvard. Score: Princeton 0, Yale 10. First Half: Goal from field by W. T. Bull. Second Half: Goal from field by W. T. Bull.

First Half: Princeton wins the toss and takes the ball. The game opens with the "V·trick," Black running therein with the ball and gaining 15 yards. On the line-up Princeton springs a new play. The end rush runs in and blocks the opposing tackle; the half and full run out and carry the opposing end out, thus splitting the line in two. Cowan goes through the opening and reaches the 10-yard line.* The play is not allowed and the ball is given to Yale. Princeton soon regains it. Stagg and Gill stop the Princeton backs for a loss and Ames drops back for a try for goal. The ball goes wide. Yale puts the ball in play at the 25-yard line. Graves and Gill make short gains, but Speer

* The origin of "boxing the tackle."

and Bovaird stop the advance and Bull punts. The play
continues in this manner for several minutes. Gill at last
gets away for a run of 30 yards, but Cowan throws McClung
for a loss on the next play and Bull is forced to punt. Ames
makes a fair catch at the 25-yard line. Princeton draws
back 10 yards and forms the V, coming forward on the
play 20 yards. But Heffelfinger makes a tackle behind
their line and Ames drops back to punt. Heffelfinger is
through and blocks the kick. Gill and McClung rush the
ball to the 20-yard line, but here sharp tackling by Irvine
and Cowan throws Yale for a loss. Bull tries a drop kick,
but misses the goal. Princeton starts from the 25-yard line
with the V, but soon punts. Yale again brings the ball
down to the 25-yard line and Bull tries unsuccessfully for
another goal. Again the V makes 10 yards, and Black and
Cowan follow it up by consecutive gains, carrying the ball to
Yale's 40-yard line. Yale holds and gets the ball. Gill
and Rhodes work it back, but Bull at last has to punt.
Princeton begins an attack on the ends, but loses the ball
for foul interference. Punts are exchanged and the two
teams are played to a deadlock, with the half nearly over,
when Princeton fumbles on the 10-yard line and Stagg
gets the ball. Bull falls back and kicks an easy goal from
the field. Princeton opens play with the wedge and then
punts. Yale, by long runs of McClung, Bull, and Gill,
carries the ball to the 5-yard line, where time is called.

Second Half: During the second half play is even for
nearly twenty-five minutes, being merely scrimmages without substantial gain, followed by punts. Wurtenberg goes
off McClung taking his place. Black and Cowan make good
gains and the ball is carried to Yale's 35-yard line. Yale
holds for downs and Bull punts. Ames returns the kick
and Harvey runs it back 30 yards. Heffelfinger adds 20
more. Cowan goes off and Riggs takes his place. Yale

bucks the line hard, but Cook and Janeway throw the runners back. Bull tries for a goal, but fails. Yale gets the
ball and kicks and Stagg gets it on a fumble. Three rushes
take the ball to Princeton's 25-yard line, where Yale is held
and Bull tries for a field goal, but the ball goes wide.
Princeton opens with a V on the 25-yard line, making 10
yards. Princeton now begins a brilliant running game.
Hodge makes 10, Channing 25, and Ames 40, but Yale gets
the ball on a foul. Heffelfinger, Gill, and McClung, by a
series of rapid line plays, take the ball back to the 30-yard
line. Only a minute is left to play. Bull, standing 37 yards
from the line and far to the side, then drops a beautiful
goal from the field and time is called.

PRINCETON VS. YALE
New York, Nov. 28, 1889

PRINCETON		YALE
B. Donnelly, '90,	Left End,	A. A. Stagg, '88.
H. W. Cowan, '88,	Left Tackle,	C. O. Gill, '89, Capt.
H. H. Janeway, '90,	Left Guard,	W. W. Heffelfinger, '91.
W. J. George, '89,	Centre,	B. Hanson, '90.
P. C. Jones, '91,	"	
J. B. Riggs, '92,	Right Guard,	A. B. Newell, '90.
J. N. Thomas, '90,	" "	L. Heyworth, '90.
W. S. Cash, '90,	Right Tackle,	W. C. Rhodes, '91.
R. H. Warren, '93,	Right End,	J. A. Hartwell, '89.
E. A. Poe, '91, Capt.,	Quarter-back,	W. C. Wurtenberg, '89.
J. S. Black, '91,	Left Half,	Lee McClung, '92.
R. H. Channing, '91,	Right Half,	P. W. Harvey, '91.
	" "	S. B. Morison, '91.
K. L. Ames, '90,	Full-back,	H. McBride, '90.

Referee: J. A. Saxe, '88, Harvard. Umpire: W. A. Brooks, '87,
Harvard. Score: Princeton 10, Yale 0. Second Half: Touchdown by
R. H. Warren, goal by K. L. Ames; touchdown by H. W. Cowan.

First Half: Yale wins the toss and takes the western goal,
backed by a strong wind. Princeton opens with the V, out
of which Channing runs for 15 yards. Black and Chan-

ning now try the Yale wings, but Stagg and Rhodes prevent a gain. Ames lifts a long punt. Yale fumbles the kick and Cowan gets it, running for 20 yards before going down beneath McClung's hard tackle. Yale gets the ball on a foul. Yale sends Harvey, Morison, and McClung against Princeton's line, but Cash, Janeway, and Cowan throw them back, the ball going to Princeton. Again Princeton loses the ball on a fumble. Yale now masses her men in a V against the tackle. The play gains 4 yards. A similar formation is tried on the opposite side and makes five yards. The ball is only 10 yards from the goal line. Yale continues to use the V, but Cowan breaks it up. Ames gets the ball and makes a long run. He tries for a field goal 40 yards away, but McBride catches on Yale's 10-yard line. Yale tries to rush it out, but Poe and Warren throw the runners back. Yale punts to midfield and the half ends.

Second Half: Yale starts the second half with a V and gains 12 yards. McClung gains 15 yards. McClung tries a drop kick, but the ball falls short. Princeton fumbles and it is Yale's ball on the 10-yard line. Three times their backs batter the line, but Riggs and Janeway stop the attack. Princeton gets the ball on downs. Ames punts to the 45-yard line and Warren gets the ball. Ames runs to the right end, but, just as he reaches the line, whirls around and makes a long pass to the left to Cowan, who runs 30 yards before being downed. Princeton fumbles and loses 20 yards, but Channing recovers the ball. On the line-up Ames tries for a field goal. The posts are missed, but the ball rolls across the line on the ground. The Yale backs fumble it and Warren, coming up like a race-horse, dives along the slippery mud and gets the ball for a touchdown. The ball is brought out and the angle for goal is wide and difficult, but Ames makes it. Only fifteen minutes are left to play. Yale launches the V with great fierceness and follows it up with fast and desperate playing. Princeton stops the advance and immediately fumbles, Hartwell getting the ball. McClung tries for field goal at 20 yards, but the ball strikes the post. Gill is through and seizes the ball, carrying it across, but it is brought back for off-side play. A moment later McBride tries another drop, but Cash blocks the kick. Princeton gets the ball and Ames starts off a phenomenal punt, which he follows up with others, keeping the ball continually down in Yale's goal. Ames tries a long drop kick, which falls short, but is fumbled by Yale. Cowan falls on the ball, but, rising to his feet, staggers across the line with the Yale team clinging to him for a touchdown. The goal fails. Yale opens with a rush and follows it up with a kick. Ames runs the ball back 30 yards, but with only McBride between him and the line, goes down, and McBride holds him at the 5-yard line. Before the ball can be sent off on the next play time is called.

PRINCETON VS. YALE

Brooklyn, Nov. 27, 1890

PRINCETON		YALE
R. H. Warren, '93,	Left End,	J. A. Hartwell, '89.
R. E. Speer, '89,	Left Tackle,	A. H. Wallis, '93.
J. N. Thomas, '90,	Left Guard,	W. W. Heffelfinger, '91.
P. C. Jones, '91,	" "	
J. G. Symmes, '92,	Centre,	W. M. Lewis, '91.
J. B. Riggs, '92,	Right Guard,	S. N. Morison, '92.
E. A. S. Lewis, '91,	Right Tackle,	W. C. Rhodes, '91, Capt.
R. Furness, '91,	Right End,	B. L. Crosby, '92.
E. A. Poe, '91, Capt.,	Quarter-back,	F. E. Barbour, '92.
P. King, '93,	Left Half,	Lee McClung, '92.
W. C. Spicer, '91,	Right Half,	P. W. Harvey, '91.
	" "	L. T. Bliss, '93.
S. Homans, '92,	Full-back,	S. B. Morison, '91.

Referee: W. A. Brooks, '87, Harvard. Umpire: S. V. Coffin, '89, Wesleyan. Score: Princeton 0, Yale 32. First Half: Touchdown

and goal by L. McClung; touchdown by L. McClung; touchdown and
goal by L. McClung. Second half: Touchdown by W. C. Rhodes,
goal by L. McClung; touchdown and goal by L. McClung; touchdown by S. B. Morison.

First Half: The game is played at Eastern Park, Brooklyn. When the teams arrive upon the field great consternation is caused by the collapse of a stand upon which are
4,000 spectators, many of whom are injured. As soon as the
confusion subsides the coin is tossed and the turn correctly
called by Poe for Princeton. Princeton opens with the V
in which Poe makes 10 yards. Homans punts to McClung,
who is tackled by Riggs on Yale's 10-yard line. Yale fumbles and Speer gets the ball. Homans tries a goal from
the field, but misses. Yale now produces a wonderful
end-interference play. The right end boxes the opposing tackle, the right half and full-back carry the opposing end out. Heffelfinger at the snap of the ball jumps from
his position in the line and, crossing between centre and
quarter-back, forms the head of the running interference,
followed by the quarter-back and the left half, the latter carrying the ball. An equally strong variation of this formation also is used against the tackle, who is carried out.
Yale sends play after play of this kind against Princeton's
line until the ball is carried to the 25-yard line. Here Hartwell, running around from end, is given the ball, and striking
in between the opposite end and tackle, plants it on the
15-yard line. King and Poe stop Yale for 2 downs without gain. On the next play McClung splits the end and
tackle for a run of 25 yards and a touchdown. He kicks
the goal. Princeton opens play with the V, but is held for
downs. Again Yale with her great interference batters
Princeton down to the 25-yard line, where McClung, led
by Heffelfinger, rounds the end for a second touchdown.
The try at goal at a wide angle is missed. Again the Prince-

ton V ploughs for 10 yards. Yale holds and gets the ball. McClung and Harvey hit the centre for short gains and the latter skirts the end for 20 yards. McClung again takes the ball over for a touchdown and kicks the goal. King makes 13 yards in the V and bucks the line for 5 more. Spicer splits end and tackle for 15 yards. King and Homans add 15 more. Here Yale holds and Homans tries for a field goal, but it fails. On the kick-out time is called for the half.

Second Half: Yale opens the second half with the V, gaining 5 yards. Thomas, Symmes, and Riggs break up the next three plays and force Yale to punt. Homans lifts a prodigious return. Yale lines up, but cannot gain, Furness, Warren, and Spicer stopping the advance. Again Yale punts and again Homans outkicks his rival, Princeton gaining 10 yards by the exchange. Yale hits the line for a short gain, but cannot make the distance S. B. Morison punts, Homans returns, and McClung gets the ball. Heffelfinger hits the line for 5 yards. McClung goes round the end for 10 more. Rhodes skirts the opposite side for an additional 10-yard gain. McClung and Heffelfinger plant the ball on the 1-yard line, King tackling and throwing both. Rhodes breaks the centre in two for the touchdown and McClung kicks the goal. Princeton's V fails to gain. King is stopped on a centre plunge by Heffelfinger and Homans punts. The ball is over the line and Yale brings it out to the 25-yard line and puts it in play by a scrimmage. McClung, Rhodes, and S. B. Morison advance the ball by slow but consecutive gains to Princeton's 35-yard line. Here King and Poe stop the Yale backs and Morison tries a drop kick. The ball goes into the crowd and is recovered by King. Homans drops back to punt, but S. N. Morison is through on him and the kick is blocked, Rhodes getting the ball on the 20-yard line. Bliss splits

FOOTBALL

the line for 5 yards, and McClung, aided by Heffelfinger, rounds the end for a 30-yard run and a touchdown. He kicks the goal. Princeton resumes play with a wedge, making 10 yards. King is thrown for a loss of 4 and Homans punts. S. B. Morison catches on the 10-yard line and runs the ball back 10 yards. McClung goes between end and tackle for 5 yards. Rhodes skirts the end for 10 more. S. B. Morison hits centre for 4. McClung rounds the end for 15. S. N. Morison breaks the line in two, and with Heffelfinger interfering, races 70 yards for a touchdown. No goal. There is only one minute left to play. Princeton sends its wedge for 10 yards and time is called.

PRINCETON vs. YALE
New York, Nov. 26, 1891

PRINCETON		YALE
R. H. Warren, '93, Capt.,	Right End,	J. A. Hartwell, '89.
A. F. Harold, '93,	Right Tackle,	W. C. Winter, '93.
J. B. Riggs, '92,	Right Guard,	S. N. Morison, '92.
J. G. Symmes, '92,	Centre,	G. F. Sanford, '95.
A. L. Wheeler, '95,	Left Guard,	W. W. Heffelfinger, '91.
A. F. Holly, '95,	Left Tackle,	A. H. Wallis, '93.
H. Vincent, '94,	Left End,	F. A. Hinkey, '95.
P. King, '93,	Quarter-back,	F. E. Barbour, '92.
J. M. Flint, '95,	Left Half,	Lee McClung, '92, Capt.
J. P. Poe, '95,	Right Half,	L. T. Bliss, '93.
S. Homans, '92,	Full-back,	V. C. McCormick, '93.

Referee: W. A. Brooks, '87, Harvard. Umpire: S. V. Coffin, '89, Wesleyan. Score: Princeton 0, Yale 19. Second Half: Touchdown by V. C. McCormick; touchdown by W. C. Winter; goal from field by V. C. McCormick; touchdown by L. T. Bliss, goal by L. McClung.

First Half: Princeton wins the toss and takes the ball. Play starts with a V, Poe gaining 8 yards. Heffelfinger stops Flint in the centre. Poe also fails to pass the centre. Homans punts and McClung catches on the 30-yard line. McClung rounds Princeton's right for 15 yards. Vincent stops a run around the left and Yale punts. Kicks are exchanged. McClung gets around the end for 15 yards. Riggs and Harold stop the advance and Bliss punts, Homans returning. Vincent throws McClung for a loss and Yale punts, Homans returning. Yale tries the line, but cannot make a gain and Bliss kicks. Princeton makes a fair catch and tries the wedge, but cannot gain. Homans punts. For the remainder of the half Princeton returns all kicks and Yale uses up three downs in trying, without appreciable gain, to make a first down. Several penalties are imposed, but the tackling is too fierce for either side to gain any advantage or come within striking distance of the goal. The half closes with a punt to midfield by Yale.

Second Half: Yale opens with a wedge, Sanford gaining 5 yards. Bliss cannot gain, Harold tackling. McClung hits the centre for 3 yards. King stops Winter with a gain of 8. McClung hits centre for 4 and Morison makes 1. Riggs breaks through and throws McClung for a loss of 4 yards. Winter hits the line twice for a gain of 5 yards on each try. McClung gets 5 more, but is stopped by Wheeler. McCormick hits centre twice, once without a gain and the second time making 8 yards. Morison goes through for 5. McClung and Winter, by short gains in three rushes, take the ball within two yards of the line. The two teams mass for a centre smash, and McCormick is forced over for a touchdown. The goal is missed. Princeton brings the ball out to the 25-yard line and starts a V, King making 2 yards. Flint goes through centre for 4 yards. McClung stops Poe on the end for 2 yards. Princeton fumbles and Hinkey gets the ball. Bliss and McClung spring a criss-cross and land the ball within one yard of the line. Winter splits tackle for the touchdown. The goal again is missed. Princeton starts the wedge at the 25-yard line, but makes no gain. Princeton punts and the ball is out of bounds at the 25-yard line. Yale loses the ball

for holding. Homans punts. Heffelfinger leaps in the air
and stops the ball with his hand, Hartwell catching it and
running around the end for 15 yards. McClung makes 8
more, and then Princeton gets the ball for holding. Homans
punts to McClung. McClung makes 10 yards around the
end. Yale gets 5 more for off-side play. Holly and Harold
stop two rushes at the line. The ball is then passed to
McCormick, who drops a goal from the 40-yard line.
Princeton starts the wedge at midfield and makes 10 yards.
Both teams hold well, requiring frequent punting. Homans
tries a drop kick at 40 yards, but the ball goes to the left.
McClung starts the wedge at the 25-yard line. Princeton
tackles sharply and forces a kick. Homans returns. McCormick runs 18 yards and is brought down by Flint. Yale
tries the line, but cannot gain consecutively and punts.
Flint tries the centre, but cannot gain. Morison downs
Homans behind the line and prevents a punt. Homans, on
the next play, gets his kick off and McClung makes a fair
catch. Yale tries the V, but loses 2 yards. Bliss punts and
Poe gets the ball. Flint makes a small gain and Homans
punts to McClung. McCormick cannot gain, but McClung
gets around the end for 15 yards. Bliss and McClung
work a criss-cross and the former gets away for a 65-yard
run and a touchdown. McClung kicks the goal. Princeton resumes play with a V at midfield and gains 5 yards.
Poe hits the line for 4 more. Poe makes 3 more, but
Morison tackles. As the teams line up time is called.

PRINCETON VS. YALE

New York, Nov. 24, 1892

PRINCETON		YALE
T. G. Trenchard, '95,	Right End,	J. C. Greenway, '95.
A. F. Harold, '93,	Right Tackle,	A. H. Wallis, '93.
F. M. Hall, '96,	Right Guard,	W. O. Hickok, '95.
D. M. Balliet, '94,	Centre,	P. T. Stillman, '95.

PRINCETON		YALE
A. L. Wheeler, '95,	Left Guard,	J. A. McCrea, '95.
L. Lea, '96,	Left Tackle,	W. C. Winter, '93.
M. P. Randolph, '93,	Left End,	F. A. Hinkey, '95.
P. King, '93, Capt.,	Quarter-back,	V. C. McCormick, '93, Capt.
J. P. Poe, '95,	Left Half,	L. T. Bliss, '93.
	" "	H. S. Graves, '92.
F. B. Morse, '95,	Right Half,	C. D. Bliss, '93.
S. Homans, '92,	Full-back,	F. S. Butterworth, '95.

Referee: W. A. Brooks, '87, Harvard. Umpire: S. V. Coffin, '89, Wesleyan. Score: Princeton 0, Yale 12. First Half: Touchdown by L. T. Bliss, goal by F. S. Butterworth. Second Half: Touchdown by P. T. Stillman, goal by F. S. Butterworth.

First Half: Princeton wins the toss and takes the west goal, with a fair wind. The Yale V makes 10 yards. C. Bliss makes 5 more. L. Bliss rounds the end and with McCormick, Winter, and Butterworth in perfect interfering formation, runs 40 yards for a touchdown. Butterworth kicks the goal. Poe makes 12 yards in the V. L. Bliss adds 4 more, but Princeton stops the advance and gets the ball. Morse, Lea, and Poe make 12 yards and Homans tries for a field goal, but the kick is low. Both teams interlock in a rushing contest, the gains being small and the ball frequently changing sides. Frequent penalties are imposed for holding. King makes a fair catch at centre. Poe breaks the centre for 5 yards. King is hurt, but resumes. Yale gets the ball on downs, but Harold and Trenchard will not let them gain. Butterworth punts out of bounds. Poe and Morse carry the ball to the 40-yard line and Homans tries for a field goal, but the ball is brought back and given to Yale for holding. Yale tries the ends, but cannot make them. Butterworth punts to Poe, and the half closes.

Second Half: Morse in the V opens the second half for 5 yards. Homans punts. Wallis, Winter, and Butterworth pound the line for short gains and C. Bliss gets around the end for 15 yards. L. Bliss doubles the other end for 20

more. Princeton gets the ball for holding. Homans drops
back for a drop kick, but runs instead. He gains slightly,
but punts on the next down. The ball changes sides on
downs. Yale drives the ball to Princeton's 30-yard line,
but is held for downs. Homans punts, but Stillman blocks
the kick and the ball bounds back over the line, Stillman
falling on it for a touchdown. Butterworth kicks the goal.
Morse makes 8 yards in the V, but Homans is forced to
kick. He lifts a prodigious punt to Yale's goal-line, where
the ball is fumbled, but Greenway gets it on the 5-yard
line. The ball is punted to Poe, who runs it back 25 yards.
King makes a great effort to round the end for a touchdown, but Butterworth stops him. Yale gets the ball on the
15-yard line. Kicks are exchanged, Butterworth running
back the kick 12 yards. He then splits the centre for 10
more. L. Bliss rounds the end for 15 and adds 5 more on
a fake kick. With Hinkey interfering, he carries the ball
to Princeton's 23-yard line. Butterworth, Graves, and C.
Bliss gain slightly, but Princeton stops the attack 7 yards
from the line. Poe makes 3 through centre. Yale gets the
ball for holding. The time is nearly up and the Yale stands
are calling for a touchdown. Trenchard throws C. Bliss for
a loss and McCormick drops back to try a drop. Lea
blocks the kick, but Hinkey gets the ball and plants it on the
5-yard line. Bliss and Graves hit the line like a battering-
ram, but Balliet, Hall, and Harold stand like a wall and
Princeton gets the ball. Time then is called.

PRINCETON VS. YALE

New York, Nov. 30, 1893

PRINCETON		YALE
H. O. Brown, '95,	Left End,	F. A. Hinkey, '95, Capt.
A. F. Holly, '95,	Left Tackle,	F. T. Murphy, '97.
A. L. Wheeler, '95,	Left Guard,	J. A. McCrea, '95.
D. M. Balliet, '94,	Centre,	P. T. Stillman, '95.

THE ORIGINAL TANDEM–TACKLE PLAY.

Princeton driving Yale to defeat with the new formation. Manhattan Field, New York, Nov. 30, 1893.

PRINCETON		YALE
K. Taylor, '95,	Right Guard,	W. O. Hickok, '95.
L. Lea, '96,	Right Tackle,	A. McC. Beard, '95.
T. G. Trenchard, '95, Capt.,	Right End,	J. C. Greenway, '95.
P. King, '93,	Quarter-back,	G. T. Adee, '95.
W. D. Ward, '95,	Left Half,	S. B. Thorne, '95.
F. B. Morse, '95,	Right Half,	R. Armstrong, '96.
	" "	E. H. Hart, '94.
J. R. Blake, '94,	Full-back,	F. S. Butterworth, '95.

Referee: W. A. Brooks, '87, Harvard. Umpire: P. J. Dashiell, Navy. Score: Princeton 6, Yale 0. First Half: Touchdown by W. D. Ward, goal by P. King.

First Half: Princeton wins the toss and takes the ball. The game opens with a flying wedge, King carrying the ball 20 yards. Yale gets the ball on a fumble. Wheeler throws Thorne for a loss of 5 yards and Butterworth punts. Ward and Morse pierce the Yale line for 9 yards, but Yale gets the ball for holding. Wheeler drops Armstrong for a loss of 2. Trenchard stops Thorne and Princeton gets the ball. A few short gains are made and the ball is kicked. Yale springs a novel play. The ends and tackles drop back for a mass play, but Butterworth punts. Half of the Yale line are down the field on Blake, but the latter makes the catch and dashes through them for 20 yards. King makes 10 yards on a double pass and punts. Butterworth gets through the line for 25 yards. Two mass plays are sent against the tackles, but Princeton gets the ball for off-side play. Blake punts, and Butterworth, after a few trials at the line by Thorne, returns the ball. Princeton now uncovers a new tackle play, running her men in the form of a tandem. In this formation, starting from the 40-yard line, King, Ward, Morse, and Blake, by short but unbroken gains, carry the ball straight down the field to the last line, where Ward is lifted on the top of a wave of striped orange jerseys and forced across the line for a touchdown. King punts out to Trenchard and then kicks the goal. Yale opens with a strong rush, Butterworth making 20 yards in the flying wedge, but Princeton soon stops the advance. The ball changes sides frequently on the 40-yard line, being punted and returned, but neither side makes a dangerous gain. The half closes with the ball on Princeton's 40-yard line.

Second Half: Yale opens the second half with a flying wedge and makes 18 yards. Princeton holds and gets the ball on downs. Morse makes 4 yards and Blake punts out of bounds. Morse makes 8 and Ward adds 3 more. Yale braces and holds for downs. Butterworth hits the centre for 4 and then punts. Blake, Morse, and Ward, in the tandem, rush the ball back 17 yards. The ball is passed to Blake, who bucks centre, but turns and passes the ball to King, who rounds the end for 20 yards. A mass play yields 4 more, and Ward and Morse plant the ball on the 5-yard line. Yale makes a spirited defence and gets the ball on downs. Butterworth lifts the ball over 65 yards. Princeton by short rushes brings the ball back to the 10-yard line, where Blake misses a difficult try for a goal from the side line. Yale cannot gain and Butterworth kicks. King catches and runs the ball back 25 yards. Again the tandem comes into play and the ball advances to Yale's 5-yard line, but Princeton cannot force it over. Thorne piles the Princeton runners up behind the line and Yale gets the ball. Thorne and Butterworth work the ball back 15 yards and time is called.

PRINCETON vs. YALE

New York, Dec. 1, 1894

PRINCETON		YALE
H. O. Brown, '95,	Left End,	F. A. Hinkey, '95, Capt.
A. F. Holly, '95,	Left Tackle,	A. McC. Beard, '95.
A. L. Wheeler, '95,	Left Guard,	J. A. McCrea, '95.
D. Riggs, '97,	Centre	P. T. Stillman, '95.

PRINCETON		YALE
J. M. Rhodes, '97,	Right Guard,	W. O. Hickok, '95.
K. Taylor, '95,	Right Tackle,	F. T. Murphy, '97.
	" "	C. Chadwick, '97.
T. G. Trenchard, '95, Capt.,	Right End,	L. Hinkey, '97.
W. D. Ward, '95,	Quarter-back,	G. T. Adee, '95.
N. Poe, '97,	Left Half,	· S. B. Thorne, '96.
	" "	H. W. Letton, '97.
A. H. Rosengarten, '97,	Right Half,	A. N. Jerrems, '96.
H. W. Barnett, '96,	" "	
G. Cochran, '98,	Full-back,	F. S. Butterworth, '95.
W. H. Bannard, '98,	"	

Referee: J. De Hart, O. A. C. Umpire: P. J. Dashiell, Navy. Linesmen: Mr. Baldwin, C. A. C., Frank Coyne, O. A. C. Score: Princeton 0, Yale 24. First Half: Touchdown by F. S. Butterworth, goal by W. O. Hickok; touchdown by F. S. Butterworth, goal by W. O. Hickok; touchdown by F. S. Butterworth, goal by W. O. Hickok. Second Half: Touchdown by L. Hinkey, goal by W. O. Hickok.

First Half: Yale wins the toss and takes the western goal. Wheeler kicks to Jerrems and the latter runs back to midfield. Princeton forms to punt, but Hickok blocks the kick and Murphy falls on the ball on Princeton's 5-yard line. Butterworth bucks the line twice, touching down on the last plunge. Hickok kicks the goal. Wheeler kicks to Butterworth and the ball is run back 20 yards. A long exchange of kicks ensues, marred by several fumbles but lucky recoveries. Princeton discloses a new system of interference. Every player but the centre rush is withdrawn behind the line. Two men start before the ball and cross behind centre, thus giving a flying interference behind which follows the runner, pushed and whirled by his associates. Yale soon solves it, and after a few trials it fails to gain. Thorne, Jerrems, and Beard buck the line for 20 yards. Butterworth circles the end for 20 more. Short line plunges now take the ball to Princeton's 5-yard line, from which Butterworth is rammed across for a touchdown. Hickok kicks the goal. Yale now opens a new interference

play. The entire team with ,the exception of centre are
formed 7 yards behind the line, the quarter playing 5 yards
behind centre. Three men start across before the ball is put
in play. Suddenly the ball is passed back to the quarter,
all backs start in motion, and a double pass is made to
confuse the opponents. Yale also produced in this game
a new method of passing to the full-back for a kick. Instead of the ball being snapped to the quarter-back and
then passed by him to the full-back, the centre threw a long
pass directly to the full-back, passing the ball between
his legs as he stood in snapping position. Yale's backs by
superior work soon force the ball well down into Princeton's
territory. Butterworth, Thorne, Jerrems, and Beard by
line-bucking reach the 5-yard line, from which Butterworth
is forced over for a touchdown and Hickok kicks the goal.
Princeton again kicks off and Yale renews its line-plunging
tactics, taking the ball slowly but steadily down to Princeton's 3-yard line, where time is called for the half.

Second Half: Yale opens the second half by kicking to
Bannard on the 25-yard line. Princeton tries for a short
gain and punts. Beard, Jerrems, and Murphy make 10
yards and Butterworth rounds the end for 15. Adee tries a
quarter-back kick, but Princeton gets it. Thorne is hurt
and Letton takes his place. Scrimmage follows scrimmage,
the ball changing sides frequently on downs and kicks.
Letton kicks out of bounds at Princeton's 15-yard line.
Yale gets the ball for holding. Letton, aided by perfect
interference, rounds the end for 15 yards. Princeton holds
for downs. Bannard punts and Yale gets it on the 50-yard
line. F. Hinkey loses 5 and Butterworth punts. Princeton
fumbles on the 10-yard line and L. Hinkey, picking up the
ball, crosses the line for a touchdown. Hickok kicks an
easy goal. Both teams resort to a kicking game. Rosengarten is hurt and Barnett takes his place. Yale catches

on the 40-yard line and puts the ball down for a scrimmage.
L. Hinkey makes 5, Butterworth adds 7 more. Jerrems
goes through for 5, and time is called.

PRINCETON VS. YALE
New York, Nov. 23, 1895

PRINCETON		YALE
L. Lea, '96, Capt.,	Left End,	L. M. Bass, '97.
S. H. Thompson, '97,	" "	
W. W. Church, '97,	Left Tackle,	J. O. Rodgers, '98.
D. Riggs, '97,	Left Guard,	C. Chadwick, '97.
P. Wentz, '99,	" "	
R. R. Gailey, 97,	Centre,	H. P. Cross, '96.
J. M. Rhodes, '97,	Right Guard,	W. R. Cross, '96.
A. C. Tyler, '97,	Right Tackle,	F. T. Murphy, '97.
G. Cochran, '98,	Right End, ·	L. Hinkey, '97.
H. M. Suter, '99,	Quarter-back,	C. M. Fincke, '97.
H. C. Armstrong, '98,	Left Half,	S. B. Thorne, '96 Capt.
A. W. Kelly, '98,	" "	
A. H. Rosengarten, '97,	Right Half,	C. DeWitt, '96.
W. H. Bannard, '98,	" "	
J. Baird, '99,	Full-back,	A. N. Jerrems, '96.

Referee: M. McClung, '94, Lehigh. Umpire: P. J. Dashiell, Navy.
Linesmen: I. McD. Garfield, '93, Williams; V. M. Coyne, E. A. C.
Score: Princeton 10, Yale 20. First Half: Touchdown by L. M. Bass,
goal by S. B. Thorne; touchdown and goal by S. B. Thorne. Second
Half: Touchdown by A. N. Jerrems; touchdown by J. Baird, goal by
H. M. Suter; touchdown by A. C. Tyler; touchdown by S. B. Thorne,

First Half: Yale wins the toss and takes the east goal.
Lea kicks off to Bass on the 25-yard line. Thorne on the
line-up returns the ball to centre. Princeton tries the line,
but fumbles, and Yale gets the ball. Thorne gets through
centre for 2. Jerrems adds 2 more. Thorne and DeWitt
on line plunges gain 15 more. Lea and Cochran throw
for losses and Thorne punts. Baird returns the kick to
Fincke. Thorne hurdles the line for 5. Thompson and
Tyler stop the advance and Princeton gets the ball. Baird
punts over the heads of the Yale backs and the ball rolls to

Yale's 25-yard line. Armstrong and DeWitt fail to gain and Thorne punts. Princeton starts a clever tandem play on the tackles and the ball steadily creeps toward the Yale goal. At midfield Princeton fumbles, and Bass, picking up the ball, aided by Murphy as an interferer, races to Princeton's goal-line and touches down. Thorne kicks the goal. Lea kicks off to Thorne on the 10-yard line. On the line-up Jerrems kicks to Baird. Rosengarten makes 15 through centre, and then Yale holds for downs. Baird drops back to punt, but H. P. Cross gets through and blocks the kick. Thorne kicks to Princeton's 35-yard line. Yale blocks the kick. Rodgers, Jerrems, and Thorne by short plunges carry the ball to the 25-yard line. Rhodes and Cochran throw back Yale for a loss and Thorne tries a drop for the goal, but misses. Princeton punts out and Thorne sends it back. Armstrong bucks centre for 11. Baird drops back to kick, but Thorne blocks it and gets the ball on the 10-yard line. The teams line up. Jerrems makes 4, DeWitt 2, and Thorne on the last down takes the ball over for a touchdown and then kicks the goal. Time is called for the half.

Second Half: Thorne kicks to Baird, who returns. DeWitt, Thorne, and Jerrems hit the line for good gains, but the ball is fumbled and Cochran gets it. Rhodes makes 4, Rosengarten 9, and Armstrong 5. Armstrong is hurt and Kelly takes his place. Princeton now starts up its tandem and the plays follow in rapid succession for short gains, taking the ball to Yale's 5-yard line. Here Hinkey and Bass throw for losses and Yale gets the ball. Thorne punts to midfield. Again the tandem starts and the ball is hammered down to the 20-yard line. Lea goes off, Thompson taking his place. Yale holds and Suter tries for a drop, but Jerrems blocks the kick. Princeton recovers the ball. Rosengarten is withdrawn and Bannard sent in. Baird punts to midfield. Thorne takes the ball on the run and

races for 45 yards before Baird stops him.   DeWitt makes
3, Thorne 3, and Jerrems takes the ball over for a touchdown.   The goal fails.   Baird kicks off to Thorne, who
returns.   Princeton takes the ball at midfield and, employing its tandem on the tackle, drives the ball steadily to the
goal-line, Baird going over for a touchdown.   Suter kicks
the goal.   Thorne kicks off, sending the ball over the line.
Baird kicks out from the 25-yard line.   Yale, unable to gain,
drops Thorne back for a punt, but the kick is blocked, by
Tyler on the 40-yard line, the ball rebounding and rolling
to Yale's goal, where Tyler falls upon it for a touchdown.
Suter's kick for the goal is low and the Yale men leap in
the air and block it with their hands.   Thorne kicks off,
and for several minutes play crosses and recrosses centre,
scrimmages and punts being intermingled.   Finally, Thorne
drops back to the 55-yard line and Yale forms in punting
formation.   Princeton throws the backs into the line to
block.   Cross sends the ball back to Thorne, but the latter, instead of punting, dashes for the end.   As he rounds
it he is met by the field of orange backs.   Dodging swiftly
in and out and shaking off tackler after tackler, he races
through them, clearing all, and with 40 yards before him,
leaps for the goal-line, which he crosses at the extreme
corner of the field for a touchdown.   The try for goal
fails.   Princeton kicks off and Yale returns.   As the teams
line up time is called.

PRINCETON VS. YALE

New York, Nov. 21, 1896

PRINCETON		YALE
H. C. Brokaw, '97,	Left End,	L. M. Bass, '97.
W. W. Church, '97,	Left Tackle,	J. O. Rodgers, '98.
E. G. Crowdis, '99,	Left Guard,	L. Murray, '97.
R. R. Gailey, '97,	Centre,	B. C. Chamberlin, '97.
H. C. Armstrong, '98,	Right Guard,	C. Chadwick, '97.
A. R. T. Hillebrand, '00,	Right Tackle,	F. T. Murphy, '97, Capt

PRINCETON

YALE

	Right Tackle,	A. H. Durston, '99.
G. B. Cochran, '98, Capt.,	Right End,	W. B. Conner, '99.
F. L. Smith, '97,	Quarter-back,	C. M. Fincke, '97.
	"	A. M. Hine, '99.
W. H. Bannard, '98,	Left Half	A. M. Hine, '99.
H. Wheeler, '00,	" "	P. D. Mills, '97.
A. W. Kelly, '98,	Right Half,	H. F. Benjamin, '99.
	" "	L. H. Van Every, '98.
J. Baird, '99,	Full-back,	L. Hinkey, '97.

Referee: M. McClung, '94, Lehigh. Umpire: P. J. Dashiell, Navy. Linesman: I. McD. Garfield, '93, Williams. Score: Princeton 24, Yale 6. First Half: Touchdown by L. M. Bass, goal by A. M. Hine; touchdown and goal by J. Baird; touchdown by A. W. Kelly, goal by J. Baird. Second Half: Touchdown by A. R. T. Hillebrand; touchdown by W. H. Bannard; touchdown by H. Wheeler.

First Half: Yale wins the toss and takes the east goal. Baird kicks off to Hinkey, who returns to Smith. Baird drops back to punt, but Rodgers breaks through and blocks the kick. A brisk exchange of punts terminates by Yale putting the ball down for scrimmage on their 45-yard line. Benjamin breaks through the centre on a trick play and runs 35 yards. Conner gains 5 and a penalty yields 5 more, with another penalty on the next play of 10. The ball is on the 25-yard line. Brokaw, Church, and Cochran throw the Yale backs for a loss and Princeton gets the ball. The signal is given for a punt. Rodgers again blocks the kick and Bass falls on the ball behind the line for a touchdown. Hine kicks the goal. Baird punts to Hinkey, who returns. On the line-up Baird again punts, Fincke catching. Yale tries the line, but cannot find an opening and Hinkey punts to Baird. Princeton tries scrimmaging without gain and is forced to kick. Hinkey returns the ball to Princeton's 50-yard line. Princeton now sets in motion a new tackle play, the "revolving tandem." It gains from 2 to 8 yards each time, the backs alternating with the ball, and without

once losing it, Baird, on the final plunge, crosses the line for
a touchdown. A moment later he kicks the goal. Hine
kicks off to Baird. Princeton at once renews its attack
with the revolving tandem, directing it continually at Yale's
right wing. Murphy goes off and Durston takes his place.
Kelly runs the end for 10, Bannard doubles the opposite
end for 10 more. Hine goes to quarter, Mills to half.
Yale gets the ball for holding. Mills splits the line for a
run of 25 yards. Yale cannot follow it up with another gain
and Hinkey punts. Baird catches on Princeton's 35-yard
line and runs through the entire Yale team, being finally
thrown by Benjamin on Yale's 10-yard line. Church makes
4, Bannard adds 1, and the revolving tandem whirls Kelly
over for the touchdown. Baird kicks the goal. Yale kicks
off, but time is called for the half.

Second Half: Benjamin kicks to Baird, who returns to
Fincke. On the line-up Hinkey punts down to Baird on the
25-yard line. Hillebrand on a fake kick makes 25 yards.
Kelly and Bannard round the ends for long gains and the
ball reaches Yale's 20-yard line, where it is lost on a fumble.
On the first play Yale fumbles and Princeton gets it. Kelly
makes 4, Bannard 7. Kelly crosses the line, but drops the
ball. Hillebrand gets it and touches down, Baird misses
the goal. Yale kicks to Princeton's 10-yard line. Princeton sends it back and gets it on a fumble. The revolving
tandem starts in motion, and Bannard, Kelly, and Baird
take the ball rapidly down the field to the 4-yard mark, where
Bannard is whirled over for a touchdown. The goal is
missed. Benjamin goes off and Van Every takes his place.
Bannard retires and Wheeler comes on. Yale kicks off
again. Princeton returns and recovers the ball on a fumble.
Once more the revolving tandem is brought into play.
Kelly, Wheeler, and Baird are whirled through the line for
short but consecutive gains. Ten minutes are required to

cover the fifty-five yards, and on the last play Wheeler goes
over for the touchdown. The goal is missed. Hinkey kicks
to Princeton's 25-yard mark. The resistless revolving tandem is set in play and whirls to Yale's 25-yard line in
twelve plays, when time is called.

PRINCETON vs. YALE

New Haven, Nov. 20, 1897

PRINCETON		YALE
S. G. Craig, '95,	Left End,	J. J. Hazen, '98.
E. G. Holt, 00,	Left Tackle,	J. O. Rodgers, '98, Capt.
E. G. Crowdis, '99,	Left Guard,	C. Chadwick, '97.
W. C. Booth, '00,	Centre,	G. L. Cadwalader, '01
I. R. Dickey, '98,	"	
W. H. Edwards, '00,	Right Guard,	F. G. Brown, '01.
A. R. T. Hillebrand, '00,	Right Tackle,	B. C. Chamberlin, '97.
G. Cochran, '98, Capt.,	Right End,	J. A. Hall, '97.
H. R. Lathrope, '00,	" "	
J. Baird, '99,	Quarter-back,	C. A. H. De Saulles, '99.
E. S. Burke, '00,	"	
H. R. Reiter, '98,	Left Half,	C. T. Dudley, '00.
A. C. Ayres, '99,	" "	
W. H. Bannard, '98,	Right Half,	H. F. Benjamin, '99.
A. W. Kelly, '98,	" "	
H. Wheeler, '00,	Full-back,	M. L. McBride, '00.

Referee: W. S. Langford, '96, Trinity. Umpire: P. J. Dashiell,
Navy. Linesmen: C. J. Howland, '94, Yale; D. Bovaird, '89, Prince-
ton. Timekeeper: E. O. Smith, '93, Wesleyan. Score: Princeton 0,
Yale 6. Second Half: Touchdown by C. T. Dudley, goal by G. L.
Cadwalader.

First Half: Princeton wins the toss and takes the north
goal. Chamberlin kicks off to Baird, who returns. Yale
cannot make first down and punts. Reiter rounds the
end for 10 yards. Hazen and Hall stop the next two
plays and Wheeler punts. On the line-up McBride punts.
Princeton fumbles and Rodgers falls on the ball at the
45-yard line. Craig and Cochran by sharp tackling hold
Yale for downs and Baird punts to the Blue's 25-yard line.

THE REVOLVING TANDEM.

Princeton whirling Reiter through Yale's line, carrying the ball momentarily out of danger. Yale Field, Nov. 20, 1897.

Benjamin and Dudley cannot gain and McBride punts. Kelly makes 5, Reiter 4, and Brown throws for a loss. Baird tries a drop kick, but the kick is low and Yale blocks it. De Saulles picks up the ball and brilliantly dodging the press of Princeton players, quickly gets under way and dashes down the field. As he runs he evades tackler after tackler. Thus 55 yards are covered. As he crosses the 10-yard line a rear tackle brings him down and closes this great run. On the first plunge Yale fumbles and Princeton gets the ball. Baird immediately punts to midfield and time is called for the half.

Second Half: Baird kicks off and McBride returns. Princeton tries the line and punts. Yale has no better success and McBride sends the ball back to midfield. Cochran and Reiter are retired and Lathrope and Ayres take their places. Kelly makes 4, Bannard 2, and Wheeler 1. Princeton punts to Yale's 20-yard line. Yale now discloses a formidable attack. Rodgers, Dudley, Benjamin, and McBride alternate with the ball and the Tiger's line is punctured for short but unfailing gains. At the 15-yard line a penalty of 10 yards is applied and it is Yale's ball on the 5-yard line. Rodgers makes 4. Dudley bursts through centre and makes the touchdown. Cadwalader kicks the goal. De Saulles kicks off and Baird gets the ball on the 20-yard line. Princeton also produces a stronger attack and Kelly and Wheeler drive the ball to Yale's 45-yard line. Here the ball is fumbled and Rodgers gets it. McBride punts. Princeton lines up for a punt, but Wheeler's kick is blocked. Yale has the ball on the 25-yard line. Four plunges take it to the 10-yard line, but here Holt and Hillebrand throw Yale back and Princeton gets the ball. Wheeler punts. Baird gives way to Burke. Yale returns the kick. Princeton again discloses a great attack. By line plunges the ball travels 55 yards, when a fumble occurs and Yale gets the

ball on their 40-yard line. The time is growing short
now and Yale puts forth every effort to score. Rodgers,
Dudley, and Benjamin hit the line in rapid succession and
the ball advances yard by yard until the 3-yard line is
reached. On the next line-up time is called and the great
game is over.

PRINCETON vs. YALE

Princeton, Nov. 12, 1898

PRINCETON		YALE
L. R. Palmer, '98,	Left End,	E. M. Eddy, '99.
M. Geer, '99,	Left Tackle,	G. S. Stillman, '01.
E. G. Crowdis, '99,	Left Guard,	F. G. Brown, '01.
M. F. Mills, '02,	" "	
W. C. Booth, '00,	Centre,	G. B. Cutten, '99.
W. H. Edwards, '00,	Right Guard,	E. E. Marshall, '99.
A. R. T. Hillebrand,'00,Cpt.,	Right Tackle,	B. C. Chamberlin, '97, Cpt.
A. Poe, '00,	Right End,	S. L. Coy, '01.
" "		G. W. Hubbell, '00.
A. V. Duncan, '01,	Quarter-back,	C. A. H. De Saulles, '99.
R. F. Hutchinson, '02,	"	M. U. Ely, '98.
J. R. Beardsley, '02,	Left Half,	H. F. Benjamin, '99.
W. H. Black, '99,	" "	A. F. Corwin, '99.
F. W. Kafer, '00,	Right Half,	A. H. Durston, '99.
H. Wheeler, '00,	" "	R. Townshend, '00.
A. C. Ayres, '99,	Full-back,	M. L. McBride, '00.

Referee: E. N. Wrightington, '97, Harvard. Umpire: P. J. Dashiell,
Navy. Linesmen: D. Bovaird, '89, Princeton; D. R. Francis, '00, Yale.
Score: Princeton 6, Yale 0. First Half: Touchdown by A. Poe, goal
by A. C. Ayres.

First Half: Yale wins the toss and takes the north
goal. Ayres kicks off to Cutten. Benjamin and Durston
try the line, but cannot gain, and Chamberlin punts.
Beardsley and Kafer plunge into the line, but are stopped
by Chamberlin and Stillman. Ayres punts. Yale fumbles and Princeton gets the ball. Unable to make any advance, however, Ayres punts. Chamberlin drops back
to punt, but Booth blocks the kick and Hillebrand falls on

the ball. In the ensuing scrimmage Princeton fumbles and Yale gets the ball and punts, Ayres returning to midfield. Yale now commences a hard attack on the line. Durston and Benjamin, alternating with the linesmen, carry the ball in rapid succession, crashing out gain after gain until the ball reaches the 12-yard mark. De Saulles calls for a mass on tackle. With a tremendous impact the wedge strikes Hillebrand and piles into a tangled pyramid. Suddenly Poe darts in from the end and wrenches the ball away from the runner. Instantly springing out, he starts at great speed for Yale's goal-line, 100 yards away, closely pursued by the Yale eleven, three men of which are close upon him. As they run, Poe draws away and crosses the line 7 yards in advance of the nearest man and touches down. The ball is brought out, carefully sighted, and the goal kicked by Ayres. A sharp exchange of kicks reopens the play, terminating in a fumble by Yale, Poe getting the ball. Another series of kicks ensues, which ends in a try for a field goal by Chamberlin, which fails. The kick-out starts another long kicking duel, closing by a fumble by Yale at midfield. Hillebrand gets the ball and runs to the 10-yard line. Stillman, Brown, and Coy throw the orange runners for no gain and get the ball. De Saulles makes 15 yards on a double pass, but is hurt. Ely takes his place. McBride punts out of bounds, giving Ayres on the line-up a chance to try for a field goal, which fails. McBride punts out and time is called for the half.

Second Half: Princeton kicks off, and Yale, catching on the 10-yard line, opens up an overwhelming attack. Durston, Benjamin, and McBride cut through the line of Orange forwards for unbroken gains and the ball reaches the 20-yard line. Suddenly out of the next scrimmage bursts Poe with the ball and, followed by three of the Princeton players, races the length of the field and touches down. The score

is not allowed, as the ball had been declared down before
Poe obtained it.   Palmer, Booth, and Crowdis throw back
the Yale runners for no further gain and Princeton gets the
ball.   Ayres at once sends a long punt far down the field.
McBride on the line-up punts back, but Wheeler, catching
the ball on the run, dashes to Yale's 15-yard line.   Yale holds
for downs and punts.   Wheeler returns, and for several
minutes a kicking duel ensues.   Yale gets the ball on a
fumble and starts another advance down the field, but is
stopped at the 35-yard line.   Wheeler kicks to midfield, Yale
fumbles, Poe gets the ball and runs to the 30-yard line, where
he is tackled, but passes the ball to Palmer, whom Ely
tackles.   Four plunges take the ball to Yale's 10-yard line,
where Yale gets it on downs.   An exchange of punts follows,
ending by Edwards blocking McBride's kick and Palmer
getting the ball on Yale's 5-yard line.   Yale makes a marvellous stand and holds for downs.   McBride punts to midfield and the game ends.

PRINCETON vs. YALE
New Haven, Nov. 25, 1899

PRINCETON		YALE
L. R. Palmer, '98,	Left End,	G. W. Hubbell, '00.
W. W. Roper, '02,	" "	
H. W. Pell, '02,	Left Tackle,	D. R. Francis, '00.
M. F. Mills, '02,	Left Guard,	F. G. Brown, '01.
S. G. Craig, '95,	" "	
W. C. Booth, '00,	Centre,	P. T. W. Hale, '00.
H. B. Bannard, '00,	"	
W. H. Edwards, '00, Capt..	Right Guard,	H. P. Olcott, '01.
A. R. T. Hillebrand, '00,	Right Tackle,	G. S. Stillman, '01.
F. V. Lloyd, '00,	" "	
A. Poe, '00,	Right End,	E. N. Snitjer, '00.
	" "	Charles Gould, '02.
R. F. Hutchinson, '02,	Quarter-back,	W. M. Fincke, '01.
E. S. Burke, '00,	"	
H. M. McCord, '02,	Left Half,	A. H. Sharpe, '02.
G. H. Lathrope, '00,	" "	

PRINCETON		YALE
H. R. Reiter, '98,	Right Half,	R. B. Keane, '02.
S. W. McClave, '03,	" "	H. Richards, '00.
H. Wheeler, '00,	Full-back,	M. L. McBride, '00, Capt.
G. M. Mattis, '01,	"	

Referee: E. N. Wrightington, '97, Harvard. Umpire: P. J. Dashiell, Navy. Linesmen: H. H. Janeway, '90, Princeton; R. J. Schweppe, '00, Yale. Timekeeper: F. A. Wood, B. A. C. Score: Princeton 11, Yale 10. First Half: Touchdown by H. R. Reiter, goal by H. Wheeler; touchdown by M. L. McBride, goal from field by A. H. Sharpe. Second Half: Goal from field by A. Poe.

First Half: Yale wins the toss and takes the north goal, with the wind. Wheeler kicks off and McBride returns. Princeton tries Yale's right tackle, but cannot gain and Wheeler punts. Yale fumbles and Princeton gets the ball. McCord breaks the line for 2 yards. Hutchinson tries to round the end on a double pass, but is thrown for a loss of 10 yards. Yale gets the ball on downs on Princeton's 40-yard line. Three times the backs are sent into the line without a gain and Princeton recovers the ball. Wheeler hits centre for 8 and McCord follows up with 1. The next play is stopped and Wheeler kicks. The ball is brought back for off-side play and Princeton given 10 yards. McCord gets through tackle for 4 yards and Reiter adds 1. Wheeler bucks the centre for 6. Reiter gets around the end for 5 yards. On the next play he again doubles the end, carrying the ball to Yale's 3-yard line. Yale stops the first crash without a gain. Hutchinson on the second attempt makes a yard. Reiter breaks the line in two and goes over for a touchdown. Wheeler punts out to Hutchinson, who heels the catch and Wheeler kicks the goal. Francis kicks off for Yale. McCord runs it back 5 yards and Wheeler and Reiter add 5 more. Wheeler punts to the 45-yard line. Sharpe catches and advances two yards before going down. Yale cannot gain and McBride punts. Princeton fum-

bles and Yale gets the ball on the 10-yard line. Sharpe
is stopped without a gain on the first down. Keane on the
second down makes 3 yards. Princeton throws the next
runner for a loss and gets the ball. Reiter doubles the end
for 20 yards. Wheeler punts to the 45-yard line. Fincke
catches, but Poe drops him. Sharpe gains 4 through tackle.
McBride makes 5 and then Princeton holds for downs.
Hillebrand tries to circle the end, but is thrown without a
gain. Wheeler dives through centre for 2. The next play
fails and Wheeler punts. The ball is fumbled and Pell
gets it. Princeton cannot gain and punts. McBride returns and the ball rolls to the 10-yard line. Reiter makes
2 around the end. The other end is tried without gain.
Wheeler drops back to punt. The kick is blocked and rolls
behind the goal-line. McBride falls on it for a touchdown.
The goal fails. Wheeler kicks off and McBride returns.
Reiter makes a yard through tackle. Wheeler adds 3 more
through centre. McCord bucks centre for an additional 5.
The next two plays are stopped and Wheeler punts. Sharpe
catches and is dropped in his tracks. McBride punts over
Princeton's goal-line. Wheeler kicks out to midfield and
Sharpe returns it 10 yards. Keane makes 2 through the
line, but on the next play is stopped without gain. On the
next play, standing on the 43-yard line and far to the side,
Sharpe drops a goal from the field. Wheeler kicks off and
McBride returns. Wheeler hits the centre for 3, Reiter
adds 12, Wheeler again breaks through centre for 7, and
Reiter goes round the end to Yale's 35-yard line. Here time
is called for the half.

Second Half: Francis kicks for Yale to Princeton's 15-
yard line, where it is fumbled, and Yale gets it. Sharpe and
Richards in two downs make only 3 yards, and Sharpe tries
for a field goal, but misses. Wheeler kicks out and sends
the ball over the heads of the Yale backs to the latter's 10-

yard line. Scrimmages ensue followed by kicks and exchanges, terminating by a fumble by Yale on the 15-yard
line. Princeton tries in vain to reach the next yard line, but
cannot make it. Sharpe makes 3, Richards 2, and McBride
4. Roper stops McBride for a loss on the next play and the
latter punts. For several minutes now the game becomes a
series of punts mingled with many fumbles. Princeton
makes one substitution after another until only three men remain of the original eleven. Princeton is on the aggressive,
and Yale is continually forced down into goal. McBride
kicks, and Mattis, after trying the line, returns to the 50-
yard line, where Yale fumbles and Princeton gets the ball.
Five minutes remain to play. Princeton lines up rapidly
and in six rushes takes the ball to the 25-yard line. Less
than a minute now is left. Poe is dropped back from end,
and the eleven forms to protect a drop kick. The ball is
passed, and Poe, standing on the 35-yard line, kicks it
squarely between the posts for a field goal that wins the
game. Only thirty seconds remain to play, and time is
called as the teams kick off.

PRINCETON VS. YALE

Princeton, Nov. 17, 1900

PRINCETON		YALE
W. W. Roper, '02,	Left End,	C. Gould, '02.
H. W. Pell, '02, Capt.,	Left Tackle,	J. R. Bloomer, '05.
R. R. Sheffield, '02,	" "	
R. G. Wright, '02,	Left Guard,	F. G. Brown, '01, Capt.
J. W. Losey, '03,	Centre,	H. P. Olcott, '01.
T. A. Butkiewicz, '04,	"	
M. F. Mills, '02,	Right Guard,	R. Sheldon, '02.
R. T. Davis, '04,	Right Tackle,	G. S. Stillman, '01.
H. Little, '01,	Right End,	S. L. Coy, '01.
	" "	C. D. Rafferty, '04.
A. E. Meier, '02,	Quarter-back,	J. H. Wear, '01.
A. V. Duncan, '01,	"	
H. M. McCord, '02,	Left Half,	W. M. Fincke, '01.

Referee: E. N. Wrightington, '97, Harvard. Umpire: P. J. Da-shiell, Navy. Linesmen: H. H. Janeway, '90, Princeton; T. B. Hull. Timekeeper: A. E. Whiting, '98, Cornell. Score: Princeton 5, Yale 29. First Half: Touchdown by C. Gould, goal by P. T. W. Hale; goal from field by G. M. Mattis; touchdown by J. R. Bloomer. Second Half: Touchdown by G. S. Stillman; goal by P. T. W. Hale; touchdown by J. R. Bloomer, goal by P. T. W. Hale; touchdown by W. M. Fincke, goal by P. T. W. Hale.

First Half: Princeton wins the toss and takes the south goal, with a slight wind. Yale kicks off to Meier, who runs the ball back 20 yards. Mattis kicks to the 45-yard line, where Hale returns the punt. Princeton fumbles, and Gould, picking up the ball, races over the line for a touchdown, in one minute of play. Hale kicks the goal. Mattis kicks off to Yale's goal-line. Wear, running behind magnificent interference, runs the ball back to the 45-yard line. Yale is set back 10 yards for a foul. Yale now plays the tackles in a tandem formation. Chadwick hits the line for 5 yards and a mass play nets 5 more. Hale punts to Mattis on the 25-yard line, where the latter is thrown. Princeton punts on the first down, Yale fumbles, and Pell falls on the ball on Yale's 52-yard line. The Tigers punch the centre, but are thrown back; a revolving mass play at tackle gains 3 yards. Mattis punts to Yale's 12-yard line, where the latter fumbles, and Princeton gets the ball. Princeton three times strikes the line, but there is no gain. Mattis drops back for a drop and sends the ball between the posts for a field goal. Hale kicks off to Mattis on the 25-yard line. Princeton tries a double pass and loses 3 yards. Reiter makes 5 around the end. Mattis lifts the leather down to Wear on Yale's 50-

yard line, the latter running 5 yards before being tackled
by Roper. Mattis drops back to punt, but the kick is
blocked, and Gould gets the ball on Princeton's 40-yard line.
Yale strikes the tackle for three yards and Chadwick hurdles
the line for 6 more. Princeton is driven back to the 10-yard
line. Roper throws Chadwick for a loss and Princeton
gets the ball. Mattis punts to Wear on the 40-yard line.
The ball is fumbled and Reiter gets away with it to Yale's
50-yard line before being stopped. Pell breaks the centre
for 2 and Mattis hits the tackle for 1. Mattis punts to
Yale's 10-yard line, where Gould catches and runs the kick
back 17 yards before going down. Yale now starts a rapid
attack on the line. The tackle-back is called into action.
Although this formation is not new, Princeton has discovered
that its execution involves some new principle which is
easily opening up the Tiger line. Yard after yard is gained
and still the tackle-back keeps on. · The ball now rests upon
the 15-yard line. Hale hurdles for 3. Bloomer makes 5,
Chadwick 3, and Hale 2. Again the tackle-back forms and
Bloomer is rammed across the goal-line for a touchdown.
The kick fails. Mattis kicks off. The tackle-back immediately starts in action, and by short but never failing
gains the ball travels to the 1-yard mark. The tackle-
back is formed for the final plunge, but time is called and
the half is over.

Second Half: Princeton kicks off to Wear, who runs the
ball back to the 45-yard line. Yale starts a vigorous attack
along Princeton's line. Fincke, Chadwick, and Hale plunge
and break through for consecutive gains, the ball advancing
steadily down the field until Stillman takes it over for a
touchdown. Hale kicks the goal. Princeton kicks off to
Wear on the 3-yard line. Again Yale commences its in-
cessant tackle-back attack, forcing the ball to Princeton's
10-yard line, where it is fumbled. Mattis at once punts back

to Yale's 50. Yale immediately puts the ball down for a scrimmage and, drawing its tackles back, hammers first on one side of the line with Stillman, and then on the opposite side with Bloomer, driving the ball down and over the goal-line, Bloomer making the touchdown. Hale kicks the goal. Mattis kicks off to Fincke, who after a short run passes to Dupee, who punts, the ball going out of bounds at Yale's 30-yard line. McClave tries the end on the line-up for a gain of 15 yards and immediately rounds the opposite side for 7 more. Reiter makes 2 through centre and then 2 through tackle. Yale stops the next rush and Mattis drops back to try for a goal, but the kick is blocked. Yale gets the ball and also a penalty of 25 yards, which takes the ball back to centre field. Yale starts its tackle-back attack in motion, and the ball creeps steadily down to the last line, where it is taken across by Fincke for a touchdown, from which Hale kicks the goal. Reiter goes off and Hart goes in. The ball is kicked off and for several minutes travels back and forth, punts following scrimmage without advantage to either. Time is called with the ball near midfield.

PRINCETON vs. YALE
New Haven, Nov. 16, 1901.

PRINCETON		YALE
R. T. Davis, '04,	Left End,	C. Gould, '02, Capt.
H. W. Pell, '02, Capt.,	Left Tackle,	G. A. Goss, '03.
	" "	P. H. Kunzig, '01.
M. F. Mills, '02,	Left Guard,	H. P. Olcott, '01.
T. A. Butkiewicz, '04,	" "	
H. F. Fisher, '01,	Centre,	H. C. Holt, '03.
J. S. Dana, '03,	Right Guard,	C. J. Hamlin, '03.
H. H. Short, '05,	" "	
J. R. De Witt, '04,	Right Tackle,	J. J. Hogan, '05.
H. H. Henry, '04,	Right End,	J. R. Swan, '02.
W. W. Roper, '02,	" "	
C. J. Freeman, '05,	Quarter-back,	J. L. De Saulles, '04.
G. H. Poe, '02,	"	

PRINCETON		YALE
W. L. Foulke, '05,	Left Half,	J. B. Hart, '02.
F. G. Pearson, '03,	" "	
S. W. McClave, '03,	Right Half,	G. B. Chadwick, '03.
C. G. Stevens, '04,	" "	
H. M. McCord, '02,	Full-back,	C. A. Weymouth, '03.
R. R. Sheffield, '02,	"	

Referee: E. N. Wrightington, '97, Harvard. Umpire: P. J. Dashiell, Navy. Linesmen: H. C. Brokaw, '97, Princeton; T. B. Hull. Timekeeper: J. H. Minds, '98, Pennsylvania. Score: Princeton 0, Yale 12. First Half: Touchdown by G. A. Goss, goal by H. P. Olcott. Second Half: Touchdown by J. B. Hart, goal by H. P. Olcott.

First Half: Princeton wins the toss and takes the north goal. Olcott kicks off to Mills on the 35-yard line. Princeton lines up and punts to Yale's 40. Hart rounds the end for 20, Goss makes 4 through tackle, Weymouth 1, Chadwick 1, a penalty advances the Blue 10 more. Chadwick gets through the line for 12 and Hart adds 4, placing the ball on Princeton's 25-yard line. On the line-up Yale fumbles, and Princeton gets the ball. De Witt punts to Yale's 50-yard line. De Saulles catches the punt and runs it back 25 yards. Weymouth and Hart make 4 and De Saulles drops back to try for a field goal, but the kick goes wide. De Witt punts out, sending the ball down to Yale's 50. Chadwick gains 10, Goss adds 6 more, Weymouth 2, and Hogan advances the ball to Princeton's 33-yard line. On the next play, Davis and Henry tackle for losses and De Saulles is forced to punt. The kick is fumbled and Swan gets the ball. Henry tackles him, saving a touchdown, but the ball is on the 15-yard line. Hart goes through the line for 1, De Saulles adds 4 more. With the tackle-back, Chadwick in four plays advances the ball 8 yards. Weymouth gets 2, and on the next play Goss is sent across for the touchdown. Olcott kicks the goal. De Witt kicks off and Yale returns. Princeton begins a scrimmage. Foulke and McClave rush the ball to Yale's 35-yard line, where it is fumbled. De Saulles punts back to midfield. A series of kicks are exchanged and the half closes.

Second Half: De Witt kicks off to De Saulles at 30. Chadwick makes 4 and Weymouth gets around the end for 30. Davis and Henry stop the next plunges and De Saulles tries for a field goal, but Pell and De Witt block the kick. Princeton punts. Yale returns and Princeton fumbles, giving Yale the ball on the former's 40-yard line. Chadwick and Hart make 15, but are stopped by Mills and Dana. De Saulles again tries for a drop, but misses. Kicks are exchanged, but De Witt gains steadily, the duel closing with the ball on Yale's 40. Yale starts a fierce onslaught on Princeton's line, running Chadwick, Hart, and Weymouth with a tackle-back for steady gains, sending the ball to Princeton's 8-yard line, where Yale fumbles and Henry gets the ball. De Witt drops back to punt, but Goss blocks the kick, Mills getting the ball. De Witt again drops back to punt and this time sends the ball down to Yale's 50, De Saulles catching and running the kick back 25 yards. Hart, Weymouth, and Chadwick with the tackle-back again plunge into the line for steady gains until Hart is shot across for the touchdown and Olcott kicks the goal. The game resumes with a brisk exchange of kicks. De Witt tries for field goal from the 45-yard line, but the kick is blocked. Princeton opens a heavy attack on Yale's left wing, carrying the ball to the Blue's 25-yard line, where it is fumbled. De Saulles punts to centre and the game closes.

PRINCETON vs. YALE
Princeton, Nov. 15, 1902

PRINCETON		YALE
R. T. Davis, '04, Capt.,	Left End,	C. D. Rafferty, '04.
K. B. Crawford, '05,	" "	M. S. Hare, '05.
E. C. Brown, '04,	Left Tackle,	R. P. Kinney, '05.
H. M. Bradley, '04,	Left Guard,	E. T. Glass, '04.

A DASH THROUGH THE LINE.

Yale splits Princeton's line in two and sends Chadwick through the opening 53 yards for a touchdown, winning the game.

PRINCETON		YALE
E. L. Rafferty, 06,	Left Guard,	
H. H. Short, '05,	Centre,	H. C. Holt, '03.
E. L. Barney,	"	
J. R. De Witt, '04,	Right Guard,	G. A. Goss, '03.
R. R. Reed, '04,	Right Tackle,	J. J. Hogan, '05.
H. H. Henry, '04,	Right End,	T. L. Shevlin, '06.
N. B. Tooker, '06,	" "	
F. G. Pearson, '03,	Quarter-back,	F. H. Rockwell, '06.
H. R. Hart, '04,	Left Half,	G. B. Chadwick, '03, Capt.
S. W. McClave, '03,	" "	
W. L. Foulke, '05,	Right Half,	H. G. Metcalf, '04.
P. M. Brasher, '06,	" "	M. Farmer, '04.
R. P. McClave, '03,	Full-back,	M. H. Bowman, '05.
J. W. Ames, '03,	"	

Referee: E. N. Wrightington, '97, Harvard. Umpire: P. J. Dashiell, Navy. Linesmen: H. H. Janeway, '90, Princeton; T. B. Hull. Time-keeper: J. H. Minds, '98, Pennsylvania. Score: Princeton 5, Yale 12. First Half: Goal from field by J. R. De Witt; touchdown by G. B. Chadwick, goal by M. H. Bowman; touchdown by G. B. Chadwick, goal by M. H. Bowman.

First Half: Princeton wins the toss and takes the goal. Yale kicks off to R. McClave on the 5-yard mark. On the line-up Princeton punts, De Witt sending the ball down to Yale's 40. The Blue fumbles and Davis gets the ball. Princeton tries the Yale line in vain, and De Witt tries a long kick for goal, but misses by inches. Yale punts out and Princeton returns. Yale makes a small gain through the line and again punts. On the line-up De Witt returns, but the kick is high. Yale fumbles and Henry falls on the ball. Hart and Foulke hit the line for short gains, but cannot make first down. De Witt therefore falls back to the 50-yard line and kicks a beautiful goal from the field. Yale kicks off to Foulke at 15. Princeton lines up and De Witt punts to Yale's 50-yard line. Yale forms a tackle-back, from which Chadwick makes 3. The tackle-back again forms and the ball is snapped. The Princeton line in some mysterious manner is split in two. Chadwick leaps through a wide gap. Side-stepping the waiting back, he races down the back field. The two defensive backs are cleverly blocked off and Chadwick, with 30 clear yards before him, leaps for the goal-line, which he crosses for a touchdown, having run 60 yards in his great dash. Bowman kicks the goal. Princeton kicks off, Yale catching on the 5-yard line and running the ball back 20 yards. Yale immediately signals for the tackle-back, and with this formation in rapid succession hits the Tiger's line. Chadwick makes 4, Metcalf 4, Bowman 2, and Hogan 4. Henry tackles sharply and Yale is forced to punt. McClave catches and Princeton lines up for a scrimmage. De Witt lifts a long punt down to Yale's 35. Yale plunges into the line twice, but cannot make an inch and Bowman punts. The wind catches the ball and whirls it down to Princeton's 15. On the line-up De Witt kicks back to Yale's 45. Chadwick plunges into the line for 4. A penalty sets Yale back 10 and Bowman punts. Hart and Foulke try to break Yale's line, but Kinney and Hogan throw them back and McClave punts. Chadwick, Metcalf, and Hogan in a series of fierce rushes work the ball back to Princeton's 48, where the latter gets possession of it on a foul. Princeton cannot make first down and De Witt punts to Yale's 20. Metcalf catches and runs back the ball 20 yards. Metcalf goes through the line for 4, Kinney adds 3. On the line-up Yale repeats its great play with Chadwick, who again dashes through a big opening in the Princeton line. Again the Tiger forwards deftly are split in two, leaving a wide opening, through which the Yale back leaps and, dodging brilliantly the back field as before, again covers 53 yards and touches down. Goal.

Second Half: Princeton kicks off and Yale immediately punts. A long kicking duel follows, neither team trying to rush the ball. Yale finally puts the ball down for a scrim-

mage on the 45-yard line. Chadwick in three plunges makes
21 yards. Princeton gets the ball for holding. Hart goes
off and McClave takes his place. Ames is substituted for
R. McClave. S. McClave makes 6, Brasher follows it up for
6, and Yale holds. De Witt punts and Bowman returns.
The catch is heeled and De Witt tries for a long place kick,
but misses. On the line-up Yale fumbles and Princeton gets
the ball on Yale's 35-yard line. De Witt falls back for a
drop kick. Kinney breaks through and blocks the kick.
Yale now commences a vigorous assault on the Princeton
line, hammering the ball slowly yard by yard until the
Tiger's 2-yard mark is reached, where Bradley and Reed stop
Metcalf and Princeton gets the ball. A long punt sends the
ball to midfield. Yale now adopts the kicking game to
keep the ball in Princeton's territory. The latter's backs
handle the ball cleanly and punt it back. Thus the rest
of the half is expended and the game closes.

PRINCETON VS. YALE
New Haven, Nov. 14, 1903

PRINCETON		YALE
R. T. Davis, '04,	Left End,	C. D. Rafferty, '04, Capt.
J. L. Cooney, '07,	Left Tackle,	R. P. Kinney, '05.
H. L. Dillon, '07,	Left Guard,	H. S. Batchelder, '05.
H. H. Short, '05,	Centre,	J. C. Roraback, '03.
J. R. De Witt, '04, Capt.,	Right Guard,	J. R. Bloomer, '05.
	" "	J. E. Miller, '04.
H. R. Reed, '04,	Right Tackle,	J. J. Hogan, '05.
H. H. Henry, '04,	Right End,	T. L. Shevlin, '06.
J. R. Vetterlein, '07,	Quarter-back,	F. H. Rockwell, '06.
T. J. Burke, '05,	"	
J. D. Kafer, '05,	Left Half,	W. L. Mitchell, '04,
A. F. King, '05,	" "	M. H. Bowman, '05.
H. R. Hart, '04,	Right Half,	H. G. Metcalf, '04.
S. Rulon-Miller, '07,	Full-back,	M. Farmer, '04.
	"	J. E. Owsley, '05.

Referee: M. McClung, '94, Lehigh. Umpire: Evarts Wrenn, '92,
Harvard. Head Linesman: E. N. Wrightington, '97, Harvard. Lines-

men: W. W. Roper, '02; T. B. Hull. Score: Princeton 11, Yale 6.
First Half: Touchdown by J. J. Hogan, goal by W. L. Mitchell; touch-
down and goal by J. R. De Witt. Second Half: Goal from field by
J. R. De Witt.

First Half : De Witt kicks off to Metcalf on the 2-yard
line. The latter advances the ball to the 15-yard line before
going down. Three rushes net 15 yards and Yale punts to
Princeton's 50-yard line. Foulke makes 3 yards. Kafer
rounds the end and reaches Yale's 30-yard line. De Witt
hits the centre for 10, but a penalty gives Yale the ball.
Mitchell kicks to Princeton's 45-yard line, where a fumble
gives the ball to Yale. Hogan hits the line twice without a
gain, but on the third attempt he breaks through for 10
yards. Off-side play costs Yale dearly, and Mitchell punts.
De Witt punts to Yale's 50-yard line. Hogan is now
brought back of the line in a series of rushes which steadily
force the ball slowly down the field and over the line for
a touchdown. Mitchell kicks the goal. De Witt kicks
off, the ball going over the goal-line. Mitchell punts out.
Kafer, De Witt, and Foulke by line plunges work it back to
Yale's 40-yard line, where De Witt tries for a field goal, but
fails. A double exchange of kicks lands the ball in Yale's
possession on their 50-yard line. Farmer drops back for a
punt, but the kick is blocked, Princeton getting the ball.
Princeton cannot punch the line consecutively and De Witt
tries for a goal from the 55-yard line, but misses. Yale
starts a heavy attack and hammers the ball down to Princeton's 20-yard line, where it is fumbled and Princeton gets it.
De Witt punts to the 55-yard line, and Yale works it back to
the 35-yard line by plunges at tackle. Bloomer, Farmer,
and Rockwell advance the ball 9 yards. Mitchell drops
back for a try at goal. De Witt blocks the kick and, picking
up the ball on the bound, runs the length of the field for a
touchdown. He kicks the goal. Yale kicks off and Prince-

THE BLOCKED KICK.

Princeton blocks Yale's kick. De Witt picks up the ball on the bound and runs 50 yards for a touchdown, tieing the score. Later he kicks a goal from the field, winning the game. Nov. 14, 1903.

ton returns. Shevlin makes 5. Rockwell sends all of his backs against Princeton's right wing, but he runs to the left, doubling the end and carrying the ball to Princeton's 25-yard line, where time for the half is called.

Second Half: Mitchell kicks off for Yale to De Witt on the 4-yard mark. De Witt runs back 19 yards before being downed. Yale on the next play gets the ball on a fumble. Mitchell goes round the end for 20 yards. Kinney makes 8 through tackle. Hogan is about to cross the line with the ball when it is taken from his arms by Princeton. De Witt immediately kicks down to Yale's 50. A few line plunges net 20 yards. Rockwell tries a quarter-back kick, which sends Mitchell with the ball to Princeton's 23-yard mark. Owsley hits the line for 7. Kinney makes 6 through tackle. Yale is set back 10 yards on a penalty. Mitchell tries for a goal, but Dillon blocks the kick. Princeton cannot gain and punts. Yale returns. Princeton gets the ball on the 40. Vetterlein hits the line for 4. De Witt kicks down to Mitchell at 15. In three line plays Yale advances the ball 7 yards. Owsley punts to Princeton's 30. De Witt on a fake kick makes 25 yards. On the line-up he punts to Yale's 30, where the latter fumbles and Henry falls on the ball. A line plunge fails to advance and De Witt tries for a field goal, but misses. Bowman punts on the first down to Vetterlein, who heels the catch at 43. De Witt drops back for a place kick from the 53-yard mark. It is Princeton's last chance. De Witt carefully sights the ball, and tossing a wisp of grass in the air finds the direction of the wind. Suddenly the ball is set down, De Witt leaps forward and the Yale line charges. De Witt strikes the ball squarely with his foot and it rises swiftly over the heads of the charging players, who vainly leap in the air to block it. Straight it travels, spinning over the 53 yards in a second and crosses squarely through the goal, still high above the cross-bar. Bowman kicks off. King makes 5 and Vetterlein adds 10. Time then is called.

PRINCETON VS. YALE
Princeton, Nov. 12, 1904

PRINCETON		YALE
K. B. Crawford, '05,	Left End,	T. L. Shevlin, '06.
J. L. Cooney, '07,	Left Tackle,	J. R. Bloomer, '05.
H. L. Dillon, '07,	Left Guard,	R. P. Kinney, '05.
O. Dutcher, '07,	Centre,	J. C. Roraback, '03.
H. H. Short, '05,	Right Guard,	R. C. Tripp, '06.
E. Stannard, '08,	Right Tackle,	J. J. Hogan, '05, Capt.
N. B. Tooker, '06,	Right End,	C. T. Neal, '05.
E. S. Ward, '05,	" "	
T. J. Burke, '05,	Quarter-back,	F. H. Rockwell, '06.
H. S. Tenney, '07,	"	
F. W. Ritter, '08,	Left Half,	L. Hoyt, '06.
W. L. Foulke, '05, Capt.,	Right Half,	W. C. Leavenworth, '06.
A. F. King, '05,	" "	
S. Rulon-Miller, '07,	Full-back,	J. E. Owsley, '05.
J. B. McCormick, '08,	"	A. R. Flinn, '06.

Referee: M. McClung, '94, Lehigh. Umpire: Evarts Wrenn, '92, Harvard. Linesman: Dr. E. O. Stauffer, Pennsylvania. Score: Princeton 0, Yale 12. First Half: Touchdown by J. R. Bloomer, goal by L. Hoyt; touchdown by W. C. Leavenworth, goal by L. Hoyt.

First Half: Princeton wins the toss and takes the south goal. Roraback kicks to the 10-yard line, Ritter running back the kick 15 yards. Stannard makes 5, Foulke rounds the end for 4, and a tackle-back fails to gain. Rulon-Miller punts. Yale tries to pierce Princeton's centre, but cannot gain, and Owsley punts. Cooney and Ritter advance the ball to midfield, but Princeton is forced to punt, the ball going out of bounds at the 35-yard mark. Hogan splits the centre for a gain of 20 yards. Cooney throws for a loss of 8 yards and then blocks Hoyt's punt. Ritter by great interference takes the ball to the 35-yard line, but a penalty sets it back half-way. Rulon-Miller punts to the 25-yard line. Leavenworth by a trick play breaks through the right wing and runs to Princeton's 42-yard mark. Burke goes out and Tenney takes his place. Hogan hits the line for 4, Bloomer adds 5, and a penalty yields 5 more. Three mass plays advance the ball to the 15-yard line. Bloomer and Hogan make five more. Bloomer in two rushes takes the ball over for a touchdown and Hoyt kicks the goal. Rulon-Miller kicks off to Shevlin, who runs it back to the 30-yard line. Hoyt on a fake-kick formation runs to Princeton's 40-yard line. Leavenworth makes 8, but Hoyt is forced to punt. Tenney catches and runs back the kick 20-yards. Princeton punts to Yale's 25-yard line. Hoyt returns the ball 50 yards to Tenney, who makes a beautiful 25-yard run before being tackled. A quarter-back run results in a loss and Rulon-Miller drops back for a kick. The pass goes over his head and Yale gets it on the 37-yard line. Hogan in tackle-back makes 5 and Yale gets 5 more on a penalty. Hoyt and Leavenworth in short gains through tackle place the ball on the 20-yard line. Leavenworth adds 5 more. Leavenworth again is sent into the line and reaches the 5-yard mark. On the line-up the ball is fumbled and Princeton gets it. Rulon-Miller falls back behind his goal-line to punt. Kinney breaks through and blocks. Leavenworth gets the ball, making a touchdown. Rockwell punts out and Hoyt kicks the goal.

Second Half: Yale kicks off to Rulon-Miller at 15, the ball being run back 10 yards. Cooney and Stannard cannot gain and Princeton punts. Yale gets the ball at 45. Crawford and Tooker throw the Blue backs for a loss and Yale punts. Dillon is through and the kick is high, Princeton recovering it on Yale's 50-yard line. Cooney plunges through the line for 5. A penalty gives Princeton 5 more. Cooney and Stannard in rapid plunges force the ball to Yale's 25-yard line. It is third down, with 1 yard to go. Yale holds and gets the ball. Hoyt punts. Tenney catches at midfield. Cooney hits the line for 6. Stannard adds 3 more. Bloomer throws for a loss and Rulon-Miller is forced to punt. The kick is returned. Tenney tries a quarter-back kick. Yale gets the ball. Foulke is hurt and King takes his place. Princeton stops Yale's advance and forces a kick. On the line-up Cooney gets away for a long run to Yale's 45, Rockwell tackling him and preventing a touchdown. Stannard makes 2. Cooney gains 2 more. McCormick takes the place of Rulon-Miller. Ward replaces Tooker. Yale stops the line-plunging by sharp tackling and gets the ball. Leavenworth circles the end for 8. Flinn hits the line for 3. Rockwell on a quarter-back run reaches Princeton's 25-yard line. The play is fast and the time is short. Leavenworth makes 5. The teams line up quickly, but time is called and the game is over.

PRINCETON vs. YALE
New Haven, Nov. 18, 1905.

PRINCETON		YALE
P. M. Brasher, '06,	Left End,	J. M. Cates, '06.
A. D. O'Brien, '05,	" "	H. H. Jones, '08.
J. L. Cooney, '07, Capt.,	Left Tackle,	R. W. Forbes, '07.
E. L. Rafferty, '06,	Left Guard,	A. G. Erwin, '07.
P. E. Waller, '10,	" "	C. W. Hockenberger, '07.
S. Carothers, '06,	Centre,	C. S. Flanders, '04.
J. B. Waller, '10,	"	
H. L. Dillon, '07,	Right Guard,	R. C. Tripp, '06.
H. D. Phillips, '06,	" "	
D. G. Herring, '07,	Right Tackle,	R. G. Biglow, '08.
N. B. Tooker, '06,	Right End,	T. L. Shevlin, '06, Capt.
E. A. Dillon, '09,	Quarter-back,	G. Hutchinson, '06.
H. S. Tenney, '07,	"	
R. A. Bard, '06,	Left Half,	S. F. B. Morse, '07.
J. R. Munn, '06,	" "	
W. H. Daub, '07,	Right Half,	P. L. Veeder, '07.
F. M. Tibbott, '09,	" "	H. L. Roome, '07.
	" "	W. F. Knox, '07.
J. B. McCormick, '08,	Full-back,	A. R. Flinn, '06.

Referee: J. C. McCracken, '01, Pennsylvania. Umpire: Evarts Wrenn, '92, Harvard. Linesman: C. D. Daly, '01, Harvard. Timekeeper: A. E. Whiting, '98, Cornell. Score: Princeton 4, Yale 23. First Half: Touchdown by R. W. Forbes, goal by G. Hutchinson. Seccond Half: Touchdown by A. R. Flinn, touchdown by R. W. Forbes, goal by G. Hutchinson; touchdown by H. L. Roome, goal by G. Hutchinson; goal from field by N. B. Tooker.

First Half: Princeton wins the toss, taking the south goal. Biglow kicks óff to Dillon, who runs back the ball 15 yards. Princeton is penalized for holding and Bard punts from the goal-line to the 45-yard line. Princeton twice fails to puncture Yale's line, and Bard punts to Yale's 30-yard line, where Hutchinson is dropped in his tracks. Flinn and Morse hit the line hard and in six rushes reach the 48-yard line where Princeton holds for downs. Yale immediately recovers the ball on a fumble. Four plunges through the line take the ball to the 15-yard line. Flinn makes 4, Morse gets 2, and Forbes reaches the 5-yard line. Forbes is again drawn back and shot almost to the line. On the next play he is again given the ball and goes over for a touchdown. Hutchinson punts out to Veeder, who catches and heels. Hutchinson then kicks the goal. Princeton gets the ball following the kick-off and Cooney makes 15 yards, reaching Yale's 47-yard mark. On the next play he makes 15 yards more outside of tackle. Yale holds for downs, but cannot gain against Princeton's line, and Veeder punts to E. A. Dillon, who dodges Shevlin, and with a clear field starts for the goal-line, but Morse overtakes him at the 48-yard line. A run by Bard and three line plunges place the ball on Yale's 32-yard mark. A mass play outside of tackle gets 5 more, but an attempt to round Shevlin results in a loss of 6. Tooker tries for a field goal, but misses, Hutchinson falling on the ball. Veeder kicks from his goal-line to the 47-yard mark. Bard makes 7 outside of tackle, but Princeton is set back 15 for a foul. Veeder is withdrawn, Roome taking his place. Princeton tries a double pass, but a fumble gives Yale the ball on the 25-yard line. Yale is penalized 15 and Hutchinson falls back to the 50-yard line for a drop kick. The ball is caught on the 10-yard line. Tooker punts to the 45-yard line. Yale fumbles and Princeton gets it. Three rushes take the ball to Yale's 45-yard line, where time is called for the half.

Second Half: Tooker kicks off to Morse. Flinn makes 5 and then 15. Princeton holds for downs and Roome punts to Bard. Princeton cannot gain and Bard punts out of bounds at Yale's 48. Roome returns to Bard. McCormick goes through the centre for 4. Daub is stopped without gain and Munn punts. Flanders runs back the kick to the 24-yard line. Yale makes a first down, but is penalized 15 yards. Hutchinson tries a quarter-back kick, which E. A. Dillon recovers. Princeton makes a first down and McCormick then pierces the centre for 10 yards. Princeton can gain no farther and Munn punts to Hutchinson, who runs back 25 yards. From the 25-yard line by mass plays Yale slowly forces the ball forward until Flinn takes it over for the touchdown. Hutchinson punts out to Morse, but the goal is missed. Tooker kicks off to Shevlin, who runs back 20 yards. The ball oscillates back and forth for some time until Hutchinson recovers a quarter-back kick and runs 65 yards, planting the ball on Princeton's 20-yard line. Hockenberger is quickly substituted for Erwin and Waller goes in for Rafferty. Yale by short rushes reaches the goal-line, Forbes making the touchdown. Hutchinson kicks the goal. Tooker kicks off, and on the first down Morse circles the end for 15 yards. Yale now begins a rapid assault upon Princeton's left wing, which by short gains without a check takes the ball to the last 5-yard line, from which Roome is shot across for the touchdown. Hutchinson kicks the goal. Tooker kicks off to Shevlin. A penalty forces Yale to punt out from behind the goal-line. Roome kicks out of bounds at 35. Tenney by a quarter-back run makes 8 yards, McCormick goes through centre for 8 more. Tibbott circles the end for 10, placing the ball on the 10-yard line. Princeton drives the ball to the last line, but is stopped on the second down, with 1 yard to make it a touchdown. Yale breaks through on the snap-back and smothers the Orange back and gets the ball on downs. Yale punts from behind the goal-line. Tenney heels a fair catch 43 yards from Yale's goal. Tooker sends a drop kick squarely between the posts for a field goal. The ball is kicked off, Princeton makes 15 yards by scrimmaging, and the game ends.

PRINCETON VS. YALE
Princeton, Nov. 17, 1906

PRINCETON		YALE
L. C. Wister, '08,	Left End,	R. W. Forbes, '07.
W. J. Phillips, '08,	Left Tackle,	H. R. Paige, '08.
H. L. Dillon, '07, Capt.,	Left Guard,	A. E. Brides, '09.
W. H. Daub, '07,	" "	
D. G. Herring, '07,	Centre,	C. W. Hockenberger, '07.
E. Stannard, '08,	Right Guard,	A. G. Erwin, '07.
J. L. Cooney, '07,	Right Tackle,	L. H. Biglow, '08.
A. N. Hoagland, '06,	Right End,	C. F. Alcott, '08.
E. A. Dillon, '08,	Quarter-back,	T. A. D. Jones, '08.
E. H. W. Harlan, '08,	Left Half,	P. L. Veeder, '07.
F. M. Tibbot, '09,	" "	
S. Rulon-Miller, '08,	Right Half,	W. F. Knox, '07.
	" "	H. Linn, '07.
J. B. McCormick, '08,	Full-back,	S. F. B. Morse, '07, Capt.

Referee: H. B. Hackett, '04, Army. Umpire: Evarts Wrenn, '92, Harvard. Linesman: F. W. Murphy, '99, Brown. Score: Princeton 0, Yale 0.

First Half: Princeton wins the toss and takes the south goal. Rulon-Miller kicks off to Jones on the 25-yard line, the ball being run back 15 yards. On the first down Veeder kicks down to Dillon on the latter's 40-yard line. Rulon-Miller gains 20 yards on a fake kick, but the ball is fumbled on the next play and Yale gets it. Veeder and Rulon-Miller exchange a series of kicks, the latter finally getting the ball on his 20-yard line, where on a foul it goes to Princeton. Two plunges fail to gain and Harlan tries a forward pass, but Yale gets it. Veeder immediately kicks to Harlan, and the latter returns the ball to Yale's 42-yard mark. Yale makes 12 yards on a quarter-back kick. Knox pierces the line for 3. Another trial is spoiled behind the line and Veeder punts to Dillon on his 40-yard line. On the line-up Princeton fumbles and Yale gets the ball. Veeder punts to Dillon on the 20-yard line, but the latter runs the ball back to midfield. Two downs fail to gain, and Harlan sends a twister down to Veeder on the 10-yard line; Wister is on him and there is no run back. On the line-up Veeder kicks to the 40-yard line. McCormick and Harlan advance the ball 12 yards, and then Harlan is forced to punt, the ball going to Yale's 12-yard mark. Veeder punts out of bounds at the 43-yard mark. McCormick makes 2 through the centre and Harlan adds 1. Dillon tries a forward pass, Biglow blocks it, but Princeton recovers it. Princeton is penalized 15 yards. Harlan tries another forward pass and Yale gets it. Veeder kicks to Princeton's 45-yard line. Harlan returns and on the line-up Veeder sends the ball to Princeton's 40-yard line, where it is fumbled, giving Yale the ball for the first time in Princeton's territory. Knox makes 8 on a forward pass. Veeder splits the tackle for 15, and the ball is near the 25-yard line. Yale is penalized and on the next line-up Veeder throws a forward pass to Paige on the 7-yard mark. The pass is foul and Princeton gets the ball. Harlan sends it to Yale on the 45-yard line. Veeder tries a forward pass, but Princeton gets the ball. Princeton fumbles and Veeder, picking up the ball, runs to Princeton's 25-yard line. Princeton holds Yale in check, and Veeder tries for a goal from the field, but misses. Princeton brings the ball out and time is called.

Second Half: Daub replaces Dillon. The game opens with continued exchanges of kicks, each team trying to plunge into the line and immediately punting. Neither side obtains any advantage, and the ball ranges back and forth between the 35-yard lines. Yale at last gets within striking distance of Princeton's goal and Veeder tries a drop, but misses. McCormick punts out to Knox. Yale now opens an attack, consisting of old-style line plays sent between Erwin and Biglow, but their opponents prevent first downs from being made. Yale fumbles and Rulon-Miller gets the ball. McCormick goes through centre for 17 yards. Yale holds and Harlan punts to the Blue's 35-yard line. Yale now commences a desperate onslaught upon the Princeton line. Yard by yard the ball is forced by terrific plunges to Princeton's 15-yard line, where time s called.

PRINCETON VS. YALE
New Haven, Nov. 16, 1907

PRINCETON		YALE
L. C. Wister, '08,	Left End,	H. H. Jones, '08.
R. C. Siegling, '10,	Left Tackle,	H. R. Paige, '08.
" "		G. Foster, '07.
P. E. Waller, '10,	Left Guard,	C. T. Cooney, '10.
W. J. Phillips, '08,	Centre,	E. C. Congdon, '08.
D. M. MacFadyen, '10,	Right Guard,	W. A. Goebel, '10.
A. E. Booth, '09,	Right Tackle,	L. H. Biglow, '08, Capt.
R. M. Brown, '08,	Right End,	C. F. Alcott, '08.
T. H. Welch, '10,	" "	
E. A. Dillon, '09,	Quarter-back,	T. A. D. Jones, '08.
E. H. W. Harlan, '08,	Left Half,	A. E. Brides, '09.
F. M. Tibbott, '09,	Right Half,	W. P. Bomar, '08.
" "		F. J. Murphy, '10.
J. B. McCormick, '08, Capt.,	Full-back,	E. H. Coy, '10.

Referee: M. J. Thompson, '01, Georgetown. Umpire: W. R. Okeson, '96, Lehigh. Field Judge: A. E. Whiting, '98, Cornell. Linesman: E. H. Young, '98, Cornell. Score: Princeton 10, Yale 12. First Half: Touchdown by A. E. Booth, goal by E. H. W. Harlan; goal from field by E. H. W. Harlan. Second Half: Touchdown by E. H. Coy, goal by L. H. Biglow; touchdown by E. H. Coy, goal by L. H. Biglow.

First Half: Princeton wins the toss and takes the south goal. Biglow kicks off for Yale and McCormick catches on the 20, running forward 18 yards before being thrown. McCormick bucks the centre for 4, Brown adds 2 more, and Harlan punts. T. A. D. Jones catches on the 35-yard line and Wister downs him without gain. Coy at once punts to Princeton's 50. Princeton tries two line plunges without gain and Harlan punts. T. A. D. Jones runs the catch back to 40. Yale forms to kick, but Bomar cross-bucks for 9. Brides adds 5 more. Biglow and Coy cannot gain and the latter punts. McCormick breaks through the centre for 31 yards. Wister does the same for 10. McCormick makes 5, Tibbott 5, and McCormick 2. Yale holds and Harlan tries a drop-kick, but misses. Coy punts out and Dillon runs the ball back 20 yards. Tibbott skirts the end for 25 yards. McCormick reaches the 22-yard line, but Princeton is penalized 15. Tibbott gets around the end for 6. Harlan tries for a field goal, but misses. Coy punts out. McCormick and Tibbott rush the ball 13 yards and Harlan again misses a goal. Coy kicks to Dillon at 45 and the latter runs back 23. Tibbott gets around the end for 5. Harlan shoots a forward pass to Wister on Yale's 35. Alcott recovers the ball on an on-side kick. Yale now adopts rushing tactics and advances the ball to Princeton's 40, where the Blue is stopped. T. A. D. Jones tries to make the down by an on-side kick. Phillips and Booth block it, and the latter, picking up the ball, runs 70 yards for a touchdown. Harlan kicks the goal. Yale kicks off. Princeton tries two rushes and Harlan punts. Yale is forced to punt and Dillon runs 19 yards on the catch. Harlan makes 6 and McCormick adds 5 more. Harlan gets around the end for 18. McCormick breaks through centre for 18. Tibbott takes the ball to' the 8-yard mark. Yale stands firm. Harlan drops a field-goal. Biglow kicks off and Dillon runs the ball back 30 .

yards. Princeton holds for downs and gets the ball on the 40. Tibbott runs 29 yards, Brown adds 4 more, and on the next play recovers an on-side kick at Yale's 25. Harlan gets off another on-side kick and Wister gets the ball on Yale's 20. The Blue holds firmly and Harlan misses a field goal. Coy kicks out. Harlan tries a long forward pass and the half closes.

Second Half: Phillips feints to kick down the field, but kicks to the right to Dillon, who catches and runs to Yale's 35-yard line. Tibbott makes 6, but Yale stops the advance and Harlan tries in vain for a field goal. Coy punts out. McCormick makes 4 and Harlan punts. T. A. D. Jones catches and runs back 40 yards. Yale is now on the 30-yard line. Coy takes the ball on every other play and on the eighth plunge crosses the line for a touchdown. Biglow kicks the goal. Phillips kicks off and Coy catches. Yale now opens a series of fake-kick formations, running Coy around the ends and thus works the ball to Princeton's 5-yard line. Coy is sent across, but the umpire brings him back. Wister stops Jones, and Yale forms for try for a goal from placement. The play is a ruse, Coy making a long forward pass instead of kicking. Alcott catches, but the ball is lost, as the play does not make the first down. Harlan gets off a fine punt and Wister tackles Jones. Yale cannot gain and again forms for a try for goal from placement. The trick play is again repeated. The Orange backs are not fooled, but Yale is fortunate in catching the ball. The goal-line is only 24 yards away. Yale cannot puncture Princeton's line, and T. A. D. Jones throws a forward pass to Alcott at 10. Coy is forced over for the touchdown. The ball is kicked out and Biglow kicks the goal. Princeton kicks off. Yale tries a quarter-back run, but the ball is fumbled and McCormick gets it. A fumble restores the ball to Yale. Yale is penalized 15 yards. Coy punts a long

spiral over Princeton's goal-line. Harlan punts out. Yale
cannot gain and Coy delivers a short on-side kick, which
Tibbott gets. Harlan kicks. T. A. D. Jones tries a forward
pass, but it is not complete. Princeton springs a long side
pass to Wister, but H. H. Jones tackles him for a gain of 3
yards. Harlan gets off an on-side kick, which T. A. D.
Jones gets. Welch takes the place of Brown. Waller stops
T. A. D. Jones for a loss. MacFadyen blocks Coy's punt,
but Alcott gets the ball on Yale's 17-yard mark. Coy punts
to Dillon at 52. Tibbott makes 8. Yale holds and Harlan
tries an on-side kick, which Coy catches and runs back 30
yards. The game closes with the ball at midfield.

PRINCETON VS. YALE

Princeton, Nov. 14, 1908

PRINCETON		YALE
H. L. Dowd, '09,	Left End,	A. Haines, '10.
	" "	W. S. Logan, '10.
R. C. Siegling, '10,	Left Tackle,	T. Lilley, '10.
	" "	H. H. Hobbs, '10.
P. E. Waller, '10,	Left Guard,	H. F. Andrus, '10.
D. M. MacFadyen, '10,	Centre,	A. A. Biddle, '09.
N. R. Cass, '09,	"	
H. G. Buckingham, '10,	Right Guard,	W. A. Goebel, '10.
A. Macgregor, '11,	" "	
A. E. Booth, '09,	Right Tackle,	A. E. Brides, '09.
F. C. Bamman, '10,	" "	
T. H. Welch, '10,	Right End,	E. H. Coy, '10, Capt.
H. W. Bishop, '09,	" "	
E. A. Dillon, '09, Capt.,	Quarter-back,	J. F. Johnson, '10.
F. S. Bergin, '10,	"	H. P. Bingham, '10.
	"	A. L. Corey, '11.
F. B. Read, '10,	Left Half,	S. H. Philbin, '10.
F. M. Tibbott, '09,	Right Half,	H. M. Wheaton, '09.
	" "	F. J. Murphy, '10.
F. T. Dawson, '10,	Full-back,	J. W. Field, '11.
T. H. Pfeiffer, '09,	"	F. J. Daly, '11.
J. M. McCrohan, '11,	"	

Referee: J. B. Pendleton, '90, Bowdoin. Umpire: J. H. Minds, '98,
Pennsylvania. Field Judge: E. K. Hall, '92, Dartmouth. Linesman:

E. H. Young, '98, Cornell. Score: Princeton 6, Yale 11. First Half:
Touchdown by F. M. Tibbott, goal by P. E. Waller. Second Half:
Touchdown by E. H. Coy, goal by H. H. Hobbs; touchdown by E. H.
Coy.

First Half: Princeton wins the toss and takes the south
goal. Yale takes the ball. Goebel kicks to Tibbott in the
south-east corner of the field. The latter runs back the kick
45 yards. Haines stops Dawson without gain. A penalty
forces Princeton to punt and Buckingham kicks to Johnson
on Yale's 25. In three plunges Yale gains 16 yards, but
can go no further. Coy punts to Princeton's 33. Dawson
goes through centre for 4. Read punts to Yale's 30. Yale
cannot gain and Coy kicks to Dillon. On the line-up Dillon tries an on-side kick, which Field catches. Yale tries
both ends without gain and Coy punts. Princeton fumbles
and Haines gets the ball. Princeton holds and Coy again
punts. Tibbott catches on the 20-yard line. A double pass
fails and Buckingham punts. Yale fumbles and Siegling
gets the ball. Princeton tries the line without gain, and
then Tibbott shoots a long forward pass to Dillon on Yale's
30. Johnson goes out and Bingham takes his place. Two
plunges take Princeton 9 yards. Here another forward
pass is tried, which Wheaton gets. Philbin makes 14
through centre. Coy tries a fake kick, but on the run is
thrown for a loss. Yale punts out of bounds at 40, but recovers the ball. The Blue cannot gain and Coy punts to
Tibbott, who runs back 12 yards. Dawson cross-bucks for
4. A forward pass fails and Princeton is set back. Read
drops back to punt, but Goebel is on him and Read runs
instead, making 25 yards. It is fourth down and Yale gets
the ball. Bingham tries a forward pass, but Princeton gets
the ball. On the line-up Tibbott gets away for a run of 45
yards. Haines saves Yale from a touchdown. Princeton
is penalized 10 yards, but Dawson regains 8. Read tries an

on-side kick and Dowd gets it at Yale's 34. Dawson makes
3 through centre. Tibbott dashes to the right and rounding
the end crosses the line for a touchdown. Read kicks out,
Dillon heels, and Waller kicks the goal. Lilley goes off and
Hobbs takes his place. Hobbs kicks off for Yale, sending
the ball over the goal-line. Read punts out. Wheaton tries
for a field goal, but misses. Read again punts out. The
kick is short and Field places it on Princeton's 32-yard mark.
Yale gets 5 more on a penalty. Yale tries a double forward
pass, but Princeton gets it. Tibbott goes around the end for
35 yards. The ball is brought back and Princeton penalized. Dawson hits the centre for 4. Dowd recovers an on-
side kick for 16, but time is called for the half.

Second Half: Waller kicks off to Field. Coy punts.
Dillon makes 5, Tibbott adds 8, and Dawson makes 4.
Princeton is set back 5. Read tries an on-side kick, which
Welch recovers at Yale's 28. Yale holds and Read tries an
on-side kick, which Philbin gets. Coy kicks to Princeton's
42. Princeton gains 15 by line-plunging and tries an on-
side kick. Goebel gets the ball. Coy punts out of bounds
at Princeton's 20. Princeton is set back to the 9-yard mark
by a penalty. Read kicks out of bounds, but Waller gets the
ball. Tibbott cannot gain and Yale gets the ball on an on-
side kick. Coy tries an on-side kick, but Tibbott gets it.
Princeton cannot make first down and Read punts to 45.
Bingham goes off and Corey takes his place. Murphy replaces Wheaton. The ball changes hands on a forward pass
and a punt, and Coy tries a drop kick from centre which
misses, but crosses the line. Read punts out. Coy runs
back 20 yards. Coy is taken from end and placed at full-
back. Pfeiffer replaces Dawson. In two attempts Coy
reaches Princeton's 8-yard mark. Cass goes to centre,
MacFadyen to guard, and Buckingham retires. Coy takes
the ball flanked by Brides and Goebel, and in two rushes it is

over for a touchdown. Hobbs kicks the goal. Waller kicks
off to Coy. Murphy and Coy hit the line for 35 yards.
McCrohan replaces Pfeiffer. Coy and Philbin continue the
advance to Princeton's 30. Princeton stops the Blue and
Coy tries for a field goal, but Booth blocks the kick. Welch
gets the ball. Daly replaces Field. McCrohan hits the
line three times for a total of 16 yards. Read tries an on-
side kick, but Hobbs gets the ball. Coy, again flanked by
Brides and Goebel, hits the line for 24 yards gain. Dillon
stops the mass, but is hurt. Bergin takes his place. Bam-
man replaces Booth. Coy again hits the line for 8. On the
next plunge, again flanked by Brides and Goebel, Coy
crosses the line for a touchdown. The goal fails. Waller
kicks off, punts are exchanged, and the game ends.

PRINCETON VS. YALE
New Haven, Nov. 13, 1909

PRINCETON		YALE
C. G. Ballin, '10,	Left End,	J. R. Kilpatrick, '11.
H. E. Gill, '10,	" "	
R. C. Siegling, '10, Capt.,	Left Tackle,	H. H. Hobbs, '10.
	" "	J. B. Spencer, 10.
P. E. Waller, '10,	Left Guard,	H. F. Andrus, '10.
I. M. Woehr, '10,	" "	W. L. Brown, '10.
F. C. Bamman, '10,	Centre,	C. T. Cooney, '10.
C. McCormick, '12,	Right Guard,	W. A. Goebel, '10.
J. M. McCrohan, '11,	Right Tackle,	T. Lilley, '10.
A. Macgregor, '11,	" "	C. H. Paul, '12.
T. H. Welch, '10,	Right End,	H. Vaughan, '11.
P. M. King, '12,	" "	T. C. Naedle, '10.
	" "	E. Savage, '11.
F. S. Bergin, '10,	Quarter-back,	A. Howe, '12.
P. P. Chrystie, '12,	"	A. L. Corey, '11.
	"	J. F. Johnson, '10.
F. B. Read, '10,	Left Half,	S. H. Philbin, '10.
	" "	P. T. Francis, '12.
W. R. Sparks, '11,	" "	
L. Cunningham, '11,	Right Half,	F. J. Daly, '11.
	" "	F. J. Murphy, '10.
E. J. Hart, '12,	Full-back,	E. H. Coy, '10, Capt.

Referee: J. B. Pendleton, '90, Bowdoin. Umpire: Carl Williams, '97, Pennsylvania. Field Judge: E. K. Hall, '92, Dartmouth. Linesman: E. H. Young, '98, Cornell. Score: Princeton 0, Yale 17. First Half: Safety by E. J. Hart; touchdown by T. Lilley, goal by H. H. Hobbs. Second Half: Goal from field by E. H. Coy; touchdown by E. H. Coy, goal by H. H. Hobbs.

First Half: Princeton wins the toss, and takes the south goal. Cooney kicks off for Yale. Welch catches and runs back 15 yards. Princeton cannot gain and McCormick punts. Yale in four smashes takes the ball to Princeton's 20-yard line, where a quarter-back run is penalized 15 yards. Coy misses a field goal. Princeton puts the ball in play on the 25, but McCormick is forced to punt. An exchange of punts gives the ball to Yale on Princeton's 50. Coy tries an on-side kick, but Bergin gets it. After two exchanges of punts Yale commences a fierce line attack which takes the ball within 3 yards of Princeton's goal. Ballin and Welch tackle behind the line and Princeton gets the ball on downs. McCormick is forced to kick from behind the goal-line. Hobbs blocks the kick. Hart gets the ball and it is declared a safety. Punts are exchanged from the 25-yard line. A punt from Coy hits the cross-bar and is declared a touchback. Princeton lines up on the 25-yard line. Cooney blocks a kick. Lilley gets the ball and races across the line for a touchdown. Goal. Corey takes Howe's place. Waller kicks off to Coy, who runs back 10 yards. Read punts to Yale's 35. Yale cannot pierce the line and Coy punts to Princeton's 20. Hart makes 10, Read adds 9 more. Yale stiffens and Read tries an on-side kick, but Yale gets the ball at 45. Coy, punts to Bergin and Kilpatrick downs him. A further exchange of punts places the ball in Princeton's possession at the 30-yard line. Read goes around the end for 12 yards. Hart goes through tackle for 5 and then through centre for 3. Philbin recovers Read's on-side kick at 50. Coy punts across Princeton's goal-line and the ball is put in play at 25. Hart makes 5 through tackle. Murphy takes the place of Daly. Two exchanges of punts place the ball on Princeton's 40. Corey attempts a forward pass, but Siegling gets it, advancing the ball 20 yards before being tackled. Read and Cunningham work a forward pass for 20 yards. Another is attempted, but Murphy gets it. Naedle takes the place of Vaughan. Lilley throws Read for a loss. Yale gets the ball and tries an on-side kick. Ballin gets it and makes 20 yards. Read tries a forward pass, but it hits the ground. Time is called for the half.

Second Half: Savage replaces Naedle. Waller kicks off to Murphy, who runs back 10 yards. Coy punts and Kilpatrick tackles Bergin at midfield. Cunningham makes 6 yards, Read makes 5. A penalty sets Princeton back, and Read tries a forward pass, which hits the ground. McCormick punts to Murphy, who runs back 20 yards. Coy goes through tackle for 6 yards. Sparks replaces Read. Coy fails to gain. Murphy gets off an on-side kick and Hobbs recovers the ball. Waller throws Philbin for a loss. Coy takes the ball plunge after plunge for nine trials and crosses the line, but the touchdown is not allowed. Coy tries a drop kick, but misses the posts. Princeton puts the ball down for a scrimmage at 25, but Sparks cannot gain and McCormick punts. Siegling tackles Murphy at midfield. Coy immediately punts. McCormick makes 12 yards on a fake kick. Hart makes 2 through centre and McCormick punts. Coy tries a fake kick, but is thrown for a loss. Coy now begins a fierce attack on the line, alternating with Murphy. Steadily the ball moves toward Princeton's goal-line; on the 7-yard mark Princeton holds for downs and Coy drops a goal from the field. After the kick-off both teams punt. McCrohan makes 10 yards on a forward pass. Cunningham tries a drop from the 40-yard line, but the kick is

short. Coy punts. Sparks tries an unsuccessful forward
pass to Bergin. McCormick punts to Murphy. Murphy
goes round the end for 12. He rounds the opposite end for
15. Coy hits the line for 20. Philbin makes 6. Macgregor replaces McCrohan. Princeton holds for downs on
the 5-yard line. McCormick punts to Murphy, who behind
fine interference runs the kick back to the 20-yard line.
Coy plunges through the line to the 1-yard mark. On the
next play he takes the ball over for a touchdown and Hobbs
kicks the goal. Paul replaces Lilley and Chrystie takes the
place of Bergin. Kicks are exchanged. Johnson replaces
Corey, and Francis goes in for Philbin. Three exchanges of
punts take place. Spencer takes the place of Hobbs and
Gill of Ballin. Coy tries a drop kick, but misses. Sparks
tries to get through tackle, but gains only 3 yards. Princeton punts. Coy tries an end run, but is thrown by Waller.
The play is repeated. Chrystie catches Coy's punt and runs
it back 30 yards. Time is called.

PRINCETON vs. YALE
Princeton, Nov. 12, 1910

PRINCETON		YALE
S. B. White, '12,	Left End,	J. R. Kilpatrick, '11.
A. Macgregor, '11,	Left Tackle,	J. W. Scully, '12.
T. A. Wilson, '13,	Left Guard,	M. E. Fuller, '11.
W. McLean, '12,	" "	
A. Bluethenthal, '13,	Centre,	E. B. Morris, '12.
C. McCormick, '12,	Right Guard,	E. W. McDevitt, '12.
C. E. Brown, '13,	Right Tackle,	C. H. Paul, '12.
E. Elsworth, '11,	" "	E. Savage, '11.
C. C. Dunlap '13,	Right End,	S. H. Brooks, '11.
G. K. Wight, '13,	" "	
V. Ballou, '13,	Quarter-back,	A. Howe, '12.
T. T. Pendleton, '13,	Left Half,	J. W. Field, '11.
	" "	R. W. Baker, '13.
W. R. Sparks, '11,	Right Half,	F. J. Daly, '11, Capt.
H. M. Sawyer, '12,	" "	
E. J. Hart, '12, Capt.,	Full-back,	E. O. Kistler, '11.
	"	R. C. Deming, '11.

Referee: W. S. Langford, '96, Trinity. Umpire: D. L. Fultz, '98, Brown. Field Judge: W. N. Morice, '99, Pennsylvania. Linesman: J. B. Pendleton, '90, Bowdoin. Score: Princeton 3, Yale 5. First Quarter: Goal from field by T. T. Pendleton. Third Quarter: Touchdown by J. R. Kilpatrick.

First Quarter: Yale wins the toss and selects the north goal. Ballou kicks off, Daly catches and runs back 10 yards, White tackling. Yale tries a line shift and gains 10 yards. Daly and Field from same formations make 16 yards. Yale fumbles and Dunlap gets the ball. A penalty sets Princeton back 15 yards and Ballou punts, Howe catching on Yale's 45. Field is thrown in a line shift for 4 yards and Howe punts. Sparks makes 5 from the 25-yard line. Pendleton makes 1 around left end and Ballou punts to midfield. Yale loses 10 yards on scrimmage plays, and Howe kicks to Ballou on the latter's 20-yard line. Princeton cannot gain and Ballou punts to centre. Yale tries a forward pass, but Hart gets it. Princeton cannot gain and punts. Yale fumbles and White falls on the ball on Yale's 20-yard line. Sparks is stopped without gain. Hart makes 5. Pendleton kicks a goal from placement. Yale kicks off. The ball is put in play on the 25-yard line. Pendleton and Sparks make 16 yards. Paul blocks Ballou's kick and Brooks gets the ball on Princeton's 18-yard line. Yale cannot gain and tries a trick play from fake placement, Dunlap throwing Field for a loss of 12 yards. Kicks are exchanged and the quarter closes with the ball in Princeton's possession on Yale's 45-yard line.

Second Quarter: Goals are exchanged, giving Princeton a strong wind. Princeton cannot gain and Ballou kicks. Yale puts the line shift in operation and advances the ball to Princeton's 35-yard line, where a penalty sets the Blue back 15 yards. Howe punts to Pendleton, who gets away for 30 yards, but is brought back upon a penalty. Ballou punts

to Howe at centre.   Field hurdles and the penalty is applied.   Howe kicks, Kilpatrick interferes with the fair catch.
Kicks are exchanged.   A hot scramble ensues for an on-side
kick on Yale's 5-yard line.   Daly gets the ball.   Deming
goes in for Kistler and punts the ball to the 35-yard line.
Hart and Sparks make 5 yards.   Pendleton tries a kick from
placement, but misses.   From the 25-yard line Deming
kicks to centre.   Pendleton shoots a forward pass to Sparks
for 12 yards.   Howe gets Ballou's on-side kick at the 31-
yard line.   Daly makes 6 yards and the half closes.

   Third Quarter: Yale takes the north goal and the wind.
Kistler returns to play, Deming going off.   Daly returns
Ballou's kick-off to the 25-yard line.   On the line shift Field
is hurt and Baker takes his place.   Howe punts to Ballou.
Ballou makes 25-yards.   Ballou makes 3 more and Pendleton sends a forward pass to White for 12 yards.   Sparks goes
through tackle for 9 yards and Ballou makes first down 15
yards from Yale's goal.   A penalty sets Princeton back.
Sparks makes 15 yards.   Pendleton tries for a goal, but Paul
blocks the kick.   Brooks picks up the ball and runs to midfield.   Howe punts, Princeton fumbles, and Scully gets the
ball on Princeton's 25-yard line.   Baker makes 2.   Howe
shoots a forward pass to Kilpatrick and the latter races 6
yards for a touchdown.   The kick-out fails.   Ballou kicks
off and Howe returns.   A punting duel ensues.   Howe gets
the ball on a fumble on Princeton's 35-yard line.   Daly tries
a drop kick, which hits the post, but goes outside.   Princeton punts out from the 25-yard line and the quarter closes.

   Fourth Quarter: Yale starts play on Princeton's 40-yard
line.   An exchange of punts gives Princeton the ball on her
45-yard line.   Macgregor throws a long side pass to Pendleton, who is tackled for no gain by Brooks.   Ballou punts.
Yale rushes 25 yards, but is stopped on Princeton's 25-yard
line.   Ballou gets off a long kick which puts the ball on

A VICTORY WRESTED FROM DEFEAT.

Kilpatrick, of Yale, catching a forward pass, leaps across Princeton's goal-line, winning the game, 5 to 3.   Nov. 12, 1910.

Yale's 15-yard line.   Yale loses 5 yards and Howe punts from behind the line.   Pendleton heels a fair catch at the 38-yard mark.   Princeton is penalized 5 yards for feinting and Pendleton misses the goal.   Howe punts to midfield. Ballou kicks to Yale's 30.   Several punts and a penalty give Princeton the ball on Yale's 45-yard line.   Sawyer relieves Sparks and makes 5 yards.   Pendleton tries for field goal from the 50.   Yale puts the ball in play on the 25-yard line and the game ends.

CHAPTER XVIII

EIGHT FAMOUS GAMES

AMHERST vs. HARVARD
Cambridge, Oct. 10, 1903

AMHERST		HARVARD
H. B. Chase, '04,	Left End,	W. T. Clothier, '04.
	" "	H. Le Moyne, '07.
F. E. Pierce, '05,	Left Tackle,	J. Parkinson, '06.
W. W. Palmer, '05,	Left Guard,	C. A. Shea, '04.
	" "	R. W. Bleakie, '04.
F. R. Behrends, '06,	Centre,	F. A. Carrick, '06.
H. R. Howard, '04,	Right Guard,	S. C. Coburn, '06.
L. G. Diehl, '05,	Right Tackle,	D. W. Knowlton, '03.
H. E. Daniels, '05,	Right End,	E. Bowditch, '03.
	" "	J. M. Montgomery, '06.
C. B. Lewis, '05,	Quarter-back,	S. H. Noyes, '05.
J. B. Shay, '04,	Left Half,	F. H. Nesmith, '06.
P. D. Storke, '04,	" "	C. W. Randall, '05.
J. H. Hubbard, '07,	Right Half,	D. J. Hurley, '05.
	" "	H. Schoellkopf, '01.
H. F. Coggeshall, '05,	Full-back,	P. O. Mills, '05.
A. M. Storke, '06,	"	

Referee: Mr. Saul, N. A. A. Umpire: Mr. Holton, B. A. A. Linesman: W. S. Hatch, '01, Amherst. Timekeeper: F. A. Wood, B. A. C. Score: Amherst 5, Harvard 0. Second Half: Touchdown by H. F. Coggeshall.

First Half: Amherst wins the toss and takes the south goal. Lewis kicks to Shea, who returns the ball to Amherst's 20. Harvard recovers the ball, but fumbles, and Lewis gets the ball. Amherst cannot gain and Shay punts to Coburn at Harvard's 10-yard line. Hurley in two plunges makes 15 yards. By a series of tackle plays, Harvard ad-

vances the ball to Amherst's 45-yard line. Here the ball is
fumbled and Amherst gets it. No gain can be made and
Shay punts. Noyes catches the ball and runs back 5 yards.
On the line-up Hurley circles the end for 26 yards. Twelve
rushes by Harvard plant the ball on Amherst's 3-yard mark.
Here Amherst holds so strong that the Crimson makes only
4 inches in 3 downs. Amherst is penalized half the distance to the line. Harvard takes the ball over, but drops it,
and Lewis falls on it for a touchback. Shay kicks out to
Harvard at the 47-yard line. The half ends immediately
with the ball in midfield.

Second Half: Harvard kicks off to Lewis at 30 and the
latter runs back 20 yards. Shay makes 8 through the line,
then punts to Harvard's 46-yard line. Nesmith is thrown for
a loss of 3 yards. A bad pass is regained by Le Moyne on
his 30-yard line. Harvard punts 39 yards. Coggeshall gets
through centre for 2 yards. Hubbard makes 6 more. Le
Moyne stops an end run and Shay punts to Palmer, who is
thrown on the 11-yard line. Le Moyne falls back to punt,
but Shay gets through and blocks the kick. Coggeshall
dives for the ball and then, with a mountain of crimson
jerseys upon him, crawls 7 yards and makes a touchdown.
The punt-out fails. Lewis kicks off and sends the ball
across the goal-line. Le Moyne kicks out and Lewis gets
the ball on Harvard's 45-yard line. Shay makes 4 yards and
Pierce adds 6 more. Pierce splits the centre for 15. Harvard stops the advance and Lewis punts. The kick is
blocked and Mills picks up the ball and with a clear field
before him starts for the Amherst goal-line. Storke overtakes him on the 40-yard line and brings him down. Before a first down can be made time is called. This game
marks the first defeat of Harvard upon Soldier's Field.

ARMY		YALE
T. W. Hammond, '05,	Left End,	T. L. Shevlin, '06.
C. K. Rockwell, '06,	" "	
W. W. Erwin, '08,	Left Tackle,	J. R. Bloomer, '05.
H. J. Weeks, '08,	" "	
T. B. Doe, '05,	Left Guard,	R. P. Kinney, '05.
A. C. Tipton, '05,	Centre,	J. C. Roraback, '03.
D. C. Seagrave, '05,	Right Guard,	R. C. Tripp, '06.
E. Graves, '05,	Right Tackle,	J. J. Hogan, '05.
A. G. Gillespie, '06,	Right End,	C. T. Neal, '05.
E. B. Garey, '08,	Quarter-back,	F. H. Rockwell, '06.
F. A. Prince, '08,	Left Half,	P. L. Veeder, '07.
	" "	L. Hoyt, '06.
R. C. Hill, '07,	Right Half,	S. F. B. Morse, '07.
A. J. Hanlon, '08,	" "	
H. W. Torney, '06,	Full-back,	J. E. Owsley, '05.

Referee: M. J. Thompson, '01, Georgetown. Umpire: J. C. Mc-Cracken, '01, Pennsylvania. Linesman: C. W. Hockenburger, '07, Yale. Score: Army 11, Yale 6. First Half: Touchdown by W. W. Erwin, goal by T. B. Doe; touchdown by H. W. Torney. Second Half: Touchdown by J. R. Bloomer, goal by L. Hoyt.

First Half: Yale wins the toss and takes the north goal. Army kicks off to Yale's 15-yard line. Two plunges into the line fail to make first down for the Blue, and Veeder falls back to punt. The Army line is through and blocks the kick. Erwin picks up the ball and crosses the line for a touchdown. Doe kicks the goal. Yale kicks off and for several minutes the play does not pass either 35-yard line, being a succession of punts and downs, without substantial advance by either team. Yale's play is marred by continual fumbling. Just as the half is closing, Yale puts the ball down for a scrimmage on the 35-yard line and by line plunges carries it to Army's 5, where the ball is fumbled. Torney gets it and runs 105 yards for a touchdown. No goal.

Second Half: Yale kicks off and Army at once returns. Both teams continue the kicking game for many minutes. Fumbles force Yale back into its goal. Torney tries twice for field goals, but misses. Yale by a long punt sends the ball to Army's 20-yard line. The latter fails to pierce the Blue line and Torney punts, Yale taking the ball at centre. The Blue now starts a rapid succession of tackle plays against the Army line, and the latter are gradually forced back. The ball reaches the 5-yard line, from which Bloomer is sent over for the touchdown. Goal by Hoyt. Army kicks off and a sharp exchange of punts follows. Yale puts the ball down for scrimmage on its 40-yard line, and the tackle-play again creeps forward line after line, until the ball rests on Army's 8-yard mark. As the teams line up time is called.

ARMY vs. YALE
West Point, Oct. 15, 1910

ARMY		YALE
J. S. Wood, '12,	Left End,	J. R. Kilpatrick, '11.
G. H. Franke, '11,	" "	
L. S. Devore, '12,	Left Tackle,	P. T. Francis, '12.
	" "	S. Glover, '12.
	" "	H. B. Van Sinderen, '11.
S. M. Walmsley, '12,	Left Guard,	H. P. Greenough, '11.
	" "	R. F. Loree, '12.
A. V. Arnold, '12,	Centre,	E. B. Morris, '12.
J. L. Wier, '11,	Right Guard,	C. L. Buckingham, '11.
	" "	M. E. Fuller, '11.
R. W. McG. Littlejohn, '12,	Right Tackle,	C. H. Paul, '12.
F. H. Hicks, '11,	Right End,	S. H. Brooks, '11.
	" "	Walter Camp, Jr., '13.
R. F. Hyatt, '12,	Quarter-back,	A. L. Corey, '11.
	"	H. N. Merritt, '12.
C. J. Browne, '12,	Left Half,	F. J. Daly, '11.
W. Dean, '12,	Right Half,	R. C. Deming, '11.
	" "	J. H. Potter, '11.

ARMY		YALE
	Right Half,	R. W. Baker, '13.
E. O. Surles, '11,	Full-back,	J. A. Reilly, '12.
A. D. MacDonald, '12,	"	J. H. Philbin, '13.
	"	E. O. Kistler, '11.

Referee: J. B. Pendleton, '90, Bowdoin. Umpire: Carl Williams, '97, Pennsylvania. Field Judge: D. L. Fultz, '98, Brown. Linesman: F. R. Gillender, '99, Pennsylvania. Score: Army 9, Yale 3. First Quarter: Touchdown by E. O. Surles, goal by W. Dean. Third Quarter: Goal from field by W. Dean. Fourth Quarter: Goal from field by F. J. Daly.

First Quarter : Paul kicks off for Yale to Dean, and the latter runs the ball back 25 yards. Army punts to Corey, who is tackled at midfield. Yale fumbles and Army gets the ball. Yale holds and Dean punts. Deming returns. Kicks again are exchanged. Corey attempts a forward pass to Kilpatrick, but Browne gets it and runs 35 yards to Yale's 4-yard line. Dean throws a forward pass to Surles and the latter goes over for a touchdown. Dean kicks the goal, and then kicks off. Kicks are exchanged and Browne goes around the end for 18 yards. Yale holds and Army kicks. Several forward passes fail for each eleven. Deming punts to Dean on Army's 40 and time is called.

Second Quarter: Dean kicks to Daly. Reilly rushes 21 yards. Yale is penalized. Dean intercepts a forward pass and kicks to Corey on Yale's 30-yard line. Deming returns. Kicks are exchanged and Army works a forward pass for 30 yards. Punts are exchanged and Reilly gets a forward pass. Reilly goes through the line for 8. Army takes the ball on downs. Dean punts and Corey runs back to the 40-yard line. Time is called for the half.

Third Quarter : Dean kicks to Reilly and Deming punts. Browne gets around the end for 35 yards. Yale holds and Army tries for a goal from placement from the 35-yard line. Dean kicks the goal. Paul kicks off to Browne. An ex-

AN END RUN FROM A FAKE KICK.

Dean, of the Army, circling Yale's end. West Point, Oct. 15, 1910.

change of punts nets 15 yards for Yale. Both teams resort to kicking. Dean at last tries an end run for 15 yards, starting from a kicking formation. Punting is resumed. The quarter closes with the ball at midfield.

Fourth Quarter: Army kicks off and a kicking duel ensues. Devore recovers a fumble on Yale's 20-yard line. Daly intercepts a forward pass and runs 30 yards and then adds 5 through the line. Yale fumbles and Army gets the ball. Punts are exchanged, the Army gaining 20 yards thereon. Surles heels a fair catch at 44. Dean tries and misses a goal from placement. Yale kicks from the 25-yard line and Kilpatrick recovers the ball on-side and runs 30 yards. Yale cannot gain and Daly drops a goal from the field at 35 yards. Dean kicks off. Both elevens resort to punts and time is called.

Brown vs. Yale
New Haven, Nov. 5, 1910

BROWN		YALE
E. A. Adams, '12,	Left End,	J. A. Reilly, '12.
	" "	S. F. Freeman, '11.
O. M. Kratz, '13,	Left Tackle,	J. W. Scully, '12.
D. H. Kulp, '13,	Left Guard,	M. E. Fuller, '11.
C. P. Sisson, '11,	Centre,	E. B. Morris, '11.
J. S. Goldberg, '11,	Right Guard,	C. H. Paul, '12.
A. E. Corp, '11,	" "	
B. G. Smith, '11,	Right Tackle,	E. Savage, '11.
R. G. Ashbaugh, '12,	Right End,	S. H. Brooks, '11.
W. E. Sprackling, '12,	Quarter-back,	E. A. Strout, '12.
	"	A. L. Corey, '11.
W. H. Marble,	Left Half,	
F. V. Young, '11,	" "	J. W. Field, '11.
	" "	R. C. Deming, '11.
G. N. Crowther, '13,	" "	E. W. Freeman, '13.
	" "	R. W. Baker, '13.
J. R. McKay, '11,	Right Half,	F. J. Daly, '11.
J. F. High, '11,	Full-back,	A. Howe, '12.
S. S. Bean, '14,	"	J. H. Potter, '11.

Referee: M. J. Thompson, '01, Georgetown. Umpire: R. G. Torrey, '06, Pennsylvania. Field Judge: A. E. Whiting, '98, Cornell. Lines-

man: J. H. Costello, '06, Cornell.   Score: Brown 21, Yale 0.   Second
Quarter: Goal from field by W. E. Sprackling.   Third Quarter: Goal
from field by W. E. Sprackling; touchdown by F. V. Young, goal by
B. G. Smith; goal from field by W. E. Sprackling.   Fourth Quarter:
Touchdown by J. R. McKay, goal by B. G. Smith.

First Quarter : Brown receives the kick-off, and after a
first down McKay punts, Yale recovering the ball on the
1-yard line.   Howe punts from behind the line and Sprackling heels the catch on Yale's 30-yard line.   Sprackling tries
for a goal, but the ball hits the cross-bar.   Kicks are exchanged and Adams recovers a fumble on Yale's 25-yard
line.   Sprackling kicks a goal from the field, but it is not allowed on account of holding.   Kicks are exchanged and the
quarter ends with the ball at midfield.

Second Quarter : Yale starts play vigorously and forces the
ball to Brown's 20-yard line.   Unable to gain farther, Daly
tries for a field goal, but misses.   Kicks are exchanged,
Brown gaining.   Brown puts the ball down for a scrimmage
and reaches Yale's 15-yard line aided by a long run by
Marble.   The Blue holds and Sprackling drops a goal from
the field.   Brown receives the kick-off and immediately
forces Yale's line for substantial gains, being at midfield
when time is called.

Third Quarter : Sprackling receives the kick-off.   Punts
are exchanged.   Brown puts the ball down for a scrimmage
and drives Yale rapidly down the field.   A long run by
Sprackling and a forward pass to Smith put the ball on
Yale's 20-yard line.   Unable to advance farther, Sprackling
drops a goal from the field.   Yale takes the kick-off, but is
forced to punt.   McKay returns and the ball rolls out of
bounds to Yale's 4-yard mark.   Yale's punt is blocked and
Brown gets the ball on the 2-yard mark.   Young bursts
through the line for a touchdown.   Smith kicks the goal.
Brown takes the kick-off and punts are exchanged.   Yale
has a kick blocked at midfield.   Sprackling sends a pretty

forward pass to McKay and the ball is down on Yale's 25-yard line. Yale tightens and Sprackling, dropping back, kicks another goal from the field.

Fourth Quarter : The ball hovers around the middle line for several minutes without advantage to either team. Many punts are exchanged. Thus the quarter is expended until in the closing minute Sprackling sends a forward pass to McKay and the latter runs 65 yards for a touchdown. Smith kicks the goal.

LAFAYETTE VS. PENNSYLVANIA

Philadelphia, Oct. 23, 1896

LAFAYETTE		PENNSYLVANIA
W. R. Worthington, '99,	Left End,	S. A. Boyle, '98.
F. H. Yost, '00,	Left Tackle,	L. J. Uffenheimer, '99.
H. C. Gates, '00,	" "	
O. F. Rowland, '95,	Left Guard,	J. Stannard, '98.
M. F. Jones, '98,	Centre,	P. D. Overfield, '01.
C. R. Rinehart, '98,	Right Guard	C. M. Wharton, '96.
G. A. Wiedenmayer, '98,	Right Tackle,	W. M. Farrar, '96.
T. B. Speer, '99,	Right End,	B. W. Dickson, '97.
W. R. Hill, '98,	" "	
C. M. Best, '99,	Quarter-back,	A. K. Dickson, '97.
G. O. Barclay, '98,	Left Half,	C. S. Gelbert, '97.
H. Zeiser, '97,	Right Half,	J. H. Minds, '98.
E. G. Bray, '00,	Full-back,	W. G. Woodruff, '97.

Referee: L. T. Bliss, '93, Yale. Umpire: W. H. Corbin, '89, Yale. Linesman: R. D. Paine, '94, Yale. Score: Lafayette 6, Pennsylvania 4. First Half: Touchdown by L. J. Uffenheimer. Second Half: Touchdown and goal by G. O. Barclay.

First Half: Pennsylvania wins the toss and takes the west goal. Rinehart kicks off to Wharton on the 5-yard line. Pennsylvania gains 20 yards in several plunges into the line, but fumbles the ball and Lafayette secures it. Lafayette cannot make first down and Bray punts out of bounds. Minds circles the end for 15. By short gains Pennsylvania with great difficulty finally works the ball to

Lafayette's 5-yard. Minds is thrown for a loss of 5 yards. On the next play Pennsylvania fumbles and Worthington gets the ball. Pennsylvania is set back 10 yards on a penalty. The Red and Blue holds for downs and gets the ball. Minds goes through the line for 2 and Gelbert follows for 2 more. A penalty also advances Pennsylvania 10 yards. Lafayette holds for downs. Two plunges into center net Lafayette 5 yards. On the next play the ball is lost on a fumble. Pennsylvania by swift, hard rushing forces the ball to the 3-yard mark. On the next play Uffenheimer goes through for a touchdown. The play is near the side line and the punt-out fails. Rinehart kicks off for Lafayette and Pennsyvlania returns the ball. Lafayette punts, Pennsylvania fumbles, and Wiedenmeyer gets the ball. The ball oscillates back and forth between the 20-yard lines, and time is called with the ball in Pennsyvlania's possession on Lafayette's 20-yard line.

Second Half: Woodruff kicks off to Lafayette's 5-yard line. Overfield stops Zeiser on a centre plunge and Bray punts to Minds at midfield. Pennsylvania by short gains reaches Lafayette's 10-yard line, where the latter holds for downs and gets the ball. Bray punts 25 yards, and Pennsylvania fumbling, Speer falls on the ball. For several minutes each team rushes for small gains and then is forced to punt. Pennsylvania tries a quarter-back kick, which Bray captures. Two plunges into the line net 12 yards. Lafayette fumbles and Boyle gets the ball. An exchange of kicks places the ball in Pennsylvania's possession on the 40-yard line. Minds falls back to punt, but Rowland breaks through and blocks the kick, catching the ball and retaining it. Lafayette tries a plunge at centre without gain. The ball is near the left side line 30 yards from the goal. Bray falls back and Lafayette forms for a drop kick. The formation is a feint. The ball is passed to Barclay, who on a

A CRUCIAL PLAY THAT WON A GAME.

Lafayette, on the defensive, with the score 4 to 0 in favor of Pennsylvania and only six minutes to play, blocks the latter's kick. In two plays Barclay carries the ball 35 yards for a touchdown, from which he kicks a goal, winning the game, 6 to 4. Franklin Field, Oct. 23, 1896.

quick opening dashes along the left side line for 20 yards,
being forced out of bounds at the 10-yard line. The ball is
brought in and Bray is sent against the centre without gain.
On the next play Barclay goes around the right end for a
touchdown. A moment later he kicks the goal. Only six
minutes are left to play. Pennsylvania kicks off and Lafayette in nine plays takes the ball 60 yards. Time is called
with the ball in the latter's possession on the 15-yard line.

LAFAYETTE VS. PRINCETON
Princeton, Oct. 23, 1909

LAFAYETTE		PRINCETON
A. A. Blaicher, '10,	Left End,	C. Ballin, '10.
	" "	H. E. Gill, '10.
A. R. Hayes, '10,	Left Tackle,	R. C. Siegling, '10.
A. R. Crane, '13,	" "	J. C. Musser, '11.
L. R. Jones, '13,	Left Guard,	I. M. Woehr, '10.
	" "	H. E. Buckingham, '10.
E. C. Foresman, '11,	Centre,	F. C. Bamman, '10.
T. S. Fillmore, '11,	Right Guard,	P. E. Waller, '10.
F. C. McCutcheon, '10,	Right Tackle,	J. M. McCrohan, '11.
E. J. Roche, '12,	" "	
W. W. Probst, '12,	" "	
R. Woodcock, '11,	Right End,	T. H. Welch, '10.
L. M. Schwenk, '11,	" "	
J. F. Moore, '10,	" "	
W. F. Dannehauer, '12,	Quarter-back,	F. Bergin, '10.
W. E. Norris, '11, `	Left Half,	F. B. Read, '10.
	" "	W. R. Sparks, '11.
M. J. Conover, '11,	Right Half,	F. Dawson, '10.
S. M. Alexander, '13,	" "	E. N. Matthews, '10.
F. H. Irmschler, '10,	" "	L. Cunningham, '11.
G. S. McCaa, '10,	Full-back,	E. J. Hart, '12.

Referee: D. L. Fults, '98, Brown. Umpire: H. M. Nelly, '02, Army.
Field Judge: C. J. McCarthy, Germantown Academy. Linesman:
S. S. Feagles, '00, Princeton. Score: Lafayette 6, Princeton 0. Second
Half: Touchdown by F. H. Irmschler, goal by G. S. McCaa.

First Half: Lafayette wins the toss and takes the north
goal. McCaa kicks to Read at Princeton's 10. Read imme-

Princeton 9. First Half: Goal from field by N. B. Tooker; touchdown by K. Whiting, goal by J. W. Wilcox; touchdown by W. L. Foulke. Second Half: Goal from field by H. H. Norton.

First Half: Princeton wins the toss and takes the goal. Navy kicks off. Princeton cannot gain and McCormick punts. Navy makes 10 yards and fumbles. Foulke and King in succession round both ends for a gain of 45 yards. Navy holds for 2 downs on the 20-yard line. Tooker falls back and kicks a goal from the field. Navy kicks off and the play for some time remains at centre. Douglas punts to Princeton's 10-yard line and the ball rolls across the line. A Princeton back fumbles and Whiting falls on the ball for a touchdown, which Wilcox converts into a goal. Princeton kicks off and Navy returns. After the kick-off King and Foulke again circle the ends for 40 yards, the latter's run ending in a touchdown at the extreme corner of the field. The try at goal is low and Navy blocks the ball. There is no further scoring in this half.

Second Half: Navy kicks off and for some time the ball surges back and forth between the 35-yard lines. Navy blocks McCormick's kick. Navy gets the ball and runs to the 25-yard line. Navy hits the line twice without gain. Norton is substituted for Wilcox and at once falls back for a drop kick. The ball goes squarely between the posts. Princeton kicks off and soon regains the ball on a kick. Princeton now advances 3 to 5 yards at a plunge, carrying the ball to the 1-foot mark from the Navy's line. The ball is fumbled on the snap-back and both teams pile up on the ball. When the mass is extricated, Ritter and Short are found to be one foot across the line and holding the ball. The official rules that the ball has been advanced without touching the second man and inflicts a penalty. Tooker tries for a field goal, but Navy blocks. Play continues in Navy's territory, Tooker once more trying for a field goal, but not succeeding. Toward the close Navy gets the ball in

HURDLING THE LINE.

Weekes, of Columbia, executing this powerful play against Princeton   New York, Nov 6, 1900.

Princeton's territory, and Norton tries for a field goal, but misses.

COLUMBIA vs. PRINCETON
New York, Nov. 6, 1900

COLUMBIA		PRINCETON
J. B. Wolff, '01,	Left End,	W. W. Roper, '02.
D. W. Smythe, '02,	Left Tackle	H. W. Pell, '02.
	" "	R. R. Coffin, '03.
C. A. Wright, '02,	Left Guard,	R. G. Wright, '02.
E. B. Bruce, '01,	Centre,	J. W. Losey, '03.
E. D. Freeman, '03,	Right Guard,	J. S. Dana, '03.
W. S. Beardsley, '03,	" "	M. F. Mills, '03.
	" "	M. F. Fisher, '03.
A. S. Austin, '03,	Right Tackle,	H. M. McCord, '02.
	" "	R. R. Sheffield, '02.
H. Van Hoevenburg, '02,	Right End,	H. Little, '01.
	" "	R. P. McClave, '03.
E. H. Sykes, '02,	Quarter-back,	A. E. Meier, '02.
B. H. Boyeson, '04,	"	
H. H. Weekes, '03,	Left Half,	S. W. McClave, '03.
	" "	H. R. Levick, '03.
W. R. Morley, '01,	Right Half,	H. R. Hart, '04.
	" "	B. B. Hodgman, '03.
C. L. Berrien, '03,	Full-back,	C. M. Mattis, '01.
	"	W. H. Underhill, '04.
	"	H. H. Henry, '04.

Referee: A. E. Whiting, '98, Cornell. Umpire: W. S. Langford, '96, Trinity. Linesman: H. H. Janeway, '90, Princeton. Timekeeper: George Goldie. Score: Columbia 6, Princeton 5. First Half: Touchdown by W. R. Morley, goal by E. B. Bruce. Second Half: Touchdown by W. W. Roper.

First Half: Princeton wins the toss and takes the upper goal. Berrien kicks off to McCord. Several punts follow, interspersed with small gains by each team. Columbia catches the ball on her 20-yard line and puts it down for a scrimmage. Wright is drawn behind the line in a formation that works havoc with the Princeton forwards. Weekes commences a spectacular but effective feat of hurdling over the Tiger line and backs. The Tigers fight desperately, but

the ball creeps by short gains down the field and in twenty
minutes of play reaches the 5-yard line. Princeton crouches
and waits the attack. Again Wright is drawn behind the
line. The ball is passed to Morley, who smashes squarely
into Princeton's centre and is rammed through and over the
line for a touchdown. Bruce kicks the goal. Mattis gives
way to Underhill. The teams resume play. The rushing is
hard and fierce, both teams playing with great vim, but
neither team comes near scoring.

Second Half: Hodgman relieves Hart. Columbia kicks
off. Princeton opens up a series of end runs, tackle-back
plunges, and straight attacks on the line that carries the ball
irresistibly to Columbia's 5-yard mark. Columbia stands
firm and takes the ball on downs. Berrien lifts it far down
the field. Princeton rushes it back to the 25-yard line, from
which Underhill tries for a goal from the field, but fails.
Columbia gets the ball and commences a scrimmage.
Weekes and Morley hit the Tiger line for good gains. The
ball reaches the 45-yard line. Here Columbia attempts a
mass on the centre. Suddenly Roper emerges with the ball.
Shaking off two tacklers he sprints at great speed for the line
and makes a touchdown. Roper brings the ball out to the
13-yard mark and holds it for Mills to kick. Three of the
Columbia players suddenly rush forward, crying that the ball
is down. One of the Columbia players falls on the ball in
Roper's hands. A dispute ensues, Princeton claiming that
the ball was not down and that the referee had not signalled.
After a long discussion the referee rules that the ball was
down and that Princeton has forfeited its try for goal.
Play is resumed. Princeton forces the ball into Columbia's
territory, from which three attempts at field goals are made
by Hodgman, which fail. Time then is called.

APPENDIX

APPENDIX

PROCEEDINGS

OF INTERCOLLEGIATE CONVENTIONS, CONFERENCES, AND SESSIONS OF RULES COMMITTEES, 1876 TO 1911*

Convention of Nov. 23, 1876, at the Massasoit House, Springfield, Mass.—Pursuant to a call issued by the Princeton Football Association there assembled at this time and place, for the purpose of adopting a uniform code of football rules based upon the Rugby Union code, the following representatives: Columbia, E. W. Price, C. D. H. Brower; Harvard, H. C. Leeds, '77, C. S. Eaton, '78; Princeton, Jotham Potter, '77, W. E. Dodge, '79; Yale, E. V. Baker, '77, J. B. Atwater, '77. Mr. Dodge was elected chairman and Mr. Baker secretary. It was voted to form an association to be known as the Intercollegiate Football Association. Yale declined to become a member, but expressed a desire to participate in the convention to the extent of adopting a code of playing rules. It was voted that the representatives of Yale should act as though members of the association, subject to the further action of the Yale Football Association. It was voted that no other institution should be admitted to membership in the association except by unanimous consent. Voted that each college of the association must play one game annually with each member of the association, and in the event of a tie, to play other games until the tie should be decided. The convention thereupon began consideration of the Rugby Union football rules, section by section, a modification thereof as an intercollegiate code being adopted as follows:

1. A drop kick, or drop, is made by letting the ball fall from the hands and kicking it the very instant it rises.

2. A place kick, or place, is made by kicking the ball after it has been placed in a nick made in the ground for the purpose of keeping it at rest.

*Copyrighted rules reprinted by permission of American Sports Publishing Company.

3. A punt is made by letting the ball fall from the hands and kicking it before it touches the ground.

4. Each goal shall be composed of two upright posts exceeding 11 feet in height from the ground and placed 18 feet 6 inches apart, with a cross-bar 10 feet from the ground.

5. A goal can only be obtained by kicking the ball from the field of play direct (*i. e.*, without touching the ground or the dress or person of any player of either side) over the cross-bar of the opponents' goal. Whether it touch such cross-bar or the posts it is called a poster and is not a goal.

6. A goal may be obtained by any kind of kick except a punt.

7. A match shall be decided by a majority of touchdowns; a goal shall be equal to four touchdowns; but in case of a tie a goal kicked from a touchdown shall take precedence over four touchdowns.*

8. The ball is dead when it rests absolutely motionless on the ground.

9. A touchdown is when a player, putting his hand upon the ball on the ground in touch or in goal, stops it so that it remains dead or fairly so.

10. A tackle is when the holder of the ball is held by one or more players of the opposite side.

11. A scrummage takes place when the holder of the ball, being in the field of play, puts it down on the ground in front of him, and all who have closed around on their respective sides endeavor to push their opponents back, and, by kicking the ball, to drive it in the direction of the opposite goal-line.

12. A player may take up the ball wherever it is rolling or bounding except in a scrummage.

13. It is not lawful to take up the ball when dead (except in order to bring it out after it has been touched down in touch or in goal) for any purpose whatever. Whenever the ball shall have been so unlawfully taken up it shall at once be brought back to where it was so taken up and there put down.

14. In a scrummage it is not lawful for the man who has the ball to pick out the ball with the hand under any circumstances whatever.

15. It is lawful for any player who has the ball to run with it, and if he does so it is called a run. If a player runs with the ball and gets behind his opponents' goal-line and there touches it down, it is called a run in.

16. It is lawful to run in anywhere across the goal-line.

* Entirely new. The Rugby Union code computed the score by goals.

17. The goal-line is in goal and the touch-line in touch.

18. In the event of any player holding or running with the ball being tackled, and the ball fairly held, he must at once cry down, and there put it down.

19. A maul-in-goal is when the holder of the ball is tackled inside the goal-line, or, being tackled immediately outside, is carried or pushed across it, and he, or the opposite side, or both, endeavor to touch the ball down. In all cases when so touched down, the ball shall belong to the players of the side who first had possession of it before the maul commenced, unless the opposite side have gained complete possession of it.

20. In case of a maul-in-goal, those players only who are touching the ball with their hands when it crosses the goal-line may continue the maul-in-goal, and when a player has once released his hold of the ball after it is inside the goal-line, he may not again join the maul, and if he attempts to do so, may be dragged out by the opposite side; but if a player when running in is tackled inside the goal-line, then only the player who first tackled him, or if two or more tackle simultaneously, they only may join in the maul.

21. Touch-in-goal. Immediately the ball, whether in the hands of a player (except for the purpose of a punt-out—see Rule 29) or not, goes into touch in goal, it is at once dead and out of the game, and must be brought out as provided by Rules 41 and 42.

22. Every player is on side, but is put off side if he enters a scrummage from his opponents' side; or, being in a scrummage, gets in front of the ball, or when the ball has been kicked, touched, or is being run with by any of his own side behind him (*i. e.*, between himself and his goal-line). No player can be off side in his own goal.

23. Every player when off side is out of the game and shall not touch the ball in any case whatever, either in or out of touch or goal, or in any way interrupt or obstruct any player, until he is again on side.

24. A player being off side is put on side when the ball has been kicked by, or has touched the dress or person of, any player of the opposite side, or when one of his own side has run in front of him, either with the ball or having kicked it when behind him.

25. When a player has the ball none of his opponents who at the time are off side may commence or attempt to tackle or otherwise interrupt such player.

26. Throwing back. It is lawful for any player who has the ball to throw it backward toward his own goal, or to pass it back

APPENDIX

to any player of his side who is at the time behind him, in accordance with the rules of on side.

27. Knocking on, *i. e.*, deliberately hitting the ball with the hand, and throwing forward, *i.e.*, throwing the ball in the direction of the opponents' goal-line, are not lawful. If the ball be either knocked on or thrown forward, the captain of the opposite side may (unless a fair catch has been made as provided by the next rule) require to have it brought back to the spot where it was knocked on or thrown forward and there put down.

28. A fair catch is a catch made direct from a kick or a throw forward, or a knock on by one of the opposite side, or from a punt-out or punt-on (see Rules 29 and 30), provided the catcher makes a mark with his heel at the spot where he made the catch and no other of his side touch the ball. (See Rules 43 and 44.)

29. A punt-out is a punt made after a touchdown by a player from behind his opponents' goal, and from touch in goal if necessary, toward his own side, who must stand outside the goal-line and endeavor to make a fair catch or to get the ball and run in or drop a goal. (See Rules 49 and 51.)

30. A punt-on is a punt made in a manner similar to a punt-out, and from touch, if necessary, by a player who has made a fair catch from a punt-out or another punt-on.

31. Touch. If a ball goes into touch, the first player on his side who touches it down must bring it to the spot where it crossed the touch-line; or if a player when running with the ball cross or put any part of either foot across the touch-line, he must return with the ball to the spot where the line was so crossed and thence return into the field of play in one of the modes provided by the following rule.

32. He must then himself, or by one of his own side, either bound the ball into the field of play and then run with it, kick it, or throw it back to his own side; or throw it out at right angles to the touch-line; or walk out with it at right angles to the touch-line any distance not less than five nor more than fifteen yards, and there put it down, first declaring how far he intends to walk out.

33. If two or more players holding the ball are pushed into touch, the ball shall belong in touch to the player who first had hold of it in the field of play and has not released his hold of it.

34. If the ball, when thrown out of touch, be not thrown out at right angles to the touch-line, the captain of either side may at once claim to have it thrown out again.

35. A catch made when the ball is thrown out of touch is not a fair catch.

36. Kick-off is a place kick from the centre of the field of play, and cannot count as a goal. The opposite side must stand at least ten yards in front of the ball until it has been kicked.

37. The ball shall be kicked off (i) at the commencement of the game (ii) after a goal has been obtained.

38. The sides shall change goals as often as and whenever a goal is obtained, unless it has otherwise been agreed by the captains before the commencement of the match.

39. The captains of the respective sides shall toss up before the commencement of the match; the winner of the toss shall have the option of the choice of goals or of kick-off.

40. Whenever a goal has been obtained the side which lost the goal shall then kick off.

41. Kick-out is a drop kick by one of the players of the side which has had to touch the ball down in their own goal, or into whose touch in goal the ball has gone (Rule 21), and is the mode of bringing the ball again into play, and cannot count as goal.

42. Kick-out must be a drop kick and from not more than twenty-five yards outside the kicker's goal; if the ball when kicked out pitch in touch, it must be taken back and kicked out again. The kicker's side must be behind the ball when it is kicked.

43. A player who has made and claimed a fair catch shall therefore either take a drop kick or a punt or place the ball for a place kick.

44. After a fair catch has been made the opposite side may come up to the catcher's mark, and except in cases under Rule 50, the catcher's side retiring, the ball shall be kicked from such mark, or from a spot any distance behind it.

45. A player may touch the ball down in his own goal at any time.

46. A side having touched the ball down in their opponents' goal shall try at goal either by a place kick or a punt-out.

47. If a try at goal be by a place kick, a player of the side which has touched the ball down shall bring it up to the goal-line (subject to Rule 48) in a straight line from, and opposite to, the spot where the ball was touched down, and there make a mark on the goal-line and thence walk straight out with it at right angles to the goal-line, to such distance as he thinks proper, and there place it for another of his side to kick. The kicker's side must be behind the ball when it is kicked and the opposite side must remain behind their goal-line until the ball has been placed on the ground. (See Rules 54 and 55.)

48. If the ball has been touched down between the goal-posts

it may be brought out in a straight line from either of such posts; but if brought out from between them the opposite side may charge at once. (See Rule 54.)

49. If the try at goal be by a punt-out (see Rule 29) a player of the side which has touched the ball down shall bring it straight up to the goal-line opposite to the spot where it was touched down, and there make a mark on the goal-line, and then punt out from touch-in-goal if necessary, or from any part behind the goal-line not nearer to the goal-post than such mark, beyond which it is not lawful for the opposite side (who must keep behind their goal-line) to pass until the ball has been kicked. (See Rules 54 and 55.)

50. If a fair catch be made from a punt-out or a punt-on, the catcher may proceed either as provided by Rules 43 and 44, or himself take a punt-on, in which case the mark made in making the fair catch shall be regarded (for the purpose of determining as well the position of the player who makes the punt-on as of the other players of both sides) as the mark made on the goal-line in the case of a punt-out.

51. A catch made in touch from a punt-out or a punt-on is not a fair catch; the ball must then be taken or thrown out of touch as provided by Rule 32. But if the catch be made in touch in goal the ball is at once dead and must be kicked out as provided by Rules 41 and 42.

52. When the ball has been touched down in the opponents' goal, none of the side in whose goal it has been so touched down shall touch it or in any way displace it or interfere with the player of the other side who may be taking it up or not.

53. The ball is dead whenever a goal has been obtained; but if a try at goal be not successful, the kick shall be considered as only an ordinary kick in the course of the game.

54. Charging, i. e., rushing forward to kick the ball or tackle a player, is lawful for the opposite side in all cases of a place kick after a fair catch, or upon a try at goal immediately the ball touches the ground or is placed on the ground; and in cases of drop kick or punt after a fair catch, as soon as the player having the ball commences to run or offers to kick, or the ball has touched the ground; but he may always draw back, and unless he has dropped the ball or actually touched it with his foot, they must again retire to his mark (see Rule 56). The opposite side in case of a punt-out or a punt-on, and the kicker's side in all cases, may not charge until the ball has been kicked.

55. If a player having the ball, when about to punt it out goes outside of the goal-line, or when about to punt-on advances nearer to his own goal-line than his mark, made on making the fair

catch, or if after the ball has been touched down in the opponents' goal, or a fair catch has been made, more than one player of the side which has so touched it down, or made the fair catch, touch the ball before it is again kicked, the opposite side may charge at once.

56. In case of a fair catch the opposite side may come up to and charge from anywhere on or behind a line drawn through the mark made by the player who has made the catch and parallel to their own goal-line; but in the case of a fair catch from punt-out or punt-on, they may not advance further in the direction of the touch-line nearest to such mark than a line drawn through such mark to their goal-line and parallel to such touch-line. In all cases, except a punt-out and a punt-on, the kicker's side must be behind the ball when it is kicked, but may not charge until it has been kicked.

57. No hacking or hacking over or tripping up shall be allowed under any circumstances.

58. No one wearing projecting nails, iron plates, or gutta percha on any parts of his boots or shoes shall be allowed to play in a match.

59. There shall be two judges, one for each side, and also a referee, to whom disputed points shall be referred, and whose decision shall be final.*

60. The grounds shall be 140 yards long and 70 yards wide.

61. The number of players shall be limited to fifteen upon a side.

1877. Columbia having defaulted in its interest in the affairs of the association, and Yale having refused to become a member thereof or to accept its rules other than provisionally, on account of an opposition to playing with fifteen men upon a side, Yale contending for eleven, and also on account of touchdowns being counted in the scoring, Yale contending for a score by goals alone, no intercollegiate convention in this year was held. An independent schedule of games, however, was played by Harvard, Princeton, and Yale.

Convention of Oct. 9, 1878, at Springfield.—Representatives: Harvard, F. W. Thayer, '78, L. Cushing, '79; Princeton, Bland Ballard, '80, G. W. Miller, '81. Yale, although not a member of the association, was represented by T. E. Rochfort, '79, and Walter Camp, '80. Yale proposed a reduction of the number of players upon a side from fifteen to eleven. The proposition was rejected.

*Entirely new. Under the Rugby Union Code the captains acted as officials.

Convention of Oct. 4, 1879, at Springfield.—Representatives: Harvard, Robert Bacon, '80; Princeton, Bland Ballard, '80. Yale, although not a member of the association, was represented by Walter Camp, '80. Mr. Camp submitted three amendments to the playing rules of the association: (1) That eleven players instead of fifteen shall constitute a side; (2) that safeties shall be counted in scoring against the side making them; (3) that the playing field shall be enlarged to a rectangle 200 feet by 400 feet. These amendments were rejected. Yale then formally applied for membership in the association. Granted unanimously.

Convention of Oct. 12, 1880, at Springfield, Mass.—Representatives: Harvard, W. H. Manning, '82, T. C. Thacher, '82; Princeton, F. Loney, '81, E. C. Peace, '83; Yale, Walter Camp, '80, R. W. Watson, '81, W. B. Hill, '81.

J. H. Stearns and W. N. Eldredge appeared in behalf of Columbia and asked for admission to the association. On motion of Yale, Columbia was admitted, but to have no vote in the conventions of the association in case of a tie, and to be subject to removal by the convention at any time upon a majority vote.

Yale moved the reduction of the players from fifteen upon a side to eleven. Passed unanimously.

Alterations in the rules were adopted as follows:

1. A scrimmage takes place when the holder of the ball, being in the field of play, puts it down on the ground in front of him and puts it in play while on side, first, by kicking the ball; second, by snapping it back with his foot. The man who first receives the ball from the snap-back shall be called the quarter-back, and shall not then rush forward with the ball under penalty of foul.

2. If the ball either fly, bound, or roll in touch from a kick-out, it must be brought back; but if it touch any player, it need not be brought back.

3. In case of a punt-out, the players of the side to which the ball is punted out must be at least 15 feet from the goal-line. The opposing side may line up anywhere in goal provided the punter has 5 feet clear extending from his scratch in the direction of touch. The punter out must not be interfered with in any way. A punt-out must be a kick from the toe.

4. If any player purposely foul an opponent when such opponent is about to try for a fair catch, the opponent's side may either have the ball down where the foul was made or take a free kick, which kick cannot score a goal.

5. The penalty for fouls when judged to be intentional by a referee, except as before provided, shall be a down for the opposing side.

6. The game shall be played by eleven men on each side.

Convention of Oct. 8, 1881, at Springfield, Mass.—Representatives: Harvard, W. H. Manning, '82, chairman; Princeton, P. T. Bryan, '82, M. Edgar, '82, E. C. Peace, '83; Yale, Walter Camp, '80, secretary; F. M. Eaton, '82, W. H. Hyndman, '84.

Rules amended as follows:

1. Disregard of rule as to on side when the ball is kicked off, or in case of a free kick, shall constitute a foul.

2. If a player be off side in the act of snapping the ball, the ball shall be snapped over again. If he be off side three times on the same down the ball shall go to the opposite side.

3. If a ball from kick-out pitch in touch three times in succession it shall be given to the opposite side as in touch at the 25-yard line.

4. The referee shall disqualify a player whom he has warned three times for intentional off-side playing.

5. In case of a tie two innings of fifteen minutes shall be played, with an interval of five minutes, the game to be decided on even innings. In case of a tie a goal kicked from a touchdown shall take precedence over a goal otherwise kicked. If the game still remains a tie the side which makes four or more safeties less than their opponents shall win the game.

6. A ball that strikes the post or cross-bar and goes inside or over the bar shall be scored as a goal.

Convention of April 12, 1882, at Springfield, Mass.—Representatives: Columbia, W. N. Eldredge, '83, B. P. Clark, '82, W. F. Morgan, '84; Harvard, W. H. Manning, '82, H. G. Leavitt, '82, E. T. Cabot, '83; Princeton, E. C. Peace, '83, D. F. Morgan, '83, C. J. Winton, '84; Yale, Walter Camp, '80, F. M. Eaton, '82, W. H. Hyndman, '84.

The session was largely devoted to discussing remedies for abolishing the "block game," but no decisive action was taken. A resolution was adopted providing that the first and second teams in a season's championship series should be entitled to play their game the following year in New York on Thanksgiving Day. An executive committee was established as follows: President, F. M. Eaton, '82, Yale; Secretary, W. F. Morgan, '84, Columbia; Committeemen, D. P. Morgan, '83, Princeton, E. T. Cabot, '83, Harvard.

Convention of Oct. 14, 1882, at Springfield, Mass.—Representatives: Columbia, W. F. Morgan, '84; Harvard, E. T. Cabot, '83; Princeton, E. C. Peace, '83, D. P. Morgan, '83; Yale, Walter Camp, '80, R. Tompkins, '84, Stanley Shaffer, '83.

Rules amended as follows:

1. If on three consecutive fairs and downs a team shall not have advanced the ball five yards or lost ten, they must give up the ball to the other side at the spot where the fourth down was made. Consecutive means without leaving the hands of the side holding it.*

2. No man shall be allowed to play in championship games for a longer period that five years.

3. The referee shall be empowered to call a game when he considers it too dark to play.

4. The decision of whether a side has made five yards or lost ten shall be left to the decision of the referee.

5. The referee shall disqualify a player whom he has twice warned for violation of the rule relating to tripping and foul tackling.

6. In punting out after a touchdown the players on defence shall not approach within six feet of the punter.

7. In scoring four touchdowns shall take precedence over a goal kicked from the field; two safeties shall be equal to a touchdown.

Convention of Oct. 17, 1883, *Fifth Avenue Hotel, New York.*— Representatives: Columbia, Messrs. Darling and Griffith; Harvard, F. L. Clark, '83; Princeton, Alex. Moffat, '84, D. M. Look, '84, secretary; Yale, Walter Camp, '80, Ray Tompkins, '84, chairman.

Amendments adopted:

Section I of Rule 5: "A side having touched the ball down in their opponents' goal, may try at a goal either by a place kick or punt-out" altered so as to read "*shall try at goal,*" the object being to prevent teams from deliberately missing goals in order to make another touchdown, which was possible under prior rules.

Rule 7, providing that "If the try be by a punt-out the opponents shall line up on the goal-line anywhere, except within the space of six feet from the punter's mark," changed to read "within the space of ten feet."

Section II of Rule 18, reading "There shall be two judges and a referee," amended by adding "each of whom shall be an alumnus."

Rule 19, providing for the disqualification of a player for two infractions of the rule prohibiting deliberate off-side play was altered so as to allow three infractions.

---

* A "fair" was the technical name of putting the ball in play from the side line when out of bounds.

A new rule added providing for numerical scoring, the values as follows:

Safety 1
Touchdown 2
Goal following touchdown 4
Goal from field 5

Convention of Dec. 5, 1883, at Fifth Avenue Hotel, New York. —Representatives: Harvard, R. M. Appleton, '84, J. Simpkins, '85; Princeton, Alex. Moffat, '84, E. C. Peace, '83, D. M. Look, '84, C. W. Bird, '85; Yale, Walter Camp, '80, Ray Tompkins, '84.

Messrs. Griffith and Stevens, of Columbia, applied for readmission of Columbia, which was granted.

The following amendments to the rules were adopted:

1. Upon a punt-out following a touchdown, no one of the defensive side shall approach within a space of ten feet from the punter.

2. The referee in all championship games of the association shall be an alumnus.

3. A player warned the third time for intentionally delaying the game shall be disqualified.

4. The referee shall take out time for all unnecessary delays.

5. The referee shall disqualify a player having been warned three times for intentionally tackling in touch.

6. The value of a touchdown shall be four points, and the value of a safety shall be two points, to be added to the score of the opposing team.

7. A player may be off side only twice during a game.

Walter Camp, '80, Yale, was directed to copyright and print the rules in behalf of the association.

Convention of Oct. 15, 1884, at Fifth Avenue Hotel, New York. —Representatives: Harvard, G. M. Kimball, '84, A. D. French, '85; Princeton, C. W. Bird, '85, J. B. Harriman, '85; Yale, Walter Camp, '80, E. L. Richards, '85.

A communication was received from Columbia, withdrawing from the association.

Rules amended as follows:

Section I, Rule 10, a new section was added as follows: "A fair catch can be made behind one's goal."

Section I, Rule 17. "A player shall be off side but twice during a game," altered so as to read: "A player at the second warning for intentional off-side play shall be disqualified."

Section III, Rule 37, relative to interference with a fair catch, was changed so as to read: "The opponents may have, at the option of the captain, a free kick or a down where the interference occurred."

Convention of Nov. 27, 1884, at Fifth Avenue Hotel, New York.
—Representatives: Harvard, G. M. Kimball, '84; Princeton, C. W. Bird, '85, J. B. Harriman, '85; Yale, Walter Camp, '80, E. L. Richards, '85. Yale appealed from the decision of Mr. R. M. Appleton, '84, of Harvard, the referee of the Princeton-Yale game, in declaring the contest no game and the score as 0 to 0. After a prolonged debate the convention voted to sustain the decision of Mr. Appleton. See page 378.

Convention of Feb. 7, 1885, at Fifth Avenue Hotel, New York.
—Representatives: Princeton, C. W. Bird, '85, J. B. Harriman, '85, secretary, C. M. De Camp, '86; Yale, Walter Camp, '80, E. L. Richards, '85, chairman, F. G. Peters, '86.

Owing to the abolition of football at Harvard by its faculty, Jan. 6, 1885, Harvard was not represented. Mr. Ellis Ward appeared and asked for the admission of the University of Pennsylvania to the association. F. D. Beattys, '85, of Wesleyan, filed a similar application in behalf of Wesleyan. On motion of Mr. Camp both were admitted.

The rules were amended as follows:

Rule 4 altered to read: "A touchdown shall be made when the holder of the ball shall carry it across the opponents' goal-line and either touch it down behind the line or in touch in goal or be there fairly held by an opponent. If the touchdown is made in touch in goal the ball shall be punted out at the intersection of the side line and the goal-line."

Rule 2, defining when a ball is down, was extended by adding the words "or when the referee has said down."

Rule 18 amended so as to read: "The contesting parties in a championship game are to decide on the referee for their game and he shall be absolute in all decisions and shall be paid."

Rule 19 altered so as to read: "The referee shall take out time for unnecessary delay. He shall decide disputed points, and shall for intentionally delaying the game or off-side play give, for the first offence, one point to the opponents, and, for the second offence, one point more to the opponents and dismissal of the offender from the field. For violation of Rules 17 or 28, relative to intentional off-side play, and slugging, the referee shall award two points to the offended side."

Rule 22 extended by adding: "If either side refuses to play within five minutes after ordered so to do by the referee the said side shall forfeit the game."

Rule 31 altered to read: "The man who first receives the ball when snapped back from a down or thrown from a fair, shall not carry the ball forward under any circumstances whatsoever."

A new rule was added as follows: "No delay arising from any cause whatsoever, shall last longer than five minutes."

Mr. Camp moved the separation of the rush-lines by a neutral zone of five yards. After a prolonged debate the motion was lost.

Convention of Oct. 10, 1885, at Fifth Avenue Hotel, New York. —Representatives: Pennsylvania, J. J. Hovey, '87; Princeton, C. M. De Camp, '86, J. P. Shaw, '86, secretary, D. Greene, '87; Wesleyan, S. V. Coffin, '89; Yale, Walter Camp, '80, F. G. Peters, '86, chairman.

A communication was received from Harvard withdrawing from the association.

Rules amended as follows:

Rules 17 and 28, requiring two warnings to precede disqualification for intentional off-side play or delay of the game, were amended so as to require only one warning and also to include unnecessary roughness.

Rule 18 was extended to supplement the penalty of disqualification as follows: "For intentional delay of the game or off-side play the penalty shall be five yards."

A resolution was adopted providing for an equal division of the net receipts in all matches.

Convention of May 5, 1886, at Fifth Avenue Hotel, New York. —Representatives: Harvard, J. B. Keyes, '77, C. S. Hamlin, '83, W. A. Brooks, '87; Pennsylvania, W. C. Posey, '86, N. W. Young, '87, F. W. W. Graham, '87; Princeton, C. M. De Camp, '86, H. S. Savage, '87; Wesleyan, J. D. Wells, '88; Yale, F. G. Peters, '86, R. N. Corwin, '87.

Harvard applied for reinstatement and same was granted unanimously. Princeton moved that the centre rush should be permitted to snap the ball without any interference from opponents. Passed. Moved to amend Rule 31 so as to require a kick-out after a kick across the goal-line, to be made either by a place kick or by a drop. Passed.

Convention of Oct. 9, 1886, at Fifth Avenue Hotel, New York. —Representatives: Harvard, C. S. Hamlin, '83, W. A. Brooks, '87; Pennsylvania, N. W. Young, '87, F. W. W. Graham, 87; Princeton, H. S. Savage, '87, R. P. Bradford, '87; Wesleyan, J. M. Stevens, '87, J. D. Wells, '88; Yale, C. L. Hare, '87, R. N. Corwin, '87.

A long debate occurred as to place of the Princeton-Yale game, finally terminating by the selection of Princeton, Thanksgiving Day.

An amendment was made to the rule permitting a team to charge as soon as the ball was in motion by changing the words "in motion" to "in play." The Lillywhite No. J ball was adopted as the official ball for all match games.

Convention of Nov. 28, 1886, at Fifth Avenue Hotel, New York. —Representatives: Harvard, E. G. Kent, '82, R. M. Appleton, '84, W. A. Brooks, '87; Pennsylvania, W. C. Posey, '86, N. W. Young, '87, F. W. W. Graham, '87; Princeton, C. W. Bird, '85, H. S. Savage, '87; Wesleyan, F. D. Beattys, '85, J. M. Stevens, '87, J. D. Wells, '88; Yale, Walter Camp, '80, F. G. Peters, '86, R. N. Corwin, '87.

Mr. Corwin moved to award to Yale the championship for 1886. Mr. Bird objected on the ground that the Princeton-Yale game had resulted in a tie at 0 to 0 because called before completion, according to the precedent established by the convention of Nov. 27, 1884. Mr. Corwin amended his motion that the championship be awarded to Yale on the basis of points scored. Mr. Bird renewed his objection that the championship could be awarded only upon results and not upon the points scored in an unfinished game. After two hours of debate the representatives of Princeton and Yale were requested to withdraw from the room in order that the motion might be decided by the non-interested representatives. The latter thereupon further debated the motion for an additional hour, at the conclusion of which the following resolutions were passed:

Resolved, That this convention cannot, as a convention, award the championship for 1886.

Resolved, That Yale, according to points scored, should have won the championship.

Convention of March 26, 1887, at Fifth Avenue Hotel, New York.—Representatives: Harvard, A. F. Holden, '88, B. W. Palmer, '88; Pennsylvania, W. C. Posey, '86, L. H. Alexander, 88; Princeton, H. S. Savage, '87, T. B. Hamilton, '88, W. J. Cook, '89; Wesleyan, F. D. Beattys, '85, J. M. Stevens, '87, H. H. Beattys, '88; Yale, F. G. Peters, '86, R. N. Corwin, '87, H. Beecher, '88.

The convention passed a resolution that the rules should be enforced rigidly by referees, and that captains should instruct their men against holding, roughing, and all other objectionable features. The 'varsity captains present supplemented this resolution by the following agreement:

We, the undersigned, captains of teams of the Intercollegiate Football Association, do hereby pledge ourselves to use all means in our power to coach our teams to stop holding in

the rush line, slugging, and all other objectionable features of
the game.

H. BEECHER, JR., Yale.
H. H. BEATTYS, Wesleyan.
W. J. COOK, Princeton.
L. H. ALEXANDER, Pennsylvania.
A. F. HOLDEN, Harvard.

Amendments to the rules as follows:

Rule 5 altered so as to compel a team to try for a goal after a
touchdown, by changing the words "shall try for goal" to "must
try for goal," the object being to prevent a team deliberately
missing the goal in order to obtain another touchdown, the ball
not being dead following the try under the prevailing rules.

Rule 7 altered so as to prohibit a team from lining up within
10 yards of the punter's mark after a fair catch.

Rule 12 altered so as to prohibit interference with the snapper-
back until the ball is in motion.

Rule 29 altered so as to make a loss of 20 yards equal to a first
down instead of a loss of 10 yards, as formerly.

A new rule was added, to wit: "In case a kick is blocked and
bounds across the goal-line the impetus shall be deemed to have
come from the kicking side."

*Convention of May 14, 1887, at Fifth Avenue Hotel, New
York.*—Representation the same as at previous session.

A new rule adopted providing for two referees, one to have jurisdiction over the men and the other to have jurisdiction over the
ball.

Messrs. Beecher, Holden, and Cook were appointed to draft
a constitution for the association.

*Convention of June 5, 1887, at Fifth Avenue Hotel, New
York.*—Representation the same as at previous session, and
Walter Camp, '80, Yale.

Mr. Camp introduced the following resolutions, which were
adopted:

Resolved, 1. There shall be an advisory graduate committee
on rules and appeals, consisting of two Harvard graduates, two
Princeton graduates, one Wesleyan graduate, one graduate from
the University of Pennsylvania, and the several acting captains of
the football teams of each year, and one graduate of any college
in the association, to be elected by the said captains as their
special advocate and advisor, elected for the term of one year only.
The other graduate members shall be elected during the commencement week by the members and ex-members of the respec-

tive university teams, absentees being allowed to vote by proxy. These graduates shall serve for the period of two years from election, except that the graduates who are to act from date until June, 1888, shall be immediately chosen by the football delegates of this year.

2. This advisory committee shall meet and propose the rules or changes in the same on the first Saturday in March in each year, and shall submit the proposed rules or changes to the secretary of the Intercollegiate Association on or before the first Saturday in April, to be forthwith transmitted by him.

A new rule was adopted providing that the referee having jurisdiction over the ball should be selected, in championship games, by the captains of the teams, but that the referee having jurisdiction over the men should be selected by the advisory committee, and that this latter official should be called umpire instead of referee.

Session of Graduate Advisory Committee, March 3, 1888, at Fifth Avenue Hotel, New York.—Representatives: Harvard, W. A. Brooks, '87; Pennsylvania. W, S. Harvey, '85; Princeton, R. M. Hodge, '86; Wesleyan, F. D. Beattys, '85; Yale, Walter Camp,'80.

The committee decided to advise the following changes in the rules:

Rule 12 to be altered so as to prevent the snapper-back from running with the ball before it had touched a third man.

Rule 14 to be altered so as to prohibit players in the rush-line from blocking with extended arms.

Rule 26 to be altered so as to permit tackling between the waist and the knee.

. Rule 35 to be altered so as to prevent any player while off side from using his hands or arms upon an opposing player.

Convention of May 5, 1888, at Fifth Avenue Hotel, New York.—Representatives: Harvard, A. F. Holden, '88, R. W. Palmer, '89; Pennsylvania, G. Q. Horwitz, '86, G. H. Frazier, '87, F. Ashurst, '89; Princeton, E. O. Wagenhurst, '88, J. R. Barr, '89, Hector Cowan, '88; Yale, Walter Camp, '80, H. Beecher, '88, W. H. Corbin, '89.

The convention vetoed the amendment advised by the Graduate Advisory Committee to Rule 12. The remaining amendments were accepted excepting the amendment to Rule 14, which was reframed and adopted as follows: " No player shall lay his hands upon or interfere by the use of his hands or arms with an opponent unless he has the ball."

Session of Graduate Advisory Committee, March 2, 1889, at Fifth Avenue Hotel, New York.—Representatives: Harvard,

W. A. Brooks, '87; Pennsylvania, W. S. Harvey, '85; Princeton, R. M. Hodge, '86; Wesleyan, F. D. Beattys, '85; Yale, Walter Camp, '80.

The committee decided to advise the following changes in the rules:

A. That time should be taken out while bringing the ball out after a safety or touchback.

B. That the penalty of disqualification for foul tackling or unnecessary roughness as provided for in one rule should be divided into two rules, of which the penalty for unnecessary roughness should continue to be disqualification, but that the penalty for foul tackling should be the loss of 25 yards only.

Messrs. Camp and Hodge were appointed a committee to compile an official list of the championships awarded by the association.

Session of Graduate Advisory Committee, March 30, 1889, at same place.—Representatives: Harvard, H. C. Leeds, '77; Pennsylvania, John C. Bell, '84; Princeton, Duncan Edwards, '85; Wesleyan, F. D. Beattys, '85; Yale, Walter Camp, '80.

The committee decided to advise the following changes in the rules:

Rule 4 to read: "A touchdown is made when the ball is carried, kicked, or passed across the goal-line, and there held either in goal or in touch in goal."

Rule 15 to read: "Both umpire and referee shall use a whistle to indicate cessation of play on fouls and downs. The referee shall use a stop-watch to keep the time. Time shall not be called for the end of the three-quarters until the ball is dead, and in the case of a try at goal from touchdown the try shall be allowed. Time shall be taken out while the ball is being brought out either for a try or a kick-out."

Rule 26 to read: "The side which has the ball can interfere with the body only; the side which has not the ball can use hands and arms as heretofore."

Rule 27 to read: "(A) A player shall be disqualified for unnecessary roughness, hacking or striking with the closed fist. (B) For the offence of throttling, butting, tripping up, or tackling below the knees the opponents shall receive 25 yards or a free kick, at their option. In case they choose 25 yards, and this would carry the ball across the goal-line, they can have only one-half the distance from the spot of the offence to the goal-line."

Rule 33 to read: "The player in a try at goal may be off side or in touch without vitiating the kick."

Session of Graduate Advisory Committee, Nov. 4, 1889, at Fifth Avenue Hotel, New York.—Representatives: Harvard, H. C. Leeds, '77; Pennsylvania, John C. Bell, '84; Princeton, Duncan Edwards, '85, E. A. Poe, '91; Wesleyan, F. D. Beattys, '85; Yale, Walter Camp, '80.

Mr. Camp offered the following resolution:

Resolved, That no one shall be eligible to take part as a player in any championship games of this association who is not a bonafide student of the college on whose team he plays, matriculated for the then current year, and regularly pursuing a course which requires his attendance upon at least five lectures or recitations a week, and in case a player's qualifications are questioned, he shall furnish to the advisory committee a certificate, signed by three members of the faculty, stating that he is a bona-fide student, matriculated for the then college year, and regularly pursuing a course which requires his attendance upon at least five lectures or recitations a week. And the player shall further furnish to the advisory committee an affidavit stating that he is a bona-fide student, matriculated for the then current year, and regularly pursuing a course which requires his attendance on at least five lectures or recitations a week, and that it is his intention to continue in said course until the expiration of the present college year. No professional athlete shall take part in any contest of this association, nor shall any player of any university or college be paid or receive, directly or indirectly, any money or financial concession or emolument as present or past compensation for, or as a prior consideration or inducement to, playing, whether the same be received from or paid by, or at the instance of, the football association, athletic committee, or faculty of such college or university, or any individual whatsoever. And any player who is specifically challenged under this section by any member of the association in writing, shall, within five days after the filing of such challenge, file with the secretary of the committee an affidavit duly verified under oath, showing that he in no way violates the provisions of this section; and upon his failure to make and file such affidavit, he shall be barred from participating in any contest of the members of this association.

And in case the sufficiency of such affidavit be questioned by the challenging party, and the committee of appeals be notified thereof, the player challenged shall submit on two days' notice to oral examination by said challenging party before said committee, who shall then and thereafter decide regarding the eligibility of such challenged player to take part in contests of members of this association.

The date of such examination shall not be set on the day of, nor within forty-eight hours of, a championship match. No challenge or protest shall in any way affect a game which has been played previous to the filing or deciding of such challenge or protest.

Mr. Edwards moved as a substitute resolution 'the following, to be treated as an amendment to Article 19 of the constitution:

ARTICLE 19.

SEC. 1. No man shall be allowed to play more than four years upon a team representing any of the colleges in this association, or on the team of more than one college.

SEC. 2. No man shall be allowed to play on a team representing any of the colleges in this association unless he be an undergraduate of the said college.

SEC. 3. No student in the department of law, medicine, or theology of any of the colleges in this association who has previous to his membership therein played upon a team representing any other college in this association shall be allowed to play on the team of said college in which he is a student.

SEC. 4. No man shall be allowed to play in a team representing any of the colleges in this association if he in any way, directly or indirectly, receive any pay for so doing. Any inducement of pecuniary value shall be held as included in the meaning of the word "pay" as used in this section.

SEC. 5. All questions of eligibility arising under this section must be investigated and decided by the advisory committee on application of any college.

Mr. Edwards and Mr. Bell argued strongly against the adoption of the first clause of Mr. Camp's resolution, contending that it was *ex post facto* legislation offered to take effect in the middle of a season, and that it could not constitutionally do so under Section 3 of the association's constitution. Upon the vote the resolution was adopted, Pennsylvania and Princeton voting in the negative on clause one. Mr. Edwards, for Princeton, then offered his resolution as a further amendment to Article 19 of the constitution.

Mr. Leeds raised the point of order that the amendment was not germane to the call for the special session. The point of order was not sustained, but the amendment was defeated. Mr. Edwards then moved that no student should be permitted to play upon any team in the association who had previously played upon the team of any other college either in or out of the association. Mr. Leeds renewed his point of order against this motion and the point was sustained. Mr. Leeds thereupon filed protests against fifteen of Princeton's players. Mr. Edwards filed protests against four of Harvard's players. The committee thereupon adjourned until November 14, ensuing.

Session of Graduate Advisory Committee of Nov. 14, 1889, *at same place.*—Representatives the same as in previous session. Answers to all protests were received, read, and filed. Mr. Leeds, moved that the committee proceed to dispose of the protests. Mr. Edwards raised the point of order that such a procedure was unconstitutional until two days had elapsed after the filing of the answers. The point was not sustained. Mr. Edwards then moved to table the protests of Harvard. Mr. Beattys asked leave to withdraw and inspect Harvard's evidence supporting their protests before voting on the motion. Messrs. Leeds and Beattys withdrew to examine the evidence. Upon their return the motion to table was carried, Pennsylvania, Princeton, and Wesleyan voting affirmatively and Harvard and Yale negatively. Mr. Edwards thereupon withdrew his protests against the four players of Harvard and the committee adjourned.

Convention of May 10, 1890, *at Fifth Avenue Hotel, New York.*—Representatives: Pennsylvania, John C. Bell, '84, T. W. Hulme, '89; Princeton, E. A. Poe, '91, A. D. Wilson, '91, Max Farrand '92; Wesleyan, F. G. Beattys, '85, S. V. Coffin, '89; Yale, G. D. Yeomans, '90, J. B. Sears, '91, W. C. Rhodes, '91. A communication was received from Harvard withdrawing from the association. Messrs. Yeomans and Farrand were appointed a committee to compile the official record of championships of the association.

Amendments to the rules were made as follows:

To Rule 3 the following section was added: "If a catcher after making his mark be deliberately thrown to the ground by an opponent he shall be given 5 yards unless this would carry the ball across the goal-line, in which case one-half of the remaining distance shall be given."

To Rule 13 was added: "Nor shall the disqualified or injured player removed from the game be permitted to return again to play."

Also the new rule: "If a player off side touch the ball inside the 5-yard line the ball shall go as a touchback to the opponents."

Convention of Oct. 4, 1890, *at Fifth Avenue Hotel, New York.*—Representatives: Pennsylvania, E. O. Wagenhurst, '91, H. Mellor, '92; Princeton, E. A. Poe, '91, A. D. Wilson, '91, Max Farrand, '92; Wesleyan, F. G. Beattys, '85, S. V. Coffin, '89, H. B. Slayback, '91, F. H. Tackaberry, '92; Yale, G. D. Yeomans, '90, J. B. Sears, '91, W. C. Rhodes, '91.

Messrs. Farrand and Yeomans filed their report upon the record of the official championships awarded by the association: "Princeton won the championship in 1877, 1878, 1879, 1885, and 1889, Yale won the championship in 1881, 1882, 1883, 1887, and 1888. There was no championship in 1880, 1884, and 1886."

Convention of May 2, 1891, at Fifth Avenue Hotel, New York. —Representatives: Pennsylvania, H. Mellor, '92; Princeton, Max Farrand, '92, R. H. Warren, '93, G. C. Fraser, '93; Wesleyan, F. H. Tackaberry, '92; Yale, J. B. Sears, '91, W. C. Rhodes, '91. The following officers of the association for the ensuing year were elected: President, Lee McClung, '92, Yale; Secretary, R. H. Warren, '93, Princeton; Treasurer, F. H. Tackaberry, '92, Wesleyan.

Richard Harding Davis, '86, Lehigh, appeared before the convention and asked for the admission of Lehigh to the association. The application was refused.

Convention of Oct. 5, 1891, at Fifth Avenue Hotel, New York.— Representatives: Pennsylvania, John C. Bell, '84; Princeton, Max Farrand, '92, R. H. Warren, '93; Wesleyan, F. G. Beattys, '85, F. H. Tackaberry, '92; Yale, W. B. Wright, '92, Lee McClung, '92.

Meeting called for the purpose of arranging schedule of championship games. Mr. Bell moved that the Princeton and Yale games with Pennsylvania should be played in Philadelphia. Motion defeated, these contests upon a succeeding motion being assigned to New York. Messrs. Farrand and Bell later transferred the Pennsylvania-Princeton game to Manheim, near Philadelphia.

Convention of Harvard and Yale at Springfield, Oct. 9, 1891.— Representatives: Harvard, George A. Stewart, '84, B. W. Trafford, '93; Yale, W. B. Wright, '92, Lee McClung, '92.

The following agreement was adopted:

"We, the undersigned, representing the football associations of Harvard and Yale, respectively, do hereby agree to play a game of football annually, in the years from 1891 to 1894, inclusive. The game in each year shall be played at Hampden Park, Springfield, Mass. The date of the game in each year shall be the Saturday immediately preceding Thanksgiving Day. The games shall be played under the playing rules of the American Intercollegiate Football Association. In the years from 1892 to 1894, inclusive, a meeting shall be held, between the captains of the two elevens on or before October 17, at which a referee and umpire shall be elected and all other matters not covered by this agreement be decided. For the year 1891 the referee and umpire shall be selected, as soon as may be, by mutual consent of the two elevens.

> B. W. TRAFFORD,
> *Captain H. U. F. B. A.*
>
> GEORGE A. STEWART,
> *For Graduate Advisory
> Committee on Football.*
>
> LEE MCCLUNG,
> *Captain.*
>
> WILLIAM B. WRIGHT,
> *President Yale University
> Football Association."*

Session of Graduate Advisory Committee, March 21, 1892, at New York.—Representatives: J. C. Bell, '84, Pennsylvania; Alex. Moffat, '84, Princeton; F. G. Beattys, '85, Wesleyan; Walter Camp, '80, Yale. The committee decided to recommend three changes in the rules: (1) If the ball is fumbled on a punt-out it shall be punted out again, and if again fumbled it shall go to the opponents at the centre of the field. (2) If a bona-fide attempt at goal is made and missed, the ball shall be put in play at the centre of the field. (3) Any person not playing attempting to coach shall be warned, and upon the second offence shall be ordered outside the enclosure.

Convention of May 12, 1892, at New York.—Representatives: S. B. Newton, '94, C. H. Schoff, '93, Pennsylvania; G. C. Fraser, '93, Philip King, '93, and J. McN. Thompson, '94, Princeton; Messrs. Gordon and Thorndike, Wesleyan; Lee McClung, '92, W. B. Wright, '92, Yale.

The following changes in the rules were adopted:

To Rule 32 was added: "If the try for goal following a touchdown be missed the ball shall be brought to the centre of the field and given to the defenders of that goal."

To Rule 34 was added: "If a punt-out from a touchdown is missed or is not fairly caught, the ball shall be taken to the centre of the field and given to the defenders of that goal."

A new rule was added: "The umpire shall warn any person coaching from the side lines. Upon second offence the offender shall be ordered behind the ropes or fence."

The application from Lehigh University for membership in the association was declined.

Convention of Jan. 21, 1893, at Fifth Avenue Hotel, New York.—Representatives: Pennsylvania, H. A. Mackey, '93, S. B. Newton, '94; Princeton, J. McN. Thompson, '94, T. G. Trenchard, '95; Wesleyan, C. H. Judd, '94; Yale, V. C. McCormick, '93.

Mr. McCormick offered the following resolution:

Resolved, That no member of a graduate department or special student or any undergraduate who has registered or attended lectures or recitations at any other university or college, or any undergraduate who is not pursuing a course for a degree requiring his attendance for at least three years, shall be eligible to play upon the football teams of the colleges of this association. Adopted, ayes, Princeton, Wesleyan, Yale; nay, Pennsylvania. An application was received from Cornell to be admitted as a member of the association. Tabled.

Session of Graduate Advisory Committee, March 4, 1893, at Fifth Avenue Hotel, New York.—Representatives: Pennsylvania, John C. Bell, '84; Princeton, Alex. Moffat, '85; Wesleyan, F. D. Beattys, '85; Yale, Walter Camp, '80.

The committee decided upon the following changes in the rules:

A. The snapper-back to have full and undisturbed possession of the ball.

B. The ball shall be brought out after a touchdown from the place where the player holding the ball is held, or where he touches down, and not where he has crossed the line. The players of the side not having the ball shall not be allowed to touch the ball until it has been put in play.

Convention of Oct. 6, 1893, at Fifth Avenue Hotel, New York.—Representatives: Pennsylvania, H. A. Mackey, '94, S. B. Newton, '94; Princeton, J. McN. Thompson, '94, T. G. Trenchard, '95; Wesleyan, C. H. Judd, '94; Yale, F. A. Hinkey, '93, E. O. Holter, '94.

Mr. Mackey moved the repeal of the "undergraduate rule." The motion, after a long debate, was lost. Mr. Mackey then moved to substitute for the "undergraduate rule" the Harvard-Pennsylvania eligibility rule as follows:

"No student who is not a regular student in the college or scientific school, and no student in each of these departments who has ever played in an intercollegiate contest upon a university or class team of any other college, shall be permitted to play until he has resided one academic year at the institution he represents and passes an examination upon one year's full work; but nothing herein shall, during the year of 1893, disqualify any one who would be eligible under pre-existing rules. No student, whether he has represented one or more colleges, shall take part in intercollegiate contests for more than four years, but this rule shall not, during the year of 1893, disqualify any one who would be eligible under pre-existing rules."

This motion to substitute also was defeated

Convention of Harvard and Yale at Springfield, Oct. 11, 1893. —Agreed that the intercollegiate undergraduate rule should not apply, but that each institution should be the judge of its own eligibility qualifications.

Convention of Oct. 28, 1893, at Fifth Avenue Hotel, New York.— Representatives: Pennsylvania, John C. Bell, '84, H. A. Mackey, '93, S. B. Newton, '94; Princeton, Alex. Moffat, '84, T. G. Trenchard, '95, J. McN. Thompson, '94; Wesleyan, F. G. Beattys, '85, E. O. Smith, '93, C. H. Judd, '94; Yale, F. A. Hinkey, '95, E. O. Holter, '94.

Princeton, Wesleyan, and Yale voting affirmatively, Pennsylvania negatively, the "undergraduate rule" was amended by the substitution of the following:

"1. No man shall be eligible for the team of any college in this association who is not pursuing a bona-fide course requiring attendance on recitations or lectures of at least six hours a week. If a graduate, he shall be pursuing a course for a degree requiring at least one year's study; if an undergraduate and not pursuing a course for a degree, he shall not be allowed to play during his first year at college.

"2. Any man who has attended recitations or lectures in any other college shall not be eligible for the team in any college of this association, unless he be a regular member of the Freshman academic or scientific class, or until he has spent one year of resident study in that college and has passed satisfactory examinations upon a full year's work.

"3. No man shall play more than four years upon any team in this association.

"4. Two weeks before each game of this association the two captains shall submit to one another a list of forty players from whom his team shall be chosen. If either captain has any objection to make to any player upon the list submitted to him he shall submit the protest within four days to the Graduate Advisory Committee and to the other captain. The Graduate Advisory Committee shall have power to decide upon the eligibility of players and shall consider the protest submitted to them within forty-eight hours of its receipt. Either captain may submit a further list of six players not later than five days before the game. Protests to any of these men may be submitted in the same manner and the Graduate Advisory Committee shall pass upon them not later than forty-eight hours before the game.

"5. The referee of any game in this association at the request of either captain shall debar from that game any man not included in the lists submitted, or who has been declared ineligible by the Graduate Advisory Committee."

Mr. Mackey offered the following amendment: "Provided that this rule shall not disqualify, during the season of 1893, any player who is eligible under the rules and constitution of this association in force in 1892 and previous thereto."

This amendment was defeated.

Convention of Nov. 7, 1893, at Hotel Windsor, New York. —S. B. Newton, '94, Pennsylvania, filed with the secretary the resignation of the University of Pennsylvania from membership in the association, as follows:

"*To the Secretary of the Intercollegiate Football Association:* At the time of the passage of the undergraduate rule and the substitute adopted therefor on the 27th ult., as amendments to playing Rule 13 and Article 10 of the constitution, we, in behalf of Pennsylvania, entered a protest against the constitutionality of the same upon the minutes of the association. Pennsylvania has since uniformly maintained the position that the legislation referred to was unconstitutional and its immediate enforcement against Pennsylvania unjust; and the board of directors of its athletic association, by resolution passed on the 28th ult., reaffirmed Pennsylvania's position in this respect, and the captain of the team was instructed to act accordingly.

"In a number of interviews and by correspondence Manager E. O. Holter, representing Yale, has insisted as a condition precedent to the playing of the Yale-Pennsylvania game, scheduled for the 11th inst., that Pennsylvania shall submit to Yale a list of her players, whose eligibility shall be decided on by the provisions of the said mentioned rule, and that Pennsylvania shall further sign a written agreement to play the game under a strict interpretation of the rules of the Intercollegiate Football Association as they now stand.

"This submission and agreement, for the reasons above given, Pennsylvania is unable to make and is therefore impelled to resign from the Intercollegiate Football Association, and accordingly hereby tenders her resignation therefrom.

"H. A. MACKEY,
"*Captain U. of P. Football Eleven.*
"S. B. NEWTON,
"*Manager U. of P. Football Eleven.*"

A communication also was received from Wesleyan, dated Nov. 5, 1893, likewise resigning from membership in the association.

Conference of Feb. 3, 1894, at University Athletic Club. New York.—Owing to the absence of an authoritative body governing football, due to the dissolution of the Intercollegiate Football Association, the University Athletic Club of New York City appointed, for the purpose of protecting the game, a committee of its members consisting of George Adee, '67, Yale; Lloyd McK. Garrison, '88, Harvard; Guy Richards, '87, Columbia; C. F. Matthewson, '82, Dartmouth, and C. C. Cuyler, '79, Princeton. This committee invited to the conference Alex. Moffat, '84, Princeton, J. H. Sears, '89, Harvard, and F. A. Hinkey, '95, Yale. The conference decided to request Harvard, Pennsylvania, Princeton, and Yale, to select one representative each to form a rules committee to govern the game, this committee to assemble February 23, 1894.

Meeting of Rules Committee, Feb. 23, 1894, at University Athletic Club, New York.—Representatives: Harvard, W. A. Brooks, '87; Pennsylvania, J. C. Bell, '84, Princeton; Alex. Moffat, '84; Yale, Walter Camp '80.

Mr. Moffat was chosen as chairman and Mr. Camp as secretary. The committee voted to increase its membership to include Paul J. Dashiell, '84, Johns Hopkins, on account of his expert knowledge of the game, and as its leading official. A public request was issued for suggestions for the reform of the game.

Meeting of Rules Committee, May 8, 1894, at University Athletic Club, New York.—The following amendments to the rules were adopted:

Rule 8 altered so as to read: "A fair catch is a catch made direct from a kick by one of the opponents, or a punt-out by one of the same side, provided the man intending to make the catch indicates that intention by holding up his hand when running for the ball, and also makes a mark with his heel upon catching it, and no other of his side touches the ball. If he be interfered with by an opponent who is off side, or if he be thrown after catching the ball, he shall be given fifteen yards, unless this should carry the ball across the goal-line. In that case he shall be given but half of the intervening distance. After having raised his hand he cannot run with the ball, but must take his fair catch if he succeed in making one."

Rule 14 altered so as to read: "The officials shall consist of an umpire, a referee, and a linesman."

Rule 15 altered so as to read: "The umpire is the judge of the conduct of the players and his decision is final regarding fouls and unfair tactics. The umpire may appeal to both the linesman and the referee for testimony regarding cases of unnecessary roughness, off-side play, or holding, but they shall not volunteer their opinion, nor can they be appealed to on these points by the captains or players. The referee is judge of the position and progress of the ball. The linesman shall use a stop-watch in timing the game. The linesman shall, under the advice of the referee, mark the distance gained or lost in the progress of the play. He shall also keep the time."

Rule 16 altered so as to read: "The length of the game shall be 70 minutes, divided into two halves of 35 minutes each, exclusive of time taken out. No delay for any cause whatever shall exceed three minutes. The captains shall toss up before the commencement of the match and the winner of the toss shall have the choice of goal or kick-off. The same side shall not kick off in two successive halves. *In all cases where the rules provide for a kick the ball must be actually kicked the distance of at least ten yards into the opponents' territory unless stopped by the opponents.*"

Rule 24 altered so as to read: "If a player when off side touch the ball inside the opponents' ten-yard line, the ball shall go as a touchback to the opponents."

Rule 25 altered so as to read: "No player shall lay his hands upon an opponent unless he has the ball. Players of the side in possession of the ball may obstruct with the body only."

Rule 30 extended so as to read: "There shall be no piling up upon a runner after he has cried down or the referee has blown his whistle. Infractions of this rule shall be penalized by advancing the ball ten yards for the offended side."

A new rule was adopted as follows: "No momentum mass play shall be allowed. A momentum mass play is one in which more than three men start before the ball is put in play. Nor shall more than three men group for that purpose more than five yards back of the point where the ball is put in play."

Convention of Oct. 5, 1894, at Murray Hill Hotel, New York.— Representatives: Princeton, E. S. Munn, '95, A. G. Milbank, '96; Yale, F. A. Hinkey, '95, B. S. Cable, '95. These gentlemen assembled as members of the old Intercollegiate Football Association. The following addition to the rules was made for the Princeton-Yale game: "There shall be an umpire, a referee, and a linesman. The referee shall judge for the ball, the umpire for the players, and the linesman's duties shall be as defined in Rule 15. No man shall act as an umpire who is an alumnus of either college."

Convention of March 16, 1895, at University Athletic Club, New York.—Representatives: Princeton, Alex. Moffat, '84; Yale, Walter Camp, '80.

It was decided in behalf of the Intercollegiate Football Association to request the University Athletic Club to invite Harvard, Pennsylvania, Princeton, and Yale to a joint conference on the rules.

During the arrangements for this conference correspondence was passing between S. B. Thorne, '96, Yale, and A. H. Brewer, '96, Harvard, terminating athletic relationships between these two universities, a severance which existed until 1897.

Meeting of Joint Conference, March 31, 1895, at University Athletic Club, New York.—Representatives: Harvard, W. A. Brooks, '87; Pennsylvania, J. C. Bell, '84; Princeton, Alex. Moffat, '84; Yale, Walter Camp, '80.

The committee was divided upon the subject of mass plays and flying interference. Princeton and Yale advocated their abolition, Harvard and Pennsylvania their retention. The committee adjourned from time to time during the spring and eventually continued its sessions into the summer, but the subjects of contention could not be adjusted. Finally the committee separated. Harvard and Pennsylvania invited Cornell to join them in the formation of an independent rules committee. This invitation was accepted, and Cornell selected as its representative L. M. Dennis, '85, Michigan, a member of Cornell's faculty. These two rule-making bodies drew separate rules upon the points of dispute, but in other respects followed the common code. The Rule Book published the latter, and then appended the rules at variance as follows:

Princeton and Yale:

1. The player making a fair catch need not signal with his hand, but must make a mark with his heel. If he makes no mark he may run with the ball.

2. The officials shall consist of an umpire, referee, linesman, and assistant linesman, any of whom may disqualify a player for violation of the rules subject to the approval of the umpire.

3. Not more than one man shall start forward before the ball is put in play and not more than three men shall group behind the line of scrimmage. Seven men must be on the line of scrimmage until the ball is snapped, except that the end rush may drop back, but must stand outside of the adjacent tackle.

Cornell-Harvard-Pennsylvania:

1. The player catching a punt may not run with the ball, but may pass it to another player, who may run with it.

2. The officials shall consist of two umpires, a referee, and a linesman.

Joint Session of Rules Committees, March 13, 1896, *New York.*— Representatives: Cornell, L. M. Dennis; Harvard, J. H. Sears, '89; Navy, P. J. Dashiell; Pennsylvania, J. C. Bell, '84; Princeton, Alex. Moffat, '84; Yale, Walter Camp, '80. The committees voted to form a single committee and thereupon adjourned from time to time. During these sessions the deliberations of the committee were participated in by E. N. Wrightington, '97, Harvard, B. G. Waters, '94, Harvard, and F. T. Murphy, '97, Yale. The committee finally agreed upon the following amendments to the rules:

A. A player trying for a fair catch shall make a mark with his heel.

B. If the forward movement of the ball is stopped, or if the runner shall cry down, the ball shall be deemed to be down. Piling up thereafter shall be penalized by the distance of 15 yards.

C. No player of the side not in possession of the ball shall touch the same until it is in play.

D. The snapper-back and man opposite may not touch the ball until it has touched a third man.

E. No player of the side in possession of the ball shall take more than one step toward his opponents' goal before the ball is in play without coming to a full stop. At least five players shall be on the line of scrimmage when the ball is snapped. If six players be behind the line of scrimmage, then two of the said six players must be at least five yards behind the line or shall be outside of the players on the end of the line.

Meeting of Rules Committee, Feb. 19, 1897, *at New York.* —Representatives: Cornell, L. M. Dennis; Harvard, R. D. Wrenn, '95; Navy, P. J. Dashiell; Pennsylvania, J. C. Bell, '84; Princeton, Alex. Moffat, '84; Yale, Walter Camp, '80. The sessions of the committee were continued from time to time until June 7, when the following changes in the rules were adopted:

A. The following shall be the values of plays in scoring: Goal obtained by touchdown, 6 points; goal from field kick, 5 points; touchdown failing goal, 5 points; safety by opponents, 2 points.

B. If the snapper-back feint to put the ball in play for the purpose of drawing opponents off side, the ball shall be considered to be in play and the scrimmage begun.

C. The referee shall arbitrarily shorten the halves when in his opinion the lateness of the game will not allow it to be fully completed.

D.   A player may be substituted for another at any time at the discretion of the captain of his team.

E.   The provisions in the rules relative to touch-in-goal were stricken out.

F.   The man who first receives the ball from the snapper-back shall not carry the ball forward beyond the line of scrimmage, unless he has regained it after it has been passed to and touched another player.

Meeting of Rules Committee, March 7, 1898.—Representatives: Cornell, L. M. Dennis; Harvard, R. D. Wrenn, '95; Navy, P. J. Dashiell; Pennsylvania, J. C. Bell, '84; Princeton, Alex. Moffat, '84; Yale, Walter Camp, '80.

The following changes in the rules were adopted:

A.   If the ball, after being kicked, strikes an opponent and then passes over the cross-bar, it still counts a goal.

B.   Whenever a side has tried a drop kick at the goal upon a first down inside the twenty-five yard line, and the result has been a touchback, the ten-yard instead of the twenty-five-yard line shall determine the position of the opponents, and the kicker's side must be behind the ball when it is kicked.

C.   In case of piling up on a player after the referee has declared the ball dead, the penalty shall be fifteen yards.

D.   For holding, unlawful use of hands and arms, off-side play, tripping, and foul tackling the penalty shall be the loss of ten yards if the side not in possession of the ball is the offender. or if the offending side had the ball, its immediate surrender to the opponents.

E.   In the case of interference of any kind with the putting of the ball in play, or unnecessary delay of the game. the offended side shall be advanced five yards.

F.   If a player trying for a fair catch is unlawfully obstructed the offended side shall receive fifteen yards and the choice of putting the ball in play by a free kick or by a scrimmage.

G.   If a player who has heeled a fair catch is thrown to the ground, unless he has advanced beyond his mark, his side shall receive fifteen yards and be obliged to take a free kick.

Meeting of Rules Committee, March 17, 1899, at New York.—Representatives: Cornell, L. M. Dennis; Harvard, R. D. Wrenn, '95; Navy, P. J. Dashiell; Pennsylvania, J. C. Bell, '84; Princeton, Alex. Moffat, '84; Yale, Walter Camp, '80.

The following changes in the rules were adopted:

A.   If the ball should strike an official it is not to be regarded as dead, but play shall continue exactly as if the ball had not touched him.

B. If the player about to kick after a fair catch advances beyond his mark the opposing side shall be permitted to line up five yards nearer the player.

Meeting of Rules Committee, April 28, 1900, at Philadelphia.—Representatives: Cornell, L. M. Dennis; Harvard, R. D. Wrenn, '95; Navy, P. J. Dashiell; Pennsylvania, J. C. Bell, '84; Princeton, Alex. Moffat, '84; Yale, Walter Camp, '80.

The following changes in the rules were adopted:

Rule I, section *d*, note. A touchdown is made when any part of the ball is on, above, or across the goal-line.

Rule 4, section *d*. A safety is made when a player of the side in possession of the ball commits a foul which would give the ball to opponents behind the offender's goal-line.

Rule 29 (new). There shall be no coaching either by substitutes or by any other person not participating in the game. In case of accident to a player only one official representative shall be allowed upon the field of play.

Rule 21, section *a*, exception. A team may not retain possession of the ball by taking it back twenty yards a second time, unless the ball in the meantime had been in the possession of the opponents.

Rule 28, exception. An off-side play by the side in possession of the ball shall not be penalized by the loss of the ball, but by the loss of ten yards, the number of the down and the point to which the ball must be advanced for first down to remain the same.

Meeting of Rules Committee, March, 1901, at New York.—Representatives: Cornell, L. M. Dennis; Harvard, R. D. Wrenn, '95; Navy, P. J. Dashiell; Pennsylvania, J. C. Bell, '84; Princeton, Alex. Moffat, '84; Yale, Walter Camp, '80.

Amendments to the rules adopted as follows:

Rule 4, add: A safety is made when the ball kicked by a man behind his goal-line crosses the side line extended behind the goal-line.

Rule 10, note: Ahead of the ball means between the opponents' goal-line and a line parallel to the goal-line and passing through the point of the ball nearest the goal-line of the side not in possession of the ball.

Rule 17, section *a* extended: Before the ball is put in play no player shall lay his hands upon, or by the use of his hands or arms interfere with, an opponent in such a way as to delay putting the ball in play.

Rule 22, section *a*, relative to putting the ball in play by a kick when out of bounds, add: "Touch it in with both hands at right angles to the side line and then kick it at least ten yards."

Rule 25, section *a*, relative to a try at goal by a place kick, add: "The referee shall signal with his hand when the ball is placed upon the ground."

Rule 28, section *d*, relative to making a fair catch, the clause prohibiting interference with a player "attempting to make a fair catch" was changed to "who has an opportunity to make a fair catch."

Meeting of Rules Committee, March, 1902, at New York.—Representatives: Cornell, L. M. Dennis; Harvard, R. D. Wrenn, '95; Navy, P. J. Dashiell; Pennsylvania, J. C. Bell, '84; Princeton, Alex. Moffat, '84; Yale, Walter Camp, '80.

Amendments to rules as follows:

Rule 13, section *a*, add: "The teams shall change goals after every try at goal following a touchdown, and after every goal from the field, and also at the beginning of the second half."

Rule 13, section *c*, relative to ball having been kicked across the goal-line at the kick-off, add: "If the ball has not been declared dead the side defending the goal may run with it."

Rule 16, section *b*, relative to being off side while snapping the ball, add: "If this occurs once more on the same down, the opponents shall receive five yards, the number of the down and the point to be gained to remain unchanged."

Rule 22, section *a*, relative to touching the ball in play from the side line when out of bounds, add: "Neither side need be on side when the ball is thus put in play."

Rule 27, add: "Only five men shall be permitted to walk up and down on each side of the field. The rest, including substitutes, water-carriers, and all who are admitted to the enclosure, must be seated throughout the game. None of these shall come upon the field of play without permission from the umpire. Breach of any part of this rule shall constitute a foul and be punished by a loss of five yards to the side whose man infringes, the number of the down and the point to be gained remaining the same."

Rule 28, section *a*, reducing the penalty for holding from ten yards: "The penalty for holding shall be the loss of five yards."

Rule 28, section *k*, note, relative to declination of a penalty by the offended side, add: "In case of a run from this play being made not more than twenty-five yards from the spot where the foul was committed shall be allowed." (The previous limit was fifteen yards.)

Meeting of Rules Committee, March, 1903, *at New York.*—
Representatives: Cornell, L. M. Dennis; Harvard, R. D. Wrenn,
'95; Navy, P. J. Dashiell; Pennsylvania, J. C. Bell, '84; Princeton, J. B. Fine, '82; Yale, Walter Camp, '80.

Amendments to rules were made as follows:

Rule 10, section *c*, add: "The man who, standing back of his
own line of scrimmage, receives the ball from one of his side and
then kicks it beyond the line of scrimmage may not put other men
on side by running ahead of them nor may he himself recover the
ball until it has touched a player of the opposing side."

Rule 13, section *a*, add: "The teams shall change goals after
every try at goal following a touchdown and after every goal
from the field, and the side just scored upon shall have the option of kicking off or having their opponents kick off. At the
beginning of the second half the teams shall take opposite goals
from those assumed at the beginning of the first half."

Rule 18, section *a*, add: "When the ball is put in play in a scrimmage at any point of the central portion of the field, that is, the
portion bounded by the two twenty-five-yard lines and the two
side lines, the player who first receives the ball when the scrimmage is within the above-mentioned territory may carry it forward beyond the line of scrimmage, provided in so doing he
crosses such line at least five yards from the point where the
snapper-back put the ball in play."

Rule 27, add: "If head protectors are worn, no sole-leather,
papier-maché, or other hard or unyielding material shall be used
in their construction, and all other devices for protectors must be
so arranged and padded as in the judgment of the umpire to be
without danger to other players."

Rule 29, section 111, add: "The linesman must penalize a side
for tripping, unnecessary roughness to a back after a kick, and
for off-side play in the line."

Meeting of Rules Committee, March, 1904, *at New York.*—
Representatives: Chicago, A. A. Stagg; Cornell, L. M. Dennis;
Harvard, R. D. Wrenn, '95; Navy, P. J. Dashiell; Pennsylvania,
J. C. Bell, '84; Princeton, J. B. Fine, '82; Yale, Walter Camp,
'80.

The membership of the committee was extended by inviting
the University of Chicago to participate. A. A. Stagg, '88, Yale,
professor and director of Department of Physical Culture at
Chicago was chosen as the university's representative.

Amendments to the rules were made as follows:

Rule 18, section *b*, to read as follows: "At least six men of the
side holding the ball must be on the line of scrimmage. If not

more than six men are on the line of scrimmage, one man of those
not on the scrimmage line must be outside the position occupied
by the man on the end of the line.   In this rule outside means both
feet outside the foot of the player at the end of the line."

Rule 18, section c, altered to read: "The first man receiving
the ball from the snapper-back may carry the ball forward, provided he crosses the line of scrimmage at least five yards outside
of the snapper-back."

Rule 22, relative to putting ball in play when out of bounds,
strike out section a, reading: "Touch it in with both hands at
right angles to the side line and then kick it at least ten yards
toward the opponents' goal."

Rule 26 altered so as to read: "Goal from a field kick, either a
drop kick or place kick, four points."

Rule 28, section E, insert: "The offended side may decline to
accept the penalty, in which case play is resumed as if no foul
occurred."

Rule 28, section G, paragraph 1, relative to interference with a
fair catch, insert: "They may receive fifteen yards, in which case
they may put the ball in play by a scrimmage; or (2) They may
receive five yards, in which case they shall put the ball in play by a
punt, drop kick, or place kick."

Meeting of Rules Committee, March, 1905, *at New York.*—
Representatives: Chicago, A. A. Stagg; Cornell, L. M. Dennis;
Harvard, R. D. Wrenn, '95; Navy, P. J. Dashiell; Pennsylvania,
J. C. Bell, '84; Princeton, J. B. Fine, '82; Yale, Walter Camp,
'80.

Amendments to the rules were made as follows:

Rule 6, add new section d, as follows: "If any player of the side
in possession of the ball other than the snapper-back makes any
deliberate attempt, by a false start or otherwise, to draw the opponents off side, the ball, if snapped, shall not be regarded as in
play, nor the scrimmage as begun."

Rule 20, add (note): "In order to prevent the prevalent stealing
of the ball, the referee shall blow his whistle immediately when
the forward progress of the ball has been stopped."

Rule 27, section b, add (note): "When a substitute is sent in he
must go directly to the referee and report himself before taking
his place."

Rule 27, section f, relative to side-line coaching, altered so as
to read: "Breach of any part of this rule shall constitute a foul and
be punished by a loss of ten yards to the side whose man infringes, the number of the down and the distance for first down
to remain unchanged.

Meeting of Rules Committee, Dec. 9, 1905, at Philadelphia.—
Representatives: Chicago, A. A. Stagg; Cornell, L. M. Dennis;
Harvard, W. T. Reid, '01; Navy, P. J. Dashiell; Pennsylvania,
J. C. Bell, '84; Princeton, J. B. Fine, '82; Yale, Walter Camp,
'80.

The following suggestions were filed for consideration:

Mr. Camp: A. Increase the yardage to ten yards; B. Increase the penalties for rough playing; C. Appoint a central
board to control officials; D. Prohibit tackling below the knees
and also hurdling; E. Limit the use of the arms by linesmen.

Mr. Bell: A. Prohibit a disqualified player from being replaced until the end of the half; B. Limit the positions of players
on defence; C. Increase the yardage to ten yards; D. Establish a central board to control officials.

Mr. Fine: A. Increase yardage to ten yards; B. Weaken
the defence; C. Modify the method of tackling; D. Appoint
two umpires.

Mr. Dashiell: A. Increase yardage to eight yards; B. Require seven men on offensive line of scrimmage; C. Introduce
forward passes; D. Prohibit substitution for disqualified player
until lapse of ten minutes.

Mr. Stagg: A. Increase yardage to ten yards; B. Establish
a modified code of rules for schools.

Mr. Dennis: Limit positions of players on defence.

The committee adjourned without action until January 12,
1906.

Conference of Colleges, December 24, 1905, at New York.—
At the invitation of Chancellor Henry M. MacCracken, twenty-eight colleges assembled to discuss reform for football, Harvard,
of the institutions represented upon the Rules Committee, being
the only one to participate. It was decided to form an independent Rules Committee, under the name of Conference Committee,
of seven members, to sit jointly, if possible, with the "old committee." The following were selected as representatives: Charles
D. Daly, '01, Harvard, and '05, Army; E. K. Hall, '92, Dartmouth;
James A. Babbitt, '93, Yale, and member of faculty at Haverford;
H. L. Williams, '91, Yale, and director of athletics at Minnesota; James T. Lees, Nebraska; C. W. Savage, Oberlin, and
F. H. Curtiss, Texas. This conference of colleges assumed the
name of National Intercollegiate Football Conference, but later
changed the name to Intercollegiate Athletic Association of the
United States.

*Joint Session of Intercollegiate and Conference Committees,
Jan. 12, 1906, at New York.*—Representatives: Intercollegiate

Committee—Chicago, A. A. Stagg; Cornell, L. M. Dennis; Harvard, W. T. Reid, '01; Navy, P. J. Dashiell; Pennsylvania, J. C. Bell, '84; Princeton, J. B. Fine, '82; Yale, Walter Camp, '80. Conference Committee—C. D. Daly, '05, Army; E. K. Hall, '92, Dartmouth; J. A. Babbitt, Haverford; H. L. Williams, Minnesota; J. T. Lees, Nebraska; C. W. Savage, '93, Oberlin; F. H. Curtiss, Texas.

It was decided that the two committees should sit jointly, under the title of American Intercollegiate Football Rules Committee, that eight members thereof should constitute a quorum, and that eight votes should be necessary to pass a motion. The rules were then taken up, and the committee adjourned from time to time.

Amendments to the rules were made as follows:

Rule 1, section *f.* The officials of the game shall be a referee, two umpires, and a linesman. Note.—The second umpire may be dispensed with by mutual agreement of the two institutions involved.

Rule 2, section *a.* The length of the game shall be sixty minutes, divided into two halves of thirty minutes each, exclusive of time taken out. There shall be ten minutes intermission between the halves.

Rule 5, section *b.* A scrimmage takes place when the holder of the ball places it flat upon the ground with its long axis at right angles to the line of scrimmage and puts it in play by kicking it forward or snapping it back.

Rule 5, section *c.* The line of scrimmage for each side is an imaginary line parallel to the goal-line and passing through that point of the ball nearest the side's own goal-line.

Rule 5, section *d.* A fair catch consists in catching the ball, etc., provided the player, while advancing toward the ball, signals his intention of making a fair catch by raising his hand clearly above his head and takes not more than two steps after making the catch.

Rule 5, section *e.* A down occurs (2) when any portion of the player, with the ball except his hands or feet, touches the ground while he is in the grasp of an opponent.

Rule 5, section *m.* A player trips another when he obstructs him below the knee with that part of his leg which is below the knee.

Rule 5, section *n.* Hurdling in the open is jumping over, or attempting to jump over, an opponent who is still on his feet. Hurdling in the line is jumping over, or attempting to jump over, a player on the line of scrimmage, with the feet or knees foremost, within the distance of five yards on either side of the point where the ball is put in play.

Rule 8, section *b*. Either captain may ask that time be called three times during each half without penalty. If thereafter, however, time be taken out at the request of a captain, his side shall be penalized by a loss of two yards for each time, unless a player be removed from the game, the down and distance to be gained to remain the same as they were before the request was made.

Rule 9, section *a*. The opponents must not interfere in any way with the snapper-back, nor touch him or the ball until it is actually in play.

Rule 11, section *c*, 1. No player of those ordinarily occupying the position of centre, guard, and tackle—that is, the five middle players of the line—may drop back from the line of scrimmage on the offence, unless he is at least five yards behind the line of scrimmage when the ball is put in play and another player of those ordinarily behind the line of scrimmage takes his place on the line of scrimmage. Note.—There shall be no shifting of men to evade this rule.

Rule 12, section *a*. Note.—Holding or unlawful obstruction by the hands or arms; side in possession of the ball includes:

1. Grasping an opponent with the hands or arms.

2. Placing the hands or arms upon an opponent to push him away from the play.

3. Circling in any degree any part of the opponent with the arm.

Session of Intercollegiate Conference Committees, March, 1907, at New York.—Representatives: Intercollegiate Committee—Chicago, A. A. Stagg; Cornell, L. M. Dennis; Harvard, W. T. Reid, '01; Navy, P. J. Dashiell; Pennsylvania, J. C. Bell, '84; Princeton, J. B. Fine, '82; Yale, Walter Camp, '80. Conference Committee—C. D. Daly, '05, Army; E. K. Hall, '92, Dartmouth; J. A. Babbitt, Haverford; H. L. Williams, Minnesota; J. T. Lees, Nebraska; C. W. Savage, '93, Oberlin; W. L. Dudley, Vanderbilt.

Amendments to the rules were made as follows:

Rule 6, add: "Opportunity to make a fair catch is where the player is in such position that it would be possible for him to reach the ball before it touches the ground."

Rule 17, section 7, insert: "In case a signal is made for a fair catch by any player who has an opportunity for a fair catch, and another player of his side who had not signalled for a fair catch catches the ball, no run shall be made nor shall the fair catch be allowed, but the ball shall be given to the catcher's side for a scrimmage at the point where the catch was made."

The referee was given jurisdiction over hurdling.

Session of Intercollegiate and Conference Committees, March, 1908, at New York.—Representatives: Intercollegiate Committee —Chicago, A. A. Stagg; Cornell, L. M. Dennis; Harvard, Joshua Crane, '90; Navy, P. J. Dashiell; Pennsylvania, J. C. Bell, '84; Princeton, J. B. Fine, '82; Yale, Walter Camp, '80.   Conference Committee—H. B. Hackett, '04, Army; E. K. Hall, '92, Dartmouth; J. A. Babbitt, Haverford; H. L. Williams, Minnesota; J. T. Lees, Nebraska; C. W. Savage, '93, Oberlin; W. L. Dudley, Vanderbilt.

Amendments to the rules were made as follows:

Rule IV, section 2.   There shall be fifteen minutes intermission between the two halves.   The referee shall cause both teams to be notified three minutes before the intermission has expired. Fifteen minutes after the close of the first half the referee shall blow his whistle in the middle of the field, and in case either team fails to appear within two minutes thereafter, the ball shall be put in play as first down by the offended side on the offending side's thirty-yard line.

Rule V.   The score of a forfeited game shall be 1 to 0 in favor of the offended side.

Rule VI, section 16, *i.*   The ball is dead when it accidentally strikes an official.   *In such case the play must be played over.*

Rule XIX, section 5, *c.*   Of the players of the side making a forward pass only the player who first legally touched the ball shall be entitled to touch or recover the ball until it has been touched by an opponent.

Rule XIX, section 7.   If the ball after having been legally passed forward crosses the goal-line on the fly or strikes the uprights or cross-bar before it has been touched by a player on either side it becomes dead and shall count as a touchback to the defenders of that goal.

Session of Intercollegiate and Conference Committees, March 27, 1909, at New York.—Representatives: Intercollegiate Committee—Chicago, A. A. Stagg; Cornell, L. M. Dennis; Harvard, C. Blagden, '02; Navy, P. J. Dashiell; Pennsylvania, J. C. Bell, '84, alternate, Carl Williams, '97; Princeton, P. H. Davis, '93; Yale, Walter Camp, '80.   Conference Committee—H. B. Hackett, '04, Army; E. K. Hall, '92, Dartmouth; J. A. Babbitt, Haverford; H. L. Williams, Minnesota; W. A. Lambeth, '92, Virginia;   W. S. Langford, '96, Trinity; W. L. Dudley, Vanderbilt.

Rule XX, section 4. Make penalty same as Rule XXVI, section 5.

Rule XVII, section 6. Official to blow whistle when forward progress stops. Side in possession may push opponents with bodies.

Rule XVIII, section 2. Strike out last clause of penalty: "Side in possession."

Rule XVIII, section 2. If player after catching ball stops with only one step or less, the ball is declared dead.

Page 205. Strike out Note 24, referring to Rule XIX, section 5.

Rule XVIII, section 2. Man ineligible to catch ball may not run into opponents.

Any forward pass, whether crossing scrimmage line or not, must be played from at least five yards back of scrimmage line.

Rule VIII, section 4. Add: "Line or line extended."

Rule III, section 2. A player disqualified for cause may not be returned to the game.

Rule IV, section 2. Penalty for player leaving field at the three-minute intermission, same as coaching from side lines.

Rule VI. If snapper-back does not hold long axis of ball as specified, ball must be put in play over again.

Rule VI, section 17 (I). If ball hits official, whether in hands of player or not, it must be played over again.

Rule VI, section 16. If player extends arms advancing ball after declared dead, it is crawling.

Rule VIII. Snapper-back may assume any position, so long as he is not off side, in putting ball in play.

Rule VIII, section 4. If end is man in motion, another must take his place on line of scrimmage, as seven men must be on this line when ball is put in play.

Rule XVII, section 6. Comrade may not lift fallen man to his feet to enable him to continue his run.

Joint Session of Rules Committees held in New York, Feb. 3, 1911.—Representatives, Intercollegiate Rules Committee: A. A. Stagg, Chicago; J. W. Beacham, '97, Cornell; P. D. Haughton, '99, Harvard; F. D. Berrien, '00, Navy; Carl Williams, '97, Pennsylvania; P. H. Davis, '93, Princeton; Walter Camp, '80, Yale. National Conference Committee: V. W. Cooper, '04, Army; E. K. Hall, '92, Dartmouth; J. A. Babbitt, Haverford; S. C. Williams, '01, Iowa; H. L. Williams, Minnesota; C. W. Savage, '93, Oberlin; W. L. Dudley, Vanderbilt.

Mr. Hall is elected chairman, and Mr. Camp secretary. The rules were amended as follows:

APPENDIX

Rule 4, section 2. There shall be two minutes intermission between the first and second periods, and between the third and fourth periods.

Rule 6, section 17. If the ball strikes an official it shall not become dead, but play shall continue.

Rule 18. All penalties under the rules relating to forward passes heretofore applied on the spot from which the pass was made, shall hereafter be applied on the spot of the preceding down.

Rule 18, section 2. Strike out the words *"and taken more than one step in any direction."* (Alteration of rule which forbade tackling or roughing the player receiving a forward pass until he had taken more than one step.)

Rule 19, section 4. If the ball having been legally passed forward and legally touched, shall then strike the ground unless having been actually caught, the play shall be considered an incompleted forward pass.

Rule 25, section c. Only three men shall be permitted to walk up and down the side lines on each side of the field.

Rule 30, section 4. The time shall be kept hereafter by the umpire.

Add a new rule: " If a foul following a first or second down is committed by the offensive side while the ball is behind its goal-line, or in flight from a kick or pass delivered from behind that line, the play shall count as a down and the ball shall be put in play upon the 1-yard line; if such foul follows a third down the referee shall declare a safety. If the defensive side commits a foul while the offensive side is running, kicking, or passing out from behind its goal-line, the referee shall declare a touchback."

The following notes were adopted:

Throwing to the ground the player carrying the ball after the referee has declared the ball dead, may be considered as unnecessary roughness.

Concealing the ball beneath the clothing of a player or substituting any article for the ball shall be considered as unsportsmanlike conduct.

Voted to incorporate in the rules the interpretations made Sept. 17, 1910.

A codification committee, composed of Walter Camp, E. K. Hall, and Carl Williams, was appointed to recodify the rules, with power to alter the verbiage thereof to accomplish simplification and clarification.

CPSIA information can be obtained
at www.ICGtesting.com
Printed in the USA
BVHW061254281021
619841BV00018B/205